S0-ATV-824

THE PAPERS
of
JOHN C. CALHOUN

John C. Calhoun

Oil portrait from late life painted by Eugenius Frans DeBlock, perhaps painted from a daguerreotype by Matthew Brady. In the collections of the Gibbes Museum of Art, Charleston.

THE PAPERS of JOHN C. CALHOUN

Volume XXVI, 1848–1849

Edited by

Clyde N. Wilson

and Shirley Bright Cook

Alexander Moore, *Associate Editor*

University of South Carolina Press, 2001

Publication of this book was made possible by a grant from the National Historical Publications and Records Commission.

International Standard Book Number: 1–57003–393–5
Library of Congress Catalog Card Number: 59–10351

Manufactured in the United States of America

This book is printed on acid-free paper that meets the ANSI/NISO specifications for permanence as revised in 1992.

CONTENTS

PREFACE

With the book in hand, a half-century's labour in creating a definitive documentary history of the great Carolina statesman/philosopher grows very near its close. A little less than eight months of life remain to Calhoun when this volume ends.

Indispensable support for this book, as for many previous, has been given by the University of South Carolina, the National Historical Publications and Records Commission, and the University South Caroliniana Society.

CLYDE N. WILSON

Columbia, June 1999

INTRODUCTION

In early 1849, in Washington, Calhoun sat to have his image recorded by the new process of daguerreotyping. The process, requiring prolonged motionlessness, could be quite trying for the sitter. Calhoun's daughter, Anna Maria, who was in America for a few short months before returning to her husband's post in Belgium, accompanied him to the session.

Some years later, Thomas Bangs Thorpe, well-known writer and publisher of "Southwestern humor," wrote an article about this sitting. It was doubtless embellished by imagination, but Thorpe's account seems to have come from someone who was actually present.

> Mr. Calhoun sat for his picture in Washington city in the year 1849—less than two years before he died. His hair, which in his younger days was dark, and stood so frowningly over his broad, square, forehead, was now long, gray, and thin, and combed away from his face and fell behind his ears. Mr. Calhoun was dressed in a suit of black, over which he wore a long cloak. Nothing in human form could have exceeded his dignity of manner and impressive personal appearance that day. He came promptly in accordance with his appointment, accompanied by his daughter, Mrs. Klempson [*sic*]. Mr. Calhoun . . . was . . . very obliging, and was constantly making some kind remark about any delay or accident that might occur. Mrs. Klempson . . . delicately arranged at times her father's hair or the folds of his cloak . . . . Mr. Calhoun [said in reply to a question from Anna Maria] . . . that the art of taking pictures by the daguerreotype was a new process, and that while the results had deeply interested him, as indicative of great advantages to the social circle and all scientific pursuits, yet he did not feel competent to explain the exact method, and with these preliminary remarks he proceeded to open up the invention by an analytical disquisition and explanation that could not have been surpassed by the most accomplished expert; and all this was done in the simplest and clearest language, that fascinated and astonished the workmen in the gallery. . . . Calhoun's eyes were cavernous, they seemed so deeply set in his head, but there was a deep blue in their depths that appeared trembling with a threatening storm; and yet there was, for all this, inconsistent as it may seem, a wonderful sense of repose.[1]

[1] Thomas Bangs Thorpe, "Webster, Clay, Calhoun, and Jackson: How They Sat for Their Daguerreotypes," in *Harper's New Monthly Magazine*, vol.

Despite escalating sectional tension, Calhoun was by this time a venerable national institution, a recognizably great figure whose deeds and words were memories from earlier and better days of the Union. A work published in 1849 said: "Considered in respect to his natural ability, acquired talents, past career, and present position, one of the most interesting and historical characters of our land, is John Caldwell Calhoun." Concluding sixty pages of description and praise, the author quoted verse to the effect that Calhoun was one of those "men whose great thoughts possess us like a passion" and "command all coming times and minds. . . ."[2]

As for the "coming times," an intimate of Abraham Lincoln remembered that "he was a great admirer of the style of John C. Calhoun." Hearing a reading of a speech of Calhoun's in reply to Henry Clay, in which Calhoun said "that to legislate upon precedent is but to make the error of yesterday the law of today," Lincoln "thought that was a great truth and grandly uttered."[3]

The New York *Herald* of July 26, 1849, published a lengthy human-interest style account of a visit to Calhoun and family at Fort Hill, parts of which were widely excerpted or commented upon in the press. This examination of "Personal Traits" was justified on the grounds that "Less is probably known to the public of the *personale*" of Calhoun "than of any of our eminent statesmen."[4]

In January 1849, Calhoun had a spell of illness that kept him from the Senate for a few days. This was widely reported and elicited respectful sympathy from the press.[5] Even the abolitionists, meeting for three days in Faneuil Hall to demand dissolution of the Union, passed resolutions commending Calhoun for "his frankness and directness . . . earnestness, consistency, intrepidity and self-

XXXVIII, no. 228 (May, 1869), pp. 787–789. There is some uncertainty as to which of the late-life daguerreotypes of Calhoun was involved here, since he had several sessions in 1849/1850, but the photographer was probably Matthew Brady.

[2] E.L. Magoon, *Living Orators in America* (New York: Baker & Scribner, 1849), pp. 182, 243.

[3] William H. Herndon, *Herndon's Lincoln: The True Story of a Great Life* (Chicago: Belford, Clarke & Co., 1889), p. 523. Perhaps it may be said that while Calhoun was interested in overruling bad precedents, Lincoln was interested in making new ones.

[4] New York, N.Y., *Herald*, July 26, 1849, p. 1, printed below. The writer was Joseph A. Scoville.

[5] Besides South Carolina newspapers, a sample: the Baltimore, Md., *Sun*, January 21; the Harrisburg, Pa., *Democratic Union*, January 21; the Alexandria, Va., *Gazette and Virginia Advertiser*, January 23, 26, and 29; the Washington, D.C., *Daily National Intelligencer*, January 25.

sacrifice in defending" what they chose to call the extension of slavery.[6]

Among the few who did not give Calhoun at least grudging respect were certain leaders of the Democratic party from the western South. Whatever disagreements men like Thomas H. Benton and Samuel Houston may have had with Calhoun over policies, their feelings toward him, even preoccupation with him, included an element of malignity that was certainly personal. Perhaps it was in part the envy of rivalry and frustration at Calhoun's powerful moral authority. "Major Jack Downing," in this case Calhoun's friend Charles Augustus Davis of New York, penned some satirical verses after a particularly ugly attack by Benton in late 1848. Called "A Senatorial Row," they picture a blustering, threatening Benton, enraged that he had been "overlook'd" for Calhoun. The latter sat serenely while his attacker roared himself into a fit and disgrace.[7]

A reporter observing the scene at Washington, wrote that Calhoun "looks remarkably well," belying the attack he suffered a month later. The reporter continued:

> . . . Mr. Calhoun and Mr. Webster came into public life about the same time—both young and ardent. Mr. Van Buren was born in the same year with them, 1782. They are all in good preservation as to body and mind. In regard to the two former, they are probably destined to a long life of activity and usefulness. Age cannot dim the fires that are fed by genius . . . .[8]

This writer's reluctance to include Van Buren among venerable geniuses is widely reflected among Calhoun's correspondents. They almost unanimously agree, Democrat and Whig, Northern and Southern, that Van Buren's becoming the Presidential candidate of the Free Soil party in 1848 was but the natural disgraceful climax to an unprincipled career.

Equality and Its Perils

Tensions over efforts to bar slave property from the Territories of the Union reached arresting levels in the last period of Calhoun's life. One of the most arresting events, then and later, was Calhoun's forthright confrontation of the doctrine that "all men are created equal."

[6] Charleston, S.C., *Mercury*, February 9, 1849, p. 2.
[7] Ms. of "unpublished" poem printed in *The Collector* (March, 1902), p. 59.
[8] Charleston, S.C., *Courier*, December 16, 1848, p. 2.

In his speech of June 27, 1848, near the end of a stormy Congressional session, he declared the proposition to be both untrue and mischievous.

Judging by his correspondence, Calhoun seemed to have struck a hidden vein of public sentiment, and not only in the South.[9] Constituting a dramatic moment in the slavery controversy, Calhoun's declaration is indelibly associated with that controversy. Apart from that controversy, however, it should also be seen as reflecting two other trends: the disappointment of many Americans over what they regarded as misdirected and failed revolutions in Europe; and the disgust of Calhoun and many others with mass politics as it had developed in the Union. After all, the two leading parties had just nominated as successors to Washington and Jefferson an undistinguished trimmer with an evasive platform and a military hero with no platform at all.

Calhoun did not make a historical exegesis of what the delegates of the thirteen States had meant in 1776 by "all men are created equal." Had he done so, it would have strengthened his case. Rather he took on directly what the phrase had come to mean in folklore. As is seen herein, Calhoun was in the process of composing his *Disquisition on Government* and his stand coincides with the opening passages of his treatise: Equality as it had come to be declared was a false principle drawn from a false premise of the "state of nature." Men were born neither free nor equal. They were born as helpless babes and they never had and never could exist free of an unequal dependence on their fellows. Not a theoretical liberty but an undoubted and unequal interdependence was man's "state of nature." By his reading, equality had come to be no longer a support for the community that was necessary for humanity but had become a hindrance and threat.

Calhoun, in his speech and in his treatise shows relatively little interest in proslavery theory narrowly defined. He never mentions the burgeoning science of racial classification, mainly a preoccupation of Northerners, except to reply politely to those who brought it to his attention. In the *Disquisition* he is not concerned with races but with the human race. Nor does he rely, except in passing, on the impressive theological case for slavery that Southern divines were elaborating. His defence of slavery as a public man is not a theory, but an exercise in what he considered the highest demands of statesmanship—the defence of a real and self-governing society. Theory

[9] See the Index entry for "Equality" in *The Papers of John C. Calhoun*, vol. 25.

was touched on to the extent that it was necessary to deal with erroneous religious and philosophical opinions that had fueled threats to his society. His basic public demand was for the moral comity necessary for a voluntary Union, another name for which is concurrent majority.

The challenge to equality would receive greater elaboration in the decade after Calhoun's death, and he could rightly be seen as its father. The next decade, with filibustering expeditions and the Ostend Manifesto, would exhibit also efforts at territorial expansion that could be linked at least partly to the "expansion of slavery." (Though a great many Americans were expansionists *per se*. The antislavery William H. Seward recommended an attack on Canada in 1861.)

In the spring of 1849, the Cuban-South Carolinian Ambrose J. Gonzales introduced Calhoun to the Cuban revolutionary leader Narciso Lopez in Washington. In a public letter written two years later, when the largest of the attempted revolutions was under way, Gonzales recalled that Calhoun had expressed sympathy for the Cuban cause and had remarked that Cuba would, with the certainty of gravitation, "eventually drop into the lap of the Union."[10]

However, Calhoun's sympathy for the white planters, merchants, and professionals in revolt against an intolerable colonial power does not necessarily suggest support for aggressive American action. He had said in the Senate that Cuba was safe for the United States as it was, as long as it did not fall to a major power. And that observation was based on considerations of national defence as well as the protection of slavery.[11] For fifteen years, and intensely in these last years, Calhoun had been preaching against militaristic expansionism. He was making a strong effort to leave to Americans a limiting interpretation of the "Monroe Doctrine," at the creation of which he had been present.

Calhoun's declaration against the pernicious effects of equality doctrine did not put him, in his opinion or that of others, on the side of General Hamilton and against Mr. Jefferson, who had been wrong on that one occasion. Though in a different situation, he remained, like Jefferson, an idealist and historicist, not a legalist or ideologist. It should not be forgotten that Calhoun was to many, as one corre-

[10] See Jesse W. Boyd, "Lopez's Expedition to Cuba," in *Gulf States Historical Magazine*, vol. II, nos. 5 and 6 (March–May, 1904), pp. 329–330. Gonzales's letter was published in the Charleston, S.C., *Mercury*, August 24, 1851.

[11] *The Papers of John C. Calhoun*, 25:410, in the Speech on the Proposed Occupation of Yucatan, May 15, 1848.

spondent put it, "still the great champion of the seperation of Government from Wealth."[12] Nor that many and substantial Northerners agreed with him on slavery and even on the rights of the slave States in the Territories.[13]

His real efforts, however, were directed at the South, to bring it to the kind of unity that would enable it to defend itself. In that goal he was making evident progress. Andrew Jackson's nephew wrote his agreement with Calhoun that the South was duty-bound and morally right to defend itself, and that slavery was the basis of liberty and equality for white men.[14]

Troubled Times

On several occasions in this period, as never before, Calhoun alluded publicly in a forthright manner to the possible dissolution of the Union. Even so, it often seems that what Calhoun wanted separation from was not the North but the two-party system which he saw as hopelessly debased. Again and again he declared that the South did not demand "the extension of slavery" but only the defensive right not to be excluded from the Territories by a Northern majority, a majority at least in part attributable to the two parties' search for marginal votes for victory in their pursuit of the spoils. Neither Calhoun nor any other Southern spokesman denied that a State could vote slavery down as an act of its inviolate sovereignty. They denied such power to the Congress and to the first squatters on the public lands.

"If worsted in that struggle [against the Wilmot Proviso], as there is great probability we will be," Calhoun told a Charleston throng on August 19, 1848, we have nothing to hope or expect from the Federal Government." This speech was made on his way home from Washington. To the students of South Carolina College on December 7, on his way back to the federal city, he said: "you are young, and must expect, therefore, to take part in the struggle, which

[12] From Abbot H. Brisbane, December 18, 1848, below. See also the Ohioan Benjamin G. Wright, December 11, 1848, and Ezra D. Pruden of New Jersey, October 4, 1848.

[13] See herein letters from Richard Rush, August 25, 1848; Caleb Cushing, August 26, 1848; George H. Thatcher, September 20, 1848; Ezra D. Pruden, October 4, 1848; Laurel Summers, October 21, 1848; John Hastings, December 28, 1848; and Fitzwilliam Byrdsall, June 5, 1849.

[14] From Andrew J. Donelson, September 27, 1848, herein.

may come, and a tremendous one it must be, pregnant with mighty consequences."

Private comments did not differ. "The argument is, indeed, exhausted," he told a long-retired former Senator from Georgia. "The question between North & South is now acknowledged by the former to be a mere question of power."[15] To a nephew he wrote, "there are storms a head" and those "who propose to take an active part in politicks must prepare to meet them."[16] To a South Carolinian inquiring about his opinion on movements in the South, he wrote that "I am of the impression, that the time is near at hand, when the South will have to choose between disunion, and submission."[17] Clearly, a majority in the South did not accept his position at the moment, but the minority was growing and in ten years a majority would be where Calhoun had been. There are perhaps few examples in history of a statesman formulating a policy so decisively for his people after he was dead.

More citizens than ever before seemed to be joining his stand. Wrote an Alabamian: "I never saw so much changing in politics and voters in my life. Truly may we exclaim—these are troublous times—and there seems to be worse a coming."[18] Said another Southerner: "let us firmly propose a compromise and settlement, final and full of this vexed and dangerous question, and present as our alternative, secession, and the establishment of an independent republic, peaceably if we can, forcibly if we must."[19] Yet another wrote Calhoun: "The public mind, is rapidly being prepared for what must come at last—the dissolution of the Union, but *we must have time*."[20]

Of course, despite forebodings, much American life went on as normal. On the day a newly designed gold coin was first struck at the Philadelphia mint, the chief engraver sent one to Calhoun as a gesture of appreciation.[21]

Calhoun, despite his publicized illness, assured his family repeatedly that he was in good health, though it was clear a milepost had been passed on the road to decline. He had to concern himself with the low price of cotton, with financial arguments between his son Andrew and son-in-law Thomas Clemson, with the dubious life-

[15] To Wilson Lumpkin, September 1, 1848, herein.

[16] To John Alfred Calhoun, October 13, 1848, herein.

[17] To John H. Means, April 13, 1849, herein.

[18] From Albert A. Dumas, September 8, 1848, herein.

[19] From Armistead Burwell, September 12, 1848, herein.

[20] From Hilliard M. Judge, April 29, 1849, herein.

[21] From James B. Longacre, May 8, 1849, herein.

style of his military son Patrick, and with the education of his other sons, one of whom, James Edward, had taken a notion to head for the California gold rush.[22] And he had now finished enough of what would become his *Disquisition* and *Discourse* to be able to discuss it with family. Whatever else history might say about Calhoun, this would be a legacy such as few who had been so active in government had left.[23]

[22] To James Edward Calhoun, January 17, 1849, herein.

[23] Recent examples of serious attention to Calhoun as a major political thinker, in political science and philosophy, respectively, are Howard Lee Cheek, Jr., "Calhoun and Popular Rule: The Political Theory of the *Disquisition* and *Discourse*" (Ph.D. dissertation, Catholic University of America, 1999), and Winston Leigh McCuen, "The Constitution of Man: John C. Calhoun and a Solid Foundation for Political Science" (Ph.D. dissertation, Emory University, 1999).

THE PAPERS
of
JOHN C. CALHOUN

Volume XXVI

AUGUST 15–DECEMBER 11, 1848

Congress adjourned August 14. Five days later, a homeward bound Calhoun, along with Senator Andrew P. Butler and Representative Armistead Burt, addressed a packed audience at Charleston's New Theatre. Calhoun described the recent triumph of the Wilmot Proviso as "a mere wanton assertion of power" by the North. He compared abolitionism to a disease which had to be arrested early or it would be fatal, and even gave a hint as to what an independent South would look like.

Farmer Calhoun remained at Fort Hill during the fall, until Congress met in December. His personal affairs had suffered from the low price of cotton, as he wrote his son Andrew on October 11, but he expected a rise. By November 25, he had to admit disappointment of this hope.

A Presidential election campaign was under way, which naturally attracted the attention of Americans. In May, the Democrats had nominated Lewis Cass at Baltimore with a platform ambivalent on the Wilmot Proviso. In June the Whigs chose the military hero Zachary Taylor at Philadelphia, with a platform silent on the Wilmot Proviso and every other issue as well. Later the same month, a new Free Soil party was formed at Buffalo, uniting the Liberty party and pro-Wilmot Democrats and Whigs. The candidate was ex-President Martin Van Buren.

Calhoun's correspondents from across the Union were eager to learn his opinion. Should they go for the nominee of the Democrats, a party which had been most friendly to Southern interests, or for Taylor, a man of character and a Southerner? Calhoun's position was clear and unchanging. Neither party promised any satisfaction. To associate with either in their race for spoils would be degrading. South Carolina should remain aloof (though the General Assembly eventually cast the Electoral votes for Cass). In November it was clear that Taylor, an unknown quantity, had won.

In December Calhoun took an unaccustomed route to Washington, stopping in Columbia. He had not been to the capital in some years and his appearance, according to the press, created a "sensa-

tion." Speaking to the students at South Carolina College, of which he had been named a trustee, he warned them to prepare for a future of struggle (with more prophecy than perhaps even he knew). Then he proceeded by invitation to the nearby State House and was invited to the floor by both houses.

Congress convened on December 4. Calhoun, very uncharacteristically late, did not take his seat until December 12. This was undoubtedly because he spent a few days with the Clemsons at their Edgefield District plantation. They had arrived from Europe in November for a short stay. It would be his last visit with Anna Maria and her children.

From Sarah Mytton Maury

Liverpool [England,] August 15th 1848

Thank you most extremely, my dear Mr. Calhoun, for the Speech [of 6/27/1848] on Slavery. I was wearying to see it, for Mr. [Charles J.?] Ingersoll had written to me, and described it as one of your noblest efforts.

I have sent several extracts to one of our leading Liverpool Journals, and have ordered a copy to be sent to you. It is very possible that the Editor may however have curtailed the matter which I forwarded.

This question, *Slavery*, begins to be much better understood, and more liberally considered than formerly. The London Times which is our most influential organ has most emphatically espoused the cause of the West India Proprietors, and as this paper is regarded as peculiarly english in its sentiments and doctrines, the effect produced by its taunts against the Abolition party have been powerful in their operation upon the public mind; more especially as the [Lord John Russell] Administration is on the horns of a dilemma in the Sugar Question. Ireland and her unhappy serfs are also a very perplexing subject for those who dare to say ["in" *interlined*] the home thrust words of Scripture, "First take out the mote from thine own eye, and then shalt thou see clearly" &.

Your reply [*not found*] to my question about the Kentucky Lady's pamphlet was so much valued by my Abolitionist friend Dr. John Sutherland of Liverpool, that he begged it from me.

This eastern world of ours is still boiling over. It was easy for a colony unacquainted with the presence of a resident Government, with the prestige of a Court, and the influences of an Aristocracy to establish a Republic; they had no ruins to clear away, before they began to build anew. But in the case of long established Monarchies turning into Republics the matter is more difficult, more protracted, and more uncertain. It *is* certain however that even should the extraordinary experiment now proceeding in Europe prove *un*successful, and new monarchical ["institutions" *interlined*] spring up, the modified forms of these restored governments, would ensure us for a time at least, against the abuses which the corruptions incident to all earthly things perforce ["are" *canceled*] engender in all systems and all codes of law. England with folded hands for the present watches, and appears externally to preserve her supreme tranquillity—but I fear that a cancer knows her heart, and the disease is so complicated that she is next to incurable. Our lower and working classes are in hopeless destitution, and unless emigration, and employment provide against such a result, our labourers and manufacturers will prove a more impracticable body than the "Ouvriers" of Paris. *They will be fed.* In the vellum copy of the "Englishwoman," you will find a curious error of the press. At page 150 of General Observations, line 3 from the top 1845 is printed instead of 1846. The error has been corrected in all the copies except two bound especially for you and Mr. [James] Buchanan. Would you oblige me by drawing a pen through the 5 and inserting a 6.

I trust you are and will be well. You are now precious indeed to America for you have no successor, and I pray that you may be permitted to die rejoicing that the question on which you dwell with such solemn and affecting fear, may be adjusted in peace, and according to your hope. That your departing hour may not be clouded by the same sorrowful apprehensions that oppressed the heart of Mr. [Thomas] Jefferson, is the true and anxious hope of her who is in heart your countrywoman, and ever your faithful and affectionate friend, Sarah Mytton Maury.

[P.S.] I cannot forbear telling you that the "Englishwoman" has received, and is still receiving extraordinary honours.

ALS in ScCleA. NOTE: "The Englishwoman" mentioned by Mrs. Maury was her book *An Englishwoman in America*, published in 1848 in London by Thomas Richardson and Son and in Liverpool by George Smith, Watts and Co.

To J[ohn] D. Wilson, [Society Hill, S.C.]

Washington, 15th Aug[us]t 1848

Dear Sir, My official engagements have been so pressing, as to prevent me from acknowledging, at an earlier date, your letter of the 4th Inst.

I am of the opinion, that neither Gen[era]l [Lewis] Cass, nor Gen[era]l [Zachary] Taylor comes up any thing like to our political standard. I regard the letter of the former to Mr. [Alfred O.P.] Nicholson [of 12/24/1847] as unsound & evasive on the important ["points" *canceled and* "subject" *interlined*] to which it relates. He is also unsound on the subject of internal improvements, and on questions relating to peace & war, and, I may add, the disbursements of the Government. I regard the latter as unsound on the veto power, and uncertain on almost all others.

Judged ["of" *canceled*] by their supporters, there is little difference between them. This session has proved, that we cannot rely, when we come to the pinch on a single supporter of either [candidate] north of ["the" *canceled*] Mason & Dixon line. They voted to a man against us in both Houses on the Oregon bill, ["which" *interlined*] embraced the Wilmot proviso to its full extent; ["on" *canceled and* "the" *altered to* "that"] is, it excluded slavery from the entire territory, without securing to the South any line below which, it should not be excluded. It asserted, and was intended to establish the broad principle, that Congress had the full & unqualified right to exclude us from every foot ["of" *interlined*] territory belonging to the United States, or that may be acquired by them hereafter. I am happy to say, that the South was alike unanimous, including both parties, against the bill, with two exceptions, both of whom were democrats, I am sorry to say, and intimate friends & supporters ["of Gen(era)l Cass" *interlined*], Col. [Thomas H.] Benton & Gen[era]l [Samuel] Houston.

Such being the facts, I am decidedly of opinion, that our true policy is to avoid a canvass between the two nominees. We cannot enter into one, without sinking down to their respective standards and dividing the State ["between" *canceled*] into two personal parties. To avoid such a result, the only way is to avoid the canvass, and to cast our vote quietly, when the time comes, where our safety and a regard to consistency may require. Be assured, that we have nothing to hope from either party at the North. Our safety rests with ourselves. The first step towards it, is Union among ourselves. It is disgraceful, when all parties are united against us at the North on the most vital [of] all questions, that we should be divided among ourselves. With great respect yours truly, J.C. Calhoun.

ALS in TxU, Waddy Thompson Letters.

From J[ohn] T. Trezevant

Memphis, Tenn., Aug. 16th 1848

D[ea]r Sir, I will thank you to send me a copy of your speech or speeches on the slavery question as it may have come up in ["any" *interlined*] of the bills before the Senate during the present session. It is one that ["is" *interlined*] regarded as all absorbing here; but the Democratic portion of our citizens in this region look upon the late movement in Charleston as singular, to say the least of it; and especially do they so regard it, when they are given to understand it has your sanction & echoes your own opinions in relation to the candidates for the Presidency.

Upon all the great questions of national policy which have divided the two parties of the country for the last half century, Gen[era]l [Zachary] Taylor gives to Congress the right to pass, without check, such laws, as, to it, may seem proper. A National Bank may be chartered; a high protective tariff passed; a system of wild, extravagant internal improvement fastened on the country, absorbing all its revenue & begetting additional excuses for high Tariffs—all these measures, against which the Democrats, from [Thomas] Jefferson's day to this, have battled, may go into effect, by a mere majority in Congress; and Gen[era]l Taylor has given his almost positive assurance that, whatever may be his opinions upon their constitutionality, the *will of Congress* shall be carried out. This is but setting up the opinions of Congress in opposition to the Constitution; and making a mere verbal law paramount to our written Constitution. If this be so, there can be no use for a body of written laws. 'Tis idle to talk about "powers delegated" & "rights reserved"; for they are both mere fancies[?], varying as the different mental complexions of Congress may vary. If Gen[era]l Taylor then can defer so entirely to the superior wisdom of Congress, in matters upon which he *must* form an opinion, as to their constitutionality; if he thus surrenders to Congress the right to pass any and all laws upon these great issues; may he not be induced to surrender a still greater ["law" *canceled*] question? May he not reason thus—That Congress does not propose to interfere with slavery in the States, or in the District of Columbia—that it simply designs to prevent its being carried to those territories where it does not now exist (as with us)—that, abstractly, it is a curse, rather than a blessing—and that the eternal agitation of the question may be thus promptly arrested—that the South has millions of acres for the employment of the slaves, without this territory, & a large majority of his countrymen wishing it, he feels it his duty to let the action of Congress take its course & not "baffle it with Presidential vetoes." I say, may not this be his reasoning? Has he given us of the South any cause, save the fact of his being a slave holder, to think he would veto a Wilmot proviso law? All that he has said, is *against* us. I see Mr. [John] Bell [Senator from Tenn.], one of his warmest supporters, though from the South & a slave holder, admits Congress has the right to pass such a law. His Whig supporters at the North, & in Congress, almost all admit this right. Why should we think Gen[era]l Taylor differs from them? These Congress Whig friends have lately shown their hands by the vote on the Compromise bill & on the Oregon bill. *There* they are for Gen[era]l Taylor, but *against the South.* The Democratic part of the House voted *with* the South; and illustrated the truth of Mr. Jefferson's assertion made years ago, that the democratic party of the North are the natural allies of the South.

All these late movements look singular; and when we look at [Millard] Fil[l]more's position, it shews a belief, on the part of the northern whigs, that, during the ensuing four years, the question may be a close one in the Senate—that it may be a *tie*, and it is all-important to have a Wilmot proviso man at the head of that body. It is idle to suppose the vote in the House will ever be *less* against slavery, than now. That strength is increasing every year. The lower House is *now* safe for their purposes—but the Senate is not. This *may* be however, in four years, and then they rely upon Taylor's not "baffling an act of Congress with Presidential vetoes." He has said that he ought not to interfere with the action of Congress on "domestic" questions; and they count upon his "holding his hand," & letting Congress act untrammelled. And we have no assurance that he will *not* do so on this question. Then let a law of that kind be passed, and if he vetoes it, it requires ⅔ to pass ["it" *interlined*]. This is more than the anti-slavery party can get in 4 years. But if he should *not* veto it, & it becomes a law, no majority will ever be raised against it, & it will never be repealed, even though we should have a President, after Taylor, who might think it odious. *His* action is not required till *Congress* acts; & that will never again be with the South.

Their want of strength in the Senate now keeps them from compromising the question. They avoid it, knowing that in a few years they'll have the strength there too—& then they ask no questions, with Taylor for President.

His warmest friends [John M.] Clayton [Senator from Del.], Bell, [Thomas] Corwin [Senator from Ohio], [John] Davis [Senator from Mass.] et al, are *against* the South here; but Gen[era]l [Lewis] Cass has voted *with* the South & against Corwin, Davis & [John P.] Hale [Senator from N.H.] upon this question. But I do not write, presuming to enlighten the mind of one so conversant with political facts as you are; nor do I write, let me further add, for parading what you might think proper to say, in the public prints; for I do not care to borrow lustre reflected in that way—though I confess I shall be gratified at hearing your views upon the claims of the two candidates, as well as upon any other subject in which, as citizens, we may all feel a common interest. With sentiments of esteem I am, J.T. Trezevant.

ALS in ScCleA; variant PC in Boucher and Brooks, eds., *Correspondence*, pp. 463–465. NOTE: The "late movement in Charleston" discussed by Trezevant became the subject of much correspondence below. As reported in the Charleston *Mercury* of 7/21 and 7/22 a public meeting of "Charleston Democrats" was held on 7/20 at which an address and resolutions were adopted supporting Taylor for President as the safer candidate for "resolving the important domestic crisis looming." The participants included James Gadsden, Ker Boyce and other friends of Calhoun, and the platform was flanked by busts of Calhoun and Taylor.

From S[YLVESTER] GRAHAM

Northampton Mass., Aug. 17, 1848

Dear Sir, Your favor of the 28th ult. [*not found*] enclosing a pamphlet form of your Speech [of 6/27/1848] on the Oregon Bill, came to hand by due course of mail. Your note has been read and your Speech reread with much interest.

I did not intend to trouble you again so soon; but in further researches in the matter of territorial government, I have fallen upon something which has created doubt in my mind, and induced me to ask your opinion concerning it.

You say in your speech (page 3d) "The Senator from New York [John A. Dix], points to the clause in the Constitution which provides" &c (see the Speech).

On first reading, I had no doubt that your views of the import of the word "*regulations*" were correct: that the clause "referred exclusively to ["the" *canceled*] territory regarded simply as public lands." But, on examining the Journal of the "Old Congress" I find that on "Wednesday September 6th 1780, Congress thought it advisable to press upon the States having claim to the Western Country, a liberal surrender of a portion of their territorial claims." And to induce those States to make such a surrender Congress, on "Tuesday October 10th 1780 fixed conditions to which the Union should be bound on receiving such cessions." (See Journal Monday April 5, 1784). The conditions were as follows,

"*Resolved,* That the unappropriated lands that may be ceded or relinquished to the United States, by any particular State, pursuant to the recommendation of Congress, of the sixth of September last, shall be disposed of for the common benefit of the United States, and be settled and formed into distinct republican States, which shall become members of the federal union, and have the same rights of sovereignty, freedom and independence as the other States. That the said lands shall be granted or settled at such times and under such regulations as shall hereafter be agreed on by the United States in Congress assembled, or any nine or more of them."

The conditions, then, "fixed" by Congress, on which the unappropriated lands were to be ceded to the United States were First: that the lands should be disposed of for the common benefit of the United States: Second, that they should be settled and formed into distinct Republican States which should become members of the federal union, and have the same rights of sovereignty, freedom and independence as the other States: and Third; that the said lands should be granted or settled at such times and under such *regulations* as should thereafter be agreed on by the United States in Congress assembled, or any nine or more ["of them" *interlined*].

Now then, the question is, not whethere [*sic*] those conditions did, or did not give Congress the legitimate power and right to prohibit Slavery in the territories; but whether the word "*regulations,*" in the third condition, does not relate to something more than "territory regarded simply as public lands"? Does it not relate to the granting, the *settling* and the *settlements* of the territories? Does not the condition give to Congress the power and right to establish regulations under which the lands shall be granted, and regulations under which they shall be settled; and regulations under which the settlements shall exist till they become "distinct republican States as members of the federal union, having the same rights of sovereignty, freedom and independence as the other States"? and did not the framers of our National Constitution, employ the word *"regulations"*—in the clause in question—in the same extended and comprehensive signification?

I pray you Sir, in considering this question, do not let the fear of consequences deter you from any conclusions to which the honest reasonings of your mind naturally lead you. For if you grant that the clause in question, does comprehend, in its true import, the government of the settlers of the territories, you have still valid grounds on which to establish your denial of the legitimate power and right of Congress to abolish or prohibit slavery in the territories.

You say in your postscript, "If an opportunity offers I will present my views of Slavery (African, as it exists among us) at large. Truth is my object and I am willing to follow its lead wherever it goes."

Sir though I regard you as having one of the best constituted minds among all our politicians, yet I should feel little respect for you, if I did not believe you to have a sincere regard for truth. It is because I believe you act according to your convictions, that, even when I cannot agree with you in opinion, I still respect your sincerity. But I know man. I know his springs of action. I know the laws by which conditions, circumstances and influences affect his springs of action and shape his opinions and determine his conduct. I can therefore regard man with sincere benevolence, even while I abhor the objects and results of his action. However sincerely you may be disposed to follow truth, the condition and circumstances of your complex nature are such, that, it is hardly possible for you to have perceptions of truth in relation to slavery, without those refractions of its light, which will, to some extent, give you erroneous impressions and lead you to erroneous conclusions. Still, I sincerely hope that an opportunity will offer, and that you will embrace it, to give your views of Slavery in full. I speak the more freely to you on this subject, because I am not one of our Northern Abolitionists. I differ from them widely in many respects, yet no man is more thoroughly *antislavery* than I am: and I regard as not one of the least of the evils of Slavery in these United States, the effect which it has on the political destiny of such men as yourself and Henry Clay.

In respect to what you say concerning the impracticableness of my presidential project, I would reason with you more at large could it be of any avail. But—"It is too late!" I say it with sorrow of heart—*It is too late*! Neither yourself nor Henry Clay nor Daniel Webster can ever be president of these United States. "Available men"—men of no political character—men of no known political capacity—

party subservients—tools—these are the materials out of which we must make presidents; while men whom nature ordained to this high destination, defeat themselves in defeating each other, and, in a great measure, waste in these efforts for mutual defeat, those energies which God gave them for the noblest services of their country. My dear Sir, you may deem my speech too free, but it gushes out from a heart full to aching.

Will you place confidence enough in me to tell me frankly what you think of General [Zachary] Taylor as a candidate for the presidency? Is he, in reality of any fixed political complexion? or is he a political chameleon? Have the South confidence in him as a whig? or only as a southern man with southern interests and sympathies? Do you not tremble at the ["popular" *interlined*] madness which selects a briefly and narrowly successful military chiefta[i]n for the supreme Magistrate of this great nation, and chains to the wheels of his triumphal car, the most learned civilians and ablest Statesmen in the land? I ask not these questions for sinister purposes, nor in idle curiosity, nor as a party politician; but as a political philosopher, who, in the retirement of his own study, wishes to mature his mind into the wisdom of a political sage. With profound respect Yours truly, S. Graham.

ALS in ScCleA; PC in Boucher and Brooks, eds., *Correspondence*, pp. 465–468.

From Ro[bert] J. Lackey

Heathsville [Va.,] August 18, [18]48

Dear Sir, I introduce myself to your honorable and distinguished self as Robert J. Lackey a young man fresh from the venerable walls of William & Mary College, but ardent in the cause of his country.

Of you, as a gentleman and a politician (or more properly statesman) I have thought most highly since first *reason* and *judgment* were planted in my brain. This is an important crisis in the history of our country and I regard you as *the man*, so permit me to ask, what course you will adopt in reference to the coming presidential election. Will you give your mighty efforts to the cause of Gen. [Lewis] Cass? Will the south be safe if Gen. [Zachary] Taylor be elected and there be a Whig majority in the House and a tie in the Senate? Would you advise a *conservative* Democrat to support the nominees of the Philadelphia [Whig] convention? Do you subscribe to the "Baltimore [Democratic] resolutions" and think they express the *true principles* upon which our Government should be administered?

My dear Sir I hope and trust that you'll pardon the *liberty* I have taken in addressing you this letter and propounding to you the above interrogatories—attribute it to the *right* cause.

I love you because of your personal character. I admire you because of your independence. I respect you because of your ability—and if Heaven would grant it I'd ask no richer boon than the head and heart of John C. Calhoun and no higher glory than to follow his distinguished course.

I hope you can reconcile it with yourself to respond to this letter—and with many apologies I subscribe myself Most respectfully Yours &c, Ro. J. Lackey.

[P.S.] Address Ro. J. Lackey, Heathsville, Northumberland Co[unty], Virginia. Any Document or paper that in your opinion might be of advantage to my humble self would be most gratefully received. R.J.L.

ALS in ScCleA.

From H[ENRY] W. CONNER

Charleston, Aug[us]t 19, 1848

My Dear Sir, As recommended in Nov. last we have done nothing further in the matter of the news paper at Washington but have quietly waited your directions.

It seems requisite however now that something should be said to the subscribers to the project.

I have rarely seen a more liberal or patriotic spirit manifested on any occasion than in the efforts amongst the people of this State to establish that paper & with a view to keep up that spirit for other occasions & to pay a proper respect to the party subscribing I would be glad to be put in possession of your views & wishes on the subject that I might as chairman of the Committee communicate it to the parties interested & I shall feel greatly obliged by your early reply. Very Respectfully Y[ou]rs &C, H.W. Conner.

ALS in ScCleA. NOTE: This letter was addressed to Calhoun as "Present" in Charleston.

From JA[ME]S GADSDEN

Charleston So. C., 19 Aug. [18]48

My Dear Sir, At the particular request of several friends, I enclose you 4 letters [*not found*] from General [Zachary] Taylor for your perusal.

The explanation which he gives of what may be called the Sanders' committal, will shew how it was brought about by a confidence in neighbours & friends, who might have considered, that the right to withdraw General Taylor's name from the Canvass was not irreconcilable with his position, that if the W[h]igs did take him they must take him *without pledges* of any kind. Such seems to have been Taylor's construction of the authority he gave Sanders & as Sanders acted under authority surely Taylor was bound in honor to admit [*one or two words changed to* "it"] and to abide the consequences. It does seem to me, too much has been made of ["an" *changed to* "a"] matter which does not affect Taylor's relations otherwise to the W[h]igs or the People. That he would not accept of a nomination upon any Platform, & that the W[h]igs so understand it, we have the authority of [John M.] Clayton [Senator from Del.] & others. But it is not my purpose to explain away this mistake, of too much confidence in friends, but simply to shew you letters which reiterate his *Independent Position* & leave you to your own judgement as to the Course to be pursued, at such a Crisis. You will find yourself in error as ["to" *interlined*] neutrality. The State are not prepared for it—and *will not receive it.* Your assuming it, with [Andrew P.] Butler [Senator from S.C.] & others will only distract us the more & leave the Combattants in the field, without the Leaders who formerly controlled harmony. Your taking your stand will produce a rally. If you decide for [Lewis] *Cass*—you ["may" *canceled, one illegible word and* "will" *interlined and then canceled, and* "will" *interlined*] carry the State, but only with a majority. But if you yield to Taylor as the safest man the Cass men will come in, and the State will present that *unanimity* which you deem so important. The ["objects" *canceled and* "objections" *interlined*] to Cass with a large party, (and your humble servant among the number) is too deep set to be reconciled to him. We *cannot*, we *will not* go—on the contrary those who affect to go for ["Taylor are only" *and a partial word canceled*] Cass are influenced *altogether* by *party ties.* Ties which have been violated by the North, & which we have ourselves repudiated. May I beg you to reflect deeply before you distract and divide us[?] Neutrality on your part will distract. A declaration for Cass as the least of evils will divide us. A yielding to Taylor as the safest man, as one of us, as with us—identified in interests & sympathies will unite the State, as formerly, in one solid falanx.

Read the letters to Butler & [Armistead] Burt [Representative from S.C.] and return them to me tonight. I will be at the Theatre. Yours truly, Jas. Gadsden.

[P.S.] I consider neutrality out of the question. By neutrality I mean throwing away our vote. It may be too late to take up one on whom we could all unite. If the contest therefore is narrowed to Taylor & Cass—Reflect on the policy of ["taking up" *interlined*] him who is not of the South & rallying on a friend & neighbour.

ALS in ScCleA; variant PC in Boucher and Brooks, eds., *Correspondence*, pp. 468–469. Note: Gadsden's discussion of "the Sanders' committal" refers to an ambiguous incident that had occurred at the Whig national convention. Judge Lafayette Saunders was a member of the La. delegation and an old friend of Taylor. There was controversy over what conditions Saunders had made in Taylor's name during a secret night meeting of delegates. Saunders had died not long after the convention.

Remarks at a Public Meeting in Charleston

[August 19, 1848]

[*In Charleston on their way home from Washington, Calhoun, Senator Andrew P. Butler, and Representative Armistead Burt were invited to address a public meeting at "the Theatre." After Butler and Burt spoke, Calhoun addressed a cheering, overflow crowd.*]

Mr. Calhoun said that his colleagues had so fully detailed the proceedings in Congress upon the questions involving the rights of the South, that he would confine himself to what he conceived to be the more immediate object of the meeting—the question of the Presidency. His attention had been early and earnestly directed to this matter, and the conclusion he had arrived at was that the proper policy of the State was to stand aloof from the contest, and in this sentiment he had the concurrence of all his colleagues of the South Carolina Delegation in Congress, with perhaps but one exception. There were several reasons for this determination—among them may be mentioned that neither of the candidates comes up to our requirements of principles or policy; and by entering into an active and heated political contest, each party abusing the candidate of their opponents and praising their own as exemplars of perfection, the State would be degraded to the level which they occupied. He had never doubted but that when the time came the State would cast her vote; but let us cast it without heat, without excitement, and in the direction which the safety and dignity of the State requires that it should be cast. As to the respective candidates, many gave the preference to Gen. [Zachary] Taylor because he was a Planter and a Southern man; others again preferred Gen. [Lewis] Cass because he was a member of the party with which they usually act. These preferences were natural and allowable, if the division to which they led were conducted without asperity or bitterness; but they would be most mischievous if their effect was to divide us at this crisis, when harmony and union among ourselves was more than ever desirable. Since I addressed you last in this place a great change has taken place in the position of parties at the North. The Abolition party, which was then a mere handful, has now grown to be a mighty party; a party above and beyond the Presidency, a party that has cast aside both the candidates of the old parties and nominated as the representative of their free soil principles Mr. [Martin] Van Buren, who was formerly the President of the United States. Such a man would never have consented to be placed in that position unless he was convinced there was a firm foundation for the movement, and saw that the North had determined to rally on this great question of sectional supremacy. He referred to the action of the Senate on the Oregon bill, and lamentable as was the defeat of the South on that question, it was still more lamentable that it was accomplished by the votes of two Southern Senators. He would name them. They should be known and deserved to be held in reprobation by every Southern man. They were Col. [Thomas H.] Benton, of Missouri, and Gen. [Samuel] Houston, of Texas. Had they stood true to the South, the bill would have been defeated. With these exceptions, the Southern men had stood side by side and shoulder to shoulder. And in this a most gratifying contrast was presented with the condition of things existing at the commencement of the session. At that time not a corporal's guard could be got together to act harmoniously. He had never witnessed so much distraction. But at the close of an arduous session, and after one of the ablest debates which he had ever witnessed, and in which the South was completely victorious, the entire South, with the exceptions above named, stood shoulder to shoulder, manfully battling for their rights.

The action of the North in inserting the Wilmot Proviso into the Oregon bill was a mere wanton assertion of power. It was universally admitted that the climate and soil of Oregon unfitted it for a slave population, but the North determined upon the assertion of the right to exclude slavery from the Territories of the Union, without conditions or restrictions. It was the first time it was so applied, and the determination is manifest so to apply it hereafter in all cases—even in Cuba, should that Island ever be annexed to our Union. In the old Confederation the Ordinance for the government of the Northwestern Territory was proposed for three years, and was only adopted then when the restitution of fugitive slaves to their owners was coupled with it as a condition. The Missouri Compromise was proposed by the North, who urged it on Congress, and sacrificed every Northern man who voted against it. But a great change has been effected in the North since that period. As they have grown in power they have increased in their exactions, and at last have boldly avowed their determination to arrest the further progress of the Slave States, by excluding them unconditionally hereafter from all the Territories of the Union.

With such a struggle at hand, how important is it that the South should be prepared to meet it with a united front. Diversities of opinion are entertained upon the subject of the Presidency. Gen. Taylor is preferred by some; Gen. Cass by others. All are equally sincere, and all, in his opinion, were equally Republicans. He did not ask that they should throw away their vote, or arrest the canvass. Things had gone too far for that. But he implored them, as Carolinians, to conduct the canvass with moderation and with kindly feelings toward each other. Do not permit the discussion so to divide or estrange you from each other as that you cannot be reconciled immediately after its termination. The time is coming when your united energies will be demanded for the struggle. At the next session of Congress the contest will be renewed for California, New Mexico, and the terrritory between the Nueces and the Rio Grande—for the North claims all that. If worsted in that struggle, as there is great probability we will be, we have nothing to hope or expect from the Federal Government. He had watched this question of Abolition for years, and from the beginning had predicted the result. There are in the body politic, as in the human system, diseases which, if not promptly arrested, become incurable and eventually fatal; and it was his opinion from the first that Abolition, if strong and decided measures were not taken to check it, would run its course, and in its progress destroy the Union and the institutions of the country. In his opinion, whichever party at the North was defeated in the Presidential election would go over to the Barnburners. With such an addition to their forces, the party will be most powerful. For defence against its policy and purposes we must rely upon ourselves alone. Hence the necessity of union, of harmony. Do not permit any mere temporary question to estrange or divide you. Remember that the Carolinian who is farthest from you in opinion is nearer to you than any Northern man of either party. If the South is united, there is yet hope of saving the Union. We can rally a great Southern Republican party, based on principles above the mere making of Presidents; and with such a party we can command our terms and control the North. So long as the South permits any candidate who claims her support to tamper with the Abolitionists for their votes, her influence will be lost, and her rights disregarded. By rallying a great Southern party that will support no man not pledged to the maintenance of the rights of the South and the guarantees of the Constitution, a party will be formed in the North who will co-operate with us. But if this fails to arrest the spirit of aggression now so manifest, and the alternative is forced upon us of resistance or submission, who can doubt the result. Though the Union is dear to us, our honor and our liberty are dearer. And we would be abundantly able to maintain ourselves. The North is rich and powerful, but she has many elements of division and weakness—Fourierites—the vote yourself a farm men—the strife of labor with capital—a spirit of anarchy and misrule already developed, which sooner or later will end in her overthrow. The South, on the contrary, has a homogeneous population, and a common bond of union, which would render us powerful and united. Wherever Southern men have been placed upon the battle field, from the closing event of our Revolutionary war down to the entrance of our army into the city of Mexico, they have shown themselves in generalship and soldiership at least equal to those of any other section of the Union. Our Custom Houses would afford us a revenue ample for every purpose, almost as great in amount as that now collected by the Federal Government. The South now exports to the Northern States more than all the exports of the North to foreign countries, and it is a well established principle that the imports of a community are based upon its exports, and that they nearly equal each other. In whatever aspect then we consider it, we will be as well prepared for the struggle as the North. He did not court it, but he would not shun it; and as old as he was, he was willing to go through his share of the contest.

From the Charleston, S.C., *Mercury*, August 21, 1848, p. 2. Also printed in the Richmond, Va., *Enquirer*, August 25, 1848, p. 2; the Washington, D.C., *Daily Union*, August 25, 1848, p. 3 (part); the New York, N.Y., *Herald*, August 26, 1848, p. 1; the Boston, Mass., *Daily Advertiser*, August 28, 1848, p. 2; the Camden, S.C., *Journal*, August 30, 1848, p. 2; the Columbia, S.C., *South-Carolinian*, September 1, 1848, pp. 1–2; the *National Era*, vol. II, no. 88 (September 7, 1848), p. 143; the Greenville, S.C., *Mountaineer*, September 8, 1848, p. 1. Variant in the Charleston, S.C., *Courier*, August 21, 1848, p. 2; the Columbia, S.C., *Daily Telegraph*, August 22, 1848, p. 3; the Washington, D.C., *Daily National Intelligencer*, August 28, 1848, p. 4. Another variant in the Charleston, S.C., *Courier*, August 24, 1848, p. 2. Note: In the *Courier* of August 25, 1848, p. 2, is a brief discussion by a reporter, "T.M.H.," of two minor textual differences in the reporting of Calhoun's speech. According to this reporter Calhoun had referred to Southerners rather than Carolinians as being closer to his audience than Northerners.

From John Heart

Charleston, Aug. 22 '48

My Dear Sir, Before this you will have looked over my report [for the *Mercury*] of your remarks on Saturday night last [8/19/1848]. No one is more convinced of its imperfections than myself, but the notes were taken at a great inconvenience, amid the pressure of a crowd and written on the top of my hat. In writing them out, however, I endeavored to preserve the spirit and tone of your remarks, and shall be most happy if they meet your approval. If you could find time to use them as notes and write out your speech in full, we should publish it with great pleasure.

The Democratic meeting last evening was for a great portion of the time a scene of perfect tumult. At length, while Mr. [Isaac W.] Hayne was speaking a glass lamp was thrown on the stage, and the indignant and withering rebuke with which he met the outrage seemed to recal[l] the rioters to a sense of propriety, and the proceedings went on to their termination without interruption. With sentiments of the highest respect believe me your friend & serv[an]t, Jno. Heart.

ALS in ScCleA.

From John W. Gordon and Others

Milledgeville Ga., August 25th 1848

Dear Sir, The Hon. H[erschel] V. Johnson [Senator from Ga.] has accepted an invitation to dine with his Democratic fellow-citizens of this city and its vicinity on thursday the 7th of September next. This compliment tendered to him, is equally due to his associates in the Senate who stood by the South in the contest there waged against her. It would afford us great pleasure, if you could be present with us on that festive occasion. Your invaluable services on the compromise bill, are duly appreciated by many of your fellow-citizens in Georgia. We respectfully ask that you will be present with us on the 7th of September. Respectfully, [Signed in one handwriting:] John W. Gordon, Richard Rowell, John W.A. Sanford, Sam[ue]l Buffington, Jr., Isaac Newell, Green H. Jordan, M.D. Huson, Alex[ande]r Jarratt, Committee.

LS in ScCleA. Note: An AEU by Calhoun reads "Invitation to MilledgeVille."

From H[erschel] V. Johnson, [Senator from Ga.], "(Private)"

Milledgeville [Ga.,] Aug. 25th 1848

My Dear Sir, The mail which carries this will also carry to you a letter of invitation to a public dinner which my fellow citizens have been kind enough to tender to me as a compliment to my course in the Senate of United States. Fearing that the distance is so great that you will not be able to attend, I take the liberty of suggesting to you, that, in the event of your not honoring us with your personal presence, it is exceedingly desirable by the committee to obtain from you a strong letter ["in" *canceled and* "on" *interlined*] the Compromise Bill reported by the Committee of eight. The course of Mr. [Alexander H.] Stephens, the representative of this District, has produced, not only here but throughout the State, considerable excitement. I enclose to you also a copy of his speech, by which you will see the grounds on which he has placed his defence and on which his party sustain his course. He has been unanimously nominated for re-election by a District Convention. He has also published a letter in the Southern Recorder, in reply to strictures which have therein appeared on his course, in which he indirectly assails all those who voted for the Bill. All this presents this bill distinctly as the issue upon ["which" *interlined*] the contest in this District is to be waged. It is believed that a strong letter from you in vindication of the Bill and in reply to the grounds assumed by its opponents will be of much service to us in Georgia; that it will go far to unite our people upon the principles upon [which] the rights of the South ought to be maintained.

Your position on the Presidential ["question" *interlined*] is well understood. It is therefore not the object of the Committee of invitation, to draw any thing from [you] upon this subject. All they desire is a letter on the Compromise bill, without any direct allusion to Mr. Stephens or others except so far as may be suggested by your own sense of propriety.

It affords me pleasure to say, that thus far, I meet with warm greetings from my friends for the part I have taken upon the absorbing question of slavery. With very sincere regard I remain y[ou]r ob[edien]t s[er]v[an]t, H.V. Johnson.

ALS in ScCleA; variant PC in Boucher and Brooks, eds., *Correspondence*, p. 470.

From Wilson Lumpkin, [former Senator from Ga.]

Athens [Ga.,] Aug[us]t 25th 1848

My dear Sir, Under the impression that you are now quietly at home, & left to calm reflection, on the extraordinary state of the world, & especially on the portentious state of affairs in our own Country, I again resume my pen, with a view to a renewal of our correspondence. Your public position has afforded me from time to time, your views on the most vital subject, connected with our national existence. My own opinions most fully coincide with yours, on every important point connected with the subject of Negroe slavery. I did ["not" *interlined*] anticipate the events, which are so rapidly hastening a final issue upon the slave question. The sectional party now consolidating its ranks, under the lead of [Martin] Van Buren & his associates, demonstrates beyond all doubt, that the argument ["of" *canceled and* "on" *interlined*] our constitutional rights upon the slave question, *is ex[h]austed.* We have to *stand by our arms*, or yield every thing, & become more degraded than our slaves. It is true, those designing & base men, who are governing the great masses of fanatics, could yet save the Country. But this they do not desire. They are under the influence of feelings of hate & revenge, they are resolved upon, *reign or ruin.*

If there be any salvation for our Union, it is in the South. If we of the slave States were a united people, we could "Conquer a peace." "Indemnity for the past, & security for the future."

But alas! a house divided against itself cannot stand. The corrupt press & office seekers of the South, are daily becoming more & more reckless, & bold in ["their" *canceled*] the prosecution of their selfish plans & objects. They are ready to sacrifice the last hope of the perpetuation of our good system of Government, upon the alter of combinations of office seekers who do not deserve the name of belonging to political parties, based upon principles of any sort. Coming events may possibly unite the South, but I fear not. When I consider the position of such men, as [Thomas H.] Benton, [Henry] Clay, [John] Bell & thousands of their inferior followers—how can I hope, to see our people United? We have thousands & tens of thousands, throughout the Southern States, whose sympathies are all against us. Look at our little *pigmy* Stevens [*sic*; Representative Alexander H. Stephens] from Georgia, & his Southern associates on the compromise Bill. Like Van Buren, they can only hope for the distinction of infamy, but they prefer that to obscurity.

If I vote at all at the coming election, I shall of course vote for [Lewis] Cass & [William O.] Butler, but I see just as clearly as you do, how little we have to expect or hope for, from any political combination, under all the existing influences & circumstances. If you see any way by which we might hope to unite the South, do suggest it, for I repeat, this is the only hope to save the Union. Shall we stand still, till we see the result of the fall Elections? Or what shall we do?

Let me hear from you soon and believe me as Ever y[ou]rs, Wilson Lumpkin.

ALS in ScCleA; variant PC in Boucher and Brooks, eds., *Correspondence*, p. 471. NOTE: This letter was postmarked in Athens on 8/24 [*sic*].

From RICHARD RUSH, [U.S. Minister to France]

Paris, August 25, 1848
63 Rue de Lille

My dear Sir, I should owe you my thanks for only your letter introducing the Izards and Hugers, (and it is not for the first time that you have made me acquainted with agreeable Carolinians since I have been here,) but having received at about the same time a copy of your speech on the Oregon bill in the Senate on the 27["th" *canceled*] of June, I must, most especially, thank you for that also. I have read it with the greatest interest, finding it replete with instruction. For myself, having long seen much to excuse in our system of slavery, and regarding it less and less as an unmixed evil, the more I see of Europe, your discussion has awakened anxious thoughts in me. I did not think the danger from the question as great as I begin to fear it may be from all you say. May Heaven avert from us the calamity of ["the" *canceled*] the breaking-up of our Union from this cause. I cannot yet believe it. Those who would think it a ["lesser"(?) *canceled and* "less" *interlined*] calamity than the existence of slavery in our new States if the people themselves choose to have that system, are in my opinion under terrible delusions.

The state of things here, is enough to baffle all reflection. In what the French Republic is to end, the wisest Frenchmen do not know. For France, the future is nothing but uncertainty. For Europe, there are perhaps more persons just now who think that things will end unfavorably to democratic forms, rather than in setting them up; though monarchies may be made more free and liberal by all that has been happening in France and elsewhere, within the present memorable year.

Thanking you again for your speech, I remain my dear Sir, in all the renewed assurances of esteem and respect, very faithfully yours, Richard Rush.

ALS in ScCleA (published microfilm of The Letters and Papers of Richard Rush, reel 21); PEx in Boucher and Brooks, eds., *Correspondence*, pp. 469–470.

From C[ALEB] CUSHING, "Private"

Newburyport [Mass.,] August 26th 1848

My dear Sir: The recent proceedings at Charleston, and the direction thus given to the political action of the State of South Carolina, embolden me to execute a purpose previously entertained, that of addressing you on the subject of the presidential election.

You will see by the speech of which I enclose a copy [*not found*], and especially by the part of it beginning at the place marked by me, that I am among those at the North who struggle for the application of just principles to the common relations of the North and South. I mention this in order to justify what I am about to say.

Parties at the North are now assuming distinctness and organisation, on the basis of one or the other of the three great Conventions of Baltimore, Philadelphia and Buffalo. Of the latter it is unnecessary to speak. As between the other two, I entertain a strong belief that it is for the interest of the South to support the nomination of the Baltimore [Democratic] Convention. The friends of that nomination at the North have assumed the grounds of equal justice to the South in the action of the Federal Government; and they alone are doing this as a party, with frankness and decision. Is it not important, then, that they should be assured of the cooperation of the South? If the Southern Democrats break away from the Baltimore nomination, will not the affect be to dishearten and disperse their best friends at the North? So it seems to me; and therefore the decision of the Charleston meeting, in favor of Gen[era]l [Lewis] Cass, gave me very great pleasure. I can assure you that the Buffalo Convention has quite neutralised the effects of the Utica Convention. Mr. [Martin] Van Buren is now regarded as the ally and agent of the Abolitionists. That is to say, the Buffalo Convention has opened the eyes of men to the true tendency & character of the Utica Convention: so that, beyond the State of New York, the democratic party is becoming reunited, instead of being further divided, by the Buffalo Convention. I have the honor to be Very respectfully & truly Your friend & s[er]v[an]t, C. Cushing.

ALS in ScCleA; PC in Jameson, ed., *Correspondence*, pp. 1181–1182. NOTE: An AEU by Calhoun reads "Gen[era]l Cushing." In a speech at Newburyport on 7/25 Cushing denied the right of Congress to exclude slavery from the Territories and deplored the effort to do so as dangerous to the Union.

From JOS[EPH] J. SINGLETON

Dahlonega [Ga.,] 27 Aug. 1848

My Dear Sir, I duly rec[eive]d yours of the 15th Inst. [*not found*] and at my earliest convenience I have attended as far as I could for the present to your request; I visited your Obarr Mine with the view of assertaining the disposition of your Lessees with regard to an abandonment of their Lease. I could not as I expected arrive at any thing conclusive on account of the absence of the two orriginal Lessees [John] Pasco[e] & [John] Hockanoll, both of whom live some 20 to 30 odd miles from this place. I have writ[t]en to them, expressing my desire to see them on business relating to their Lease; I expect to see them in a few days, immediately after which I will write you again, and by which I shall be better prepared to give you their determination with regard to the continuation of said Lease. They cannot be forced to abandon their Lease short of a troublesome lawsuit, should they be disposed to hold on to it. Should it continue desireable with you to lift their Lease, the best plan in my opinion will be to urge a strict compliance on their part with the terms of the Lease under the penalties of the law, or its immediate abandonment, and this without their knowing any thing of your contemplated sale, lest they might [*one word canceled*] seek an advantage on that account. I think they will prefer the lat[t]er proposition; if so, I shall acceed to it, unless I am otherways instructed by you, at least this is the plan I have marked out to myself when I see them.

They have not employed the necessary means as yet, to develop the full resources of your mine as required by their Lease, and which was your object no doubt in granting the Lease, which will be the ground I shall take when I see them. They have erected no machinery, employed no capital of consequence, nor have they given that personal attention which was expected by you on giving them the preference at reduced terms to that which you had been offered.

They took into copartnership another individual who has had the management of the concern in a small way ever since the commencement of the Lease. He has done his best no doubt, and has acted honestly I am equally certain, and who is now nearly ready to make another small Deposite in the Mint. On reference to my book I find subject to your order $55.03; in a short time I presume there will be more added.

Tomorrow week our superior court sits, when I anticipate some interesting scenes between political combatants, some for [Zachary] Taylor, some for [Lewis] Cass, some for [Martin] Van Buren, none agree. Ask a Whig which he would prefer Cass or Van Buren. The reply is invariably Van Buren. Ask a Democrat which he would prefer Taylor or Van Buren and the reply is just as certain to be Van Buren. Now if you feel much interest in the contest, you will have it ["in" *interlined*] your power to do much good by coming over, even, if upon a mere visit ["upon" *canceled and* "of" *interlined*] business, as I hope you will, before long, as promised. I have the honour of being yours very Respectfully, Jos. J. Singleton.

ALS in ScU-SC, John C. Calhoun Papers.

From THO[MA]S Y. SIMONS

Charleston, Aug. 28th 1848

Dear Sir, I feel in addressing you this letter & asking your Consideration of the Report, adopted by our State Medical Convention—that I am somewhat intruding ["fro" *canceled*] upon that retirement from great intellectual efforts—which has been the admiration & profound respect ["not only" *interlined*] of all good men in our Country irrespective of party—but of the Civiliz'd World. But knowing as all in our Common Country do, that ["in" *canceled and* "with" *interlined*] you *Self* is never consider'd ["but" *canceled*] when ["good whether in private or public is consider'd" *canceled and* "the welfare of a community or your country is concern'd" *interlined*] May I then ask your Serious Consideration of the Report Sent. The principles of which are So admirably & practically carried out in many portions of Europe for the promotion of the Cause of humanity & which I firmly & Conscientiously believe—carried out with us in the respective States, would tend to great & important blessings morally[,] intellectually & physically—& Such as you will perceive is the opinion of the Combined wisdom & experience of the medical gentlemen of the U. States as expressed in Convention.

The great difficulty in a government like ours—absorb'd So much in political Considerations is to get them to a Calm Survey of Subjects promotive of Hygiene, or as I may properly express it Medical philanthropy—Promote the health ["morally" *canceled*] physical & moral of a people & ["in any(?)" *canceled and* "a" *interlined*] community—& we will find[?] progressive prosperity & happiness the result. Medical men in Europe & America believe this can be done by the plans propos'd ["viz" *canceled*] To Have a proper register of ["Birtth" *canceled*] Births[,] Marriages & Deaths—& proper metereological observations which would [*word missing*] proper Statistics of the real condition [of] different portions of the Country—& the means of correcting existing evils & creating good So far as Health ["in" *canceled*] is concern'd. I have experienc'd its great good in

Charleston—& if in your leisure hours you Could advance the Cause of your Medical Constituents it would add another to the many Causes of respect to one who has been identified with all that is noble & good to his whole Country & Carolina in particular. With high respect I am dear Sir your obed[ien]t S[er]v[an]t, Thos. Y. Simons, M.D.

ALS with En in ScCleA. NOTE: Simons enclosed the *Report of the Committee on the Registration of Births, Marriages and Deaths, to the Medical Convention of South-Carolina, Held in Charleston, in February, 1848* (n.p., n.d.), a 12-pp. pamphlet, which endorsed legislation for the registration of vital statistics.

From JULIUS N. GRANGER

Manchester Center, Ontario County, N.Y.
[*ca.* August 1848]

Respected Sir, Having learned by the papers that you have recently delivered a Speech on the Oregon question in the Senate [on 6/27], I feel an anxiety to read it, that I cannot well describe to you; I have long been in the habit of considering your views on great questions affecting our national interests as entitled to more reliance than any of the great compeers of your day: Therefore, not expecting to obtain a perusal of your views of the question, from any means within my immediate reach, I would respectfully ask the favor of you to send me a copy of the same. Yours with great Respect, Julius N. Granger.

ALS in ScCleA. NOTE: An AEU by Calhoun reads, "Mr. Granger."

To [JOHN HEART, Charleston, S.C., *Mercury*]

Fort Hill, September 1, 1848

My Dear Sir: Your report of my remarks, considering the circumstances under which it was made, was as good as could be expected.

It will not be possible for me to write out my remarks in full, as you desire. I find my engagements, during the short interval until the next session, are such as will fully engross all my time, and leave me no leisure for relaxation, which I greatly need and desire. Among others, I have a speech [of 8/12/1848] to write out from notes I brought with me from Washington, which will, in part, embrace the views I took in that I delivered in Charleston.

There is, I think, but little excitement as to the Presidential question in this quarter. I fear it is not the case with you. I see, after all the pains I have taken to be distinctly understood as to my position, I have not escaped misconstruction; which I attribute to party zeal. If my friends, on both sides, would regard me as taking no part between the two candidates, and as standing on independent ground, ready to support or oppose the successful, as his measures may or may not accord with the principles and views of policy which have long governed me, they would avoid all misapprehension. I see too much to condemn and little to approve in either candidate. Yours truly, J.C. Calhoun.

PC in the Charleston, S.C., *Mercury*, September 5, 1848, p. 2; PC in the Columbia, S.C., *Daily Telegraph*, September 6, 1848, p. 2; PC in the Columbia, S.C., *South-Carolinian*, September 8, 1848, p. 1; PC in the Petersburg, Va., *Republican*, September 8, 1848, p. 2; PC in the Richmond, Va., *Enquirer*, September 8, 1848, p. 2; PC in the New York, N.Y., *Herald*, September 11, 1848, p. 3; PC in the Alexandria, Va., *Gazette and Virginia Advertiser*, September 12, 1848, p. 2; PC in the Boston, Mass., *Daily Advertiser*, September 13, 1848, p. 2; PC in the New Orleans, La., *Daily Picayune*, September 13, 1848, p. 2; PC in the Athens, Ga., *Southern Banner*, September 14, 1848, p. 1; PC in the Philadelphia, Pa., *Pennsylvania Freeman*, September 14, 1848, p. 3; PC in the Greenville, S.C., *Mountaineer*, September 15, 1848, p. 1; PC in the Jackson, Miss., *Mississippian*, September 22, 1848, p. 2; PC in the Tuscaloosa, Ala., *Independent Monitor*, September 22, 1848, p. 2; PC in *Niles' National Register*, vol. LXXIV, no. 1916 (October 18, 1848), p. 247; PEx in *The Liberator*, vol. [XVIII, no. 38] (September 22, [1848]), p. 150. Note: The *Mercury*, in publishing this letter, commented that Calhoun "defines his position so explicitly, as to leave no possible chance for opposing parties to draw conflicting conclusions. It is the position which we had supposed and maintained to be his real one, and it is the one of all others which we prefer to see him occupy."

To Wilson Lumpkin, [Athens, Ga.]

Fort Hill, 1st Sept. 1848

My dear Sir, Your opinions so entirely accord with mine, that I would but repeat yours, should I attempt to give mine, on the various subjects touched on in your last. The argument is, indeed, exhausted. The question between North & South is now acknowledged by the former to be a mere question of power. The pretex[t] of bettering the condition of the Slave is laid asside. The only alternative left us is, shall we resist, or surrender, & thereby in fact change conditions with our Slaves.

Our condition is hopeless, unless we should become far more United than we are at present. With Union, we could certainly save ourselves, and possibly *the Union.* I say possibly, for it is to be doubted, whether the disease has not already progressed too far for that.

You ask me how is Union among ourselves to be brought about? I see but one way; to make manifest our danger & to expose the folly of the two parties in attempting to hold together with their respective Northern associates, when it is manifest, that neither party there can be relied on. A good deal was done towards this end at the last session; and I hope much more may be at the next. Nothing that I see can be done between this & the presidential election, but to moderate, as far as possible, the asperity between the two parties, by showing how little we have to hope from the success of either candidate. What madness to divide among ourselves, when our Union is essential to our safety, & to quarrel about two men, from whom, & their Northern supp[ort]ers, we have so little to expect!

After the election is over, the next & important step, is to adopt such measures as that every Governor of every slave holding State, & and [*sic*] all their Legislatures shall take the highest grounds, in reference to the Slave question; so that their members of Congress shall be assured, they will be backed & sustained at home in a manly discharge of their duty. The rest must be left to them. The session will be a short one, and the great question between North & South will come in issue on all points. If we shall be defeated, as in all probability we shall, nothing will be left, but for the South to meet in convention, & to take our defense into our own hands, and their members of Congress, must move in that. One ought to be called, in the case supposed, if the meeting should be even partial. It would give an impulse. Even an effort would be better than to settle down in hopeless despair.

You have one or two sound papers in your State. One I see frequently, the Macon Telegraph. If you have leisure, two or three strong communications to it from your pen, discussing the vast importance of the present juncture to the South, could not but do much good.

You propose to yourself the proper course as to the Presidential election. As to myself, I stand aloof on independent grounds, ready to support the democratick or whig candidate, which ever may succeed, so long as he goes right, & oppose him when he goes wrong.

With kind regards to Mrs. [Annis Hopkins] L[umpkin] & your family. Yours very truly & sincerely, J.C. Calhoun.

ALS in DLC, John C. Calhoun Papers.

From Cha[rle]s N. Webb

Halifax, N.C., September 1, 1848

My Dear Sir, I have read extracts from a Speech recently made by you to your fellow citizens of South Carolina—from which I am unable to learn who you would like to see President of the United States. You seem to object to all of the Candidates in the field—and one would infer from your speech that you had made up your mind to take no part in the Election.

In the face of this however, it is asserted here, by Democrats—(by what authority I know not) that you will support [Lewis] Cass and [William O.] Butler, and that they will get the vote of your State. Can it be possible that an individual so much wedded to the South, and her institutions as you have ever been, will support a man who in every respect is opposed to her interest—a man who is North in location and North in feelings—a Wilmot Proviso man beyond doubt? I am unwilling to beli[e]ve it.

James K. Polk, has given the Country a stab to its very center, by his signature to the Oregon Bill, with the Wilmot Proviso attached to it. The Northern people hail it as a great triumph, and will hold it up as a precedent for future Legislation. It is said that James K. Polk signed the Bill to advance the interest of Cass at the North. What are we coming to? A Southern President taking sides with the North, and Mr. [Martin] Van Buren, who was elected President on account of his being a "Northern man with Southern feelings," running as the Northern Candidate for the Presidency, is enough to alarm us. It is enough [to] make us have misgivings about almost any and every man's firmness.

Now that the North has organized a Northern party, with Mr. Van Buren at their head, sanctioned by Cass and Polk so far as principle is concerned, what seems to be the duty of Southern men? Is it not their duty to go for that man who is Southern in location and Southern in feeling if one is to be found who is trust-worthy?

In whom sir do you think the South can rely mostly ["in" *canceled*] for the protection and safety of her institutions—General

[Zachary] Taylor or Lewis Cass—one a Southern man—and the other a Northern man? What is your plan for meeting the crisis which is fast approaching between the North and the South which will shake the Union to its very center?

I address you this letter through the best of motives with the hope that you will give me your views for publication. Your friend, Chas. N. Webb, Editor of the "*Roanoke Republican*."

ALS in ScCleA; PC in Boucher and Brooks, eds., *Correspondence*, p. 472. NOTE: No reply has been found, but see below Calhoun's published letter to an unknown person dated 9/9/1848.

From AND[RE]W P[ICKENS] CALHOUN

Tulip Hill [Marengo County, Ala.,] September 2nd/48

My dear Father, I have not written in some time, for we have been going again through the ordeal of the worm, and I disliked to raise unnecessary apprehensions on the subject of the crop. The latter part of July and the first part of August was very wet, and the consequence was the worm made a terrible onslaught upon the cotton—for awhile I never saw them worse. About the middle of August it cleared off, and has been hot and dry—the result is the worm has *entirely dissappeared*, and we can again form a definite idea of our prospects. We will make a *large crop* still, under some contingencies, *a fair one under any*. There are spots in the cotton as fine as I ever saw, and then again others destitute of bolls but filled with squares and blooms. We count upon every bloom making a mature boll to the 15th of this month. If then no accident happens we will make from our worse cotton a heavy *top crop*. Our crop is very forward, and had it not been for the worm we would have made a *bale* to the *acre*. I never took so much pains with a crop, and even in spite of the worm, as I said, we will make an average crop. I sent a bale to market on the 4th of this month. It ranked fair, and sold for 7 cents. We have out now *90 bales*, the largest number I have ever had out at this season. The picking is superb. We are getting at this picking *800* lbs. to the acre. Our fields on the ridges are as white as snow, and the under crop of the stems—where our injury principally lies—is a heavy one. I will make no calculation of what we will make yet awhile for I have had so much experience about these matters that I know the inaccuracy of any prediction based upon appearances at this early period. If the weather is fair I will get out 160 bales this month—my picking is 7 bales a day—many of our hands are getting 300 lbs. every day. We have seen nothing like it since 1845. Well now that we will make some cotton—how stands the prospect for *price*[?] We have just got the Cambrias news, and it seems the Irish rebellion will be easily put down. Should affairs in England settle down peacefully cotton will go to 8 or 10 cents I think for I scarcely think affairs on the continent of Europe will effect to any great extent the cotton market *in the face this year of a short crop.* For altho' I speak favorably of our crop, *the crops generally* are indifferent in this section, and the *Southwest generally*, so far as I have heard. At all events what would you advise, to sell *now* at 6½ cents, or run the hazard of waiting[?]

What is Carolina about that she is arraying herself for a plunge in the presidential canvass[?] She really loses my esteem by supporting [Lewis] Cass—an old force bill man—one who played the sycophant to [Andrew] Jackson when all the purity in the country was ostracized—a didapper politician who nobody could tell where he would come up, but all knew he would come up and *float*, and by this very *duc*tility ["he" *canceled*] he has worked his way to nomination and leadership. And So. Carolina is bowing the cringing knee to such a man. It is well perhaps that the stern times that envelope us, should come, to bring her back to her faith, for the ordeal that is coming must either *make* or *undo* us. Gen[era]l [Zachary] Taylor has made such a granny of himself that I shall not waste powder by saying what I think of him. If your life can only be spared, the time is rapidly coming when you will occupy a position truly sublime. You who have always foreseen, foretold, and tried to avert, the terrible issue, now rushing with electrick speed upon us; you will be looked to as the pillar of fire to guide us thro' the angry elements gathered up on every side, ready to envelope us.

We are *all perfectly* well[,] not a soul complaining on the place, nor has the services of a physician been called upon this year.

I wanted to write upon many matters but my paper is filled. All join in love. Your affectionate son, Andw. P. Calhoun.

ALS in ScU-SC, John C. Calhoun Papers.

To John W. Gordon and Others, [Milledgeville, Ga.]

Fort Hill, (S.C.), 2d Sept., 1848

Gentlemen: I hasten to acknowledge your note of the 25th of last month, (received late last evening,) inviting me to attend a dinner to be given to your Senator, the Hon. H[erschel] V. Johnson, by his political friends of Milledgeville and its vicinity on the 7th inst., in approbation of his conduct during the last session of Congress, on the most vital of all questions to the South, and the Union. I regret to state that the great distance and my engagements compel me to decline the invitation.

The conduct of your Senator well deserves the honor you have tendered him. I was a close observer of his course during the whole of the eventful struggle, maintained by the South, near the close of the session, in defence of her rights and equality in the Union as it relates to the territories belonging to her in common with the North. It was throughout able, patriotic, and faithful to his trust. Always at his post, he stood in the front ranks of her defenders, fearless, eloquent and argumentative.

But in bestowing due praise on your Junior Senator, it would be unjust to withhold what is due to his colleague your Senior Senator [John M. Berrien]. His course too, is deserving all praise on that eventful occasion. They both deserve the approbation not only of their own State but the entire South. Indeed, Georgia may well be proud of the conduct of her Senators throughout that memorable and momentous contest. No State was more ably and faithfully represented, and had every other Southern State been equally so, victory, instead of defeat, would have been inscribed on the banner of the South. With great respect, I am yours, &c. &c., J.C. Calhoun.

PC (from the Savannah, Ga., *Georgian* of unknown date) in the Charleston, S.C., *Mercury*, September 18, 1848, p. 2; PC in the Alexandria, Va., *Gazette and Virginia Advertiser*, September 28, 1848, p. 2. Note: Other members of the committee addressed by Calhoun were Richard Rowell, John W.A. Sanford, Samuel Buffington, Jr., Isaac Newell, Green H. Jordan, M.D. Huson, and Alexander Jarratt. The Savannah *Georgian* reprinted from the Milledgeville, Ga., *Federal Union*. Andrew P. Butler's reply was also published.

From M[ARCUS] C. M. HAMMOND

Near Hamburg [S.C.,] Sept[embe]r 6, 1848

Dear Sir, I regret exceedingly that your time was so limited, on your way home, that I did not have the honor of a visit from you, and missed seeing you altogether. It would have been very gratifying to have heard your views of public affairs, more minutely than they were reported in Charleston. And I would have been glad to ["have" *interlined*] given you some points of information, which possibly might influence you somewhat in the ["present" *canceled*] Presidential controversy. As these have multiplied & magnified very recently, I take the liberty of writing you on the subject. Not to make suggestions to you, whose knowledge generally is as broad, and whose vision is more extended than that of any other man. But to call your attention to facts which perhaps, have not been written to you, & which the press has not noticed. As preliminary I will state my belief, that the existing division in the State has arisen mainly from two causes. First, your silence respecting the merits of the Candidates, and next the general impression that the Mercury was your Organ. Standing pre-eminently first, ["almost" *canceled*] as it were alone in South Carolina, had you expressed an early preference for either Candidate, the State would have been almost as one man in support of your choice. There would have been no division, and being, as she certainly was, predisposed in favor of Gen. [Zachary] Taylor, had you chosen him, there would not have been a whisper for [Lewis] Cass within ["our" *altered to* "her"] borders. You did not like either, & hoping no doubt as ["most" *canceled and* "some" *interlined*] of us did, that a more acceptable man would yet be offered, you would not take either. It was therefore thought, by a few who fancied they had hints, that you secretly preferred Cass and they adopted him. It was believed by another class that you inclined to Taylor—as the choice of evils—and this, allied itself at once to him. The Mercury at first denounced Gen. Cass in unmeasured terms & the latter party were confirmed in their conviction. It then changed & advocated him, & the former rallied more ardently to his support. Your speech at Charleston undeceived neither faction. But the several interpretations of a remark of yours, confirmed both. If you said that any Carolinian was nearer to us than any Northern man, with a view to mitigate exasperation, you were non committal. If however you said that every *Southern man* & *slaveholder* was nearer, it was an avowal for Taylor. The Mercury endorsing the former & avowing a ["char" *canceled*] preference for Cass, encouraged that party. While the Taylor men swore to the last expression & maintained their ground. The contest is growing more heated daily, & threatens to engender bitter animosities. It will in time spread thro' out the State. From intense interest in events & with ample lights before me I ["can" *interlined*] assure you this is the true origin & progress of parties among us. And there can be no adjustment of differences—no relinquishments of preferences, until you speak decidedly. When you do give an opinion, it will paralyse all opposition. Those who ["maintain" *canceled and* "hold" *interlined*] a different one now, which was imbibed from the conviction that it coincided with yours, will quietly abandon it, & gradually come to the support of yours. I know this from various sources. I have seen it done. I know an instance of a person who adhered to Cass, thinking you did, & afterwards being convinced that you preferred Taylor, he has adopted him. Your word was never more powerful in this State than at this crisis. The confidence of the masses never so full & implicit. There has been a small faction opposed to you for some time—not loud mouthed—not openly. You know some of them of course, & you know equally ["as" *canceled*] well that those in whom I have interest *are not of them.* These last are true friends & ardent admirers. My words therefore will not be misconstrued.

But what I desired especially to bring to your notice is, the weight ["that" *canceled and* "of" *interlined*] your opinion ["has" *canceled*] elsewhere, as well as at home. Eminent in the Country & preeminent in the South, its influence is not confined to party. I never go into Georgia that I am not beset by Whigs & Democrats to learn something of your views. I have seen letters from Fla. & Ala. expressing the same interest, and declaring it to be general. I have seen travellers from the West within a few days, who say, it is the same there. And I am of the decided belief, that an expression of your preference for the Presidency, will not only *unite* our State, but will *certainly* decide elections in Georgia & Florida, & tend to the same effect in Ala. while its influence will be felt, in every Southern State. I am not alone of this impression. Many have expressed it to me. My brother [James H. Hammond] has been some weeks on the Geo. Rail Road & met travellers & persons from all quarters, and he gave it as *his conviction.* You are claimed every where by both parties, & that one which can impress the belief of your alliance with it, increases in that quarter.

It is true that you are particularly partial to neither candidate, and believe that the Presidential struggle is of subordinate importance, & care not to mingle in it. But nearly all have taken sides &

nearly all believe that slavery is involved in the contest. There are few neutrals. There are fewer eminent men neutral. The opinions of these last have a magic influence, & the country is entitled to them. And I honestly think & say ["it" *interlined*] candidly, with all deference to your superior judgement that neutrality, under the circumstances, will not strengthen your hold on the affection & confidence of the South. It must weaken both I fear, tho' of course only temporarily.

I am aware that Gen. Cass is obnoxious to you personally & politically. He has perhaps always been so. Yet to show you what effect may be expected from your decided preference, if you have new lights which induce you to believe him more safe & altogether better suited for the South, *I will yield my opposition & will silence one battery* (press). If however you prefer Gen. Taylor, as bound to us by indissoluble ties, & as more honest & independent, I am sure the Cass men will yield full as readily as I would. And if you do incline to the last as I have been led to think from many hints, I will say for him, that I have heard from a personal friend who is equally intimate with Gen. Taylor, that he will veto the Wilmot proviso & all kindred measures without hesitation, & that he advocates the Missouri Compromise ["And" *canceled*] That [John J.] Crittenden & the Whigs cannot influence him in the least, as the former tried it on one occasion & signally failed—that he is entirely independent—& that he has not promised any appointment whatever & will not before he is elected.

I beg that you will receive these, as the honest impressions of a decided friend personally & publicly—of one who under all vicissitudes, from earliest youth, has maintained an unshrinking support of you, who expects to do it always. With best respects to Mrs. [Floride Colhoun] Calhoun I am with high respect y[ou]r mo[st] ob[e]d[ien]t Ser[van]t, M.C.M. Hammond.

[P.S.] The opposition to Mr. [Armistead] Burt is not of much force.

ALS in ScCleA. NOTE: This letter is written on stationery that has a letterhead portrait of Gen. Zachary Taylor, the slogan "Gen[era]l Taylor never surrenders," and names of Mexican War battles. An EU reads: "M.C.M. Hammond[,] bro[ther] of Gov. Hammond." M.C.M. Hammond (1814–1876) had graduated from West Point in 1836 and left the Army, after service in Seminole campaigns, in 1842 to become a planter.

From Eustis Prescott

Hudson N.Y., 6th Sept[embe]r 1848

My Dear Sir, When in New York [City] a few days since I had the pleasure of receiving the "Patent Office" Report which you were so kind as to forward and am extremely obliged for. Your esteemed note of 15 July with the copy of your speech was forwarded me some time since.

Our political position has since that period very much changed, and I have this morning forwarded to my friends in Louis[ian]a all the information bearing upon the election and prospects of parties which I have picked up in an extensive eastern tour.

The Amalgamation, Free soil, and checkered party of John Van Buren is drawing more largely upon the Whig than Democratic ranks. The Whigs in this State[,] Mass. & Connecticut are all dissatisfied with the Philad[elphi]a nominations, and many of them will abstain from voting. I think that [Lewis] Cass & [William O.] Butler have now the best chance for this State. Mass. will probably not elect by the people and a little energy by the Democracy in Con-n[ecticu]t would carry that State.

The South must be united also on Cass & Butler to defeat [Millard] Fil[l]more—the most objectionable man in the Whig ranks, a protective tariff, Bank, Internal improvements advocate, and *Abolitionist.*

The Democratic party as now constituted will sustain the south, and we must sustain it. Union alone is required to have a strong party based on principle. The Whigs in rejecting their leader, and as Mr. [Daniel] Webster said taken up "Gen[era]l Availability" are afloat without compass, and if beaten now must amalgamate with the barn burners, abolitionists, Socialists, Reformers, Antirenters, and all fractions of parties—such a union will be of short duration as each party seeks only its own aggrandisement, and their strength will be frittered away. We must however bear in mind that all—with the exception of the Democrats *proper*, and a few high toned noble individuals are opposed to the extension of slavery, and in favor of its abolition in the District of Columbia.

You have my dear Sir pointed out the only course for the South to pursue after this election, an entire and cordial union—regardless of names, planting themselves on the Constitution—this done, and there will be aid enough from the North to render such a party invincible. I remain my dear Sir Very truly & respectfully your friend, Eustis Prescott.

P.S. I hope to be in New Orleans early in Nov[embe]r.

ALS in ScCleA.

From William [Ross] Wallace

New York [City], September 7, 1848

Dear Sir, Please accept from me this copy [*not found*] of my poem as a testimonial of my respect.

Perhaps you may remember me as the young man that you were so kind as to talk at in the lobby of the U.S. Senate last March. You often left your seat to meet me. Your kindness I shall never forget. The great pure man of my Country bestowed on me, a young man but little known, many hours of his invaluable conversation. Those hours I mark the brightest in my life.

I also send you the prospectus of my new magazine on which you are registered "*free*." If you would send me an article for the first number it would make the periodical at once. Of course I know you too well to *urge* you to do it. But I hope you will. Your friend, William Wallace. Address Berford's[,] No. 2 Astor House.

ALS in ScU-SC, John C. Calhoun Papers. Note: William Ross Wallace (1819–1881), a native of Ky., lived in New York City most of his life. He published *Alban the Pirate* (1848) and *Meditations in America, and Other Poems* (1851).

From A[lbert] A. Dumas

Dayton[,] Marengo Co[unty,] Ala., Sept. 8th 1848

Sir, Although I have not the pleasure of an acquaintance with you—yet I hope it will not be considered an intrusion for me to address you asking your autograph. I write not to you for the purpose of knowing your late political Sentiments in regard to this, that, or the other question that may have shaken this beloved Republic from its very foundation. I am a Whig and have the honor to edit a Whig Paper, but I hope you will not object sending your Autograph on that account—for I consider the Veriest Democrat in the South as nearer and dearer to me—by a thousand ties than the most ultra Whig of the North. We are now beginning to see the effects of being too much attached to party. Consider me Sir—if you please—with a cup of cold water to my lips quaffing a bumber [*sic*; bumper] to you and H[enry] Clay—as two of the most honest and safe politicians of any age or clime. For the Chief magistracy of this Union—H. Clay is my first choice and you are the Second—and when the Northern fanatics commence to trample our rights in the dust as now they are about to do—I prefer you—honored Sir—above all others. The Whigs of Alabama next to H. Clay—would sooner cast their Suffrages for you than any other Statesman living. I think as the contest now lies—that [Zachary] Taylor will carry Alabama or very near do it. We cannot trust Lewis Cass and I never saw so much changing in politics and voters in my life. Truly may we exclaim—"these are troublous times—and there seems to be worse a coming." I saw your son A[ndrew] P. Calhoun Esq. only two days since. He is quite well and has a most excellent [crop]. I think he will make about 600 bales of Cotton—he has out—112 Bales.

Sir I do hope you will not neglect to send me your autograph. I should like you would write as much as possible—but simple [*sic*] the glorious name of—J.C. Calhoun—will be most highly appreciated. Address me if you please at Dayton, Marengo Co[unty], Ala.

Wishing you a long life of health and prosperity and hoping that you may long be spared as the advocate of the South and of the whole Union I remain your most Ob[edien]t S[er]v[an]t, A.A. Dumas.

ALS in ScCleA. Note: An AEU by Calhoun reads "Mr. Dumas."

From J[acob] P. Reed

Anderson C[ourt] H[ouse, S.C.,] 8th Sept. 1848

Dear Sir, I have the honor to acknowledge the receipt of your note of the 3d Inst. which did not reach me till this moment.

Herewith inclosed you will receive a copy of the "Anderson Gazette" containing the letter desired.

I beg to thank you for the kindness shown me by that letter, and more particularly, for the benefit it has been, to the enterprize referred to, & which I have So deeply at heart. The prospect of the early Success of the Rail Road is flattering ["in" *canceled*] in every respect & I can but hope, now that you have a Short Season of relaxation from the turmoil of politics, that we may avail ourselves of

Some further expression of your Views, in refference to the Rail Road, either written, or orally, at a meeting to be held at this place on the Subject, on the 27th of this Instant, of which you will receive due notice.

The paramount question for the South at this Juncture is to devise means for the preservation, of the equality of her political position in the Union, and for her defence if driven by fanaticism to assert her rights. Rail Roads I regard as a very great means of defence to a country & hence politically, (every other consideration aside) the construction of our Road is of vast importance to South Carolina, and whilst looking intently & constantly to the gathering Storm, I feel that our leisure Should be devoted in Some degree, to an enterprize that will not only aid us in resisting its force, but confer in every respect very great benefit upon our gallant old State.

Beg[g]ing that you will pardon this digression I have the Honor to Subscribe myself Very Respectfully &c, J.P. Reed.

ALS in ScCleA. Note: An AEU by Calhoun reads, "Mr. Reed. Relates to the rail road." Due to a scarcity of extant files of the *Anderson Gazette*, the En mentioned in the second paragraph cannot be identified with certainty. However, see below Calhoun's letter of 9/24 to citizens of Anderson.

To ——

Fort Hill, 9th Sept. 1848

Dear Sir: I cannot better answer your letter, than by transmitting the enclosed [speech]. I have only to add, that I have no hope of arresting abolition through the Presidential election. Instead of affording a remedy, it is that which aggravates, extends, and perpetuates it; and which, finally, will give it a fatal termination, unless, in the meantime, an effective remedy of some description be applied. With respect, J.C. Calhoun.

PC in the New York, N.Y., *Herald*, October 5, 1848, p. 3; PC in the Boston, Mass., *Daily Advertiser*, October 6, 1848, p. 2; PC in the Charleston, S.C., *Mercury*, October 9, 1848, p. 2; PC in the Alexandria, Va., *Gazette and Virginia Advertiser*, October 10, 1848, p. 2; PC in the Columbia, S.C., *South-Carolinian*, October 13, 1848, p. 2; PC (from the Baltimore, Md., *American*) in the Tuscaloosa, Ala., *Independent Monitor*, October 19, 1848, p. 2. Note: It is possible that this is an excerpt of a letter written by Calhoun in reply to the letter from Charles N. Webb above dated 9/1/1848.

To ——

Fort Hill, 9th Sep[tembe]r 1848

Dear Sir, I accept with pleasure the honorary membership confer[r]ed on me by the Newton Literary Institute of Baltimore, accompanied by [a] sincere wish for its success. With great respect I am & &, J.C. Calhoun.

ALS in ScU-SC, John C. Calhoun Papers.

From Jos[eph] J. Singleton

Dahlonega [Ga.,] 10th Sept. 1848

My Dear Sir, Since my last to you, I have seen Messrs. [John] Pasco[e] & [John] Hockanoll. They came to see me as p[e]r my request. I informed them that you desired a strict compliance with the terms of their lease, or an abandonment of the lot, at their own discretion, that you wished to avoid any, or all difficulties whatever. Their reply was that they had recently been at some considerable experimental labor in searching for the old, or proper vein, which they wished to continue to the end of this year. Should they prove successful, they would "erect the necessary machinery, employ an adequate force &c. for its development"; other ways, they would give up their lease.

Their intentions heretofore, no doubt, was to make the best of a hard bargain, as is the custom of the country. But on finding that their bargain had to be complied with however hard, they now, I think make a fair proposition, and I also think that you have no alternative short of a tedious lawsuit; to avoid which I would advise, on the ground of uncertainties.

They are legally bound to comply with the terms of their lease, but according to the customs of the Country it is very doubtful whether any thing could be recovered in the event of an effort to do so.

The terms of their lease are that they agree to "erect the necessary machinery, and employ an adequate force to develope the full resources of your mine," for which I have from the first contended, and which they have wa[i]ved until the present crisis. So[?] the end of the present year will determine, accordingly you know best the course to to [*sic*] be persued in accordance to whatever obligation you may be under in your proposed terms of sale.

Another small deposite has been made since my last, of which $35.12½ is now in my hands, in addition to the am[oun]t mentioned in my last letter. We should be very much pleased to see you over with us, and especially so, if accompanied by Mrs. [Floride Colhoun] Calhoun. Let it be so now, simply by way of recreation from her arduous duties during your continued absence. The best of wives may be overburthened. Yours as usual, Jos. J. Singleton.

ALS in ScU-SC, John C. Calhoun Papers.

From A[RMISTEAD] BURWELL

Vicksburg [Miss.,] Sept. 12, 1848

Sir: The present seems to me, to be an important crisis, so far as the Southern States, and especially the institution of slavery are concerned. The public mind is disturbed, agitated, I may say, alarmed, at the advances which opinion is hourly making, in opposition and open hostility to *our* institutions. Discussion, and declamation are openly encouraged, upon a subject which in better and purer days, was not considered proper for public debate.

I am incapable of the vanity of an effort to instruct you, by referring to events and indications, which prove that the south never was in such eminent peril before.

Constant agitation on this question (I mean the slavery question without reference to the Territories) must it seems to me, produce evil effects in the south, incalculable in their extent.

How long will agitation and discussion continue, and in what, will they result? If we have seen but the beginning of the end, it becomes southern men, to look to their own interests, aye to their own safety.

Discussion of this delicate subject, must be ended: from it, the south has every thing to lose, nothing to gain. The slaves hear and comprehend much more of the speeches and letters, which are delivered and written, than is generally supposed: and I know that it is very generally understood among the slaves, that a great movement is now being made on their behalf; the objects to be accomplished not precisely defined, but by which their condition is to be affected.

The important enquiry, "how can discussion & agitation be prevented?" must be answered, some day or other. The propriety and expediency of taking up this subject *now*, and acting upon it boldly, yet calmly and deliberately, must in some form be brought to the consideration, and decision of Southern men. We may desire, and who does not, to postpone it indefinitely, if that can be safely done, but we are not worthy of the name of freemen, if we fear to vindicate our rights, and *protect our safety*, because this vindication and protection present an aspect of danger. But we cannot postpone this question if we would. It is *pressed* upon us; it meets us at every stage of our affairs: it is thrust into every public ["debate" *interlined*] and private conversation, and is now the rallying point of more than half the Union. Will we of the south be better prepared a year hence to defend ourselves than we are now: will we have then more of the elements of safety, than we have now? Will the north be more friendly, less disposed to interfere with, to encroach upon us, than now, or have less ability to do it? I can answer none of the questions, in such manner, as to induce a wish to delay action on the part of Southern men.

You, Sir, on another question, many years ago, assumed a bold position, and against the most powerful odds maintained it: technically it may be said, that you failed, but the results of your exertions then, claim for you, the lasting gratitude of all who truly love their country, and especially of the South.

The fear of a dissolution of the Union, inspired men with its love, on terms *endurable by and safe for the South.* No other motive seems to be sufficiently powerful. Northern men calculate the value of the Union, and to them, the balance will be found in its favour. It is time for us of the south, to make some calculations, and with coolness, deliberation and courage!

Is the mere Union, (for it is fast becoming a mere Union, without community of feeling or mutual interest and advantage) worth to us of the south so much, that, for the apprehension of danger by its dissolution, we ought to incur the "*certain hazard*" of ruin, by permitting our most delicate relations to be the subject of unending debate and agitation and I may add of calumny and abuse?

The southern States can form an independent confederation, which can sustain itself against the world. An independent government and ["perhaps" *interlined*] nothing but that, can and will put an end to dangerous and insurrectionary agitation. The north needs the south: derives greater benefits from the Union than the south: and as a last resort, (but the only one left to us), let us assume a bold,

I will not say threatening attitude; ["but" *canceled*] one which at every hazard we will maintain: let us firmly propose a compromise and settlement, final and full of this vexed and dangerous question and present as our alternative, secession, and the establishment of an independent republic, peaceably if we can, forcibly if we must. Northern men may again make calculations, and we may have peace and security for ourselves and our posterity.

It is not a pleasant or enviable condition even for the bravest, to live over a magazine of gunpowder, with the knowledge, that an enemy is daily attempting to explode it: or that a friend is wantonly, thoughtlessly, using fire about it. For one, I much prefer, to meet danger in the open field: to seek it out; it then loses its terrors: it is disarmed.

If a disease attacks the limb, how idle to defer amputation, until it spreads th[r]ough the system, or encroaches so near to the vitals, as to defy the surgeon's skill. The sooner, the knife is resorted to, the smaller the part of the body, it will be necessary to cut off: if the operation is deferred, it may be performed at great loss, perhaps of the life itself. The application of these similes is too plain to escape notice.

The eyes of quiet citizens, men who have no political aspirations, begin to turn towards you, as a beacon light, for guidance & safety & desire this subject to be brought, plainly and practically to your notice. Measures will be taken for southern security: not so much as regards, the area and territory of slavery (for these I regard as minor considerations) but against agitation and the fearful results, which may flow from it. Who so capable as ["of" *canceled*] yourself, of giving direction and effect to these measures, and combining with them that prudence and firmness, without which evil only can result from their attempt? The crisis in our affairs calls upon your patriotism, your firmness, your knowledge, and consummate skill in affairs of state, to meet it.

Is the emergency so pressing, as to require a convention of Southern States in imitation or opposition to the free soil assembly? what is the proper course to pursue? to act decisively, or to remain quiescent? to assert our safety boldly, and meet the danger fearlessly, or to wait until we are more defenceless, and the enemy are upon us?

For myself, and I believe I but echo the *real* not the *party* opinion, of most of our citizens, I am not disposed to act rashly, or to defer action, when deemed necessary, though it may be attended with danger. I am willing to submit to your judgment, and hope you will not overlook these suggestions, because of their humble source. With profound respect I am your ob[edien]t ser[van]t, A. Burwell.

ALS in ScCleA; PC in Boucher and Brooks, eds., *Correspondence*, pp. 473–475.

To Mrs. P[LACIDIA MAYRANT] ADAMS, [Pendleton]

Fort Hill, 13th Sep[tembe]r 1848

Dear Madam, I received your note of the 23d of May last [*not found*], giving me notice according to the terms of our bond to you, that you would want $1200 or $1500 in October next. I did not answer it, because I did not think it necessary, as I expected to make payment in conformity with the terms of the bond, at the end of six months, ["that is" *canceled*] from the time of the notice; that is the 30th of May, when ["the" *canceled*] your letter was received.

I would cheerfully advance the money now but am not in funds, owing to the low price at which my cotton was sold, and my heavy expenses last year. I have written to my son [Andrew Pickens Calhoun] to remit the amount, as soon as he is in funds from the sale of our crop, and expect to receive ["it" *interlined*] at, or before, the the [*sic*] expiration of the notice. It will be paid as soon as received. With respect I am & &, J.C. Calhoun.

[P.S.] The six months expires on the 30th Nov[embe]r next. J.C.C.

ALS owned by Mr. Holbrook Campbell.

To A[NDREW] P[ICKENS] CALHOUN, [Marengo County, Ala.]

Fort Hill, 13th Sep[tembe]r 1848

My dear Andrew, Yours of the 2d Inst. was brought me by the messenger who took my last to you to the office. It releived me greatly, both by informing me, that you were all well and ["that" *interlined*] the prospect of the cotton crop ["was" *interlined*] so good. We have really been fortunate in the health of our place. The combination of so much health, with such fertility, in so low a latitude & new a country, is a phenomonon.

Never was a good crop so important to us, as just at this time. The low price & the failure of the last two years, were bringing our pecuniary affairs to a crisis; and putting our credit to a ["test" *canceled and then interlined*]. The present will enable us to meet them I trust without any serious embarrassment, even should the price be moderate; for from what you state, combined with the fine fall, I anticipate it will be among our best crops. Never had we finer weather, thus far, to mature a ["the" *canceled*] cotton crop & to harvest it. This time last year, I just began to pick; now I have about the 4th of what I expect to make, picked, and one third of my crop opened. It still continues fair with a prospect of a long & open fall, which, if it should prove to be the case, will, I hope, make our Alabama crop from what you state, ["to" *canceled*] one of the best we ever made.

As to selling, I am of the impression we ought not to hesitate to sell at 6½, if we cannot get more. There is danger of another scarce year in England from the failure of the potato crop. In addition, there is almost a certainty of a visit from the colora [*sic*]; and the chance more than equal of continued dependance on the continent. I am of the impression, we ought to sell as fast as we can get out & send down, and apply ["our" *canceled*] the proceeds to our debts. It will keep down interest. Among our early applications, should be a payment, say of at least $1000 on [Ker] Boyce's judgement. Mrs. [Placidia Mayrant] Adams has given notice, that she wants one thousand dollars on our debt to her. The bond requires six months ["interest" *canceled*] notice, which will be about the Middle of November next. You must bring it, or remit ["it" *interlined*]. If you can, I would rather you would remit a draft to me in advance of the time. I shall also want the amount due to me for the carriage & horses before I leave for Washington, to meet my engagements & expenses here. I am in arrears to John E[wing] Bonneau & cannot draw on him. In addition our bank debts will have to be attended to punctually. It would be desirable to pay something more than the mere discount on the renewal on the 1st Jan[uar]y, but this & the others ["debts" *interlined*] can be the subject of consideration, when we meet in November to settle with Mr. [Thomas G.] Clemson. If you should sell more than is necessary to meet these arrangements, before you leave, the surplus that ["can" *interlined*] be spared ought to be applied to Boyce's judgement.

I greatly regret that this State has gone into the canvass; but I am happy to state, that there is little excitement out of Charleston. The

[mail] bag is about starting to the [Pendleton] Village, & I must close, and reserve politicks for another occasion.

We are all in perfect health. Love to Margaret [Green Calhoun] & the children [Duff Green Calhoun, John Caldwell Calhoun, Andrew Pickens Calhoun, Jr., and Margaret Maria Calhoun]. Your affectionate father, J.C. Calhoun.

ALS in NcD, John C. Calhoun Papers.

To "Col." JA[ME]S ED[WARD] COLHOUN, [Abbeville District, S.C.]

Fort Hill, 13th Sep[tembe]r 1848

My dear James, I am not certain whether I answered your last letter, received with its enclosure just before I left Washington. I had the letter ["enclosed" *interlined*] forwarded [through] the Prussian [Minister, Friedrich von Gerolt] to Bremen to the person to whom it was addressed.

I had the pleasure on my return home to find all well, a good crop of corn & cotton & the place in good order.

My principal object in now writing is to express the hope, that you will visit us at some early period during the fall. I want to see you much on several accounts and among others to consult you on a subject of interest to me. The journey would be of service to your health at this fine season of the year; and it would afford all of us great pleasure to see you. I hope you will not fail to come. Let me hear from you whether I may expect you on the receipt of this; and if so, when, that I may make my arrangement to be at home at the time.

I enclose a Cuba paper received the mail before the last, which ["may" *interlined*] contain something interesting to you. Yours affectionately, J.C. Calhoun.

ALS in ScCleA.

From A. P. Stinson, "Private"

St. Joseph [Mich.,] Sept[embe]r 13/48

My dear Sir, So vauge & uncertain are the Rumours which Reach us as the Position of S. Carolina & your own on the *Presidential Question,* I am Induced to trespass on you for a Solution of the Question. I know well the feelings which Animate you on the Oregon Bill, I said *Animate* I would say *Excite.* I Still believe, Indeed I know, you misapprehend the *feelings* & *motives* of many Northern Democrats (& Indeed most as I believe) on the "Free Soil question." That the Rights & Interests of the South would be as *Safe* in the Hands of Mr. [Martin] *Van Buren* as with *G[e]n[era]l* [Lewis] *Cass* Exercising the Office of President I believe. There is a Deep feeling of *Indignation pervading* the *Democracy* of the *Country* at the *means* resorted to & *measures adopted* by which *G[e]n[era]l Cass* was placed before them for the Office of President, & Hence to a great extent this "*Free Soil*" *move* with which to "*head him off.*" Thousands of as good Democrats as Ever lived in Every "Free State" will vote for *Gen. Taylor* & many who Call them Selves "Free Soil" men! A Determination to *Defeat Cass,* at all Hazards Lies quite as Deep with many, as the "*Free Territory*" *question* & I Predict If the *South* Drop Gen. Taylor & give their Support to *Cass,* they will find when too Late, they reckoned without their Hosts. Had *Levi Woodbury* been the Nominee, this "*General out Breake,*" would never have had an Origin. As It is, I know not where It may End. In the Western States there is no telling what will be the Result. *Van Buren* is gaining on *Cass Astonishingly* & It is believed by many, Stands as good a Chance in *this State, Ohio, Ind., Ill., Iowa* as Cass & a far better one in *Wisconsin*! I desire never to see *Cass* Elected. Let him be *defeated* & there will be an End of this Corrupt & Corrupting System of Caucuses & Conventions. My friend *Hon. Jno. Norvell* U.S. Dist[rict] Attorney & former *U.S. Senator* is out in "full blast" for Old "Rough & Ready." I believe he would make a good President Infinitely better than *Cass.* I hope Sir, you will Enlighten me as to your views & wishes & I "pledge my Honor as a man" to keep *Inviolate* the Same if So desired & this you will please Consider as for your Eye & Ear alone & believe me to be as I am Your friend faithfully, A.P. Stinson.

ALS in ScCleA.

To [Marcus C. M. Hammond]

Fort Hill, 13th September 1848

Dear Sir: I would have accompanied Mr. [Armistead] Burt [Representative from S.C.], and spent a night with you, had I not found, on calculation, I would miss the stage arrangement at Abbeville, and lose two days.

I have read your suggestions and reflections with attention, and appreciate the friendly motives in which they originate; and, let me add, I have a high respect both for your opinion and your brother's [James H. Hammond]. But I cannot but think you greatly overestimate the weight attached to my opinion in reference to the Presidential election. Be that, however, as it may, if I had a preference, and if I thought its expression would tend to unite and strengthen the South for the coming contest, I would express it, regardless of consequences as to myself. But such is not the case. My conviction is deep that we can gain nothing, and must lose much, in taking a part in the present canvass—lose, I mean, in reference to the great struggle which must come for our liberty and safety—lose by dividing and distracting the State—and lose by inducing us to look to the Presidential election as the means of arresting Abolition, when, in fact, it is the great cause of exciting and perpetuating it. I not only believe that there is not the least hope of arresting or retarding its progress through it, but that the first step towards the only means by which it can be arrested—I mean, to take the remedy into our own hands—to rely on ourselves and not it, or the Federal Government—is to cease to take any interest in the Presidential election.

Notwithstanding this impression, if General [Zachary] Taylor had stood as an independent candidate and refused to accept the nomination from either party, I would have given him my decided support, as is well known. I openly expressed myself to that effect. I would have done so, because I regard it as the most effectual way to break up nominations by what are called party conventions; what I consider as constituting the ligatures by which the Southern portions of both parties are bound to their respective Northern portions so strongly, that Abolitionism, with its certain destruction to us, cannot rend asunder. But as he has chosen to take a different course, I cannot see any way to give him my support, consistently with what I believe to be the only means left us to arrest the progress of a disease, which, if not arrested, will prove fatal.

With great respect, yours truly, J.C. Calhoun.

PC in the Charleston, S.C., *Mercury*, October 30, 1860, p. 1. NOTE: The *Mercury* published the above letter with the following introduction: "A friend has handed us for publication the following letter of Mr. Calhoun. It exhibits the nature of the struggle in which we are engaged, and the sole remedy—not success in Presidential elections, but in resisting and putting an end to Northern aggressions." The addressee of this letter was not identified, but it could well be a reply to Marcus C.M. Hammond's letter of 9/6 above.

From GEO[RGE] H. THATCHER

Ballston Centre [N.Y.], Sept. 20th 1848

Hon. Sir, Your last is received, & right glad I am that you are desireous of having *all* the facts & phases of this great political, or rather *politico-religious* movement before you. In my judgement the signs of the times indicate a mightier upheaving of the social, political, & religious elements, all of which are involved in this great question, than any we have passed through since the foundation of our Republic. This is an age of *radical crusades*, in which, by a strange conjuncture, religion under the form of political puritanism, & infidelity go hand in hand. Elements diametrically antagonistic coalesce with wonderful ease. In this crusade against slavery we see representatives of every shade of opinion. Side by side on the same platform stand the grave divine & the Fourierite—the ambassador of the Prince of Peace & the disciple of Voltaire & Fanny Wright. When such a combination takes place—when all the passions of our nature good & bad concentrate on a given point—what else can we expect than a general crusade of this kind? To reason with men in such circumstances is a waste of time. Picture to yourself a calm reasoner standing before the hosts that rallied at the magic call of Peter the Hermit, just as they were starting for the Holy Land, & attempting to argue ["with" *interlined*] them. Politico-religious fanaticism has no ears for argument—it desires & consequently listens only to what will agitate the passions. It cannot have escaped you that the *religious sentiment* has given birth to many of these modern crusades, & you are sufficiently versed in history & the science of human nature to know that when this sentiment voluntarily surrenders itself to the guidance of politicians it loses its discretion while it retains & augments the virulence of its impulses. Were I to give a definition of fanaticism I would call it Religion *without discretion.* There is any amount of this mingled up with the present movement. But it is not my design at present to trace out its bearings on this movement. Another subject will furnish material for this letter.

There is one phase of this movement which, I am confident, is not generally known at the South. Perhaps *you* may have discovered it, but I doubt whether others have. If you have examined the Buffalo platform [of the Free Soil Party] you have observed one resolution relating to the election of the civil officers of the general government. It is as follows: "That we demand the election by *the people* of *all* civil officers in the service of the ["Government" *interlined*] *so far as the same may be practicable.*" If you ask how far it may be "practicable"? they will tell you that it would be practicable to elect the President, the Members of the Cabinet & Senate—Custom-house officers, assistant measurers[?], Postmasters & Judges by a *direct ballot.* Custom-house officers & Postmasters & all other district officers could be elected in the districts where they are located. Senators in the States sending them, but the President, Vice President & Cabinet by a *direct vote* of the people throughout the Union. This resolution, Sir, unless I greatly mistake its design, contains the germ of a mighty agitation, & perhaps, revolution. To fully appreciate its import it will be necessary to take into consideration some of the political changes in our State. One of the questions which occasioned the present division in the Democratic party was that of a reform of our State Constitution. A portion of that party were in favour of reforming the Constitution so as to take away from the Governor & Senate the power of *appointing* most of the inferior officers—such as Secretary of State, & Comptroller, & also Judges, & canal commissioners & ca & give their selection *directly* to the people. This brought on a severe struggle, & out of it grew the party names—Barnburners, & Hunkers. The former were called Barnburners, because, being in favour of this reform they were deemed *radicals* & *levelers.* They retorted by calling their antagonists Hunkers—i.e. those who cling to old abuses for the sake of the spoils. By the aid of the Whig radicals, the Barnburners succeeded—a new Constitution was adopted containing the desired alterations. Accordingly all these officers are elected. Now the makers of the Buffalo platform will strive to bring about a similar reform in the Constitution of the U.S.A[?]. Their *ultimate* object you will discern if you will for a moment suppose this plan carried out. What will be the effect? If the people elect the President by a direct vote, where will the great majority of the voters reside? In the free or the slave States? Those of the free States will preponderate, & in ["their" *altered to* "this"] state of things it will be more easy to concentrate their suffrages on an anti slavery candidate. Then such a candidate would have the advantage of gathering the suffrages of the minorities in the slave States who are opposed to slavery. Take Virginia for an example. So far as Slavery is concerned, the minority in that State have no voice at all in the selection of President; for by the present plan electors are chosen who represent different sentiments. But, if the President were elected by a direct vote of the people, the votes of this minority would count: &, if you add to the votes of the free States, those of the minorities in Virginia, Maryland, Kentucky &c, it would give the free States an overpowering elective supremacy. In this way they would secure all the prominent officers. As a consequence that powerful Executive patronage which, the North complains is so constantly wielded against them, & by means of which it is alleged that a pro-slavery party is *kept up* at the North, would be done away. By this decentralization of political power they hope to destroy executive patronage & thus remove the chief obstacles which now oppose them. They would extend this reform to the Judiciary for their Resolution says "so far as is practicable." In their view it is as "practicable" to elect the Judiciary of the U.S.A[?]. as that of the State of New-York. If they can thus bring about this alteration of the Constitution, they expect to combine *all the branches* of the Government against Slavery. With a government, all the branches of which co-operate to discourage & annoy the institution of slavery, both by their administrative policy & the moral influence of their station, they hope the more speedily to effect its overthrow. Should they succeed in their plan, they will *ultimately* attempt to disturb slavery in the States—though they now disclaim any such intention. At all events they will endeavour to do it by *indirection*. What would be easier than for the general government to "give aid & comfort" to an abolition party that might start up ["in" *interlined*] any of [the] slave States? Especially would this be done were such a party to become strong in numbers & influence as will probably soon be the case in Virginia, Maryland & Kentucky. But it is needless for me to point ["out" *interlined*] results which your own mind will foresee at a glance. This project will not be made prominent in the present canvass. The question of slavery-extension will answer all present purposes for making political capital. Nor do they expect to accomplish it speedily—it will be the work of years. So much the better. *It will serve the purpose of future agitation & to keep the party now forming firmly united.* In the Buffalo Convention there were *long* heads & *cool* heads as well as *hot* heads. These men saw the importance of making a platform that ["would" *interlined*] embrace more permanent & *comprehensive* issues than that of mere slavery-extension. That issue might be settled in a year or two, & hence, if they organized *only* on that, its settlement would, ipso facto, disorganize them. Through the instrumentality of the great question now pending they intend to prepare the way for the successful agitation of the other. That the project will be a *popular* one in the free States I have no doubt. It would be, if it had no bearing at all on the institution of slavery—much more when it can be made a dagger to give that institution its death-wound. When the reform of our State Constitution was under discussion, though it was opposed by some of the most influential men & papers in the State belonging to both the old parties, it was carried by an overwhelming majority. So, in my opinion, will it be in regard to this matter, in all the free States. Indeed the movers of this project do not anticipate much trouble in getting *all the free States* to declare in its favour. Counting these States, to start with, they expect in a short time to gain enough of the moderate slave States to make out the requisite two thirds. Mean time it will serve as an admirable electioneering resource for '52. This & the abolition of slavery in the D[istrict of] C[olumbia]—Land Reform—River & harbour Improvements &c—will make the Buffalo platform a thing not to be sneered at. If free-trade becomes popular that too will be added. Before 3 years shall have passed, men who now ridicule the prediction you made at Charleston will see cause to change their tune. The mouse will by that time grow to a lion. The vote for Mr. [Martin] Van Buren this fall will astonish them.

In regard to this contemplated reform of the Constitution, the arguments that will be offered will fast gain the popular favour. It will ["be" *interlined*] urged that to elect a President in this way will be—1st More Democratic. For by the present method a candidate may have a majority of electors while the popular vote is vastly against him—& thus the will of the *people* is defeated. 2nd The people can just as well choose directly a particular candidate as to appoint others to do it for them. 3d It will save a needless expense. 4th If the other officers be elected likewise, it will break up the present system of central cliques & prevent expectants of office from influencing parties in their respective States. A candidate cannot start in the canvass with an army of Postmasters, Custom-house officers &c to aid in electing him. 5th To these will be added the weightier considerations relating to the institution of slavery. 6th

It will be further urged that a similar reform has been made in State governments & worked well, & why would it not respecting the General Government.

Now for the evidence that this project is seriously entertained— 1st I adduce the Buffalo platform itself. 2 The men who moved it were Mr. Van Buren[']s friends & were the *very ones* who went ahead in the change of our State-constitution. 3d Mr. Van Buren indorses the Buffalo platform. In his letter accepting the nomination he says: "I have examined & considered the platform adopted by the Buffalo Convention, as defining the *political creed* of the 'Free Democracy,' with the *attention due to the grave subjects* which it embraces, and the interesting circumstances under which it is presented. It breathes the right spirit, and presents a political chart which, with ["the" *interlined*] explanations I am about to make, I can, in good faith, *adopt and sustain.*" 4th The Language of the [Washington, D.C.,] National Era. In reply to the [Washington, D.C., Daily] National Intelligencer which stigmatised this resolution as a "contemptible appeal to the Demagogue Spirit &c" the Era remarks—

[Appended Clipping]

This "contemptible" clause, is a declaration in favor of the policy of electing all civil officers in the service of the Government by the People, *as far as practicable*. Very good. For one, we would have the President and Senate elected by the People, and other civil officers, *so far as practicable*. The more popular responsibility you introduce into a republican government, the less parties, and conventions, and electoral colleges, and legislatures, and other intermediate bodies, stand between the People and their agents, the better. That is a sound principle.

Of course it ["is" *interlined*] as yet in embryo—a future convention of the party may, & doubtless will, speak out in plainer terms.

As to the present Canvass. I think Mr. Van Buren has been gaining strength ever since the Buffalo Convention. Present appearances indicate that he will carry New York, Vermont, Massachusetts, Ohio, & Wisconsin. In a certain contingency, however, he may carry neither. The Hunkers, rather than permit him to carry these States, may, when the election comes, throw votes enough for Taylor, to give them to him. They want, if possible, to defeat Van Buren *at all hazards*. The [Albany] Argus has already intimated the propriety of such a course. I do not much think they will do it. For it might secure Taylor's election by the people & destroy the forlorn hope of Gen. [Lewis] Cass, which is, the House of Representatives. That would be paying too great a price for the mere gratification of personal spite. However I *know* some of that party who avow their determination so to do. But if they vote for Cass, Van Buren[']s chances in these States are the best. Unless therefore, the Southern States go very strong for Taylor, the election will be thrown into the House. As to the South I cannot judge. My opinion is that the [Henry] Clay Whig movement in our State will operate in Van Buren's favour. Willis Hall who presided at the Clay meeting in New York is *personally intimate* with the Van Burens, & he declared on that occasion that he would rather vote for Van Buren than Taylor. Hall is a very strong Free Soil man.

But the *great* effort of the North will be made on Members of Congress. It will be difficult for any but Wilmot Proviso men to get elected in any part of the North. Even the adherents of Cass are afraid to oppose it. At their recent Convention for nominating State officers they had to equivocate on the subject in one of their resolutions. They declare that the assertion ["('accusation')" *interlined*] of the Barnburners & others that they are in favour of extending slavery is "a libel alike upon *truth* and *justice*." You see *even they* fear to oppose it. Wherever it will be necessary, in order to secure a Wilmot Proviso man for Congress, the Whigs and Barnburners will unite. [Horace] Greeley of the [New York] Tribune, expresses the general feeling on that subject. In a recent number he says:

[Appended Clipping]

> We speak not now of party or parties; we ask none to vote for this or the other Presidential candidate or the supporters of such candidate: but we ask freemen of every party to take care that not one Member of Congress shall be chosen from a Free State who is not reliably devoted to the preservation of the New Territories from the pollution of Human Bondage. If possible, let men be chosen who have been ever faithful to Freedom, whose hearts are in the cause, and who may be trusted without pledges as well as with them; but elect any body who is for Free Soil, no matter of what politics, rather than any one who is against it. Other issues, however important intrinsically, can wait; this cannot. Presuming that Gen. Cass will not be in the White House to veto any barrier against Slavery Extension which Congress may pass, and that no one else will dare if any can wish to do so, we believe that every vote cast for a Member of Congress will be a vote directly for or against Freedom on the overruling issue. What Northern freeman will shut his eyes to this issue and vote to connive at the Extension of Slavery?

I believe I have now given you a fair statement of the course events are taking. If I could afford the expense I would take a hundred or so of our Northern papers, & keep you apprised of all important movements. But this I cannot do. I will, however, write you when I discover any thing of importance. I am at present unemployed in my vocation, & for the reason that I cannot submit to the degradation of making the pulpit a rostrum for pandering to the taste of those religionists who would have me forego the gospel & preach abolitionism, or ultra-temperance or other similar isms. Thanks to a kind Providence I have a moderate income to support me. If I had not, I have hands & I *can "dig."*

There is a story going the rounds of the papers that one of your slaves recently attempted to poison Mrs. Calhoun. Such things are seized upon at the North as *arguments* ["against" *interlined*] slavery. How is that? Your poor head has to take it here at the North. They bend no small share of their attacks upon you. If you live you will soon participate in events of far more importance than you have yet gone through. The tone of the North is getting bolder & bolder daily.

I wish you could find time [to] write more at length & let me know more of the state of things at the South—but I suppose you are very much employed. You will, however, please acknowledge my letters that I may know you receive them. I direct this to Pendleton because yours was post-marked there though dated at Fort Hill. Will you favour me with a copy of the speech you are preparing for the Press? With unfeigned respect, I am Hon. Sir, yours, Geo. H. Thatcher.

P.S. I have just seen another letter from Gen. Taylor—which I suppose is "*positively the last.*" I think this letter will help him very much at the North. That is, it will preserve to him most of the Whigs. For the last 3 or 4 weeks they have been deserting him by thousands. His acceptance of the Charleston nomination to run with [William O.] Butler for Vice President played the mischief with him here—the entire Whig party of this State came very near casting him overboard. If he stops with *this letter* he will gain ground I think—tho the ultra C[l]ay Whigs will hardly support him. Mr. Clay I see has also written a letter in which he says he will give no countenance to any attempts to run him—but he preserves "ominous silence" as to Gen. Taylor. Those who got up the meetings in his favour did not *expect* him to countenance them, nor did they *care*. They had *one object* to accomplish, which was in my opinion to help Van Buren. So long as Mr. Clay maintains his *present attitude* towards Gen. T[aylor] the more ardent of Mr. Clay['']s personal friends will either stand aloof from the contest or else go for Van Buren out of spite. Whether Gen. T[aylor] will gain enough from the Democratic parties to make up his Whig loss is as yet difficult to determine. He will, however get many moderate Democrats. I see in his last letter he intimates his determination not to proscribe office holders for opinion's sake. I think many of the Democratic office holders will catch at that bait & perhaps give him their vote or ["their" *interlined*] secret support at least. You undoubtedly know enough of our New York politicians, to be aware, that, though possessed of the *usual* infirmities of modern patriotism, they nevertheless, have such a *disinterested love* for the *dear people* that they could not have the heart to *refuse* to serve them in any *lucrative* office. Well, "nous ver[r]ons" as Father [Thomas] Ritchie says. A few days more, & I will be able to tell better how this last letter of Gen. T[aylor']s will affect the Canvass. How do you think the Southern States will generally go? As I have already intimated to you, you are at liberty to make any use you choose of my letters, if you deem them of any importance at all, with this "Proviso," that my name is known only to yourself. I have now no party attachments. I try to be an *eclectic* respecting political principles & measures. In so doing I must follow my judgement & that will not permit me to adopt all the doctrines of any party. What you said recently of the two Candidates I can say of the two parties "I see much to condemn, & little to approve in either." Your independent, &, as I believe, honest & patriotic conduct in the recent trying circumstances relating to our policy with Great Britain & the war with Mexico, has awakened in me a *strong personal* attachment towards yourself. You have a mightier influence with the reflecting portion of our people than you are aware of. If I do not mistake the signs of the times it will be soon thrown into your power to affect the destinies of our Republic to a greater extent than at any former period of your life. Hence my solicitude that you may be possessed of *all* the *facts* & *aspects* of political movements at the North. That you will act for the good of the *whole country* I have no doubt. Please remember & send me a copy of the speech you have or are about to publish. As soon as any thing occurs to affect the prospects of either candidate I will write you again. I hope in the mean time you will find time to write me briefly at least in return. Yours truly, Geo: H. Thatcher.

ALS in ScCleA.

J[OHN] Y. MASON, [Secretary of the Navy], to J[ohn] C. Calhoun, A[ndrew] P. Butler, [Senators from S.C.], and Others

Navy Department, September 21st 1848

Gentlemen, Transmitted herewith for your information is a copy of a letter addressed to the Department by George Law Esq[ui]r[e] of New York assignee of Albert G. Sloo the contractor for the line of mail steamers between New York [City] and New Orleans. Also a copy of his reply under date of 13th instant. I am respec[tfull]y yours, J.Y. Mason.

[Enclosure]

J.Y. Mason to George Law, New York [City]

Navy Department, August 29th 1848

Sir, Enclosed herewith is a copy of a communication addressed to this Department, by the Delegation in Congress from South Carolina, dated the 7th instant [*not found*].

The appropriation made by Congress, with authority to make advances on your Steamers after they shall be launched, has attached to it a proviso, which evinces a wish on the part of Congress that in your trips to and from New Orleans, your vessels shall touch at Charleston. The importance of this City in a commercial point of view, the high respect I entertain for the Gentlemen who have made to me the enclosed communication, and my strong desire that the Steamers contracted for on this line, shall render as extended benefits to our country as may be practicable, induce me to urge on you the agreement proposed of making Charleston one of your regular points of approach and communication. I am strongly persuaded that the interests of yourself and associates will be promoted by this arrangement. You will be pleased to inform me whether you are willing to make it a stipulation of the contract, that you shall stop at Charleston as proposed. I am respec[tfull]y yours, J.Y. Mason.

[Enclosure]

George Law to J.Y. Mason, Secretary of the Navy

New York [City,] Sept. 13th 1848

Sir, Your Letter of the 29th ult. enclosing a Copy of a communication to the Navy Department from the Delegation in Congress from South Carolina dated 7th August reached this city while I was absent in the country, otherwise it would have given me pleasure to reply at an earlier date.

I am fully sensible of the importance of the City of Charleston in a commercial point of view and appreciating the desire expressed in your Letter, that the Steamers which I am building for the line designated in the Contract with Mr. [Albert G.] Sloo shall render as extended benefits to our Country as may be practicable, allow me to say that my own interest will be best promoted by whatever will conduce to that result.

In prescribing the class of vessels to be employed under this Contract, the Government have had in view not only capacity for Mail and Commercial service in time of peace, but adaptation to service as War Steamers should it become necessary to convert them to that use—and to the latter end they have prescribed a strength and consequent weight which was wholly unnecessary for merely commercial service along our coast. While therefore the proviso contained in the Law mentioned in your letter may perhaps seem to indicate a wish on the part of Congress that the Vessels shall touch at Charleston, the language of the proviso no less clearly indicates that this wish is subordinate to the important condition that the vessels shall be of a size and strength in all respects suitable to the other purposes contemplated. The same may also be said of the same proviso as contained in the Contract itself and in the Law under which the Contract was made.

It may no doubt be true in the language of the communication enclosed to me that "strong and Sea going Steamers which have been built since the Contract was made find it practicable to go in and out of Charleston Harbor" but it is not yet ascertained so far as I am informed, whether Steamers constructed so as fully to meet the requirements of the Government in relation to this line, will find it practicable or not, and I may add with the most sincere respect to the Hon. Gentlemen who have addressed you on this subject, that they must be aware of the refusal of Congress after protracted debate to make the touching at Charleston peremptory, lest in so doing they might compell the Contractors to sacrifice in the power or strength of the vessels, objects deemed by the Government of greater importance.

In determining the size, model and mode of construction of these vessels it has been an object of most earnest solicitude so to combine the required power, capacity and strength as to comply with all the conditions of the Contract with a draft of water which should render it practicable to touch at Charleston. If this shall be accomplished the vessels will in all respects be better adapted to all the purposes for which they are designed, the interest of the owners will be largely promoted &[?] the public interest best subserved.

In this endeavour I flatter myself that a degree of success has been attained hitherto unequalled in Naval construction. In the Contract a capacity of not less than fifteen hundred tons and Engines of one thousand horse power are required and reference is made to one of the large Steam Ships recently built by the United States as a guide in re[*margin crumpled*] to other particulars. I have no hesitation in stating my belief that in the construction of the vessels already launched every valuable quality contemplated by the Law and by the Contract has been fully secured with such improvements in the form and structure as will render the draft of water at least three feet less than that of the Steam Ship referred to in the Contract and the vessels in all respects superior to any now built or building. Indeed I believe that the draft of these vessels when loaded will be found from three to six feet less than the draft of any vessel, of the capacity and power stipulated in the contract, and adapted to the purposes of war or conversion into war Steamers which have yet been constructed in this country or in Europe.

I most sincerely hope that the result of the endeavours made to secure a light draft of water will prove so successful that touching at Charleston will not only be practicable but easy. I have no doubt that my own interest as well as the wishes of yourself and the gentlemen addressing you the communication enclosed to me will be promoted by such a result.

Under these circumstances I submit to you as I think I might safely submit to the Honorable Gentlemen whose communication I have referred to that it would not only be unjust to the Contractors but improper in every view, to make that a peremptory condition, which Congress would not consent to—such absolute condition if compliance with it has not been attained already by the endeavours I have made might render it impossible to comply with the other conditions of the Contract which have, in all the Legislation on the subject, been deemed indispensable. I certainly cannot voluntarily consent to any thing which possibly might lead to such a result.

I may add moreover that it may well happen in the course of the period specified for the service to be rendered, that such changes may occur in the situation of the Bar off the Harbour of Charleston as will render the Harbour at times more and at times less difficult of access and in such case the Proviso as contained in the Law would be reasonable and just.

I prefer for all reasons that the provisions of the Contract on this subject be made no more stringent than at present.

Believing that the interest and wishes of all parties fully concur in the result to be sought I remain very Respectfully Your ob[edien]t s[er]v[an]t, George Law.

FC (of letter and first En) in DNA, RG 45 (Naval Records), Miscellaneous Letters Sent by the Secretary of the Navy, 1789–1886, 30:374, 413 (M-209:15); LS (of second En) in DNA, RG 45 (Naval Records), Miscellaneous Letters Received by the Secretary of the Navy, 1801–1884, 93 (M-124:238, frames 124–125). NOTE: In addition to Calhoun and Butler, this was addressed to S.C. Representatives J[oseph] A. Woodward, D[aniel] Wallace, R[ichard] F. Simpson, R[obert] B[arnwell] Rhett, A[rmistead] Burt and I[saac] E. Holmes. A Clerk's marginal interpolation on the first En reads, "This letter was received by me on the 4th October too late for proper place." EU's on the second En read, "Enclose copy of this & of my letter to which it is a reply, to the Gentlemen, who addressed me—under cover to Hon. Mr. Calhoun" and "Done Sept. 20."

From HENRY R. SCHOOLCRAFT

Washington, Sept[embe]r 23rd 1848

My dear Sir, You will, I dare say, appreciate my views & feelings, [*two words interlined and then canceled*] in the enclosed ["paper, as paying a" *interlined*] tribute to the administration, ["on the frontiers," *canceled*] of a friend, to whom, with yourself, I am indebted for ["the earliest" *interlined and then altered to* "early"] aid and countenance. The ["few" *interlined*] introductory remarks, are by Mr. Allen.

In this sketch, in which I embrace, the reminiscences of many years, passed in the depths of the wilderness, on a very remote frontier, I but express the natural impulses of my heart, without any attempt to mislead, or over-estimate character. For, I sincerely believe, that there is no man, on that wide theatre of action, who has evinced ["an equal" *canceled and* "a superior" *interlined*] degree of energy & decision of character, united with an ["equally" *interlined*] comprehensive mind, and so true ["& high toned an" *interlined*] American feeling. He went to that quarter of the Union, early in life, without means or friends, and has risen steadily, but slowly, ["but" *altered to* "by"] his own unaided energies, & without the prestege of hereditary wealth, or honor. ["Had he remained in Ohio, & not removed to Michigan, he would have been in the U.S. Senate, years ago" *canceled.*]

Mr. [Daniel] Webster, in his recent speech, has, perhaps, but *charicatured* a truth. Gen. [Lewis] Cass is doubtless a "progressive," in the spread of our American institutions & principles; but is imbued with deep conservative ["principles" *canceled and* "spirit" *interlined*], and an ever abiding ["axiom" *canceled and* "determination" *interlined*], to keep the expanding States & Territories strictly within the plain, acknowledged, republican limits of the Constitution. This, ["I have ever observed," *canceled and* "may be observed in all his writings & speeches" *interlined*], notwithstanding his sometimes *florid*, & always *warm* style of writing. And it is from this consideration, that I think, southern democracy may have the surest reliance on him, in relation to the new territories. ["A territory which, in my view(?), like the seed, that is growing, cannot be invested with new power, but must yet abide the proper time, to unfold itself" *interlined.*] If the "free soil" movement, so called, ["but really gag rights(?) party" *interlined*] is defeated by the election of Gen. Cass, southern & western democracy, will build itself, upon this triumph. It is easy to foresee, that after this triumph, the "free soil party" will, ["for a while," *interlined*] spread & strengthen itself, by ["further" *interlined*] imbibing factious elements of all sorts, till ["the question of" *interlined*] New Mexico & California ["are admitted by leaving them the inherent power" *canceled and* "is favorably settled" *interlined*] as they now are, ["that is," *interlined*] free & untrammeled by the theoretic chains of pseudo-politicians, ["who, deny co-States of such rights" *interlined*], like [David] Wilmot, or mere cunning & ["astute" *interlined*] demagogues, like [Martin] Van Buren. And at this point, the free soil party will culminate & expire, for the very want of nutriment, to subsist on. I shall rejoice at such a result the more, because it will ["eventually" *interlined*] place you on a platform whence you will fulfill the just & long entertained wishes of your friends by [*one or two words canceled and* "occupying" *interlined*] the Presidential chair.

I beg you to pardon me, for the liberty of these remarks, which have been thrown out, from a mere impulse, in transmitting you a brief political tract ["issued by" *canceled and* "which I have prepared for" *interlined*] the Congressional committee. I am sir, ever, with unaltered respect & attachment y[ou]r most Ob[edien]t Servant, Henry R. Schoolcraft.

Autograph draft in DLC, Henry Rowe Schoolcraft Papers, vol. 24. NOTE: Schoolcraft published *Outlines of the Life and Character of General Cass* (Albany: Joel Munsell, 1848). On 4/25/1850, Mary Howard (Mrs. Henry) Schoolcraft wrote to Calhoun's niece, Martha Calhoun Burt, expressing her condolences on Calhoun's death: "I shall ever esteem it, an *honour to have known him*, an *especial* privilege too, that he was the first man, who encouraged, and started my husband, in his literary career, and never afterwards ceased to manifest the most kind appreciation of his works, an an author." She enclosed a poem by Henry R. Schoolcraft on Calhoun. ALS with En in ScCleA.

From Augustus Fischer[lue?]

New Braunfels, Comal Co[unty], Texas
Sept. 24/48

Dear Sir, Will you have the goodness to send me a copy (or several if you have them to spare) of your late speeches on the subject of slavery.

We have a large German settlement here, (say from 6, to 10,000) introduced under one of the Colonization contracts, with the late Republic of Texas. These Germans, a great portion of whom have become citizens, under the Republic, have a large & powerfull political influence, which is growing daily, as they are made Citizens. It becomes therefore a matter of great importance, that the intelligent portion of them should properly understand, the issues, of the conflict, in which they, too, must engage, or which at any rate, they must help to decide.

These, Sir, are my views of the position of my countrymen, & under these circumstances you will surely excuse me, for troubling you. The position, which Gen[era]l [Samuel] Houston has taken, is very much calculated to mislead them. I feel therefore an anxiety to see proper information disseminated among them.

Should you have any former speeches of yours at your hands on this or any other subject of general interest I shall feel glad to receive them for the use of our people here. With sentiments of the highest respect & admiration I remain very respectfully y[ou]rs, Augustus Fischer[lue?].

ALS in ScCleA. Note: An AEU by Calhoun reads, "Send Speeches. Augustus Fischerlue."

To J[ames] W. Harrison, J[acob] P. Reed, and A[rchibald] Todd, [Anderson, S.C.]

Fort Hill, 24th Sept., 1848

Gentlemen:—I regret that I have an engagement on hand, which will not permit me to accept your invitation to attend the Rail Road mass-meeting and barbecue at Anderson on the 27th inst.

I avail myself of the opportunity of expressing my undiminished confidence in the favorable location of the road. Indeed, the more fully and minutely I become informed in reference to it, the greater is my confidence, both as to the facility of constructing the road and the extent of trade and travel it will command. But I go further, and avail myself also of the opportunity to express my increased confidence in the successful and early completion of the road, not only from my increased confidence in its favorable location, but from the spirited and judicious beginning that has been made. I learn, that the whole of the grading from Anderson to Columbia is already under contract and in the course of execution, with the exception of a few miles, and that the contracts have been taken by the stockholders, under an arrangement which gave them the preference. Nothing could be more judicious, than such an arrangement. There is in the country at this time, much more surplus labor than surplus money. It will be far more easy for the stockholders to pay their subscription in the former, than the latter. By extending the same arrangement to all other descriptions of labor, that can be well done by the stockholders, a large portion of the whole expenditure may be met with very little diminution of income on their part.

So spirited and judicious a commencement augurs well. It gives grounds for assurance that good sense, economy and skill will govern in the construction and management of the road, and that the work will be cheaply, speedily, and well executed.

I shall not undertake to enumerate the many and great advantages of the road to the State, and especially our section. I have already expressed myself pretty fully on that point in a letter to one of the Committee, and shall content myself with adding, they are so numerous, that some will be omitted in the most careful enumeration, and that so great will be its convenience, that we will wonder, after the road is in operation, how we got along at all without it.

In conclusion permit me to offer the following sentiment:

The President, Directors and other Officers of the Rail Road: Their good management thus far entitle them to the thanks of the Company, and give reasonable grounds for belief, that the great enterprize, of which they have the charge, will, as far as it depends on them, be early, economically and faithfully executed. With great respect, I am, &c. J.C. CALHOUN.

PC in the Charleston, S.C., *Courier*, October 3, 1848, p. 2; PC in the Greenville, S.C., *Mountaineer*, October 13, 1848, p. 2 (from the Anderson, S.C., *Gazette*, September 28, 1848); PC in the Charleston, S.C., *Mercury*, October 14, 1848, p. 2.

From A[NDREW] J. DONELSON, [U.S. Minister to Prussia]

Frankfort [Germany,] Sep[tembe]r 27, 1848

My dear Sir, I was greatly obliged to you for the copy of your able speech on the Territorial bill, which reached me in Switzerland. It was ineffectual I see in the vote of the House, but I trust its moral influence on the country will be useful.

I concur with you in saying that Mr. [Thomas] Jefferson, in the famous ordinance for the Government of the Territory North of the Ohio, yielded to a feeling of Philanthropy, what all his political doctrines would now compel him to withhold. If now alive he would see that the free soil party instead of proposing to relieve the burdens of slavery, aimed to punish the white man in the South for having done what was his duty under the circumstances of his situation.

It will not do for the North to say they have abolished slavery. They have only banished the black man from their Territory, who has found an asylum in that of the South. To give themselves credit for such an act is to reverse the law given for our imitation in the case of the good Samaritan. How many are the Blacks who are to enjoy the benefit of the free soil claimed by the Buffaloe Convention? Does not every body ["know" *interlined*] that the North Western Territory contains comparatively no blacks, and never will? Is not therefore the practical effect of all such Legislation an idle boast, not benefitting the Black race, but punishing the white man who has had the humanity to protest it[?]

It is not by such pretentions that the impartial eye of our posterity will be swayed when they trace the events of our history. The best[?] historian will see that the South have done their duty.

My residence in Europe has satisfied me that this institution of ours, called slavery, has had an agency in shaping our institutions which few of us in the South ["even" *interlined*] sufficiently appreciate.

The presence of the black race in the United States enabled the white man to treat as his equal all his own race. A basis was thus formed for liberty as broad as the population: and hence popular sovereignty was a reality, not a fiction. The absence of such a basis in Europe is the secret of the failure of all its attempts to found popular institutions.

But I have not the space here to argue such a question, and if I had I could not hope to say any thing new to one so familiar with the subject as you are. To give you in a few words, however, my idea of the service which the slave institution has rendered us, allow me to say, that it is my firm conviction if all the inhabitants on the American continent were suddenly swept away, and if its vast solitudes were thus offered to the inhabitants of Europe for their occupation, settle[me]nt, and Governme[n]t, the institutions they would establish would be no better than those they are now attempting to reform. This is only saying that in my judgement, if slavery be an evil as recognised by us in the South, it is one which has been sent by Providence, and ["it ought to have convinced" *canceled*] our No[r]thern friends ["ought long ought long (*sic*) ago to have learned" *interlined and* "long since" *canceled*] that their remedies for it, even if successful would only doom them as well as ourselves to dangers far more threatening to our common liberty and prosperity.

You are aware that I am here as a Minister. You m[a]y desire to know then what I think of the destiny of this Government. The Arch Duke [John of Austria] is a man of sense. He means what is right, and deserves credit for throwing himself into the torrent of convulsions which are pouring over his country. Crisis after crisis overtakes him until he is at last forced to protect the national Assembly with a guard of 12000 regular Tro[o]ps, to declare the city of Frankfort in a state of siege, and to enforce his orders at the point of the bayonet. Yet you must not conclude that his Government is hopeless, or that he aims to acquire power at the expense of liberty. These extreme measures were necessary to save the lives of the Assembly, and the city of Frankfort from pillage & murder.

The question which brings up this crisis is one that we should have regarded in the United States as anterior to the existence of a Federal Government. I mean that of the powers conferred by the seperate states. In the Armistice made by Prussia with Denmark a part of the Assembly alleged that Prussia had not followed the mandate of the Assembly and thus denied the Treaty power to the central Government. This rouses the jealousy of Austria and puts in motion the rivalities of all the Kings that are parties to the confederation. Hence the close vote in the Assembly, the people out of doors sympathising with the Left, and pushing their discontent into a revolt because they dread the military ascendancy of Prussia.

Fortunately at the same moment the local contests at Berlin & Vienna render the separate action of either of those courts dangerous if not impossible. Should the power therefore which the Arch Duke is obliged to exercise not wound too deeply the national feeling he will still hold the advantage in the game, and thus ["affords" *can-*

celed] afford a hope that a constitution may be formed under which the political education of both the Kings & the people of Germany may be improved. By such a slender thread suspends the chance that this Govt. may bring better days to the German people. And yet it was on this slight hope that I advised the President to recognise the central power. Faint as it is it is better than that afforded by the independent action of the state Governments, where if the Kings regain their former power the people will suffer [*one word canceled and* "more" *interlined*] than ever.

France under the flag of the Republic does even worse than Germany. There the press has been muzzled whilst what is called a free constitution is manufactured. And France even looks with jealousy at the German project of union, and menaces Austria out of excessive love of freedom. I need not say to you that I turn sick from such scenes, and am almost ready to give up the hope of seeing the world governed by popular institutions. No one here looks into the future without trembling and none look[s] back without seeing that old institutions are undermined, and must be succeeded by others having a different basis. What shall be this basis?

But if I turn from Europe to look at home, I am almost as much afflicted when I see the changes which have been wrought in the last two years, in the party relations of our public men. The war with Mexico has increased our military glory, but it increases the emigration from Europe, which is itself a danger—it multiplies our points of contact with Foreigners—it forces us abruptly on m[an]y untried questions at home, among which this of slavery is not the least.

I take consolation only from the hope that our statesmen, adopting the spirit of your Territorial speech, will study more closely the Constitution, and respect more cordially the spirit of compromise on which all our success rests. I am very respectfully y[ou]r ob[edien]t s[er]v[an]t, A.J. Donelson.

[P.S.] Your young friend [Edward W.] Geddings is here with my son. They have run away from the cholera, which I hope will be so far terminated next week that we may go back with safety, for I still consider Berlin my head quarters. A.J.D.

ALS in ScCleA; variant PC in Boucher and Brooks, eds., *Correspondence*, pp. 475–477.

From H[ENRY] W. CONNER

Charleston, Sept[embe]r 28 1848

I have just returned from the North where I went soon after I saw you in Charleston & found your letter of the 25th ult. on my arrival.

I notice particularly what you say in regard to the paper & will communicate the views to the parties interested as opportunity offers.

A great change has come over the people of the North since my last annual visit amongst them. Free soil is now *the universal sentiment of the whole North & East* & has already swallowed up both parties & all orders & classes of people & I can conceive of no sentiment stronger than the determination evinced ["there" *interlined*] to eradicate slavery from the whole continent of North America & they mean to do it & will do it regardless of all consequences unless we meet & defeat them before our strength is undermined.

From what I saw I verily believe [Martin] Van Buren would have been elected upon the free soil movement if both the whig & democratic parties had not at once wrested his ground from him & occupied it themselves. They both now alike claim free soil as being always their true & legitimate ground & are endeavouring to force the Van Buren[ites] off upon the ultra ground of abolitionism & liberty party.

The plan as I understand it with the free soil party is to exclude us from all Territory henceforward & a large portion of the democratic party, consisting of the masses[?], now largely composed of emigrants, & the politicians are intent upon the absorption of all Mexico, Cuba & Canada. The South is of course to be excluded from all, while ["a" *canceled*] constant approaches are to be made upon slavery in the frontier States as Kentucky, Missouri, Virginia, Maryland, North Carolina & Tennessee with the expectation of the people themselves being brought to emancipate by their own Legislatures under an amendment of their constitutions under a Convention of the people & they quote Kentucky & point to Virginia in confirmation of what they propose. But what gave me most concern was to perceive an increasing disregard & disrespect of the South. In truth they are fast loosing [*sic*] all fear & all respect for us for they see us wasting our energies upon petty—& pitiful issues when day by day the Factions of the North are drawing the cordon closer & closer around us. Indeed I was told over & often that you were not the exponent of the feeling & sentiment of the South on the subject of slavery and that the people were not with you & would not sustain you in your defence of the institution.

I find a good deal of excitement here about [Zachary] Taylor & [Lewis] Cass—but not a great deal of acrimony. But for the ill temper & indiscretion of a few there would be no great bitterness felt by any. After the election is over I hope differences may be healed.

I leave on Saturday for Georgia & as far as Montgommery Ala. to return in 10 days & thought I might as well give you the result of my observations at the North.

As well as you understand the condition of things you would be amazed at the state of feeling now existing North. Yours, H.W. Conner.

ALS in ScCleA; variant PC in Jameson, ed., *Correspondence*, pp. 1182–1184. NOTE: Calhoun's AEU reads, "Conner."

From LEWIS E. HARVIE

"Elk Hill," Amelia Va., Sept. 29th 1848

Dear Sir, I beg leave to trespass on your indulgence in asking your attention to the following communication upon a subject mutually interesting to both of us.

In taking part in the discussion of the political ["contest" *altered to* "canvass"] that is now agitating the country I have thought proper to treat the contest that is going on between the two parties for the presidency as trivial & secondary in importance, when compared with that waged by the North against the South & my views have met a cordial response from the people in my county.

On yesterday after a discussion in a meeting of the Democratic party which turned on the position of the two candidates in reference to the slavery question, a proposition was submitted ["& unanimously adopted by the meeting," *interlined*] by a highly respectable whig to call a meeting of the people of the county irrespective of party to take into consideration the propriety of adopting an address and resolutions, declaratory of our views on this subject & for the purpose of instructing our delegates to the Legislature & Congress as to their action next winter. From the utter indifference felt in the presidential election & the keen interest manifested on this subject I hope that this meeting may be the forerunner of many others, if we act wisely & with prudence. I am sure that our people are sound, ["&" *canceled*] but equally sure that they require to be roused in anticipation of the coming storm. It is important that in taking action they take proper action & such is the stringency of party drill that I am at a loss with whom to consult without imposing on your time & (permit me to say) known fidelity. I wish you to prepare a short address & resolutions placing us on the position that the South must occupy next winter keeping aloof from this miserable party scramble for the Presidency. It is much that I am asking, more than I would feel justified in asking in reference to any matter less vitally important. You will not be known in the matter at all, & we shall then be sure to do no mischief in our effort to sustain our rights. My object is to take advantage of the present feeling & to make an effort to prepare the public mind for the coming storm & to show in advance to the party hacks what they must expect in case they persevere in trading upon this delicate & dangerous question. I do hope that you will lend me your aid in this matter; & at all events write me your views ["in time for the meeting, to be held on the 4th Thursday in October," *interlined*] if you do no more. I am deeply impressed with the conviction that if the South yeilds once more, that all is lost, & without popular action, I feel no confidence in the courage or fidelity of our representatives in Congress. So far as the Presidential question is concerned, I believe it will decide nothing pro or con. [Lewis] Cass has come as near to us as he thought necessary to secure our votes & having secured them we will have lost all hold on him. [Zachary] Taylor trusting to his Southern location & ownership of slaves is openly bidding for the support of our opponents, & his Southern friends are sustaining him openly on the ground that he ought to go into the presidency uncommitted, to act as arbitrator & compromise the question. When he entered into the Canvass he had my respect at least as a man of character & patriotism, now I hold his character & intellect in equal contempt. Having not the least confidence in either candidate I shall yet support Cass as the least objectionable of the two. Occupying the position in the country that you do, I think you are clearly right for supporting neither & applaud you for it. With great respect I am Most truly Y[ou]rs, Lewis E. Harvie.

ALS in ScCleA.

To "His Ex[cellenc]y Gov[erno]r" [David] Johnson

Fort Hill, 1st Oct[obe]r 1848

My dear Sir, I take the liberty of enclosing you the Pendleton Messenger, containing a corrected copy of my letter addressed two or three years ago [11/1846], to a part of the delegation of this district, on the subject of the proposed change of the manner of appointing [Presidential] electors. The subject, it is probable, will be again aggitated at the approaching session of our legislature. In my opinion, few subjects have ever come under its consideration of more vital importance to the well being of our State. I cannot be mistaken in asserting, that the adoption of the General Ticket System would end in a total and disasterous change in our State Government.

Should you take the same view, I do hope you will throw the weight of your Authority & influence against it in your annual Message. Our present system has worked well, and has given a stability to our legislature, and a weight and control in the federal Government never enjoyed by any ["other" *interlined*] State of the same population. I solemnly beleive, that on preserving our State Government as it is, depends, not only ["our" *interlined*] safety, but that of the entire South.

I feel assured you will excuse me, in availing myself of the opportunity of making a few remarks on the other vital question to us: I mean abolition.

I am thoroughly convinced, that it has reached a stage in its progress, when there is no longer any reason to hope, that it will ever be arrested through the presidential election, or the federal Governm[en]t. To rely on either will most assuredly prove fatal to us in the end. To arrest it, the South must look to itself. To lay aside all party strife and to be united among ourselves is the first step towards arresting it. We have a far deeper interest in restoring harmony among ourselves, than in pursuing party ["harmony" *canceled and* "relations" *interlined*] with either party at the North. Nor have we any time to lose in restoring harmony, if we desire to save ourselves. The presidential ["election" *interlined*] will soon be over, and the next session of Congress will decide what reliance we can place on the North. If nothing effectual should be done, & the South should fail to take some decisive step to arrest the further progress of the disease, & to cause our rights to be respected, we shall be in eminent danger. In my opinion, in that case, the next summer should not be permitted to pass without a Convention of the South;

if to do no more, to proclaim what our rights are & our solemn determination to maintain them and fixed resolution to hold no party relation with any ["who are" *canceled and* "at the North which is" *interlined*] not prepared to stand by us in maintaining them. The more prompt and decisive our course, the safer for us and the Union. If the disease is permitted to progress much farther, it will be beyond the control of any remedy, and must end in emancipation in its worst form, or the dissolution of the Union. I speak from a thorough investigation and Knowledge of the subject.

I am very happy to hear that you are recovering from the terrible injury you received, and sincerely hope you may be speedily restored to the ["full" *interlined*] use of your limbs. With great respect yours truly, J.C. Calhoun.

ALS in ScU-SC, John C. Calhoun Papers. NOTE: An AEU by Johnson reads, "Hon. J.C. Calhoun, 1st Oct. [18]48. Ans[were]d 16: Oct[obe]r [18]48 [*not found*]. Copy enclosed."

From R[APHAEL] J. MOSES

St. Joseph [Fla.,] 1 Oct. 1848

Dear Sir, I took the liberty of forwarding to your address, by the last mail—my defence as a Delegate to the Baltimore Convention. I am aware that the probability is—that in the many more important calls upon your time, you will scarcely find leisure to glance at it.

But my respect for your opinion, and my gratitude to you for your kind approval of my course at Baltimore, prompted me to forward the address. I assure you sir that the few kind words said to me by you in W[ashington] have sustained me through an ordeal more severe than I had ever expected to pass. The maintenance of my position has subjected me to the most bitter denunciations and that virulent abuse which political partisans treasure in their vocabulary to be hurled against those who are unwilling at the sacrifice of principle to yield submissive obedience to the dictates of party. Every politician including my colleagues at Baltimore ["have" *canceled*] are (I learn) supporting the nominees. Mr. [David L.] Yulee [Senator from Fla.] wrote to me by the last mail that he had written an address to the people of Marion [County, Fla.] advising the support of [Lewis] Cass & [William O.] Butler: so that I stand *alone* supported through the State by perhaps 100 voters who will have independence enough not to cast a vote at all.

My impression is that our State ticket will be beaten in endeavoring to carry Cass. In my own county [Calhoun] the Dem[ocratic] Ticket will be elected. I did all I could for its success, for my anxiety was to carry the State Ticket thus showing our Dem[ocratic] strength, and then by with[h]olding a majority vote for the Presidency, the *reason* would be more apparent to North Democracy. South Carolina's abandoning her neutral position has been a severe blow to those Southerners who were endeavoring to make a rally against the Tyranny of party. Had she stood firm I believe we should have succeeded in making an organization in this State favorable to her views. Excuse my troubling you with this communication & believe me to be with sentiments of the most profound respect, your ob[edien]t Serv[an]t, R.J. Moses.

ALS in ScCleA. NOTE: Raphael Jacob Moses (1812–1893), a native of Charleston, was a lawyer, merchant, land speculator and later a Confederate supply officer.

From KER BOYCE

Kalmia [S.C.,] Oct[obe]r 2d 1848

My dear Sir, I have to apoligise for [not answering] your letter of the 19th of August [*not found*]. I was not present when it Came to hand and It happened to [be] put in the Book Case and fell over and I only found it today. They told me that a letter had been received from you, which I presumed was a[n] answer to Myne [*sic*]. I will allow the debt to stand over as you have requested.

I have felt much, on account of the affairs of our Countray [*sic*] alltho[u]gh I have retyured[?] from publick life, but I feel much and deeply to see the warmth that is getting up through the Southern Countray on the Presidential Election and peculare[?] for [Lewis] Cass, who cares no more for the South than any other politician of the North for our Interest. They have no respect for us and thear only object is to see the Negroes Cut our throghts [*sic*; throats], and I feel alarmed to see such men as [Robert Barnwell] Rhett Coming out and making warm and inflametary speeches in his favor and against [Zachary] Taylor. I look upon Taylor [as] a[n] honest man and If he should happen to fall into good hands will make a good President. If in bad hands he will make a bad one I fear. But Cass will not make a good one under any circumstances. You will see that I would vote for Taylor if I had a vote as he must be sound on the Main Question. His being a Southern Man and a slave holder give assur[anc]es beyond doubt. Still I would not take trouble to have him Elected as I think him a weak man and in bad Company, So you will see that I am not so [a]fraid of Names[?] as to be drawn in to the nominee of the Baltamore Convention. Which was denounced by those who now, are warm in his Cause and denounce all those who do not go for that Nominee. Sir I feel the most alarming feature in this Canvass is that party [comes] first and our rights and libertyes next. I feel that we must [*one letter canceled*] be disgraced and when I see men like [William L.] Yanc[e]y who had a platform, made by the State of Ala. and because he like a Patirot [*sic*] stood up to that, that he is now denounced and at the meeting at Attilanta [*sic*] where one of the speakers said that Yanc[e]y is [and] was denounced and de[a]d in Ala. that expression brought forth the greatest applaus[e] that was produce[d] by any of the party. This alarms me when a man stands up for the South that Partisans have him denounced. This is what, I feel to be alarming. Y[ou]rs Most Sincarely, Ker Boyce.

ALS in ScCleA. NOTE: This letter was mailed from Graniteville, S.C., on 10/4. "Kalmia" was the summer home of the manufacturer William Gregg.

From JOHN A[LFRED] CALHOUN

Eufaula [Ala.,] October 2d 1848

D[ea]r Uncle, When in South Carolina this summer I paid a flying visit to your family, expecting to have met with you on your return from Washington. I was sorry, that your unexpected detention at Washington, deprived me of the pleasure which I anticipated at once more meeting with you. I assure you my disappointment was great, and nothing but the most urgent business could have induced me to have left as soon as I did. My determination, however, to return to Abbeville compelled me to hasten back to this place in order to arrange my business for my return.

There were many matters upon which I desired to converse with you. In the first place it was my desire to have consulted with you as to my return. I regret very much the necessity which compels my return. Not that my attachment to my native State, has been in the slightest degree diminished by my absence from it. On the contrary I appreciate her, and her high position, even more than I did when I left there. The contrast between the high toned bearing of South

Carolina, and the miserable partizan condition of things as they have existed here has caused me to cling with more than common tenacity to the Carolina position. The regret which I feel arises from the fact, that having taken a bold stand here, in opposition to the servile system of *Party tactics*, and fought manfully for the ascendency of sound principles; And having to a great extent, accomplished a radical change in the tone of public sentiment, I am compelled to leave, just as my condition enables me to take a lead in political matters. I feel well assured, from abundance of evidence, as well as from the assurance of numerous friends here ["that" *canceled*] if I were to remain here, that not all the power of party could prevent me from occupying a commanding position, in opposition to the mere party leaders. As an evidence of my power here, I am assured by numerous friends ["since my return" *interlined*] that to my individual exertions, alone, is to be attributed the prostration of both the [Zachary] Taylor & [Lewis] Cass clubs. They each, had but one meeting, when the fource [*sic*; "of" *interlined*] public sentiment was such as compell[ed] their discontinuance. The most prominent men of both parties (the demagog[ue]s excepted) have told me that they regard my leaving them as a great calamity. Do not set all that I have said on this subject to personal vanity. I confess that all this is flatt[er]ing to my self esteem. But it is all true, and in relating it to you, I hope you will consider it, as it is intended, for your eyes only. I have uncovered[?] myself fully to you, as to the true cause of my regrets at leaving this place. I confess that prudential considerations, alone, have restrained my political aspirations; and now that my circumstances, no longer render it it [*sic*] improper for me to restrain myself I acknowledge to you, that I have a strong desire to play the politician (not the demagog[ue]). Your [career?] in political life, is the one I should like to copy—and though it has been beset with [many?] trying scenes, and has been but illy reward[ed] yet I should choose a similar one, with all its trials, and little reward; in preference to one of the most brilliant success, with less elevation. I fear, however, in the move which I now feel somew[h]at compelled to make, in defference to the wish of my Father-in-law [Williamson Norwood], I am risking the loss of all chance to gratify my wishes. I will have to begin anew ["to" *canceled*] in Abbeville, and fear that the peculiar situation which I will occupy (having Mr. [Armistead] Burt ahead of me) will prevent me from regaining my former position. Write me at your earliest convenience. Your nephew most affectionately, John A. Calhoun.

ALS in ScCleA.

From JAMES H. TAYLOR

Charleston, October 3d 1848

Respected Sir, I have the honor to hand you a receipt of one Box containing two pieces of Cotton cloth—Manufactured at the Charleston Cotton Manufacturing Company's mill, in this City. These Clothes are made from the first Bale of New Cotton received in this place this season and are pretty fair samples of the Goods we make being perhaps a little improved by extra dressing and brushing. Our Factory now employs about 100 operatives (all white) and their pay is from $2 to $6 per week payable in cash monthly. 17 of these operatives are from the north and are well acquainted with the business. The rest are new hands collected from this City, and suburbs. As a general thing our Southern Girls do as well as the same class at older manufacturing establishments and will without doubt make as good operatives in time. The value of the raw material in our goods is about 2¢ per yard the remainder of its price is divided between Labor and Profit—Labor being 2¢ per yard more, and gross profits aside from Commissions and Interest about 1½ to 2½% per yard, according to width. Our small mill will pay per an[nu]m about $50,000 for Cotton and Labor and in dividends to stockholders about $16 to $18,000. We regard our ["(experiment as setling the)" *interlined*] question in relation to Manufacturing Cotton into Cloth to advantage by *Steam*, in our Southern Cities, and I have the strongest hope that in a few years the manufacture of our own *great* staple will add to the Southern States incalculable wealth and prosperity. I send you Sir ["these" *canceled*] these two pieces merely as a specimen of goods which cannot be surpas[s]ed in the same grade by any manufactory in the United States. I am Sir with profound Respect Your ob[edien]t S[ervan]t, James H. Taylor, Agent, C[harleston] C[otton] M[anufacturing] Co.

ALS in ScCleA; PC in Boucher and Brooks, eds., *Correspondence*, p. 478. NOTE: Taylor's letter was written on stationery with a letterhead that depicted the Charleston Cotton Manufacturing Company's mill. An AEU by Calhoun reads, "Charleston factory."

From EZRA D. PRUDEN

Morris Town N. Je[r]sey, Oct. 4, 1848

Honourable and Dear Sir, Permit me sir to refer to your notice a subject of great importance as connected with party politicks here at the north in regard to the sin of slavery. This point sir is what furnished them with their most powerfull weapons, on this basis stands their ["most" *canceled*] impregnable fortress And indeed sir this is by no means remarkable. It results from early prejudice. It grows with their growth and strengthens with their strength, and it is incorporated in the elements of their early education and inst[r]uctions and at length becomes with most a mater of faith and Conscience and would be considered next to blasphemy to assert that slavery was no sin. I frankly confess sir that I was formerly of this opinion and confirmed in it by Dr. [Samuel H.] Cox of N. York and Dr. [William R.] Weeks of Newark where I then resided. They semed to me to be pillars in the Church and as I had sat for some years when a boy under the preaching of Dr. ["Cox" *canceled*] Cox I considered ["that" *interlined*] whatever he said was law & gospel to[o]. This of course setled the question with me without an investigation and I presume that this is the case with most of us here at the North. They never have examined the subject and they are confirmed in their prejudices by a thousand humbug storys about the suffering of the poor slave and in this way thousands of honest men are deceived. Nothing here sir to rebut these calumnies or to enlighting the public mind on this important subject. On the contrary nearly all the Religious Journals advocates Anti slavery and especialy that engine of Hell the N. York Evangelist published by an asociation of (gentlemen). How can it be posible sir that honest men can be so deceived as not to perceive that the spirit that would sow swords[,] firebrands[,] arrows and death broad cast over the land sow disunion[,] distrust and divide the churches cannot come from Heaven. I had concluded that there was no danger to our union arising from the Abolitionists But now under the mask of free soil[,] land distribution[,] slave representation &c the Bait is easily swalowed and spreads like wild fire in these parts. There is nothing in circulation here to expose their base hypocrisy and therefore thousands of honest men easily swallow the bait and when once swalowed there is no hope for them. The most of them ["appear to me like Judus after he had swalowed the salt" *canceled*] they are infatuated their reason is blinded and their will perverted and some of them are shut up to all sympathy but that of the poor slave. They can see a poor man laboring and toiling with feeble health to support a large family of children and will extort the last cent from them though his children should be in want of bread (and then mourn about the poor slave). They will even oppress the widow and fatherless children turn them out in the street if their rent is not paid (and then mourn about the poor slave). I protest before God sir that my wife whose health has been feble for 10 years and daughters is obliged to make mens thick shirts for 72 cents per day, and if not made in the best manner they are sent back on their hands to ["do" *altered to* "done"] over again and then obliged to trade out every cent. Nor one sponfull of flour can they get without money though it be due them and after deducting out their exorbitant proffits the making does not cost them over 4 cents a piece. This seem to me like requiring brick without giving straw. I have been to the south sir I spent a half a year in Augusta & Savanah Ga. 1831–32 and I can say that I have seen greater suffering here among our white slaves than than [*sic*] i seen there amongst the blacks. I love the South sir. I have tasted of their warm friendship and hospitality unknown here at the north. I might refer to Names in Agusta who are an honor to their country. My name can be found on the church record there. The happyiest hours of my life I spent there and I have long mourned over the treachery[,] basness and folly of a part of my countrymen. I fear sir that a collision between the North & south is near at hand and to all appearance inevitable and when I saw the Authority of the bible and the Prince of peace used to head a conspiracy or mob a thousand times worse than Judus headed in the garden of Gethsemane I could hold my peace no longer. I sat down and wrote a challenge to a presbyterian clergiman of a [*mutilation*] congregation ["who preached Abolition &c" *interlined*] to point out the chapter and verse that clearly condemnd slavery as a sin and it would settle the question with me forever. After waiting 2 weeks without an answer I resolved to ["give" *canceled and* "puplish" *interlined*] the result of my own investigation in a course of numbers and accordingly wrote 2 numbers and took them to the editor who promised to publish them the next week. After waiting 2 weeks I took them away to annother editor who also agreed to publish them but after another week he intimated to me that many of his customers were of that class and feared it would injure his paper but through the influence of a friend I obtained the first editor[']s consent to publish it if the whole argument were reduced to a sheet of paper which i immeadiatly endeavoured to do—a copy of which I here enclose which I am informed is to be answered next week and I have the promise of the editor fair play in his colums and I trust your honor will see that I have not taken the field without weapons.

My motive in writing to you sir is to offer you my service if I can any way se[r]ve your cause even should it cost my life. Yea if I had a hundred lives I think I should feel willing to sacrifice them all in the cause of truth. I have no desire sir to outlive the disgrace and ruin of my country. I do not write this sir to solicit the honor of your name but if you should percieve that the subject is worthy of notice and appoint one of your friends to communicate with me and furnish a small donation to enable me to get pamplets ["printed," *interlined*] and circulated to hire some of the leading journals to insert the argument and if it does no more than raise a doubt in the minds of the north whether slavery is or is not a sin it will do more for the cause of the south than hosts of Armed men. I think I speak from experience in what i have already observed in my weak efforts in the cause. There are honest men here sir hosts of them. Even the gentleman through whose influence I obtained the use this publick paper told me that unless they proved from scripture that slavery was a sin he would ["not" *interlined*] patronise free soil altho his sons and all of his work hands are hot Abolitionists and I know that it can never be proved from scripture. See their wicked attempt at the last meeting of the Missionary Board at Boston Sept. 13th and there in the face of no proof assert that slavery was a sin and a great evil and that it lay directly across the Misionary path and must be met and then set about establishing the inquisition over the Missionaries to the Indians for hireing slaves (consistency where has thou fled). Why is it sir that the south does not attempt in some way to counteract this conspiracy at the north. Why sir the paper that I before aluded to has for more than 18 years exausted all the powers of eloquence[,] Philosiphy and Sophistry under the Mask of Religion to prejudice the minds of the north against the south. They have used every art that ingenuity could divise to circulate there paper over the Union and from 1833 to '43 if i am not mistaken they have used every stratagem to circulate their paper ammong the slaves by enclosing them in boxes of merchantdise for the south[,] boxes of medicine &c till numbers ["lost" *interlined*] their southern custom by it. I repeat it why does not the south retaliate. Are the presses musled here at the North. If so would it not be well to sound the alarm.

I am under the conviction sir that this Anti slavery principle originated in france with Voltaire in his secret password Crush Christ and aimed at the foundations of all governments and first introduced in politicks by Bonyparte in his Decree to abolish negro slavery and the slave trade June 1815. I now submit this subject to your consideration. No eye but my own has seen or heard a word of this letter. I stand alone ["I stand alon" *canceled*]. Even my nearest Brother a Justice of the peace and a leading Whig has turned over to the Abolition party and i believe the most of them are merging on the [Martin] Vanburen platform.

I sincerly hope sir that my fears are groundless but I feel that what is done in this cause must be done without delay. I feel confident sir that there will be a strong reaction here when this affair results in blood. They will find that they have not counted all their men and should I recive any assistance in this cause directed to Morris Town N.J. I pledge my self to be accountable for every dollar I recive ["from" *canceled and* "to" *interlined*] any name given and observe the strictest secrecy if required. If poverty be a crime sir I plead guilty to its full extent but I allow no man ["to call me" *canceled*] to call me dishonest. I believe sir that I can pull aside the mask of this free soil hypocrisy and hold it up to publick view by procuring pamplets printed cheap and circulate them by the paper carriers and employ those public journals that will insert it for a small fee.

I hope your honor will pardon me for trespasing on your time and my bad writing for I wrote in haste. Your humble servant till Death, Ezra D. Pruden.

P.S. My motive Sir in puting forth the argument in this method as you will see in the slip was to tempt discusion. What I consider the strongest point is not here aluded to. E.D.P.

ALS with En in ScCleA. NOTE: Pruden enclosed an article clipped from the Morristown, N.J., *Jerseyman* of an unknown date, entitled "Is Slavery a Sin? answered."

From W[illia]m Pinkney Starke

Hamburg S.C., October 5th 1848

Dear Sir, When we parted at Abbeville you expressed a wish to be informed of the effect of the water-cure upon General [George] McDuffie's health—how far it might tend to relieve the symptoms of his case. The General, likewise, on my taking leave of him last Saturday, desired me to write to you. He is at the "Milledgeville Water-cure Institute"—and I am happy ["at" *canceled*] in being able to write that the beneficial results already obtained by the use of cold water encourages the hope of a very considerable amelioration of his health if the treatment be persisted in long enough. It were folly to think of repairing a constitution so wofully shattered by the wear and tear of twenty years of toil, excitement and mismanagement in the space of a few months; but that there is sufficient to justify the expression of hope will be made evident by referring to the symptoms of improvement already manifested.

The first effect of cold water rightly applied as a remedial agent is in a salutary action upon the general system; its influence over local disorders is secondary and resultant. Mr. McDuffie's declaration of increasing strength and sense of well-being would serve to show its constitutional action in his case to be beneficial, ["had" *canceled*] even had we not other proofs in the evident return of blood to the surface and in his manifestly improved appetite. Sleep is being coaxed back by degrees as nervous excitement is allayed; and the wondrous power of water in calming nervous irritation has not been more marked than its happy effect in stimulating and strengthening those nerves which move and distribute animal life. The viscid mucous hardly supplied by his salivary glands has increased in quantity and become so much diluted as to allow him the privilege long denied of *spitting*, while his paralysed limb, so long ["entirely" *interlined*] powerless I have seen him elevate to the height of six inches. The General is very comfortably situated and barring a little humbug of manner, the physician is an agreeable man, and evidently understands his business. How is your health? Your habitual temperance ["combined" *canceled*] with an occasional *dash* of cold water will, I trust, preserve long unimpaired your mental and physical energies. I shall not soon forget the rare intellectual treat the lucky accident of my trip to Abbeville, ["at the time" *canceled and* "as" *interlined*] it occurred, threw before me. With Great Respect Your Obedient Servant, Wm. Pinkney Starke.

ALS in ScCleA. NOTE: An AEU by Calhoun reads "Mr. Stark. Send Letter & the Speech to be published."

From I[SAAC] E. HOLMES, [Representative from S.C.]

Charleston [S.C.,] Oct[obe]r 6th 1848

My Dear Sir—I am most maliciously attacked by an anonimous Writer who signs himself "an Independent Voter"—an attempt is made to impugn my veracity in the relation I gave ["in my Speech" *interlined*] of the interview between y[our]self, Mr. [Robert M.T.] Hunter [Senator from Va.] & myself upon the night of y[ou]r arrival in Washington, during the pendency of the Oregon Question. That Speech you told me you had read.

May I ask you to say whether I was not correct in my narrative.

You may remember that the very morning my Speech appeared in the [Washington Daily National] Intelligencer I, asked you the same question in the Senate & you then told me that ["it" *interlined*] was.

I regret to trouble you but the base attack in the [Charleston] Courier leaves me no other alternative.

My respects to Mrs. [Floride Colhoun] Calhoun. With great respect y[ou]rs Truly, I.E. Holmes.

ALS in ScCleA.

From J[ACOB] P. REED

Anderson C[ourt] H[ouse S.C.,] Oct. 7, 1848

Dear Sir, Your letter to Gen. [Joseph N.] Whitner on the Subject of the Rail Road, in his absence, was handed to me by Mr. Kennedy with a request that I should answer it, and I take the earliest convenient moment to do. There has been no arrangement made by the Direction for takeing Subscriptions of stock, on the terms proposed by you, altho, I have heard the matter spoken of; I can only give my opinion therefore as an individual as to its propriety. That opinion is, that, whilst subscriptions in the usual way would certainly be preferred, I can see no material objection to such as you suggest. A Single Subscription of that kind has already been made by Mr. John Smith of Laurens, who gave his Bond to the company obligating himself to pay at one instalment *$5,000* so soon as the Road shall be constructed to the Saluda River, and I have no doubt such subscriptions will be cheerfully received by the company. It is however a matter proper for the determination of the stockholders themselves in Convention and it will be settled at their meeting in November. As to the form of subscription, it does not matter what it is, so it is Legally binding. But I would suggest that the most desirable mode would be the execution of a Bond or Bonds payable in one or more instalments upon the happening of the condition annexed. Such subscriptions might be made immediately available to the Company, when one in the ordinary way could not. Perhaps the better plan if it is satisfactory, would be to make the sums subscribed payable in two instalments & upon the performance of two conditions—One half to be paid when the road crosses the Saluda River and the other half when it is completed to Anderson C[ourt] H[ouse]. You will perceive that persons who take stock in this way will have a decided advantage, over the original ones. In the first place they run no risk as to its construction, and Secondly they loose nothing in the way of interest, whilst stockholders in the ordinary form are subjected to both of these disadvantages.

Our great object however is to construct the road as speedily as practicable, and if possible without incurring any other debts than we may have the means in reserve to pay, and hence I am decidedly in favor of receiving Subscriptions, upon any available terms.

As a member of the Company and of the Board of Direction I feel myself greatly indebted to you for the interest you have taken in our enterprize, and am much gratified at the favorable change in the public feeling about Pendleton. I trust we may yet, through your instrumentality, receive a very handsome Subscription in and around that Village, upon such terms as your Judgment may approve.

The Company will meet in Convention in Columbia on the Friday after the 4th Monday in November, when I hope to be able to report the Subscription from your neighborhood. I have the honor to remain Your Obedient Servant, J.P. Reed.

ALS in ScCleA. Note: An AEU by Calhoun reads "J.P. Reid [*sic*]. Relates to rail Road."

From Osee Welch

State [of] Illinois[,] Galina, Oct. 7, 1848

D[ea]r Sir, Allow me to trespass upon your attention a few moments. My object is to get your opinion on a new proposition started in our community, which is deemed of sacred importance to our whole country, and your views will be held in high respect by every democrat in this ["part" *interlined*] of the north, at least by all those who have considered your pollitical course, and views on all subjects vital to our national weal, and the powers of the Federal government, as new issues are starting throughout the north, your friends ["friends" *canceled*] feel themselves ["entild" *canceled*] entitled to your views on so grave a subject as I beg here to present.

It is believed by the most considerate Democrats, ["that" *interlined*] the principle danger to which our institutions are now exposed, is the assumption of powers by the federal government never confered by the Organic law, or the more subtle enlargement of the powers confered beyond all constitutional limit, and that there is a dangerous tendency to this kind of usurpation in the Congress of the United States at this time, and to such an extent that every true patriot should take the alarm, hence the legitimate ["province &" *interlined*] powers of the federal government cannot be to[o] soon agitated and defined. That strange proviso of Mr. [David] Wilmot, adverse to all the guarantees of the Constitution, has aroused the attention of many, to an investigation of the real powers of the government.

We desire to get your opinion with reference to the power of the federal government (*Congress*) to exercise *any jurisdiction whatever over her territories* other than merely to survey[,] sell and dispose of the land, and to protect the settlers by sending their Soldiers to the frontier to protect the citizens from invading enemies, and I beg to submit the following resolutions that you may see more clearly the proposition.

1st. Resolved that thier [*sic*] is no power confered upon the federal congress giving them jurisdiction over the territories not even to appoint Governors or Judges for any territories belonging to the United States.

2[.] Resolved that Congress has no right to pass any law giving her jurisdiction or power to appoint Judges or Governors in her territory, unless that power be confered by the Constitution.

3[.] Resolved that the exercise of the right of jurisdiction over the Territories, and the appointment of Governors and judges is a usurpation of power on the part of the Congress of the United States.

4th Resolved that the public domain and all the territories can only be held by the Federal government in trust for every citizen of the United States.

5. Resolved that it is the privilledge of any and every Citizen of the United States to settle upon the public domain in the territories,

elect thier Governors[,] Judges and other Officers and make such rules & regulations as their domestic convenience require, and the Federal Government according to the guaranties of the Constitution is pledged to sustain and protect them in the enjoyment of these privilledges.

6[.] Resolved that the inherent right of the government to acquire territory can give her no right to the soil, other than a mere possessory-trust-tittle for the benefit of every Citizen of the United States who may choose to occupy said lands or territories.

Mr. Calhoun will confer a great favor upon some of his [*manuscript torn*] political friends, If he will spare time to consider these propositions and favor us with an answer—he will do a favor to the common cause in which we all are interested. With high respect I am Y[ou]r Ob[edien]t S[er]v[an]t, ["Welch & McQuillan" *erased*] Osee Welch.

ALS in ScCleA; PC in Boucher and Brooks, eds., *Correspondence*, pp. 478–479. NOTE: This letter was addressed to Calhoun at Charleston with a note to the postmaster "If Mr. C[alhoun] is not [at] Charleston, forward to his Residence."

From JOHN TYLER, *"Confidential"*

Sherwood Forest
Ch[arle]s City County Virginia
October 10, 1848

My Dear Sir, I reciev[e]d a few days since from Mr. [John Y.] Mason, a letter asking my permission to furnish Mr. [James K.] Polk with a statement of ["the" *interlined*] facts which transpired during the last days of my administration, upon the subject of Texas annexation, and by way of inducing such consent, setting out at large his recollection of them. I replied by stating my dissinclination to have statements volunteer[e]d to private contraversialists, but at the same time express[e]d my readiness to furnish to Mr. Polk, if he should request it, a full and authentic statement made under my own name, after corresponding with each member of my late Cabinet, thus avoiding as far as practicable all diversity of statement. I then proceeded to point out an obvious error into which he had fallen, as an inducement to the course whch I had indicated. That error, which it is not necessary to specify in this communication, has seem[e]d to me to render it ["necessary"(?) *canceled and* "desirable" *interlined*] that a well authenticated statement of the facts should be made out, whether ask[e]d for by Mr. Polk or not, for the purpose of securing the accuracy of history, and with this view I have drawn up the enclosed narrative, and request you to assist my memory, if it be defective, by such suggestions as may occur to you!

Asking your early attention to this matter I am D[ea]r Sir with true regard, y[ou]rs &, John Tyler.

ALS in ScCleA. NOTE: This letter was addressed to Fort Hill, "Pendleton County [*sic*]." An AEU by Calhoun reads: "Ex P[resident] Tyler."

To A[NDREW] P[ICKENS] CALHOUN, [Marengo County, Ala.]

Fort Hill, 11th Oct[obe]r 1848

My dear Andrew, I am glad to learn by your's received the last mail, that you are all well, and that you have made such good progress in harvesting your cotton. It is very early to have half harvested by the last of September. The weather still continues fine, and should this month prove as fine as the last, you will have but little left for harvesting after its termination. I have harvested about two thirds of mine & will finish getting in all my corn today. I can finish the rest of my cotton in two, or three weeks. I am much encouraged with the success of manuring. I manured about 30 acres, which has yeilded well.

I agree with you, that there is little prospect of cotton rising and that we ought to sell without waiting for a rise even at the present price. We have heretofore lost by holding back, both by our sales & the rising[?] on of interest.

Mr. [Thomas G.] Clemson is now on his way from Europe with his family & will be here in November. I will apprise you of his arrival, and you must be prepared to come in to meet him & to make arrangement in reference to what we owe him.

We have had, indeed, to contend with great difficulties ["to contend with" *canceled*] in consequence of low prices; and I fear they are not yet at an end; but we must not be discouraged. If we have not made much, we have held our own. Take ["altogether" *interlined*] debts, property, & improvements and capacity for production, & we are as well off, & better, than when we purchased.

I wrote you, that I had to have a note discounted ["with" *canceled and* "by" *interlined*] the bank of the State [of South Carolina] to meet a remittance to Mr. Clemson, & the advance to Patrick [Calhoun]. The exact amount is $1660 & it will fall due the 10th of Nov[embe]r. I hope you will not fail to meet it. The pressure on the money market was such, that it was favour to get it. If any accident should prevent you, let me know in time, in order that I may explain the reason why it was not paid, but I hope there will be none.

We are all well, and all join in love to you, Margaret [Green Calhoun] & the children [Duff Green Calhoun, John Caldwell Calhoun, Andrew Pickens Calhoun, Jr., and Margaret Maria Calhoun]. Your affectionate father, J.C. Calhoun.

ALS in NcD, John C. Calhoun Papers.

From C. W. Jacobs

Berlin[,] Worcester Co[unty]
E[astern] S[hore] Md.
Oct. 12th 1848

Dear Sir, It has become a prominent question, with candid men of both parties, to know, whether in the event of the election of either of them ["Gen. (Zachary) Taylor or Gen. (Lewis) Cass" *interlined*] to the office of President—they would sign a bill, giving to California & New Mexico Constitutions trameled by the Wilmot Proviso or any other Provisos embodying those principles.

A knowledge of this question satisfactorily obtained, ought and doubtless would determine the Electoral vote of this State, and as one most likely to know, and in whom we can place entire confidence I, in behalf of others & myself address you this letter.

The North can out vote us, at least in the House [of Representatives], and Gen. Taylor has declared in one of his letters to J.S. Al[l]ison dated April 22nd 1848—"that the Veto should not be exercised except in cases of *clear* violation of the Constitution or *manifest* haste and want of consideration by Congress." Again in same letter "The personal opinions of ["the" *interlined*] individual who may happen to occupy the Executive Chair ought not to control the action of Congress upon questions of *domestic policy*, nor ought his objections to be interposed," &c etc.

The North, from that letter and a knowledge of their power, are induced, so far as they do, to support Taylor; While the South from his connection with the Institution of Slavery, his location, and consequent presumptive predilection towards the Institution; might safely trust him—but for that letter and the comments on it by such men as [Daniel] Webster in his late Marshfield Speech, & [Robert C.] Winthrop in his later Speech at the *Mass.* Convention.

These reflections too combined ["combined" *canceled*] with Gen. Taylor's expressed preference for Mr. [Henry] Clay & Mr. Clay's Lexington Speech, and the favor that speech met with at the North, all go to excite suspicion and distrust as to what course Gen. Taylor would take on this question [were] he elected.

Nor are we any more certain of what Gen. Cass would do on this subject, in the event of being elected, as both North & South claim in him an advocate of their peculiar interests.

If not asking too much we would regard it as a special and lasting obligation confered on us to know your views on this matter.

As to party, Whether Whig or Democrat, neither can have our votes as such merely—but only as they conform to our interests and the principles of ["they" *altered to* "the"] Constitution and Safety of the Union.

Should you feel disposed to give us the benefit of your views, it shall meet with that confidence and delicacy at our hands which is so justly due to yourself and the subject.

Asking your indulgence for this long letter we beg to subscribe ourselves your sincere and Most Ob[edien]t S[er]v[an]ts, C.W. Jacobs for himself & others.

ALS in ScCleA; PC in Boucher and Brooks, eds., *Correspondence*, pp. 479–480. NOTE: An AEU by Calhoun reads, "Mr. Jacobs."

To J[OHN] A[LFRED] CALHOUN, [Eufaula, Ala.]

Fort Hill, 13th Oct[obe]r 1848

My dear John, I greatly regret, that I missed seeing you, when you were in last. I arrived at Anderson in the stage the same morning you left there, and not more than an hour, or two after you had taken your departure.

I have read your letter with much pleasure. And I am gratified to learn, that you have taken so bold a stand against the old party organization, in your portion of Alabama, & with such success. After having accomplished as much as you have it is certainly greatly to be regretted, that you should fail to reap the fruits of your success, and yet, I doubt not, you have decided right in returning to your native State. I hope even ["there" *canceled and* "here" *interlined*] the door will not be closed to the hopes of your political asperation. Mr. [Armistead] Burt, I am inclined to think, does not wish to continue in political life. I say this, however, in strict confidence. By pursuing the same independent course, accompanied with prudence, you may be, ["as successful" *interlined*] I doubt not, in establishing a well founded popularity in this State, as you have been in Alabama. You may have some disadvantages, that you have not had, where you are, but you will also have advantages you have not had there.

I know it will not discourage you to say, there are storms a head, and that those, who propose to take an active part in politicks must prepare to meet them. The government and people have become corrupt. Those who look to spoils, have the control of both. The existing party organizations are held together entirely by their cohesive power. In the meane time, the South & the North are rapidly becoming alienated & hostile to each other. Disorder, confusion & collision must be the result, but to what they ["may" *interlined*] lead no man can say. I have long stood up against the course of events, which has led to the present state of things, but in vain; and am prepared to do my duty let what may come, & be the consequences, what they may. It is high time for the South to look to its liberty & safety. They are in great danger.

Miss Calhoun & family join their love to you, Sarah [Morning Norwood Calhoun] & family. Yours affectionately, J.C. Calhoun.

ALS in CtY, Sterling Library, Rabinowitz Collection.

To A[NDREW] P[ICKENS] CALHOUN, [Marengo County, Ala.]

Fort Hill, 15th Oct[obe]r 1848

My dear Andrew, I have just received your letter covering one from Patrick [Calhoun], which I have read with pain; & I now write, without a moment[']s delay to say, that if he draws for the amount stated, it must be meet [*sic*]. He is at a critical point, and I cannot but hope, if he gets through his present difficulties, he will see the necessity of a reform in his habits & expenses! He has good sense & many excellent qualities. His misfortune is, his fondness for pleasure.

I must make arrangement to meet a part of our demands to the amount, either the sum Mrs. [Placidia Mayrant] Adams' wants or an indulgence on our smaller debt to the Bank of the State.

I will write to Patrick on the subject and avail myself of the opportunity of urging a reform in his expenditures in the most solemn manner. He will be nearer to me during the winter, which I hope will enable ["me" *interlined*] to establish a control over him.

I shall charge him with all the large advances I have made him, as a part of his portion of $7,000, that I allow all my children, when they settle in life. They amount already with this to upwards of $4,000.

I wrote you so lately that I have nothing more to add. Your affectionate father, J.C. Calhoun.

ALS in NcD, John C. Calhoun Papers.

From Jos[eph] J. Singleton

Dahlonega [Ga.,] 15th Oct. 1848

My Dear Sir, Yours of the 1st Inst. by Mrs. J[ohn] E[wing; that is, Martha Maria Davis] Colhoun, (who is now in our village, & with whom I spent most of yesterday very pleasantly) is received, and in reply to which, I will say 1st, that I handed her $90.15/100 am[oun]t Due you from toll from your Obarr mine. Nothing doing on s[ai]d mine more than I have heretofore mentioned to you by letters. Still a nonperformance of orriginal contract. They have recently cleaned out the old works, and say if they cannot do better by so doing they are willing to give up their lease. I so understood Mr. Hockanall [*sic*; John Hockanoll] in a conversation I had with him since my last letter to you. I am inclined to think that their lease will be given up at the end of the present year without much difficulty. So much for the Obarr mine. 2d. I called on R.B. Lewis in regard to 817, who informed me that he had about $60.00 toll from that mine, which he would send you by ["Mrs." *interlined*] C[olhoun] and that there had been no operation on said mine "for a year or so." 3d. So far as regards your mines at the confluence of Pegionroost, there has been nothing doing since the termination of Messrs. [Robert H.] Moore & [William G.] Lawrence's lease.

Yours of the 10th Inst. by mail was rec[eive]d yesterday, with its accompan[y]ing envellop[;] from the character, and proposition of

Mr. James Anderson, I should judge him to be a respectable man. I do not know him, but will endeavour to find out his character, and if successful, I will immediately inform you. I have heretofore heard too many such tales about the Obarr lot, as well as my own lots, to place much confidence in them; I would of course doubt they be all true. Should you have more proposals to purchase Gold mines than you really want, be pleased to refer the applicants to your humble servant, who can furnish any quantity, variety, or quality which may be desired.

I was much in hopes to have seen you with us this fall; but believing as I hope, that you are more profitably engaged for our common Country, I am content. I have the hon[our] &C., Jos. J. Singleton.

[P.S.] God save the Republic.

ALS in ScU-SC, John C. Calhoun Papers.

To F[RANKLIN] H. ELMORE, [Charleston]

Fort Hill, 16th Oct[obe]r 1848

My dear Sir, Now that the presidential election is over in our State, as far as the popular vote is concerned, it is time, that those, who look to the peace[,] stability & prosperity of the State [turn] to what, in my opinion, is a far more important question; the proposed change in the electoral law of the State. I cannot be mistaken. To adopt the general ticket system will utterly overthrow the State Constitution, & will introduce party organization & machinery, & with it, discord, confusion[,] corruption and the debasement of the character of the people & the State. For my reasons, I refer ["you" *interlined*] to my letter on the subject, published some years since [11/1846] with no other change than the many & gross errors of the press in its first publication, which in many places marred its sense. I herewith enclose a copy.

It is a gross delusion to think, the election, as they call it, can be given to the people directly by adopting the General Ticket, ["wholly" *imperfectly erased and* "&" *written over it*] unworthy of the intelligence of the State. I would prefer the election by districts to any other mode, if other States would adopt it, and have steadidily [*sic*] advocated an amendment of the Federal Constitution to that effect. It would be, in my opinion, a most salutary change. I have gone farther, and advocated the dispensing altogether with electors, and for the voters to vote by electoral districts, direct for the Pres[i-den]t & V[ice] Pres[iden]t; the plurality of votes in each district to count one, and am still in favour of such an amen[d]ment. My only objection to districting the State is, that its vote ["by" *canceled and* "might" *interlined*] be divided, when all others would be united, & that it would finally lead to that most mischevious & anti Republican of all delusions, a general ticket.

I see it objected to the present mode, that it is unconstitutional. The objection is utterly without foundation. The language of the Constitution is; "Each State shall *appoint* in such manner as the legislature ["shall" *canceled*] thereof may direct, a number of electors equal to & & &." If you will turn to the 5th Art[icle] of the old [Articles of] confederation you will find the expression is borrowed from the provision for selecting members of Congress under it. The language used is; "delegates shall be annually *appointed* in such manner as the legislature of each State shall direct, to meet in Congress & & &." The language is nearly verbatim. Now ["as" *interlined*] it is notorious, & was well known to the framers of the Constitution, that the usual mode in which they were appointed was by the legislatures of the States, & that when the present Constitution went into operation, it was the mode ["generally" *canceled*] adopted by ["the States" *altered to* "this State"] and many others; & ["that" *canceled and* "as" *interlined*] their votes have been received without ever being objected to in a single instance, there can be no rational doubt of its Constitutionality. Indeed, the term appoint of itself showes [*sic*] it was intended to be left to the Legislature without [*one word altered to* "restrictions"], as to the manner. Had it been intended to restrict it to popular election, the language used ["by the Constitution" *interlined*] in providing for the appointment of the members of the House of Representative[s] would be used; "to be chosen by the people," or elected by the people, as the legislature shall direct.

I do not know your opinion on the subject, but I hope it accords with mine. Your position gives you a commanding influence in reference to it; and whether our opinions accord or not, I do not think, we can possibly disagree, as to the importance of av[o]iding the ["agitation of the" *interlined*] question for the present, when there is so urgent a necessity for union among ourselves, and to have our whole attention directed to the one all important & vital question. I fear the recent election has done much to divide & distract the State, and that the agitation of the question of the electoral law would add greatly to it. I trust, that the prudent & patriotick on all sides, will unite to postpone it. There will be ample time the next four years to decide, what is to be done, deliberately & ca[l]mly[?]. The present election out of Charleston did not turn on it, and there, it was started suddenly, to bear on another question.

If you concur with me, I hope you will use your influence to have it passed by for the present. As the letter was so erroneously printed, when first published, I would be glad, if you would have it published in the [Charleston] Mercury, &, if it can be done, in the other city papers.

I wrote out since my return, from the manuscript report, a speech I delivered [on 8/12] on the Oregon bill from the House, just before the close of the last session. It will appear in the next [Pendleton] Messenger. I have gone farther into the abolition question than I ever did before, as you will see. Let me hear from you. Yours truly, J.C. Calhoun.

ALS in ScC; photostat of ALS in DLC, Henry Workman Conner Papers.

To "A Prominent Gentleman in Georgia"

Fort Hill, Oct. 16, 1848

My Dear Sir: I cannot give you better proof of my entire approbation of your course, than by enclosing a copy of a speech, delivered by me just at the close of the last session, and which I wrote out from the manuscript report, since my return home. The leading objects were to show the origin of abolitionism, and that the cause of its growth and great and dangerous progress is to be traced to the Presidential election, and that it must continue to advance until it accomplishes its end; unless we cease to look to it, and look to ourselves for a remedy. Entertaining these views, I cannot but approve your course, and regret that this State, Florida and the other Southern States, did not take the same course. It is to my mind clear that we must give up our slaves, or give up our political connection with all parties at the North, unless one should rise up, who shall in good faith observe the compromises of the Constitution, and join us to put down abolitionism.

I see from indications, that the Whigs will in all probability elect [Zachary] Taylor, and that the Democrats will be signally defeated. They will deserve it; and if they should be defeated, it will be because they do deserve it. They have utterly departed from the old State Rights creed, by means of which they rose to power; and have rewarded those who led in the departure, and neglected and denounced those who resisted and warned them of their danger. Defeat was indispensable to reform the party—if, indeed, there be soundness enough left for reformation.

I would be glad to have my speech extensively circulated through your papers. With great respect I am, &c., &c., J.C. Calhoun.

PC in the Charleston, S.C., *Mercury*, May 2, 1860, p. 1; PC in David Rankin Barbee, ed., "A Sheaf of Old Letters," *Tyler's Quarterly Historical and Genealogical Magazine*, vol. XXXII, no. 2 (October, 1950), pp. 89–90.

To H[enry] W. Conner, [Charleston]

Fort Hill, 18th Oct[obe]r 1848

My dear Sir, I have read your letter with the attention its contents so well deserve. The result of your observations, as to the state of publick opinion at the North, in reference to the slave question, singularly accords with the impressions, I have entertained, as you will see by perusing the enclosed copy of a speech, delivered on the Oregon bill from the House, just before the close of the last session of Congress. I brought the report of it with me in manuscript from Washington, & had it written out & placed in the hand of our [Pendleton Messenger] Editor, before I received your letter. I mention these facts, as you might otherwise suppose from the similarity of views & even expressions that I had received your letter before I had prepared my speech for the press.

There now can be no rational doubt, that the time has arrived, when we must make up our mind, to give up our slaves, or give up all political connection & association with either of the existing parties at the North, and rely on ourselves for protection. The reasons I have assigned, in my speech for coming to this conclusion, are unanswerable. The only real practical question is; What should be done to bring the South to the same conclusion, & to rally in support of her domestick institution?

My speech was intended to lead the way to the former; but it will have little effect, unless it should be duely noticed & receive a wide circulation. The first step towards that will be to have it printed in all the city papers with proper comments, to effect the object in view. Now is the time, before the meeting of the Southern

Legislatures. Its publication in the city papers will cause it to be published in the country papers, & to be printed, I hope, in the Georgia papers and ["those of" *interlined*] the States further to the West & South west, especially, if aided by ["the" *interlined*] exertions of you & other friends in Charleston. I will have it published in the [Washington Daily National] Intelligencer & the [Washington] Union.

If the South can be brought to see, that there is no hope from the Presidential election, or the federal government, unless backed by union among ourselves, & that speedily, all would be safe; but until that is done, nothing ["is" *canceled and* "will be" *interlined*] done. In addition to what has been stated, & to give effect to the views I have presented in my speech, and ["every" *canceled and then interlined*] other measure to rouse the South to a sense of her danger, it is most important to ["establish" *canceled and* "start" *interlined*] the paper at Washington, even temporarily, for the next session, or a year, if it can be done with any thing like a general concert among the South[ern] members of Congress. That, however, I cannot decide on, until I arrive at Washington; but it is important towards effecting it, that I should be ["prepared" *canceled and* "authorised" *interlined*] to say, that our State will be prepared to advance the requisite funds to start a paper at once, with the assurance of co-operation from the other States. And I do hope, that the principal subscribers to the paper will be so far consulted, as to enable me to give such assurance, when I arrive at Washington. I can be informed, whether I may, or not, as I pass through the city, on my way to Washington. The sum of $5,000 or 6,000 would be sufficient, I would suppose for that purpose.

With its aid, & a decided & vigorous course on the part [of] the Southern Legislatures at their next sessions, the sound portion of the Southern delegation in Congress may take a stand on higher grounds, than they have yet ever ventured to take, in defence of our peculiar institution, and ["thereby" *interlined*] bring the question at once to an issue. My hope is, that a sufficient number, if not all, may be brought before the end of the session to call a convention of ["the" *interlined*] Southern people, for the purpose of consulting & determin[in]g what should be done. [*One illegible word and* "to" *imperfectly erased.*] To that point in my opinion, all our efforts should be bent. In whatever we do, we must act in good faith, to save the Union if we can, consistently with our liberty & safety; but, if not, to save ourselves at all events.

In the trying scenes before us, we must make up our mind, that this State must take the lead, if any thing is to be done, that will be effectual. For that purpose, we must have harmony among ourselves. I fear the late canvass has done a good deal to distract your city. It has had little, or no effect of the kind with us; and not much, as far as I can learn, out of Charleston. The schism with you in the city must be healed, and the good & patriotick of both parties must take the lead in ["doing it" *altered to* "bringing"] it about.

I saw, with regret, an attempt made just before the election to agitate the question, of changing the manner of appointing electors. My views are well known in reference to it; but if I was ever so much in its favour, instead of being decidedly hostile to it, I would be opposed to acting on the subject at this time, when union was essential to our safety. Its agitation at this time by the Legislature, would contribute much to aggravate and perpetuate whatever schism ["grew" *canceled*] may have grown out of the late canvass. There will be ample time to act on the subject in the next four years, if by our united efforts, we can place ourselves, where we can stand ["in honor" *canceled and* "con-" *interlined*] sistently with our honor & safety in the Union; but, if not, a [*sic*] matters little ["in" *interlined*] what manner our electors may be appointed. Indeed, any great Zeal about it, at this time, would indicate not a little indifference about the question, which ought ["at this time" *canceled and* "now" *interlined*; to] absorb all our attention, if we regard our liberty & safety. With these impressions, I hope the good & patriotick will unite, in using their influence, to postpone any action on the subject ["for" *altered to* "at"] the present session of the legislature.

I took the liberty of furnishing an extract from your letter to our editor, which will probably appear in his next paper, without, of course, using your name, or identifying my name with it. I did it, because I believed it would strengthen the views I took, and the conclusion to which I came. Yours truly, J.C. Calhoun.

ALS in ScC; photostat of ALS in DLC, Henry Workman Conner Papers.

From David Johnson, [Governor of S.C.]

Lime Stone Springs [S.C.,] 18th Oct[obe]r 1848

My dear Sir, I have the pleasure of acknowledging the receipt of your favour [of 10/1] on the subject of the election of Electors of President and Vice President and the Pendleton Messenger containing your letter to a part of the Pendleton delegation on the same subject. Entertaining the same views with yourself I brought the subject before the Legislature at the last Session supposing they would act upon it then and regret that I had not had access to the Messenger as it would have supplied [*one word canceled*] many valuable suggestions that did not present themselves to my mind. If arguments can avail any thing your letter has covered the whole ground and I fear that my personal influence will avail but little in such a question—but I would willingly use it for what it is worth to prevent what I should regard as a great evil to the State. The natural tendency of Republican forms of Government is towards Radicalism and I should regret very much to see our Parish Representation deranged as I have always regarded it (although sufficiently Republican) as our principal Conservative power. It was I observe made something like a test question in Charleston at the late elections and from what I can collect from the news papers there seems to be a disposition there to conciliate the Parishes by adopting the District system in the appointment of electors and it may be that this will take and that I apprehend is the real danger.

Knowing as I do your devotion to the interests of the South and that with the best means of information and untiring zeal you have thoroughly investigated the subject of Abolition in all its bearings I am deeply impressed with your remarks on that subject. Indeed a casual observer [*partial word canceled*] cannot fail to observe that it has taken such deep root at the North & North West that there is no reasoning with it. A few of the more considerate are willing to abide by the compromises of the Constitution and the merchants as a class are opposed to it from interest—but the great mass cherish it from feeling and I am charitable enough to suppose that they think on principle [*several words canceled*]. However this may be they will at no distant day make their influence felt through every department of the Government and I agree with you that we have nothing to hope or expect from them—nor have we more to look for from Presidential power if indeed we should remain any thing but a blank ["to" *canceled and* "in" *interlined*] the appointment. The veto was certainly intended as conservative, but it is a dreadfull despotism to be obliged to depend on the will of one man as a security for our most important rights—more especially when interest and ambition conspire to seduce him to forbear the exercise of the power and I turn with disgust from being obliged to select between the two prominent candidates for the Presidency—having no confidence in one and ["in nei" *canceled*] nothing past or present to aid me in judging what is to be expected from the other.

I have been willing to flatter myself that the present excitement grew in a great degree out of the Presidential Election and that it would pass of[f] with it. That perhaps is hardly desirable for we shall be obliged to meet the question at no distant day and the sooner I think the better. We cannot calculate on any accession of strength under the present operations of the Government, whilst there is great danger that the border slave holding States will yield to the pressure of Circumstances. How long will Maryland, Western Virginia[,] Kentucky, Eastern Tennessee and even the Western part of No. Carolina feel it their interest to retain slaves—they are already unproductive as laborers & their sympathy would not weigh a feather against their interest & their prejudices in another scale. Throwing them out of the question, if unhap[p]ily my apprehensions should be realized, there will be yet strength enough in the remaining States to make their rights respected if they can be brought to act in concert. A Southern Convention is the only means of accomplishing this and the very first movement of the Government of the United States, improperly interfering with our rights ought to be seized on to call it into action. It will at least have my hearty concurrence.

I am very much obliged by your concern about my affliction. I have not yet entirely recovered but with the aid of Crutches I am able to get about the house and adjacent grounds without inconvenience or pain and I am flattered that I shall be able to attend the approaching ["Sess" *canceled*] extra Session of the Legislature. I am with great regard and esteem very sincerely Yours &C, David Johnson.

ALS in ScCleA; photostat of ALS in ScU-SC, John C. Calhoun Papers; PEx in Boucher and Brooks, eds., *Correspondence*, pp. 480–482. Note: An AEU by Calhoun reads "Gov[erno]r Johnson."

From Cuyler W. Young

Armenia[,] Scriven Co[unty] Georgia
19 Oct. 1848

Dear Sir, The undersigned, who is now, and ["here" *canceled*] who was heretofore, (except in 1840 and 1844 when [Martin] Van Buren and [Henry] Clay were candidates) *with* you and *for* you, begs leave to address you. I need not recur to the year 1839, when you answered a letter of enquiry from me respecting the Doctrine of Instructing. I hold to the same doctrine now. I am also for Free

Trade, as you will see from several articl[e]s of mine published in the Charleston Mercury, I think about 1st of April last, dated at Macon Ga. over the signature of Macon, respecting a Rail Road from Halcyondale Ga. to Charleston S.C. I addressed a crowd of some 10,000 men in Philadelphia at the [Whig] convention, ["where" *canceled*] where I was for Clay, and expressed my preference of yourself to either [Zachary] Taylor or [Lewis] Cass. Of course I am a Whig in the sense in which you defined that term ["when" *canceled*] in [Andrew] Jackson's time. It is the opposite of Tory. May I take the liberty now to say that I believe that in Tho[ma]s H. Benton and his Hunkers, you may recognize your bitterest political enemies? Claiming to be friends to the South, they are secret enemies to the South and to Southern talent and honesty. Because you voted against a wicked war, had they nominated yourself, and a respectable candidate north for the Vice presidency, I would have been foremost in your support. I hope you will pardon me for saying that I believe that the Benton, [James K.] Polk and [Henry S.] Foot[e] cliques with others, are the worst of knaves—all for office—perfectly unprincipled. It was long after the Philadelphia convention before I could make up my mind to vote for Gen. Taylor, supposing that Clay had been sacrificed. But I have since formed a better resolve; to vote for Benton's nominee, never; and knowing that Southern influence defeated Clay at Philadelphia by reason of some abolition letter he had written, I turned with hope to Taylor. I did not like [Millard] Fillmore, but without him or other northern candidates Taylor must be defeated. And now I am decided to vote for Taylor & Fillmore reserving to myself the ["pr"(?) *canceled*] right to oppose their administrations if they prove false to duty and the country. And what a glorious state of things, allow me to say we should have, could we have Taylor for president, and if you would consent to act as Secretary of State, and settle all our differences by establishing for ever non-interference with Southern Rights, low duties, no extension of territory to strengthen anti-slavery power—honorable peace—and a final compromise of the Wilmot proviso squabble by adopting the Missouri Compromise or some other. I have a letter from Gen. Taylor in which he flatly denies any agency in causing his nomination—but Gen. Cass cannot say so much. Now I have heard that Gen. Taylor if elected will urge yourself to enter the State Department. I believe he is for Free Trade and opposed to the bank, and how small seems the difference ["if any" *interlined*] that divides you and the Whigs. Will South Carolina vote for Gen. *Cass*, who I consider is no better than V[an] Buren, and the tool of Benton and others. I will not believe she will. But I am impertine[n]t I fear, and trust your pardon for these remarks, written by an humble & obscure friend to one of the world[']s statesmen. I beg you will write me your views fully, at your leisure. Very sincerely your friend & Ob[edien]t Ser[van]t, Cuyler W. Young.

[P.S.] Address me at Armenia, Ga.

ALS in ScCleA.

From Laurel Summers

Parkhurst, Scott Co[unty] Iowa
Oct. 21st 1848

Dear Sir, Although a citizen of a remote corner of the Union and an entire stranger to you, I nevertheless have taken great pains to study and understand your views upon the various Constitutional questions that are now, and have been for some time agitating the public mind; some of which are shaking our glorious Union to its very centre.

I am what we here call a democrat, and of course believe in a strict construction of the Constitution, and nowhere can I find in that time honored instrument any power delegated to the General Government to charter a Bank; to Legislate upon the subject of Internal Improvements, either *general* or *special*; to pass what is called a *protective* tariff act, or Legislate upon the institution of *slavery*. This latter question, as you are aware, is now exciting the public ["mind" *interlined*] more than all others, and [is] unquestionably the most dangerous to the safety of the Union of these States. To my mind, a question, more foreign to legitimate Legislation by the *General* Government, has never been sought out by the fruitful brains of political demagouges.

I have viewed your course with greater care from the fact, that you seem to form your opinions independant of that blind devotion to men that actuates and seems to be the ruling passion of too many of our public men. Upon many questions of public policy advocated by you I have been compelled to differ with you; but generally upon great Constitutional questions your views to my mind are sound. Well, my object in writing to you at this time is to make the inquiry, what power has the General Government to *compromise* the subject of slavery? I hold that it is *not* a question upon which Congress can constitutionally Legislate. I believe that you hold to the same doctrine. My opinion, then is that Congress should not only *frown* down the *Wilmot Proviso*, but the *Missouri Compromise* line also; for if they have power to pass the one they have power to pass the other also.

Should ["you" *interlined*] find time and feel so disposed I should be pleased to hear from you in answer to the above inquiry at your earliest convenience. You may rest assured that the democrats of Iowa are sound to the *core* of this subject. The Whigs are for Gen. [Zachary] Taylor *and the Wilmot Proviso.* What inconsistency! Respectfully, Laurel Summers.

ALS in ScCleA; PC in Boucher and Brooks, eds., *Correspondence*, pp. 482–483.

From J[OHN] H. HOWARD

Columbus [Ga.,] Oct[obe]r 22nd 1848

My Dear Sir, Many of your friends desire (that for the present good of the country, as well as the ultimate triumph of republican principles in the administration of the government) a letter from you expressing your preference for the democratic candidates. They believe as I do that it in [*sic*] this doubtful election, you would by such a letter place yourself securely in the affections of that party. You must remember that the strong tendency of a vote for [Zachary] Taylor is to make that voter a whig. There are many democrats in Georgia, but more in Alabama who are very much under the influence of your opinions and if the letter I propose for you to write, could be published immediately in some paper on a rail road line where it could command a rapid transit to all quarters of the country, the election might possibly be saved. I believe that we shall carry Georgia. I am going through the lower part of the State to rally the democracy. I think that of course there is no doubt of Alabama, but I wish you to be impressed with the truth that every vote for Taylor running as he does exclusively upon whig principles must add to the strength of the whig party, which party we all know you have as little disposition as any of us to advance. I do hope that you will write the letter I request of you as I think it is due to your position to do so. If you write it it is well worth a special messenger, to Augusta to give it immediate publication. Your friend personal & political, J.H. Howard.

ALS in ScCleA.

From E[PHRAIM] M. SEABROOK

Edisto Island [S.C.], Oct. 22d/48

Dear Sir, Knowing the interest you feel in all questions relating to our State Govt., I take the liberty of writing you, and soliciting your views on ["so" *canceled*] a subject which has impressed me as being very important to the purity of our State Govt.

The constitution of our State makes all elections not only by the people, but also by the General Assembly, to be determined by ballot voting. During the short time that I have had the honor of a seat in the Legislature, I have been struck with the impolicy of this mode of voting by the General Assembly: however well it may answer in popular elections.

It has struck me as wrong in theory and bad in practice. The Gen[era]l Assembly is a representative body, and as such is responsible for the faithful discharge of the whole of its duties. The election of public officers is as much a part of its duty, as the making of laws; and in some cases, a most important one, as in that of Judges and also of Senators. Now the secrecy which attends the voting by ballot, in a measure does away with the responsibility, which ["should" *canceled*] belongs to the Representative character of the General Assembly; in as much as it enables the Representatives to act, without the responsibility which necessarily grows out of the ["fact" *canceled and* "consciousness" *interlined*], that their acts are open to the public gaze and to public judgment.

The election of good public officers is essential to good govt.; and to secure the election of good public officers, the Representative must be made to feel his responsibility; and to effect this, publicity in voting is necessary.

As far as practice is concerned, the most superficial observer, must have seen even in our State Legislature, the injurious effects of this mode of voting. It gives rise to a system of logrolling ["and" *canceled*] which is truly demoralizing and corrupting. I have been so impressed with the necessity of a change in the present mode of voting by the General Assembly of our State, that I have it in contemplation to bring in a bill at ["the c" *canceled*] it's coming session, for the purpose of altering it to that of viva voce.

I should be pleased to have your views on the subject ["for my private instruction" *interlined*], if you can find time and inclination. Allow me at the same time to thank you for your letter on the subject of the Presidential Election in the early part of the summer.

The excitement of a canvass has only infected Charleston and

Georgetown—the parishes of the low country have been indifferent and have generally elected Representatives without pledges. With considerations of esteem & respect, I remain your ob[e]d[ien]t serv[an]t, E.M. Seabrook.

[P.S.] Please direct to the care of John Fraser & Co: Charleston.

ALS in ScCleA.

To Col. FRANCIS H. SMITH, [Superintendent, Virginia Military Institute, Lexington, Va.]

Fort Hill, 22d Oct[obe]r 1848

Dear Sir, I understand, that Maj[o]r D[aniel] H[arvey] Hill, now of the United States Army, is an applicant for a professorship in the Virginia Military Institute.

I am not personally acquainted with him, but I take pleasure in stating, that, from what I have learned of his character & qualifications, from a reliable source, I believe him to be well qualified to fill the place for which he applies. His connections I know to be highly respectable. His grand farther [*sic*], Col. William Hill, who resided in York district in this State, was an ardent & influential whig, in the War of the revolution; and rendered important services to the cause of the country. With great respect I am & &c, J.C. Calhoun.

ALS in Nc-Ar, Daniel Harvey Hill Papers; photostat of ALS in NcU, Daniel Harvey Hill Papers; microfilm of ALS in ArU, Daniel Harvey Hill Papers.

From H[ENRY] W. CONNER

Charleston, Oct[obe]r 24, 1848

Dear Sir, I last night rec[eive]d your fav[our] of the 18th with the paper enclosed.

You pay me an unmerited compliment for seeing—what you have long foreseen in the state of the abolition question at the North.

I have read your speech with great interest. It appears to me it could not have come out at a better time.

The Evening News has commenced its publication. The [Charleston] Courier will insert it tomorrow or next day—all in one paper [*marginal note*: "and the Mercury in a day or two."] I will have it republished in Columbus Geo., Montgomery Ala.[,] Mobile[,] New Orleans & Nashville & in the New York Herald—if I can. I believe I can have it done at all the other points named & some others. It will require no notice but will speak for itself.

I will see & confer with the old subscribers to the paper but lapse of time—long silence & a changed condition of things will I fear have cooled down the ardour of many. Still it seems to me that if the sum you name—[$]5000/6000—be sufficient to start it, there can be no dificulty in making up that sum. It were well for you to write [Isaac W.] Hayne, [Franklin H.] Elmore & others of the original promoters of the scheme & amongst us we will be prepared to speak definitely as you come along.

I was in hopes & so said I believe that the electoral question would not be mixt up with the present contest. Altho of a different opinion 6 months [ago] I came to the conclusion before the election that it would not be disturbed but it was brought up at the last moment. The opinion here is almost universal now in its favour & its friends say great unanimity prevails in the country. Of this I am unable to speak. I entirely agree in the opinion that it ought not to be approached at present but if what I hear be true there is but little hope of staving it off but you know best.

I returned home from the west the last day of the election & was concerned to find greater excitement & worse feeling involved in the contest than was called for & I was pained to find much of it had been produced by persons & from quarters where it was least to be expected. We are trying however to get it all right again.

A meeting of the democratic [Zachary] Taylor party will be held on Monday night next (the last that will be held by it ["as a" *canceled*] under that designation) and a preamble & resolutions will be adopted that I hope will meet your approbation. We shall lead off on the broad Southern ground—going for a Southern convention & pledging ourselves to cooperate & unite with any & every other portion of the South irrespective of party in a joint effort to maintain the rights & equality of the South & I should have been very, very glad to have had your views fully on the whole subject before we acted but there has not been time since it was determined on to get an answer from you. I may remark however that in the outlines of the resolutions in preparation we cover exactly the ground you set forth in your letter & I trust we shall be fortunate enough to carry all through right.

Except taking hold of a labouring oar when necessary or doing that which others were unwilling to do I have always avoided being placed in any prominent position in public matters—particularly of a party character. My connexions with the Bank [of Charleston]—my great infirmity in defect of hearing & my own sense of propriety under the circumstances seemed in my estimation to render such a course on my part highly proper. There has a condition of things arrived however when it will become every man of the South to take up his position boldly & decidedly & to maintain it firmly & fearlessly. To the full extent of all my power I have firmly resolved to do both & the only question I shall henceforward have to settle with myself will not be one of rank or precedence but where & how can I be most useful.

In what we do or say we shall as regard[s] others, particularly our democratic Brethren, be governed by temper[,] moderation & respect & one amongst other reasons for my taking prominent part in the measures in contemplation will be to reconcile difference—promote harmony & unity & effect union & concert of action—if possible.

In Georgia & Alabama I found the people almost as united & determined in their spirit of resistance to the Wilmot proviso & other kindred measures—as the Free soil advocates are on the other side. A great & gratifying change has come over Georgia in this respect within a year past & in Alabama about Montgommery they are always true.

With proper means & proper exertions I have no doubt the whole South can be united on a common course of action for their common peace & safety & we should know no peace until it is done.

If the Taylor & [Lewis] Cass men would compromise the matter at the called session by dropping both & throwing away their vote or voting for [George M.] Dallas—[John A.] Quitman[, later a Representative from Miss., Levi] Woodbury [Associate Justice of the U.S. Supreme Court] or some one else, I think it would go far towards reuniting the present division in the democratic party. The Taylor party here would readily agree to it I believe.

You could accomplish it—if desired—especially if present at the Legislature. Yours &C, H.W. Conner.

ALS in ScCleA.

From CHA[RLE]S G. DELAVAN

Baltimore, 24th October 1848

Sir, Like yourself I am a South Carolinian; born, bred and educated within the limits of the State, it will be readily admitted that all my sympathies, my deepest attachment is to my native State; born within 20 miles of the City of Charleston my widowed Mother removed near to Statesburg and I was reared under the immediate supervision and control of the late Gen. [Thomas] Sumter. This will be taken at all times at least in So. Carolina, as a voucher of my politics. My Father in his youth had sustained his part during the Revolutionary War, and the deep scars of a British Sabre on his head & shoulder testified to his fidelity and services; But no more of that. Whilst a young man I emigrated to Tennessee with many other So. Carolinians, and have since been part of my time in Missouri & Arkansas, and occasionally in the middle States where I happen to be at present, and from whence I address you.

My present object is to assure you, that the opposition you have made and are making to the Election of Gen. [Zachary] Taylor to the Presidency is unfortunate, and is founded on a misconception of his character. Had you known him as I know him all your Heart would have been with him, and all your energies exerted in his support; I know him well, and I know his antagonist Gen[era]l [Lewis] Cass *much better* than you do; and readily admitting the claims of Gen. Cass to being a man of Education, intelligence, and in politics a sound unwavering Democrat at least within the last 20 years, there are fundamental objections to him which in my estimation disqualify him for the Executive Office; He is deficient in moral courage—he has neither the firmness, nor decision of Character so indispensable to the incumbent of that Office, when the nation should have arrived at some great Crisis, and to illustrate this I could relate you an anecdote ["that" *canceled*] of what occurred whilst he was Sec[retar]y of War under Gen. [Andrew] Jackson, and may do so hereafter. Not so with Gen. Taylor, besides his being a man of clear head, a fund of practical common sense, *which is wisdom*, and much better than scholastic discipline without wisdom—he is calm, decided, energetic and firm—not so ready perhaps as Gen. Jackson to "take the Responsibility" but equally decided and free to do so, on all proper occasions, and as firm in maintaining his position when it ["was" *canceled and* "is" *interlined*] taken. And then his habits, his Education, his sympathies, his interests are all with the South, and he will guard with untiring zeal, and unwinking vigilance all the interests of the South. What though Gen. Taylor has said "*I am a Whig*"—I know him in politics to be as truly democratic as I am—aye or as truly so as Mr. Calhoun himself. In days gone by when Mr. [Henry] Clay led the Democratic party of the West, of which Gen. Taylor was a member, and Col. [Richard] Taylor his Father a leading[,] a distinguished member, the latter mainly contributing as I have always understood to the passage of the Lexington resolutions, the basis of nullification, ["and" *canceled*] an attachment was formed and a confidence bestowed on Mr. Clay which has continued to the present day—and without undertaking to investigate the soundness of every principle and the tendency of every measure of policy of which Mr. Clay in latter days has been the advocate—Gen. Taylor recollecting merely what their views were, when cooperating in years long past, he placed on a remote frontier and occupied with matters ["of" *canceled*] very different from politics, and remembering Mr. Clay *as he was*, says "had I voted it would have been given to Mr. Clay" and understanding that in the classification of parties in the present day that Mr. Clay is the Magnus Apollo of that party he says "I am a Whig" meaning no more thereby than as he would vote for his old friend and compatriot Mr. Clay—he must *quo ad hoc* be a Whig. I feel entirely confident from all I hear and see that Gen. Taylor will be our next Presid[en]t and that under his Administration the South and Southern interests will receive ample and just protection, and from him the new party just starting into open view (the free Soil party) will receive a check, a rebuke that may perhaps drive it back into the dark recesses where it has been hatching for the last 10 years. I had an opportunity of seeing and hearing some of the trickery of that celebrated Buffalo Convention, which brought forward that unprincipled intriguer Mr. Martin Van Buren, and by which he will only be exposed and crushed—for one so cautious and wiley it is surprising that he suffered himself to be caught so readily—his overweening ambition had made him impatient, and he lent himself to the movement certainly with but slight hopes of success in the present struggle—but intending to lay the platform in advance for 1852—["with" *canceled and* "without" *interlined*] adverting to the fact, that all the principles of the free Soil party, being the very principles upon which the *Northern* Whigs ["based" *interlined*] their opposition to the South in years long gone by, and at a time when this very Mr. Van Buren was stigmatized as "*the Northern man with Southern principles.*" You see in the published addresses of Messrs. [Daniel] Webster, [Rufus] Choate, [Charles] Hudson, [George] Ashmun &ca. &ca. with what bitterness Mr. Van Buren is attacked, denounced and exposed. And in all of which they declare that the free Soil party have under a new name usurped the ground long since occupied by the Whigs of the North who are the true original free Soil party according to the Buffalo platform. Still Mr. Van Buren will answer a purpose—he will set the ball in motion, and be easily pushed aside by Mr. Webster four years hence, who is even at this time, the selected ["the" *canceled*] Candidate of the *Northern Whig* party embracing within its range, free Soil, and to be pushed as far as Abolition if they dare do so. It is in such an emergency that Gen. Taylor would be wanted. In men as in Horses I pay some regard to blood—I admire and have confidence in a good stock. Col. Taylor father of the General was an officer in the Virginia line during the Revolutionary War, and after peace removed to Kentucky; He there stood forth in opposition to the general policy pursued and the arbitrary measures of the Elder [John] Adams; He was a [Thomas] Jefferson Elector a [James] Madison Elector a supporter of the War of 1812 and stood shoulder to shoulder with the democratic party. And thus was Zachary Taylor, cradled, nursed and bred—he cannot prove recreant to his lineage and breeding. And mark me Sir—In less than 12 months after his Election, Whigs, free Soil and all will be in opposition.

I prefer Gen. Taylor because he is Southern by birth, Southern in habits & taste, Southern in Sympathy and interests—whilst Gen. Cass is north, in all of this—and deficient in moral courage he might in a serious Crisis, from his Education, habits, connections and local position be induced to throw his weight in the scale ag[ain]st us. With great respect your most Obed[ien]t Serv[an]t, Chas. G. DeLavan.

ALS in ScCleA; PC in Boucher and Brooks, eds., *Correspondence*, pp. 483–485.

From Henry G. Wheeler

Jersey City, N.J., October 24th 48

Sir, I was honored by the receipt of your letter [*not found*].

The address [to the Memphis Convention] in the "Detroit Free Press" was two columns long—spoke in the first person, & bore, I thought, a strong cathedral impress. The last sentence, however, differs from that which your letter gives as the authentic one. I had no alternative but to omit the address, which I was not willing to do, or to go to press without it. If it should be found that the published copy is not the true one, the requisite correction in the stereotypes shall certainly be made hereafter. I regret that you did not find it convenient to send me the copy you speak of, as, even in the event of its loss, against which I would have taken every precaution, the perfect word would always have been found in my volumes. I am now in the hands of the binder, & waiting only for the election to pass over before I publish.

I was, of course, familiar with your Report in the Senate on the Memphis Memorial. Satisfied that I could present no adequate summary of its arguments, I felt constrained to transfer it, entire, to my pages, as I had done John C. Spencer's Memorial on behalf of the Executive Committee of the Chicago Convention. With Great respect, Your obedient Servant, Henry G. Wheeler.

ALS in ScCleA. NOTE: In 1848 Wheeler published *History of Congress . . . Comprising a History of Internal Improvements* . . . . 2 vols. New York: Harper & Brothers.

From L[AURENCE] M. KEITT

Orangeburgh C[ourt] H[ouse, S.C.], 25th Oct. 1848

My Dear Sir, I have just received your very kind and obliging letter, and beg to return you my most grateful acknowledgements. I recollect reading your discussion of the proposed "change in the mode of appointing Electors" when I was reading law in the office of my friend Mr. [Henry] Bailey—and my mind has ever since retained a distinct and luminous ["im" *canceled*] conception of the argument and its conclusiveness. I regard the present session of the Legislature as pregnant with grave and weighty topics, and the Political horizon rife with gathered and boding storm clouds. I deeply fear the manner in which I think, these questions will be met by the present Legislature. The Hurricane is syllabling[?] its voice here as in Europe, and Demagogues here, as ["in" *canceled*] there, are courting its hot breath. They are ["demol" *canceled*] demoralizing the popular instinct in every direction. Oily wrigglers between miserable resorts are climbing into power—Change is their rubric. I am afraid I shall be thrown into a minority upon several important questions.

I am eminently *conservative*, because ["are" *canceled*] our institutions are worth preserving. Upon the Electoral question I am with you heartily. The support of the Low Country upon that measure is preposterous and suicidal. I am afraid also that I shall stand alone from my delegation upon that measure. Major [John M.] Felder ["st" *canceled*] has stampeded from his old ground, and gone over ["it" *canceled*] to it, upon the infamous pretext that it is popular. I have succeeded in my election against his indefatigable ground moling & hostility. His issues are protean, Down with the College—Down with the Bank in any way—Down with the election of Electors by the Legislature—Power stealing from the many to the few. In my canvass I clung to the old anchorings of the State, and I shall do it in the Legislature, I shall enquire whether a measure is *right* or *wrong* not whether it is *popular*. To the change in the Electoral Law I shall give the most emphatic and unflinching opposition. Upon foreign questions I shall take the ["op"(?) *canceled*] sharpest course. I will cooperate to ["put" *interlined*] the State into an immoveable attitude of hostility to all aggressions, come whence they may. The boldest ["State" *canceled*] course I prefer if the State stands alone. Yet I am willing to take a conciliatory policy if it does not sacrifice principle—and will succeed in uniting the South, or the State. Divided we fall—for we can no more stand in division, than the pulsations of the heart can exist save when all the animal parts are locked into one organization. I should be very glad also to have your opinions upon the vote of the State for the Presidency. I want them to illustrate my own course. They shall be perfectly private if you desire it.

Be kind enough to extend my compliments to Mrs. [Floride Colhoun] Calhoun and accept them yourself. I am with great Respect your obe[dien]t Serv[an]t, L.M. Keitt.

ALS in ScCleA.

From J[ACOB] P. REED

Anderson C[ourt] H[ouse, S.C.,] Oct. 26, 1848

Dear Sir, Altho I regard it as settled that the [electoral] vote [of the State] will be given to [Lewis] Cass & [William O.] Butler, I should be pleased to learn your opinion as to the course South Carolina should pursue in the Presidential Election. I am aware, that you have hitherto declined to express a prefference between the nominees, and I take it from your speech recently published, that the proper course for the State in your Judgment, would be to stand aloof from the contest, and refuse to vote for either. Am I right in this conjecture?

If, as I apprehend Cass electors should be appointed at the approaching extra session of the Legislature, would it or not, in your opinion, be proper to accompany their appointment with the passage of resolutions, protesting against his known opinions, and those of his party, at the North, on the Territorial & slavery questions and clearly defineing the ground the State intends to occupy upon these questions? Or would it be better to wait till the regular session before we assume our final ground? Or should the Legislature forbear to act upon this subject at either the extra or regular session this winter, pursuing still further the "wait and watch" policy if I may use the expression?

I shall be grateful to you for your opinions upon these points, as my position will require me to act upon the matters referred to, and I desire to do so understandingly.

And may I ask, if in your opinion the State should take her position finally, through the Legislature, at either of the approaching sessions, that you will embody the substance of what you regard the proper position for her to take, in the form of Resolutions, with permission to use them, as I may think proper? To be right is my great desire, ut[t]erly discarding all party names and associations, and aid the State as far as I may be able in getting right as a Unit, and continuing so. Aside from this, which if I know myself is the great object of my heart, the questions involved being vastly important, I confess I desire to take a position high, as possible. One that I may or may not be able to maintain, and hence my desire to avail myself of your opinions and suggestions.

Be so good as to pardon the liberty I have taken, and do me the honor, if convenient, to let me hear from you between this and Thursday next, when I shall leave for Columbia. I have the Honor to remain Your Obedient Servant &c, J.P. Reed.

ALS in ScCleA.

From W[illiam] F. Van Amringe

Montgomery[,] Orange Co[unty,] N.Y., Oct. 26, 1848

Dear Sir, Your acceptable & much valued letter of 12th inst. [*not found*] is received, & [I] am much gratified with the opinion you have expressed of my Natural History of Man. My estimate of your judgment is so high, that it would have been gratifying to know in what respects you are "not prepared to yield your assent" to some of my propositions or arguments; because, in a second edition, should it be called for, it would be very desirable to correct the errors that may be discovered; and certainly no suggestions, from any quarter, would receive more attention than from you. But although it would have been pleasing, I know it was not to be expected, & am therefore much obliged by your kind approbation of the main feature, & arguments of the work. With assurances of great esteem & respect, I am Your Mo[st] Ob[edien]t S[er]v[an]t, W.F. Van Amringe.

ALS in ScCleA. Note: Van Amringe addressed this letter to "Hon[ora]ble Jno. C. Calhoun L.L.D."

From "Taylor of Caroline, No. 1," published at Richmond, 10/27. This pseudonymous writer, identified as "one of the most distinguished political writers in the State" of Va., begins a series of lengthy public letters addressed to Calhoun. He addresses Calhoun because the position he occupies between the two parties of the country makes him "almost the arbiter of that country's destinies," whose vote will be followed by "hundreds of thousands." The writer, evidently a Whig, laments that Calhoun has used his great influence for the past twelve years to keep the Democratic party in power. The Democratic party, he believes, represents Federalist principles and Presidential usurpation. After battling nobly against Andrew Jackson, Calhoun withdrew from the ranks of the good and "enlisted under the banner of modern Democracy." The writer considers himself a follower of the true State rights principles and that Calhoun has been mistaken in believing that the Democratic party best represented those principles. He elaborately defends the position of the Whig party on internal improvements and the protective tariff. PC in the Richmond, Va., *Whig and Public Advertiser*, October 27, 1848, p. 4.

From "Taylor of Caroline, No. 2," published at Richmond, 10/27. The pseudonymous writer continues his public letters to Calhoun by elaborately defending the Whig party history and positions and attacking the Democratic party history and positions in regard to distribution of the proceeds of the public lands, internal improvements, banking and currency, and executive patronage. PC in the Richmond, Va., *Whig and Public Advertiser*, October 27, 1848, p. 1.

From F[RANCIS] LIEBER

Columbia S.C., 29 October [18]48

My dear Sir, Have you any spare copy of your Letters on Parliamentary Law, signed Hortensius? And if not, can you direct me to any person who might be able to give them to me?

I have always ma[i]ntained that a wise parliamentary law is more than half a constitution; that it is far the most important part of the British Common Law, and that the states of antiquity as well as the people of the European continent show the grievous impediment in the career of developping liberty, resulting from the absence of sound parliamentary rules. What I had thus believed and known was strikingly illustrated to me by the German parliament during my recent visit, and many of the most prominent men urged me to write a brief work on this all-important subject. I now occupy myself with it, and, naturally, converse on one or the other point with Mr. [William C.] Preston. It was during one of our late conversations that he informed me of your newspaper correspondence with Mr. [John Quincy] Adams on the position of ["the" *interlined*] presiding officer of the Senate and told me that I must by all means get the Hortensius Letters.

Have you read Mr. [Alphonse de] Lamartine's shallow, flimsy speech on the uni-cameral principle? He says we Americans want a senate to represent our "imperfection" viz. the confederative principle, that still clinging to the most melancholy idea that unitary centralisation is perfection (while liberty is impossible with it), and besides not knowing that we have two houses in every single State!

Unfortunately every single item I predicted of the French so-called republic (but it is merely a kingless ["state" *with the first* "t" *interlined*] of things) at the time of the expulsion of L[ouis] Ph[ilippe] comes to be verified.

I would most ["gladly" *canceled and* "willingly" *interlined*] give you an account ["of the" *canceled*] of the German affairs, in which you must feel deeply interested, but I could indeed not do it without writing an essaylike epistle. That poor country will be obliged to go through a grave civil war. I am, my dear sir, with the highest respect Your very obed[ien]t, F. Lieber.

ALS in ScCleA. NOTE: In referring to Calhoun's letters on parliamentary law, Lieber means the 1826 essays written under the name "Onslow" (not "Hortensius").

From W[illia]m H. Chase

Chasefield, near Pen[s]a[co]la, Oct. 30 1848

My dear Sir: After a long service on the Gulf of Mexico, indeed, since 1818, and in a country which, whilst it received all my devotion and sympathy, was deemed by most of the officers of the Corps as a sort of "Botany Bay" I have ["been" *interlined*] ordered on a Branch of E[n]g[i]neers & Naval officers to the Pacific Coast, to perform duties that will require two years of one's life to perform.

The early part of my service on the Gulf and whilst I was yet a young lieutenant was performed under your watchful eye when Secretary of War, and amongst the pleasant things I have to remember is your approbation of my services expressed at several times, one of which I am sure, you will be happy to recollect on reading the following extract from a letter of the E[n]g[i]neer Dept. dated November 30, 1822, addressed to Lt. W.H. Chase U.S. E[n]g[i]neers.

"The Secretary of War having examined your tabular report exhibiting an analysis of the operations at the Rigolets affording a view of the progress and actual condition thereof with the drawing illustrative of it was pleased with them, and although informed that the approbation of the Dept. had been already expressed to you, directed that, in the next letter to you in addition to any thing that might have been stated from the Department, that he considered your report to be creditable to your talents for the manner in which it was executed and to your zeal for the promptness with which it had been furnished."

Such a testimonial from such a source amply repaid me for my services and has served since to stimulate me to all honorable exertion.

Perhaps I might have been more useful, if I had resigned and entered into political life, but whilst remaining in service I have not been unmindful of my political duties. The extraordinary relations of the South towards the north requiring every son, native or adopted of the former, to be constantly on the watch.

At this particular time I especially desire to remain on the Gulf of Mexico. To remain always, at least until *you can rise in the Senate and say that the rights of the South and consequently the Union are safe.* I have an abiding confidence that you will be able to say it, but until it is said I desire to remain at my post.

I desire not to go upon the pacific coast mission. There are many officers of the Corps as well qualified ["as I am" *interlined*] and better entitled to go ["*by less service*, there(?) than I am" *canceled*].

The object of this letter is to request that you would address me a letter at Wa[shin]gton, to which place I shall go tomorrow, expressing your wish that I may be permitted to complete my mission on the Gulf, authorising me to use the letter, with the President, the Secretary of War or General [Joseph G.] Totten, or, if you would prefer it, to write directly to either of those functionaries. I am with high Respect Very truely Your friend & Ser[van]t, Wm. H. Chase.

ALS in ScCleA. NOTE: An AEU by Calhoun reads "Maj[o]r Chase."

From W. B. Townsend

New York Express office, 30 Oct. 1848

My Dear Sir, The Telegraph will long before this reaches you bear the tidings ["of the death" *interlined*] of our mutual friend Dixon H. Lewis. It was my lot to witness the sepperation of soul & Body—& well knowing your close intimacy with the deceased, I presume it will be most acceptable to have the fuller detail of his sickness.

He arrived here on Monday three weeks since ["with Mrs. (Susan Elmore) L(ewis) & his son John" *interlined*]. The next day he complained of Fatigue, Wednesday he asked me to send for a Physician & called in Dr. Neilson, one of our most respectable Physicians, of the old Practice; He Bled him & gave a dose of calomel, on Thursday he was better & took a ride with me, through the City. On Saturday & Sunday was quite smart. On Monday he complained considerable. On Tuesday He said to me "Townsend I have sent for a Hom[e]opathy Physician—I will let him play with me, you know they can do no harm." On Wednesday he kept his room for the first time, on Thursday still ill. On Friday a very sick man, with a constant drowsiness. On Saturday a little better & Sunday quite ill. On Monday Mr. Cozel[?] arrived, He was with me not, pleased with the course of Practice[?], but as Mr. Lewis was as Mr. C. said not near as sick as he had often been, we hoped all would go well, & Mr. C. left for Home. On Tuesday it was evident that Mr. Lewis was sinking. I then asked Mrs. Lewis if she was satisfied with her Physician. She said Perfectly, & so was Mr. Lewis, & that if I sent for any other, she did not believe Mr. Lewis would see him. On Tuesday night Mr. Lewis was alarmingly ill, so much so, that his extremities were cold & it was with great difficulty, Perspiration could be restored. On Wednesday Morning, he revived a little, But poor Mrs. Lewis who had not left his Bedside during his sickness five minutes at a time, told me she gave him up. The Physician hearing the remark, told us, that Mr. L[ewis] was in no immediate danger, & that he did not despair at all of his getting up. The words were hardly out of his Lips, when the countenance of Mr. L[ewis] became purple, he rolled up his Eyes, & the Thread of Life was severed for ever.

The scene was most distressing, Mrs. Lewis gave way to Paroxisms of Grief. The sudden change, that came over Mr. Lewis had every appearance of Apoplexy, & so the Physician pronounced it. From the First the great feature of his complaint seemed to be drowsiness, constant sleep. He could hardly be roused to take his medicine. He suffered but little from Pain. Dr. [John A.] McVickar who attended him, is one of our most eminent Physicians, of his school & attended to his Patient night or day seldom leaving his sick Room. Mr. Lewis had very little consciousness of his situation, he alluded two or three times to his position, & said that a man with his habits was allways in danger, But I think had no idea that his end was near. His Physician Pre[s]cribed for an inflam[m]ation of the chest, & for a secretion of the Kidneys. Having no knowledge of Hom[e]opathy, I cannot judge of the Practice. Mrs. Lewis is perfectly satisfied with the Physician, & that everything was done that could be.

The Common Council the moment the event was known, Resolved to give him a Public Funeral, which was carried into effect, & every demonstration was made that became the City & the man. His remains were interred in a Leadon[?] coffin & deposited, in a most judicious spot in Greenwood Cemetery.

It is a source of satisfaction, that in his illness & death he was surrounded by his Family & Friends & that everything was done that could be. I need not speak of his virtues or his character[,] they are known to the world. Let us imitate his example. Mrs. Lewis left to day for Home attended by her son. I am with great regard Your O[bedien]t S[ervan]t, W.B. Townsend.

ALS in ScCleA.

From W[illia]m Pinkney Starke

Hamburg S.C., Oct[obe]r 31st/48

Dear Sir, I have to thank you for the reply you did me the honour of making to my letter in relation to Mr. [George] McDuffie's case, as well as for the speech sent with it.

Your speech, I read with, the interest attached to everything emanating from your pen and, the pleasure one always feels in ["reading" *canceled*] viewing an argument, connected, clear, and unanswerable. The editor of the Hamburg paper to whom I gave your corrected copy promised to publish it in his next number, and it will also appear in the Augusta papers. I see by the Courier that it has reached Charleston and will thus, I hope, soon find its way over the South. It is growing time for us to decide upon the extent of contumely and insult the blessings of the Union may justify us in submitting to, and how much a Constitution in shreds is worth.

When your letter on ["the" *canceled*] changing the mode of electing electors was made public, I must have been in Europe, as I have never had the pleasure of seeing it. You would place me under another obligation by forwarding it to me. It should be published again as, to judge by the close struggle on that question in the last Legislature, an important change may soon be operated unless something ["preventive" *interlined*] be done, in the formal part of our State constitution.

Dr. Coyle in his last letter to me gives a most cheering account of Mr. [George] McDuffie's situation. According to him the General is in fine spirits—confident of a cure and ["that" *canceled*] the symptoms of his case are every way satisfactory. He sleeps eight or nine hours; and rides ten miles daily for exercise. I sent Mr. McDuffie an extract from that portion of your letter in relation to him, and joined with you in the hope that he would persevere.

You would hardly be inclined to credit me if I told you that yesterday I was labouring under a severe attack of fever. At ten o'clock ["A.M." *interlined*] my pulse beat 102 strokes per minute. The ["process of cure" *canceled*] treatment was most simple: a wet sheet followed by a bath, friction and copious water drinking. This repeated three times has entirely relieved me.

Mine is the second case in ["the yard" *canceled*] our ["ho" *canceled*] family treated in this manner ["and" *canceled*] cured, within two weeks. Yours with gr[ea]t respect, Wm. Pinkney Starke.

ALS in ScCleA.

From "Taylor of Caroline, No. III," published at Richmond, 10/-31. The pseudonymous essayist continues his series of elaborate public letters addressed to Calhoun. He excoriates Andrew Jackson, Martin Van Buren, James K. Polk, and all the actions of the Democratic party for twenty years, which Calhoun has abetted, as corrupt and Jacobinical in contrast to the Whig party which, he avows, represents the true State rights republican principles of Thomas Jefferson. PC in the Richmond, Va., *Whig and Public Advertiser*, October 31, 1848, p. 4.

From [John R. Mathewes]

[Charleston?, early Nov. 1848?]

My Dear Sir, I was in hopes to have had the pleasure of seeing you this fall on the South Side of the Togoloo [*sic*] but here I am & no such agreeable event has happened. If I knew how I could possibly meet you on your way to Washington business should be put aside to do so. The fact is that I wish to suggest one or two moves in the event of the success of the free soil party which I consider as the enslavement of the South—["even" *changed to* "If"] ever it does happen. The idea of leaving the Southern seats vacant in Congress would only ["be" *interlined*] pouring oil upon a raging fire—it would be confessing defeat & weakness & strengthening the means of the robber to pursue his purpose. If you remember in a letter some time ago I referred you to the ["suicidal" *interlined*] fate of the Girondists under similar circumstances—and we know that a weak army retiring before a strong one invites & encourages pursuit—perhaps annihilation. What effect had the retirement of [Isaac W.] Hayne & [James] Hamilton [Jr.] and I believe [George] McDuffie on the Hounds that pursued their track[?] Why to stimulate renew'd action & we got the force Bill to ride the Tariff on—but enough of this. The present movement of Massachusetts & Co. is to divert the attention of their *workers* from their sufferings (& which will one day be aroused against their Capatalists [*sic*]) to sympathize with the negro assumed or misrepresented ["evils of" *interlined*] Slavery. Their leading men [Daniel] Webster & Co. are thus diverting for the present the attention of the enemy they dread at home & would turn them loose upon us to save themselves. The moment the Slave Question meets the fate of the Tariff then comes the tug of war at the north Greek against Greek. Well these people have been seeking our ruin long enough, they are fast subsidizing our Southern men & presses—Self preservation is the first Law of nature—can not some Northern fanatick be found as well as a [Alexander H.] Stephens, who could be induced to touch upon the propriety of improving the Labouring Classes condition at the North? an object more worthy of Southern action & sympathy than that of northern & eastern tears over the fat, contented & well treated African[?] My idea is to carry the War into Africa & cease this unavailing wringing of *our* hands whilst ["the" *interlined*] enemy is preparing to wring our hearts. Well, I have another defensive proposition—a rabid abolitionist can be found to *Stephenize* for us, there are of this party who are daily praying for a dissolution of the Union—get one of these to move his desire & let the South United say amen—depend upon it, if the Union is to be preserved & we are to be allowed our equality & constitutional rights—these two movements will bring the Ag[g]ressors to a pause & reflection. They will ["then" *interlined*] count the value of the Union, which to them alone has been a blessing and to us poverty, & at present degradation. I have much to say. This [Zachary] Taylor Democratic Whig association here I fear is only a beginning of the curse of the South so long practiced with success. Divide & conquer—I hope I may be wrong. I have thought when reflecting on this pretended intervention and [*one word changed to* "sympathy"; "for" *interlined*] negro suffering, why a comparison has never been drawn between the *free* Indians (from Cape Horn to the polar Esquimaux) progress towards civilization, temperance, religion, morality & learning, & that of the African *Slave*—the Indian has had the *advantage* of Freedom over the latter, ["also" *interlined*] proximity & free intercourse and every tender of Education made to them. The Slave has had a master, is the Indian to be compared as a member of a civilized community in any way, form, or manner with the African Slave; in a Domestic way he is useful, laborious, orderly & promotes the welfare & subsistence ["of himself" *interlined*] & master & nationally affords to Government the most valuable productions of commerce & consumption. The Indian on the contrary wastes & distroys himself and all the rest of God[']s creation. His Bump of distructiveness concentrates to its purposes all others. I leave here tomorrow for Columbia to observe a little of the wire workings at the Election of President—Georgia I think will go for the Democracy but it is hard to say positively the martyrdom of Stephens by the unfortunate move of [Francis N.] Cone (a Yankee Demo[crat]) subdued the intended action of the Geo[rgi]a Whig Senator when ["he" *interlined*] saw him in a Barouche, 4 horses, arm in sling, face tied up & all his wounds gaping wide like dead Caesars he was more ready to enact Mark Anthony before 7 or 8 thousand of Stephens worship[p]ers than to speak in justification of himself—so he went to Atlanta—and then came back again & very lately ["to" *canceled*] at Da[h]lonega made a long speech in favour of Whig[g]ery, Taylor & [Millard] Fillmore.

This was after hearing the news of the Charleston Whig victory & the clapping of hands & loud boasting of their success in Pen[n]syl-v[ani]a & Ohio. A Georgia Demo[crat] wrote me on the occasion exclaiming, "Oh these vultures how quick they follow the scent of the carcass." I was amused and at the same [time] gratified to hear your name & authority quoted & mentioned in the most respectful manner by both parties in that State. Rumour says Mr. [Thomas G.] Clemson & family are expected home shortly—if so, and you see him, do remember me most kindly to himself and Lady [Anna Maria Calhoun Clemson] and that I shall be happy to hear from him. Make my best respects to Mrs. [Floride Colhoun] Calhoun & your family and I remain as ever y[ou]rs most respectfully & truly [John R. Mathewes.]

[P.S.] If any thing occurs at Colum[bi]a I will close this with it there. Every thing here in the shape of business is at a stand & produce declining.

[P.S.] Columbia 7 Nov[embe]r. Mr. John Middleton elected [speaker of the S.C. House of Representatives]. I believe he received the vote for his consistency in Democratic faith whilst his colleagues went the other way. The [Electoral] vote for [Lewis] Cass & [William O.] Butler is 129[;] for Taylor 27. [*Marginal interpolation:*] 8 Blank votes and some scattering.

ALU in ScCleA. Note: This letter is in the handwriting of John R. Mathewes.

Testimonial to Dr. Isachar Zacharie, 11/——. Testimonials by Calhoun, Henry Clay, Lewis Cass and other prominent political figures were published by Zacharie, a chiropodist, in a promotional pamphlet *Corns, Operations on the Feet* (n.p.?, n.d.?). Calhoun's testimonial stated "I take pleasure in saying that Dr. Zacharie extracted my Corns without the slightest pain, and to my entire satisfaction." Quoted in Charles M. Segal, "Isachar Zacharie: Lincoln's Chiropodist," in the *American Jewish Historical Quarterly*, vol. XLIII, no. 2 (December, 1953), p. 77, note 18.

From C[hristopher] Hughes, Baltimore, 11/1. Hughes transmits a copy of the Brussels, Belgium, *L'Independance*, dated 10/2/1848, with an appended note: "I obey my Friend Frank Corbin & send this paper to Mr. Calhoun joining Corbin in my best wishes & respects for Mr. Calhoun, & adding my best wishes for the happy & speedy arrival *at Home* of Mr. & Mrs. [Thomas G.] Clemson." The newspaper reported Clemson's departure the previous day for the U.S.

on a six months' leave of absence from his post as Chargé d'Affaires at Brussels. A note of 10/2 from Corbin, at Brussels, to Hughes reads "Send this paper to Mr. Calhoun, with my best wishes & respect." ALS (written on newspaper) in ScU-SC, John C. Calhoun Papers.

From H[ENRY] W. CONNER

Charleston, Nov. 2, 1848

I wrote you on the 24th [of October] & we have since had our meeting, proceedings of which you will see in this morning[']s papers.

The 11th resolution was added at the instance of Col. [Christopher G.] Memminger & Col. [Franklin H.] Elmore. They saw me the day before the meeting & expressed a great desire for unanimity on the part of the State. I said the first & most effectual means of producing it was to abandon both candidates for President & vote unanimously for a third—but it was rejected. They sketched off then each of them—the form of resolutions to be presented to the Legislature on Monday next. I sketched off something also, not very different. They said if our resolutions would cover that ground they would form on our platform. I then said it was exactly the ground our resolutions would take except that we had not pledged ourselves to stand by the State of So. Ca. tho there was not a man of us now but what would do so to the death in the last resort tho we considered any seperate or independent action of the State—at least for the present or until all efforts for a joint action of the slave States had failed, as fatal to the very object we were all aiming at. I immediately got our committee together & the overture was met in a becoming spirit & the 11th resolution was the consequence.

It embraces all that Col. Memminger & Elmore required I believe & I hope it may be considered as the first & successful step towards a harmony amongst us all.

At the same time I must express my belief that there has been & probably still is a design to revive the old Bluffton move & with the same motive & end. [*Marginal note*: "I do not think Col. Memminger or Col. Elmore favours it—at least not as a present mode of action—but (Robert Barnwell) Rhett & others do."] I do not think it will obtain favour. *I should regret it exceedingly if it did* for I believe the only means efficient & practicable for our purpose is a convention or cooperation by some Joint action on the part of all the slave States & *I do feel* great confidence in the practicability of such a combination *if the labour & management proper for it is put in play.*

I have with a view of at least giving due energy & industry to the object taken the place of chairman of the corresponding Committee & now have to beg the favour of you to give me your views as to how we should proceed. I wish to start fair & start right & when I have my chart before me I will put on the sail. Pray write me freely & fully (& in private if you please). I think we may do much if we start right towards producing concert & union amongst the slave States.

About the 1 Dec[embe]r I expect to go to Georgia[,] Alabama[,] Mobile & New Orleans & Apalachicola [Fla.] & I may do much by personal intercourse.

I will not omit attention to your suggestions as to the paper before I go. Very Truly y[ou]rs &, H.W. Conner.

ALS in ScCleA; variant PC in Jameson, ed., *Correspondence*, pp. 1184–1185. NOTE: The Charleston meeting discussed by Conner received considerable attention. It was held on 10/31, among its participants were a number of close associates of Calhoun, and it was described as a meeting of "the Democratic Taylor party," leading to an impression that Calhoun or South Carolina were endorsing Taylor for President. The proceedings of the meeting, as described in the Charleston *Mercury*, November 2, 1848, pp. 2–3, had more to do with opposition to the Wilmot Proviso than with Presidential endorsements. The 11th resolution declared that the members of the meeting would support whatever decision was made by the people of South Carolina. The General Assembly met a few days later and cast the State's electoral vote for the Democratic candidates Cass and Butler.

From "Taylor of Caroline," published at Richmond, 11/3. In the last of his public letters to Calhoun, the pseudonymous writer argues that Calhoun has never drawn any benefit from his collaboration with the Democratic party. In fact, Calhoun's friends in Virginia have been punished by the Democratic organization. Zachary Taylor will become President and will be "the second saviour of his country" who will arrest "the alarming and downward course of events." PC in the Richmond, Va., *Whig and Public Advertiser*, November 3, 1848, p. 1.

From ELLWOOD FISHER

Cincinnati, 11 mo[nth] 5, 1848

Dear Friend, I have been prevented from answering thy last letter dated at Washington by an absence from home which continued until a month ago and by sickness which has attended me ever since. I made a trip up the vallies of Wabash and White Rivers in Indiana where fevers abound and returned with a severe one which is only yet reduced to an intermittent.

I have had to day the pleasure of seeing in the [Washington] Intelligencer thy last speech on the Oregon question pending an amendment to the bill. The views it presents concerning the sentiments of the North on the South and on Slavery are precisely applicable to these North Western States where both parties are at length clamorous to be considered antislavery men—which was never the case before this canvass. It is perfectly correct[?] also as thee maintains that this sentiment does by no means go so far as to contemplate or tolerate a dissolution of the Union. But proceeds on the assumption that the South will give way.

This belief here has been much confirmed by Kentucky Whig speakers of eminence who are ready to abandon the South on that question, and by the growing prevalence of the policy of emancipation in that State.

The reigning theory of the natural rights of man to which thy first speech last session on the Oregon bill gave so great a shock does now indeed for the sake of the liberty and peace of our own country as well as Europe demand the most searching and serious scrutiny. But the current is setting both there and here with alarming rapidity in a wrong direction. I do not find among the people whom I meet and converse with one out of twenty who questions ["the natural equality of man or" *interlined*] the absolute power of a numerical majority—but regard ["it" *canceled and* "them" *interlined*] as the [*partial word canceled*] corner stone of free institutions. And who are to contend against this error[?] The South all except thyself slumbers in apathy, or bargains with the enemy for a little longer delay. The Press is in the North, and in the enemies['] interest.

I suppose the Southern members of Congress will of course present a united vote against a flagrant encroachment on the rights of their constituents. But in debate three fourths of them yield the moral argument, and I think it is in vain to rely on the fidelity of the Federal government to its proper sphere where a majority can accomplish a scheme of plunder and pretend it to be a moral and christian duty.

Thee will have seen by the papers long ago the effect of the [Martin] Van Buren movement in this State. But one must be present to realize the dismay of the Whigs as the returns of the election are coming in to find how completely they have been bereft of power in the State by that faction—although they professed themselves all the time to be much better antislavery men than the abolitionists. Of course thee will learn the result of the Presidential vote here before this letter arrives, ["but" *canceled*]. The Whigs, many of them, expect to lose the State by some ten to fifteen thousand votes which would indicate the Van Buren strength with both parties to be about thirty thousand.

In Indiana the Abolitionists do not much abound and the Van Buren movement has no effect there. [Lewis] Cass will get the State probably by five thousand majority.

Of course you already have Telegraphic notice of a movement of Cass's (and the story is to me probable enough) of sending off to [David] Wilmot to announce his re-adhesion to the Proviso and I hope it will have the effect, (if otherwise there was danger) of preventing South Carolina from giving him her vote. And as the ["Presidential" *interlined*] vote threatens to be very close I hope ["it" *canceled and* "that of Carolina" *interlined*] will be given to thee as in that event ["the election might go into the House and" *interlined*] either party in the House would prefer thy election to the other and the country I am quite certain would be satisfied.

I have heard great numbers of *both* parties express their preference for thee as a second choice and their readiness to acquiesce in thy election most cheerfully.

I hope that my health and engagements will permit me to be at Washington this winter.

Please present my regards to thy family. Thy friend, Ellwood Fisher.

ALS in ScCleA.

From RICH[AR]D K. CRALLÉ

Lynchburg [Va.], Nov[embe]r 6th 1848

My dear Sir, I received by the last mail your favour of the 23rd Ult., together with the newspaper containing your Speech, which I have read with much satisfaction. It contains all that a Patriot should feel and say on such a subject in times like these. I shall, as soon as the election is over, cause it to be published in the newspapers here with such comments as may seem to me pertinent.

The subject discussed is, in my view, become so controuling in its character, and involves consequences so momentous in respect to the Union and the safety of the South, that, however opposed warmly to Mr. [Lewis] Cass, whose position appears to me more dangerous than that of the Provisoists themselves, yet I do not regret that you have maintained, and still maintain a neutral and independent stand. It best befits both your character and the cause itself, as it enable[s] you, after the electioneering conflict is over, to take high grounds in respect to both parties; and, *by possibility*, to control, to some extent, the action of both, when the great question comes up at the next Session. I say, *by possibility*, for I am by no means sanguine. It seems to me that the South has become so thoroughly broken down—so utterly degraded by the baneful influences of Party-organization, that you will be unable, even on this great issue, to rouse their energies, or even open their eyes to their honor and interests. Already I see you are assailed by the Whig Organ at Richmond; and I doubt not that the Democratic Press will follow the example as soon as the election is over. [Lewis E.?] Harvie may succeed to some extent in his County, and, perhaps, the district, but I much fear Virginia will never again be roused from her slumbers, if the Spoils Party remain in power. I have already sounded some of the chief Leaders here as to a call on both Parties to rally on this question immediately after the election; but they have got the cue, and are ready to raise the cry of "*Disunion*"! on the very first move. They know Cass to be unsound, but they are just as well prepared to sustain his action on this subject as they were any of the usurpations of [Andrew] Jackson. In my opinion the only hope is in the Whig Party, especially if Cass be elected. They might be brought to unite in the movement proposed, as it would indicate hostility to the Administration. Many of their Leaders here, indignantly denounce the Editor of the [Richmond] Whig for his pitiful assault on you. The whole Party has, I think, been seriously alarmed by the pretensions set up in Cass' letter [of 12/24/1847] to [Alfred O.P.] Nicholson, and if the Leaders of the West and East can be brought to cooperate, a very powerful organization might be effected, and the spoils Party driven out of power in the State. But the Western portion of the State is strongly infected with the spirit of abolitionism; and some difficulty will be felt in bringing them to unite cordially with the East. I will, however, as soon as the election is over—which takes place tomorrow, test the feelings of both Parties in this section and let you know the result, soon after you reach Washington. I will now, however, briefly state my own views—which I am sure you will pardon for doing.

If Cass be elected, it is vain to hope that Virginia *can be* brought to oppose him on *any question.* The Party is too well drilled, and too corrupt to expect this. I say this on the supposition that the State will go for him. This, however, may possibly not be. If she votes for [Zachary] Taylor, I am confident, unless he should prove to be himself unsound, that the State may yet be roused in feeling, and placed on high *Southern* ground. But assuming that she votes for Cass, and *that he be elected,* and you may, with perfect confidence, anticipate the reacting of those scenes of mean[n]ess, servility and treachery which you witnessed in 1832, & 3. The Leaders will not offend Cass, will not hazard their hopes of preferment, for all the soil acquired under the Treaty with Mexico. There is not the least display of interest—the least evidence of concern amongst the Party, either in reference to Polk's sanction of the Proviso in the Oregon Bill—or the position of Mr. Cass in reference to the Territories. I have not seen the slightest indication of any feeling or interest on the subject. Indeed, Sir, they approve both—and do not hesitate to defend them. If then you throw yourself in the breach in opposition, you may rely on it, not only that you will receive no support from them, but that you will be assailed with the utmost virulence. Nor will this, in my opinion, be the worst. If South Carolina cast her vote for Cass, the act will be attributed solely to you; and the entire Whig Party, I fear, will, from a feeling of revenge, if for nothing else, unite as one man against you. You will thus, I much, fear, lose the support of both. Such are my *well considered* opinions, tho' I am by no means capable of forming as correct a judgment as yourself.

Such will be, as it appears to me, the Consequences if Cass should be elected by the vote of Virginia & *South Carolina.* On the other hand, if Taylor should be elected, and *prove to be unworthy,* I feel the fullest assurance that the entire South could be rallied against him; and a Party organized on this question alone which would be *irresistible.* He could not, in such case, retain the support of a single slave-holding State; whether he adopted the principles of the Wilmot proviso, or the yet more dangerous theory of popular sovereignty in the Territories.

So strongly am I persuaded of the correctness of these views that, if Cass be elected, I shall indeed, not only despair of the Union, but of the possibility of saving the South, however earnest and able be your efforts. These efforts, combined with others already on our records, may—nay, *must* cause you to be ever remembered as the first, the purest and greatest of our Statesmen, but they will assuredly make you, *for the present,* the prominent object of bitter hate and denunciation. The simple fact that you are the leading opponent of a *Northern* President, elected by *Southern* votes, will, as Parties are at present organized, be enough to secure you the condemnation of both *North* and *South*—And, (I will not ask what will be your own personal condition, for where duty calls, I verily believe that question is far more interesting to me than to yourself—) what will become of the issue? What will be our fate in the South? South Carolina will doubtless maintain her chivalrous character; but will a single Southern State come to her assistance? The history of 1832 and '3 gives me the answer. The Politicians, looking to the favour of the Federal Government, will be content with the limits of Slavery as they are at present. New Mexico & California will be declared sterile, unsuited to Slave labour—and the whole question, with all its momentous sequences, will be denominated a "*mere abstraction*"—and you will be made the victim, while the South will gain nothing in return.

Such are my views. They are written with the freedom of one who has never wavered in his affection or his confidence, and who will be the last to forsake you—nay, who will not forsake *at all*. I was prepared, from the published remarks of Messrs. [Andrew P.] Butler and [Armistead] Burt, to hear that the State would vote for Mr. Cass; and the fact grievously disturbed me. I had hoped that, *if her vote would elect Taylor* it would be given to him; if not, that it would be thrown away. This hope was merely *instinctive*—and grounded on no knowledge of public sentiment; but simply on the past conduct and present position of the State in relation to the two Parties. The views of Messrs. Butler and Burt are not to me satisfactory; for whatever may be said of the relations of the State Rights to the Whig Party, it can certainly claim but slight kindred with that denominated *Democratic*. The meanness, treachery and malignity of its Leaders, the profligacy of its measures—and its utter destitution of all fixed principles entitle it to no favour from an honest and high-minded people. I would far rather see the State throw her vote away entirely than to give it to Cass, whether considered as a public man merely, or as the Leader of a Party.

But I leave the subject—with a hope that Divine Providence will so order things as ultimately to advance the cause of truth, justice, and the public welfare.

Mrs. [Elizabeth Morris] Crallé and Mary unite with me in affectionate regards to yourself, Mrs. [Floride Colhoun] Calhoun and Miss [Martha] Cornelia [Calhoun]. We hope yet to see you at our mountain home whither we expect to remove permanently during the next summer. Say to Mrs. Calhoun that our *little Floride*, promises to be the ornament, as she is the pride of our Household. Parental partiality aside, she is, by all her see her [*sic*], put down as a "*very remarkable child;*" not a very definite phrase, it is true, but in this case literally true. We call her Floride Calhoun, instead of Anna Floride, which Mrs. [Anna Saunders] Preston positively objected to, in as much, as she declared, I had more respect to Mrs. [Anna Maria Calhoun] Clemson than to herself in the selection. With highest regard and respect ever Truly yours, Richd. K. Crallé.

P.S. I have just heard of the death of poor [Dixon H.] Lewis. It has filled my heart with the deepest sorrow—for he was a true friend both to you and to me. I fear he has left his domestic matters much deranged, as he wrote to me not long since, that his Commission merchants—having his whole crop of the last year in their hands, had failed.

ALS in ScCleA.

From JOHN B. FRY

Washington, Nov[embe]r 6th 1848

My Dear Sir: I trust that you will pardon me, who am comparatively a stranger to you, for the liberty I take in writing this letter. During the last session of Congress, about the time of the death of the late Senator [Chester] Ashley, of Arkansas, I hand [*sic*] the honor of an introduction to you, in the Senate Chamber, by the Hon: Mr. [William] Upham of Vermont. On that occasion, we held some little conversation relative to your public career—your son Major P[atrick] Calhoun—the place of my nativity (Delaware County N. York) &c. I allude to this, for the purpose of awakening your recollection of me.

I intended, before you left Washington, to have availed myself of your polite invitation to call and see you at your lodgings; but engagements which then pressed upon me prevented. The object of my desire was to hear from your own lips, in familiar conversation, the views which ["you" *interlined*] entertained in regard to our public affairs. From your present attitude, I think I cannot be mistaken in the conjecture that you, in common with the more sound and reflecting portion of our citizens, must regard the standard by which the pretensions of Presidential candidates are graduated, as having been lowered to a very humiliating point. Mental endowments the most extraordinary, experience the most enlarged, and consecrated by fervent patriotism and unquestioned probity are made to yield, it would seem, to every fitful breeze of popular excitement; until, at last, we ["have" *canceled*] witness with complacency the elevation of men to the chief magistracy, who possess but meagre abilities, and whose reverence for *party* greatly transcends their love of Country.

From my youth (and I am yet young) I have regarded yourself, Henry Clay and Dan[ie]l Webster as incomparably the greatest of living Americans; and, for the renown of our Republic, have cherished the pleasing anticipation that you all might, in turn, occupy the Presidency. Your respective ages admonish me, that I should dismiss my hope in this regard. I take the admonition with painful regret, and look upon it as the announcement of a great public calamity. This, I firmly believe, will be the universal feeling and sentiment before another generation shall have passed away.

I am aware that the views entertained by yourself and Clay and Webster upon matters of public policy are widely at variance, in many respects; but I am persuaded that you will allow the classification to stand. Unrivalled by any of your co[n]temporaries, you enjoy full equality with the first American Statesmen who have preceded you. I have fulfilled the object of my letter. It was to give utterance to the warm sentiments of esteem, friendship and pride with which your transcendant talents and great public services have inspired me.

If agreeable, and not inconvenient to you, it would afford me extreme gratification to receive a letter from you. I would attach high and lasting importance to your present impressions of public affairs; and would preserve them among my choicest relics. I have the honor to be, Sir, Your friend & Ob[edien]t Servant, John B. Fry.

ALS in ScCleA.

To John Y. Mason, [Secretary of the Navy]

Fort Hill, 6th Nov[embe]r 1848

Dear Sir, The object of the applicant, to whom the enclosed [*not found*] relates, is to obtain the place of Assistant Surgeon in the Navy. I am not acquainted with Dr. [William H.] White, the applicant; but do not doubt, from the high character of Dr. [John Edwards?] Holbrook as a man & physician, & the highly respectable character of Mr. [*sic*; Dr. Marmaduke T.?] Mendenhall, that he is well qualified for the place for which he applies, and hope, when the Board of Physicians again meet to pass on candidates, that his name will be among those selected for examination. I am much obliged to you for informing me in reference to the meeting of the last Board. I did not avail myself of the information, because my son [John C. Calhoun, Jr.] had changed his mind. With great respects I am & & &, J.C. Calhoun.

ALS in IGK. NOTE: No "Dr. White" entered the U.S. Navy in the subsequent few years. John C. Calhoun, Jr., had received a medical degree from the University of Pa. in 4/1848.

To [Mary Ho]ward Schoolcraft, [Washington]

Fort Hill, 10th Nov[embe]r 1848

My dear Madam, I am much obliged to you for informing me, that Mrs. Lennox desires to rent her house; but my arrangement will depend a good deal on Mr. Ar[mistead] Burt, [Representative from S.C.,] and [*mutilated*] at all pr[*mutilated*] we shall [*mutilated*] house [*mutilated*] a short session. I cannot give Mrs. Lennox the least encouragement, that we will take her house.

With kind regards to Mr. [Henry R.] Schoolcraft & your brother, if with you. Yours truly, J.C. Calhoun.

ALS (*mutilated*) in DLC, Henry Rowe Schoolcraft Papers, vol. 24.

From John Cuningham

Charleston, 12 Nov. 1848

Dear Sir, The pressure of business and of private affairs has hitherto prevented my acknowledging the receipt of your letter of the 16th ult. Your speech both from its subject matter and the juncture of its delivery and publication, has and will produce a profound and general impression on the public mind of the South, and neutralize to some extent the injurious influences of the past election. These last have done much, in that section at least, to rivet upon us party discipline, and give us as controlling guides and tests, party ties and purposes. Nothing can now arrest so well this fatal tendency as a concerted effort by the leaders of both parties at the South to get up a Southern Convention, in compliance with their understanding at Washington and the necessity of the crisis. You have no doubt observed that our party here (those who preferred [Zachary] Taylor to [Lewis] Cass) have since the election reorganized as a "Southern State Rights Republican" party, with a view to such effort, and to break down among ["our"(?) *canceled*] ourselves those party influences which were shackling our free and manly resistance as an insulted and injured people.

I regret that I cannot entirely agree with you as to the electoral question. ["The people of" *interlined*] This State are certainly not represented ["as among(?) themselves" *interlined*] in the election of electors, according to the federal relations, and upon the federal basis of representation. I have inclined to the opinion also that the present mode of appointment in this State ["or this feature of it" *interlined*] was not only not contemplated ["in this" *canceled*] by the Constitution for this reason, but because, in view of the representation of both the popular numbers and of the State sovereignties in the Presidency, the people should have a direct choice, at least in proportion to their direct share in that representation. It is in addition a fact that ["the" *changed to* "our"] people now desire and will insist upon having the appointment of the electors. Waiving then the question of constitutionality dependent upon the words of the Constitution, I gave my consent at the last election for the above reasons to the proposed change. I did so reluctantly however, as I admire and would cherish the conservative working of the present system in our State. But as to the time of the change I am uncommitted and feel no urgency. If it will at all interfere with our entire concentration of mind and purpose upon the great issue as to slavery and our rights, it should by all means be postponed. I shall certainly not urge it immediately, and shall aid in keeping down all excitement and wrangling as to it. But there will probably be none, even if urged at each ensuing session of the Legislature.

The majority in the House of Representatives is so large and fixed in favor of the change, that action will be taken without debate. I am informed there is also now a majority in the Senate, and that it will take the same course. No popular agitation will probably occur under four and at least not under two years. A proposition for the change will be brought before the next Legislature. I think it will be impossible to prevent it. Nothing, but the danger now threatening Southern institutions and a fear of distraction, could do it. But I am also satisfied that the deep conviction of the necessity of Southern action and union, is so strong in our people, that nothing can distract them from pursuing with prompt vigor any course that may appear to them as proper and effective, and of which they are duly advised. The late Congressional elections at the North warn us that the Wilmot Proviso will be applied to our entire territory; and that if we resist successfully we must do so now.

Floride [Noble Cuningham] was confined with a son a fortnight since. Both are doing well. She joins me in the kindest regards to yourself and family. We hope to see you soon, as you pass on to Washington.

It would give me great gratification and assistance to hear from you as to any of the questions, general or local, that may agitate the State or Nation. Yours most sincerely, John Cuningham.

ALS in ScCleA; PC in Jameson, ed., *Correspondence*, pp. 1185–1187.

To Richard Rush, [U.S. Minister to France]

Fort Hill, 13th Nov[embe]r 1848

My dear Sir, This will be presented to you by John B. Morris of the city of Baltimore, to whom I take pleasure in introducing you.

Mr. Morris is intelligent & well educated, and of highly respectable character & family.

His object in crossing the Atlantick, is to make the tour of Europe.

Any attention you may extend to him, or facility, in effecting the object he has in view, will place me under personal obligation to you. With great respect Yours truly, J.C. Calhoun.

ALS in ScU-SC, John C. Calhoun Papers.

From John Tyler

Sherwood Forest, Ch[arle]s City C[oun]ty, Virg[ini]a
Nov. 13, 1848

My Dear Sir: I addressed you a letter on the 10th of October enclosing a statement of my recollection of the closing scenes of my administration on the Texas question, to which I invited your attention and [“requested” *interlined*] any suggestions of amendment which you might see cause to make. From your long silence I am led to apprehend that my letter has been lost upon the wayside, and feeling an increasing interest in [“possessing” *interlined*] a just and authentic account of that proceeding, I have deem[e]d it best to enquire into the fate of my communication, so that if it has fail[e]d to reach you I may forward another copy. I have design[e]d to submit my reminiscences first to yourself, because of their reaching back to the day preceding the Cabinet meeting and relating to what transpir[e]d between ourselves. I have sought to do you the fullest justice in the statement, and if in this I have fail[e]d I pray you to believe my readiness and even anxiety to place it right. With sentiments of true respect Y[ou]rs &c, John Tyler.

ALS in ScCleA.

From J[ohn] Y. Mason, [Secretary of the Navy]

Navy Department, November 15th 1848

Sir, In reply to yours of 6th instant I have the honor to inform you that a permission has been sent to Dr. [William H.] White to present himself before a Board of Surgeons now in session at Philadelphia. Should the time however be too short to allow him to make preparations for his examination, upon his signifying to the Department his wish to appear before the next Board when it may meet, permission will be given him so to do. I am respec[tfull]y yours, J.Y. Mason.

FC in DNA, RG 45 (Naval Records), Miscellaneous Letters Sent by the Secretary of the Navy, 1798–1886, 40:495 (M-209:15).

To Laurel Summers, [Parkhurst, Iowa]

Fort Hill, 16th Nov[embe]r 1848

Dear Sir, You are right. Consolidation is shaking this government to its center, and will overthrow it, unless we abandon a loose and latitudinous construction of the Constitution, and return to the old & rigid construction, which brought the Republican party into power.

You ask me; what right has Congress to compromise the subject of Slavery? I answer none at all. That it is a subject, that does not fall within its province, except to pass such acts as may aid in car-r[y]ing out the Compromises of the Constitution in reference to it, including the delivering up fugitive slaves, & the apportionment of direct taxes, and of representation in the House of Representatives, and to secure the just equality of the citizens in all places where ["they" *canceled and* "it" *interlined*] has exclusive jurisdiction, & in reference to all subjects falling within its jurisdiction. It can make no discrimination between the citizen of one State and another, on account of their local institutions or from any other cause.

But while I hold that Congress has no power to pass a compromise line or to prohibit the citizens of the South to emigrate with their slaves into the territories of the U. States, I at the same time hold, the inhabitants of the territories have no such right, until they are authorised to form a State & to enter the Union as one of its members. The Sovereignty over the territories is exclusively in the people of the Several States, composing the Union, in their federal character, as such; and it is the greatest of ["absurdity" *altered to* "absurdities"] to suppose, that the inhabitants of a territory before they are authorised to form a State, can perform an act, which involves the high exercise of sovereign power. With respects, I am & &, J.C. Calhoun.

ALS in Ia-HA; PC in "A Pro-Slavery Letter by John C. Calhoun," in *Annals of Iowa*, 3rd series, vol. 2 (1894), p. 235.

From "A Friend of the Union"

Wallingford [Vt. or Conn.?], Nov. 18, 1848

Sir, The voice of an unknown & private individual appeals to you as the Guide & champion of the South not to countenance these meetings of the people in S. Carolina & elsewhere *Resolving* what they will do & what their Representatives in Congress *must* do if the north insist on preventing the extension of Slavery into Territory now free—do you wish to be placed in the predicament you occupied in 1832? do you imagine there will be any way to escape from such a predicament in regard to the above Question? Do you suppose it possible the nonslaveholding States will ever *compromise* this question to your satisfaction? It were a pity you could not live a few months in our midst, here, & learn how *difficult* it would be for northern men to submit, to what they would conceive to be in this age, the height of national dishonor & crime. But what do my feeble words avail! My object is just to point your attention to the enclosed paragraph [clipping]. The North will as yet consent to let the Slave Holding States alone (altho' they feel that the time *must* come when this national Stain of Slavery can no longer be tolerated) but they cannot, *will not*, consent to any thing more. Do you imagine it to be *possible* that they should? be undeceived! be wise & wary—assent to the Wilmot proviso & thus secure to yourselves immunity for the past & present, but dream of nothing more. As yet you occupy equal & fair ground. The north, altho opposed to Slavery, as you would be to polygamy, or the Slavery of our white citizens—have yet elected a Slave Holder for President of the United States. You see in this that we know how to discriminate between the man who *consents* tacitly to the existence of a wrong he *cannot* remedy, & him who would *extend* & *perpetuate* that wrong. We would not ostracise men because they are born under fortuitous circumstances. I voted for Gen[era]l [Zachary] Taylor. I believe he would sign a Bill containing the Missouri Compromise as well as one with the Wilmot Proviso—but we know you cannot but by bribery & fraud obtain the passage ["(or if it passes it cannot *stand*)" *interlined*] of the Missouri Compromize this winter. Protest & oppose as much as you please—this you can do & be ["comparatively" *interlined*] blameless—but don't try to carry the matter any further. It is *impossible.* You might as well destroy or attempt to destroy the Constitution itself. The people will *never* permit it. You cannot nullify at the South. It were greater madness to attempt it than any yet exhibited by any people. Think you the north will ever consent ["or allow" *interlined*] a few Slaveholders to set at defiance the laws of the Union—They *will* be *enforced*! The Union cannot be dissolved on *such* a *question* as the *extension of Slavery.* Neither God nor man, will consent. Avoid the *pit* such a *thing* as nullification or treason would dig for you. Very respectfully, A friend of the Union.

P.S. Often have I beheld in imagination the sublime picture of patriotism & virtue that such an act as the following would present:

"The acknowledgement by Jno. C. Calhoun that he had occupied a false position in some respects hitherto in regard to the Question of Slavery & is now satisfied that in this age ["& country" *interlined*] it would be impracticable ["in this Country" *canceled*] to do any thing to perpetuate or extend an Institution in regard to which there is so much opposition, whether wise or unwise—& that therefore he is ready for one, in order to avoid the immense evil of a dissolution of the Union or a Civil War, to accede to the principle contained in the Wilmot Proviso—that henceforward he will make to it no opposition."

What a sublime spectacle would such a manifesto present! How would all this great people cry "Honor, the highest we can bestow, & blessing be to the name of J.C. Calhoun!" How it would put[?] to rest the wave of strife and civil broil! and how would the great tho' now troubled Spirit of J.C. Calhoun revel in the luxury of having contributed more than any other man of this age to the ["Peace &" *interlined*] glory of his Country, & how *peacefully* would that Spirit leave a world it had so much contributed to bless, whenever God should call! Oh that we would be wise! that we would but *consider*!

ALS in ScCleA. NOTE: The author appended a clipping from an unknown newspaper quoting a speech at Memphis by Meredith P. Gentry, Representative from Tenn., in which he stated that the Wilmot Proviso was "the only hope and only alternative of saving this great and glorious Union." An AEU by Calhoun reads, "Anonymous."

To T[HOMAS] G. CLEMSON

Fort Hill, 19th Nov[embe]r 1848

My dear Sir, I hasten to answer your's of the 11th Inst. [*not found*], received by the mail of yesterday.

Owing to the great length of the last Session of Congress, and the uncertainty of the time, I would leave Washington & be at Aiken on my way home, I could not make arrangement for my carriage to meet me there, and was in consequence prevented from taking your place [in Edgefield District] in my way home from the want of conveyance, and am not informed what has been done towards finishing your House since I was there this time 12 months. At that time, the House was so far advance[d] towards finishing, that it required not much additional work to ["close it in &" *interlined*] make it comfortable.

As to the articles you may need, I understand from Mrs. [Floride Colhoun] Calhoun, that she has written to Anna [Maria Calhoun Clemson] on the subject. You will find all you left; and, if you have a list of them, by looking over it, you will be able to decide, what additional you may need.

Mrs. Calhoun will leave day after tomorrow for your place, & will send the Carri[a]ge to meet Anna at Aiken. I hope it will be in time. I will follow a few days after, & take your place in my way.

Your letter was not received in time to address you at Philadelphia, as well as at Charleston, as you desired; and I am affraid this will be too late to meet you in Charleston, as there will be no downward mail before the 22d Inst. Your affectionate father, J.C. Calhoun.

ALS in ScCleA.

From W[ILLIAM] A. HARRIS

Buenos Ayres, 20 Nov[embe]r 1848

My dear Sir: You have just passed through the ever exciting, and very important process of a presidential election. The result is probably at this moment known to you; but, as the appliances of steam and magnetic telegraphs, are not yet known in these latitudes, we must be content to wait the slower and more uncertain means of wind and sails, to bring us this intelligence. Perhaps, by the last of January, we may hear the result of the election. At this great distance from the scene of action, I can have no means of judging from the opinions of leading men, or from the tone and opinions of the public press; I can only reason upon general principles, look at general operating causes, and thus infer results. In thus examining the subject, therefore, I am brought irresistably to the conclusion, that the democratic party is, or ought to be, stronger now than at any period since its origin; and, being so, that it has the most impressive motives that ever influenced it, to exert itself to the utmost, to attain success—not the mere success of men—but success of its principles. I can scarcely doubt, therefore, but that the men who most nearly reflect these principles, will be—or rather, have been—elected by a very great majority. I feel well assured, then, that [Lewis] Cass and [William O.] Butler, in spite of free soil factions, abolitionism, and the whigs, have been elected by the people—as I have just said—by an immense majority.

I cannot deny, however, my high estimate of the character and services of Gen[era]l [Zachary] Taylor. My admiration and feelings were greatly excited in his favor. But, his many irreconcilable letters, and the use which the whigs appear to be making of him and them, show the impolicy of attempting to make a man president, who professes little other qualification, than that of military eclat. Patriotic intentions and martial fame, are scarcely sufficient, in the present situation of our country, and the agitated and disturbed condition of the world, to qualify a man properly to discharge the momentous duties of the presidency of our great Republic. It may be, however, that Gen[era]l Taylor, if elected, will indeed call to his aid such men of experience and ability, as with his own patriotic purposes, may enable him to conduct the political affairs of country, with great success. I do not think, however, that the contingency will probably arise, to illustrate his patriotism in this respect.

Much less can I suppose, that the shameless, malicious, and wicked apostacy of Mr. [Martin] Van Buren, can defeat the wishes of the democratic party. His motives are too diabolical. His purposes too distructive and selfish, to enable his fanatical troop of partizans to rise to the dignity of a party, or to attain the objects of his wicked ambition. It may be, indeed, that his ability and corrupt management, may give a shape and direction to abolitionism, which may hereafter occasion much embarrassment and trouble. If the whigs of the south, as well as the democrats, do not stand by the guaranties of the Constitution, and resist unitedly these unjust encroachments upon those sacred rights which it has secured, the final results of this movement, may be truly disastrous. And this the more certainly, if the *whole* South is not true to itself—to its rights—to its vital interests. And I know from my own personal observation, and from association with northern men, that it is only by the south presenting a united front in the question, without regard to parties, that it can calculate on the assistance of the democratic party of the north. Yet, after all, I can but believe that his purposes will fail. Neither his ambition nor his malice will be gratified. So far from his being able to defeat his former friends, I think it will—it certainly ought—to inspire them with new zeal, and the most cordial and perfect union throughout the country.

As to the ultimate effects of the question, they may indeed, ["m" *canceled*] be more serious than I now apprehend. But, not if the whigs of the south, are faithful to themselves and to the Constitution, rather than to the requirements of party. This I think, they finally will be; and thus Mr. Van Buren and his miserable and motly faction, will at last fail, and be dispersed. But, we shall see.

But, really it was not my purpose to bore you a moment upon the subject of politics, but only to say a few words to you about some seeds of these ["countries" *canceled*] countries which I have been collecting, and now send to you.

These seeds are chiefly from Paraguay, with some few from Corrientes. The most important of course, are the two specimens of cotton, and cotton seeds. Both these specimens are from Paraguay. The white appears to me to be, from its seed and and [*sic*] long silky staple, a species of our Sea Island cotton. In Paraguay and Corrientes, it grows on upland, as their alluvial lands are all subject to overflow. And that it is a cotton, ["that" *canceled*] which, whilst it seems to possess some of the good qualities of the Sea Island, yet will grow on lands other than Sea Island, appears to me to be one of its advantages. With a fibre, perhaps, more silky, ["and" *interlined*] a staple nearly as long, as our best qualities of Sea Island, if it will thrive and mature on our bottom lands, or the usual cotton lands of our southern country, it will surely be an advantageous kind to cultivate.

I am informed, that it is usually planted about six feet apart, each way. It bears the first year, and the plant, or small tree, is perpetual. It attains about the size of the Quince tree, and requires no cultivation, except the occasional cutting off the top, to prevent it growing too high. At least, such is the mode of treating it in Corrientes and Paraguay; yet, I have not a doubt, that a more attentive and careful cultivation of the plant, would produce the usual advantageous effects. *You must remember that frost, is absolutely unknown in Corrientes and Paraguay.* And whether the plant is adapted to the climate of our southern States or not, can only be determined by experience. I think, however, that it will succeed; though, our soil and climate, may perhaps soon assimilate it to our common upland cottons.

If you think proper, you might give a few seeds to be tested in other localities than your own. Be pleased to say to my friend, the Hon. Dixon H. Lewis, that Mr. Audley H. Gazzam of Alabama, who was recently here, procured a portion of the same seeds, which he has probably delivered to him ere this.

The seed and specimen of nankeen cotton now sent, are also from Paraguay; but, I am unable to say, in what particular, if any, it differs from the other. You will of course manage it, as in your judgment may seem best.

In regard to the other seeds, I need say nothing; except that I would suggest that you distribute a small portion of the Paraguay Tobacco seed, to the members from Missouri and Kentucky, or Tennessee—or perhaps more southern States would be better—so that it might have a fair trial. The Tobacco is of a light kind, very much like the Havana tobacco, but not quite so good, though it is very much used here for Cigars.

I shall send the box containing the seeds to the care of some one in New York—Mr. De Forrest or Mr. Zimmermann—with directions to send it on to you at Washington, by Adams's express. I will address it to the care of Asbury Dickens Esq., so that sh[oul]d you have left the City, he will forward it on to you, by some means. The box is quite small. It is possible, however, that it may reach you in Washington, as soon as this letter. Should you have the kindness to wish to send me any document or other matter, you can readily do so, by sending them to the care of Robert C. Wright & Co., Baltimore; or to B. De Forrest & Co., New-York.

However, if the whigs succeed, I shall probably have but a brief period to receive documents here; although Gen[era]l Taylor declares himself not an "ultra whig." As matters are now, I sh[oul]d prefer to remain a few years longer; but, nevertheless, if I am recalled, it is all right. I w[oul]d willingly exchange my present position, for a less responsible employment nearer home. Believe me, my dear Sir, with the sincerest regard & respect, y[ou]r friend & ob[edient] serv[an]t, W.A. Harris.

ALS in ScCleA. NOTE: Harris was U.S. Chargé d'Affaires in Argentina and a former Representative from Va.

From William Sloan

Tranquilla [Pendleton, S.C.,] Nov[embe]r 23d 1848

Dear Sir, I solicit your influence to obtain for my Son David U. Sloan a situation at West-Point.

My Son has evinced a decided predilection for the Army, and I am persuaded possesses those qualities necessary for a Soldier, in a higher degree than for aney of the ordinary pirsuits of life. When the requisition was made upon the State of So. Carolina for a Reg[i]ment for the Mexican service he volanteered, but the company was not formed in time to be received.

My son entered his nineteenth year last Feb[r]uary he is 5 feet 8 Inches high of a robust constitution.

His Grand Father David Sloan emigrated from Ireland before he reached his twentieth year, enlisted in the continental army and served to the close of the war. His ["Great" *interlined*] Grand Father on the mothers side Maj. Samuel Taylor was also a revolutionary soldier, and rendered important services to his country. I mention these facts with a view to strengthen his claims to admission. Verry respectfully your ob[edien]t servant, William Sloan.

ALS in DNA, RG 94 (Adjutant General's Office), Application Papers of Cadets, 1805–1866, 1848, 262 (M-688:173, frames 343–345).

To A[ndrew] P[ickens] Calhoun, [Marengo County, Ala.]

Fort Hill, 25th Nov[embe]r 1848

My dear Andrew, The last mail brought me yours of the 15th Inst.; and I deeply regret to learn, that little Andrew's hip is so seriously effected. I hope Dr. [Josiah C.] Nott will be able to releive him. I shall be anxious to learn, whether such has been the case, or not.

In reference to Patrick [Calhoun], I said nothing in my letter, which could by possibility be construed as the sligh[t]est reflection on you, or the least approbation of his course. On the contrary, I expressly approved of your course, & said that you could not act otherwise than you did, & expressed myself in strong, but not unkind termens [*sic*], of disapprobation of his course. I shaped my course, with the view to control him, & to save him from the certain ruin, that awaits him, unless he should reform. But I wrote you so fully ["(a few days since)" *interlined*] in reference to him in my last, which I hope you got, that I will not add more. You did right, in expressing yourself, in strong terms, in reference to his course. I hope, combined with the course I have taken, it will do much good. It is proper, he should be made to feel sore, but not to be alienated.

The low price of cotton is, indeed, alarming. As low as the price ["is" *interlined*] in Charleston, it is still lower in Mobile. You quote the best at 4¾. The last Mercury received, yesterday, quotes it in Charleston from 5 to 5 15/16 as the extremes, and the average ["sale" *canceled*] from 5 to 5½. In New York [City], it is quoted at 6 and upwards. Mobile is certainly one of the worst cotton markets in the Union. I learn today in our Village, that there has been another arrival, & that cotton had advance[d] an ⅛ [*sic*], which will probably raise the price to 6 in Charleston. It does strike me, ["by making" *canceled and* "it would be advisable to make" *interlined*] an arrangement to ship our crops to some strong, ["&" *interlined*] safe House in New York. In addition to getting a better price, we might, I think, make it the bases of getting a loan. [James] Edward Boisseau, I am sure, would gladly oblige us, by taking a general superintendence of our interest there, should we make the arrangement.

Mr. [Thomas G.] Clemson arrived early in the month with his family in New York [City]. They encountered a most terrifick storm, and were well near being lost. Every sail was carried away, but one, & that one, saved them. They are expected to be at their place on the 28th Inst.; and your Mother [Floride Colhoun Calhoun], John [C. Calhoun Jr.,] & [Martha] Cornelia [Calhoun] left day before yesterday to meet Anna [Maria Calhoun Clemson] & the children. Mr. Clemson goes on from Aiken to ClarksVille [Ga.], to attend to his interest there. I shall leave tomorrow, or next day, for Washington, taking Mr. Clemson's place in my way, but think it doubtful, whether he will have returned in time from ClarksVille for me to meet him. It is, of course, too late for you, him, and myself to meet at this time, or even for you & me to meet at Aiken or Charleston as you propose. He will probably go on to Washington, to be there by the time Gen[era]l [Zachary] Taylor will arrive, say middle of January, as he desires to continue in his present post. If we are to meet at all, ["it" *canceled*] in case he should be continued, I suppose it will have to be there. In that case, you could go on to New York [City], if you should think with me that it would [be] advisable to attempt to make the New York arrangement, I have suggested. I will write you so soon, as I learn what Mr. Clemson's movements will be. I shall take all the papers with me necessary to make a settlement with him.

The arrangement, you suggest in reference to our debts & my property in Alabama, would require more reflection, than I can give it at this time. You may rest assured, my dear son, that I have entire confidence in you, and duely [*sic*] appreciate the skill, judgement & industry, with which you have managed our joint concern. I know your devoted attachement [*sic*] to me, and I attach no blame whatever to you in making the purchase of the place, or the embarrassments to which it has led. They are ["to be" *canceled*] attributable to causes, which could not have been foreseen. Nor can I say, that I regret ["it" *canceled and* "the purchase" *interlined*]; for I know not, what better could ["have" *interlined*] been done, than was, & I do not dispair of our going through ["with it" *interlined*] successfully yet, & laying the foundation of a good estate for you all. I live only for my family & country; and regard no trouble, or difficulty, where they are concerned.

As to yourself, I feel, that I owe it as a duty to you, to place you in as safe and unembarrassed ["a" *interlined*] position as possible, in reference to our Alabama concern. I do not think, the feeling, you suppose, exist[s], on the part of your brothers or sisters. I have never heard either of them utter a word, that would indicate it. On the contrary, they always speak in kind terms of you, & they all know how unreasonable your mother is, when under excitement; for they have all, like you, individually felt it. What has occur[r]ed to me, as the best means of effecting what I intend, is to set a part [*sic*] the portion of my estate in Alabama, land & negroes, under your control & superintendence, jointly with your own, and to apply the ["net" *interlined*] proceeds, after a deducting [*sic*] a moderate fixed sum for the support of the family, including yours & your family expenses, for the extinguishment of the debt, when, ["& not before" *interlined*] my part, shall be subject to a division. I have not yet mentioned my ideas, & will not decide on my course, until I have reflected more fully & consulted with you.

Something decisive must be done about [Ker] Boyce's debt. If you can make the ["one" *canceled and* "arrangement" *interlined*] you suggest, it would, I doubt not be satisfactory. Cannot you get the delay of one year, on the next Cuba instalment & apply that to his debt? I hope ["to" *interlined*] be able to meet, what Mrs. [Placidia Mayrant] Adams requires. I saw her this evening, & let her have $152 to me[et] her immediate wants, &, I think, there is a fair chance, that Dr. [Ozey R.] Broyles will raise enough to meet the residue she requires, by the time it will be needed. If such should be the case, & the cotton should sell even at 5 cents, there would be ["sufficient to" *canceled and* "left after" *interlined*] meeting Patrick's drafts, & to [*partial word canceled*] paying bank discounts & the interest on [Ann Mathewes] Ioor's debt, & [*sic*] a considerable residue to apply to Boyce's debt. You must not fail to transmit money in time to renew our notes in bank, & pay the Ioors interest. If you can get 5 cents sell, & that I think, you can almost certainly [get]. I will send our notes in blank in time to the banks to be renewed. To conclude; let me entreat you to write me fully and often, & keep ["me" *canceled*] me early informed of all remittances you may make, or arrangements you may make, in reference to our debt, and the sales you may make of our cotton & the funds that ["is" *canceled and* "are" *interlined*] or will ["probably" *interlined*] be at your disposal. In reference to all these, you have been negligent; which has embarrassed me much, & crippled my ["in my" *canceled*] efforts to support our credit. You need not fear, that you will occupy too much of my time by writing me ["too" *canceled*] often & ["too" *canceled*] fully; or that you will make me anxious by making me fully acquainted with the utmost extent of our difficulties. I would always rather know the worst. I am not easily disheartened.

I shall expect to hear from you shortly after I arrive at Washington fully on all points.

Love to Margaret [Green Calhoun] & the children. Your affectionate father, J.C. Calhoun.

[P.S.] Have you sold any of the crop of cotton? & if you have, how much & at what price?

ALS in NcD, John C. Calhoun Papers.

To Dr. R[ALPH] E. ELLIOTT

Fort Hill, 26th Nov[embe]r 1848

My dear Sir, I intended to deliver to you the documents refer[r]ed to in the enclosed note [*not found*], & in reference to which I spoke to you, & also to return the money paid for the rock salt you were so obliging to order for me, but neglected it at the time. I was mortified after my return from a trip to the mountains ["to learn" *interlined*] that it was too late, as you had left for below. I would send the documents by mail; but the weight is above my frank. I hope, however to have the pleasure of delivering them to you when you come up next summer. Yours truly, J.C. Calhoun.

ALS in ScU-SC, John C. Calhoun Papers.

From Z. L. NABERS

Carrolton Ala., Nov. 29th 1848

Sir: The spirit & manner in which the late presidential canvass was conducted in reference to the question of slavery in California & New Mexico; the result of that canvass; the silence of Gen. [Zachary] Taylor on the Wilmot Proviso; his opposition to the Veto power; the known majority of the Free Soil party in Congress; are facts which indicate that our country is rapidly approaching a crisis, when the rights of the South & South West are to be disreguarded, or our glorious confederacy dissolved. At such a time our country has none to whom she can look for counsel & advice with more confidence than yourself. Your opinion therefore upon the present duty of the slave-holding States; the propriety of holding a Southern Convention to adopt such measures as will protect our rights; & the time the convention should be held; would be read & cheerished with a deep interest by every Southern man, as well as by every lover of the Union in the North. With sentiments of high regard I am your obed[ien]t Serv[an]t, Z.L. Nabers.

ALS in ScCleA; PC in Boucher and Brooks, eds., *Correspondence*, pp. 485–486.

From Nathan Gaither

Columbia (Ky.), Dec[embe]r 2nd 1848

Dear Sir, My great anxiety for the fate of the Union has prompted me to ask you for information upon the subject. I see our fate clearly if the free soil doctrine is pressed to consummation. The Union is gone beyond redemption. I know the South can do as well without the North as the North can without the South yet I greatly prefer the Union as it is and if the South will stand firm[,] yield nothing in principle all may yet be well. Kentucky in 1824 received a Northern stain by the junction of two opposite bodies that has given political complexion to the State for the last fifteen years & confidence in its durebility gave boldness to the party upon the slave question. We have at hand a Convention to revise the Constitution & gradual emancipation reared its head with the Northern party. It will not take & the effort will prepare the State to act with the South upon the free soil doctrine. Upon the slave question you have much able matter which would be most acceptable to me in the approaching contest & I will be under lasting obligation to you for it.

The election of [Zachary] Taylor disappointed me much but I hope no great evil will result from it. The crisis of the slave question will be brought on earlier & our fate will be the sooner over. What part Taylor will play time only can determine. The present administration is marked with astonishing results by the force of circumstances more than the power of the statesman for I look upon the heads of affairs as a jumble of politicians with a slight tinge only of the statesman. I did not intend to trouble you with my own notions. I only wanted a peep into the political future from you and matter to assist us in the approaching State struggle on slavery. If you can spare the time to give me on each subject I shall be yours &c[?]. Respectfully, Nathan Gaither.

ALS in ScCleA. NOTE: An AEU by Calhoun reads "Dr. N. Gaither[,] Ken-[tuck]y."

From JOSEPH E. LATHROP

Middletown C[onnecticu]t, Dec. 2d 1848

Dear Sir, I inclose to you, a communication, which I have been induced to write, for reasons therein specified.

Whatever may be your opinions, in regard to the sentiments, which ["it" *interlined*] contains, I trust you will pardon me, for thus intruding upon your patience, whilst I assure you, I am actuated by no other motive, than a sincere desire to see the government of this country, administered according to the principles of the Constitution, fairly interpreted, as a whole, and applicable to the whole.

I wish to see Congress legislating, directly and incident[al]ly, for the general interests of the whole country, so far as those general interests are constitutionally committed to ["their" *canceled and* "its" *interlined*] care; and not legislating directly for one section, and incident[al]ly for an other.

Were this principle kept in view, and the action of Congress directed accordingly; it appears to me, the affairs of the nation would be better attended to, Congress would have less trouble, less excitement, and a far better general influence, and there would ["much" *canceled*] be much less occasion for trying to prevail on the Executive to evade his duty, in one instance, and to go beyond it, in another, than there now is.

Looking upon these United States, at the ["presen" *canceled*] present time, as the center of an influence, that is exerting and extending itself over the countries of Europe; I would hope for good; my sincere wish is, that nothing may take place, calculated to lessen that influence abroad, or to disturb its equanimity at home. Most Respectfully Your Ob[edien]t serv[an]t, Joseph E. Lathrop.

[Enclosure]

[Joseph E. Lathrop] to John C. Calhoun

Connecticut, December 1848

It is hoped the sentiments contained in this communication, will not be deemed altogether ["altogether" *canceled*] beneath your notice, or unworthy of your attention, emanating as they do, from a private individual; a large part of whose life has been spent, in the laborious pursuits of agriculture or mechanical business; and therefore without any pretensions to profound intellectual attainments, or political science. But nevertheless, they are from one, who looks with favor, upon the course which you have maintained, in reference to many of the most important subjects, which have, at different times, agitated the councils of the nation, during the last few years.

I am induced to write, not from a vain idea of enlightning your understanding, or of imparting any views, not already familiar to your own reflections; but, from considerations which have sprung up in my own mind; prompted by some of the peculiarities, connected with the late Presidential election, and the singular position of the President elect; not only in regard to the different political parties into ["which" *interlined*] the people are divided; but in regard to his own action, upon questions which may arise, of vast importance in themselves, and involving, at the same time, the most important, and even the vital interests of this great Republic.

In the election of [18]44, I took an active part, and was one of the first, if not the first, in this vicinity, to advocate the peculiar measures, which resulted in the election of President [James K.] Polk, but in the late election, I took no part, except to put my vote into the ballot box. I saw, or thought I saw, in the letters and demeanor of General [Zachary] Taylor, evidence of an honest and well disposed mind; and I hold myself ready to give to his Administration, an honorable and hearty support, if in its developments, it shall comport, with what, I conceive to be for the best interests of the country at large.

General Taylor declares himself to be "a whig," "but not an ultra one." Now this phraseology imparts no idea to the mind, either of principles or measures; and if repeated a thousand times, it would still be perfectly insignificant. Had he said he was a Democrat, or a Republican, "but not an ultra one;" this would convey to the mind, at ["leas" *canceled*] least, the idea that he was in favor of popular institutions.

But perhaps it will be said, the term Whig, is the name, by which a powerful political party is known. Be it so. Take from the whig party, ["of the No" *canceled*] especially the whig party of the North, all its ultraisms; and there would be no whig party left.

In 1840, the Whigs declared themselves, the advocates of what they called "great whig measures"; upon the carrying out of which, they said, the "salvation of the country depended." At the extra session of '41, Mr. [Henry] Clay summed the whole, in a bank of the United States. Subsequently, Mr. [Daniel] Webster declared the bank had become an "obsolete idea." Mr. Senator [Reverdy] Johnson of Maryland, at a political harangue, about a year ago, in New York, (if correctly reported) said he pronounced the whole "an obsolete idea."

In [18]48, the excellence of the whig party, and its strength too, appears to consist, in the abandonment of all "old issues," and substituting no new ones; unless it be a new Candidate; and a horror stricken dismay at the "one man power" of the Constitution.

The whigs are in favor of a banking system; but they would have that system so arranged, as to give to ["that" *canceled*] the money power, a controlling influence, over all the concerns of the country.

They say they are in favor of a revenue tariff; but in adjusting it, their ultra notions of protection, must have the first place, and revenue the last.

They go for a system of internal improvement, at the expense of the national treasury; but are entirely unwilling to confine their appropriations to objects truly national.

They profess a great regard for the Constitution, but are continually racking their inventive powers to make it speak a language, that it was never intended to countenance. Indeed, ultraism appears as naturally to follow all their important movements, as fruit does the blossom.

It is not intended to say, that there are no ultraisms in the Democratic party. It is scarcely possible, that in a contest for ascendency; such as has characterized the political parties of this country, for the last twenty years, nothing of an ultra nature, ["shoul should" *canceled*] should spring up in its progress. But ultraism is not so much the natural element, nor so conspicuous a characteristic of the Democratic, as it is ["of" *canceled*] a certain production of the whig, or Federal party.

According to news paper reports, Senator [John M.] Ber[r]ien of Georgia, called upon the people of the South, to support General Taylor, for the Presidency, because he was a Southern man, was of the South, and therefore was known to be with the South. If this be so, it is a whig ultraism of the South, and entirely reprehensible.

If it be claimed, that the election of General Taylor, is a verdict of the people, in favor of the ultra measures and exploded theories, brought forward by the whigs, during the last 20 years, as is now set up, by the leaders of that party; it is, to say the least of it, entirely inconsistent, with the position, which that Gentleman occupied, during the recent election.

But if it be claimed, that the result of the late election is a decision of the people, in favor of the views, taken by Southern politicians, in regard to these questions; then are there thousands of Northern Democrats, who will acquiesce in the assumption, and who will willingly give their aid, in sustaining the coming Administration, although they may not have cast their votes, for the President elect; and there are thousands of northern Whigs, who voted for him, that will turn against him, if in the progress of his Administration, they shall find their ultra views and notions are not to be sustained by the Executive.

Many however, will flatter themselves, that in case they do not succeed, entirely, during the next four years, they will, at least acquire such an ascendency, as will enable them to dictate terms, in [18]52, carry out all their plans, and establish all their hitherto defeated, but still cherished measures.

"The veto," or as the whigs call it, the one man power, has been the great weapon, say these Gentlemen, that has killed all our schemes, heretofore; but we have got a man now, who is pledged not to interpose, ["it," *interlined*] not even to prevent the passage of the "Wilmot proviso."

Whatever may have been the views, feelings or apprehensions, by which the framers of the Constitution, were induced to clothe the Executive with ["the" *canceled*] power to veto the doings of Congress; the beneficial effects resulting from its exercise thus far, have been sufficient to satisfy me, both of its propriety and utility; and I would fain hope, that a Southern President will not be the first, to pursue a course calculated to bring its use into disrepute.

Had it not been for the application of the veto, ere this day, the destiny of these United States, had been in the power of a National Bank, "a Fiscal Agent," or some other money working machine. A National Bank, with fifty or a hundred millions capital, would be a "Monster," altogether too powerful, for the partizan and mercenary politicians of the present day.

Had it not been for the application of the veto, the National Treasury, ere this day, would have been rendered bankrupt, by an enormous expenditure for internal improvements.

Some of the most important instances, in which, the Executive veto has been interposed, have been to sustain measures and principles, advocated by Southern Gentlemen; and should a Southern President be the first, to discountenance its use, it would go much farther to bring it into disrepute, than if the same had been done, by one from the North.

The doctrine, strenuously advocated by some, viz. that the President ought not to exercise legislative functions, appears to me, not well founded; in as much, as the same organic law, which defines the duties of Representatives and Senators requires that all their acts shall be reviewed by the Executive, before they can become the law of the land. And who? it may be asked, can be better situated, to judge correctly, and to act discreetly, ["than" *canceled*] upon the doings of legislators, acting not unfrequently, under the heat of a stormy debate, partizan zeal or sectional feelings, than the President?

No one, at all acquainted with the real designs and evident intentions of the whig leaders, especially the Northern Whigs; can fail to be satisfied, that they are still, strenuously bent upon fastning upon the nation, another national bank, and with it, all their other, at present, dormant projects. If they can acquire a permanent ascendency, in both Houses of Congress, their secret intentions will soon show themselves. But not knowing into whose hands the Executive power may fall, the ultraists are peculiarly anxious, if they cannot destroy the veto power, at least, to render its use, not only unpopular, but obnoxious. I cannot believe the hero of Monterey and Buena Vista will be the first, to countenance their heart cherished but iniquitous designs. No one, who does not see and hear for himself, can well imagine the air of triumph, which now prevails among the whigs, as they ["proc" *canceled*] proclaim to one another, that they have now got a President that will not veto the doings of Congress.

It is very difficult to conceive how any discreet man can, (as it is claimed General Taylor has) pledged himself, in advance, that he will approve of all the doings of Congress, unless per chance, it be some palpable and unmistakable violation of the Constitution; and I therefore will not believe he has, until I shall see some better evidence for it, than any I have as yet seen.

Previous to entering on the execution of his office, the President is required to take the oath prescribed by the Constitution. A part of which, is, that he will "preserve, protect and defend the Constitution of the United States."

Now the Constitution says, "Every bill which shall have passed the House of Representatives and Senate, shall, before it becomes a law, be presented to the President of the United States; if he approve, he shall sign it, but if not he shall return it, with his objections." How then, can the President approve or disapprove, without careful and deliberate investigation?

Under these circumstances, is the President at liberty to say in advance, he will approve of every thing, that ultraism, and "log rolling" may work through Congress? Surely this would be an ultraism, not to be expected from a high minded Southern Executive.

The Constitution, for which the ["whigs" *interlined*] pretend a most sacred regard, plainly enjoins a duty upon the Executive, in reference to the acts of Congress; and the Executive, under the solemnity of an oath, promises to discharge that duty. Can he, consistently with his duty, act an indifferent, or neutral part, and throw the responsibility upon Congress?

It is pretended, that the President, by his veto, can nullify the action of one third of both Houses of Congress. This is not the truth, for it requires more than three sixths, to pass a law, under any circumstances—and it requires only four sixths to do it, under the veto. So that its effective influence is less than one sixth.

But what has the effect of the veto to do with the discharge of the President's duty? The veto power was not placed in the Constitution, by his agency, nor can it be expunged by his neglect. Away then! with that ultraism that would bring into disrepute, one of the most important provisions of the Constitution, by Executive infidelity.

The following language upon this subject, is from a letter written by Hon. Millard Fillmore and published in the Buffalo Commercial Advertiser. Speaking of the future action of Congress and the Executive, he says, "Where Congress has the Constitutional right to legislate, the will of the people, as expressed through their Representatives in Congress, is to control; and that will is not to be defeated, by the arbitrary interposition of the veto power."

Thus, in the estimation of the Vice President elect; for the President to discharge a duty, imposed upon him by the Constitution, and enjoined upon him by solemn oath, deserves no milder name, than an arbitrary act.

What language could be more contemptible? coming as it does, from one, who owes his own election, to the fact, that he was run upon the same ticket with General Taylor; and yet, before he is inducted into office, he is exerting himself to embarrass the President, in the exercise, not merely, of a Constitutional right, but in the discharge of Constitutional duties. Duties as clearly defined, and as imperatively enjoined, as any pertaining to the members of Congress. Why may not the action of the Vice President, when he gives the casting vote in the Senate, be termed an arbitrary act; with as much propriety, as the act of the President, when in the discharge of a duty, enjoined upon him by the Constitution, and enforced by the solemnity of an oath, he signifies his dissent from certain acts of Congress;

Every year's experience and observation, serves more and more to convince me, both of the wisdom and utility of the Executive veto. It may, ["doubtless" *canceled*] doubtless, be abused; but any wanton abuse of it, can easily be corrected by Congress. Remote then, be the day, when it shall be stricken from the Constitution, or its exercise be rendered obnoxious, by the efforts of ultra politicians. President Taylor may never have occasion to interpose his veto, upon any of the doings of Congress; but I will not believe, he will lend his influence to bring its exercise into disrepute. The time may, not only come, but it may be near at hand, when it may be the means of saving this great Republic from disruption; and of preventing incalculable mischief, both in this country and throughout the world.

It is not to be denied, that many Democrats at the North, have been disappointed, at the result of the late election. Whilst disunion has done much to defeat their Candidates at the North, several of the Southern States, heretofore accustomed, almost uniformly, to sustain the nominees of the Democratic party; have, at the late election, pursued a different course; apparently indicating, that sectional feeling had much influence in deciding the contest.

Still, there is a very prevalent disposition, to entertain favorable views and feeling, towards the President elect; and should his course of action and policy, be such as many believe it will be, it will go far, to mittigate the asperity of party feeling; and to induce a willing and cheerful support of his administration, even from many, who felt an ["ardent" *canceled*] ardent desire, for the election of General [Lewis] Cass.

Among the whigs, many misgivings are already showing themselves. Some are fearful that there will not be a general turning out of office, in order to make room, for the victors. Others are apprehensive, lest the new Administration will not give such support to the ultra notions and projects of former days, as they are desirous to have carried out. Others still, are afraid, that, after all, General Taylor is not so much of a modern whig, as they supposed him to be; and possibly he may be too much tinctured, with Old Virginia Democracy, to make a good whig President.

Without speculating upon the present result, or what may be, or what may not be the final effects of the late election; a few things may be inferred, as immediate and natural consequences.

If the President elect shall be induced, to exert his influence and opinions, in opposition to the use of the veto; he will do much to inflict a deep wound upon the Constitution, and to encourage ultra politicians, in their efforts to carry out measures, not only in violation of the true spirit of the Grand Charter of our liberties; but dangerous to liberty itself; to the true welfare and peace, of this, now great, and happy Republic.

At a time like the present, when the nations of the Old World are staggering under the weight of accumulated evils, brought on by bad government, when the eyes of the whole civilized world, are turned to these United States, for a mddle [*sic*] of good government, and of civil institutions, adapted to the wants of human nature; any thing ["that" *canceled*] that looks like bringing the requisitions of our glorious Constitution into discredit, will be ["haile" *canceled*] hailed with joy, alike, by the despots of the old, and the ultraists of the new world.

As to myself, I am satisfied, that if the ["preset" *canceled and* "present" *interlined*] institutions of our country, are to be maintained; they must depend, chiefly, for their support, upon the agricultural sections of the South and West. I have no doubt, of the honorable views and honest intentions of General Taylor; and it matters not with me, whether he hail, as whig or democrat; If I see him clinging to the Constitution, determined to sustain its provisions, to discharge the duties it enjoins, regardless both of the blandishments and sneers of artful politicians; I shall be ready to do my part, in supporting his administration. And my confidence, that he will do this; is much strengthened, by the fact, that he is from the South.

I sincerely hope, that General Taylor will be found, exactly fitted for the present crisis, both of our own country, and also of the world.

There will, doubtless, be a great rush for appointments to office, after the fourth of March. It will tend much to the credit of President Taylor's administration, if those who may receive appointments, at his hand, are such as carry with them, the confidence ["of" *canceled*] and esteem of the communities in which they dwell.

It is not to be denied, that within the last few years, many executive appointments have been made, discreditable to the appointing power. Men have been thrust into important stations, apparently, without regard to their qualifications, personal character or demeanor. The sentiment has been inculcated, that qualifications and personal demeanor, were of little consequence, provided there be a clerk in the office, competent to do the business. By these means, the moral sense of the community, has, in many instances been outraged. I do not know that these evils can be entirely remedied, but I am confident they may be in some measure. Many deserving individuals, whose appointment would be, not only creditable to the appointing power, but would exert a favorable influence in its support, are forced to stand at a distance, rather than engage in the disgraceful scramble, necessary ["to" *canceled*] for success in their application. [Joseph E. Lathrop.]

ALS with En in ScCleA.

From Jos[eph] J. Singleton

Dahlonega [Ga.,] 3d Dec. 1848

My Dear Sir, This is in reply to yours of the 14th Ult. [*not found*]. The delay has been occasioned under two heads. 1st. The enquiry with regard to the character of Mr. James Anderson, the person who wrote you some time since for a lease upon the Obarr lot. I have recently assertained that he is a clever man and one who may be relied upon as a man of truth & veracity, but poor.

2d. As ["it" *canceled*] regards the determination of your present Lessees ["upon s(ai)d lot" *interlined*] I cannot yet find out. They will not say what they will do, but still appear obstinate; their pledge however is out, and I will soon have an opportunity of attending to its consummation, which you may rely on.

I can but admire your determination to compare the gold business with that of cotton raising, and sincerely hope you may be enabled to realize the difference in your small way sufficient to enlarge profitably. I know it to be the best business. Yours Truly &c, Jos. J. Singleton.

ALS in ScU-SC, John C. Calhoun Papers. Note: This ms. contains an AEU by Calhoun reading: "Copy of the Lease to [John] Pascoe & [John] Hockanol."

From John C[ustis] Darby

Lexington Ky., 4th Dec[embe]r 1848

Dear Sir, In the year 1838 I took the liberty to write you a letter on another subject, to which you did me the honor to reply. It was in reference to a speech of yours, & one of Mr. [Henry] Clay upon the Bank, Treasury Note Bill, & ["an" *interlined*] Independent Treasury. I must congratulate you upon the final triumphant success of the views & plan expounded & advocated by you as early as the session of 1833–4, when *you, first* broached the idea of separating the Government from the Banks. I sincerely trust that it will be a perpetual separation.

Now to the object of this communication. We are next year to elect men to form a new Constitution for the State of Kentucky. A predetermined & concerted effort will be made to introduce a clause abolishing slavery in this State. According to my humble ability I shall oppose it in toto. Knowing your thorough acquaintance with the whole subject I thus take the liberty to request you to refer me to the best works upon the subject; & to send me any documents you may have at command. What I particularly want is an abstract (if there is any such) of the reports which have been made to the British Parliament within the last few years ["upon Africa & the slave trade" *interlined*]. There was a report made by a Captain Harris (I think is the name) from which I have seen an extract & which I should very much like to see entire. I have been endeavoring for a year past to collect facts; but knowing as I do the amount of talent, learning, & ability which will be concentrated upon Kentucky by the Abolitionists from all quarters, I, as well as others, should be forewarned of the necessity of a thorough preperation. Already have they commenced: In "the Examiner" an out & out Abolition Paper, published at Louisville, nos. 76, 77, vol. 11 there is a long article "By a committee of the Synod of Ky." signed John Brown Esq[ui]r[e]; John C. Young Secretary. Rev. J.C. Young D.D. is the President of Centre College, Danville Ky. & is also the son-in-law of Gov. J[ohn] J. Crittenden. That article, (which by the way, has not yet appeared in the Presbyterian Herald, the organ of the P[resbyterian] Church & of the Synod of Ky. which is also published at Louisville) is a fair exposé of the men & the kind of argument, we have to contend against. Nothing, as you will see, has ever emanated from an abolitionist of the north more ultra or fanatical. The Paper is no doubt taken in Washington & you can see it.

I have commenced a series of articles under the signature of Moses, which I also publish in "The Examiner." My first article appears in the number (77) of Dec[embe]r 2d [18]48. The Editors sent me the number (76) before that, which was the first one I had seen of the Paper. I considered that the antidote, so far as I could make one, had better appear with the poison. Feeling assured that my articles will have the greater weight & influence if it is not known who writes them, I must beg the favor of you not to make it known that I am the writer of the articles signed "Moses." Considering the importance of the subject to us all, & the obligation which rests upon every lover of his country to resist this pseudo philanthropy & revolutionary movement I know that you will consider that no apology is needed for thus troubling you. With every sentiment of regard & consideration I am Dear Sir your friend & ob[edien]t Serv[an]t, Jno. C. Darby.

ALS in ScCleA.

From J[AMES] WISHART

St. Louis, Dec[embe]r 6th 1848

My Dear Sir, Since you favored me, last summer, with your speech on the Oregon Bill, now the law of the land, a revolution has come over the country. Gen. [Zachary] Taylor, the first southern whig, who ever filled the executive chair, is elected. On the whole, I believe it is best he should occupy that position, from the fact that a crisis, in the confederacy, has taken place. This crisis I expected, but not so soon. But, since come it must, I rejoice it has not been longer postponed. Your anticipations and warnings have been regarded as idle bravado, but no intelligent, unprejudiced, upright statesman, in the north, could close his eyes on the coming evil. But the partizan and *selfishness* in the *demagogues who rule all, for gain,* ["has" *canceled and* "have" *interlined*] done it.

Trusting, rather to the interests, sympathies, associations and location of Gen. Taylor, than the pledges, against all these, of Gen. [Lewis] Cass, and believing him rather a partizan demagogue than a patriotic statesman, I prefered the election of the former. Whig and democrat exist no longer. It is north and south. Slave and free soil will now form the party lines. Believing that patriotism called, although I have not taken an active part in the election, I have acted, in a matter relative to yourself, as I felt unwilling to trust any other man in the exigency that exists. What I have done may be, and probably will be disregarded, and may not meet your approbation—But fearing the clearness of Taylor I urged the appointment of yourself as his secretary of state, for this among other reasons, that you were, on this especially, as well as other questions, the champion of the south. If he is the man I take him to be, my letter will bring an answer. If it does not, it will, be to me, a criterion of character.

If the south is prepared to submit to the Oregon Bill, she is also ready to relinquish the confederacy. No compromises will now serve. The federal government must retrace her steps, otherwise the constitution is no protection to any State, nor possesses power to confine the action of that government ["with" *altered to* "within"] any other limit than a law of congress, which seems now to be too generally regarded ["the" *interlined*] organic and supreme law of the land. It seems, from the infatuation of the people, or the gross ignorance or baseness of *that class who control the entire government* that a simple repeal of that bill would not be a sufficient protection to the south, for the same aggression will be repeated in a few years. Nothing short of an explicit and positive prohibition against the interference of the general government with the subject of slavery either in the States or territories, will protect the south against the incendiary spirit of northern fury.

I have also stated my views, in reference to the novelty of his position, and that it is now north and south, not whig and democrat. That this will remain till this question is settled, as it was by the constitution at first, and amendments prohibiting the federal gov[ernment] from interfering with this question any where. That this or a northern and southern republic will spring from the disruption of the confederation, or a consolidated despotism, will be erected on the ruins of popular government.

My opinions as to the origin of all our evils, are peculiar perhaps to myself. In 45 or 46 I think I stated these opinions to a gentleman who was connected with you, when secretary of state, Mr. Crawlle [*sic*; Richard K. Crallé]. These opinions I entertain still, and have expressed them to Gen. Taylor, to show that the selection of "military chieftains" to the presidency, is not the pressing evil of the country. Sixteen thousand men, moved by a common impulse, who fatten on convulsions, credit systems, banking systems expansions and contractions, public and private indebtedness, revolutions, popular and commercial vicissitude, and distress, overtrading and in a word, whose interests are antagonistical to the interests of all other classes, and yet control the entire political power of the country, is an evil seen by but few, and yet pregnant with destruction to popular government. I refer to political lawyers, which embraces, directly and indirectly, nearly the whole number. This class took a fee from me, and then trafficed [*sic*] me, all for political and private interest. "*Hine illae lachrymae.*" But I am not alone in this process, for thousands annually share my fate, and though they are ranged on both sides of the political question, as they are on both sides of a law case, for a fee, the leading object and inquiry, with them, is, by what process, in giving direction to the executive, legislative, and judicial departments of the country, they can extract the greatest amount of money from all. United by a common interest, and the esprit du corps, against all other classes, they assist each other in filling all places of honor and profit, both at home and abroad. They make all our candidates for office, and put up and put down whomsoever they please. They give direction to canvasses for elections. Make all our political, judicial, and legislative speeches, for the printing, and the time consumed in delivering these Buncom speeches, hundreds of thousands of dollars are, annually, extracted from the people, which finds its way, at last, into their pockets. Constantly before the eyes of the people, they have become the fac totum of the country. They are the government, and the reason you are not a favorite with them is, that you have refused to join the clique. By their profession they legitimately wield one third of the poli[ti]cal power, and they have usurped the control of the other two thirds, in the executive and legislative departments. It is thus a great complicated machine, that silently and unseen, drains the life blood of the country. All this may be a necessary evil, but if it is, it is paying immensely for a popular government. Hence we are governed, for the benefit of sixteen thousand vampires.

I send you a new theory of matter and form which I have developed, and on this theory have explained phenomena in the laws of nature, hitherto supposed to be inexplicable, and have positively fixed, and limited the origin of aerial poisons, human and other animal viruses, miasm[a]s from chemical decomposition, by laws as definite and specific as the laws which govern animal and vegetable generation.

The basis on which the positions taken in the essay I sent you last summer, rests, is seen in this, as well as the claim to an important discovery in the laws of nature, established, and I have at least the consolation of knowing that I have added some valuable ideas to the stock of human knowledge, which will be durable as mind itself. In it will, I think, be seen, more originality and greater grasp of thought—More exact discrimination, and power of analytic investigation, and synthetic ability, than has been displayed by any or all the members of the profession, now or formerly resident here, although there is also evidence of careless and hasty composition.

In you I have found a closer correspondence, in the several habits of perception, of thought, of feeling and of general mental conformation than in any other with whom I have had intercourse, and however inferior in degree, the organisation may exist in me, it nevertheless forms a psycological ligament of union, and confidence which I highly prise. But my dear sir, although I have been successful as a physician and I have, by my own exertions, placed myself in the first class, among hundreds of physicians and two medical colleges—though I feel myself equal to the achievment of mental labor of a high order, there is hardly a motive for exertion. For with all this the composer of a twattling song for the piano, in which there is not a valuable idea, mental, moral or physical can secure, for the copy right, five hundred or a thousand dollars, ["while" *interlined*] mine will not procure me a red cent; and it is with the utmost difficulty, I am able to procure food and raiment for my family, or comfortable clothing for myself. I hope the time has come when it will be impossible to succeed without mind. Yet it is doubtful how far Gen. Taylor will see the cause, character and remedy for the crisis, as I do. For it seems to be the character of the American mind, if not of the age, that an agent purely physical, with no more mind than a steam engine, is held in higher estimation, than the mind that put it in motion, or the most elevated scintillations. If therefore you can, without affecting the relation in which you wish to stand with all others, see how I could be more profitably employed please inform me, and believe me respectfully &c. Any documents or letters will give pleasure, J. Wishart.

ALS in ScCleA.

Remarks at South Carolina College

[Columbia, December 7, 1848]

[*Calhoun was escorted into the college chapel on the arm of President William C. Preston at 11 a.m. The chapel was crowded with students and townspeople for commencement exercises. William H. Wallace, a member of the senior class, made a welcoming address, to which Calhoun responded:*]

Young Gentlemen, Students of the South Carolina College: I feel deeply grateful to you for the reception which you have been pleased to give me; and rest assured that I properly appreciate the warmth of the greeting with which I have been honored. It is not my intention to deliver you an address, but I would say to you, one and all, that during your connection with this institution, if at any time the temptations and seductions incident to a College career should assail you and draw you from your duties, that you remember that you are South-Carolinians, and that much is expected of you. You, sir, (to Mr. Wallace) have alluded to the crisis now most certainly approaching—which it is your duty to be prepared to meet. During the term of my life its end may not be—but you are young, and must expect, therefore, to take part in the struggle, which may come—and a tremendous one it must be—pregnant with mighty consequences. Again, then, I repeat, be diligent in the acquisition of knowledge, that you may become good citizens, able and ready to protect the Constitution of this Union, by asserting and maintaining at *all hazards*, the rights of the South, and the dignity and honor of all its citizens.

From the Columbia, S.C., *Daily Telegraph*, December 8, 1848, p. 2. Also printed in the Pendleton, S.C., *Messenger*, December 15, 1848, p. 1; the New York, N.Y., *Herald*, December 16, 1848, p. 4. NOTE: The *Telegraph* reported that after these remarks, the students "pressed forward to grasp" Calhoun's hand and he exchanged "cordial greetings" with them. Upon leaving the college, Calhoun went to the capitol. According to the Washington, D.C., *Daily National Intelligencer*, December 15, 1848, p. 3, (reprinting an unidentified S.C. paper), Calhoun visited the Senate chamber at 1 p.m. "and shortly afterwards was conducted to a seat in the House by the committee appointed for that purpose. The House was crowded to excess, many persons never before having seen Mr. Calhoun . . . . It has now been several years since he visited Columbia, and his present visit created quite a sensation." The *Telegraph* said that its report of Calhoun's remarks gave the "substance," but "his words we do not pretend to give." William H. Wallace was subsequently a Brig. Gen. in the Confederate army and speaker of the S.C. House of Representatives.

From C[HRISTOPHER] G. MEMMINGER

Columbia, Dec[embe]r 9, 1848

My Dear Sir, Your engagements prevented you from appearing at the Bible Convention held in this place, and as that left them without sufficient speakers, I had to be impressed in your place. So that you will more readily excuse my apparent negligence in not calling in the evening to converse with you as I had promised. I collected your views from others who had seen you, and I think the action which we have determined upon in a Caucus last night will meet your views. We pass a single Resolution declaring the time for discussion as to our exclusion from the Territory acquired from Mexico has passed, and that we are ready to cooperate with our Sister States in resisting the Principles of the Wilmot Proviso, at any and every hazard.

I rejoiced to see you looking so well, and earnestly hope that you may be preserved in the service of the country many years. With much respect & esteem Very truly Y[ou]rs, C.G. Memminger.

ALS in ScCleA; PC in Boucher and Brooks, eds., *Correspondence*, p. 486. NOTE: By chance, this letter and the one immediately below were written by the two future successive Secretaries of the Treasury of the Confederate States.

From G[EORGE] A. TRENHOLM

Charleston, Dec[embe]r 11, 1848

My dear Sir, I have long since made the following reflections upon the Act of 1834 altering the value of Gold, and will be glad to know if you have ever regarded it in the same point of view, and what your opinion is as to the correctness of the conclusions I have arrived at. To spare your time as much as possible I shall condense what I have to say & reduce it to distinct propositions.

1. That previous to the Act of 1834 nearly all the Gold produced by the U.S. was exported to Great Britain because it was more valuable there than here.

2. That to the extent to which we added to her stock of Gold we strengthened and expanded her currency; and that the steadiness and expansion of her currency, added materially to our wealth by raising in the same proportion the value of our chief staple (cotton) of which England fixed the price for the whole world.

3. That an expanded currency in G. Britain, tending to elevate the price of Cotton, and a contracted currency at home reducing the price of manufactured Goods, were conditions highly favorable to the South.

4. That the Gold Bill therefore of 1834 was in its effects highly injurious to the Cotton growing region—by the following operations

1. Whenever the balance was in favor of this Country and had to be brought home in coin, we drew Gold out of the vaults of the Bank of England—for every Guinea we drew she contracted the currency three Guineas and by this violent contraction produced a sudden & ruinous decline in Cotton.

2. Whenever the balance was against us we exported Silver

(while it lasted) which gave no relief to Great Britain where it is not a legal tender, and is not used as a circulating medium or as the basis of circulation.

3. That the Silver being all gone a struggle began between the two Countries for the Gold, which has resulted in making the same quantity of metal that would now perhaps ["no more than" *interlined*] suffice for the commerce of G. Britain alone, supply the wants of both Countries to the injury of both, and chiefly to the injury of the Cotton Planter.

Much more might be said in elucidation of this view of the subject, but it would consume your time unnecessarily; enough has been said to secure your attention to the subject, if the views advanced are sound, and too much if they are not. I will be very glad to receive a line from you in reply.

Mr. [Henry W.] Conner has gone down to New Orleans; he left a letter for you which will reach you through the mail; I would have delivered it in person had you passed through ["the" *canceled*] Charleston. I was very glad to find that it was your intention to give Gen[era]l [Zachary] Taylor's Administration a fair support while he continued to deserve it.

I learned today that it was the intention of Mr. Secretary [of the Treasury Robert J.] Walker to refer the selection of the site of our new Custom ["House" *interlined*] to the two Senators of the State. The Merchants are unanimously of opinion that it should be on East Bay and any other decision would occasion great disappointment. The Chamber of Commerce have addressed two Memorials to the Sec[retar]y in favor of East Bay. With great respect y[ou]r mo[st] ob[edient] S[ervan]t, G.A. Trenholm.

ALS in ScCleA; PEx in Boucher and Brooks, eds., *Correspondence*, pp. 486–487.

From B[ENJAMIN] G. WRIGHT

Belmont [County,] O[hio,] Dec. 11th/48

Dear Sir, As a number of the Democrats here think that you will most likely be tendered a place in Gen. [Zachary] Taylor[']s cabinet, I have thought it not unfriendly to say, that your acceptance woul[d] give general satisfaction & be hailed by the party in this region as a guarantee that the country would be safe under the new administration.

An implicit confidence in your patriotism & integrity seems to be every where felt whenever danger is to be apprehended from Whig rule. Such being the fact it is certainly strange how the party can pass by such a man for President whilst its members so highly appreciate his worth in times of danger & defeat.

For my part I can see no good reason for you to refuse if such a tender should be made by the President elect. An acceptance would enable you to render invaluable service to the country, & though it would be an humble[r] station than your old State Rights friends could wish you to occupy, yet they would feel proud to know that your great talents & long experience would give tone to an administration which without the aid of your wise counsel might endanger popular rights. Believe me as ever, Dear Sir, Your humble Servant, B.G. Wright.

ALS in ScCleA. NOTE: This letter was postmarked "Morristown, Ohio, Dec. 13."

DECEMBER 12, 1848–JANUARY 31, 1849

The first weeks of the second session of the 30th Congress were eventful. Southern members caucused several times and determined to issue an Address to their constituents on the status of the "free soil" question. A committee of five was appointed to draft the Address, with Calhoun as chairman. Eventually, on January 22, the caucus adopted Calhoun's draft, with slight modifications by John M. Berrien, Georgia Whig. Forty-eight members of the House and Senate signed. Whigs, whose President was to take office in a few weeks, were notably absent, as was one wing of the Democratic party, that led by Thomas H. Benton and Sam Houston. The Address reviewed the grievances of the outnumbered region of the Union and, most importantly, made a plea for firm unity among the Southern people as the first step towards defence.

Toward the end of this strenuous episode, on or about January 19, Calhoun had an attack of some sort, or a fainting spell. Abundant newspaper accounts disagreed on the exact day, whether there had been one or two incidents of the sort, whether it or they occurred in the chamber or the lobby of the Senate, and whether he was carried to his lodging or revived in the Vice-President's room and went home under his own steam. The reports had in common the impression that the attack was largely the product of over-work and a sincere concern for one who was now something of a venerable national institution. He tried to return the next day but had to leave before adjournment. He was back in the Senate in a few days, however, ignoring doctor's orders for long rest.

From Eustis Prescott

New Orleans, 12th Dec[embe]r 1848

My dear Sir, It strikes me very forcibly that in the division of parties under a new Administration our little band—which you have for so many years so gallantly lead—may hold an important position in the balance.

If it can be used to compromise the vexed question which the North seems determined to push upon us, and to keep in check the Ultras of other parties, it may save the country.

I have no confidence in the Whigs and feel confident that in possession of power they will push their old issues of the U.S. Bank, Protective Tariff, Internal improvements &ca. As there is no surplus, of course the division of spoils must be postponed. But in the spoils of Office, they may be shipwrecked. Unless Gen[era]l [Zachary] Taylor places himself entirely in their hands there will be a rupture with him in less than two years, and he will be thrown upon the Democratic party for support.

The Gen[era]l is honest, but obstinate to a fault. Here he is surrounded by a bevy of brawling politicians whose only aim is to obtain offices for themselves and friends.

I had hoped to have been in Washington this winter, but as my health is very nearly restored, I have concluded not to venture into a cold latitude, until I may have the strengthening influence of another season.

I took the liberty last winter of asking you as an old friend to enquire the progress of a claim before the Senate from *E.P. Calkin & Co. of Galveston Texas*, for damages on goods seized by the Texian Govt. *after* annexation.

My friend Gen[era]l [Thomas J.] Rusk [Senator from Texas] informed me as he passed thro here, that just at the close of the Session it was reported upon *favorably* by the Committee on claims and would come up with the unfinished business. May I again tax your memory with a thought of it and aid in pushing if necessary. Gen[era]l Rusk will inform you how it stands.

It is my only hope of getting something out of a debt due me for $5,000 as I had to pay for all the goods.

If you have time & any thing interesting occurs in the winter I should be much gratified to hear from you and remain My dear Sir Very truly & respectf[ull]y Y[ou]r friend, Eustis Prescott.

ALS in ScCleA. Note: An AEU by Calhoun reads, "Mr. Prescott[,] see Gen[era]l Rusk."

Remarks on the Petition from New Mexico

[In the Senate, December 13, 1848]

[*Thomas H. Benton presented a petition "of the people of New Mexico, assembled in convention." Among other things, the document asked Congress to organize a territorial government, prevent the "dismemberment" of territory in favor of Texas, and protect the petitioners from the introduction of domestic slavery. Benton moved that the petition be printed and be referred to the Committee on the Territories.*]

Mr. Calhoun. Mr. President, I rise to make no objection to the motion of the honorable Senator from Missouri; but I rise to express my opinion that the people of this Territory, (New Mexico,) under all the circumstances of the case, have not made a respectful petition to this Senate; but, on the contrary, that they have made a most insolent one. I am not surprised, however, at the language of this petition. That people were conquered by the very men they wish to exclude from that Territory, and they know that. I enter my protest, sir, at once against being governed by a consideration presented under such circumstances as that petition has been upon this subject.

[*Benton said that Calhoun had applied a "gratuitous and unfounded" epithet to the petition.*]

Mr. Calhoun. It is not at all strange that the Senator from Missouri (Mr. Benton) should consider the charge of insolence against the petition gratuitous, looking upon the matter as he does, nor that I should make the charge, looking upon it as I do. I look upon the rights of the southern States, proposed to be excluded from this territory, as a high constitutional principle. Our right to go there with our property is unquestionable, and guarantied and supported by the Constitution. The Territory belongs to us—to the United States. It belongs to the States of Carolina and Virginia as much as it does to New York and Massachusetts. The Senator from Missouri differs from me upon this point, and therefore he does not consider it insolent on the part of the people of that Territory to ask that we should be excluded from it. But these are my convictions, and I repeat that I consider the petition to be insolent.

[*Thomas J. Rusk questioned the document's assertions about the territorial claims of Texas. Benton declared that he had merely acted in a parliamentary manner in introducing the petition, and that in reference to slavery, it resembled a petition made by Virginia to George III before the American Revolution.*]

Mr. Calhoun. I made no charge against the manner of presenting the memorial. My objection was to the petition itself. The Senator sees in that petition no disrespect to one-half of the people of this Union; but I see the greatest disrespect. The Senator endeavors to assimilate it to the case of the petitioners of George III; but they are antagonistic; they bear no comparison. Sir, we of the southern States claim the right, under the Constitution, to go into that Territory with our property. These memorialists are a conquered people—conquered by the arms of the United States, and especially by troops drawn from the southern States; and for them now to turn round and propose to exclude us, it is the very height of insolence, if the Senator from Missouri does not see it.

Mr. Benton. I wish to know what the Senator means? I will give him time to reply.

Mr. Calhoun. My meaning is clear to every Senator. I do not interfere with the Senator from Missouri. I have stated the ground upon which I consider the petition disrespectful. It is disrespectful, coming from a conquered people, and because it infringes our constitutional rights. If the Senator does not see that there is foundation for my opinion, it is no fault of mine.

[*Benton declared that the Senate was debating over nothing and repeated that terming the petition insolent was "gratuitous and unfounded."*]

Mr. Calhoun. The Senator ought to understand that I rose to make a remark against the petition itself, not against its reference or printing, nor the manner of presenting it. I had a right to remark on every part of that petition. There is nothing unparliamentary or unusual in my course. But he seems to think that himself and the Senator from Delaware (Mr. [John M.] Clayton) [who had also received a copy of the petition] are responsible for every word and expression that it contains. That is not my view of it at all. I did not say the petition was unconstitutional; for petitions may be presented here, constitutional or unconstitutional; but I do say that the petition undertakes to exclude one-half the Union nearly from territory that belongs to the States collectively; the Constitution declares the territories to be the territories of the United States—the States in their federal capacity. And I say such a petition, coming from a people recently subdued by our arms, and under our control, is insolent; and whether the Senator from Missouri thinks so or not, it is to me a matter of perfect indifference.

[*James D. Westcott, Jr. of Fla. said the importance of the petition was being overrated. It did not really represent the people of New*

Mexico, a point which Benton disputed. Clayton hoped that Calhoun would reconsider the charge of insolence.]

Mr. Calhoun. Mr. President, I rise to say one word in reply to the Senator from Delaware (Mr. Clayton). It is impossible to change my opinion that this petition is disrespectful to the Senate. The Senator (Mr. Clayton) says that the rule of the Senate is, that when the petition is disrespectful to a Senator, it should not be received. Granted. Well, he says if it is disrespectful to our constituents, the same rule applies: it is disrespectful to the Senate and ought not to be received. Well, sir, I took the same view as the Senator from Delaware now takes when abolition petitions were first presented here. That was my ground. The Secretary (of the Senate) [Asbury Dickins] will very well remember that I called upon him to pull out three or four of those petitions and read them to the Senate. They were disrespectful to the South in the extreme, calling us thieves, and everything else that was distasteful. I then appealed to the gentlemen on the other side of the Chamber that those petitions were disrespectful to our constituents, and, therefore, disrespectful to the Senate. I appealed to the gentlemen, but my appeal was in vain. They voted me down and received those petitions.

Sir, I hold that this petition ought not to be received, for the very reason that it is disrespectful to the constituents of one-half the members of this body. But I do not wish to make the point here. I rise here to express my sentiments, and I shall ever rise when any imputation is cast upon the rights or honor of those whom I represent.

It is highly insolent when a people, recently subdued by our arms, to the accomplishment of which the southern portion of the country contributed more than their full share by a great deal, come here and pray the American Congress to exclude one-half the States of this Union, to which this very territory belongs as States. It does not belong to us as a Congress. It does not belong to the North as the North, nor to the South as the South. It belongs to the thirty States of this Union. And can there be a higher piece of insolence than to come here and present such a petition? Sir, had I taken the ground which the impulse of the moment dictated, I would have moved to lay this petition upon the table, as has been the fate of all petitions of this kind.

[*Benton dared Calhoun to make such a motion.*]

Mr. Calhoun, (in his seat.) I shall make no motion, sir.

[*Debate continued over the representativeness of the document until the presiding officer called the question, which was the motion to print.*]

Mr. Calhoun. I shall certainly oppose this motion. I entirely concur with the views taken by the Senator from Mississippi [Henry S. Foote] and the Senator from Florida [Westcott], that this whole affair is an imposition. We have no evidence going to show that the paper is anything but the petition of those persons whose names are attached to it. It is hardly probable that, in any convention, a part of the members would sign their memorial, whilst others would not. Under this belief, I do not think it should be taken as the petition of the people of New Mexico; and therefore I cannot give my vote to print the paper.

[*The Senate agreed to the motion to print by a vote of 33 to 14.*]

From *Congressional Globe*, 30th Cong., 2nd Sess., pp. 33–37. Partly printed in the New York, N.Y., *Herald*, December 16, 1848, p. 1; the Philadelphia, Pa., *Pennsylvania Freeman*, December 21, 1848, p. 2. Variant in the Washington, D.C., *Daily Union*, December 14, 1848, p. 2; partly printed in the Alexandria, Va., *Gazette and Virginia Advertiser*, December 16, 1848, p. 3. Another variant in the Baltimore, Md., *Sun*, December 14, 1848, p. 4; the Charleston, S.C., *Courier*, December 18, 1848, p. 2; the Petersburg, Va., *Republican*, December 18, 1848, p. 2. Another variant in the New York, N.Y., *Herald*, December 14, 1848, p. 2; the Boston, Mass., *Daily Advertiser*, December 15, 1848, p. 2. Note: The Alexandria *Gazette and Virginia Advertiser* commented on this occasion in regard to Calhoun and Benton: "Both Senators were very earnest and personal, particularly Mr. Benton." (December 14, 1848, p. 3).

From J[ohn] B. Jones

Philad[elphi]a, Dec[embe]r 14th 1848

Dear Sir, From the indications at Washington, as well as in the North, North-West and East, one may conceive apprehensions of a settled purpose on the part of the strongest combination of the States, to nullify the Constitution, and to usurp a tyrannical supremacy over the weakest party. On this side of Mason's & Dixon's line, the terms of the Compact are not understood, and all arguments which tend to uproot the prevailing prejudice, founded in ignorance, are doomed to ["be" *canceled and* "remain" *interlined*] unheard and disregarded. This is the work of party-leaders. They have succeeded in putting in motion a fearful ball, which I believe no human agency ["as at present constituted" *interlined*] can arrest. The barriers of the Constitution cannot stop it—and it must inevitably roll on in its course, increasing in weight and impetus as it proceeds, ["until" *canceled*] and crushing and desolating all before it.

And thus the generosity of the slave-holding States is repaid! At first the strongest party, how could they suppose that out of their generous grants and provisions (I allude to the N.W. territory) would grow an overshadowing evil, first to humiliate, and finally to destroy them? They aided the North in attaining a political equality—and now the North would doom them to a degrading inferiority! It cannot be. Intelligent and honorable men will not bear it. If our forefathers were justifiable in the sight of God, in opposing forcible resistance to their brethren and kindred in G[rea]t B[ritai]n who resolved to tax them without representation, and otherwise oppress them, the same justification exists for the South at this day, in the same manner, to use every means in its power to resist a similar, certainly an equal oppression.

For my very humble part, I would rather be one of the oppressed than one of the oppressors. But I would never submit to an injustice as long as there was a remedy. In the serious difficulty which I think ["I perceive" *canceled and* "is" *interlined*] about to be fully developed, my convictions and sympathies are all on the side of the weaker party; and I shall be prepared to contribute my means and services whenever and wherever it may be deemed they can be useful.

The pernicious sentiments which now prevail so generally in the non-slaveholding States, have been, I think, chiefly disseminated from the principal cities. These cities, and indeed all the flourishing manufacturing towns, as you are aware, owe all their prosperity and wealth, to the profits realized from customers and consumers in the slave holding States. This city, ["as well" *canceled and* "particularly" *interlined*] would be utterly ruined, if southern resentment should ever go so far as to produce a cessation of communication. Similar effects would be felt in the other cities. And yet the chief papers here and elsewhere, supported by the merchants, are constantly teeming with fulminations against the south. It seems to me that if the Representatives from the South would utter a few just denunciations against these cities, indicating that a time may come when those they represent, may cease to have intercourse with those who vilify them, that ["those" *canceled and* "the merchants" *interlined*] whose reason cannot be affected, might at least have their cupidity startled.

The people here seem to think that S.C. alone will never submit to their meditated movement. And they affect to believe that it might be as well for S.C. to be detached from the union. Such is their hallucination!

I supported Gen[era]l Taylor for the Presidency mainly because he was a Southern man, and I was persuaded he was constitutional and Southern in principle. If I ["should" *canceled and* "shall" *interlined*] be disappointed, I cannot be the friend of his Adm[inistratio]n. But if I should not be disappointed, then there will be great disappointment among his northern supporters. They are irrevocably committed to the Wilmot Proviso.

I pray heaven that your efforts, and the efforts of all good men, to avert the blow ["threatened" *canceled*] now aimed at the Constitution, may yet be successful, without the necessity of a reorganization of the political system. But I almost despair of such a consummation, without the miraculous interposition of Divine Providence. Believe me truly and sincerely Your faithful, ob[edien]t s[er]v[an]t, J.B. Jones, 124 S. Ninth Street.

ALS in ScCleA; variant PC in Boucher and Brooks, eds., *Correspondence*, pp. 487–489.

To A[NDREW] P[ICKENS] CALHOUN, [Marengo County, Ala.]

Washington, 15th Dec[embe]r 1848

My dear Andrew, I arrived here on the 11th Inst. I took Mr. [Thomas G.] Clemson's place [in Edgefield District] & Columbia in my way. I was delayed at the former two days, waiting the arrival of Mr. Clemson & the family, and remained two days with them after their arrival. They are all in fine health. Anna [Maria Calhoun Clemson] is much improved in appearance. She is full & plump without being fat. The children [John Calhoun Clemson and Floride Elizabeth Clemson] are well grown; very good looking, & smart. They are quite comfortably fixed in a new House & will remain at the place until some time in February, when Mr. Clemson & the family will come on here, on their return to Europe, should he be continued. He will, however, not leave until some time in April. I left your Mother [Floride Colhoun Calhoun], [Martha] Cornelia [Calhoun] & John [C. Calhoun, Jr.] with them. The two former will remain until they leave. John expected to set out in a few days after I left on his way to New Orleans. He will take MilledgeVille [Ga.] in his way, in order to look at a water cure establishment there, & may probably remain a few weeks there. He intended also to take your residence in his way. I trust he may succeed in his profession [medicine]. His inclination & aptitude lie that way. Speak encouragingly to him.

I remained two days in Columbia. My reception was warm & all I could desire. Willie [William Lowndes Calhoun] had just passed examination, & entered the Sophmore class. He passed, I am told, an excellent examination, & I hope will do well. James [Edward Calhoun] is studious & steady, & stands high in College. They both are disposed to be economical.

The papers this morning announced the arrival of the Canada Steamer. Cotton was still on the rise. It had risen an ⅛. Bread-s[t]uff[?] low & on the decline, specie plenty & interest low; all of which are favourable, but the Continent bore a disturbed appearance. If you have not sold, I think you should seize the favourable state of the Market & sell. You ought, under circumstances, get 6, or nearly 6 round, which would enable us to meet the pressure on us. I hope you will not fail to make remittance to meet our bank engagements in time. It is very important, that they should be punctually meet.

If you can possibly, I hope you will make your arrangement to be here to meet Mr. Clemson in February, say about the 20th, in order to close our accounts. I have brought all the papers necessary for the purpose with me. It will be at a season at which you can better leave home, than any other, & it will afford you an opportunity to see Anna & her children, who will be glad to see you, and ["also" *interlined*] to visit N. York [City], to make arrangement to put our debt on some permanent & better fotting [*sic*]. I think the times will be propitious for the purpose. The extraordinary deposites of gold found in Calafornia, the plenty of specie in England & the low rate of interest there; & the great rise in the price of stocks here & low rate of Exchange on England (8½ per cent, that is 2 below par) all indicate a state of expansion to be at hand. Indeed, if the Calafornia deposites continue to yield as they have even up to this time, it is difficult to say how high prices may rise, or expansion extend; that is, to say how much money may depreciate. In such a state of things, I have much confidence, that you may by visiting New York negotiate a loan to answer our purpose, for 6 per cent with some of the large factors or commission Merchants by connecting it with an arrangement to ship our cotton crop to them, ["which" *canceled*] which in the shape of commissions for selling would in reality add so much to the interest. It is at least worth the trial. A saving of one per cent would be important; and, as to sales, I am sure we cannot do worse in New York, than in Mobile. I hope you will take the same view & make your arrangements accordingly. Let me know your determination as early as practicable, ["so" *canceled and* "in order" *interlined*] that I can inform Mr. Clemson, if you should conclude to come, so that he may make his arrangement to meet yours, as to the time.

Congress, as yet, has done little. The indication is, that the slave question will be brought to issue early in the session. The South has been forced back to the Wall, and the only alternative is, shall we resist, or submit. Our people are slumbering over a volcano.

I hope Dr. [Josiah C.] Nott has relieved Andrew [Pickens Calhoun, Jr.]. I have been, and am, uneasy about him, & shall be so, until I hear from you. My love to Margaret [Green Calhoun] & the children. Your affectionate father, J.C. Calhoun.

ALS in NcD, John C. Calhoun Papers.

From W[ILLIA]M SMITH, [Governor of Va.]

Richmond, Dec. 17, 1848

My dear Sir, Yours of the 15th was duly received.

Mr. [John S.?] Barbour's letter was addressed to you to Petersburg to the care of the President of the Railroad, supposing it would thereby, certainly reach you at that place. I should have been happy to have had [you] as my guest.

I do not understand Douglass' [*sic*; Stephen A. Douglas's] bill. Does it not surrender every thing for which we contend? I confess my mind is full of apprehension. Had I my way, I would surrender nothing; we have no constitutional right to do it. I would directly put to our Vampires, the issue of Disunion or our Rights.

But, I shall ["soon" *interlined*] be off the stage, my connection with the parties of the country except as a voter, sundered forever. I have never felt to the South a craven or a treacherous thought, would that I could think so, of thousands among us. Wishing you health and happiness, I remain Yours truly, Wm. Smith.

ALS in ScCleA. NOTE: An AEU by Calhoun reads, "Gov. Smith, Va."

From A[BBOTT] H. BRISBANE

Charleston, 18th De[cembe]r 1848

My dear Mr. Calhoun, I should be cautious how I write to you when I call to mind your silence on the subject of my little work & my long letter in fartherance of your most favorable opinion. It would be safer perhaps if I placed this letter to the score of duty, for the subject that I would draw your attention to is of the same nature—Viz, the creation of this new "Interior Department," for the first time mentioned here in our papers this evening.

It is said by the Washington Correspondent [of the Charleston, S.C., *Courier*?] to be favorably received there, and will probably be organized this session. May I say to you in the most expressive language 'God forbid.' I ask, may I say to *you*, for we hail you still the great champion of the seperation of Government from Wealth in any of the many shapes & forms it may be presented in. What has the *municipal power* of government to do with Agriculture, the main element in the productive economy of the country? Why did it not at once incorporate manufacture, so as to complete the productive department of Wealth?

I see Mr. Calhoun in this new office a most dangerous function introduced into the administration of federal affairs. Give to the *Political* government of the country an appointment which takes cognizance of *production*, and what must follow—Transportation & Exchange—the other two divisions of Wealth. And with these what may we not expect? internal improvement of course as an element in Transportation; and a Bank as an element in exchange.

Since I wrote you Sir on the subject of a seperation of Wealth from Government as as [*sic*; an] essential Southern move, and indispensible to the continuance of the Confederacy, we have been active in the promulgation of our views, and the elaboration of our principles, corresponding through responsible committees with Messrs. [Langdon] Cheves, [James H.] Hammond and others, touching the propriety of taking our industrial interests entirely from Congress and organizing them ourselves. Mr. Tho[ma]s Bennett, our venerable Ex governor, is chairman of our Charleston correspondence, and when I add such men as Messrs. [Jonathan] Lucas, Poyas, [William Izard?] Bull[?] &c members, you may well believe us in earnest.

You will ask what we mean by organizing our industrial interests ourselves. We answer, our platform is, "every nation is entitled to *all the values* of its peculiar soil & climate as exhibited in its raw material *worked up* for exchange." To effect this important movement in the economy of national Wealth—in other words to make *Wealth distributive*, as the principles of our Government are distributive, we will introduce machinery into the daily operations of Southern industry—we will make the spinning jinny [*sic*] & the loom as indispensible to the cotton growing region as are the hoe & plough. The soil shall not produce its rich fruits, and these be trafficked from us in their crude states, to be increased in value hundreds of folds by an industry trivial in character and consuming no time, while we are looking on, scarcly conscious of the theft.

But you will again ask, why cannot this change be effected in silence and among ourselves? We answer, "because it is too late." The fury[?] of the federal government is upon us—in four years, as Mr. [Martin] Van Buren says, we shall not have power to erect spinning jinnies, nor build rail-roads, ["not" *altered to* "nor"] carry on trade. "These States are divided into *Producing, Manufacturing* & *Commercial* States, and you belong exclusively to the producing department—you are doomed to till the soil for twelve *long months* for the raw material which we are in twelve *short hours* to work up and distribute to the world at our own prices—paying you the minimum of course. No, the Southern & Western States are the producers, we, the States of New England are the manufacturers, and New York city the great commercial mart." Is not this the language of Van Buren, [Daniel] Webster, and their joint conver[sa]tion? Was it not the language, Mr. Calhoun, of our Old England masters, when we were collonists [*sic*], as we are again becoming, unless we organize our Wealth before the eyes of the world—aye—organize it as *independent States*, over this province of action at least? It is too late sir, to act upon this great question in a corner—it is too late to act upon it, if we allow the federal government to forestall us in the action—"to prohibit our manufacture—prohibit our shipping—striking an arrow into the very sapling of our forest, that it might be doomed to profitless old age, rather than be hewn down and brought into market." Allow not, Dear Sir, this office of "Interior Secretary"—*and write us*, that *you will aid* in organizing the Wealth of the South as soon as it can be done with prudence, & in view of the interests of the world. Yours with sincerest regard, A.H. Brisbane.

P.S. Gen[era]l Hammond has just answered us by last mail, entering heartily with us in our measures, *within alluded to*. Mr. Cheves *declines* from age and infirmity. He says that, "he is 73, and we want younger men for so great an effort." We will write to Gen[era]l [Jefferson] *Davis*, next [to writing to?] you, in a few days. I mean, [the Senator] from *Mississippi.*

My dear Sir, A young friend—a recent graduate of our State military school (the head of his class) has just requested me to procure for him an appointment in the surveying parties that will probably be sent out by government for California. Gen[era]l Hammond will also write for him from this State & Ex Gov[erno]r [William] Schl[e]y from Georgia. If it will not inconvenience you too much do move in his favor. His name is [H.] Oliver of Edgefield district. Y[our]s &c, A.H.B.

ALS in ScCleA. Note: A register of graduates of the Citadel, Military College of S.C., lists "H. Oliver" as a member of the Class of 1848. He was a civil engineer and died in 1853.

Resolution of a Southern Senators' Caucus

[Washington, December *ca.* 20?, 1848]

Resolved That a committee of five be appointed to ascertain who amongst the Southern members are willing to unite in an address to the Southern people advising ["resistance" *canceled and* "firm, prompt, & manly opposition" *interlined*] to the Wilmot proviso in the event of its being applied by law to the territory acquired from Mexico South of 36° 30′ and that the said committee be empowered to ["convene" *canceled and* "call" *interlined*] a meeting of the Southern members when in their opinion it is proper to do so. The Committee will consist of Messrs. [Robert M.T.] Hunter [of Va.], [Henry] Johnson of Louisiana, [Thomas J.] Rusk [of Tex.], [John M.] Berrien [of Ga.] & [Henry S.] Foote [of Miss.]. [Signed:] Jeff[erso]n Davis, J.C. Calhoun, S[olomon] W. Downs, R.M.T. Hunter, A[ndrew] P. Butler, D[avid] L. Yulee, H[erschel] V. Johnson, D[avid] R. Atchison, Tho[mas] J. Rusk, William R. King, H.S. Foote, Ben Fitzpatrick, J[ames] D. Westcott Jr., W[illiam] K. Sebastian.

Draft (in Hunter's hand) in Vi, Robert Mercer Taliaferro Hunter Papers; PC in Charles H. Ambler, ed., *Correspondence of Robert M.T. Hunter*, p. 104. Note: The ms. is undated. An approximate conjectural date has been chosen.

From Peter Von Schmidt

New-York [City,] Decemb[e]r 21st 1848

Honored Sir! Knowing Your great interest you take in promoting the common benefits of our Co[u]ntry, I take the liberty to submitt to you the accompan[y]ing memorial, with the respectfull request, to be pleased and to present the same at an early day, to the Senate—said memorial containing suggestion, calculated to benefit Government and the mining population of California.

I do not hesitate to believe, You will consent to my request, and at the same time, giving your sup[p]ort and recommandation to the said memorial; *provided*, You should find nothing Containing in it, contrary to common interrest of our Country.

I already have originated 3 mining Companies destined for California, and one more in progress, we think to leave New York as soon the necessary machin[e]ries, and other arrangements ar[e] made, which may be, in 3 or 4 weeks time; but, before I leave N.Y. I have to visit Washington on privat[e] business, where I will have the pleasure to pay my respect and a trist farewell, to Your honor, in person.

To give an Ideea of our arrangement of assosiation for mining purposes, I enclose hereby the artickles of Assosiation—also a hand-bill for the organization of the two last Companies—now in progress. With high respect and consideration I have the honor to be Your Ob[e]d[ie]n[t] Servant, Peter von Schmidt, Civil and mining Engineer, No. 11 Barclay Str. N.Y.

[Enclosure]

New-York [City,] December 21st 1848

To the Honorable the Senate and House of Representatives of the United States, in Congress assambled

The Memorial of Peter von Schmidt civil and Mining Engineer, respectfully represents:

That Your Memorialist has originated and formed two Mining Companies destined for the Gold region of California; and that he is about to organize two more, numbering in all about eighty members.

The object of Your Memorialist is, the introduction of Mining operations in a Systematic form, through Machinery and other arrangements necessary to success. He is also impressed with the importance of Government protection, and of the manner, in which the revenue may be secured to the Country.

The difficulty to protect the Miners by a regular Military force, is, under the circumstances, to him apparant, unless attended by extraordinary expence. From the number of imegrants already on the spot, with the incalculable progres[s]ive increase, will necesserily bring on tro[u]ble or Collision, of one kind or other, between the troops and the Mining population, and to avoid these difficulty's; Your Memorialist begs respectfully to submit some outlines or Suggestions, which appear to him, will satisfy all concerned, insure a vast revenue to Government, and enco[u]rage and protect the Mining population, without incurring expense.

1st. It is his belief, that Government should appoint an Engineer whose duty shall be, immediat[e]ly to fix the Meridian near San Francisco, and from such point proceed East, and locate every Mile, by permanent Mark.

2d. Competent Surveyors should then be appointed, whose duty it shall be, to divide from said fixed line the entire region into Miles or Sections—Each Surveyor to have two Square Miles under his direction, and again, Sub-divide such division into Acr[e]'s, or 1280 parts. Then, after establishing the corner Marks of each Acre, to act as Collector, and lease for a certain time, each Acre, to Citizen of the United States, (at all times giving preference to Squatter) who may apply.

3d. Each lessee, after paying to the Surveyor or Collector *ten* ounces of Gold, shall recieve his licence, and be permitted to proceed in his Mining operation, as he may think best.

4d. The Surveyor or Collector, for every *ten* ounces of Gold recieved, to pay into treasury, *two* ounces. The balance to be a full compensation for his Services, during of his appointement.

5d. Each lessee to pay to the United States, *one tenth* of the proceeds of his Mining operation, to be collected weekly or monthly, by the Surveyor or Collector.

6d. No person shall be permitted to lease, or work more than *two* Acres at a time.

7d. Should it be discovered, that any lessee had conceeled any part of the proceeds of his Mining operations; with a view, to defroud the Government, he shal[l] forfeit his lease and possession, and forever, be deprived of the right to Mine in the region.

8d. All leases should be given under the Condition, that the lessee should embody himself in a Voluntar or Military Regiment, under the organization and Command, of the Governor, with the understanding, to protect all the right of the United States—to suppress all disorders—Arrest deserters—and prevent any person from diggin[g], mining, or otherwise interfering with the public property without licence.

9d. Each district of *two* Square Miles, to Cho[o]se their own justice of the peace, Constable &c; who shall be authorised to settle all difficulties arising in the Mining district.

10d. Each lessee should be permitted to build on his leased Acre of land, such Shanties, Houses, Stores, &c. as may be necessary to his business. But, at the expiration of his lease, or at the reletting, if he did not avail himself of the preference, which in all cases shall be given, he may sell, or dispose of, his improvements, as he shall think proper.

Your Memorialist is of opinion that such arrangement would be practicable without injuring to Government—that all would be permitted to work the Mines for a time, perhaps sufficient, to make themselves comfortable, and by a sistemamatic Rotation, no one would be disappointed, and Speculation on a large scale, would positively be precluded.

He is also of the Opinion, that a large Military force would not be introduced with advantage to the district. To bring force, in aid of the Collectors, has never been successfull in anny Country, and in *this*, where the *will* of the Government, is the interest of the people, no Collision should be enc[o]uraged or excited.

Your Memorialis[t] is further of the opinion that his Suggestions, or rules of a similar import, should be introduced before the emigration are largely increased, particularly from foreign Countries—The division of Land, the leases, armed Companies, Regiments & Brigad[e]s, would more readily meet the views of the parties on the spot, than when augmented by foreigners, and all would be interrested in protecting the Government. The region would present a Mining Military Colony, where the rights of the individuals and the Government would be equal[l]y secured.

With such arrangement and such a revenue Your Memorialist believe, the construction of a Rail Road accross the Isthmous, or the gigantic project from New-York to San Francisco may be readily accomplished from the proceeds of the Mines. If each Square Mile is divided into 640 parts, and each part paying into the treasury two ounces of Gold, or $32, the amount for *one* square mile would be $20,480. Then take only the present Estimated number of emigrants at 6,000, and each occupant should become a lessee, the amount would be $192,000. But should the proceeds of these 6,000 diggers amount to $10 per day each, or $60,000 in the aggragate, and multiply this by 300 days in the Year, the amount would be $18,000,000, of which *ten* per cent would be paid to the Government, the proceeds for the first Year would be from the entrance mon[e]y and per centage $1,992,000. But, should the business be carried on Systematical[l]y—in the manner intended by Your Memorialist, then, the revenue to Government may be Estimated with great probability, at do[u]ble, or triple, the amount.

Your Memorialist therefore, respectfully aske Congress, to adopt the earliest Measures for the protection of the operating Miners. Your Memorialist will ever pray as Your most Obed[ient] Servant, Peter von Schmidt, Civil and Mining Engineer.

ALS with En in DNA, RG 46 (U.S. Senate), 30A-H20. Note: On 12/26 Calhoun presented this petition to the Senate; it was referred to the Committee on Territories. The enclosed articles and handbill have not been found.

From James Chapman

Charleston, 22 December 1848

Dear Sir, Last summer I had the pleasure of travelling on our Rail Road in Company with yourself & Judge [Andrew P.] Butler, and we talked of the steamer Isabel which was then preparing to run as a mail Boat from here to Havana—for which service she gets the enormous sum of *Fifty Thousand Dollars*, which I contend is just so much money of the people thrown away. The Boat of course will get a good deal for letters, But that is no ground to prove that the Government makes money by it. My own idea is that her whole mail will not exceed 10 to $12,000 per annum. Now she ["pay"(?) *canceled*] gets 50,000$ from the U.S. and returns probably 10 to 12,000$ while the entire 50,000 is a loss to the U.S. Vessels sail to the West Indies and particularly Havana and Matanzas every day in the week and the same from Cuba. I own *4* and others here own a dozen more which now constantly ["run" *interlined*] to Havana—besides transient vessels from here & there, Thus affording constant opportunities of sending letters to Cuba—or from Cuba to the U.S. Besides there are a number of fine packets from New York[,] Philadelphia & Baltimore—so that these vessels trading from all parts of the U.S. took and brought letters by the 100 and 500—for which *the Government get the Postage*, same as the steamer now gets while the vessels get nothing—as many letters of course come by sailing vessels—only not in such large numbers as the steamer. But the Government get as much *money* and did not call them mail Boats. But what I wish to bring to your view is this—which I write to *you* Because the Post Master Gen[era]l [Cave Johnson] get[s] himself entangled with the contract and he will never inform the members of Congress of the Real State of things. I am ["decidly" *canceled and* "decidedly" *interlined*] opposed to manopoly and discrimination. Our Government certainly ought not to grant a manopoly to one vessel merely because she has steam over sailing vessels both trading in the same articles. Now Sir—here are facts which I state plainly. The Isabel takes the mail to a *foreign Country* for the enormous sum of $50,000—and not content with so much of the People[']s money, carries 2 to 300 Tierces Rice and has man[a]ged to be admitted into Havana, on most unequal terms over sailing vessels with the same cargo. For instance if one of my sailing vessels takes *one Tierce* of Rice she has to pay her *full* Ton[n]age and port charges—say the full *capacity* of the vessel—being 114 Tons—she pays $350 in Havana. This sum *has* to be paid, whether the vessel has one Tierce or 300—while by *some* means or *other* the agents of the *Isabel* merely because she has the *pretext* of having a mail, carries any quantity of goods and *pays only* on the quantity of goods she has *in* So if she carries 300 Tierces Rice twice a month *she* nearly consumes the trade and why; because she pays only 280–300$ while she ought on the principle of all nations is [*sic*] that when vessels, steam or sail, have *cargo in*, then they are liable to the Port charges. Where is the Justice in giving a vessel because she has *steam* any priviledge over the *same flag* under *canvass*. She is 1100 Tons and even allow her liberally for coal & Engine, 500 Tons—she would be liable to pay on 600 Tons—which would be on the same footing we sail. Our vessels pay by the measurement from stem to stern, cabin[,] Forescuttle & depth of hold, every part is included in her Ton[n]age.

Therefore how can we compete with such a manopoly as is enjoyed by the steamer over sailing vessels[?] The steamer can supply the Havana market entirely with Rice and thus drive sailing vessels out of the trade entirely, but only because she is allowed to sail on such unequal terms.

Now I can hardly think that our government can let the matter rest so, and I write that you may do us the favor of representing the matter & have the Cuba authorities to put sailing vessels of the U. States on the same footing as steam vessels carrying cargo. I own 4 vessels which I have employed constantly in the Cuba trade and being of a kind adapted to that trade can be of no use to me in any other and several of our merchants are like myself, must sacrafice our vessels & lose 15000 to 20,000$ because a steamer is fed on Government Pap by the Post Master General, to the injury of *individuals* in favor of a *corporation* of rich men, who seek protection in their enterprise of [$]50,000, from Government and then to seek such unfair terms in Cuba. I am sure your principles of free Trade will at once point out the *injustice*. Discrimination & Protection, are terms I abhor. The Isabel too is owned by some 10 to 12 persons here—*not one* of whom are engaged in the Cuba or West India trade except Mr. [Moses C.] Mordecai the agent & he I presume owns a part merely to get her business.

I beg if consistent with your views that you may make an early move in the matter. I am Dear Sir Your Ob[edien]t Serv[an]t, James Chapman.

[P.S.] The Isabel pays on the quantity of goods she has on board, be it only 20 Tierces Rice or 300 Tierces and *only half* the usual Port charges—while if I have one Tierce Rice, I pay on the *whole* Ton[n]age of the vessel and the *full* Port charges. Is this equality and Justice[?] J.C.

[P.S.] I would further state that the mail by the steamer is a Tax on the people of the U.S., Because before we can *mail* a letter from here, we have to pay the Postage 12½¢ for each single letter, while before she ran All letters went free of Postage—so we have to pay on our letters from here—and then *also* on all letters which come by her from Cuba, as the parties writing from there are ["not" *interlined*] required to *pre*pay the Postage. Thus the Postage both ways falls on the People of the U.S. *Is this fair*[?] The Boat is also owned by parties no doubt in Havana. One House there, the agents of the Boat I know ["I" *canceled*] took great interest in getting her up and I feel sure, own a large share in her—and an English merchant residing here (*who is not a Citizen*) owns a share. All this is contrary to ["the Laws of" *canceled*] the Navigation Laws of the U.S. This boat being a manopoly injures our own merchants and does more to depress the price of Rice than anything that could have been done. The certainty with which she carries supplies always prevents the dealers in Havana from buying other cargoes even if they get in 1 or 3 days before the steamer. Rice is always sold *afloat* in Havana—& they know that the steamer is to be there every 10 days with Rice and that *she* can[']t keep her cargo on board to try & get a fair price—being obliged to sail in three days her cargo must be landed & sold at once, Thus injuring the interest of the whole trade. Surely the U.S. ought not encourage a vessel by having a mail & paying such a sum as to enable the Boat to run free of expense to the owners. They can carry Rice on so much better terms than we can who receive no pay from the U.S. I am sure it will lessen the revenue for except we can take out Rice we can[']t go to bring Sugar[,] Molasses

&c. Rice is our main article from here. Mr. I[saac] E. Holmes of our own City did all he could to obtain a steam Boat to carry a mail. But he could not have thought of the *interest* of *others* he was *sacraficing* in getting it—& Besides what advantage is she to this city[?] All her Coal is brought from the *north*. Her Captain belongs to the north, and her officers too—and then she is manned by some 15 to 20 negroes also from Baltimore. She can sail, so manned much cheaper than we can as we have to employ white seamen. Because our vessels go to the wharf at Havana, while she lays in the stream at anchor & can keep them (Black crew) on board which we can[']t do going to the wharf.

If she drives us all out of the trade which she must do very soon, It will take annually from our city at least $100,000, which the West India vessels now lay out in wages, stores & &. When we look at things as they ought to ["be" *interlined*] viewed, she is an evil to the place & no benefit. She hurts this place & Savannah in the Rice trade by throwing ["giving" *interlined; sic*] the whole export of Rice in the hands of her agent here. She hurts no interest at the north because their exports do not conflict with ours.

If she carries the mail, and passengers let her do so. But if she carries cargo then we think our Government ought to require the Cuba authorities to put the same flag on the same footing, when they have cargo. This seems but Justice.

I say put an end to manopoly & protection. Again, J.C.

ALS in ScCleA. NOTE: Chapman was an experienced Charleston commission merchant.

REMARKS AT A MEETING OF SOUTHERN MEMBERS OF CONGRESS

[Senate Chamber, December 22, 1848]

[*Eighteen Senators and 51 Representatives convened pursuant to the call of the five-member committee appointed a few days before. Thomas H. Bayly, Representative from Va., offered resolutions strongly denying the power of Congress "to impair or destroy the right of property in slaves either in the States, the District of Columbia, the Territories, or any other place whatever." He called for the members to address their constituents on the matter. Alexander H. Stephens, Representative from Ga., moved that a committee of one member from each of the fifteen slave States be appointed to consider the whole question, including Bayly's resolutions.*]

[Calhoun said:] The resolutions of the gentleman from Virginia (Mr. Bayly) are good, and, considering the length of time which he has had to prepare them, do him great credit, but they are not perfect. They are defective in several particulars—I am, therefore, less unwilling to agree to the motion of the gentleman from Georgia (Mr. Stephens). Another consideration strongly impels to the same course. I am thoroughly impressed with the necessity of harmonious and united action, both on our part and on the part of the southern community.

I am opposed, however, to too great delay, and consequently would prefer that the committee should report to a meeting to be held on the 10th instead of the 15th of January. The Legislatures of several of the Southern States are now in session, and it would be well that our address should reach them in time to be acted on by them before their adjournment.

I consider the address indispensable. Whatever action is taken must proceed from the slaveholding States. If the Constitution be violated, and their rights encroached upon, it is for them to determine the mode and measure of redress. We can only suggest and advise. We are on the theatre of action—the witnesses of the alarming encroachments which have been going on upon the rights of the slaveholding part of the confederacy—we see them plainly, we feel them deeply; they are rapid and alarming; for who believes that propositions which have, within a few days past, commanded the support of a majority of the Lower House of Congress, would even three years ago have been tolerated by any respectable portion of either House.

We are in the midst of events scarcely of less import than those of our revolutionary era. The question is, are we to hold our position in this confederacy upon the ground of equals, or are we to content ourselves with the condition of colonial dependence.

Sir, it will be worse than colonial dependence; for who would not prefer to be taxed and governed, without pretence of representation, than, under the forms of representation, to be grievously oppressed by measures over which we have no control, and against which our remonstrances are unavailing. It is undeniable that the encroachments upon our rights have been rapid and alarming. They must be met.

I conceive that no Southern man can entertain, for one moment, the idea of tame submission. The action of the South should be united, temperate, but decided—our positions must be taken deliberately, but held at every hazard. We wage no war of aggression. We ask only for the constitution and union and government of our fathers. We ask of our Northern brethren to leave us those rights and privileges which our fathers held, and, without securing which for their children, all know they would not have entered into this Union. These we must maintain.

It appears to me proper that we, who are here on the theatre of action, should address our constituents of the slave-holding States, briefly and accurately portray the progress of usurpation and aggression, vividly exhibit the dangers which threaten, and leave it in their hands to mark out the proper line of action. What that should be it is needless here to discuss. Whatever it is, should be temperate, mild and decided.

Having expressed these views, I have to say that I make no objection to the motion of the gentleman from Georgia (Mr. Stephens) to refer the whole matter to a select committee, to consider maturely and report to a future meeting, but I would rather prefer an earlier day for that meeting than the 15th of January. I am, above all, for union, harmony, and decision on the part of the South.

From the Baltimore, Md., *Sun*, December 27, 1848, p. 4. Also printed in the Alexandria, Va., *Gazette and Virginia Advertiser*, December 28, 1848, p. 2; the Boston, Mass., *Daily Advertiser*, December 29, 1848, p. 2; the Richmond, Va., *Whig and Public Advertiser*, December 29, 1848, p. 4; the Charleston, S.C., *Courier*, December 30, 1848, p. 2; the Charleston, S.C., *Mercury*, December 30, 1848, p. 2; the Camden, S.C., *Journal*, January 3, 1849, p. 2; the Edgefield, S.C., *Advertiser*, January 3, 1849, p. 2; the Greenville, S.C., *Mountaineer*, January 5, 1849, p. 2. NOTE: The meeting appointed a committee of fifteen, including Calhoun, to draw up an address to their constituents. The committee of fifteen met on 12/23 and appointed a subcommittee of five to prepare an address to the Southern people. The subcommittee consisted of Calhoun, John M. Clayton of Del., and William R. King of Ala., Senators, and Bayly and Charles S. Morehead of Ky. from the House of Representatives. Bayly's resolutions are printed in *Niles' National Register*, vol. LXXV, no. 7 (February 14, 1849), pp. 100–101. It had been agreed that no reporters could attend the caucus of 12/22, but apparently the correspondent of the Baltimore *Sun* was able to obtain an account of the meeting including Calhoun's remarks above. All other newspaper reports originated with the *Sun*, which on December 25, p. 4, reported that Calhoun's remarks on this occasion were "one of his ablest and most eloquent speeches, moderate for him in its tone . . . ."

From Anna [Maria Calhoun] Clemson

Christmas Day, Canebrake, [Edgefield District, S.C.] 1848

All the best wishes of the season to you, my dearest father. I will not begin by excuses for my delay in writing, because I am sure you never attribute my silence to want of inclination to write. The fact is housekeeping at the Canebrake, is no sinecure, not from the actual *key carrying*, that *mother* [Floride Colhoun Calhoun] does for me, but from the necessity of thinking, planning, & arranging, to get along without things to keep house with. This keeps my mind constantly occupied, to try & prevent any one wanting anything, & this together with some one always co[ming &] going, & [the] regularity with which all [*ms. torn; several words missing*] has made me delay from day to day.

William [Lowndes Calhoun] goes to Edgefield tomorrow[;] however I am determined he shall not go without a letter from me. We all get on very happily. Mrs. [Elizabeth Clemson] Barton has joined us. Her cough is entirely finished, & I think with moderate care she is perfectly safe. She tells me that she lost the cough, & soreness in her chest immediately on coming south. I hope to send her home entirely renovated. She is a charming woman & full of talent, & I am sure you would like her. She was in Sumterville, when you passed through Columbia, & says had she known you were there, would have gone to see you, she is so anxious to make your acquaintance.

We expect the boys every moment. Tom did not go for them so soon as he should have done because Mr. [Thomas G.] C[lemson] had to go to Sumterville for his sister & took the carriage as far as Aiken to bring them back.

Mr. Clemson has gone by invitation to eat his Christmas dinner with Col. [Francis W.] Pickens. He (the Col.) was here while Mr. C[lemson] was away so he has not seen him yet & as he starts for Alabama in a few days it is necessary they should meet on account of business. [By] the way I think it my duty to give you an a[ccoun]t of a conversation I had wi[th] him w[*ms. torn; one or two words missing*] indeed of his whole man[ner.] When he [saw?] mother & myself he *burst into tears*[,] kissed me several times & told me no brother could [be] happier to welcome me home than he was. The next morning he took the opportunity when we were alone to commence by saying "Oh Anna dreadful changes have taken place since you were in Europe. Artful persons have disunited your father & myself["] & then went on to give me an account of all the occurrence.

He was deeply agitated & affected & again shed tears & if not sincere in what he says is the greatest actor & hypocrite that ever existed. Do not misunderstand me. I do not doubt that he was led away by ambition, desire to prove his independence of you, bad counsels, & the excitement of the moment to say even perhaps what is stated but *I do believe that he does not know it himself.* This may appear a paradox to you but our powers of self deception are wonderful & I have seen instances of it infinitely beyond this. His account of the matter is this. He denies ever making the statement or using the words attributed to him. Says they were given in a letter not signed but written by [Louis T.] Wigfall to injure him because he had refused going his security. That Wigfall was a disgraced man whose word went for nothing in Edgefield. Th[at he?] had been [advi]sed[?] to leave there & was at[*ms. torn; one or two words missing*] Texas [bu]t before going had apologised [to him?] before several witnesses & retracted all he [had] said before going. I told him that I was authorised to say nothing. That you had never mentioned the subject to me but I would tell him frankly that I had spoken to you of it. I then mentioned briefly the statement you had made me & said that as I understood the difficulty of restoring your relations had arisen from his never having made a public denial of a public offence. To that he replied that he had never denied it in the papers because he never denied anonymous statements as you never did yourself but that had the letter been signed or had he seen a[n] editorial he would have denied it over his name & that he had written a letter, (to whom I do not recollect, but I think either Mr. [Richard F.] Simpson, or Judge [Andrew P.] Butler,) containing his refutation, which letter he had authorised him ["(the person)" *interlined*] to make what use he chose of & that he had denied it *before witnesses* to yourself personally, & that when he went to your house he thought the whole affair settled. He then spoke of the pain his reception gave him. I said I was sure *you* had not failed in politeness. No he said but you were cold to repulsiveness. I told him I thought he was mistaken but he said he could not be as Judge Butler had w[ritten?] him at your request after you went to [Washing]ton that the coldness in your reception [was i]n *deference* to your son. I [told?] him I w[as s]ure the word was ill chosen on the Judge's part. He said what had most pained him was the manner in which Mr. [Armistead] Burt in Abbeville & Andrew [Pickens Calhoun] in Alabama had spoken of his treatment at your house on their return home. He repeated to me several times "*so help me God*! I had no allusion to your father." & said that when he went to Fort Hill he had papers to show you which would have proved his innocence but that after his reception his pride would not permit him to show them. This is a short statement of a long conversation which proves at least his repentance. I have only room to say that all are well & send much love. [John] Calhoun [Clemson] has recovered entirely & rides alone on horseback. Your devoted daughter, Anna Clemson.

ALS in ScCleA.

From JOHN HASTINGS, [former Representative from Ohio]

New Garden, Col[umbiana] C[ount]y, Ohio
Dec. 28, 1848

Well, my dear Sir, I see that the slave labor game has commenced in Senate and House. In forming the Unional Compact, it was an error of great magnitude, permitting any thing less, in the slave labor States, than the whole population being a basis of representation; an error, out of which has arisen all the Ununional interferences up to the present hour. It was a compromise for the sake of forming a Union: well, it was so, but it was unfortunate as it has turned out; and if interunional justice in the body politic had, at that day, been rightly understood, Unional right would not have been thus compromised. However, it cannot now be helped; and, like all deviations from equality in right, involves a constant litigation in wrong—offence and defence.

I do not know what was exactly the understanding at the time of forming the Constitution; but I understand that the sovereignty of the States is represented in the Senate, and that labor, which involves population, and has to support the body politic—the government, is represented in the House, therefore the representation should have been based on population in its entire integrity, without any reference to the ["nature" *canceled*] nature of the labor. The compromise outraged a sound principle, where a union of sovereign States for better protection and defense, was the object. But it is one of the many pernicious results of sliding from the solid basis of equality of rights among the States, (this equality the perpetuative of the Union) into abstractive theoretical discussions—discussions, which it was a pity that the great men of that day entertained; and we experience the consequences.

It is somewhat of a solecism in political economy, to see that $3/5$ of the exports are from the slave labor States, and that $3/5$ only of their lab[o]rers are represented in the Unional government; while the whole of the population, irrespective of color, is represented in the non slave labor States! And this too, in presence of the fact—that the exports induce the imports, and that the taxation which supports the Unional government is procured through the action of the imports!

Much, very much, could be said upon this subject, that would disabuse the minds of well meaning people of the false impressions imbibed from the immolative[?] schemery of venal office aspirants, but it is difficult to get truthful, honest matter to the people. Yet, in such way, chiefly, can the harmony of the Union be improved, and Unional justice more nearly arrived at. Last winter I sent two essays of this character, to be followed by others, to the Washington Union, but they did not publish them. I intended, as I told the editors, that the matter was for New York more immediately; and as the sentiments and reasonings were dispassionate and impartial, I hoped, from them some good. The first I sent through Mr. C[ave] Johnson, and the other through Mr. [Robert Barnwell] Rhett. I never heard from Mr. [Francis W.] Pickens any thing about them: I felt at the time, that they were much better calculated to be listened to with more favor in New York, than some other matter published in the [Washington] Union.

I have little, indeed I may say, no hope (judging from the past, as well as present indications) of Unional right from Congress. It has become a despot in its conduct; for through the unjust decisions of its majorities, it sets at defiance the rights of the States, and the inviolability of the Constitution: it seems to be governed by any thing but dispassionate thought: to much of its important action may be attributed ignorance, stupidity, prejudice, hypocrisy, venality—a total absence of patriotism, honor, and public virtue. This is a deplorable and true exhibit. It may be asked, why this ["is" *interlined*] so? why so much animalism[?] in Congress? As far as my observation serves, it is owing to electioneering immorality; office aspirant's misleading, in the canvas[s] as it is called, the people[']s free will, resorting to all conceivable arts no matter how base, manufacturing public opinion, keeping back the truth from the people, using false issues—vide Wilmot proviso, &c, fraud and chicanery—any resort to procure a nomination, perfectly un[s]crupulous in subserving the public good to their own private views[?] and interests—vilenesses these, that honest, patriotic men will not stoop to, and the hackneyed electioneerers are ["elect" *canceled*] elected. Hence, so many unprincipled, worthless men in Congress. Hence, it is not of frequent occurrence that the wisest, most patriotic and able citizens in the Congressional districts are selected for Congress. This fatal evil may be remedied in time, but I cannot at this moment conceive how; nor can I conceive when the Constitution will become strictly the guide of those to whom the States and people delegate their power in the Unional government. From all this—the necessity of a virtuous, wise, firm, *truly Unional* President, who will vote *Unionally* ["for" *canceled*] (his signature or veto, being his vote as one ["bran"(?) *canceled*] estate of the government, for or against) on all measures that pass the legislative branches.

The only hope now is, that true patriots in both Houses will fearlessly do their duty to the Union; and that if the territorial matter should come before the next President, that he will veto any thing in it whatever that shall violate the spirit of the Unional compact—that he will religiously adhere to the Constitution in spirit and in truth.

I will be glad to hear from you what the prospect is, or may be. Most truly yours, John Hastings.

ALS in ScCleA. Note: An AEU by Calhoun reads, "["Mr. Wishart" *canceled*] Hon. Mr. Hastings."

From [Governor] Whitemarsh B. Seabrook

Edisto Island [S.C.], Dec. 28, '48

My Dear Sir, I brought with me from Columbia, and have deposited in the Bank of the State of So. Ca., a sword, which the State designs to present to Gen. [James] Shields. As I know not how to put him in possession of it, (if I knew his post-office, I would write to him on the subject) will you have the kindness to make such inquiries in relation to the matter, as will enable me quickly to accomplish the object I have in view. The Senator or Representatives from Illinois are perhaps the proper persons to whom to apply.

My predecessor [David Johnson] addressed a letter to Gen. Shields concerning the sword about five weeks ago, but no answer as yet has come to hand. Perhaps one of the members from his State will consent to deliver it to him. If so, there will be no difficulty I suppose in getting it to Washington.

The political atmosphere is becoming more and more threatening. I am prepared to meet the crisis, and I think you may rely with confidence on the State, in despite of its *frothy* resolution so recently adopted. Very respectfully yours & &, Whitemarsh B. Seabrook.

[P.S.] Have the kindness to send me a copy of the President's [James K. Polk's] message with the *accompanying documents.*

ALS in ScCleA. Note: An AEU by Calhoun reads, "Gov[erno]r Seabrook."

From "Tranquillus," [Francis Lieber, South Carolina College, Columbia, 1849]. Using a pseudonym, Lieber drafted five letters (apparently never sent nor made public) "to the Hon. John C. Calhoun on the present Slavery Question." He addresses Calhoun "because you represent, at this period, the most uncompromising portion of the ["the" *canceled*] Southern people." Lieber argues that the South has no right to demand the extension of slavery into U.S. territories. This right is nowhere granted and cannot be assumed, because slavery is a municipal institution and must be established by municipal law. This fact does not, however, exclude Southern citizens from settling in newly-acquired territories after having sold their slaves any more than U.S. law prohibits a Turkish citizen from living in the U.S. because of Turkish laws on polygamy. Slavery must change with the times, and Lieber feels that leading politicians like Calhoun must open their eyes to the true nature of their peculiar institution and assist in making necessary changes, if ultimate violence is to be avoided. Autograph drafts in CSmH, Francis Lieber Papers; PEx's in Thomas Sergeant Perry, ed., *The Life and Letters of Francis Lieber*, pp. 229–237.

From M. D. Cardwell

Dresden Ten[nessee,] January 2nd 1849

Sir, The important and distinguished position you have so long occupied before the American people I deem a sufficient apology for this letter. While I I [*sic*] know and have long been an observer of your course upon great National questions and especially upon questions affecting Southern rights, I have looked around for some individual to whom I could look for advice and instruction in regard to the position that should be taken by the South upon ["the absorbing" *canceled*] the all absorbing question of Southern rights in regard to the newly acquired ter[r]itory from Mexico. Should the North inforce the Wilmot Proviso upon the South what course should the South take? Shall we tamely submit to the fanatical domineering of the North or Shall we [*partial word canceled*] assert our rights? And in what way? For my part my mind has been long since made up. It is this, so soon as the north forces the Wilmot Proviso through Congress—to call a convention of Southern States, and show the north that we have rights and that we intend to enforce them. But having long been an admirer of your course upon questions of this kind, I have taken this liberty of addressing you upon this subject. Being a candidate for the Legislature at our next election, I wish to be prepared to take such ground as will be acceptable to the South—and I know of no one whose opinions would have more weight than your own. Should you feel at liberty to address me your views upon this subject, you would place me under obligations to you.

Your views are not desired for the public eye unless by your permission but I do think that it is time for the South to begin to understand their true position, so that when we have to act, we may be united upon some plan. With assurances of my high regard I am &c, M.D. Cardwell.

ALS in ScCleA. Note: An AEU by Calhoun reads, "Mr. Cardwell. Send Address."

From John E. Carew, [Editor of the Charleston *Mercury*]

Charleston, 2 Jan. 1849

My Dear Sir, Your Esteemed favor, covering proceedings of the Meeting of Southern Members of Congress, has been received and you will have noticed ere this, that we had anticipated your wishes by publishing in the Mercury. We also published a report of your remarks taken from Baltimore Patriot which we thought bore marks of genuineness. ["We" *altered to* "I"] trust that your expectations of a happy result may be realized, tho I confess I am not without my fears, when I see such a man as [Alexander H.] Stephens at the head of the Committee.

I have considered it prudent for the present, when Virginia and N. Carolina are exhibiting Symptoms of Vitality on this Subject, that the *Mercury* should be Comparatively quiet, tho my individual opinion is decidedly favorable to the action of our own State *alone* if no other can be brought to Cooperate.

I would esteem it a great favor if you would permit us to hear from you occasionally when your engagements will permit.

I know I am asking a great deal from one whose time is so much taken up with important business, but I feel that if you could favor us with your Views on all questions bearing on this, to us, all important issue, we might render efficient service to the South.

We have no news in the City. Some Apprehension of Cholera. I remain Sir Yours with great respect, Jno. E. Carew.

ALS in ScCleA.

From J[OHN] T. TASKER

Boston, Mass., Jan[uar]y 2, 1849

Dear Sir: I persuade myself of your pardon in obtruding this upon your notice, from the fact, that I trust you will see it is dictated in a spirit of patriotism—and ardent attachment to the Union of these States. I have ever ranked myself among the supporters of your principles in the main, and for evidence of this I may ["refer" *interlined*] to the files of the "N. Hampshire Gazette" in the years 1843–'44 & '5, and also to my speeches during the recent presidential campaign, in this State, some of which have been published in part. I am prompted *to presume* upon your notice *at this time*, in consequence of the dark & portenteous cloud that seems to be gathering over us—threatening the integrity of this Union—and because I think I see a safe course between Scylla & Charybdis.

You Know, Sir, that in the late election the supporters of Gen. [Lewis] Cass in the North, as a whole, were, by the action of that most unprincipled of politicians (Martin Van Buren) brought squarely up to the work on the slavery question, and boldly & manfully took and defended the ground of "no jurisdiction in Congress"—["that" *canceled*] that Gen. Cass would not only veto the "Wilmot Proviso," but also any act authorizing the *extension* of Slavery into our newly acquired territories. On the other hand, the Whigs of the North took the ground that Gen. [Zachary] Taylor would *not* veto the Wilmot Proviso, or any other measure which had heretofore been sanctioned by Congress—(which of course included all their old measures of Bank—Tariff &c. &c.): They even pretended to have received letters from him, of a private character, to this effect. This, with Van Buren's base conduct, lost to the Democrats of the North Pennsylvania & New York—(but what lost us Georgia & Louisiana I don't exactly know.)

I regret, and have regretted sincerely, that Gen. Taylor did not by himself remove this ground of fraud upon either the North or South—and I foresaw, as you did, that, should the Democratic nominee be defeated (and I feared he would be) the proper settlement of this question would be much more difficult if not hazardous. Because the Democrats of the North, believing that Gen. Taylor *would veto* the Wilmot Proviso, and ["therefore" *changed to* "thereby"] expose and sunder the Whig party—would go in *for* the measure *for this very purpose*—and that they might not then be able so easily to retrace their steps. And besides, they regard a National Bank & a high Protective Tariff, the darling measures of the moneyed & corporate aristocrats of the north, as tending, in reality, to enslave themselves, and as unconstitutional, in fact—as you of the South regard the interference of Congress in the Slavery question. Again, they say if the South will form an alliance with the Whigs of the North, (who are known to be openly committed to the Wilmot Proviso), then let them look to that party for support on the slavery question, especially when, by silence, they suffer a Northern Democrat to be beaten by a Southern Whig, since that office, for so long a time, has been filled by Southern gentlemen.

Sound or not sound, this is the way they reason. I am on terms of friendship and intercourse with many leading Democrats in N. England—(& among them Gens. [Caleb] Cushing—[Franklin] Pierce, of N.H.—[Robert] Rantoul, et. als.)—and know in the reasons (?) above mentioned is to be found the apparent caving in, on the part of the Democrats of the North.

Now, how can this question be *amicably* settled? that is the question. I confess I can see but one way—and that I believe, you gentlemen of the South, *if united* can bring about. If we get along in this matter without *dissolution* (Oh! what a horrible idea)—I think there can be no doubt but that the essential features and principles of our present revenue and financial systems, will, in the end, become firmly established: their change will be injurious: they may be somewhat modified in detail—as occasion and the real good of the country may require. To this, I think, the *Whigs* of the South *ought* to assent, for the sake of ["the" *interlined*] Union—at least, for the present. With the present complexion of the Senate, they probably cannot be changed for the next two years. If this can be fixed upon in your meeting to be had on the 15th inst., then, it seems to me the way is open for a settlement of this matter. Gen. Taylor is not supposed, generally, to be under any pledges to any party, but I have no doubt, he will yield to the general wish of the South. Now, suppose, in his inaugural address, he should, protesting against any desire to influence the legislation of Congress—squint pretty strongly at an approval of Democratic Republican principles—and, in the organization of his Cabinet, should select sound conservative men of the South, and such sound conservative men of the North as [Stephen A.] Douglas, [Levi] Woodbury, [William J.?] Worth, or [Daniel S.] Dickinson—or [William L.] Marcy of N. York or others of the Democratic party—sending the more talented and moderate of the Whigs of the North abroad, and observing, generally in his appointments, at the North, a prudent and cautious course, of nominating to office the moderate and influential of both parties—having regard to this great question. In this way I sincerely believe, support from the North, sufficient with the united front of the South may be secured to settle amicably this difficult question. If this disappoint the Whigs of the North, why so be it—they richly deserve it. They cannot justly complain of treachery either on the part of Gen. Taylor or of Southern Whigs, because of their utter disregard to truth and Southern principles upon this very measure, in the recent election. If they do, it will avail nothing—they can do nothing. Such a policy on the part of Gen. Taylor, while it would tend to erradicate the corruptions that have existed in the machinery of the Democratic party, would lay ["a" *canceled*] deep and sure ["the" *interlined*] foundation for a great constitutional Republican party that will ride over all obstacles, and grind up all factions of northern fanatics, as a peppercorn between the upper and nether millstones. We shall have then, in this party, the great body of the South, and of the Democrats of the North, together with the patriotic, wise & unselfish of the Whigs of the North.

If you of the South, as a whole, can agree upon and recommend to, Gen. Taylor a course of policy of this or a similar character, I cannot doubt its success.

Let me not be understood as having any particular preference to the names I have mentioned. Though formerly on the most friendly terms with Judge Woodbury, in April last I was somewhat offended with him, and still am, (perhaps wrongfully) from the manner in which he saw fit to conduct in a very important case in which Mr. [Robert] Rantoul Jr. & myself were engaged on the same side, as counsel, and the Hon. R[ufus] Choat[e,] B[enjamin] R. Curtis, the Judge's son, & two others from N. York, upon the other. But this does [not?] prevent me from supporting him when I think he may benefit the Country.

I hope and trust our Southern brethren will neither be hasty nor rash—but sincerely pray God, you may by prudence and caution, and a proper exercise of the influence of your position upon Gen. Taylor—in whose hands, in my opinion, are committed the destinies of this Republic in a greater degree, owing to the circumstances, than they ever have been to any one man since the days of [George] Washington—bring about such a state of things as shall carry our beloved Country, in its integrity, along in its high way of liberty, to glory & renown.

I trust I need not say to you, that I am utterly opposed to placing the African race, on this Continent, upon an equal footing with myself, or that I prefer the Bill reported at the last Session by Senator [John M.] Clayton, for the settlement of this question, to any other proposition yet made to my knowledge. I have no sort of sympathy with the Abolition politicians of the North, of whatever hue &, with those *pseudo philanthropists*, who, while they strain every nerve to grind down the honest industry of the *North*, assume to dictate to Southern taskmasters not more severe. I have the Honor to be Sir with the highest respect your o[be]d[ien]t Servant, J.T. Tasker.

P.S. I have hastily glanced at the above copy as made by my clerk—and it has struck me, that inasmuch as you never descend to party *tacticks*—and as, since the death of my esteemed friend the Hon. Dixon H. Lois [*sic*; Lewis]—I could not well presume to address any other Southern gentleman, from want of a personal introduction—I might suggest to you, if you saw fit—to pass this to Senator Wescoatt [*sic*; James D. Westcott, Jr., of Fla.] or [David L.] Yulee or such other friends, as you may see fit. Of course I should a little prefer others that [*sic*] real Northerners. Most respectfully, J.T. Tasker.

LS in ScCleA; PEx in Boucher and Brooks, eds., *Correspondence*, pp. 489–492. NOTE: An AEU by Calhoun reads, "Mr. Tasket[,] relates to Slavery question."

From John Tyler

Sherwood Forest
[Charles City County, Va.] Jan. 2, 1849

My Dear Sir: Your letter of the 6 Nov. [*not found*] covering the statement which I forwarded you of our last hours on Texas annexation reached me in due season, and I made your suggestions of change the basis of a new statement to the other members of the Cabinet. I feel satisfied that you are mistaken in fixing on Sunday as the day of our first interview after my approval of the resolutions. The Cabinet council was held on Sunday, and our interview was on Saturday. But in the new statement I have adopted the use of the *day* of the month in place of the *day* of the week—thus—"The resolutions reached me on the 1 day of March, 1845. My official term expired on the 4th day of the same month. After my approval had been given to the resolutions Mr. Calhoun the Secretary of State call[e]d on me, &c &c" and what follows is made to conform throughout. I enclose you the reformed statement which you will find to be modified according to your suggestions. [George M.] Bibb, [John] Nelson & [Charles A.] Wickliffe substantially concur. From [John Y.] Mason and [William] Wilkins I remain to hear. By the by Wickliffe gives me a fact of which I was ignorant—viz. that Mr. [James K.] Polk without loss of time after his inauguration wrote [Andrew J.] Donelson [then U.S. Minister to Texas] to suspend all action on our instructions until he ["D." *interlined*] should receive further instructions. He says Donelson shew[e]d him the letter when he W[ickliffe] was in Texas, and doubts not but that it would be found among the Texan archives of Legation. He states his belief that the letter was not mark[e]d confidential, but still does not wish his name to be mention[e]d in connexion with it. Had you any knowledge of this? Yes My D[ea]r Sir it was "the midnight messenger" that secur[e]d annexation. Anson Jones is a potent witness to establish the fact. The fact is that that movement controul[e]d two Cabinets, that of the U.S. and that of Texas.

I perceive that the Abolitionists are in the lead among you in Congress, and how matters are to terminate the future will disclose. One thing is quite obvious[:] that old parties are changing their affinities and that Legislation is in future more to be controul[e]d by sections than principles. Tendering you the congratulations incident to the season I am D[ea]r Sir Truly Y[ou]rs, John Tyler.

[Enclosure]

"(A statement of what transpired after the passage of the joint resolutions for the annexation of Texas to the United States.)"

The resolutions reached me, and received my approval, on the 1st day of March, 1845. My official term expired on the 4th of the same month. After my approval had been officially given to the resolutions, Mr. Calhoun, the Secretary of State, called on me, and the conversation immediately turned to the subject of the resolutions. Mr. Calhoun remarked that the power to make the selection between the alternative resolutions rested with me, and that he hoped I would not hesitate to act. I replied that I entertained no doubt in the matter of the selection; that I regarded the resolution which had been moved and adopted in the Senate, by way of amendment to the House resolution, as designed merely to appease the discontent of some one or two members of that body, and for no other purpose; and that my only doubt of the propriety of immediate and prompt action arose from a feeling of delicacy to my successor. We both regarded the opening of a new negotiation, as proposed by the Senate resolution, as destined to defeat annexation altogether,—that Texas, in consequence of the defeat of the late treaty by the Senate, would listen reluctantly to any new proposition for negotiation; that this reluctance would be greatly increased by reason of the very small majorities in Congress by which the resolutions had passed, which might well create a doubt whether a two-thirds vote could be obtained for the ratification of a treaty, and that these doubts might very wisely incline Texas to throw herself upon the good offices of Great Britain and France, with a view to obtain the recognition of her independence by Mexico, in preference to relying on the uncertain contingency of a new negotiation. Upon the point of delicacy to my successor, Mr. Calhoun urged strongly the necessity of immediate action, which he regarded as sufficiently great to overrule all other considerations. It was enough that Congress had given me the power to act by the terms of the resolutions, and that the urgency of the case was imminent. I give the substance of what transpired, not the words. The conversation terminated by my requesting him to summon a cabinet for the next day.

The next day the whole cabinet assembled; every member gave a decided preference to the House resolution over that of the Senate. I stated to the gentlemen that the only doubt that could exist as to the propriety of immediate action by me might be found in the fact that, as my term of office expired on the Tuesday following, it might bear the appearance of indelicacy to my successor, and imply a want of confidence in him I did not feel, if in the last hours of my official term I anticipated his action; and that it was mainly on this point I desired their advice. All concurred in the necessity of immediate action. Mr. Polk and his cabinet would necessarily require time to look around them after he and they were installed in office, and that, if Texas was lost by delay, the censure would fall on my administration. The same considerations for prompt action which have already been mentioned as having occurred in the interview with Mr. Calhoun the day before were again repeated. In their force I fully concurred, and suggested, as an expedient that would save the point of delicacy, that Mr. Calhoun should wait on Mr. Polk, inform him of my action on the subject, and explain to him my reasons therefor. The suggestion was fully approved. Mr. Calhoun waited on Mr. Polk, after the meeting of the cabinet, and reported to me the substance of the interview the next morning, which was, that Mr. Polk declined to express any opinion or to make any suggestion in reference to the subject. The instructions to Mr. Donelson, being submitted to and approved by me, were dispatched on the same day.

ALS in ScCleA; PC in Jameson, ed., *Correspondence*, pp. 1187–1188; PC of En in Lyon G. Tyler, ed., *Letters and Times of the Tylers*, 2:364–365. NOTE: Tyler's statement edited here was enclosed with a letter of 11/27 from Tyler to William Wilkins, former Secretary of War. Tyler commented therein to Wilkins, "I have already submitted the statement to Mr. Calhoun, who concurs in it as now presented."

From WILSON LUMPKIN

Athens [Ga.,] Jan[uar]y 3d 1849

My dear Sir, I pass by unnoticed, all other subjects, however important they may be, for the purpose of dwelling for a moment, on the subject of the slave question, in its present aspect. It must now be obvious to every informed person, that the argument upon this subject is entirely ex[h]austed.

The people of the slave holding States, must submit to degradation, inequality & the most flagrant injustice: or resist, as best they may, the arrogant strides of an unconstitutional & despotic majority.

A few days will give the result of your Southern Congressional meeting. What will be the *tone*, & *harmony* of that meeting, I shall impatiently await to know.

Much depends upon the course which may be taken, by Southern men, who are now members of Congress. Every patriot of the South, ought at this time, to throw aside all former *party* shackels, & stand firmly on the Constitutional rights of his constituents.

We have already yielded so much on this subject, for the sake of peace & Union—that we ["have" *interlined*] lost the respect of our oppressors, & to no small extent, our self respect.

I presume some of the most extravagant measures of the majority, on the slave subject, will be checked by Mr. [James K.] Polk[']s Vetoe, for the present—but this will only add fuel to the flame of infatuation, which is daily increasing in the non slave-holding States. Nothing now can quench this fire of *Hell*, but the united resistance of the South. And now the great question is, will the South patriotically unite upon this subject? I regret to say, I have strong doubts. On this subject, I have not entire confidence in any State in the Union, except South Carolina. Beleive me when I assure ["you" *interlined*], that our own beloved South, has many, very many—anti-slavery people in her bosom. People whose sympathies are with our vilest Enemies. Nevertheless, in all the slave States, a majority will act with us, if we take decided ground, & act promptly & energetically. And thus, a decided course taken without delay—would silence, if not overwhelm, the leaven of disaffection, dispersed throughout the South. We have every thing to loose [*sic*], and nothing to gain, by a longer agitation of the slave question. Our opponents know, that time & agitation, is rapidly consummating all that, they desire. The gold excitement in California, will exclude slavery from all that region. Not because negroes are not superior laborers for mineing, but because slave holders, will not under existing circumstances run the risque of loosing their slaves. For myself, I prefer any thing, that could befal me, to submission, to such Tyranny, as is decreed against the South, by the non slave holding States. I have confidence in God, in his truth and justice—and now nearly 66 years old, I would sho[u]lder my muskett & die in the field like a man, rather than wear the chains forged for my hands, by a people, who of all others, deserve to be destested by God & man, for their want of good faith to their confideing brethren. Your friend & Serv[an]t, Wilson Lumpkin.

ALS in ScCleA; PC in Boucher and Brooks, eds., *Correspondence*, pp. 492–493.

From Louis T. Wigfall

Marshall [Texas,] January 4, 1849

My dear Sir, I take the liberty of sending y[ou] a copy [*not found*] of a Preamble and Resolutions adopted ["by" *canceled and* "at" *interlined*] a public meeting in this place. I trust that they will be responded to in other portions of the State. If they are not I am pursuaded that twill be only because the people are not aware of the dangers impending. The Resolutions were opposed both in the Committee and at the meeting by Mr. Hall on the ground that they contained an attack on Gen[era]l [Samuel] Houston and Mr. [James K.] Polk and yet he was sustained by only three persons. Judging from the feelings of the people here, in this county I mean, I infer that Texas is ready whenever the occasion arrises to hazard as much for the Constitution of [17]87 as She did for that of [18]24. I have endeavoured, as you will see from the Preamble and Resolutions, to draw the public attention to our rights *under the Constitution* and recognise *only* the *Compromises which it contains.* If we admit the propositions that our only hope of safety is in Union & that members of Congress can, under the name of Compromise, alter the Constitution, the South is doomed. It seems to me that our only and last hope now is to stand upon the Constitution and declare that whilst we are willing to preserve the Union of [17]87 we will enter into no other nor allow its existence.

Texas would probably not take the lead in opposition to the application of the [Wilmot] Proviso to the Territories of New Mexico and California; but would follow willingly and almost unanimously the lead of any other State. I see from the papers that South Carolina is thinking about "United Southern action." I trust that 'tis not all that she thinks of. The South I have heretofore thought could not be united for a blow—but when the blow is struck would unite for defence and stand as one man. There must be a Wat Tiler to Knock down the excise man. I shall be disappointed if South Carolina does not on this occasion strike the blow. Upon the Boundary question Texas will act boldly and promptly. She claims to the Rio Grande and will beyond doubt maintain that claim at all hazards.

I see from the papers that a proposition has been made to admit California and New Mexico at once as a State. If such a proposition has been made with any prospect of being acted upon I should be glad to know your views. I believe there is nothing *in the Constitution* which fixes either the population or size of a Territory applying for admission as a State. If Congress has the *legal* right to make a State of California & New Mexico; the want of equity would be so obvious as to warrant us in objecting [at] all hazards. The object is manifestly to exclude Slavery and it is a matter of but little importance to us, practically, how we are deprived of our share of the common conquest and purchase.

I trust, my dear Sir, that you will excuse the liberty I take in addressing you at all and particularly the freedom with which I write. I thought that it might not be without interest to you to Know the feeling of the people in this Section upon the engrossing topics which are agitating the whole country and have therefore sent you our Resolutions which I trust will meet your approbation. Gen[era]l [Thomas J.] Rusk will tell you that the Committee & officers of the meeting are of the most respectable of our population. Your own views I have taken the liberty of asking because of the confidence I feel in them. I will only add that they are asked for my own guidance only. It seems to me that the time is rapidly approaching when the South will have to act and I desire to be in the right position when She does. I trust that my motives will be a sufficient excuse for my addressing you in a manner and with a freedom which the difference in our ages and positions might forbid. I am, my dear Sir, Very Respectfully, Louis T. Wigfall.

ALS in ScCleA; PC in Boucher and Brooks, eds., *Correspondence*, pp. 493–495.

From A[NDREW] J. DONELSON

Berlin, 5 January, 1849

My dear Sir, I think it my duty to express to some friend who may be in a situation to communicate them to the proper source some considerations that may be material in determining the question of my being continued [as] Minister in Germany. In selecting you for this purpose I hope I trespass upon no restriction imposed on yourself, although I am aware I have no such claim to your friendship as would authorise me to expect your aid on a question of appointments if you had an influence which you were disposed to exert on such a subject.

In regard to the office which I fill there is nothing to prevent my saying that I desire to hold it until the negotiations rendered necessary by the recent changes in the German Government can be closed. Up to this time these negotiations have been kept back until the constitution of the Central power became perman[ent.] But whatever may be the future union of these states it is qui[te] certain that their present legislation must be altered so as [to] permit the introduction of uniform customs duties and the establishment of a common navy. This will render necessary Treaties with them and will make inapplicable those we now have with the states not in the Zollverein. These last Treat[ies] were not of a character to secure us permanent benefits, since the states with which they are formed contain not one sixth of the German population. I have devoted much study to the subject and if Gen. [Zachary] Taylor can confide to me the negotiation I hope to bring it to a conclusion beneficial to our country.

My creed has always been that the office holder owed it to himself and to the country not to mingle with the course of the elections. I predicted when Mr. [James K.] Polk sent our armies to the Rio Grande that the effect of the war would take the Presidency from the hands of the Democratic party as then organised, and it was soon evident that Gen. Taylor was the individual that would verify this prediction. Those who know him as I have, could have no other wish than that he may be as fortunate in the Cabinet as he has been in the camp. He has been elected by neither of the great political parties. He takes hold of the national ship free to consult the experience of all his predecessors: and I doubt not that this experience is already accepted by him so far as it accords with the old republican doctrines as expounded by [Thomas] Jefferson and [James] Madison.

My hope and belief is that Gen. Taylor will dispose of the Slavery question, on the principles of the Senate bill of the last session, or at least leaving the subject with the people of the territories acquired from Mexico, uninfluenced by the action of Congress. If he does, we, in the South, may well give him in advance all the confidence which is due to his eminent services, and to his spotless character as an honest man who will have no motive to mislead him as the President of the country.

I shall be obliged to you to make known these personal views of mine to Gen. Taylor, whom I desire not to be mistaken in respect to my feelings. If he removes me I shall make no complaint, but in this event it will be important to me to know his intentions, in order that I may make my arrangeme[nts] here as little injurious as possible to my private affairs.

Prussia and all Germany are for the moment quiet. Great difficulties however yet remain to be adjusted before we can say that the revolution is finished. It will not surp[rise] me if there is a general war in six months. I am very truly your most ob[e]d[ien]t serv[an]t, A.J. Donelson.

[P.S.] Your young friend Mr. [Edward Wyatt] Geddings continues well, and promises to make a fine scholar. A.J.D.

LS in ScCleA. Note: This letter is slightly frayed in the right margin of the first page, leading to the loss of a few parts of words. Calhoun's AEU reads, "Maj[o]r Donelson."

From John S. Lorton

Pendleton [S.C.,] January 7th 1849

Dear Sir, I was at Anderson a few days since and enquired of the commissioner in Equity what the prospects were for collecting the money belonging to the Estate of [Chester] Kingsley and he informed me that there was no prospect of getting any shortly, perhaps none this year.

Mr. R[obert] A. Maxwell requested me to say to you, that he expected during this month, to receive between Three & Four Thousand Dollars, and if so, he wished to invest the amount in bonds, and would like very much to let you have it for a term of years, as it belongs to [the] Estate of Mays, and he is the guardian of the Children. You can either write me or Mr. Maxwell if you conclude to take it. I saw Mr. Fred[e]rick[s] the other day and all were well then. Yours Respectfully, John S. Lorton.

ALS in ScU-SC, John C. Calhoun Papers. Note: An AEU by Calhoun reads, "J. Lorton, Informs me that R.A. Maxwell desires to place certain funds in my hands. Wrote Mr. Maxwell I would accept his offer & authorise Mr. Lorton to receive & receipt for it for me."

From Jeremiah Clemens

Huntsville, Ala., Jan. 8th 1849

D[ea]r Sir, I hope you will pardon the liberty I have taken in addressing this letter to you. I am desirous of obtaining some information which I believe you better able to supply than any one else.

It is my purpose to urge upon the people of Ala., during the next summer, the propriety of passing a law, to prevent the further introduction of slaves into the State, because such a law would, to some extent, prevent the States nearest the free States, (Maryland, Virginia, Kentucky & Missouri for instance) from pouring that Class of their population upon us, & then, when they are no longer interested in maintaining the institution of Slavery, becoming allies of the Abolitionists, or at least very uncertain friends to the planting States. As aids in this purpose I wish to obtain, or be refered to, such documents as contain a history of the "rise & progress" of Abolitionism, & also such Statistical information as may be of use, in relation to the migration of the Slave population from the States refered to, or from other States now free, to a more Southern latitude.

I have ventured to address you in the belief that you could readily furnish me with the documents alluded to. If I am mistaken, however, & if it will put you to any inconvenience, I beg that you will not trouble yourself about the matter. I can probably obtain them from other sources.

Either of the Senators from Alabama [William R. King and Benjamin Fitzpatrick] will give you any information you may desire in relation to myself, or any assurance of the uses to which I shall put such documents as you may forward. Very Respectfully Yours &c, Jeremiah Clemens.

ALS in ScCleA; PC in Boucher and Brooks, eds., *Correspondence*, p. 495. NOTE: Clemens became Senator from Ala. in 11/1849 to fill the vacancy created by the death of Dixon H. Lewis. An AEU by Calhoun reads, "J. Clement. Send Address."

From RUFUS A. FRENCH

Giles Courthouse [Va.,] January the 8th 1849

My dear Sir, We have established here a Lyceum, embracing some of our most intelligent citizens. The following question was at its last meeting proposed and accepted, & will be *publickly* discussed. "Which of the two distinguished gentlemen, is the better entitled to the admiration and gratitude of the American People, John C. Calhoun or Henry Clay." My prepossessions, my heart, my judgment are with my old friend, and to maintain myself effectively in the discussion, must have data, upon which to rest an argument. Can you send me by mail Mr. "Calhoun's life" prepared by Hon. R[obert] M.T. Hunter? I once had it, but it is not now forthcoming. The Speeches of the same gentleman upon the war of 1812, the Proclamation and force bill, and the Veto power, His reports in favour of increasing the Navy, Also a history, if it can be had, of the rise & progress of the fires of Abolition, not forgeting the Missouri Compromise, The Names of those gentlemen, Cook & others who when repudiated by their constituency, were appointed to places of honor & profit, under the administration of Mr. [John Q.] Adams. Upon the subject, of the Bank & Tariff, I trust I am clearly informed. I should like to have a *Statisticks* of the exports and imports since the organization of the government, shewing the articles exported from the North, as well as from the south in their proper columns, together with the valuations attached thereto. This I regard as a very valuable document, & important to the discussion. I should also wish to have Mr. Clay[']s speech delivered at Lexington upon the Subject of the Mexican War, and should like much to see a eulogy pronounced some years ago, upon the life and character of my distinguished friend by the Hon. Mr. [Isaac E.] Holmes of your State, & such other Matter as you may consider pertinent to the discussion. If I can have a thorough preparation, I shall not fear the result.

Can a proper and amicable direction be given to the Slave question, during the present session? If not, what will be the result? Where and how will stand the President elect [Zachary Taylor] upon the question? I trust he will ["fall" *interlined*] right. Who will constitute his Cabinet? Much in my opinion depends upon its *complexion.* I will not trouble you further, but must beg pardon for this intrusion. With high consideration, I remain My dear Sir Your friend & H[um]ble Serv[an]t, Rufus A. French.

ALS in ScCleA. NOTE: An AEU by Calhoun reads, "Mr. French. Send Speeches."

From HENRY O'RIELLY

[January 8, 1849]

Copies—*for the Hon. John C. Calhoun*

(from Mr. [James] Monroe's manuscripts.)

A paper endorsed "*Interrogatories, Missouri—March 4, 1820. To the Heads of Departments and Attorney General.*"

Questions (on opposite page.)

"Has Congress a right, under the powers vested in it by the Constitution, to make a regulation prohibiting Slavery in a territory?

Is the 8th section of the act which passed both Houses, on the 3rd instant, for the admission of Missouri into the Union, consistent with the Constitution?"

With the above is the original draft of the following letter, in President Monroe's handwriting, on half a sheet of paper, but not endorsed or addressed to any one. There are interlineations, but the text, as left by the writer, is as follows:

"Dear Sir: The question which lately agitated Congress and the Public, has been settled, as you have seen, by the passage of an Act for the admission of Missouri as a State, unrestrained, and Arkansas likewise when it reaches maturity, and the establishment of the 36° 30′ north latitude as a line, north of which Slavery is prohibited, and permitted to the south. I took the opinion, in writing, of the ad[ministratio]n, as to the constitutionality of restraining territories, ["and the vote of every member was" *canceled*; "which was" *interlined*; "unanimous and" *interlined and then canceled*] explicit in favor of it, and as it was that the 8th section of the Act was applicable to territories only, and not to States when they ["became such" *canceled*] should be admitted to the Union. [*Marginal interpolation by O'Rielly*: "The original draft is thus interlined, and words ("are" *interlined*) scored out as above."] On this latter point I had ["at first" *interlined*] some doubt ["at first" *canceled*], but the ["opinions" *changed to* "opinion"] of others whose opinions were entitled to weight with me, supported by the sense in which it was viewed by all who voted on the subject in Congress, as will appear by the Journals, satisfied me respecting it.

I have never seen a question so fraught with serious menacing to our Union, or pursued with such persevering obstinacy, since that agitated, in 1786, for shutting up the Mississippi. [*Canceled*: "The object was the same as in the former, the establishment of a permanent control, over the Union, in one section of the Union."] [*Canceled marginal interpolation by O'Rielly*: "The words 'Turning, too, on the same principle, that of power, in those who brought it forward, supported, too, by the whole body of the people in the non-slaveholding States, in principle sound abstract, for reasons which were favorable to success, or which had much prospect of success,' are here erased, in this manner, in the original draft."]

The object in both attempts was the same, that of power, by the establishment of a permanent control over the whole Union in one section of it. The ["expedient" *interlined*] *means* might also have been the same dismemberment by the Allegheny, I always thought, was that contemplated by the first project, being satisfied ["that" *canceled*] had the measure been adopted that such would have been its consequences, if dismemberment of another kind had not ensued.

Such being the state of affairs, I leave it entirely to yourself whether you had better retire at present or remain in the service. I well know that whereever you may be, that you will always be ready to obey the call of your country in any extremity.

I have always wished that you should remain in the service, and retire when I did.

Whatever your decision may be, be assured that my perfect confidence and most friendly and affectionate regards will always attend you." [James Monroe]

Washington, Jan. 8, 1849

I certify the foregoing to be a correct copy (fac-simile, as far as practicable) of the paper that it professes to re-produce—the original being in my possession. Henry O'Rielly.

DS in ScCleA. NOTE: See *The Papers of John C. Calhoun*, 25:652–654 for the letter of 8/7/1848 from O'Rielly to Calhoun concerning James Monroe's papers.

From John Hastings

New Garden, Col[umbiana] C[ount]y, Ohio
Jan. 9, 1849

My dear Sir, The Southern Members are (some of the papers say) to hold an adjourned meeting the middle of this month. On the result, much will depend: guided, I do hope it will be, by wisdom and firmness; and if entire, energetic unanimity should be present, the influence will be the more efficient.

I trouble you at this moment with some ideas; for the evident determination of a majority in Congress, as again commenced this session, to pertinaciously interfere with the equal rights Unionally, of the States and the People, makes me uneasy and anxious. Through all the tumult of factionalism so far, I have had no doubt of the Union; but I must confess that the vote in the House [of Representatives] on the 18th Ult. for entertaining Mr. [Joshua R.] Giddings's bill, has staggered my confidence: 79 representatives sustaining such a glaring outrage on the Unional Compact and its Constitution, as that bill proposed, is astounding to all who love the Union and the free self government which it secures.

The truth is: political corruption, ["chiefly through office seeking," *interlined*] has become so common [through] out the Union, that there may be fears for the future. Indeed it may be a question, from what we see at this hour, whether man is capable of perpetuating rational liberty? for there never has prevailed so extensive a departure from Unional good faith, from patriotism, from "do as you would be done by" between States and people politically, as exists at this moment. Still, if the yeomanry of the Country could get the truth, Ununional factionism would be rendered less noxious. It is probable there is as much political profligacy in Ohio, in proportion to population, as in any State in the Union; yet if the people ["could" *interlined*] get the honest truth, they would, in general, oppose any interference with the rights of the States and People as in the Union, whether offered through the Territories, District of Columbia, or other mode. But as in my late letter—how can the truth be got to the People? If the press were not so demoralized politically, it could be done.

I do fear for the future. Has not Congress become a despotism? For a majority that ["in its enactments" *interlined*] goes wilfully, and repeatedly, ["out of the" *canceled*] and perseveringly, out of the Constitution, torturing it into Unional wrong, evincing a total [*one word canceled and* "absence" *interlined*] of Unional good faith—of Unional justice, aberrating from truth and honor, showing in its action that it will be amenable to no responsibility—is virtually a despotism. However, States that are wronged by the unconstitutional interference ["of Congress" *interlined*] with slave labor will, should be, firm in adhering to and determining their rights; the integrity of the Union, if nothing else, demands it: and there is a saving power, I think, in some of the other States—Pennsylvania and the North western ones, ["at least," *interlined*] that will, particularly if the truth be fearlessly explained to them, side with Unional right.

I observe that there is a proposition offered in the House, to retrocede to Maryland her part of the District [of Columbia]. Let it be done at once: it will deprive the factionists of one pretense for carrying on their disloyal labors; and one of the many follies—one of the many innovations on practical good sense, which the Union indulged in, [*partial word canceled*] the body politic will be finally relieved from.

I am looking forward most anxiously to the determinations of your meeting; devoutly hoping that they will be impartial and just, purely patriotic, and firm—offering to all, constitutional concord and consequent Unional harmony. Yours as ever, John Hastings.

ALS in ScCleA.

From E[DWARD] P. PITTS

Richmond, 11th Jan[uar]y 1849

Dear Sir: Will you be so good as to send me a Copy of a Speech you made some short time ago, I believe last winter, on the "Wilmot proviso." The subject of Slavery & the powers of Congress over the subject are now before the Virginia Legislature and I desire as much light on the subject as I can obtain. Is it the doctrine of the South that Congress has no power over the subject in the District [of Columbia] and in the Territories? It seems to me that if the action of Congress can be regarded as fixing its powers, the question is settled as far as the Territories are concerned. The Missouri question as well as the late Oregon Bill seems to surrender the power. If I am not trespassing too far upon your time I should be obliged to you for any information you can give upon these subjects. I am a member of a ["joint" *interlined and then erased*] Committee of the Senate of Va. which has this subject before it, to report resolutions for the adoption of the Legislature & should like ["to" *interlined*] sustain Southern Grounds. With great respect Y[ou]r ob[edien]t S[er]v[an]t, E.P. Pitts.

ALS in ScCleA. NOTE: An AEU by Calhoun reads, "Mr. Pitts. Send Address."

From H[ENRY] W. CONNER

Charleston, Jan[uar]y 12, 1849

I reached home last night & hasten to give you the result of my observations South & West.

The people of Georgia of both parties are up to the mark & ready to act but may not take the lead but they consider the issue as inevitable & the sooner it is made the better. Savannah & Augusta [are] less true than the country owing to the Northern population.

Alabamma, the Eastern part of it are sound & to the point. Their leading men as [George T.?] Goldthwaite, [William L.] Yancey,

[John A.] Elmore, [James E.] Belser & others understand the subject & the remedy well. The northern part of Alabama & the west I can speak of only from hearsay. The north I think is a good deal governed by party. The west are with us[.] So are the south except at Mobile where they ["are" *interlined*] divided[?], the northern population being as they always are against us. The people of Alabama as a whole are with us in every thing but the difficulty is with the politicians & the parties. What one side proposes the other opposes.

I fear for Louisiana. New Orleans is almost Free soil in their opinions. The population is one half Northern agents—another ¼ or ⅓ are Foreigners—the remnant are Creoles who cannot be made to comprehend their danger until the negroes are being taken out of the fields. They would then fight furiously. The Theory there too is that by restricting slavery to its present bounds the Lands & negroes of Louisianna would be enhanced in value. I was told however by some persons whose oppinions I had great respect for (they were of the Senate of that State & planters) that the country was sound & altho they would not make any noise by resolutions or otherwise they would be found in line when the time for acting came. Louisianna will be the last if at all to strike for the defence of the South.

In Florida I was no where but at Apalachicola. They are all Northern agents there but Florida is right.

The cities all of them are becoming daily more & more unsound & uncertain & all for the same reason; the infusion of Northerners & Foreigners amongst them & their influence is being felt in the interior[?]. The draymen & labourers of New Orleans are all white & Foreigners—& they will not let a negro drive a dray. He would be mobbed or killed. The steam Boats are all employing white Servants & their captains mostly Northerners & the [*one word canceled*] issue of Free labour against slave labour will soon be made at the South.

Our own people many of them are desponding. They begin to think that the Institution of Slavery is doomed. That all the world is opposed to it & that we ourselves will not or cannot do any thing to avert it. As yet it has been all talk & no action & the majority at the North becoming daily more & more decided.

Here to my mind is *the only danger* of the South & I have heard & seen the feeling of despondency expressed with shame & sorrow. I blushed for my countrymen when I saw them ready to cower before the storm. Our slaves themselves are becoming arrogant from the knowledge of this feeling & will soon be troublesome. The feeling is not general however but it is on the increase.

From all I have seen & learned *I am more convinced than ever of the vital importance of prompt*[,] *decided & efficient action on the part of the South.* The mode of action the wise & the patriotic must determine[?] on. Whatever is done should be ca[l]mly[,] considerately & wisely considered ["its execution" *canceled*] & its plan of execution well arranged but above all in the execution, the action should be *bold, determined & decisive.* This is necessary to give confidence. It is necessary every way for success & without it we are lost. We must show ourselves able & willing to defend ourselves before we can obtain the support of our friends or the respect or fear of our adversaries.

My whole theory so far as I am concerned is [*three words canceled*] wise & deliberate—but bold & determined action & with the least possible delay.

My movements have been so rapid that I have fallen behind the current of events. I see however that the Southern members held a meeting on the 15th. Whatever is determined on each member should exert himself to procure a prompt response from his own district—a simultaneous movement can be obtained in that way. I may write soon again regarding ["again" *canceled*] Gen[era]l [Zachary] Taylor. Y[our]s, H.W. Conner.

ALS in ScCleA; PC in Jameson, ed., *Correspondence*, pp. 1188–1190.

J[ohn] C. Calhoun and Others to President [James K. Polk]

Senate Chamber, 13th Jan[uar]y 1849

The President of the U.S.

We recommend David W. [*sic*; U.] Sloan, as well qualified and as having strong claims to fill one of the places of Cadets at large to be appointed by the Executive. As evidence of his qualification & claims, we enclose the certificate [dated 11/25/1848] of his teacher [J. Leland Kennedy] & the letter [of 11/23/1848] of his father [William Sloan]. His father is a neighbour of ours; and is a gentleman of high respectability. What he says of the revolutionary services of his ancestors are facts familiarly known to the Neighbourhood. With high respect We are & &, J.C. Calhoun, R[ichard] F. Simpson.

Turn over.

We concur in recommending David W. Sloan for the place for

which he is an applicant. A[ndrew] P. Butler, D[aniel] Wallace, Sign at the request of Mr. Simpson—R[obert] B. Rhett, J[oseph] A. Woodward, I[saac] E. Holmes.

LS with Ens in DNA, RG 94 (Adjutant General's Office), Application Papers of Cadets, 1805–1866, 1848, 262 (M-688:173, frames 343–349). NOTE: Except for the signatures and the phrase "Sign at the request of Mr. Simpson," which was written by Rhett, this letter is in Calhoun's handwriting.

REMARKS AT A MEETING OF THE COMMITTEE OF FIFTEEN

[Washington, January 13, 1849]

[*The Address which Calhoun had prepared was presented. Thomas J. Rusk of Texas objected that the statement went too far.*]

Mr. Calhoun said I [Rusk] certainly could not have read the address[,] that there was nothing in it which could possibly bear the construction which [I] was putting upon it.

[*Rusk said he had not read the Address but had heard part of it read, and argued against its assumptions about the future hostile actions of the North.*]

Mr. Calhoun said the address also said that if the North backed out from their pretensions that we should avoid such a state.

[*Rusk reiterated his confidence in the "Patriotism of the great mass of people at the North."*]

Mr. Calhoun replied that he was astonished at the course taken by the gentleman from Texas[;] he must say that he was deeply ["mortified" *canceled*] wounded by it[;] That he would sooner have expected a blow at the South from any other quarter than from Texas[.] The gentleman must be aware of the course pursued by the South towards Texas[;] he must be aware of her positions in regard to the subject of annexation and he should also remember that Texas ["yet" *canceled*] has vitally important questions yet unsettled.

[*Rusk replied, in part, that Texas appreciated the services of the South and of Calhoun in regard to annexation. "I have more than this to remember I shall never forget nor cease to be grateful to the gentleman from South Carolina for his personal kindness to myself when I was a boy [in his neighborhood] . . ." He reiterated his opposition to issuance of the Address. By a vote of 8–7 the committee recommended submission of the Address to the full Southern caucus on 1/15. The nay voters were all Whigs except for Rusk.*]

Two ADU's (memoranda by Rusk) in TxU, Thomas Jefferson Rusk Papers. NOTE: The two documents by Rusk, one of nine pages and one of three pages, are undated. It is possible that he may have conflated discussions of 1/13 in committee with those of 1/15 in the caucus. Also among Rusk's papers at TxU is a draft letter of 1/30/1849 to an unknown correspondent justifying his course, declaring his allegiance to the Union and "the rights of every member of this Confederacy," and reiterating his faith in the patriotism of the North.

From [Governor] WHITEMARSH B. SEABROOK

Executive Department
Charleston, Jan[uar]y 13th/49

The following joint resolution of the Legislature of South Carolina was directed to be transmitted by the Executive to their Senators and Representatives in Congress—Resolved that the time for discussion by the Slave holding States as to their exclusion from the territory recently acquired from Mexico has passed and that this General Assembly representing the feelings of the people of the State is prepared to cooperate with her sister States in resisting the application of the principles of the Wilmot proviso to such territory at any and every hazzard. Whitemarsh B. Seabrook.

Telegraphic transcript in ScCleA. NOTE: This telegram was sent via the "Washington Office of the Washington and New Orleans Telegraph Line" to Petersburg, Va., and mailed from there to Washington, D.C. It is the earliest document transmitted in this form found among Calhoun's extant papers.

From L[AURENCE] M. KEITT

Orangeburgh C[ourt] H[ouse, S.C.]
14th Jan. 1849

My Dear Sir, You will excuse this ["tress" *canceled*] trespass for the object contemplated, and the ends intended to be subserved. Preliminary to the last session of our Legislature a large Public meeting was convened at our Court House, to take into consideration the agitation of the question of Slavery by the North, and to ["devise" *canceled and* "enquire" *interlined*] what, if any, checks could be devised, to protect ourselves against the incendiary machinations of Northern fanatics. The meeting was unanimous and enthusiastic in the adoption of a set of resolutions, expressing a fixed and unswerving determination to resist aggression and maintain our equality at every cost and hazard. These resolutions were merely initiative. They contemplated, and so I stated to the Legislature, in the event of the alleged contingency, prompt ulterior measures. I avowed emphatically that they were preparatory to Secession, should that alternative be forced ["up" *canceled*] upon us. We would not stray from our path to seek ["to seek" *canceled*] it but much preferred it to a surrender ["of" *canceled*] of our rights and a compromise of our equality and our honor. Under any other view the Resolutions were infantile and meaningless. My District has come up to the mark, and intends to stand there. I am satisfied that the whole State is up to the mark. 'Tis the Politicians among us who are timid and hysterical. I have met ["fe" *canceled*] but few, who ["do" *interlined*] not admit to the full, the nescessity of prompt and definite action on the part of the State. They patter about taking a high course through apprehension that the People *may* not sustain them. Their constituents are in the advance. Be that as it may, however—popular opinion must be ripened and strengthened, if it is unsteady, and indeterminate. One State can make the issue with the General Government, and a wavelet can eddy the waters throughout the State. My District is mailed and sworded, and means to continue her opposition with her flag above her, and her beaver up. In our judgement one State must make the issue. The very character & nescessities of an agricultural people forbid, or at least greatly encumber, concert in preliminary measures. The weaker members of no confederacy have ever combined in advance against the stronger. The Battleflag rallies, and the battlefield wedges them together. 'Tis immaterial what State runs up the flag, for we are embarked in the same vessel, and must prosper or sink together. Our State ought ["to" *interlined*] have spoken "trumpet-tongued" for fortunately she is more united than any other. Yet it is not too late, and efficient measures should be speedily adopted to assign her a definite position. We are looking anxiously for your report, and hope it will propound to us some determinate and specific action. If in a general report however, you judge it impolitic to propose anything specific, ["wh" *canceled*] we will be ready to demonstrate our support of your suggestion if you think it advisable ["in any" *canceled*] to take any ground or carry out any specific measures in support ["of" *canceled*] and establishment of the general propositions contained in such report. With great Respect Your Ob[e]d[ien]t Ser[van]t, L.M. Keitt.

P.S. Would it not be wise or expedient to have an expression of opinion in primary assemblies consequent upon your report. L.M.K.

ALS in ScCleA. Note: An AEU by Calhoun reads, "Keitt."

To G[eorge] W. Barton, [Philadelphia]

[Washington, *ca.* January 15, 1849]

My dear Sir, I hasten in reply to your letter just received [*not found*] to say, that I am of the opinion, that it would be the most advisable for the suggestion to your Senator or Mr. [Stephen A.] Douglas ["should" *canceled and* "to" *interlined*] come from you instead of me.

I am much gratified to learn from your letter as well as from mine from Mr. [Thomas G.] Clemson's that Mrs. [Elizabeth Clemson] Barton's health has so much improved. Yours truly, J.C. Calhoun.

ALS in ScU-SC, John C. Calhoun Papers. Note: Barton's letter to which this was a reply probably concerned an effort to upgrade the Belgian diplomatic post of his brother-in-law Thomas G. Clemson. An approximate date has been provided for this undated document.

Memorial of Lt. Isaac S. Keith Reeves, presented by Calhoun to the Senate on 1/15. He petitions that the pay and emoluments of officers serving as adjutants at the Military Academy be made equal to those of adjutants of regiments. The petition was referred to the Committee on Military Affairs. ADU in DNA, RG 46 (U.S. Senate), 30A-H9.

Remarks at a Meeting of the Southern Caucus

[Senate Chamber, January 15, 1849]

[*More than eighty Southern members from both houses gathered. The address which had been prepared by Calhoun "with Mr. [Thomas H.] Bayly's assistance" was submitted by the Committee of Fifteen and read by Abraham W. Venable, Representative from N.C. Much discussion and parliamentary maneuvering followed, during which Whig members attempted to kill the address. Charles S. Morehead,*

Representative from Kentucky, stated that the address hinted at breakup of the Union.]

Mr. Calhoun rose, afterwards, and said that he was for the Union, but if that could not be preserved he was for taking care of the South. If the gentleman from Kentucky (Mr. Morehead) should insist on a vote on his [substitute] resolutions, he would offer an amendment to them, declaring "that disunion was preferable to emancipation in the States."

[*Robert Toombs, Whig Representative from Ga., argued strongly against the address, asserting that Congressional legislation was necessary to authorize slavery in the new territories. In reply:*]

Mr. Calhoun went into a short argument, to show that the South could take their slaves into California and New Mexico, and that Congress was bound, by the usual acts of legislation, to protect this property and to put it on the same footing with other property. It required no law of Congress to authorize slavery there. Mr. Calhoun was calm and dispassionate, and in his earnest appeals to the South for unanimity, he is represented as using language replete with eloquence and pathos.

[*At the end of the meeting, which went past midnight, by a close vote the draft address was recommitted to a reconstituted Committee of Fifteen to report on 1/18.*]

From the Alexandria, Va., *Gazette and Virginia Advertiser*, January 22, 1849, p. 2 (reprinting from the Baltimore, Md., *Patriot*) and the Columbia, S.C., *South-Carolinian*, January 24, 1849, p. 2. Variants in the Baltimore, Md., *Sun*, January 17, 1849, p. 4; the New York, N.Y., *Herald*, January 17, 1849, p. 2; the Pendleton, S.C., *Messenger*, January 26, 1849, p. 2; the Boston, Mass., *Daily Advertiser*, January 19, 1849, p. 2; the Petersburg, Va., *Republican*, January 19, 1849, p. 2. NOTE: The meeting was closed to reporters, and the reports of Calhoun's remarks, which have been above combined from two sources, must be taken as second-hand. Five of the opposed members of the Committee of Fifteen asked to be excused and were replaced by more sympathetic members. The Address was recommitted to the new Committee of Fifteen for revisions which Calhoun expressed a willingness to accept. (See below Calhoun's letter to Venable of 2/2/1849.)

To "Prof[esso]r" [MATTHEW J.] WILLIAMS

Washington, 15th Jan[uar]y 1849

Dear Sir, The enclosed [*not found*] is the answer of the Secretary of War [William L. Marcy] to my application in your favour.

It is due to him to say, that he expressed a desire to meet your wishes, and that he was only prevented from the belief, that there was a legal impediment in the way. It will not exist at the next selection, when I hope your wishes will be met. With great respect I am & &, J.C. Calhoun.

ALS in ScU-SC, John C. Calhoun Papers.

To A[NDREW] P[ICKENS] CALHOUN, [Marengo County, Ala.]

Senate Chamber, 17th Jan[uar]y 1849

My dear Andrew, I received your last letter by the mail of yesterday; and I ["hope" *interlined*] you will not think of leaving home, until all danger from the c[h]olera is passed. As important as it is to meet our engagements, it is still more so ["to attend to the health of your family & the place" *interlined*]. I hope, however, that the danger will pass in time for you to come on before the termination of the session.

I wrote you pretty fully a few days since & have nothing additional to add. I am happy to hear that you all continue in health. Love to all. Your affectionate father, J.C. Calhoun.

ALS in NcD, John C. Calhoun Papers.

To J[AMES] ED[WARD] CALHOUN, Jun[io]r, [Columbia, S.C.]

Washington, 17th Jan[uar]y 1849

My dear James, I am so much engaged at this time, and am so much behind with my correspondence, that I have very little more time at my command, than to acknowledge the receipt of your letter, written after your return from your visit to Mr. [Thomas G.] Clemson['}s.

You must give up all idea of going to Calafornia. The mines may be rich, ["and" *canceled*] but more will be ruined by them, than will make fortunes. Nothing is more uncertain than gold mining; but if you should be ever so successful, the enormous prices of every thing there will take away the greater part of your profit. Besides, the danger of violence, sickness & loss of life is great; to say nothing of the great expense and the fatigue & difficulty of going there. It would suit persons of hardy constitution, and of desperate circumstances to go there, but not any one, who has a reasonable prospect of doing ["reasonable" *canceled*] well here. I trust, you will give up all idea of going, & stick to your studies, which will be of vastly more advantage to you in the end, than you could get ever by going to Calafornia.

The Committee of one from each State reported to the adjourned meeting of the Southern members an Address to the people of the South. I prepared the Address. It gave rise to much discussion, which continued to a late hour. The meeting adjourned to meet on Monday next, when it is probable the address will be adopted by a pretty decided Majority. The Whigs with some exceptions are opposed to any action. They rely on General [Zachary] Taylor, as they say, but their real object is to keep the two wings of their party, North & South, together.

Say to William [Lowndes Calhoun] I have got his letter & will answer it shortly. I hope he is getting along well. My love to him & kind regards to James Rion. Your affectionate father, J.C. Calhoun.

ALS in NcD, John C. Calhoun Papers.

From H[ENRY] L. HEISKELL

Surgeon General's Office, January 17, 1849

Sir: Your letter of the 15th Instant [*not found*] to the Secretary of the Navy [John Y. Mason], covering a letter of recommendation in behalf of Doctor Milner Boggs, who is desirous of an appointment in the Medical Department of the Army, has been referred to this Office.

In reply to your request to be enabled to answer the communication, I have the honor herewith to enclose a printed Circular for the information of persons desirous of entering the Medical Department of the Army; and beg leave to state that Doctor Boggs will be invited to present himself before the first Medical Board that shall be convened for the examination of Applicants for appointment. With great respect I am, your ob[edient] S[ervan]t. By Order, H.L. Heiskell, Surgeon, U.S.A.

FC in DNA, RG 112 (Surgeon General), Letters and Endorsements Sent, 1818–1889, 19:364.

From Jos[eph] Saul

New Orleans, 18th Jan[uar]y 1849

Dear Sir, I was much disappointed by not having had the pleasure of seeing you, on your visit to New Orleans in 1847. It wo'd have afforded me great satisfaction to have extended to you, the humble hospitality of "Saulsbury"—but I was not apprised of you[r] visit, until after your departure from the City, or I should have paid my respects to you.

We shall very soon commence a new Administration. Gen. [Zachary] Taylor has been elected by the vote of the Whigs, assisted however by votes from the opposite party, under the impression, that he will not be bias'd by the ultra views of either. I most sincerely hope ["it" *interlined*] may be the case. I warmly supported his election upon that ground; but to place you in possession of my views, & the principles which actuated me, I send you an article which I had publish'd in one of our City papers, "the Argus," during the canvass for the Presidency. The Editor omitted a portion of my manuscript, which I have subjoin[e]d; I have every confidence that Gen. Taylor will faithfully act up to his professions. That his Cabinet will be composed of Men of the highest standing & talents in the Country, & that no decidedly ultra partizan will compose any part of it—"mais nous verrons." I am however fearful, that under the new order of things an attempt will be made to rivive the "Bank of the Un. States. I infer so from signs which I have noticed, particularly from the Hon[ora]ble J[ohn] P. Kennedy[']s [former Representative from Md.] Maryland Speech, during the Presidential canvass. From my intimacy with that Gentleman, I have communicated to him, my entire views on that subject—how far my opinion may have weight with him, I cannot say, for it is too often the case "That the enthusiast in Politicks, is like the fanatick in Religion—to argue with either has seldom any other effect, than to rouse into further action, those prejudices which stifle both reason, & reflection—I will however do Mr. Kennedy the justice to say, that in all my frequent interchange of opinions with him, I have ever found him (altho very energetick in his views) quite liberal, & at all times disposed to respect, & weigh dispas[s]ionately the opinions of others.

A part of the grounds which I have taken ["with Mr. K(ennedy)" *interlined*] I will recapitulate to you—viz. "I am not disposed at this time to enter into a disquisition as to the Constitutionality of a Bank charter, eminating from the Federal Government; But its connection with the Government Deposites, I have no difficulty in making up my mind," that it is decidedly unconstitutional for the Government to place its funds at the disposal of a company of Stockholders, to be loaned out by Discount or otherwise &c. I have not the Constitution of the United States at hand, to refer to, but I well remember, "that one Section of it, positively prohibits any monies being drawn from the Treasury "otherwise than for appropriations by Law." Now if the funds of the Government are placed at the disposal of money dealers, who lend it out by discounts or otherwise, Is it not virtually drawn from the Treasury? The shadow may remain upon the Books of the Bank, to the credit of the Treasurer; but the substance may be found wanting, (which has heretofore been the case) when the Government may most require its means. But we will suppose, that a charter of a Bank by the Gen[era]l Government to be constitutional, is the connection of the Govt. with it, or the privileges granted in the charter, expedient—I answer No! It produces the very baneful effect, which it is contended the Bank is calculated, and intended to check, viz. "overtrading—The Notes being received by Law in payments to the Government, gives to them an unlimited circulation—thereby not only encouraging, but materially aiding the credit system upon a ficti[ti]ous capital. It may be said that the issues of a Bank, are limited according to its capital; of what is the capital of a Bank composed? Why principally upon the credit of its issues. For instance, charters generally state, That as soon as a certain amount of the Stock is subscribed, the Bank may go into operation. The payment of the first instalment on that portion Subscribed, may possibly be paid in specie; but all future payments on Stock, will be paid by Bank accom[m]odation granted upon means raised by their paper circulation, and deposites—making the alledged capital a mere moonshine, nearly altogether ficti[ti]ous. This is a true picture, no fancy sketch. Then why should the Government place its funds as a guarantee for the ability of the Bank to meet its engagements, when they can have no direct Controul, or security against a mal Administration of its affairs.

But it is contended that a charter may be safely granted with certain restrictions and limitations, & by making the entire stock pay[a]ble in specie. That wo[ul]d all sound well in theory, but to those who have studied the subject, & examined it in all its bearings, or who like myself has had a long practical knowledge of the operations of a Bank—must be convinced of the impossibility of framing a charter, that it cannot; nay, I will say more "will not be evaded.

It is not the charter, but the administration of it, that produces the good, or evil; but even with an honest Administration, & the Bank

Stock all paid in specie—still it is not that capital alone ["upon" *interlined*] which Banks trade. The object of Stockholders is to make the Bank profitable, but if they were restricted to trade alone upon ["their" *changed to* "the"] capital paid in—(Their loans & Discounts being restricted by the charter to 6 p[er]/[centu]m[?] per ann[um]) their Dividends wo[ul]d of course be minus of 6 p[er]/[centu]m[?] by all the expences, & casualties of the Institution. It is therefore evident, that Stockholders contemplate, & depend upon the credit system to make a Bank profitable, the Specie Capital is soon diminish'd by an extended circulation, & loans, far beyond a prudent, or safe amount. A Bank charter limits the responsibility of the Stockholders to the amount of Stock held by them, which clearly indicates, that a risk is created by the credit operations of the Bank. Then I again ask, why should the Government mingle, or jeopardise its funds with Individual operators, & whose responsibility is limited by Law?

Those who advocate the renewal of the Bank Un. States, ought also to bear in mind that Bank Directors are not now as formerly, chosen from that class of high minded Men whose long standing, & propriety of conduct gave a tone to society, and a guarantee for a faithful discharge of the trust reposed in them. Such men have long since been superseded by reckless Traders, fortunate Speculators, stock jobbers, money Brokers &c., & such is now, & has for Years back, been the universal spirit of speculation prevalent in all classes of society, that these Men for Years to come, will be the principal operators, & managers of monied Institutions. I am satisfied "that if a Bank Un. S. is again charter[e]d, with whatever restrictions, it will not be long out of the hands or control, *at least*, of an objectional class. I am therefore most clearly of opinion, "That even admitting that a Bank Un. S. is constitutional, that under present circumstances the re-establishment of it, wo[ul]d not only be objectional, but decidedly improper, inexpedient, and injurious to the Country. It is highly essential to the future prosperity of the United States, that Bank Un. S. is again charter[e]d, with whatever restrictions, it will wo[ul]d go far to check the baneful effects of ["an" *interlined*] unboundless credit system, & I know of, but one effectual mode of doing it—which is for the Government to collect the Revenue in specie, to be deposited in the Treasury—any Commercial man must be as blind "as those who will not see" not to ["have" *interlined*] perceived, that the Collection of the Revenue has already (particularly in Commercial Citys) had a salutary effect. The Notes issued for the Government according to my plan, will at all times be payable in Specie, therefore merchants, and others will be enabled to draw the Specie with the Notes for commercial, or other necessary purposes; It will stop the cry of the Government locking up the Specie, which is as rediculous, as the cant of the "Sword & purse," or "Log Cabin & hard Cider." When the Government gives into the hands of a Bank its funds, it not only puts them at risk, but parts with the only means of restricting the Circulation of all Banks within their proper limits."

I am aware Sir you & I differ in our opinion ["as" *interlined*] to the policy of the Government issuing Notes to serve as a circulating medium. I may be mistaken as to the necessity, or expediency of it; but my conviction of its utility is based upon many Years observation and reflection on the subject. I commenced Banking in 1795 & continued as Cashier, or Director of Banks until 1836. However ["whatever" *interlined*] system may ultimately be adopted, I sincerely hope, that it may be divested of all party consideration, & carried into effect with such unanimity by the patriotism, & virtue of the Representatives of the nation, as to disarm future opposition on party grounds.

I feel more than common solicitude on this important subject, which must plead my excuse for intruding upon your valuable time. But I with many others look with solicitude to your efforts on this, & the Slave question—those judiciously & justly settled, and there is no calculating the future prosperity, & grandure of ["the" *interlined*] Nation. I am Sir, with sentiments of the highest consideration Y[ou]r Ob[edient] S[ervan]t, Jos. Saul.

ALS with En in ScCleA. NOTE: The enclosed newspaper clipping deprecates the evil effects of party influence in American politics, especially in regard to appointments to office and abolition, and praises Zachary Taylor as an honest man who professes independence from party control or manipulation.

From A[LEXANDER] BOWIE

Fife, Tal[ladeg]a [County, Ala.,] 19 Jan[uar]y 1848 [*sic*; 1849]

My dear Sir, I was much gratified to learn, through Mr. [Franklin W.] Bowdon [Representative from Ala.] a few weeks since, that he left you at your post, enjoying excellent health, and evincing all the vigor of your earlier days. If the anxious wishes of your numerous friends (of whom I claim to be one of the earliest, warmest & most constant) could perpetuate this condition of health, vigor & usefulness, you would never be otherwise. I have been long desirous of possessing your opinions & veiws on some matters of political interest, ["and" *canceled*] which I cannot well obtain otherwise than by a free conversation; and therefore, I am more than ever anxious to see you at my house. I have your promise to come this way on your next visit to Alabama, unless you should travel under circumstances which will compel you to take another route. As next summer will be your long vacation, I have great hopes of seeing you then.

We are looking with intense interest upon the proceedings of your present session. What will be the end of the agitation of the Slave question? Till now, I have never dreaded it much; because I beleived that we had the power & the will to arrest it whenever it became absolutely necessary to act. *Now*, I greatly fear I have miscalculated the energy & spirit of our people upon this subject. If the question should, at this moment, be made, between submission to the claims of the abolitionists and the ["continuance" *canceled and* "dissolution" *interlined*] of the Union, I am by no means sure that our people would not give up their unquestionable rights, to preserve a union which would then become a curse instead of a blessing. At all events, I am confident there would be much division amongst us, even upon that question. You & I know, whatever others may beleive, that the Nullifiers of '32 were the truest friends of the Union, although regarded by many, as its worst enemies—because we sought to perpetuate the Union by preserving the Constitution. I have long beleived that if the Slave States would, unitedly & firmly, take the position that they must be *let alone* on this subject, or they would secede in a body, all agitation, at least all worth regarding, would instantly cease. I beleive so, because I know that our friends in the free States are too much alive to their own interests, and too acute in perceiving where they lie, to be willing to surrender the advantages they derive from a union with us, for any advantage they could reasonably hope to obtain from continuing the agitation. I should like to have your veiws upon the probable result of this question, and particularly your opinion as to what will be the proper course for us to pursue, if the question shall be pushed to extremes. I can see no remedy but secession. I see by the 'papers that you have written the report to be made to the meeting of the Southern members on this question, and ask the favor of you, if it is printed in pamphlet, to send me a copy. Please also send me (or ask [former] Gov. [Benjamin] Fitzpatrick to send me) a copy of Mr. [Robert J.] Walker's report on the ware-housing system.

Shall we have a renewal of Whig measures with the incoming Whig administration? If so, you will have to fight over again your old battles; and the Democratic party will once more learn to speak laudingly of you because they will have use for you. Whilst I always feel proud of your position of independence, I often feel depressed on account of its difficulties. To be a politician & an honest man at the same time, is now the most difficult character in the world to maintain. I ought not, however, to rank you as a politician—your aim is to be a statesman, & it is the only virtuous aim. I should like, above all things, to talk with you about Mr. [James K.] Polk's administration. With one exception (the Mexican war) it appears to me to have been about the best we have had for a long time. At least, he has come nearer fulfilling the pledges with which he went into office, than has been common of late days.

I did not intend when I sat down, to trouble you with so long a communication. But I find myself, often now, afflicted with the proverbial garrulity of old age, and when I begin to write I hardly know when to quit. I know you will excuse me for making this draft on your patience, while I assure you of the sentiments of sincere regard, with which I am Your old & constant friend, A. Bowie.

ALS in ScCleA; PC in Jameson, ed., *Correspondence*, pp. 1157–1158.

The Address of Southern Delegates in Congress, to Their Constituents

[Adopted January 22, 1849]

We, whose names are hereunto annexed, address you in discharge of what we believe to be a solemn duty, on the most important subject ever presented for your consideration.* We allude to the conflict between the two great sections of the Union, growing out of a difference of feeling and opinion in reference to the relation existing between the two races, the European and African, which inhabit the Southern section, and the acts of aggression and encroachment to which it has led.

The conflict commenced not long after the acknowledgment of our independence, and has gradually increased until it has arrayed the great body of the North against the South on this most vital sub-

* *Editor's note*: The following passage by Calhoun at the end of the first sentence was deleted by the Southern caucus from the official version: "not excepting the declaration which separated you and the other united colonies from the parent country. That involved your independence; but this your all, not excepting your safety."

ject. In the progres[s] of this conflict, aggression has followed aggression, and encroachment encroachment, until they have reached a point when a regard for your peace and safety will not permit us to remain longer silent. The object of this address is to give you a clear, correct, but brief account of the whole series of aggression and encroachments on your rights, with a statement of the dangers to which they expose you. Our object in making it is not to cause excitement, but to put you in full possession of all the facts and circumstances necessary to a full and just conception of a deep-seated disease, which threatens great danger to you and the whole body politic. We act on the impression, that in a popular government like ours, a true conception of the actual character and state of a disease is indispensable to effecting a cure.

We have made it a joint address, because we believe that the magnitude of the subject required that it should assume the most impressive and solemn form.

Not to go further back, the difference of opinion and feeling in reference to the relation between the two races, disclosed itself in the Convention that framed the Constitution, and constituted one of the g[r]eatest difficulties in forming it. After many efforts, it was overcome by a compromise, which provided in the first place, that Representatives and direct taxes shall be apportioned among the States according to their respective numbers; and that, in ascertaining the number of each, five slaves shall be estimated as three. In the next, that slaves escaping into States where slavery does not exist, shall not be discharged from servitude, but shall be delivered up on claim of the party to whom their labor or service is due. In the third place, that Congress shall not prohibit the importation of slaves before the year 1808; but a tax not exceeding ten dollars may be imposed on each imported. And finally, that no capitation or direct tax shall be laid, but in proportion to federal numbers; and that no amendment of the Constitution, prior to 1808, shall effect this provision, nor that relating to the importation of slaves.

So satisfactory were these provisions, that the second, relative to the delivering up of fugitive slaves, was adopted unanimously, and all the rest, except the third, relative to the importation of slaves until 1808, with almost equal unanimity. They recognize the existence of slavery, and make a specific provision for its protection where it was supposed to be the most exposed. They go further, and incorporate it, as an important element, in determining the relative weight of the several States in the Government of the Union, and the respective burden they should bear in laying capitation and direct taxes. It was well understood at the time, that without them the Constitution would not have been adopted by the Southern States, and of course that they constituted elements so essential to the system that it never would have existed without them. The Northern States, knowing all this, ratified the Constitution, thereby pledging their faith, in the most solemn manner, sacredly to observe them. How that faith has been kept and that pledge redeemed we shall next proceed to show.

With few exceptions of no great importance, the South had no cause to complain prior to the year 1819—a year, it is to be feared, destined to mark a train of events, bringing with them many, and great, and fatal disasters, on the country and its institutions. With it commenced the agitating debate on the question of the admission of Missouri into the Union. We shall pass by for the present this question, and others of the same kind, directly growing out of it, and shall proceed to consider the effects of that spirit of discord, which it roused up between the two sections. It first disclosed itself in the North, by hostility to that portion of the Constitution which provides for the delivering up of fugitive slaves. In its progress it led to the adoption of hostile acts, intended to render it of non-effect, and with so much success that it may be regarded now as practically expunged from the Constitution. How this has been effected will be next explained.

After a careful examination, truth constrains us to say, that it has been by a clear and palpable evasion of the Constitution. It is impossible for any provision to be more free from ambiguity or doubt. It is in the following words: "No person held to service, or labor, in one State, under the laws thereof, escaping into another State, shall, in consequence of any law or regulation therein, be discharged from such service or labor, but shall be delivered up on claim of the party to whom such service or labor may be due." All is clear. There is not an uncertain or equivocal word to be found in the whole provision. What shall not be done, and what shall be done, are fully and explicitly set forth. The former provides that the fugitive slave shall not be discharged from his servitude by any law or regulation of the State wherein he is found; and the latter, that he shall be delivered up on claim of his owner.

We do not deem it necessary to undertake to refute the sophistry and subterfuges by which so plain a provision of the Constitution has been evaded, and, in effect, annulled. It constitutes an essential part of the constitutional compact, and of course of the supreme law of the land. As such it is binding on all, the Federal and State Governments, the States and the individuals composing them. The sacred obligation of compact, and the solemn injunction of the supreme law, which legislators and judges, both Federal and State, are bound by oath to support, all unite to enforce its fulfilment, according to its plain meaning and true intent. What that meaning and intent are, there was no diversity of opinion in the better days of the Republic, prior to 1819. Congress, State Legislatures, State and Federal Judges and Magistrates, and people, all spontaneously placed the same interpretation on it. During that period none interposed impediments in the way of the owner seeking to recover his fugitive slave; nor did any deny his right to have every proper facility to enforce his claim to have him delivered up. It was then nearly as easy to recover one found in a Northern State, as one found in a neighboring Southern State. But this has passed away, and the provision is defunct, except perhaps in two States. [*Footnote*: Indiana and Illinois.]

When we take into consideration the importance and clearness of this provision, the evasion by which it has been set aside may fairly be regarded as one of the most fatal blows ever received by the South and the Union. This cannot be more concisely and correctly stated, than it has been by two of the learned judges of the Supreme Court of the United States. In one of his decisions [*Footnote*: The case of Prigg *vs.* the Commonwealth of Pennsylvania.] Judge [Joseph] Story said: "Historically it is well known that the object of this clause was to secure to the citizens of the slaveholding States the complete right and title of ownership in their slaves, as property, in every State of the Union, into which they might escape, from the State wherein they were held in servitude." "The full recognition of this right and title was indispensable to the security of this species of property, in all the slaveholding States, and, indeed, was so vital to the preservation of their interests and institutions, that it cannot be doubted, that it constituted a fundamental article without the adoption of which the Union would not have been formed. Its true design was to guard against the doctrines and principles prevalent in the non-slaveholding States, by preventing them from intermeddling with, or restricting, or abolishing the rights of the owners of slaves."

Again. "The clause was therefore of the last importance to the safety and security of the Southern States, and could not be surrendered by them without endangering their whole property in slaves. The clause was accordingly adopted in the Constitution by the unanimous consent of the framers of it—a proof at once of its intrinsic and practical necessity."

Again. "The clause manifestly contemplates the existence of a positive unqualified right on the part of the owner of the slave, which no State law or regulation can in any way regulate, control, qualify, or restrain."

The opinion of the other learned judges was not less emphatic as to the importance of this provision and the unquestionable right of the South under it. Judge [Henry] Baldwin, in charging the jury, said: [*Footnote*: The case of Johnson *vs.* Tompkins and others.] "If there are any rights of property which can be enforced, if one citizen have any rights of property which are inviolable under the protection of the supreme law of the State, and the Union, they are those which have been set at nought by some of these defendants. As the owner of property, which he had a perfect right to possess, protect, and take away—as a citizen of a sister State, entitled to all the privileges and immunities of citizens of any other States—Mr. Johnson stands before you on ground which cannot be taken from under him—it is the same ground on which the Government itself is based. If the defendants can be justified, we have no longer law or government." Again, after referring more particularly to the provision for delivering up fugitive slaves, he said: "Thus you see, that the foundations of the government are laid, and rest on the right of property in slaves. The whole structure must fall by disturbing the corner-stone."

These are grave and solemn and admonitory words, from a high source. They confirm all for which the South has ever contended, as to the clearness, importance, and fundamental character of this provision, and the disastrous consequences which would inevitably follow from its violation. But in spite of these solemn warnings, the violation then commenced, and which they were intended to rebuke, has been full and perfectly consummated. The citizens of the South, in their attempt to recover their slaves, now meet, instead of aid and co-operation, resistance in every form; resistance from hostile acts of legislation, intended to baffle and defeat their claims by all sorts of devices, and by interposing every description of impediment—resistance from judges and magistrates—and finally, when all these fail, from mobs, composed of whites and blacks, which, by threats or force, rescue the fugitive slave from the possession of his rightful owner. The attempt to recover a slave, in most of the Northern States, cannot now be made without the hazard of insult, heavy pecuniary loss, imprisonment, and even of life itself. Already has a worthy citizen of Maryland lost his life [*Footnote*: Mr. (James H.) Kennedy, of Hagerstown, Maryland] in making an attempt to enforce his claim to a fugitive slave under this provision.

But a provision of the Constitution may be violated indirectly as well as directly; by doing an act in its nature inconsistent with that which is enjoined to be done. Of this form of violation, there is a striking instance connected with the provision under consideration. We allude to secret combinations which are believed to exist in many of the Northern States, whose object is to entice, decoy, entrap, inveigle, and seduce slaves to escape from their owners, and to pass them secretly and rapidly, by means organized for the purpose, into Canada, where they will be beyond the reach of the provision. That to entice a slave, by whatever artifice, to abscond from his owner, into a non-slaveholding State, with the intention to place him beyond the reach of the provision, or prevent his recovery, by concealment or otherwise, is as completely repugnant to it, as its open violation would be, is too clear to admit of doubt or to require illustration. And yet, as repugnant as these combinations are to the true intent of the provision, it is believed, that, with the above exception, not one of the States, within whose limits they exist, has adopted any measure to suppress them, or to punish those by whose agency the object for which they were formed is carried into execution. On the contrary, they have looked on, and witnessed with indifference, if not with secret approbation, a great number of slaves enticed from their owners, and placed beyond the possibility of recovery, to the great annoyance and heavy pecuniary loss of the bordering Southern States.

When we take into consideration the great importance of this provision, the absence of all uncertainty as to its true meaning and intent, the many guards by which it is surrounded to protect and enforce it, and then reflect how completely the object for which it was inserted in the Constitution is defeated by these two-fold infractions, we doubt, taking all together, whether a more flagrant breach of faith is to be found on record. We know the language we have used is strong, but it is not less true than strong.

There remains to be noticed another class of aggressive acts of a kindred character, but which instead of striking at an express and specific provision of the Constitution, aims directly at destroying the relation between the two races at the South, by means subversive in their tendency of one of the ends for which the Constitution was established. We refer to the systematic agitation of the question by the Abolitionists, which, commencing about 1835, is still continued in all possible forms. Their avowed intention is to bring about a state of things that will force emancipation on the South. To unite the North in fixed hostility to slavery in the South, and to excite discontent among the slaves with their condition, are among the means employed to effect it. With a view to bring about the former, every means are resorted to in order to render the South, and the relation between the two races there, odious and hateful to the North. For this purpose societies and newspapers are everywhere established, debating clubs opened, lecturers employed, pamphlets and other publications, pictures and petitions to Congress, resorted to, and directed to that single point, regardless of truth or decency; while the circulation of incendiary publications in the South, the agitation of the subject of abolition in Congress, and the employment of emissaries are relied on to excite discontent among the slaves. This agitation, and the use of these means, have been continued with more or less activity for a series of years, not without doing much towards effecting the object intended. We regard both object and means to be aggressive and dangerous to the rights of the South, and subversive, as stated, of one of the ends for which the Constitution was established. Slavery is a domestic institution. It belongs to the States, each for itself to decide, whether it shall be established or not; and if it be established, whether it should be abolished or not. Such being the clear and unquestionable right of the States, it follows necessarily that it would be a flagrant act of aggression on a State, destructive of its rights, and subversive of its independence, for the Federal Government, or one or more States, or their people, to undertake to force on it the emancipation of its slaves. But it is a sound maxim in politics, as well as law and morals, that no one has a right to do that indirectly which he cannot do directly, and it may be added with equal truth, to aid, or abet, or countenance another in doing it. And yet the Abolitionists of the North, openly avowing their intention, and resorting to the most efficient means for the purpose, have been attempting to bring about a state of things to force the Southern States to emancipate their slaves, without any act on the part of any Northern State to arrest or suppress the means by which they propose to accomplish it. They have been permitted to pursue their object and to use whatever means they please, if without aid or countenance, also without resistance or disapprobation. What gives a deeper shade to the whole affair, is the fact, that one of the means to effect their object, that of exciting discontent among our slaves, tends directly to subvert what its preamble declares to be one of the ends for which the Constitution was ordained and established: "to insure domestic tranquility," and that in the only way in which domestic tranquility is likely ever to be disturbed in the South. Certain it is, that an agitation so systematic—having such an object in view, and sought to be carried into execution by such means—would, between independent nations, constitute just cause of remonstrance by the party against which the aggression was directed, and, if not heeded, an appeal to arms for redress. Such being the case where an aggression of the kind takes place among independent nations, how much more aggravated must it be between confederated States, where the Union precludes an appeal to arms, while it affords a medium through which it can operate with vastly increased force and effect? That it would be perverted to such a use, never entered into the imagination of the generation which formed and adopted the Constitution, and, if it had been supposed it would, it is certain that the South never would have adopted it.

We now return to the question of the admission of Missouri into the Union, and shall proceed to give a brief sketch of the occurrences connected with it, and the consequences to which it has directly led. In the latter part of 1819, the then territory of Missouri applied to Congress, in the usual form, for leave to form a State Constitution and Government, in order to be admitted into the Union. A bill was reported for the purpose, with the usual provisions in such cases. Amendments were offered, having for their object to make it a condition of her admission, that her Constitution should have a provision to prohibit slavery. This brought on the agitating debate, which, with the effects that followed, has done so much to alienate the South and North, and endanger our political institutions. Those who objected to the amendments, rested their opposition on the high grounds of the right of self-government. They claimed that a territory, having reached the period when it is proper for it to form a Constitution and Government for itself, becomes fully vested with all the rights of self-government; and that even the condition imposed on it by the Federal Constitution, relates not to the formation of its Constitution and Government, but its admission into the Union. For that purpose, it provides as a condition, that the Government must be Republican.

They claimed that Congress has no right to add to this condition, and that to assume it would be tantamount to the assumption of the right to make its entire Constitution and Government; as no limitation could be imposed, as to the extent of the right, if it be admitted that it exists at all. Those who supported the amendment denied these grounds, and claimed the right of Congress to impose, at discretion, what conditions it pleased. In this agitating debate, the two sections stood arrayed against each other; the South in favor of the bill without amendment, and the North opposed to it without it. The debate and agitation continued until the session was well advanced; but it became apparent, towards its close, that the people of Missouri were fixed and resolved in their opposition to the proposed condition, and that they would certainly reject it, and adopt a Constitution without it, should the bill pass with the condition. Such being the case, it required no great effort of mind to perceive, that Missouri, once in possession of a Constitution and Government, not simply on paper, but with legislators elected, and officers appointed, to carry them into effect, the grave questions would be presented, whether she was of right a Territory or State; and, if the latter, whether Congress had the right, and, if the right, the power, to abrogate her Constitution, disperse her Legislature, and to remand her back to the territorial condition. These were great, and, under the circumstances, fearful questions—too fearful to be met by those who had raised the agitation. From that time the only question was, how to escape from the difficulty. Fortunately, a means was afforded. A Compromise (as it was called) was offered, based on the terms, that the North should cease to oppose the admission of Missouri on the grounds for which the South contended, and that the provisions of the Ordinance of 1787, for the government of the Northwestern Territory, should be applied to all the territory acquired by the United States from France under the treaty of Louisiana lying North of 36 30, except the portion lying in the State of Missouri. The Northern members embraced it; and, although not originating with them, adopted it as their own. It was forced through Congress by the almost united votes of the North, against a minority consisting almost entirely of members from the Southern States.

Such was the termination of this, the first conflict, under the Constitution, between the two sections, in reference to slavery in connection with the territories. Many hailed it as a permanent and final adjustment that would prevent the recurrence of similar conflicts; but others, less sanguine, took the opposite and more gloomy view, regarding it as the precursor of a train of events which might rend the Union asunder, and prostrate our political system. One of these was the experienced and sagacious [Thomas] Jefferson. Thus far, time would seem to favor his forebodings. May a returning sense of justice, and a protecting Providence, avert their final fulfilment.

For many years the subject of slavery in reference to the territories ceased to agitate the country. Indications, however, connected with the question of annexing Texas, showed clearly that it was ready to break out again, with redoubled violence, on some future occasion. The difference in the case of Texas was adjusted by extending the Missouri compromise line of 36 30, from its terminus, on the western boundary of the Louisiana purchase, to the western boundary of Texas. The agitation again ceased for a short period.

The war with Mexico soon followed, and that terminated in the acquisition of New Mexico and Upper California, embracing an area equal to about one-half of the entire valley of the Mississippi. If to this we add the portion of Oregon acknowledged to be ours by the recent treaty with England, our whole territory on the Pacific and west of the Rocky mountains will be found to be in extent but little less than that vast valley. The near prospect of so great an addition rekindled the excitement between the North and South in reference to slavery in its connection with the territories, which has become, since those on the Pacific were acquired, more universal and intense than ever.

The effects have been to widen the difference between the two sections, and to give a more determined and hostile character to their conflict. The North no longer respects the Missouri compromise line, although adopted by their almost unanimous vote. Instead of compromise, they avow that their determination is to exclude slavery from all the territories of the United States, acquired, or to be acquired; and, of course, to prevent the citizens of the Southern States from emigrating with their property in slaves into any of them. Their object, they allege, is to prevent the extension of slavery, and ours to extend it, thus making the issue between them and us to be the naked question, shall slavery be extended or not? We do not deem it necessary, looking to the object of this address, to examine the question so fully discussed at the last session, whether Congress has the right to exclude the citizens of the South from immigrating with their property into territories belonging to the confederated States of the Union. What we propose in this connection is, to make a few remarks on what the North alleges, erroneously, to be the issue between us and them.

So far from maintaining the doctrine, which the issue implies, we hold that the Federal Government has no right to extend or restrict slavery, no more than to establish or abolish it; nor has it any right whatever to distinguish between the domestic institutions of one State, or section, and another, in order to favor the one and discourage the other. As the federal representative of each and all the States, it is bound to deal out, within the sphere of its powers, equal and exact justice and favor to all. To act otherwise, to undertake to discriminate between the domestic institutions of one and another, would be to act in total subversion of the end for which it was established—to be the common protector and guardian of all. Entertaining these opinions, we ask not, as the North alleges we do, for the extension of slavery. That would make a discrimination in our favor, as unjust and unconstitutional as the discrimination they ask against us in their favor. It is not for them, nor for the Federal Government to determine, whether our domestic institution is good or bad; or whether it should be repressed or preserved. It belongs to us, and us only, to decide such questions. What then we do insist on, is, not to extend slavery, but that we shall not be prohibited from immigrating, with our property, into the Territories of the United States, because we are slaveholders; or, in other words, that we shall not on that account be disfranchised of a privilege possessed by all others, citizens and foreigners, without discrimination as to character, profession, or color. All, whether savage, barbarian, or civilized, may freely enter and remain, we only being excluded.

We rest our claim, not only on the high grounds above stated, but also on the solid foundation of right, justice, and equality. The territories immediately in controversy—New Mexico and California—were acquired by the common sacrifice and efforts of all the States, towards which the South contributed far more than her full share of men, to say nothing of money, and is, of course, on every principle of right, justice, fairness, and equality, entitled to participate fully in the benefits to be derived from their acquisition. [*Footnote*: Total number of volunteers from the South—Regiments 33, Battalions 14, Companies 120. Total number of volunteers from the South 45,640. Total number of volunteers from the North—Regiments 22, Battalions 2, Companies 12. Total number of volunteers from the North 23,084. Being nearly two on the part of the South to one on the part of the North. But taking into consideration that the population of the North is two-thirds greater than the South, the latter has furnished more than three times her proportion of volunteers.] But as impregnable as is this ground, there is another not less so. Ours is a Federal Government—a Government in which, not individuals, but States, as distinct sovereign communities, are the constituents. To them, as members of the Federal Union, the territories belong; and they are hence declared to be territories belonging to the United States. The States then are the joint owners. Now it is conceded by all writers on the subject, that in all such Governments their members are all equal—equal in rights and equal in dignity. They also concede that this equality constitutes the basis of such

Government, and that it cannot be destroyed without changing their nature and character. To deprive, then, the Southern States and their citizens of their full share in Territories declared to belong to them, in common with the other States, would be in derogation of the equality belonging to them as members of a Federal Union, and sink them, from being equals, into a subordinate and dependant condition. Such are the solid and impregnable grounds on which we rest our demand to an equal participation in the territories.

But as solid and impregnable as they are in the eyes of justice and reason, they oppose a feeble resistance to a majority, determined to engross the whole. At the last session of Congress, a bill was passed, establishing a territorial government for Oregon, excluding slavery therefrom. The President [James K. Polk] gave his sanction to the bill, and sent a special message to Congress assigning his reasons for doing so. These reasons pre-supposed that the Missouri compromise was to be, and would be, extended west of the Rocky Mountains, to the Pacific ocean. And the President intimated his intention in his message to veto any future bill that should restrict slavery south of the line of that compromise. Assuming it to have been the purpose and intention of the North to extend the Missouri compromise line as above indicated, the passage of the Oregon bill could only be regarded as evincing the acquiescence of the South in that line.* But the developments of the present session of Congress have made it manifest to all, that no such purpose or intention, now exists with the North to any considerable extent. Of the truth of this, we have ample evidence in what has occurred already in the House of Representatives, where the popular feelings are soonest and most intensely felt.

Although Congress has been in session but little more than one

* *Editor's note*: The preceding four sentences did not appear in Calhoun's draft, but were substituted apparently in the revisions made after the meeting of 1/15. At the same place, the following passage of Calhoun's draft was deleted: "At the last session, they passed a bill to establish a territorial government for Oregon, containing a provision to exclude slavery, unaccompanied by compromise, or by making any concession or equivalent to the South. It was so passed, professedly to assert the unlimited control of Congress over the subject. It was the first bill of the kind ever passed, and marks an important stage in the progress of aggressions and encroachments in reference to the territorial aspect of the subject. It has given a new and powerful impulse to the abolitionists. Instead of resting satisfied with so great a step in their progress, they are now urging with greater zeal than ever towards the accomplishment of the object they have in view."

month, a greater number of measures of an aggressive character have been introduced and they more aggravated and dangerous, than have been for years before. And what clearly discloses whence they take their origin, is the fact, that they all relate to the territorial aspect of the subject of slavery, or some other of a nature and character intimately connected with it.

The first of this series of aggressions is a resolution introduced by a member from Massachusetts [John G. Palfrey], the object of which is to repeal all acts, or parts of acts which recognise the existence of slavery, or authorize the selling and disposing of slaves in this District [of Columbia]. On question of leave to bring in a bill, the votes stood 69 for and 82 against leave. The next was a resolution offered by a member from Ohio [Joseph M. Root], instructing the Committee on Territories to report forthwith bills for excluding slavery from California and New Mexico. [*Footnote*: since reported to the House.] It passed by a vote of 107 to 80. That was followed by a bill introduced by another member from Ohio [Joshua R. Giddings], to take the votes of the inhabitants of this District, on the question whether slavery within its limits should be abolished.

The bill provided, according to the admission of the mover, that free negroes and slaves should vote. On the question to lay the bill on the table, the votes stood, for 106, against 79. To this succeeded the resolution of a member of New York [Daniel Gott], in the following words: "Whereas the traffic now prosecuted in this metropolis of the Republic in human beings, as chattels, is contrary to natural justice and the fundamental principles of our political system, and is notoriously a reproach to our country, throughout Christendom, and a serious hindrance to the progress of republican liberty among the nations of the earth. Therefore,

"*Resolved*, That the Committee for the District of Columbia be instructed to report a bill, as soon as practicable, prohibiting the slave trade in said District." On the question of adopting the resolution, the votes stood 98 for, and 88 against. He was followed [*sic*; preceded] by a member from Illinois [John Wentworth], who offered a resolution for abolishing slavery in the Territories, and all places where Congress has exclusive powers of legislation, that is, in all forts, magazines, arsenals, dock-yards, and other needful buildings, purchased by Congress with the consent of the Legislature of the State.

This resolution was passed over under the rules of the House without being put to vote.

The votes in favor of all these measures were confined to the members from the Northern States.* True, there are some patriotic members from that section who voted against all of them, and whose high sense of justice is duly appreciated; who in the progress of the aggressions upon the South have, by their votes, sustained the guarantees of the Constitution, and of whom we regret to say many have been sacrificed at home by their patriotic course.

We have now brought to a close a narrative of the series of acts of aggression and encroachment, connected with the subject of this address, including those that are consummated and those still in progress. They are numerous, great, and dangerous, and threaten with destruction the greatest and most vital of all the interests and institutions of the South. Indeed it may [be] doubted whether there is a single provision, stipulation, or guaranty of the Constitution, intended for the security of the South, that has not been rendered almost perfectly nugatory. It may even be made a serious question, whether the encroachments already made, without the aid of any other, would not, if permitted to operate unchecked, end in emancipation, and that at no distant day. But be that as it may, it hardly admits of a doubt that, if the aggressions already commenced in the House, and now in progress, should be consummated, such in the end would certainly be the consequence.

Little, in truth, would be left to be done after we have been excluded from all the Territories, including those to be hereafter acquired; after slavery is abolished in this District and in the numerous places dispersed all over the South, where Congress has the exclusive right of legislation, and after the other measures proposed are consummated. Every outpost and barrier would be carried, and nothing would be left but to finish the work of abolition at pleasure in the States themselves. This District, and all places over which Congress has exclusive power of legislation, would be asylums for fugitive slaves, where, as soon as they placed their feet, they would become, according to the doctrines of our Northern assailants, free; unless there should be some positive enactments to prevent it.

Under such a state of things the probability is, that emancipation would soon follow, without any final act to abolish slavery. The depressing effects of such measures on the white race at the South, and the hope they would create in the black of a speedy emancipation,

* *Editor's note*: A final clause to this sentence in Calhoun's version was deleted before adoption: "and consisted of those of both parties." In the next sentence the passage after the semicolon was apparently added by committee to Calhoun's draft.

would produce a state of feeling inconsistent with the much longer continuance of the existing relations between the two. But be that as it may, it is certain, if emancipation did not follow, as a matter of course, the final act in the States would not be long delayed. The want of constitutional power would oppose a feeble resistance. The great body of the North is united against our peculiar institution. Many believe it to be sinful, and the residue, with inconsiderable exceptions, believe it to be wrong. Such being the case, it would indicate a very superficial knowledge of human nature, to think that, after aiming at abolition, systematically, for so many years, and pursuing it with such unscrupulous disregard of law and Constitution, that the fanatics who have led the way and forced the great body of the North to follow them, would, when the finishing stroke only remained to be given, voluntarily suspend it, or permit any constitutional scruples or considerations of justice to arrest it. To these may be added an aggression, though not yet commenced, long meditated and threatened: to prohibit what the abolitionists call the internal slave trade, meaning thereby the transfer of slaves from one State to another, from whatever motive done, or however effected. Their object would seem to be to render them worthless by crowding them together where they are, and thus hasten the work of emancipation. There is reason for believing that it will soon follow those now in progress, unless, indeed, some decisive step should be taken in the meantime to arrest the whole.

The question then is, Will the measures of aggression proposed in the House be adopted?

They may not, and probably will not be this session. But when we take into consideration, that there is a majority now in favor of one of them, and a strong minority in favor of the other, as far as the sense of the House has been taken; that there will be in all probability a considerable increase in the next Congress of the vote in favor of them, and that it will be largely increased in the next, succeeding Congress under the census to be taken next year, it amounts almost to a certainty, that they will be adopted, unless some decisive measure is taken in advance to prevent it.

But, if even these conclusions should prove erroneous—if fanaticism and the love of power should, contrary to their nature, for once respect constitutional barriers, or if the calculations of policy should retard the adoption of these measures, or even defeat them altogether, there would be still left one certain way to accomplish their object, if the determination avowed by the North to monopolize all the territories, to the exclusion of the South, should be carried into effect. That of itself would, at no distant day, add to the North a sufficient number of States to give her three-fourths of the whole; when, under the color of an amendment of the Constitution, she would emancipate our slaves, however opposed it might be to its true intent.

Thus, under every aspect, the result is certain, if aggression be not promptly and decidedly met. How it is to be met, it is for you to decide.

Such then being the case, it would be to insult you to suppose you could hesitate. To destroy the existing relation between the free and servile races at the South would lead to consequences unpar-all[el]ed in history. They cannot be separated, and cannot live together in peace, or harmony, or to their mutual advantage, except in their present relation. Under any other, wretchedness, and misery, and desolation would overspread the whole South. The example of the British West Indies, as blighting as emancipation has proved to them, furnishes a very faint picture of the calamities it would bring on the South. The circumstances under which it would take place with us, would be entirely different from those which took place with them, and calculated to lead to far more disastrous results. There the Government of the parent country emancipated slaves in her colonial possessions—a Government rich and powerful, and actuated by views of policy, (mistaken as they turned out to be,) rather than fanaticism. It was besides, disposed to act justly towards the owners, even in the act of emancipating their slaves, and to protect and foster them afterwards. It accordingly appropriated nearly $100,000,000 as a compensation to them for their losses under the act, which sum, although it turned out to be far short of the amount, was thought at the time to be liberal. Since the emancipation, it has kept up a sufficient military and naval force to keep the blacks in awe, and a number of magistrates, and constables, and other civil officers, to keep order in the towns and on plantations, and enforce respect to their former owners. To a considerable extent, these have served as a substitute for the police formerly kept on the plantations by the owners and their overseers, and to preserve the social and political superiority of the white race. But, notwithstanding all this, the British West India possessions are ruined, impoverished, miserable, wretched, and destined probably to be abandoned to the black race.

Very different would be the circumstances under which emancipation would take place with us. If it ever should be effected, it will be through the agency of the Federal Government, controlled by the dominant power of the Northern States of the Confederacy, against the resistance and struggle of the Southern. It can then only be effected by the prostration of the white race; and that would necessarily engender the bitterest feelings of hostility between them and the North. But the reverse would be the case between the blacks of the South and the people of the North. Owing their emancipation to them, they would regard them as friends, guardians, and patrons, and centre, accordingly, all their sympathy in them. The people of the North would not fail to reciprocate and to favor them, instead of the whites. Under the influence of such feelings, and impelled by fanaticism and love of power, they would not stop at emancipation. Another step would be taken—to raise them to a political and social equality with their former owners, by giving them the right of voting and holding public offices under the Federal Government. We see the first step toward it in the bill already alluded to—to vest the free blacks and slaves with the right to vote on the question of emancipation in this District. But when once raised to an equality, they would become the fast political associates of the North, acting and voting with them on all questions, and by this political union between them, holding the white race at the South in complete subjection. The blacks, and the profligate whites that might unite with them, would become the principal recipients of federal offices and patronage, and would, in consequence, be raised above the whites of the South in the political and social scale. We would, in a word, change conditions with them—a degradation greater than has ever yet fallen to the lot of a free and enlightened people, and one from which we could not escape, should emancipation take place, (which it certainly will if not prevented,) but by fleeing the homes of ourselves and ancestors, and by abandoning our country to our former slaves, to become the permanent abode of disorder, anarchy, poverty, misery, and wretchedness.

With such a prospect before us, the gravest and most solemn question that ever claimed the attention of a people is presented for your consideration: What is to be done to prevent it? It is a question belonging to you to decide. All we propose is, to give you our opinion.

We, then, are of the opinion that the first and indispensable step, without which nothing can be done, and with which everything may be, is to be united among yourselves, on this great and most vital question. The want of union and concert in reference to it has brought the South, the Union, and our system of Government to their present perilous condition. Instead of placing it above all others, it has been made subordinate, not only to mere questions of policy, but to the preservation of party ties and ensuring of party success. As high as we hold a due respect for these, we hold them subordinate to that and other questions involving our safety and happiness. Until they are so held by the South, the North will not believe that you are in earnest in opposition to their encroachments, and they will continue to follow, one after another, until the work of abolition is finished. To convince them that you are, you must prove by your acts that you hold all other questions subordinate to it. If you become united, and prove yourselves in earnest, the North will be brought to a pause, and to a calculation of consequences; and that may lead to a change of measures and the adoption of a course of policy that may quietly and peaceably terminate this long conflict between the two sections. If it should not, nothing would remain for you but to stand up immovably in defence of rights, involving your all—your property, prosperity, equality, liberty, and safety.

As the assailed, you would stand justified by all laws, human and divine, in repelling a blow so dangerous, without looking to consequences, and to resort to all means necessary for that purpose. Your assailants, and not you, would be responsible for consequences.*

Entertaining these opinions, we earnestly entreat you *to be united*, and for that purpose adopt all necessary measures. Beyond this, we think it would not be proper to go at present.

We hope, if you should unite with any thing like unanimity, it may of itself apply a remedy to this deep seated and dangerous disease; but, if such should not be the case, the time will then have come for you to decide what course to adopt.

R[obert] M.T. Hunter,	*Virginia*	S[olomon] W. Downs,	*Louisiana*
James M. Mason,	"	J[ohn] H. Harmanson,	"
Archibald Atkinson,	"	Emile La Sere,	"
Thomas H. Bayly,	"	I[saac] E. Morse,	"
R[ichard] L.T. Beale,	"	T[imothy] Pilsbury,	*Texas*
Henry Bedinger,	"	David S. Kaufman,	"
Thomas S. Bocock,	"	Solon Borland,	*Arkansas*
William G. Brown,	"	W[illiam] K. Sebastian,	"
R[ichard] K. Meade,	"	R[obert] W. Johnson,	"
R[obert] A. Thompson,	"	Hopkins L. Turney,	*Tennessee*
J[ohn] R.J. Daniel,	*North Carolina*	F[rederick] P. Stanton,	"

* *Editor's note*: Here the final published address deleted a sentence of Calhoun's draft: "It would be for them, and not for you, to count the value of the Union. Without your rights, it would be worse than useless—a sword to assault, and not a shield to defend you."

A[braham] W. Venable, "
A[ndrew] P. Butler, *South Carolina*
J[ohn] C. Calhoun, "
Armistead Burt, "
I[saac] E. Holmes, "
R[obert] B. Rhett, "
R[ichard] F. Simpson, "
D[aniel] Wallace, "
J[oseph] A. Woodward, "
H[erschel] V. Johnson, *Georgia*
Alfred Iverson, "
Hugh A. Haralson, "
David L. Yulee, *Florida*
D[avid] R. Atchison, *Missouri*
William R. King, *Alabama*
B[enjamin] Fitzpatrick, "
John Gayle, "
F[ranklin] W. Bowdon, "
S[ampson] W. Harris, "
S[amuel] W. Inge, "
Jefferson Davis, *Mississippi*
Henry S. Foote, "
P[atrick] W. Tompkins, "
A[lbert] G. Brown, "
W[infield] S. Featherston, "
Jacob Thompson, "

P.S. Since this address was prepared a motion to reconsider Mr. Gott's resolutions has passed the House of Representatives, and they are now the subject of further proceedings.

PC in *The Address of Southern Delegates in Congress, to Their Constituents* ([Washington:] Towers, Printer, [1849]), a 15-pp. pamphlet; PC in the Washington, D.C., *Daily Union*, January 28, 1849, pp. 2–4; autograph draft in NcD, Bedinger-Dandridge Family Papers, a 14-pp. ms.; PC in the Baltimore, Md., *Sun*, January 29, 1849, p. 1; PC in the New York, N.Y., *Herald*, January 30, 1849, p. 1; PC in the Charleston, S.C., *Mercury*, January 31, 1849, p. 2; PC in the Alexandria, Va., *Gazette and Virginia Advertiser*, January 31, 1849, p. 2, and February 1, 1849, p. 2; PC in the Boston, Mass., *Daily Advertiser*, February 1, 1849, pp. 1–2; PC in the Columbia, S.C., *Palmetto-State Banner*, February 1, 1849 ("extra"), p. 1; PC in the Charleston, S.C., *Courier*, February 1, 1849, p. 2; PC in the Columbia, S.C., *South-Carolinian*, February 2, 1849, p. 2; PC in the Petersburg, Va., *Republican*, February 2, 1849, pp. 1–2; PC in the Richmond, Va., *Enquirer*, February 2, 1849, p. 1; PC in *Niles' National Register*, vol. LXXV, no. 6 (February 7, 1849), pp. 84–88; PC in the Philadelphia, Pa., *Pennsylvania Freeman*, February 8, 1849, pp. 1–2; PC in the Pendleton, S.C., *Messenger*, February 9, 1849, pp. 1–2; PC in the Greenville, S.C., *Mountaineer*, February 9, 1849, pp. 1, 4; PC in the St. Louis, Missouri, *Republican*, February 14, 1849, p. 2; PC in the Charleston, S.C., *Southern Baptist*, February 14, 1849, pp. 1–2; PC in the Vicksburg, Miss., *Weekly Sentinel*, February 14, 1849, pp. 1–2; PC in the Jackson, Miss., *Mississippian*, February 23, 1849, p. 2 (weekly); PC in the Washington, D.C., *Daily National Intelligencer*, June 19, 1849, p. 2; PC in *American Quarterly Register and Magazine*, vol. III, no. 1 (September, 1849), pp. 276–287; PC in Crallé, ed., *Works*, 6:290–313. Note: Official minutes of the caucus meeting at which the address was debated and voted on during the night of 1/22 are in the Washington, D.C., *Daily Union*, January 28, 1849, pp. 2–4, and January 30, 1849, p. 2. (Reporters were barred from the meeting.) About forty percent of the members from the slaveholding States signed, two-thirds of the Democrats and only two Whigs, members of a party whose President-elect would take office in a few weeks. The textual evolution of the Address is complicated and cannot be entirely reconstructed. The ms. draft in Calhoun's hand looks like a first draft and not the submitted "paper" referred to in Venable's statement of 2/4/1849 below. It is heavily canceled and interlined, but the changes appear to be revisions during composition rather than during committee amendment. On 12/23/1848 the Committee of Fifteen appointed by the Southern caucus met and appointed a committee of five, with Calhoun as chairman, to draft an address. On 1/15 the Fifteen met again, and the address which had been drafted by Calhoun was read by Venable. The address was then returned to a new drafting committee for revisions, which Calhoun expressed his willingness to accept. On 1/20, the Committee of Fifteen, which had been reconstituted, met and adopted the revised document, and on 1/22 the address was adopted by the caucus by a narrow vote after a softer substitute document by Senator John M. Berrien of Ga. had been voted down. Calhoun was absent from the 1/20 and 1/22 meetings from illness. The revisions made in Calhoun's draft were subsequently subject to a press controversy initiated by Senator Thomas J. Rusk of Texas, as is indicated below by Calhoun's letter to Venable of 2/2/1849. The Washington, D.C., *Daily Union*, February 4, 1849, p. 2 (copied in the Charleston, S.C., *Mercury*, February 7, 1849, p. 2) printed a statement by Venable and a version of the address furnished by him showing changes in Calhoun's version before adoption that are reproduced in the Editor's Notes above. For press reports of the proceedings on the adoption of the address, see the New York, N.Y., *Herald*, January 24, 1849, p. 3; the Alexandria, Va., *Gazette and Virginia Advertiser*, January 25, 1849, p. 1; and the Charleston, S.C., *Courier*, January 27, 1849, p. 2. The *Herald* reporter concluded with this observation: "The reporters were excluded, though one or two remained at the keyhole. In ordinary cases we would condemn such eavesdropping; but although in this instance, as in others not exactly suited to the taste of your reporter, he does not consider it objectionable in this business on the part of those who listened at the door. In such caucuses, we should consider any means of obtaining a hearing, as perfectly honorable and praiseworthy." Berrien's defeated substitute is printed in *Niles' National Register*, vol. LXXV, no. 7 (February 14, 1849), pp. 101–104.

To T[homas] G. Clemson, [Edgefield District, S.C.]

Washington, 22d Jan[uar]y 1849

My dear Sir, I wrote a few days since to Mrs. [Floride Colhoun] Calhoun, and explained why my correspondence has been so much inter[r]upted and delayed for some time passed. With other reasons, I stated my health had been indifferent of late. Since then it has been still more so; I ["have" *canceled*] in consequence was attack[ed] with momentary fainteness in the Senate, owing principally to the bad air & heat of the room. It passed in less than a minute, and left me as well as usual, with a regular pulse. It has been the subject of much exaggeration in the papers, which [I] fear, if it should reach you & the family will cause much uneasiness. If so, I hope what I state will expel it. Dr. [James C.] Hall was called in. He attributed it to a dera[n]gement of my stomach & a want of tone in my system; & says that there is not the least danger. He advises to keep quiet for a few days & to live a little more generously. The indisposition originated in a cause the reverse of apoplexy.

I am now free from all disease, and as well, as ever, except a little weak. My cold has almost entirely left me, and my cough is a great deal better.

I received a letter from Mr. [George W.] Barton a few days since on the subject of raising the Belgian mission to the grade of a minister resident. He suggested the propriety of my moving in it, or, if I thought more advisable, he would write to one of his Senators, or Mr. Douglass [*sic*; Stephen A. Douglas, Senator] of Illinois to do so. I advised the latter. Since then I have seen Mr. [James] Buchanan; who informed me, if called on, he would make a favourable response.

My own impression is against the movement at this time for two reasons. The first is, I do not think it will succeed, and the next is, if perchance it should, it would raise up competitors against you, which would greatly endanger your return. Should ["you" *interlined*] agree with me, write me without delay, so that I may stop or prevent action on the subject.

I also saw Mr. Buchanan shortly after I received your letter in reference to the extension of your leave of absence; and suggested ["to him" *interlined*] to extend it to a period sufficiently long after the 4th of March to enable Gen[era]l [Zachary] Taylor's administration to act on it. I know not whether he has done it, nor do, I think, [it] very material. The Gen[era]l will not be here until about the 15th of Feb. and I am of impression, that it is not important for you to be here before the end of the month.

I wrote to Andrew [Pickens Calhoun] long since to meet you here, and I expect him to leave home in order to be here, so soon as the dread of the Colara has passed away.

The Southern delegates will meet tomorrow night to take final action on the Slave question. There is much diversity of opinion as to what ought to be done, but ["none" *canceled*] all seem to agree, as to the necessity of resistance should the aggression be continued.

I send you the news papers pretty regularly. I hope you receive them.

My love to all, including Mrs. [Elizabeth Clemson] Barton, as one of the family. Your affectionate father, J.C. Calhoun.

ALS in ScCleA. Note: Calhoun's statement that the Southern delegates would meet "tomorrow night" suggests that he may have written the letter on 1/21 or in the early morning hours of 1/22.

To A[nna] M[aria Calhoun] Clemson, [Edgefield District, S.C.]

Washington, 24th Jan[uar]y 1849

My dear Anna, I was happy to learn by your letter, that you were all spending your time so agreeably, at the Cane Brake. I feared, that you, with all your philosophy, would find the change between Brussels & so retired a place, too great to be agreeable; especially with all the vexation of house keeping, where supplies are so limited and little diversified.

I gave, in my letters, written a few days since to your Mother [Floride Colhoun Calhoun] & Mr. [Thomas G.] Clemson, an account of the state of my health. Since then it has been improving, and I now feel fully as well as usual. The day is fine & I will take my seat again in the Senate. The slight attack of fainteness, which passed off in less than a minute, was caused by several acts of imprudence, and among others, by doing what has not been usual with me, sponging my body all over as soon as I got up. The morning was cold & my system did not react, as I hoped it would. I must be more careful hereafter & not tax my my [*sic*] mind as heavily as I have been accustomed to do.

I had a letter from John [C. Calhoun, Jr.,] a few days since. He is under the operation of the water cure, & says that he already feels much benefitted. He writes, that Mr. [George] McDuffie has been so far restored as to be free of the dyspeptick & nerveous symptoms, but that the paralized limbs remain unreme[d]ied.

The meeting of the Southern members took place again last Monday night [1/22]. My address was ["voted" *canceled and* "adopted" *interlined*] by a decided majority. You will see a brief account of the proceedings in the [Washington Daily] Union, which goes with this. It is a decided triumph under circumstances. The administration threw all its weight ag[ai]nst us, & added it to the most rabid of the Whigs. Virginia has passed admirable resolutions, by an overwhelming vote. The South is more roused than I ever saw it on the subject.

I shall postpone the reflections, which your statement of the conversation of Col. [Francis W.] Pickens gave rise to, until I shall see you, with a single exception. He has constantly endeavoured to hold me in the wrong by attempting to make the impression, that I have been influenced in my course towards him by the artful mannagement of persons hostile to him. There is not the least foundation for it. No attempt of the kind has ever been made; and no man knows better than himself, how far I am above being influenced by such attempts: for no one has ever done as much to ["endeavour to" *interlined*] influence me that way, as himself, and as he knows without success. I have never regarded the course, which has led to the present relation between us with any other feeling but that of profound regret, on his account.

My love to all. Your devoted father, J.C. Calhoun.

ALS in ScCleA; PC in Jameson, ed., *Correspondence*, pp. 761–762.

From Bertha C. Gentry

Shelbyville[,] Shelby C[oun]ty, Mo.
Jan. 25th [18]49

Hon. Sir, I will commence my Epistle by asking you to pardon the intrusion, which doubtless such a man as I believe you to be will do, when you peruse, and find that it is from a fond and doting Mother. When quite a Child (my Father taking a very active part in political affairs) I was led to admire the general Character of certain distinguished Political Gentlemen, among whom was the Hon. John C. Calhoun, whose Character and Talent I most admired. So much so that having grown to womanhood, married, and become the Mother of a very Sprightly and promising Boy, I Called him by your name. He is now Six years Old, can read very well, is an uncommon handsome and Sprightly Lad. He takes great delight in reading the Proceedings of Congress, in Order that he may find your Name. When he does so he is in ecstacys, and says Mother do you hear what Mr. Calhoun says. His Father is poor but intends to labor daily to procure means to Educate him. If he should be blessed in his efforts, it ["is" *interlined*] not at all impossible that his Son may fill the place of ["the" *interlined*] Hon. Gentleman for whom he has been named, when he is gone. My object in writing this is to ask a *Boon*, to make a request which I hope you will grant. You may think it weakness, ay[e], presumption in me but I feel assured that it will ["be" *inter-*

lined] pardoned. The Treasure I desire is, the Likeness or Portrait of the Hon. John C. Calhoun. I desire it not only that my little Boy may see, (as well as hear from) the distinguished Personage for whom he has been called, but I desire it as an O[r]nament to my little Cottage[.] Feeling assured that I have by this time worried your patience and greatly in hopes that you will grant my request, I subscribe myself A sincer[e] Admirer of Your Character and Talents, Bertha C. Gentry.

ALS in ScCleA.

From Geo[rge] B. Butler

New York [City,] January 26, 1849

My dear Sir, You may see in the Journal of Commerce some of the articles editorial and in the shape of communications in relation to yourself and be curious to know their author. They were written by me. The first was a leading Editorial over a fortnight ago, the 2d a letter from Washington signed Viator written at Mrs. Hills in relation to y[ou]r admin[istratio]n of the war department, The third the article enclosed [*not found*]. The public sentiment is somewhat improved on this subject, but I am amazed at the indifference manifested here (except by a few) and regret to think that nothing but a shock will set men to thinking on the subject.

My arduous duties as Attorney of the Hudson River Rail Road Co. and Secretary of the Board, prevent much attention to any other subject. The signature "Fordham" is the place of my Country residence in Westchester Co[unty]. The President of our Board is the late Comptroller of this State Mr. A[zariah] C. Flagg who is quiet about politics, though connected with Mr. [Martin] Van Buren & his policy.

I found a letter a day or two ago written by Silas Wright on the subject of interfering with Slavery in the District, and he cautions those to whom it is addressed to beware of the men who attempt to disturb it. I shall publish it soon with some remarks.

I am much rejoiced to hear of your return to the Senate Chamber, and to good health and beg to be remembered to Mr. & Mrs. [Armistead] Burt and your St[ate] representatives to whom you introduced me. The Journal of Commerce I am glad to see is doing good service in promoting harmony between the North & South. With great respect Y[ou]r truly good friend, Geo: B. Butler.

ALS in ScCleA; PEx in Boucher and Brooks, eds., *Correspondence*, p. 496. NOTE: An AEU by Calhoun reads, "Mr. Butler of N. York."

From CH[ARLE]S EDMONDSTON

Charleston Chamber of Commerce
26 Jan[uar]y 1849

Dear Sir, It becomes my duty as President of this institution to forward to you the accompanying proceedings—and to request your aid in using them in that way most conducive to the object to be attained, And Oblige Yours Respectfully, Chs. Edmondston.

[Enclosure]

Charleston Chamber of Commerce
Charleston, 23d January 1849

At an Extra Meeting of the Chamber held this Evening at the Charleston Reading Room, the following were part of the proceedings which took place.

On motion of Mr. H[enry] Gourdin, seconded by Mr. [Smith] Mowry [Jr.], the following Resolutions were unanimously adopted.

Resolved, that the Chamber of Commerce of Charleston have heard with peculiar gratification, that the Coast Survey which has produced benefits of such magnitude to other sections of this Union, has at length been commenced upon the Coast of South Carolina and in the Harbour of Charleston under directions of the present very efficient and scientific head of the Coast Survey Professor [Alexander D.] Bache.

Resolved, that this Chamber consider this Survey as a work of more utility and importance to Charleston and the extensive Country of which it is and will be the port, than any work the General Government has ever undertaken for it, and that we shall watch its progress and early completion with the deepest interest.

Resolved, that the examination of the Harbour and all its approaches, the accurate ascertainment of the Currents and Channels, the volume, force and speed, of the Waters that flow and reflow through them, the exact locality and influence of the natural and artificial Banks, shores or obstructions which control or affect them, and which do or may be so made as to bear upon the Channels or Outlets to the sea, so as to widen and deepen them, will be of such value to the City as to call upon this Chamber to give to the Survey every aid and assistance in its power, for which purpose a standing Committee of Members shall now be appointed, to be at all times in communication with the Officers engaged in such survey, and to extend to them every information, aid and assistance they may require, within the ability of this Chamber to extend.

Resolved, that the Surveys which have been made with so much scientific and professional ability under the present able Head of the Coast Survey Professor Bache, is warrant that if carried on and completed for our Coast by him, nothing will be omitted which will render the work as perfect as it is capable of being made.

Resolved, that the General Government having already expended more than One and a half Millions of Dollars in surveying and preparing accurate Charts for the great Commercial ports of the North and its Sea Coast, and also for Partial Surveys and examinations of the Coasts of Texas, Louisiana, Alabama, Mississippi and Florida, that those of Georgia and the Carolinas, ought also to be completed; and that to repeal the Acts of Congress authorising this Survey before its benefits have been extended to those who have not yet had them, would not be just.

Resolved, that a Copy of these Resolutions be forwarded to our immediate Representative in Congress, and to each of the Senators from South Carolina, requesting them to make such use of the same as they may deem most judicious—also that a Copy be sent to Professor Bache.

Resolved, that the number of the standing Committee to be appointed under the foregoing Resolutions be fixed at Five, and that the President be requested to appoint the same at his leisure.

The President has appointed the following Gentlemen on the standing Committee.

Messrs. H. Gourdin, James Welsman, G[eorge] A. Trenholm, M[oses] C. Mordecai, S[amuel] Y. Tupper.

Extract from Minutes. William B. Heriot, Secretary.

LS (in Heriot's handwriting) with En in DNA, RG 46 (U.S. Senate), 30A-H3.1. Note: Calhoun presented this memorial to the Senate on 1/30, and it was referred to the Committee on Commerce.

From J[ACOB] C. LEVY

Savannah, 26 January 1849

Dear Sir, The phrase of "the common property of mankind" was applied to Fenelon by the hostile Allies of France, from the great purity of the archbishop[']s character. I may at least view you as the common property of the South, and as a South Carolinian myself trespass on your time for a few minutes in relation to the subject of domestic Slavery, which I very much fear is producing more wear and tear on you than any other question thro' out your political career; and altho' the views of unknown and perhaps obscure individuals put forward thus, generally are unbecoming and subject the writers to rather unfavorable impressions, still I hold it, the duty of every man of the South, however insignificant may be his position, however humble his means, to assist for the preservation of our common safety by word, and if necessary by deed. With this apology for intrusion, I wish to bring to your view the resolution of the Society for the Suppression of the Slave trade passed in London a few months ago as worthy your notice the following "Resolved that the extent and activity of the African Slave trade, tho' in some degree affected by foreign interference, and at times restrained by the exertions of the governments of Cuba and Brazil, *have been mainly governed by the demand for the products of Slave labor in the markets of Europe.*["] Such a resolution solemnly coming from such a quarter must be allowed by their opponents to be incontrovertable, I presume even by our Northern Saints, including the Cottonocracy (excuse this coinage) of the New England States. It follows then, that if there were no demand for Rice, Cotton, Sugar[,] Tobacco[,] Coffee &c productions of Slave labor that Slave holders would cease to hold slaves, that it is the demand abroad and in the free States, which gives vitality to domestic Slavery. I do not think sufficient stress has been laid on this important truth. The demand for this labor then dipends as our planters and merchants know, on the extent and activity of the Capital carried out by the skill & activity of the working population of England, Continental Europe and the North, and in proportion to the amount of this capital and skill, increasing said population, must be also the increased demand for slave labor and slave products. And when wages are even at the minimum point, a part of the earnings from the indestructible habits of mankind must go to purchase these indispensable necessaries of life with the sole exception where they are too poor (as in Ireland during Famine) to have anything to give for these wants. So it follows that the domestic institutions of Slavery must increase, with the increase of population and that it is stimulated with the increase of wealth. It is for these reasons that the productions of Slave labor have progressively increased to the present extent since the return of peace in Europe, and the giant strides of population & wealth in our own country. You have not failed to notice what a large segment in the circle of European & American industry, the Slave labor contributes—how every increase of wealth but stimulates, and as it were holds out a bounty for the products of Slave labor and how this increase of wealth & population acts to increase its demand, and reacts to swell that wealth & population. The very Moralists who denounce Slavery almost in the same breath urge the use of its products to counteract the vile habits the lower classes are addicted to[.] "There would be an End of turbulence in Ireland say they, if every man used 30 pounds of Sugar a year."

It follows then, that if the sources of national wealth, skill the progress of Science—must ["go" *canceled*] all go, from the *unalterable and indestructable* habits of civilized man, to promote and increase the demand for this Slave labor (and these supplies cannot be had from any other source) that to carry out the anti-slavery schemes, they must *commence by destroying the industry wealth and means by which this black labor* is supported and stimulated, which Europe ["& our own Northern States" *canceled*] unites in doing, ["as such" *canceled*] as much as the loud mouthed maker of domestic Negro Cloth, Negro Shoes, Cotton gins and agricultural implements, who makes a merit of denouncing Slavery; but he is not more inconsistent than the great Reformers of England, who endeavor to destroy with one hand, while they seek to build up with the other.

If purity of motive (Hell they say is paved with good intentions) is sufficient to excuse the Evils brought on Society, it would be virtuous to wish a revival of the Slave trade, if only to abate the dreadful fate of the poor wretches illegally or illicitly transported and the frightful cruelty attending it. The African creed ["by" *canceled and* "might" *interlined*] truly be "The Lord deliver us from the assistance of our friends." And the reasoning above applies with equal force, to the trade as to the institution of Slavery and the effects of its labor on the necessities & the habits of mankind. When & where have men ceased to seek these productions, that cannot be had by other means. In all ages these productions have been sought in barter for the productions and the labor of countries having different institutions. The sweat of the brow is part of both, perhaps is least among those provided for by the master and if the illicit Slave trade from unconquerable causes increases, is it not a Compromise with Error or something worse to persist? Is it not due to humanity to readopt and again legalize the trade, bringing the power of an Enlarged humanity to aid the moralist and making humanity concur with policy, to carry out, what the power of nations cannot prevent? And thus fulfill the designs of a higher power in civilizing an inferior race by the only practical means we know—not one of whom, under the worst condition was ever willing to return to the Savageism of his own Continent.

The same reasoning applied will shew, the folly of Legislating or restricting the institution, in the acquired territories[.] The Soils adapted to this Labor—if the demand requires it will be cultivated despight [*sic*] of regulations. If not adapted for Slave Labor no regulation could force it—whether it was this or the other side of the 36 parallel of Latt[itude].

It may have struck you that the best arguments against the course of the abolitionists are to be found in the English Journals and well they may, for they have learnt wisdom from Negative examples. What refers to Europe equally refers to our own Country[.] Withdraw Slave Labor from supporting the Capital, Skill Labor and Industry of the North and it is not necessary to point out what would be the condition of those who every moment of their lives, look to stimulate it; whether in making Cloth, Shoes, Machines, Engines or building Ships[.]

Craving your pardon & indulgence for trespassing on your valuable time, & trusting that your health will be equal to the discharge of the great and serious duties entrusted to you—I beg you to believe me D[ea]r Sir With great respect, J.C. Levy.

ALS in ScCleA. NOTE: Jacob Clavius Levy's daughter, Phoebe Levy Pember, was a noted hospital administrator for the Confederate army.

From ANNA [MARIA CALHOUN] CLEMSON

Canebrake, [Edgefield District, S.C.,] Jan. 27th 1849

My dear father, We were all made very miserable yesterday, by the receipt of the papers mentioning your illness, for tho' mother [Floride Colhoun Calhoun] received a letter from you dated the 14th, yet as the date of the papers which mentioned your illness was the 17th, that was not much consolation. I shall be very uneasy till we hear again. Unfortunately, in this out of the way spot, it is almost impossible to hear from Washington under two weeks, which in our state of anxiety is terrible. Do my dear dear father, take care of yourself. How I wish I were there to nurse you. You are too careless of yourself, I know, & I am sure were the truth known, your indisposition is to be traced to your too great exertions in this Southern meeting, & your distress at seeing the sordid egotism & time serving it has brought to light on the part of the Southern members. Let us hope the people are sounder than their representatives seem to be—but above all preserve your health. Setting aside your family, your [*sic*] are too important to the whole country, & the South in particular, not to feel your health a sacred deposit. What will become of the country if you, who appear to be the only really honest & fearless politician, are not there to give them timely warning of the breakers towards which they are rushing? I do hope this letter will find you perfectly recovered but you should continue careful & come home as soon as possible. From what I hear the winter is uncommonly severe & that should render you more cautious. Mother is very uneasy about you. She would have written today but finding I was doing so said she would delay a few days.

Mr. [Thomas G.] Clemson, mother, Mrs. [Elizabeth Clemson] Barton, Mr. Jolly, & sister [Martha Cornelia Calhoun], are going down to Edgefield next week. I shall stay to take care of the children. Col. [Francis W.] Pickens was here the other day, with his wife [Marion Antoinette Dearing Pickens]. She seems a very pleasant person, but not to compare, I should say, to poor cousin Eliza [Simkins Pickens]. Susan [Pickens] has moved to Florida, & the other children are in Georgia at school, so I did not [see a]ny but the little child by this wife [Jennie M. Pickens], who is the [ex]press image of her grandfather cousin Andrew Pickens.

Mr. [William A.] Harris still wishes to buy this place. I do hope he will, for I am more & more convinced Mr. C[lemson] is utterly unfitted for living here, & ought to sell even at a sacrifice.

Mrs. Barton was much pleased at your remembrance of her in your letter to mother, which she begs to reciprocate. I hope her health is entirely restored. She has no cough, & is apparently very well in every way, & in excellent spirits. She is a woman of sterling worth & much talent & a great favourite of mine.

Mother is very well & very contented. She keeps house which gives her occupation. Sister is looking uncommonly well, & seems to enjoy herself. She is very fond of Mrs. Barton, who finds means to make her talk & laugh more than any one else. Mr. C[lemson] is also very well, & quite busy building & manuring. The children [John Calhoun Clemson and Floride Elizabeth Clemson] are pictures of health, & are developing much in this healthy country life. Calhoun, in particular, is becoming really square shouldered. He begins to ride on horseback very well, & is very manly. Oh! how I wish we could have had you here with us. It is very hard after so long an absence, to see so little of you, especially if we return [to Europe] in April which Mr. C[lemson] seems bent on doing. I who love you [more] than any one else in the world loves you, I [d]o believe, see less of you than any one. I am so afraid sometimes, you will get used to doing without me, & miss me less. Love me I know you always will, & appreciate my affection for you.

There is a good deal of sickness I believe throughout the country. Tho' we are perfectly healthy here. Willy [William Lowndes Calhoun] writes he has had a severe attack of Pneumonia, but was recovering. Col. Pickens has lost twelve negroes from it, at his home place, in the last two months. I do hope it wont come here.

The winter on the whole has been severe, tho' we have had many fine days, & Mrs. Barton & Mr. Jolly are enchanted with the climate & well may they be, on comparing it with the excessive cold, of which all the accounts from the north tell us. Warm as it is, we sometimes find the house very cold & open, tho' a great deal has been done, since you left, to make us comfortable. It seems, however, to agree with us, for no one, not even Mrs. Barton, takes cold, & we eat, drink, & sleep, to admiration.

Tom has been to Pendleton since I wrote. All were well & doing well there. Fredericks wrote he was filling the ice house & coming on very well in everything.

And now, my dear father, do write us often & if you have not the time to write more than two lines write us those two. [*Ms. torn; one word illegible*] take care of yourself. Wrap up warm—keep your feet dry, & dont exert yourself too much. Direct, & make others work for you. You have worked all your life & deserve holliday now.

All send much love & the children many kisses to dear grandfather of whom they speak often. Calhoun said the other day to Mimi "they say my hair & head is like grandfather's. I only hope the inside will be like him, for they say he is a great man" & I mean to try & be a great man too!"

Mother & sister join me in love to cousin Martha [Calhoun Burt] whom we beg to take care of you in spite of yourself. Your devoted daughter, Anna Clemson.

ALS in ScCleA.

From V[an] d[e] V[astine] Jamison

Orangeburg [S.C.,] Jan[uar]y 29th 1849

My dear Sir, According to promise, I write to remind you, that I will be more than obliged to receive all your speeches delivered in Congress and elsewhere, that have been published. My object is to have them bound and to keep them as a memento.

I have been exceedingly mortified to see that you have not been able to maintain that unanimity in the Southern members which was so desirable at this period. I am constrained to believe that those *dissenting Politicians* are not aware that the People are far in advance of them on this most vital question, and when ever the issue is made, and soon it will be from our apparent division, they will find to their sorrow, that it will be too late to stem the current.

The whisperings, such as a Southern confederacy, with Mr. Calhoun for President, is becoming more loud and energetic amongst us, and if the issue is made, and such a state of things occur, your prophecy years ago, that "the Grass would grow in the Streets of New York" will become comparatively true. The North should not be deceived in this matter. Every Southern man knows the advantage which the South would derive. The only objection which could be urged, would be, that the South would continue to break into other limits, and rend this whole Union into Atoms. I for one am prepared for any and every emergency, rather than submit to the degrading position we now occupy.

Excuse this my dear Sir, as I know you must be annoyed with many such communications, but if you knew my regard for your public and private character you will forgive me.

I am truly glad to hear of your recovery, and I trust in a Merciful God that your useful life may be long spared to us, in this, the most eventful period of our Political existence. With sentiments of the highest regard, I am my dear Sir very truly and sincerely Yours[,] V.D.V. Jamison, Orangeburg C[ourt] H[ouse] So. Ca.

ALS in ScCleA.

From C[ASWELL] R. CLIFTON

Jackson, Miss., Jan[uar]y 30, 1849

Sir, I visited Washington last winter, to attend to some cases, in the Supreme Court. One of them, the case of Harris vs: Wall, was not reached. Not being able, from a variety of causes, to get off in time to attend to it, in person, this winter, as I apprehended, I have, some days ago, forwarded a printed argument. I know not if the case is yet submitted. I do not suppose, however, I violate any rule of propriety, in circulating a few extra copies, which I had struck off for that purpose. I take the liberty, therefore to forward to you one, by to-day's mail.

The question, mainly, discussed is a politico-legal one–involving the doctrine of State Rights. It is placed on the true & only safe ground. It would afford me great pleasure to know that the views presented, met your approbation. The conduct of the Supreme Court, in this particular, deserves more attention, it seems to me, than it has attracted.

Allow me to add that the settlement of the slavery question ought not to be postponed. We are much stronger now, than we shall be two or five years hence. Let the extreme South be urged to pass laws, immediately–prohibiting the introduction of slaves–& thus force Virginia, Maryland, Kentucky & Missouri, to stand their ground, & make common cause with us. If not otherwise, it could be effectually checked, if each State would declare who should be slaves–that is–those who now are such, within their limits–& the descendants of the females, thereof; tho' this would require reflection. I have the honor to be, with the sincerest respect, Y[ou]rs most truly, [Judge] C.R. Clifton.

ALS in ScCleA; PEx in Boucher and Brooks, eds., *Correspondence*, p. 496.

From JAMES HARRIS

Philad[elphia,] 31st Jan[uar]y 1849

My Dear Sir, My eyes are open thank God, and I intend to keep my deaf years [*sic*] unstopped, your address has convinced me of facts I never before believed on account of not paying the proper attention to the origin of our beloved Constitution.

Keep at it my dear fellow let nothing dismay you. Justice humanity and religion are on your side, and in spite of abolition Free soil, that God who has inspired you to give the country those plane Facts, will reward you in time, and *eternity*.

And thousands after you are gone will call you *Blissed* [*sic*]. I wish I had a personal acquaintance with you that I might ask a letter to lay long side of other letters for my two sons to look at when I am gone.

Your address will be read in this Northern climate by honest h[e]arts, and my word for it, will have affect.

Many here want to charge you with trying to dis[s]olve the Union, it is all false, they want to do it. If you will read [James G.] Bennett[']s Herald of Tuesday last Ex G[overno]r [William H.] Seward[']s address at Cleveland Ohio proves the fact.

Accept my sincere regards, James Harris. No. 97 Market St. Philad[elphia].

N.B. Mr. [James A.] Pearce of the Senate [from Md.] is well acquainted with me.

ALS in ScCleA.

FEBRUARY 1–MARCH 23, 1849

During the last weeks of the 30th Congress, Calhoun's correspondence was heavy—from all parts of the Union. The main concern was response to the Southern members' Address to their constituents and all the issues which had brought it forth and to which it was related. The tone of most writers was not optimistic of the future.

Perhaps not feeling well, Calhoun did not speak as often in the Senate as was his wont, though he was there every day, and, as always, spoke when needed against unnecessary expenditures and bad precedents. Notably, he crossed swords with Webster on February 24 in a grand Constitutional debate over the power of Congress in the Territories. And on the day the Congress expired, March 3, he spoke unsuccessfully against the creation of a new federal Department of the Interior. Meanwhile, in early February, a three-day convention of abolitionists in Faneuil Hall declared for dissolution of the Union.

The new President, General Taylor, was inaugurated the next day. As was customary, the Senators whose terms had not expired stayed in Washington a few more weeks to consider the nominations to office by the new Chief Magistrate of the Union. The Senate adjourned March 23. Henry Clay had been reelected to the Senate after a period of "retirement" and would join the next Congress. Daniel Webster would remain in the Senate past Calhoun's end, and himself die a bit later while Secretary of State. James K. Polk visited Charleston on his way home and was given a reception there on March 9. He would die in little more than three months. Martin Van Buren had lost his last election and was in permanent retirement from public office if not from mischief. He would live until 1862.

From F[ITZ]W[ILLIAM] BYRDSALL

New York [City,] Feb[ruar]y 1st 1849

Dear Sir, I have read the address adopted by the convention of Southern members of Congress to their constituents, as published in the New York Herald, of which if published in pamphlet form, I shall look to you for a copy. From the commencement of the movement in Washington, all the newspapers here have been using all the worst arts of the press to decry it and misrepresent the motives of those concerned in it; for it is a lamentable fact that most of the Editors, correspondents and owners of the public press, are men who have little or no regard for truth, impartiality, or personal honor. But notwithstanding all the charges of treason, conspiracy, denunciation, contempt and abuse that have been published, the address will perform an important mission to the confederacy. I bless its appearance and hail it with hopefullness. It has my hearty approval.

The calm statement of wrongs, sustained by the facts adduced, clearly demonstrates that nothing less than patriotic union amongst the Southern people ["can preserve them" *interlined*] from the tide of encroachment upon their rights, encreasing year after year in magnitude. The address will go before the constituents of those who have endorsed it & those who opposed it, and this ordeal will decide the fate of the Southern States. I cannot suppose that the people of the South will prove recreant to their rights, their interests and their honor. The supporters of the address must come out of the trial before the people triumphantly. Give us a victory in all the slave States and then the issue will come up before the people of the free States, broadly clearly and mightily, that Wilmot provisoes, abolitionism and all other aggressions and insults upon the South, must cease or the Union is dissolved. Bring such an issue home to the heads and hearts of the north; make it as clear as the noontide sun, and at once the whole pack of incendiaries, Demagogues ["and" *canceled*] venal politicians and unprincipled presses, will be abandoned and left to merited odium, detested by every patriot. This is the true way of preserving the Constitution and union of the States.

The very anxiety to create prejudice in advance against the Southern movement, the base charges one day, the ridicule on another, the denunciation afterwards, with the avidity to sieze on every little incident adverse to it, and the praise bestowed on those who endeavored to frustrate it, or turned the cold shoulder upon it, are decided evidences of alarm, shewing clearly that whether the Southern members do or do not understand the pith value and mighty consequences that would follow a union of the Southern States in a common cause, that northern cunning fully comprehends what would ensue in this part of the Union. They dread it.

The existence of secret organizations in the free States to aid the escape of runaway negroes, is so self evident, that no one north of the Potomac would deem it necessary to ask for proof. Yet this is not all, for there is self evidence of the existence of funds for the furtherance of the same object, for in no case that I ever heard of, where a runaway negro was brought up before any court, did there appear any lack of means or lawyers to aid and assist the runaway. But the case is different as regards poor white people. A late presentment of a grand jury of this county demonstrates that many hundreds were ["held" *interlined*] imprisoned on Blackwells Island ["a few weeks ago," *canceled*] because they had not money nor lawyers to maintain their rights.

I know of no constitutional or political right of the Southern people clearer than their equal right of settling in the new territories with their property and families. If they cannot maintain this right, what other right can they maintain against a majority becoming every year more formidable? Depend on this that come what may, the South has got to manifest a universal spirit of determination to preserve every right that belongs to them intact, or their rights of property will be invaded when they are comparatively less able to resist. Already the right of property in persons held to labor is violated though the Constitution provides for it. The father of a child who is seduced away from his roof brings his action for loss of the services of his child, because he has a property in those services. The owner of a slave who was born in his household or who was acquired from another in whose household he ["the slave" *interlined*] was born, has a property in the slave or in other words the labor of the slave. Hence the Constitution by the words "persons held to labor &c" recognizes the property of the owner in the labor of the slave and necessarily in the slave himself unless there is a law in the State from whence he has fled, to the contrary. A master mechanic has the ownership of his apprentice during the term of his apprenticeship–A parent the ownership of his child untill it comes of age–and the proprietor of a slave the ownership of the slave during life. In short, to be owner of a slave and not of his labor, would be a burthen no way desirable, but to be the owner of his labor, is essentially and truly the ["whole" *canceled*] ownership of both.

According to the unanimity of the South will changes take place in popular sentiment at the north–Surely, surely the ["retributive" *canceled and then interlined*] visitation of the Southern people must come upon those who desert the cause. May God preserve you many years! Yours &c &c, F.W. Byrdsall.

[P.S.] The newspapers are rejoicing that the address is published as they state "*annonymously.*" I trust a large edition will be issued all over the Southern States in pamphlet form, with the names of the members of Congress who approve it, attatched to it. This is highly necessary for many good reasons. The crisis has come and he who has not nerve to come up to meet ["it" *interlined*] with moral and political courage should be uncovered to his constituents that they may displace him with a better man. This, the first great move which should have been made long ago, cannot now be receded from without incurring greater peril and disgrace. If but thirty names are signed, let them be attached, the honor will be the greater to the fewer in number. Every act of courage and determination now on the part of Southern Representatives is an act of *prudence* in fact.

ALS in ScCleA; PEx in Boucher and Brooks, eds., *Correspondence*, pp. 496–498.

From E[LISHA] MITCHELL

University of N[orth] Ca[rolina], Feb[rua]ry 1th 1849

My Dear Sir, Mr. [Thomas L.] Clingman of the House of Representatives who will at my request put this into your hands and Messrs. [George E.] Badger and [Willie P.] Mangum of the Senate will if inquired of inform you that I am a man of respectable character and decent capacity and not altogether unworthy of your attention[.]

The question of slavery has as you know assumed an aspect almost exclusively religious, and when religion and politics become mixed and involved with each other, the case, as the history of Europe for three centuries shews becomes one of the most unmanageable that the statesman can have presented to him. He becomes dependent more or less on the mere theologian.

It appears to me that the Southern people have been too neglectful of the warfare that has been waged upon their social condition for some years at the north, too careless about repelling assaults—and that where a defence has been attempted the wrong ground has been taken.

I have been led to prepare and ["pridt" *and* "prist" *canceled*] print in the first instance for the use of a few relatives at the north an argument on the matter of slavery wherein the only ground is taken which is in my judgment tenable and and [*sic*] whose strength northern men will be compelled to feel and acknowledge[.]

It is approved by a few persons of no mean capacity who are about me here. You have thought more deeply and intently upon the subject than any person of whom I know, and although I ought not perhaps in the impaired state of your health to ask such a favour, I should be glad to have you take so much cognizance of my pamphlet as to be able to form an opinion upon its merits.

If it shall by a few intelligent men like yourself be regarded as mischievous or worthless—I shall without any murmuring direct the larger part of the impression to be burned. If you shall on the other hand think it may do good can you by any means aid in giving it such notoriety as shall cause it to be read more or less at the north—for which especially it is intended. That region is now nearly as impervious to apologies for slavery as the south is to abolition publications. Beyond this I have no favor to ask. I am with great respect Your obedient Servant, E. Mitchell—Professor in the University of N. Ca.

P.S. Since writing the foregoing I have read the address of the Southern delegates. It is said ["in it" *interlined*] that many people at the North "believe the institution of slavery to be sinful and the residue with inconsiderable exceptions believe it to be wrong.["] There are many religious people at the South who have strong misgivings on this head and are likely to prove lukewarm friends. These latter are even more dangerous than the other. Both need that this matter of human rights should be examined to the bottom and the like law of nature and the teachings of the New Testament ascertained. This has not hitherto been done. At least I have met with no apology for slavery that was satisfactory to my own mind[.] Yours, E.M.

ALS in ScCleA. Note: An AEU by Calhoun reads, "Prof[esso]r Mitchell." To settle a controversy over the height of Mount Mitchell, the highest peak in the U.S. east of the Rockies, Mitchell (1793–1857) made his fifth expedition to that region in 1857. While crossing the mountain during a storm, he fell into a creek and drowned. Mitchell's printed "argument" sent to Calhoun was *The Other Leaf of the Book of Nature and the Word of God* [No place: 1848].

From W[ILLIA]M C. PRESTON, [President of South Carolina College]

[Columbia, S.C., *ca.* February 1, 1849]

My dear Sir, You will not read with greater pleasure than I write my hearty commendations of your son Willie[']s [William Lowndes Calhoun's] conduct in college. In some late disturbances he has signalized himself by the propriety of his demeanour & by a prompt and bold expression of just and honourable sentiments thus obtaining for himself the approbation of the Governors of the Institution and the respect and esteem of his fellow students. In short my dear Sir he is a very noble youth, and if God spares him he will be a great comfort and delight to you. It is a very particular pleasure to Mrs. [Louise Davis] Preston & myself to be able to give you this assurance. I am D[ea]r Sir Y[ou]r ob[edien]t Serv[an]t, Wm. C. Preston.

ALS in ScCleA.

To H[ENRY] W. CONNER, [Charleston]

Washington, 2d Feb: 1849

My dear Sir, I received, in the due course of the mail, yours of the 12th Jan[uar]y and read it with much interest. Your opinion, as to the feelings of the South, and the necessity of promptly meeting the aggressions of the North, accorded very much with my own.

We have done all we could do here to unite the South on some common ground in resistance to them. Our success has not been nearly as complete as we at one time hoped it would be, but nevertheless much has been done, all things considered. We found it impossible to draw in the whig supporters of Gen[era]l [Zachary] Taylor beyond a very limited extent. I conversed freely with them, and gave every assurance, that our object was to support him, if he would support the South, by rall[y]ing with his supporters and uniting the whole South in support of him & his administration. But it all proved in vain, through the narrow views & party attachments of a few leaders, who professed to believe that General Taylor, with their aid ["would be able" *interlined*] to put all things right. They drew off with them the whole party, but two; so that we had the almost entire weight of the party to contend with.

But that was not all. The [James K. Polk] administration took a decided & active part against us; & succeeded in keeping all the thorough going hacks of the party from signing the Address, after failing to substitute [John M.] Berrien[']s in its place. Under such circumstances, it was doing much to get 49 [*sic*] signers ["of" *canceled and* "to" *interlined*] it, consisting of a large majority of the party and the most talented & influential of its members.

I send you a copy of the Address, having the names of the signers appended. As far as we have heard, it has been well received, even in the North by the considerate & patriotick. No man here doubts the truth of the Nar[r]ative, & the correctness of the conclusions drawn from the facts set forth. All admit it to be decerous [*sic*]. The wonder is, that any Southern man should with[h]old his signature.

We trust that the South ["in primary meetings" *interlined*] will give it & the Virginia resolutions a hearty response without distinction of party ["& that our friends" *canceled*]. Now is the time to take our stand. A powerful impression has already been made on the North. Let all Unite on this vital issue however much they may be devided [*sic*] on other questions, & we may yet save the Union, or failing to do that, the South & its institutions.

I will write to [Franklin H.] Elmore & [Isaac W.] Hayne. Acting in concert you ["with them" *interlined and then changed to* "three"] may give an impulse that will extend over the whole State. Yours truly & sincerely, J.C. Calhoun.

ALS in ScC; photostat of ALS in DLC, Henry Workman Conner Papers.

From Rich[ar]d K. Crallé

Lynchburg [Va.,] Feb[ruar]y 2nd 1849

My dear Sir, The Papers here gave us, nearly on the same day, an account of your late indisposition and partial recovery; allowing, however, a sufficient interval for anxiety and concern. I fear you have overtaxed your strength in order to meet the late emergency, growing out of [Daniel] Gott's [Representative from N.Y.] Resolution. The matter is, indeed, one of the highest moment; but I do not think that you ought to have been required to do more than dictate the course proper to be pursued; while the labour of preparing the address should have been devolved on others. Yet I have very little doubt that both the mental and manual labour have been performed by you. It is very strange nay, it is unpardonable on the part of

[Robert M.T.] Hunter, [James M.] Mason [Senators from Va.] & others, if this shall have been the case. I have not seen the Address; though I have no doubt its preparation has required much labour and reflection; and that your recent attack is owing, in a great measure, to overwrought faculties, mental and physical. Permit me to remonstrate with you against this *incessant* labour of mind and body. It is not just to yourself, nor yet to the public—for there is other work before you of greater importance even than this; if I am not much deceived. [William] Pitt, one of the most laborious men of his age, would never consent to waste his energies on mere manual work, yet, even with this precaution, he fell a victim of overwrought energies before he reached his forty-eig[h]th year. I would to God that I could be with you to take the burden of manual occupation off your hands; for I suppose it is not considered compatible with *Senatorial* or *Representative* dignity to do this.

I see to day that the Address has been published, but it has not yet come to hand. I shall look for it to night with much interest. The country is beggining, at length to be roused, and I have very little doubt the strongest grounds will be sustained. This feeling, however, is *against* the wishes of the leading Politicians, at least on the Whig side. *They* would still continue to rely on palliatives and promises; but they are forced by the increasing force of the popular feeling, to yield a reluctant support to the position assumed by the Legislature. This is every day becoming more evident; and I am now clearly of the opinion that two Parties will hardly be found in the State on this question. [Robert E.] Scott, the leader of the Ultra Whigs has been thoroughly put down; and both Parties unite in his condemnation. The passage of the Resolutions of the Joint Committee—and the election of [John B.] Floyd as Governor, leave no doubt as to the soundness of the State; and give full assurance that it will stand or fall by the principles avowed.

What will be the effect on the North? The late proceedings in the Legislature of Massachusetts would seem to indicate that Puritan pertinacity still remains as it ever has been. It never had any other rule of action than its own heady and unteachable self-will. New Hampshire too, and New York, Illinois and Michigan, I see, are pledged to the same insane policy. Should the other Free States follow in the train—and I have no doubt they will—there will be nothing left us but *separation*. This I shall regret as a great calamity, but by no means the *greatest*—and such I believe is the common sentiment of the Country around me. Many men here speak openly in favour of *dissolution*; for the course of the northern States has goarded [*sic*] them on to this. The pitiful attempts of the Richmond Whig to weaken the force of your Address by attributing to you a fixed purpose to dissolve the Union, have brought upon the contemptible simpleton the curses of his own Party in this section. Even his Colleague the Editor of the Patriot here, has been compelled to come out in his last Paper, and reads his Richmond Associate a severe lecture for his recklessness and audacity. Moseley's rhapsodies will have no effect any where. The country is prepared to sustain you, and will do so effectually.

I am much surprised at the course of [John M.] Berrien, [Alexander H.] Stephens and the Whig members of Congress generally. Does this course indicate [Zachary] Taylor[']s *wishes* or *purposes*? Is it possible he will sustain the Proviso, or any other kindred measure? If so I shall be greatly disappointed and mortified. I had hoped he was made of different materials. If he maintain the same grounds I trust in Heaven he may go down with the curses of the whole South. I am becoming more and more doubtful of him. His purpose to bring around him a *Whig* Cabinet *exclusively*—for so I interpret his late letter—is ominous of the future. I did hope that he was a man of different materials, and that the State Rights Party would have had a voice in the public councils. If none but Whigs are to be heard, it is not difficult to foresee what is to be the event. [John J.] Crittenden, [Andrew] Stewart, [George E.] Badger, [Truman] Smith, [Abbott] Lawrence &C &C. will prove to be only *pall-bearers* to the Republic. They are, one and all, totally unfit for the crisis; and if Taylor constitute his Cabinet of them, or such as them, we may as well "*roll up the map of the United States*," as Pitt said after the receipt of the news of the battle of Austerlitz. There is not one man amongst them of ordinary political sagacity—to say nothing of Statesmanship.

If my health allow I shall go to Richmond on Monday next, on some business connected in part with our proposed Rail Road; and if I can command the time will try to be in Washington for a day. But it is doubtful whether I shall be able to leave home—as I have been confined for the last ten days with the prevailing influenza which is just leaving me with a "Church-yard cough." The whole community here has suffered much with this disease—and some of the strongest constitutions have yield[ed] to its attacks. My family have all suffered, more or less, but are now recovering.

Should your address appear in Pamphlet I should like to get a copy to have bound with your speeches, which I have carefully preserved. Very respectfully and truly yours, Richd. K. Crallé.

ALS in ScCleA.

Tho[mas] J. Rusk to A[braham] W. Venable

Senate Chamber, February 2, 1849

Dear sir: I addressed a note to you on the 29th ult., requesting to be furnished with a certified copy of the address of the southern delegates, reported to, and adopted by, the committee of fifteen, which you were kind enough to say, verbally, you would furnish me with as soon as you had leisure, as others opposed the address as well as myself; and as it is deemed due to all who did so that the original should be published, I respectfully request you, as the secretary of the meeting, to publish the address as agreed to by the committee of fifteen, reported to and acted upon by the meeting in the Senate chamber on the 15th ultimo, or furnish me with a copy for that purpose. Very respectfully, yours, Tho. J. Rusk.

PC in the Washington, D.C., *Daily Union*, February 4, 1849, p. 2; PC in Crallé, ed., *Works*, 6:285.

To A[braham] W. Venable, [Representative from N.C.]

Washington, Feb. 2, 1849

Dear sir: I am in the receipt of your note of this instant, in which you request me to answer the following questions:

Was not the paragraph in my address, relating to the Oregon bill of the last session, struck out with my consent the evening the report was made [1/15], whilst it was under consideration, and before it was recommitted?

Was not the substitute, as it stands in the address, made with my consent, and accepted by me?

Were not the two sentences in the conclusion, which stated that it was for the North to calculate the value of the Union, struck out with my consent, and by my direction, the same evening, and before the recommitment?

And were not the subsequent modifications, of any importance, all made with my consent, and under the general declaration made by me in the meeting, that I would consent to any modification coming from those disposed to sign the address which did not affect the truth of its narrative, or materially change its character?

To all the foregoing questions I answer, yes.

No one was bound to sign the address unless he individually approved of it. The object was to unite on some common ground against aggressions and encroachments on our rights, as far as it might be practicable within the limits above stated. For that purpose, I readily consented to all the modifications proposed which did not go beyond.

Very truly yours, &c., &c., &c., J.C. Calhoun.

PC in the Washington, D.C., *Daily Union*, February 4, 1849, p. 2; PC in the Charleston, S.C., *Mercury*, February 7, 1849, p. 2; PC in the St. Louis, Mo., *Missouri Republican*, February 14, 1849, p. 2; PC in Crallé, ed., *Works*, 6:288–289.

A[BRAHAM] W. VENABLE to the Washington *Daily Union*

[Washington, published February 4, 1849]

In compliance with the desire of Gen. [Thomas J.] Rusk [Senator from Texas], a member of the committee of fifteen, on its first organization, I with great pleasure publish the original address reported from that committee to the meeting of the southern members of Congress on the 15th of January. The modifications and changes appear by a comparison with that published in your paper of the 28th. It will be seen that many are merely verbal and unimportant, whilst none materially affect the spirit or character of the address.

The subjoined letter [of 2/2] from Mr. Calhoun will explain them most satisfactorily. Two, which are deemed most important, were made on the evening of the 15th, after the address was read, and before it was recommitted. This was done in accordance with the declaration of Mr. Calhoun, its author, that he would consent to any modifications which would not impair the truth of the narrative, or materially change the character of the address. One modification consisted in striking out the paragraph which referred to the Oregon bill of the last session, and another paragraph was inserted the next morning, by his consent; another, the striking out of two sentences near the conclusion, which declared that, under certain circumstances, it was for the North to calculate the value of the Union; a third, the expansion of a clause which referred to the northern members of Congress who had uniformly sustained the rights of the South. There are some other alterations of minor importance, but all made with the approbation of Mr. Calhoun.

The three modifications alluded to above were made or consented to by the author on the evening [1/15] when the address was reported, and before its recommitment. It was placed by me in the hands of Mr. [John M.] Berrien [Senator from Ga.] with those alterations on the face of the paper, and a slip which contained the substituted paragraph. Mr. Berrien's [substitute] address was considered in committee. He returned Mr. Calhoun's address to Mr. [William R.] King, the chairman, and he reported to the meeting on the 22d Mr. Berrien's address and that of Mr. Calhoun, with a recommendation that Mr. Berrien's should be adopted as a substitute. It was the identical paper containing Mr. Calhoun's address with the above-named modifications, made before recommitment, which was voted upon in connexion with that of Mr. Berrien at the meeting of the 22d.

The address of Mr. Calhoun was not read to the meeting of the 22d, because its reading was not demanded. That it had been modified was a matter of notoriety. It was equally well known that the author declared in the meeting of the 15th that he would consent to such modifications.

When the vote was about to be taken at the meeting of the 22d, some members hesitated to vote, because they had not read the address with sufficient care. There was a general annunciation that objectionable passages, not affecting the matter and character of the address, might be stricken out at the suggestion of its friends. Then there was passed a resolution proposed by Mr. [Alfred] Iverson [Representative from Ga.], that the secretary suspend the publication of the address until directed by a meeting of those who should sign it. This gave an opportunity to all parties interested maturely to consider it; and in order to facilitate that purpose, eight private copies were printed and given to persons desiring to read it.

After this, and at the instance of some of the signers, a passage was stricken out of the introductory paragraph, in the following words: "Not excepting the declaration which separated you and the other united colonies from the parent country. That involved your independence; but this your all, not excepting your safety." There were, besides, some slight modifications, almost wholly of a verbal character.

The original is now before the public; and I would take occasion to remark, that if the journal of the votes contains mistakes, those who have been unintentionally misreported can, and doubtless will, inform me of the fact, and it shall be corrected.

You will please publish the annexed letter of Governor [Thomas] Metcalfe [Senator from Ky.], whose official statement places before the public the facts in relation to the retention of Mr. [John M.] Clayton [Senator from Del.] on the committee, who had asked to be excused. I have thus given the facts connected with this whole transaction. A.W. Venable.

PC in the Washington, D.C., *Daily Union*, February 4, 1849, p. 2; PC in Crallé, ed., *Works*, 6:285–288. NOTE: Prefaced by this statement, Venable made public the letters of 2/2 to himself from Rusk and Calhoun and the original reported version of Calhoun's proposed address.

From [Governor] WHITEMARSH B. SEABROOK

Edisto Island [S.C.], Feb[ruar]y 5 '49

Dear Sir, Some time ago I received a letter from you, informing me, that one of the Senators from Illinois had consented to take charge of the sword, presented to Gen. [James] Shields by the State of So. Ca. Since then, the Gen. has informed me by letter, that he desired the sword might be entrusted to the keeping of Mr. [James] Buchanan, until he wrote for it, or called in person for it.

When last in Town [Charleston], I asked Mr. [Charles M.?] Furman to forward it by Mr. [Robert B.] Rhett's son, or any other person who would take charge of it. At the same time I put in his possession my letter to the Sec. of State, in which was enclosed one to Gen. S[hields].

I learn that it is probable that Mr. Hart [*sic*; John Heart?] was the bearer of the sword to Washington. If so, be kind enough to request him to deliver it to Mr. Buchanan—whether he took with him my letter to that gentleman, I am uninformed.

I greatly deplore the state of things at the Capitol. The great question must be taken by the people out of the hands of politicians, who, as a body, are utterly corrupt. The Whig party, or rather their representatives in Washington, are inflicting a severer blow on the rights and interests of the South than the fanatics of the North. The position of Virginia is the proper one. If I am Governor at the time,

South Carolina shall be with her in the hour of trial. Respectfully y[ou]r Ob[edient] & &, Whitemarsh B. Seabrook.

[P.S.] Judge [Andrew P.] Butler or Mr. Rhett will explain, why the resolutions in relation to the Wilmot proviso, adopted by our Legislature, were not transmitted at an earlier day.

ALS in ScCleA.

From Henry B. Goodwin

Newport, Charles county Maryland
Feb. 6th 1849

Dear Sir, I, a stranger to yourself have taken the liberty of addressing a letter to yourself in manuscript, on nine sheets of paper which I mail herewith under cover of two separate envelopes. I place the same at your disposal. I also mail herewith a pamphlet containing five letters written ["by myself" *interlined*] some time ago. I am a native of Massachusetts, and was never out of New England till after I attained the age of twenty-three. I have seen nearly every State in our Union. I have be[e]n a slaveholder during sixteen years last past. I visit New England every year. I have had opportunities for knowing what I have written. Allow me to refer you to my friend and representative, the Hon. John G. Chapman, for further information respecting me. I am a clergyman of the Protestant Episcopal Church, and sign my proper name hereto. With great respect, I am, Sir, Your friend, Henry B. Goodwin.

[Enclosure]

Dea[r] Sir, Your Speech delivered in the Senate of the United States, on the 10th of August 1848, as it came to me in the [Washington] National Intelligencer newspaper of the 2d of November last, is before me. I approve of it entirely. I adopt it bodily. Every cause which you mention, has existed; and every effect which you have attributed to some certain cause has, to some extent at least, resulted from that cause.

I have not the honor of your personal acquaintance. Suffer me to send herewith, a copy of a series of five letters, which, some three years ago, I did myself the honor to address to the Hon. George P. Marsh, the distinguished member of the House of Representatives of the Congress of the United States, from Vermont.

I feel much reluctance to offer for your perusal, so poor a performance. As what I am about to write, implies what is there written, I ask you to know me thro' those letters.

They contain a partial analysis of society, showing it to be diverse in the North and South of this country. I proceeded no further than to state the most prominent law which I found in each—Puritan morality in the North, Manners in the South.

There is, Sir, a complete code of unwritten laws, which govern every civilized community. Under christian civilization, there is no article in the code of any community, which is not found in the codes of all other communities. Diversity results from the circumstance of priority, and from variety in general collocation.

Every individual community which we may choose to contemplate, forms an entire and consistent whole, as are the well regulated individual minds of which it is composed, entire and consistent wholes. There are no solecisms in society.

The phases which any given community presents, are to be accounted for, by considering the code which that community has adopted, and the relations which the individual members sustain to that code. Man is both a devotee and an evader of such laws.

Since writing the letters above refer[r]ed to, I have read "Democracy in America, by M. [Alexis] De Tocqueville." In that masterly chapter, whare [*sic*] "Honor is the subject of his story," he regards the two states in which I find Southern and Northern society to be, as consecutive states of one and the same community of men: the transition depending upon the circumstance of the individuals of that community virging towards a state of equality in condition. According to this author, the laws of honor obtain where the distinction in the grades of society is considerable; the law of right and wrong takes their place in a community of equals.

Doubtless De Tocqueville's idea of a highly civilized community of equals, was never so nearly realized as is the case in the New England States. And his position, as applied to them, is unimpeachably philosophical, exact and compleat [*sic*], tho' he makes no mention of christianity, as the source whence the knowledge of right and wrong is derived. They take the Bible, "as they understand it," as their standard of right and wrong.

Our civilization was derived from Great Britain. The misfortune is, if indeed it be a misfortune, that coexistent elements underwent an analysis. Equality of condition, with its right and wrong, (doubtless obeying the polarity of climate,) was attracted to the North. Aristocracy, with its primogeniture and laws of honor, was congenially located in the South.

Our author predicts that the civilization of the North will pervade the whole Union. The North, from natural causes, pours its population into the South. If our Union lasts, (and, God grant it may,) intercommunication, accelerated as now, by steam and lightning, in addition to the "immunities" of our Constitution, there must, in time, result from the action and reaction of these elements on each other, a civilization as goodly, as is our domain vast and unrivaled. There is sublimity in the war[r]ing of the Northern and Southern elements as they now conflict.

Of the three terms, Manners, Law of Honor, and Chivalry, I select the term, Law of Honor, as best adapted to designate what I have now to say about the primary law in the civilized code of the South—Puritan Religion will, for present purposes, well designate the primary law of the North.

Sir, the North are disposed to prescribe limits and restrictions to the peculiar institution of the South, which we are not disposed to agree to. And the question is, how shall their aggressions be met? I shall suggest a remedy, and I propose to deduce this one only remedy, and the motives for applying it, from the philosophy of society.

Puritan religion stands foremost—is the first and great commandment in the code of Northern civilization. Honor is with them "A trim reckoning."

Puritanism itself is, to some extent at least, fanaticism. It is, as its name imports, superlative purity, at least in its own estimation. It was, in its infancy, so pure, that it asked the mother who held it in her bosom, to purify herself. And because the Church of England would not consent to become as pure as Puritanism required her to be, because she would not consent to unchurch herself, away fled Puritanism to Holland. Thence went she to the rock of Plymouth, to enjoy religious and civil liberty; and has met with no hindrance but such as she has vanquished, to this hour. Political ["dis" *canceled*] phases do indeed attend the disease, as it is presented for the consideration of the South. But these are only incidents. The disease is fanatical puritanical religion, and nothing else—A meer[?] instance in which "Mortal man" essays to "be more just than God—a man to be more pure than his maker."

Puritan religion established itself at an early day, as the primary law in New England civilization. It stands first and is precedent to every thing else, to this day. From prescriptive usage, it rides triumphantly over every other matter. It is the privileged question, and like the question of adjournment in the Houses of Congress, is always in order. It takes precedence of every other question, and hence it is, that we must now consider it.

It is in the particular of prescriptive precedency, in puritanical fanatical religion, and in no other fact whatever, that it presents itself in its present formidable array. It is no more to the solid massive strength of the North, than I to Hercules. It is religious, and therefore from immemorial usage is precedent. The solid mass of the common sense of the North lies under it. ["It" *canceled and* "This common sense" *interlined*] was overpowered at first, and has remained quietly in its place to this hour, and there will it remain, in obedience to the law of habit, and in obedience to its own gravity, until some means other than have hitherto been employed, are resorted to, to rouse it into action, and compel it to assert its supremacy.

Sir, I adopt the philosophy of fanaticism which is indicated by yourself. It always arises out of that class of minds, where the passions are greater than the reason. I shall denote all other mind by the term common sense.

It is not difficult to perceive, how, under the known circumstances, the religion of the Puritans came to establish itself as the primary law of the civilization of the New England States. How it continues to hold ascendency under the vast increase of common sense mind, might seem to require some explanation.

The Puritans came to Plymouth for no such purpose as to eat and drink and live like other men. These things they did. But they were only incidental to their primary purpose; which was to free themselves from the political and religious trammels which enthralled the inhabitants of the old world, and to try if religion, freed from all control, would not take effect on the minds of men to a degree commensurate to their ideal standard.

In pursuance to their plan, they took religious power out of the hands of the clergy, and divided it up among the laity, to the ladies and gentlemen, "share and share alike."

The distinction between fanatical and common sense mind obtained then as now. But fanatical mind prescribed the law. Common sense perceived exag[g]eration and excess in its doings, and it could not go all lengths with what was in vogue. It had no redress, so shut its mouth. Pursuits apart from being extravagantly religious, invited its attention. And it was permit[t]ed in a submissive and covert way, to engage in the acquisition of wealth and other worldly pursuits, but only as it paid court to the primary law, and acknowledged religion to be the one thing needful.

A compromise came to exist between extravagance and common

sense, by which it was stipulated that fanatical mind might go on unmolested in its excesses, provided that gain, and worldly well-being might, as liege subjects, be left in silence to ply their avocation. "Ample room, and verge enough" being thus secured to fanatics, they have more and more taken religious matters into their own hands, till new systems, and new-fangled theories sweep, like devastating hurricanes, over the face of society, and common sense, in all its variety, lies condensed into one compact, uniform, immovable mass beneath. Abolitionism is a religion, is one instance among many.

The common sense masses of the North, give their passive consent to the issues which fanaticism has made up; and thus the North appear before us, as tho' in solid phalanx.

The non-slaveholding States present to our observation a consistent, philosophical, concrete whole, enveloped in a thin covering of abolition fanaticism.

The remedy to check the assaults which the fanatics are making upon us, must be ["such" *canceled*] one which will effect an analysis of the elements of Northern society. The common sense masses must be reached, and to such an extent, as will compel them to assert and maintain their supremacy.

The capital, the wealth, of the North represents a large portion of common sense, of the strongest and most unmistakable kind. Fanaticism and wealth are not conjoined. "The fool and his money soon parted."

Sir, that portion of your speech which shows that the North have profited by our slaveholding, whether we have grown poor by it or not, seems naturally addressed to the mercantile, manufacturing, and monied interests of the North.

It did not reach them. They neither said aye, yes, nor no, tho' they may have laughed. If their actions, which are said to speak louder than words, might be interpreted, the language would be somewhat to the following effect.

"You should have known that we are subjects of Puritan law. Religion speaks first, and it generally says enough to save us the necessity of saying any thing. We only laugh when we see an individual so apparently uninformed about us, as not to know that questions of religion must needs first be disposed of. If slaveholding is wrong, there is an end of the matter. We were compelled, at an early day, to crouch under, or be crushed by, this Juggernaut. And we have done it so long, and find that we derive so many advantages from so doing, that we have come to be not only satisfied with our position, but positively like it. The mighty engine of religion which is hurled along over our heads, is conducted by other hands. We are in league with it. We have made a covenant of perpetual peace and amity with it. We are its subjects, upon this one condition alone, which it has never yet insufferably (we are enduring,) violated; that it should let us alone." Now, Sir, the remedy which we apply, must be such as will excite these masses to action.

You forcibly enumerate the grievances under which we labor, to this effect. "As bad as the Wilmot proviso is, it is not the worst or most dangerous of its (abolitionism's) assaults, and the only effect of arresting it would be to concentrate and give increased vigor to its attac[k]s on more vulnerable and vital points. Movements have been made in the other House, towards abolishing slavery in this District, to be followed, no doubt, in time, by like movements to abolish it in all the forts, arsenals, navy yards, and other places over which Congress has exclusive power of legislation. It would open every where throughout the entire South asylums to receive our fugitive slaves, who would, as soon as they entered, cease to be so. How long could slavery continue in the other portions of the South under such a state of things? But these are not the only vulnerable points. Through Congress—through the legislation of the Northern States, we have been assailed. There is scarcely a single Northern State that has not passed laws which, in effect, annulled the stipulation" in the constitution. "They, indeed, have practically expunged it from the constitution."

The remedy ["to be" *canceled*] resorted to by us, must be ["such as" *canceled and* "of a kind that" *interlined*] will cure these evils. What shall it be? Supposing that, in Congress assembled, the North should contract with the South, that the Missouri compromise line should be extended to the Pacific Ocean; are the same high powers competent to contract, that their constituents shall not be religious fanatics, and act as such? Have they the power, supposing them to have the disposition, to contract that no more unconstitutional laws, to deprive us of our slaves, shall be enacted by the legislatures of the non-slaveholding States? And should they so contract, would they be able to fulfill their engagements? Can stipulations entered into in Congress prevent Northern fanatics from "doing right, and leaving consequences to God?—from obeying God, rather than men?"

The North hold in their bosom, and uphold the fanatics who have created this disturbance. They consider themselves bound to do so, as guardians of civil and religious liberty. They must be brought to repudiate them, to cast the accursed thing from their bosom. The remedy we apply must be such as will produce an analysis that will separate the precious from the vile.

Sir, an issue must be made up, by which the North will be inevitably forced to one of two things, either to fight us, or to recede from their present position. Our position must be chosen with statesmanlike wisdom and discretion; but it must involve this indispensable condition, it must be a palpable, unmistakable aggression upon the present advanced position of the North.

We must plant ourselves on literal localities. If we choose to defend, what is termed the slave-trade in the District of Columbia, tell them so. Tell them solemnly that we will not permit it to be abolished, till we are first abolished. That we will cross the Potomac, and defend whatever of our institution we have in Washington, and will never recross that river, but as conquerors.

Or if it is deemed wise to abandon this post, and take armed possession of as much of the ter[r]itory of New Mexico and California as we choose, at least so much as will suffice to vindicate our honor, and show the North that we hold slaves by a tenure that asks no favors of them, let us loose [*sic*] no time in fitting "the action to the word."

Let us take possession, and invite them to abolish slavery therefrom.

We must take possession in such manner as will convince them that we consider that our honor is to be vindicated, and that in marching against us, they will be marching to "that undiscovered country, from whose born no traveler returns."

Sir, I would not advocate the application of so severe and caustic a remedy, if any less one would suffice. But no less a remedy will have the slightest effect. It is religious fanaticism we have to deal with. Meet it promptly; and crush it, or be crushed by it. To reason with it is folly, to tamper with it is death.

I suggest this remedy, not with a desire to make war, but as the only possible means of preventing war. You will never have occasion to break a lance with the North, if you procede [*sic*] in this way. They will not take up the gauntlet so politely flung down by you, till they have considered well of the matter. "With good advice they make war." Their characteristic unimpassioned reflection, renders it certain, that so grave a matter will be coolly and deliberately weighed. They will retract, because they will perceive themselves to be in the wrong. The puritanical fanatical religious humbug, which now beclouds their vision, will be rent away by the first touch of this caustic remedy.

The common sense mind of the North, will be reached. Money and men, sufficient to abolish the white race of the South, in their own country, will be perceived to be the least condition upon which the campaign can be undertaken, without the inevitable certainty of its ending in defeat and disgrace to the North. And, what is not less material in the matter, success, upon the only terms on which it could be purchased, the abolition of the white race in the South, would purchase for themselves the eternal reward of self contempt.

Nothing short of the issue which I propose, will "hold the mirror up to nature," and compell the North to look its own image in the face. Upon no less a condition, will the North be brought to a knowledge and expression of its real sentiments on slavery.

The North are not cowards, as many a well fought battle both by sea and land, in all the past history of our country, may testify. "Tis conscience that makes such cowards of us all." They fear God, and dare not march to their final doom, with the ["impious" *canceled*] fals[e]hood on their lips, "it is a sin to hold slaves."

In the exigency supposed, the common sense clergy of the North, will see cause to speak. A far abler amount of slaveholding defence, from the sacred scriptures, resides in the clergy of the North, than in the clergy of the South. This may appear a paradox, but ["this" *canceled and* "it" *interlined*] nevertheless is so. Motives sufficient in their own estimation, prevail on them to keep silence in the present posture of affairs. But when the question of a civil war stares the country ["full" *interlined*] in the face, they will not be slow to tell the North, that "the Lord of hosts will not go forth with their armies," in a contest against slaveholding. That, as for the South, "The Lord his God is with him, and the shout of a king is among them."

The distinction between christians and infidels will then become apparent, and it will be found that abolitionism consists of infidels, fanatics, and fools.

The common sense of the North once compelled to be a party in this matter, will see itself, for the first time, held to its accountability—will see that an apology from itself is due, not to the South particularly, nor because the South, actuated by their laws of civilization, expect ["it" *canceled*] such an apology; but because their own sense of character demands it at their hand. They will say, and say the truth when they say, that they were unawares inveigled by the fanatics into the present awkward position, in which they find themselves—That while they left the fanatics to do good, and continued to mind their own business, it never once occur[r]ed to their minds that they themselves could be made parties to their doings. Least of all did it appear to their minds, that it was their duty to check the fanatics, and put them down. But now they perceive that it was even their duty to have done so, before matters came to such a pass. That they have never departed from the faith of their ancestors, but have now an abiding conviction of the truth of the doctrine, that man is capable of self government, and that the South are fully competent to make laws for the regulation of their own affairs, without any assistance from the North. That they never had the least notion of fighting the South to prevent them ["from" *interlined*] holding slaves, nor have they now any such notion.

Thus will the North repudiate fanaticism, in view of the "battle of the warrior, the confused noise, and garments rolled in blood," and not in view of any amount of motive short of this.

Thus situated, the common sense of the North will put down fanaticism in such a way, ["as" *canceled*] that it will stay down. It will assert its ["supremmacy" *changed to* "supremacy"], and consistency, united with interest, will compell it for the future, to hold the reins of its own destiny in its own hands.

The North, both clergy and laity, both representatives and constituency, when once you break the spell, and rouse them from their nightmare, and they stand erect in the majesty of their strength, will be ever-lastingly obliged to you for the favor confer[r]ed.

Sir, I deemed it important to show what I have shown, namely, that it is religious fanaticism, and nothing else, which constitutes the disease which this country is now laboring under. The political attitude which it has assumed is not natural to it. It is one which it has been forced into; and what is from necessity is not of choice. It took refuge and intrenched itself in the constitutional question, only because there were no seats reserved in the Houses of Congress for religion to occupy. And yet, all the attempts to enforce the theory; that religion is an entirely separate thing from political government, have never prevented saints from preaching, and fanatics from prating in the halls of legislation. Treat its political symptoms. It is well to do so. Only remember that all this is preliminary. Religious fanaticism, in its naked identity, has got to be met.

Sir, the character which the South has established for herself, indicates what is to be done. In the eye of the North she has a character, from which it is dangerous for her at this time to deviate. Pursuant to the law of honor, the South have always promptly resented affronts. By virtue of this trait in her character alone is it, that she is standing at this hour.

Since the period alluded to by yourself, the year 1835, when "a widespread circulation of incendiary publications all over the South," took place, there has elapsed no one succ[e]ssive period of six months, during which, writers from the North, wielding "the pen, mightier than the sword," would not have located themselves in the cities of the South, and have produced a servile war, were it not for the prompt dealing which the South manifested on that occasion.

Aspirants of this class, rising up in the North, guage [*sic*] their ideas of "the freedom of speech, and of the press," by Northern practical estimation, and are indignant at the abridg[e]ment of liberty under the Constitution, which the South imposes. This class of gentlemen have not since been idle. They have worked systematically ("their madness has method in it,") towards a definite end, to wit, the end of involving the whole of the non-slaveholding States in their quarrel—are now the rereward [*sic*], and are forcing Congress and the Constitution into our faces.

The law of honor is the first commandment in the civilized code of the South, "and the second is like unto it," the religion of the Bible, both the Olde and new Testaments. There are no commandments in our code, "greater than these." The position which the North has assumed, is an affront to ["bothe" *changed to* "both"] of these. They say that we shall not buy and sell slaves in Washington, and that we shall not hold slaves in New Mexico and California. This is a direct assault on our honor. And when, at any time, did a southern man "count his life dear unto himself," when his honor was at stake?

Our religion is also assaulted. We are told that it is a sin to hold slaves, when we know that the direct reverse is the truth—that it is a christian thing to hold slaves. Let us avenge our honor, by making haste to do the exact thing which we are told, we shall not do. Without "being careful to answer the king in this matter," let us actually hold slaves on the forbidden ground, and let us be ready and waiting to add the highest sanction known to religious faith, since the Christian Era, to our religion. God has not left himself without a witness. His law has backers. Test the law, and it will appear whether it is in force or not. These indignities, if the North persist, must be washed out in blood.

"I call upon the right reverend, the most learned, and upon all orders of men among us, to vindicate the religion of their God, and the honor of their country."

The condition of being an actual slaveholder constitutes a distinction which we do well to consider. We stand alone, except that God is with us. In various degrees, this our relationship separates us from all other men. If we listen to the siren song of our most nearly allied friends, well meaning tho' they are, when they say, "no rash measures, no hasty, violent proce[e]dings," and all that sort of language, right tho' their propositions in terms are, yet profoundly wrong in their application to the occasion on which they are introduced, we shall every hour loose strength to resist aggression. While our relationship is so peculiar that it constitutes even our friends unsafe advisers, if we look to ourselves, we at once see in what our great strength lieth. There exist not on this earth an equal number of men, so firmly allied as we. "We all speak the same thing, and there are no divisions among us. We are perfectly joined together in the same mind and in the same judgment." 1st Corinthians, 1st chap. 10th v.

We find ourselves not only in a state of obedience to what St. Paul here enjoins, but we find this one other preeminent grace of the spirit of christianity within us, a readiness to die in attestation of our religious faith.

We are in number, some say two, some say three millions. Vastly greater, at the lowest estimate, than God ever consented to employ when He was about to make bare his arm, to vindicate himself, in the eyes of the nations. We are moreover, freemen in such a sense as could not be predicated of any race of christian slaveholders who have preceded us. Our predecessors have been themselves the slaves of kings and potentates. God has raised us up, and made us free. "We are with him—are called, and chosen, and faithful." We owe no allegiance, in the matter of slaveholding, and will acknowledge none, but to "the throne of God, and Him that sitteth thereon."

Sir, the North will not fight us to prevent us from holding slaves on the ter[r]itories belonging to the United States, any where that we please. I say they will not fight us. Is this evident? Yes, to a demonstration. In the first place they say they will not. But as you say, we can rely only upon their "acts," "we have been too often deceived to rely on promises or pledges," let us look at what would appear most likely to be the course of their "acts," in an attempt to raise an army to go against us. Suppose them to call for volunteers.

The Quakers are the oldest, most respectable, and consistent antislavery sect among us—have not, to my knowledge, furnished more than their average quota to the ranks of fanaticism. They should, in all courtesy be first invited to form the line of battle. Alas, their faith happens to be of that peculiar ["kinde" *changed to* "kind"] which "is without works" meet for the occasion—"dead." The "Garrisonians," "Conscience Whigs," all, all, have adopted nonresistance as a part of their religious creed.

A trial of faith more precious than golde, to the future welfare of this country, would thus be had. The common sense of the North will not fight, just because of that one reason most commendable to their understanding, because they have nothing to fight for. They will see that a cheaper way of setting themselves right before the South, and before the world, will be to sacrifice the fanatics, whom they already abhor, paradoxical as it seems. This they will do. They will "cast this Jonah into the sea. Then will the sea be calm unto them."

Sir, it has occur[r]ed within a few years past, that a line defining our possessions from those of Great Britain, has been drawn from the Atlantic across the continent of North America in the breadth thereof, to the Pacific Ocean. The South stood by the North, and backed her utmost pretensions. Yourself, Sir, with the blood and bearing of a statesman, and with a zeal for the honor of your whole country, which consumed you, stood for the northern limit of Oregon as now settled, while you well k[n]ew that the possession of the same must redown [*sic*] to the empire of the North, as overbalancing the South; while in the high post which you filled, had you been capable of being a mere sectional man, a mere Southern man, you might have connived at the pretensions of Great Britain, and have got rid of a large portion of that ter[r]itory. You knew your country, your whole country, and nothing else on that occasion.

When the balance in the Senate Chamber was about to turn irrevocably to Northern preponderance, you rose and asked, Are we not to be protected? A silence—sullen as death, was the eloquent response to your interrogatory.

The North now tell you that by their numerical power, they will pass a law which will exclude us from settling slaves on the territories contiguous to, and even south of some of the slaveholding States. The South stand, still asking, are we not to be protected?

According to the truth in this matter, which my philosophy discloses, the bone and muscle, the sinews and stamina of the North answers in a tone of seven thunders, "Put your own shoulder to the wheel, and then call on Hercules."

Sir, the slaveholding States, in unison of action, ought to send a deligation of slaveholders, with their slaves, from each State, forthwith, on to the territory where we are told we shall not go. In that case, the very ground on which they stand will be holy and consecrated in the estimation of the Northern masses. If such a colony needed any defence, Northern valour would see a cause worthy of its steel, and would rush to its rescue.

They expect you to do so, and will uphold you in trampling the Wilmot proviso under your feet, if it should become a law. The very members of Congress who will vote for the proviso, will throw cold water on any attempt to enforce it, provided we have spirit enough to trample upon it. If it does, however, become a law, this solemn humbug will be consecrated to an indefinite existence, and there will be an interminable talk in Congress about your holding slaves where the law says you shall not. I am, with high consideration, Your friend, A Northern man, with Southern citizenship.

ALS with En in ScCleA.

From John Hastings

New Garden, Col[umbiana] C[ount]y, Ohio
Feb. 7 1849

I have just read the proceedings of the Convention, as published in the [Washington, D.C.] Union. Your report, my dear Sir, is repleat with truths that cannot be questioned—truths, as justly portrayed by you, of solemn import to those who appreciate the value of the union, to the whole American people[.]

But how can the report be got to the people of the non-Slave States? If it could be got fairly before them, I feel confident there would be a salutary change. There may be a few—but very few—fearless, patriotic Editors that may publish it; but on the other hand, the presses of the factions will garble it to subserve their sinister designs[.]

You observe that many people of the North think that the slave labor system is a sin, and that many think it wrong; having the inference, that these sentiments induce violations of the Unional Compact, and persecutions of the Slave States. But if this is to be the deduction, I do not, as far as my observation serves, view it in the same light: I think that electioneering device to get into office has caused, substantially, the reckless interferences with the rights of the slave labor States that exist at this moment—the device of using, misleading, the anti-slave labor feelings of the people of the non-slave States, to climb into distinction and its influences[.]

The Quakers ["have" *interlined*] always ["give" *altered to* "given"] their testimony—as they called it, against slavery: but a faction, based on this protest, calling itself anti-slavery, arose, increased, and (encouraged no doubt, more or less by England, if she did ["not" *interlined*] assist ["in" *canceled*] mainly in originating it) worked itself into unconstitutional action against the Union. Nevertheless, the body of the people of the non-slave States continued to respect in ["the principle of" *interlined*] good faith the Unional Compact and its Constitution, until office aspirators, commencing with the opponents of the democracy, made inroads on this principle through their operations in subserving the anti-slavery action to their greed of power, place, and aggrandizement. However, as I have stated to you heretofore, I believe, that if the people of this State, Ohio, could get the truth honestly explained to them, then would—notwithstanding all the efforts of malcontents—["be" *canceled*] vastly more than a majority of them oppose effectively, all aggressions on the unional rights of the States through violations of the Constitution[.]

I know that through this Country, many, very many of the most substantial of its yeomanry, are, on principle, utterly opposed to any interference whatever through Wilmot Proviso, free soil, or other violation of the Unional rights of States and people—will faithfully support the Constitution of the Unional Compact[.]

It is deplorable that as many of the members of the Convention have been so blind to the necessity of unanimity. It is to be feared that place and power have been too much in view—Poor human nature! How few statesmen soar above circumstance!

If your Report should get into pamphlet, will you please to frank it to a few, as below, of those I have alluded to? Yours, my dear Sir, as ever, John Hastings.

John M. Jenkins—["Esqr." *interlined*] Wellsville, Col. Cy. Ohio
John Bush — — Greenford — " — "
James Graham Esqr. — — New Garden — " — "
Joseph Goulbourn Esqr. — — Salem — " — "
George Burns, Esqr. — — Salem — " — "
Job Cook — — Salem — " — "
Emmas T. Weaver Sen[io]r — — Salem — " — "
John Blackburn — — Salem — " — "
Thomas Santee — — Benton Mahoning Cy. Ohio
Clement L. Vallandigham Esqr. — Dayton
Montgomery Cy. Ohio

Mr. Vallandigham thinks highly of you. He edits the Dayton Empire, and will probably publish your Report.

If you cannot send to all—frank by all means to Mr. Vallandigham, Mr. Jenkins, Mr. Graham, and Mr. Burns: but to all if possible[.]

ALS in ScCleA.

From DAVID G. BURNET, [former President of the Republic of Texas]

San Jacinto, Texas, Feb[ruar]y 10h 1849

Sir, In the winter of 1830–31, I had the pleasure to be introduced to you, in the Senate Chamber, by my brother Jacob Burnet. This incident, although it has probably escaped your recollection, prompts me, in part, to take this liberty. But I presume you are so accustomed to similar applications, that an apology is quite superfluous.

H[iram] G. Runnels Esq[ui]r[e], the present Collector for the Port of Galvezton in this State, informed me sometime ago, that he intended to resign that Office at the close of the then ensuing quarter. I propose making application for that vacancy and if I can receive your favorable consideration I shall be exceedingly gratified, irrespective of the issue.

I am altogether sensible of the influence which is usually and for the most part, properly conceded to the opinions of Senators from the State from which an application for office is made. Should my name come before the Senate, I know full well, that the nomination will receive the most virulent opposition of Gen[era]l *Sam Houston.* He will throw upon it his utmost ingenuity in slander and villification—and if he has one *Superior* trait of intellectual character, it is of this and other kindred qualities. He will denounce me as anything—but—an honest man. Sir, he *lies* instinctively—it is his familiar habit. If I were a juror, acting under oath, and he was presented as a witness I would not regard *his* oath as worthy the slightest credit, had he *any* motive of ambition, avarice, vanity or revenge, to induce a falsehood—indeed, it requires a base motive to extract the truth from him.

I am sensible, Sir, that this is harsh and unseemly language to use to you and of one who occupies a seat in the same Chamber where only the honorable, the pure and the talented should appear. As there was a Judas among the twelve, it is not very marvellous, that his type should be found among sixty select ones of this age.

My opinions of that most unprincipled man are no secret and I am by no means careful to conceal them. They are congenial with the opinions of almost every honorable and intelligent man in Texas, who has known and observed him long enough to penetrate the veil which his *cunning*, the highest quality he posses[s]es, usually throws around his acts. But I will not trespass further on your patience, for the subject is, in itself, highly disgusting. I have ventured thus far because I wished some gentleman of the Senate, to understand the relations that subsist between that man and myself. With great respect Your mo[st] ob[edien]t Serv[an]t, David G. Burnet.

ALS in ScCleA. NOTE: An AEU by Calhoun reads, "Mr. Burnet, relates to Gen[era]l Houston."

From H[ENRY] W. CONNER

Charleston, Feb[ruar]y 12, 1849

Your fav[ou]r of the 2nd came to me under an envellop with a copy of your address. It so happen[e]d that I rec[eive]d two other of the address the same day—& put up the same way. Having opened one & seen that it contained but a printed address I did not open yours—but placed it away to be refer[re]d to in future.

Two days ago Pereneau [*sic*; Henry W. Peronneau] & [Isaac W.] Hayne came to me to speak about a public meeting & refer[re]d to a letter from you in which you spoke of having written me. It flashed upon me at once that there might be a letter from you under the envellop with the document & on referring to it I found it so. I feel mortified at the mistake but know ["not" *interlined*] how to better explain it than to tell the truth about it & express my regret that it happened so. I knew you were sick & in fact did not expect you to write. I am glad to perceive however by the papers that you are recovering.

[Franklin H.] Elmore is not here—[he] is in Alabamma. Hayne & Pereneau are moving[?] & authorise me to say that a meeting will be held this week. I am of course, as ever, ready to do any thing I can. We will say but little but that little will be to the point.

I am exceedingly pressed with my duties just now—it being our busiest [banking] season—but shall work an oar.

The people begin to feel that the time for talking much is past & that they would rather act.

If Virginia will only by her Legislature—take a bold & decided position—the demonstration would be made at once & the issue be joined.

The politicians stood up to you even better than I expected at your convention of Southern delegates & a great object was accomplished in getting the address put forth as it is—but the hope & reliance of the South is upon her own people through their own acts in primitive assembly or by the States in their Legislative capacity I think. The proceedings here whenever a meeting is held will be—briefly to endorse the address & the Virginia resolutions & pledge ourselves to stand up to both—temperately but determinedly. Y[ou]rs very Truly, H.W. Conner.

ALS in ScCleA.

Remarks on a point of order, 2/12. During consideration of a Naval appropriations bill, a motion to strike out a provision was proposed to be amended by a motion to strike out and insert. This created a discussion on parliamentary procedure. Calhoun said: "I would suggest that, in order to amend the amendment which proposes to strike out, the proposition must relate to striking out only, and that no amendment which proposes the insertion of a new proposition will be in order. The amendment to the amendment must confine itself to the nature of the original amendment." Later Calhoun said: "According to my conception of the rule, there is no amendment in order, except it pertain to the words of the proviso. You cannot move to amend by inserting something entirely new. I hold the parliamentary rule to be clear that, upon a motion to strike out, no amendment can be moved for the insertion of new matter." After further discussion the offending motion was withdrawn. From *Congressional Globe*, 30th Cong., 2nd Sess., p. 508. Also printed in the Washington, D.C., *Daily National Intelligencer*, February 15, 1849, p. 1. Variant in the Washington, D.C., *Daily Union*, February 13, 1849, p. 1.

Remarks on the proposed abolition of flogging in the Navy, 2/12. During a long discussion, Calhoun was asked by a Senator what had been the effect of the abolition of flogging in the Army. In imperfectly reported remarks, Calhoun replied that "it has had a pernicious effect. In lieu of whipping, the ball and chain has been substituted, which is a more degrading punishment, and Mr. Calhoun contended that it was inexpedient to abolish flogging in the Navy."

From the New York, N.Y., *Herald*, February 14, 1849, p. 1. Variant in the Washington, D.C., *Daily Union*, February 13, 1849, p. 2.

From W[ILLIA]M P. DUVAL

Tallahassee, Feb[ruar]y 13th 1849

My dear [Sir], I was deeply distressed to see announced in the public prints the sudden attack, which assailed you in the Senate, and I pray to god your health did not materially suffer, by its continuance. I believed at the time, (as I now do,) the sudden attack resulted from the distressing and alarming & perilous condition of the union. The deep anxiety and the awfull consequences—springing from a settled determination of the enemies of the South, to violate the constitution, to the distruction of our sacred rights no doubt was the cause of your illness.

I have just risen from a bed of sickness—and my mind and blood are cool and temporate. I would do much to preserve the union but cannot submit to the degradation and insult, and the violation of southern rights—to preserve a disgraceful confederacy. I have read more than once your report recently made to the meeting or convention of the southern members of congress. It is all it should be clear, forceable and temperate. It is such a report as will stand the scrutiny of the wisest heads of the nation. I have given strict attention to Mr. Berrian's [*sic*; John M. Berrien's] report, which is in fact your's, with the strength, and spirit extracted, so as to leave little better, than stale beer. The time has passed for conciliation, this has too long been the mistaken policy of the South. For one I am ready to meet the worse that can now Occur. My native State Virginia has stood forward, nobly and under her lead the South will rally in spite of the tra[i]tors that have stolen into her confidence and now like scorpions are stinging her bosom. Virginia has an im[m]ense store of arms and she will distribute them to sustain the South. When the time shall come (and I fear it is near) I will return to my native State, and leave nothing undone to procure 1200 stand of arms for a corps that I will raise & command in this State and hold ready to march to any point where their services may be required.

If our slaves must wrongfull be taken from us, we will try and settle them in the north, we will give them freedom and let them conquer our enemies, and give them their cities ["&" *canceled*] and country that they may win by their arms. The coloured race will have much to encourage them in this attempte[d] freedom, a country they can call their own, wealth and honor the result.

Able leaders, discipline and arms will carry that distruction & ruin to our enemies that they are preparing for us. The fanc[i]ed security of the north may be shattered by a volcano—over which they little dream they are preparing for themselves. I rejoice to see so many of the Southern members uniting on your report, and if further action is determined on by our Southern friends, I am ready to act with them at all hazzard.

I see Mr. [Henry] Clay is elected to your senate, he goes there I fear for evil—for good, he has never sought for ["in" *interlined*] the last 20 years. Gen[era]l [Lewis] Cass too is reelected. I am glad of this, as he will now shew whether his professions are as sincere as I believe them to be—I sacrificed my election to congress, to sustain him, from the conviction he stood firmly by the constitutional rights of the South. Could I have sustained Gen[era]l [Zachary] Taylor, no man in this State, could have defeated my election. I have never sacrificed principle for office, I go for my country & her honor & rights, and prefer defeat on principles, than honor, and office, without them.

Let me hear of your health, and let me also have your opinion of the *hope* or *prospect* of any compromise of the all engrossing question of slavery.

I trust providence will preserve your health and enable you to bring to a favorable issue the agitating and dangerous controversy that so seriously threatens the perpetueity of our union. Your friend, Wm. P. Duval.

ALS in ScCleA; PC in Jameson, ed., *Correspondence*, pp. 1190–1192. Note: An AEU by Calhoun reads, "Gov[erno]r Duval."

To J[ames] H. Hammond

Washington, 14th Feb. 1849

My dear Sir, I have no copy with me of your letter referred to in the enclosed [*not found*] and know not where one can be got except from yourself. If you have a spare copy, I would be obliged to you for enclosing it to me, & to return the letter [*not found*] of Mr. Jackson with it.

I enclosed you a copy of our Address, which I hope you have

received, & that it meets your approbation. I trust it will do something to unite the South, and to prepare our people to meet & repel effectually & forever the aggressions of the North. Already the stand taken here, & in Virginia, N.C., our State & Florida has made a deep impression on the North. Missouri is about to take a firm & decided stand & Kentucky will, I learn, put down effectually the attempt ["in favour of emancipation" *interlined*] proposed to be made in the Convention to be held this year in that State. It is said, there will not be three members of the body in favour of it. But this and all other favourable symptoms, so far from relaxing, ought to add new energy to our efforts. Now is the time to vindicate our rights. We ought rather than to yield an inch, take any alternative even if it should be disunion, & I trust that such will be the determination of the South. Yours truly, J.C. Calhoun.

ALS in DLC, James Henry Hammond Papers, vol. 16; PC in Jameson, ed., *Correspondence*, pp. 762–763. NOTE: By "your letter" Calhoun was probably requesting a copy of Hammond's letter of 6/21/1844, while Governor of S.C., to Thomas Brown, Moderator of the Glasgow Presbytery. This letter on Southern slavery had been published.

From GEO[RGE] W. MATTHEWS

Port Tob[acc]o [Md.,] 16th Febr[uar]y 1849

D[ea]r Sir, The circumstances which prompt this communication, I trust will excuse the liberty I take. Since your correspondence, some twenty years ago, with Gen[era]l [Andrew] Jackson, when you unveiled the intrigue, which sac[r]ificed the integrity of the democratic party, very few with myself, in this section of Country, (where, up to that period, your popularity was universal) did not yield to the influences which distempered the public mind, crippled the South, & led to the crisis which is now upon us. The press, which would not become the instrument of gambling politicians, could not be sustained at the seat of government. You, to whom *we* looked, as the, only, hope to awaken the public mind to the dangerous assaults, daily, made upon the Constitution, were, as often, misrepresented; & what you said or wrote, only, came to us, in a mutilated form. At this time, however, I am happy to know, there is a disposition, here, favorable to wholesome impressions; & we are anxious to improve it. You will oblige us by assisting, in sending any of your speeches or publications & those of others, (which you find convenient to let us have) on the subject which, now agitates the Country. We, particularly, wish to have your letter [of 8/12/1844] to Mr. [William R.] King. Very respectfully y[ou]r ob[edient] S[ervan]t, Geo: W. Matthews.

ALS in ScCleA. NOTE: An AEU by Calhoun reads, "Mr. Mathews. Send [Ellwood?] Fisher's Lectures & Speeches of Mr. [Albert G.?] Brown[?] & [*illegible name*]."

From SETH SALISBURY

Harrisburg, Pa., February 16/49

My dear Sir: I have read the *whole* proceedings of the United States Senate, under the new Administration, and I may be allowed to say, Sir, that your course has my entire approbation.

Your late able, and, in my opinion, unanswerable Speech will be published in the "Harrisburg Argus." May I, Sir, be allowed to commend this Paper—the "Argus" to your *special* confidence.

I return to my home "East Smithfield," Bradford County, this evening—where *John C. Calhoun* is strong in the respect, and confidence, of the honest-hearted Democracy.

Sir; I agree with you, that, there is not independence enough in the character, and conduct of our public men.

Col. [Thomas H.] *Benton* united—yes, Sir, *he*, in "union and harmony" with the whig party, at the opening of the *new* Congress, under the new Administration, defeated a *known* and *devoted friend* of *yours* from Pennsylvania. With great respect, am faithfully yours, Seth Salisbury.

ALS in ScCleA.

To Professor [ELISHA] MITCHELL, [University of North Carolina, Chapel Hill]

Washington, 18th Feb: 1849

My Dear Sir, I am obliged to you for affording me an opportunity, through Mr. [Thomas L.] Clingman [Representative from N.C.], of reading your publication on the great & exciting question of the day.

I have perused it with attention. It is well executed, & is calculated to make a strong & salutary impression on the portion of the Union, for which it was mainly intended, by showing clearly, that they cannot carry out their doctrines in reference to us, without being involved in gross inconsistency, unless they should also carry them out in reference to themselves.

But in commending your publication to this extent, I must in candour say, I do not agree in your interpretation of either the Book of Nature, or the Word of God, in this connection. I hold the view, which regards the individual state of man, that is the state he is suppose[d] to exist [in] prior to the social & political, to be his *natural* state, to be utterly untrue. That he was formed for the social state, & that his race can be perpetuated & improved only in that state, no sane mind will deny; and surely ["that" *canceled and* "a" *interlined*] state repugnant to his nature, & in which his race cannot be preserved, cannot be his natural state. But I go farther. The Social cannot exist without the political; ["that is" *interlined*] without a power to protect against violence and anarchy; and hence the conclusion is irresistible, that the political, and not the individual, is the natural state of man. It is the state, in which the race of men is ever found, & in which individuals are born, live & die, with scarcely an exception. But the political state implies subordination, and that, restrictions and inequality, varying in degree, in different communities, according to the different degree of intelligence[,] morals, patriotism, and other circumstances, ["according" *interlined*] as they may require ["a" *canceled*] less subordination and restriction, or greater, to preserve the community against violence & anarchy. To that extent, subordination & restriction must of necessity exist in every community. No community can have more equality or liberty, than they deserve, all things considered; & few, in the ["end" *canceled and* "long run" *interlined*] have less. Instead of coming into the world, ["that is" *canceled and* "or" *interlined*] being created, or born free & equal, to use the common phrase, infants come into it subject not only to the inequality & restrictions, to which their parents are, but also subject to their control; & instead of losing their equality & liberty, which they brought with them into the world, as the phrase would import, they acquire by growing to manhood, all that the political institutions of the community allow. To attempt to carry liberty & equality in any case beyond the ["degree" *canceled and* "point" *interlined*] of subordination & restriction necessary to preserve order in the community, will ever end, if successful, in anarchy, to be foll[ow]ed by despotick power. So reads the book of Nature.

With this the Word of God, in my opinion accords. The grant

to Adam & Noah, which you quote, is to the race, as you correctly state; but I cannot agree with you, that what was given to the race, can be construed to be given to each individual composing it, so that each is entittled to an allotment. In the former sense, it has been ["litterally" *canceled and* "strictly" *interlined*] fulfilled. The earth, in its fullness, has been subject to man, but in most unequal portions, both as between communities & communities & individuals & individuals composing the different communities. In all, where it has been devided, it has been left with ["fewer" *canceled*] more or less restrictions, to ["the" *interlined*] operation of the laws, which regulate the distribution of other property; nor can I see any thing in the grant to Adam, or Noah, which ought to make it an exception.

I am ["aware" *canceled and then interlined*], that the view, which you take both of "the Book of Nature & the Word of God" is the prevalent one at the North, but with my impression, I cannot recommend its circulation at the South.

I feel assured, in expressing myself with the candour I have, I but meet your ["wishes" *interlined*] in honoring me with a copy. With great respect I am & & &, J.C. Calhoun.

[P.S.] I send by the mail that takes this a copy of the Southern Address, which you please accept as a mark of my respects.

ALS in ScU-SC, John C. Calhoun Papers.

From J[AMES] H. HAMMOND

Silver Bluff, [Barnwell District, S.C.] 19 Feb. 1849

My Dear Sir, I enclose you a copy of my letter [of 6/21/1844] to the Scotch Presbytery & also return you Mr. Jackson's letter [*not found*] which I thank you ["for" *interlined*] sending me that I ["might" *interlined*] see his agreeable compliment to me.

I have read with great satisfaction your very judicious & forcible Address to the Southern People & am sanguine that it will have a more salutary influence among them than it had with a portion of their Representatives. Living in the woods here & passing a great portion of my time in the heart of swamps I am reclaiming as a forlorn agricultural hope, I hear less than almost any one of what is said even among our own people & know little more of public sentiment here than you do at Washington. But my opinion has long been that the discussion of the abolition question has eased nearly every conscience in the South about holding slaves, & that self-interest will prompt us almost to a man to go through any struggle & risk any change rather than emancipate them in any way, much less on our own soil. The few trading politicians of the South, who have sold themselves & would of course without hesitation sell us & our wives & children for their own promotion, will therefore have a fearful reckoning when it becomes apparent to *all* the people that the crisis has actually arrived. Your Address is well calculated to awaken them, & the conduct of the abolitionists in Congress is daily giving it powerful aid. I look with perfect certainty to see the storm rise before long & when it does rise there can be but one result—a dissolution. For the Free States can then hardly be brought to give us those stringent & humiliating guaranties to keep the peace which we shall imperatively & *imperiously* demand. I know that the value of the Union is now calculated hourly in every corner in the South, for I rarely get into ["a" *interlined*] cotorie even in the streets of Augusta—a Yankee town you know—but it is discussed. The conviction too is growing rapidly, if I may judge by what I hear from time to time in these discussions[,] that the Union has always been & always will be a disadvantage to us & that the sooner we can get rid of it the better. I have thought this myself for twenty years, but where I met one five years ago who agreed with me, I now meet fifty. These are indubitable signs. I did think that if there could be an organization of the Southern Members of Congress [*two words canceled and* "& an" *superimposed*] agreement to act there in concert ["with" *canceled and* "on" *interlined*] this subject, it might alarm the North & even arrest abolition movements for a long time to come. If this could be done, rather than have a Revolution, I would be willing to tolerate the Union for my time: & having occasion to write to Judge Bayley [*sic*; Henry Bailey] last summer I strenuously urged him to attempt such an organization. I will own that the result of your late effort has surprised me. I had been startled by the treachery of some Southern Members both Whigs & democrats at the close of the last Session. But I would not allow myself to believe though I feared & sometimes said, there was considerable defection among our politicians. I knew too that no Southern man could maintain out & out the essential Whig principles of [Henry] Clay & the North, without being wholly false to the South. But that the Whigs in a body & so many democrats too should *desert* us on *this* question so palpably & promptly I did not expect. But I see through it. The fate of the Union is sealed. It is the order—the decree of Providence. Looking as for sometime past I have done altogether to generals & not details in political affairs, it appears to me that this signal failure to adopt the only measure which could give us security in the Union reveals the design of God to sever the Union—to rescue us from the licenti[o]us Sodom of Northern Mobocracy & raise us to that position which our vast resources physical & moral will enable us to maintain. If this is not His design, then the knell of *our* fate has tolled. Disunited & distracted it is we who are to bow our heads to the destroying angel. But I do not believe that such is our destiny. We have not merited it. Its consummation would throw civilization backwards a century or more. In the midst of the daily strife & high excitement of your position you will probably smile at a semi-superstitious philosophy like this. But I will candidly own that I have come to the solving of all great Moral Problems by tracing through them as well as I am able, the Designs of a Power far above ourselves. I look calmly therefore at the events in Washington & do not doubt that they will prove the means of working good. Let the abolitionists press forward. It is our duty so far as we can see *clearly* to oppose them at every step. But we must not be disheartened by *apparent* defeats, but address ourselves to the greater & daily more obvious duty of preparing to shake them off altogether. Very Sincerely yours, J.H. Hammond.

ALS in ScCleA; PC in Jameson, ed., *Correspondence*, pp. 1192–1194.

From W[ILLIAM] GILMORE SIMMS

Woodlands, Feb. 19, 1849

Dear Sir, I am indebted to you for a pamphlet copy of your admirable address to the Southern States, for which you will please recieve my acknowledgments. That it did not recieve the unanimous signature of the Southern Delegates, is, I apprehend to be ascribed only to the demoralizing influences of party organization, the very worst of the evils which, it appears to me, threatens our section. Still, its effects will be measurably beneficial. It will lessen the insolence of our enemies, in alarming their fears. It will put off the day of evil, and contribute considerably towards preparing our people for it. By the way, I am greatly disposed to think that our people of the Southern States are in advance, on this subject, of their halting representatives. I do not doubt that they will have to pay a heavy penalty yet to the popular feeling for the selfish coldness & indifference which baffled your efforts at unanimity—the only thing which is necessary towards the complete triumph of the South in regard to this vexing question. While on this subject, permit me to draw your attention to another which may be made tributary to it. I have been honored by the patrons of the Southern Quarterly Review with its future Editorial conduct. Regarding [this] periodical as an important vehicle for political writing, as well as that which belongs to General Literature, I am desirous of securing some contributors, who may be relied on, as much for their sympathy with us & good faith, as well as for their experience in political affairs. I should greatly like, for example, at this very juncture, to get from Washington an article reviewing the two addresses—yours & [John M.] Berrien's [Senator from Ga]. They would furnish an admirable text for the development of the whole subject, the encroachments of the North, the dangers of the South, the modes of combat, and the general prospects of the struggle, with ["such" *canceled*] a ["proper" *interlined*] running accompaniment of warning notes, particularly in regard to the subsidizing influences of the national parties, in buying up our leading politicians. Articles of spirit and sense, of warmth and justice, could be written here: but not with that degree of intelligence which can only be derived from such a knowledge of details as belongs to you in the Federal City. Is it possible to get such a contributor or contributors? Are there not Southern men in Washington, thus endowed, & having the leisure, who would be pleased to take up the cudgels through such a medium as the Southern Review? The work greatly needs assistance of this sort, and the results would amply repay it, from the circulation which it possesses among that class of independent and intelligent population in the South, who would prefer receiving their views from this organ, ["rather" *interlined*] than through the usually doubtful & suspected medium of newspaper & speech. If your eye could single out such persons, as writers, a hint might secure their cooperation & industry. Your own views freely expressed in conversation would suggest all the necessary clues to the argument. You will soon witness the change of administration. I feel sure that [Zachary] Taylor means well & will [*partial word canceled*] design and desire honestly. The question with him, as in the case of Queen Elizabeth—will he choose good counsellors? I trust, at all events, that in entering office, he will not allow himself to forget that he really owes his election to Democrats. The whigs could not have elected him by themselves; and nothing but the revulsion which honest men of the Democratic party necessarily felt, at the gross uses to which that party has been put, and the base hands into which it had fallen, could possibly have lost them the ascendancy. With great respect & very truly Y[ou]r ob[edien]t serv[an]t &c, W. Gilmore Simms.

ALS in ScCleA; PC in Oliphant, Odell, and Eaves, eds., *The Letters of William Gilmore Simms*, 2:482–483; PEx in Boucher and Brooks, eds., *Correspondence*, pp. 498–499.

From Jo[hn] C. Weems, [former Representative from Md.]

Tracys Landing P.O., Loch Eden [Md.,] 19 Feb[ruar]y 1849

My Dear Sir, Saturday[']s mail brought me the Southern address or rather the address of the truly honourable Southern Delegates in Congress to their Constituents drawn up by you and signed as I perceive by 48, would to God the other Southern Delegates ["had all done likewise" *interlined*]. (I will not say could have seen ["and felt" *canceled*] as did the 48 because I can not believe otherwise than that they do see i.e. the whole of them) but a servile fear of their loss of Popularity, *Their Idol* alone prevented. And Poor Old ["Mary" *canceled*] Maryland stands it would seem at the head of the disgraced List, not one individual[']s (Whig or Democrat) name on the List and why is it so? It does not require a Prophet or the Son of a Prophet to give the Answer. So nearly equal do the Parties Stand in Md. That a very few votes taken from Either side and given to the other so compleatly Elevates or depresses the Beam of Party scales as to induce such Pittyfull political miscreants rather to commit purjery (as all inevitably do who sware to support the Cons[t]itution) than to chance the consequence of ["the loss of" *interlined*] a few Abolition votes. But still Sir I will not disspare. I am unwilling to believe that there ["not" *canceled*] are not as many righteous persons in this Country in propo[r]tion to the whole population as would have save[d] Sodom, where had there been only ten righteous persons The Lord would have for their sakes ["have" *canceled*] spared The City and the Inhabitants, as is to be seen by referance to the 18 Chap. of Genesis 17 vers[e] to the end of said Chapter, and "Surely our God is unalterably the same from Generation to Generation—and if so as He uses man as an Instrument to carry out his Purposes, I trust Sir that you & those 47 who signed with you, said address, will be found as such determined to go ahead, without looking back, as did Lott[']s wife, and thereby accomplish your Object. The Same that our Revolutionary Fathers intended by the Compact entered into ["for" *interlined*] "the better security of Life Liberty & property." It is not to be believed at least by me That the unprecedented Blessings and advantages we enjoy as a People so highly favoured and so prosperous and Happy as to draw the Eyes of all the different Tribes of all the Earth to us and our Institutions as precedents for them. To be deprived of all by the dareing acts of comparatively but a few, Abolitionists and those worse even than they "If ye had not seen ye would not have sin[n]ed but now ye say we see your Sin abideth" i.e. such for Instance as my Immediat[e] Representative Gen[era]l J[ohn] G. Chapman. But [*one word canceled*] in this perhaps I may be mistaken. He may be so very weak (as in most matters he surely is) as litterally to "see with out seeing and hear without understanding." Be it so or not I feel assured in my mind now that the work (permit me to say) of that real "protection, of our lives Liberty and Property" that should have progressively gone on from the session of 1819 has been revived by the Glorious 48 under a conviction produced by The reiterated acts of aggression on the Part of the North & East against the South so clearly and forceably set forth by your address. ["It" *canceled and* "We" *interlined*] will not be found submissively disposed to yeald another Inch to such Ishmelites as the South must ["be" *canceled*] now th[r]ough your Instrumentality soon be induced to look upon the governing part of our Eastern & Northern misnamed Confederates, who with their Idol or in their own words "their God like Daniel" at their head misconstrue our most generous acts and Noble forbareance in all time past, to a Cowardly Fear, of what they are pleased to term an overwhelming and greatly to be dreaded Evil in our midst, which if now an Evil has been rendered so by their Hellish advice and intermed[d]ling, and the great folly of some few slave holders among us who have for Party strength in days gone by joined in the declimation ["viz" *canceled*] "That Slavery was an Evil," viz. Henry Clay, John Randolf [*sic*], and indeed many others, both of us could name, who I consider have done more injury thereby, than all their ["other" *interlined*] acts and 10000 times as many more of a different Charactor will ever make amends for. But Sir I agree with you & the Noble 47 that have acted with you "Leaving all that has past behind and looking only to what now Exists in open day light before our Eyes, it is high time to unite in a determination to act for the Salvation not only of our Property" "removeable as Chattles from the Globe" ["to" *canceled*] of our lives and the lives of ["our" *interlined*] Wives & our Children more dear to Southerners than ["their"(?) *changed to* "our"] own, such a determination Possitively formed and as positively adheared ["to" *interlined*] is now our only security, and will very soon after being so Established induce such Ishmelites whose hands have been so long raised against us; that their own best Policy will be, to lower them and that forthwith and for Ever thereafter, nothing else, *no no other* policy now on the Part of the South can Effect the perpetuation of our otherwise most glorious Union. I was on Saturday at Galesville (where our Steamers Land and take of[f] Passengers and Freights &c where I met with some 18 or 20 gentlemen slave holders i.e. Whigs too, who in conversation with me on this all engros[s]ing subject, expressed a great desire to see The Address of Southern Delegates in Congress *to their Constituents* Having seen it published only in detached parts in different nos. of the news Papers they take (Whig) some saying they Had read Mr. [John M.] Berrien[']s as addressed to the People of the U.S. but would like to see Mr. Calhoun[']s. Now I do not know how they can be gratified in Md., not a Representative in Either ["Branch" *canceled and* "House" *interlined*] of Congress from Md. haveing signed said address, of course all such nos. thereof as may come into their possession will be suppressed. If I could furnish the cost which I am unable to do, I would have thousands of coppies struct, of said address and send them out myself to the slave Holders of Maryland, ["which" *canceled*] and I would be fully satisfied with the result evinced by the next Congressional Election. Now or never I believe is the time to save old Maryland, if overlooked or lost the 2d step after this first on the Part of those who now misrepresent Maryland i.e. the Slave Holders of Md. will be Abolitionist with or without their consent ex necessitate; Excuse so long and, I will not say tiresome a letter but uncalled for Knowing and believing as I do that you & your Friends who think with you will leave nothing undone That you can honourably and safely Effect to save the Union and with it all that is dear to Southerners at all Events the latter even at the loss of the Union If necessary. Very Respectfully your Ob[edien]t Serv[an]t and Sincere friend, Jo. C. Weems.

ALS in ScCleA; PEx in Boucher and Brooks, eds., *Correspondence*, p. 498.

Remarks on a Point of Order

[In the Senate, February 20, 1849]

[*During consideration of the main government appropriation bill in Committee of the Whole, John Bell of Tenn. offered an amendment to an amendment, which raised a point of order. The amendment called for the immediate admission of California to the Union. The Chair ruled that the amendment was in order, a ruling that was appealed.*]

Mr. Calhoun. I do not intend to argue the constitutional part of this question at this time; but surely there ought to be some principle by which to regulate the question of the congruity of an amendment with the original proposition. I think the rule is laid down by Mr. [Thomas] Jefferson. Although the Chair cannot decide the question of congruity, it is in the power of the body to decide it. It comes to the body to decide, now that the appeal has been taken from the decision of the Chair. I appeal to this Senate, that if there ever was a case of incongruity, this is one.

[*Bell called Calhoun out of order.*]

Mr. Calhoun. I am sure that the Senator from Tennessee has not understood me. I stated, that if my memory served me, Mr. Jefferson lays it down that, although the Chair cannot decide the question of incongruity, it belongs to the body to decide it.

[*Bell argued at length against Calhoun's interpretation of parliamentary order.*]

Mr. Calhoun. Mr. President, what I said was, that when a question of this kind is brought to the Chair, and the Chair decides that it is not out of order, and an appeal is made from that decision, it belongs to the Senate to say whether it shall waste its time in combining measures so directly opposite in their character as these; whether we shall waste our time at this late period of the session, in discussing one of the most momentous questions that can be brought before us in an appropriation bill; and especially since, when we have taken a position, the bill itself may be lost, or coercion may be applied to Senators to vote in favor of a measure which, under other circumstances, they would not vote for. Now, sir, I have no doubt that every Senator will admit the entire incongruity, and that they will vote at once upon the subject, and not waste our time, and reserve their vote until after the discussion.

[*After long discussion the Senate adopted a motion to lay the appeal on the table, the effect of which was to sustain the decision of the Chair.*]

From *Congressional Globe*, 30th Cong., 2nd Sess., p. 562. Also printed in the Washington, D.C., *Daily National Intelligencer*, February 21, 1849, p. 1; the Washington, D.C., *Daily Union*, February 21, 1849, p. 1.

J[ohn] C. Calhoun and Others to "Gen[era]l" Zachary Taylor, "President elect of the U. States"

Washington, 20th Feb[ruar]y 1849

Sir, The undersigned, the delegation from South Carolina, having heard that the office of Commissioner of Patents will soon become vacant, and that Mr. [James D.B.] DeBow, of New Orleans, (late of South Carolina[)], has been recommended for that office, take pleasure in adding ["our" *altered to* "their"] testimony to his eminent qualifications. Mr. DeBow, is a gentleman of high character, talents and fine attainments. ["We" *altered to* "They"] doubt not he would do great credit to the office, and good service to the Country. [Signed:] Armistead Burt, J.C. Calhoun, R[obert] B[arnwell] Rhett, Jno. McQueen, Dan[ie]l Wallace, A[ndrew] P. Butler, J[oseph] A. Woodward.

LS in NjP, Andre DeCoppet Collection. Note: The letter was written in Burt's hand. Calhoun and Butler were the Senators from S.C. and the other signers comprised five of the seven Representatives from the State.

From James Davis

Enon Grove[,] Heard C[oun]ty
Georgia, Feb. 21, 1849

Dear Sir, I have just risen from the persusual of your address—to your Southern Constituents, and I am truly Gratified at the high ground you have taken, while I am sorry to find div[i]sion, growing up with the Southern delegation on so vital a question. Patrio[t]-ism[?] and the true interest of both races ought, ever to rise superior to all mere party distractions[.] And I do most fervantly pray that the day may not be far distant when the South as one man will stand, shoulder to shoulder, prepared to do and dare all in the cause of Southern rights and Southern Institutions. I thank you most kindly for the address—which has my unqualified approbation. In the last campaign I was at a great loss—which way to go. But after long and mature reflection, I concluded to vote for Gen. [Zachary] Taylor. If I erred It was the error of the Head and not the heart, as it was under all the circumstances, a choice of evils—And I could not give my vote to Gen. [Lewis] Cass who I regard as a wild and reckless politician, and more one too who had taken shuch an open stand against your wise views in refference to the Mexican war. If any man on earth could led me astray, it would be you. But Sir as much as I love you and admire your wisdom and profound knowledge of human affairs I will ["not follow" *interlined*] any man, only as I approve his views on any subject.

Enclosed I send the prospectus of the Masonic Journal A work, which I have recently comme[nce]d. The first Number is out it is a neat ["pha" *canceled*] pamphlet of 24 Octavon ["pages" *interlined*]. I would like to enroll your name as a Subscriber, and Secure your influence among Masons, to give it circulation in South Carolina. It is the only work of its kind in the South. We intend to make it of utillity and interest to the Fraternity and a welcome, visiter to the parlor, the fire side, and the family circle. I have since the publication of the first Number secured the services of Dr. J.B. Randall the Editor of the Helicon[.] will you in your Leisure moments this appro[a]ching Summer write us a few articles on the moral limits[?] of the Bible[?] Direct all communications to Marietta Cobb County Ga. I am as ever yours in high &, James Davis.

ALS in ScCleA. Note: An AEU by Calhoun reads, "Rev[eren]d Davis."

From J[ames] K. Paulding

Hyde Park, Duchess County [N.Y.]
February 21st 1849

My dear Sir, I thank you for the copy of the address you were so kind as to send me. The statements it contains are too true, and the arguments uncontrovertible. But Fanaticism neither reasons nor listens to reason; and hypocrisy is still more invulnerable.

Matters are certainly verging towards a crisis in relation to the interests of the South; and though forever withdrawn from all active participation in Politics, I can and do still take a deep interest in Public affairs. The Free Soilers, as they call themselves, have thrown a Firebrand, and the two Parties of Foxes are striving to whose tail it shall be tied. They are struggling for the Bone of Fanaticism, and seem determined to go all lengths to obtain the support of those, who in an evil hour were discovered[?] to hold the balance in New York and Ohio.

But where, were the rest of the Southern Representatives, that their names are not to the address? Do they think they can protect themselves from the wolves, ["by" *canceled*] like a flock of sheep, by all running different ways; or like a covey of Partridges by hiding their heads in a Brush heap? Have they forgot the Fable of the Bundle of sticks? United, they can, and will maintain their right to an equal participation in what they were equal instruments in obtaining. The refusal of this is a virtual dissolution of the confederacy which is based on that principle alone. The Partnership is dissolved when any one of the members is refused his just share of the profits. I confess myself astonished at the absence of so many names of the Southern delegation, from an address so reasonable and temperate; nor can I conceive any motive which ought to be strong enough to neutralize them at a crisis like the present. All ["other" *interlined*] interests combined are trifles compared with that now at issue. When the North combines against the South, the resistance of the latter is simply self-defence, which supersedes all other considerations. The People here have been made to believe that the South is not in earnest in resisting the principle of the Wilmot proviso; but were they convinced that a perseverance ["of" *canceled and* "in" *interlined*] those measures of ["aggression" *canceled and* "hostility" *interlined*] would end in a dissolution of the Union, I feel assured, not one of them, with the exception of the hot-brained Fanatics, and those leaders who make them their tools, would persevere in this system of aggression. They will not risk the Union for all the woolly heads in existence; and the moment they believe it really in danger, will start back in dismay.

I hope you are entirely recovered from your temporary indisposition. You must take care of yourself, for you are wanted in these times. You should give yourself a long holiday next summer and let your mind remain in abeyance. I cannot expect to tempt you among the Foxes with Firebrands at their tails, but if you could persuade yourself to visit the North, and stay sometime with me at one of the most healthy and beautiful spots on the Hudson, you would by [*sic*] heartily welcome. I am my dear Sir, Yours very truly, J.K. Paulding.

ALS in ScCleA; variant PC in Aderman, ed., *The Letters of James Kirke Paulding*, pp. 492–494.

To W[illiam] C. Preston, [President of South Carolina College]

Washington, 21st Feb: 1849

My dear Sir, I am much gratified with the contents of your note, and am under great obligation to you for giving them.

I have had a favourable opinion of Willie's [William Lowndes Calhoun's] correct & honorable feelings, which I am happy to have confirmed by yours after witnessing a display of them on a trying occasion.

I hope your health is better, and that it will be speedily wholly restored. My son James [Edward Calhoun] expresses great regret at the prospect of losing the advantage of your instruction in consequence of your indisposition. With kind respects I am yours truly, J.C. Calhoun.

ALS in ViU, William James Rucker Collection.

Remarks on a Mexican War Claims Bill

[In the Senate, February 22, 1849]

[*Under consideration was a bill to compensate Manuel X. Harmony, a trader on the Santa Fe Trail, for goods lost during the war.*]

Mr. Calhoun. Mr. President, the determination of Senators to press through this bill, as it now stands, seems to be so strong that I do not know that the letter which has just been read [from the Secretary of War, William L. Marcy], will have any influence at all; but it does appear to me that the Secretary of War goes as far as he ought to go under any circumstances. That American traders, knowing that a war existed between Mexico and the United States, should undertake to go into that country for purposes of traffic, seems to me to be one of the most extraordinary things in the world. It was an act of folly as well as of temerity, and it was very fortunate, and they ought so to consider it, that they were stopped. I think the officer had the right to stop them. I cannot perceive, if they had proceeded, how they would have escaped being captured, the whole property taken, and perhaps themselves imprisoned. The officers of the Government, in my opinion, acted for the best. Col. [Alexander W.] Doniphan could not have done less than he did. He was obliged to put them in the rear. He was right in organizing them and placing them in the public service, and he would have done right if he had ordered them back.

Sir, it is highly probable that, if these traders had not been stopped by Colonel Doniphan, they would have been captured by the Mexicans, their whole property destroyed, and their own lives placed in jeopardy. Besides, it is treasonable to hold any such intercourse with an enemy in time of war. This man was fool-hardy to engage in an expedition which might have led to such a catastrophe; which might have resulted in the loss of all his goods, and put his own life in hazard. He engaged in the expedition with a full knowledge of its dangers, and now to come here and ask for a remuneration for his losses, I consider to be an impudent act. I consider the precedent a very bad and a very dangerous one, and I hope the Senate will not pass the bill with the amendments proposed.

[*Other Senators stated that Calhoun was mistaken in believing that the expedition had started after war was declared.*]

Mr. Calhoun (interposing.) Not at all. That makes not the slightest difference. The question is, whether a man is authorized under any circumstances to trade with the enemy during a time of war? There is no authority whatever to support the affirmative of that question, and if an individual enters into any intercourse with them, he not only exposes his property to confiscation, but jeopards his life.

[*Senator James M. Mason asked if Calhoun had asserted that the expedition was "an unauthorized act in its inception."*]

Mr. Calhoun, (in his seat.) Not at all.

[*Several Senators discussed the case in detail, stating that Doniphan had failed to provide protection to the goods of an American citizen.*]

Mr. Calhoun. Mr. President, if I have been mistaken in relation to the facts of this case, all I can say is, that I drew all my knowledge of the facts from the remarks of my honorable friend from Maine, (Mr. [James W.] Bradbury.) And I might say that my friend from Virginia (Mr. Mason) would not have exhibited such excitement if he had listened attentively to what I said. I never said that the incipient stage of this expedition was wrong. That would have been absurd. Nor did I say at any time that the petitioner should not receive compensation to the extent of the property used. On the contrary, I expressly stated that he should receive compensation to the extent recommended by the Secretary of War. Now, for any thing beyond that, the case appears to me to be exceedingly plain. When this trader was overtaken by the officer of the United States, between Independence and Santa Fe, he had his option to return or go on. As a prudent man I think he ought to have returned, but he decided to go on. That was legal. I make no objection to that. He fell into the rear of the army, and made as much a part of the army as the sutlers of the army, and had precisely the same right to protection as they, while he was with the American army, and confined himself to the scope of the army, to the duties of the army; while he was under the dominion and authority of the officer commanding the army. This was legal, and hence, according to my conception, all was legal up to the time of his arrival at Santa Fe. Now, whether or not these military duties could be rightfully imposed upon him, is a question which is not involved in the present case, and, therefore, I pass it over. He had a right to stay at Santa Fe so long as the American army had possession. But he was not contented. He wished to move forward, and did move forward—not prohibited by Gen. [Stephen W.] Kearny, it is true, but not permitted to move by Gen. Kearny. He ought to have asked and obtained the positive written permission of Gen. Kearny, then commanding. Had he applied, Gen. Kearny would not have given his permission, and I suppose he knew it, and therefore did not apply. Now, sir, he commences this illicit trade, and proceeds towards Chihuahua. He halts to see if it was safe to go on. The American officer informed him that it would not be safe to go forward, but that he could proceed at his own risk and hazard. He proceeds. In the mean time Colonel Doniphan overtakes him and makes him fall into his train—makes him fall in his rear. He (Mr. Harmony) must take all the consequences of this movement. There is not the slightest responsibility, as far as I have heard, upon the American Government for all that followed, except to the extent to which the property was seized and used.

In my opinion this is a question that involves many consequences. There is not a sutler of the army, there is not an American trader during the whole of this Mexican war, if you allow this case, that may not come forward and present precisely such a case as this, or perhaps a stronger one. We should be careful, therefore, how we set a precedent so dangerous as, I am persuaded, this will prove.

From the Washington, D.C., *Daily National Intelligencer*, February 23, 1849, pp. 1–2. Variant in the Washington, D.C., *Daily Union*, February 23, 1849, pp. 2–3.

From John S. Lorton

Pendleton [S.C.,] February 24th 1849

Dear Sir, Dr. O[zey] R. Broyles as the Guardi[a]n of the heirs of Chester Kingsley, has this day paid over to me for you, One Thousand nine hundred Dollars, and requests me to say to you that he thinks by the middle of March, he can let you have the amount promised you. I have paid Mrs. [Placidia Mayrant] Adams['s] order you accepted, in the hands of Mr. E[noch] B. Benson, amounting to Twelve hundred & twenty three Dollars & fifty six cents, including one month & 1/4 of a month's interest, from the time of your acceptance, having previously paid the balance in my ["hands" *interlined*] out of the amount received from Mr. R[obert] A. Maxwell, after paying a note of my own as per statement below. Yours Respectfully, John S. Lorton.

Recd. of R.A. Maxwell $1000
" of Dr. O.R. Broyles 1900

$2900

Paid J.S. Lorton in a note $ 712.63
" Mrs. Adams order & Int. 1510.93

2223.56

Balance in my hands $ 676.44

Leaving a balance in my hands of Six hundred & seventy six 44/100 Dollars, subject to your order.

ALS in ScU-SC, John C. Calhoun Papers.

Remarks in Debate with Daniel Webster on the Constitution and the Territories

[In the Senate, February 24, 1849]

Mr. Calhoun. Mr. President, I rise, to detain the Senate but for a few minutes with a view to make a few remarks upon the proposition advanced by the senator from New Jersey, (Mr. [William L.] Dayton,) endorsed in full by the senator from New Hampshire, (Mr. [John P.] Hale,) and partially endorsed by the senator from Massachusetts, (Mr. Webster,) that the constitution of the United States does not extend to territories. Now, sir, I am very happy to hear this proposition, for it will have the effect to narrow to a great extent the controversy between the North and South as regards the slave question in connexion with the territories. It is an implied admission on the part of these gentlemen, that if the constitution extends to the territories, it will protect the slave property of the South within their limits. It will place it under the shield of the constitution, and you can put no other interpretation upon the opposition which gentlemen have made to the extension of the constitution over the territories of the United States. Then the simple question is, does the constitution of the United States extend to the Territories? Why, sir, the constitution interprets itself; it pronounces itself to be the "supreme law of the land."

Mr. Webster, (in his seat.) What land?

Mr. Calhoun. "The land." The land belonging to the United States, or the territories of the United States as a part of the land. Not the supreme law of the States only; wherever our flag goes, wherever our authority goes, the constitution, in part—in all its suitable parts—goes. Why, sir, can we have authority beyond the constitution? I put the question to the honorable gentleman—if the constitution does not go there, how do we go there? Are not we subject to the constitution? Is not the existence of Congress itself dependent upon the constitution? Would it not be annihilated with the constitution? And shall we, the creature of the constitution, pretend that we have an authority beyond the reach of the constitution? Sir, I was told a few days since, that the Supreme Court of the United States had made a decision that the constitution did not extend to the territories but by act of Congress. I was incredulous, and I am now incredulous, that any tribunal pretending to have a knowledge of our system of government should announce such a monstrous absurdity. Such a decision as that would be a significant omen. But, sir, I for one say it ought not, and never can prevail. The territories belong to us. They are ours, as representatives of the States of the Union. We are the representatives of the States of this Union, and whatever authority the United States can exercise in the constitution must be exercised by us. It is by the authority of the constitution that they have become ours. Sir, there are some questions that do not admit of argument. This is one of them. The mere statement carries with it the conclusion.

I rejoice, then, to hear gentlemen by implication acknowledge that if the constitution be there, we are under its shield. The South want no higher or stronger position to stand upon. You have put us upon high grounds. You have admitted that the only means of defending your claims, and refusing ours, is to deny the existence of the constitution in the Territories. The gentleman from Massachusetts, I said, only partially acknowledges it. He acknowledges that the great fundamental principles of our government may be carried there. He is right in that; he is right in that. Now, sir, is there a more fundamental principle than this—that this is a federal Union; that the States, as parties to the Union, are States to which the territory belongs in their federal capacity? Is there a more fundamental principle than this—that there is a perfect equality between the members of the federal Union in all respects? There can be none, sir. The constitution forbids all discrimination which would subject one portion of the Union—nearly half the entire number—to the other portion, upon any question.

Sir, I will not dwell upon this longer. I am ready to listen, if gentlemen choose to go on and show us by what ingenuity they can make out their case. It is a mere assertion to say that the constitution does not extend to the territories. Prove that proposition. Prove that it does not extend; that it is incapable of being extended.

I hold the whole course of this debate to be triumphant upon this point. We are put upon higher grounds. It has narrowed the difference, and reduced it to a single point. The true difference will be more easily understood by the community when it is admitted that we can only be ousted by ousting the constitution.

[*Webster asked Calhoun what he meant by recent Supreme Court decisions asserting that the constitution did not extend to the territories.*]

Mr. Calhoun. I said that I was told of them, but I was incredulous of the fact.

[*Webster replied that the Supreme Court had made such decisions for thirty years, that the Constitution, of itself, did not extend U.S. laws to the territories but that statutes and the constitution were "the supreme law of the land."*]

Mr. Calhoun. The laws of Congress made in pursuance of its provisions.

[*Webster remarked that British authority over colonies was established by military power and governance was later extended by statute. Their colonies belonged to England, but were not a part of England.*]

Mr. Calhoun. I will be very short, and I trust decisive, in my reply. The senator's first objection is, as I understand it, that I show no authority by which the constitution is extended to the territories. Well, sir, I ask the senator if I did not inquire how did Congress get any power over the territories?

[*Webster quoted the provision of the Constitution relating to Congressional regulation of the territories.*]

Mr. Calhoun. Then to that extent at least the senator admits that the constitution extends to the territories, in direct contradiction to the assertion that it does not extend to them.

Mr. Webster. To be sure it does; the power to make laws.

Mr. Calhoun. The senator says, in making laws. I answer, not laws in reference to the government of the territory, but in reference to it as property; for it expressly unites territory with other property of the United States, showing that it regards territory simply as property, and gives Congress only the power of regulating it as such. Now, I ask the senator where does he get the power to establish a territorial government, if the constitution extends to territory only to the extent of regulating it as property?

Where, then, do you get your legislative power over territories? I repeat, how do you extend the authority of Congress to the territories, when the existence of Congress depends upon the constitution? Can any one answer me? And yet the senator said I assigned no reason for it. I assigned the strongest reason—that if the constitution does not extend there, you have no right to legislate there.

His next point is that the constitution is confined exclusively to the States, and he was surprised to hear from me the rule I laid down upon the subject. He stated that the constitution of itself cannot execute itself; it requires the government. I never asserted that the constitution could execute itself without a government. It can no more execute itself within the States without a government, than beyond the States without a government. It requires human agency to support it everywhere. I say nothing as to that.

His next objection is that all the provisions of the constitution do not extend to the territories; and he mentions the case of judges. He says judges are appointed for a term of years in the territories, and the constitution requires that judges of the Supreme and inferior courts shall hold their tenure during good behavior. He says that this proves that these judges do not come under the provisions of the constitution.

Mr. Webster. So far as an appeal lies from them, they are inferior courts.

Mr. Calhoun. So an appeal lies from the State courts, and many of the judges of the State courts do not hold their tenure for a term of years. Are they, too, inferior courts within the meaning of the constitution? Now, sir, whether the Congress of the United States has a right to fix the legal tenure of the judges or not, I do not pretend to say. It may be that Congress has stretched its power beyond the constitution, or it may be that the courts have decided erroneously. That is a question unnecessary for me to decide. I never asserted that the whole constitution extends itself to the territories. Many of its provisions are inapplicable to the territories. The greater portion was intended to provide for the special legislation of the States composing the Union. But many provisions do extend to the territories.

He says there is nothing in my argument declaring that constitution to be the supreme law of the land, because it also provides that laws made in pursuance of it are also the supreme law of the land; and in illustration of that position, he asserted that if such was the case, it would be unnecessary to establish custom-house laws in California as this bill proposes, as the existing custom-house laws would be extended as a matter of course. In reply, I state that, according to my impression, all the custom-house laws have a local character, and are enacted in reference to particular places by name. Am I right in this impression? (Several Senators. "Yes.") They, then, from their nature, cannot be extended to California without special legislation for the purpose.

I do not remember whether the senator has made any other objection. I have noticed them all, I think. If I have not, I shall be very glad to be reminded of any other, for I listened attentively to his remarks.

I do not need to make out a case. No, sir, the proposition that the constitution of the United States extends to the territories, as far as it can be applicable to them, is so clear that even the great talent of the senator from Massachusetts himself (Mr. Webster) cannot maintain the opposite.

It may be, indeed, doubtful what particular provisions of the constitution are or are not extended to the territories in many cases. But there is one entire class in reference to which there can be no doubt. I refer to those provisions which prohibit Congress from enacting certain laws in any case whatever. Among them, I ask the senator whether Congress has the power to make any laws with respect to religion in the territories, which the constitution expressly forbids? It also forbids the establishment of an order of nobility. I ask, can Congress establish such an order in the territories? I might go on and repeat many such questions, to all of which there can be but one reply—that it cannot. This class of restrictions, then, upon the power of Congress, must be admitted to extend to the territories; and if they may, why may not the powers of Congress, when applicable, be also extended? No good reason can be assigned.

Sir, I do not deem it necessary to dwell longer upon the point. I should be happy to hear any explanation from the senator.

[*Webster asserted that a territory "when it remains in a territorial state" was not a part of the United States. However, they are subject to the government of the U.S. according to the Constitution's powers to regulate them.*]

Mr. Calhoun. The senator has undertaken to reply to my answer by maintaining that the territories form no part of the United States. I had supposed that all the territorial possessions that we have were within the limits of the United States, and constituted a part.

Mr. Webster. Never!

Mr. Calhoun. The constitution expressly declares they belong to the United States.

Mr. Webster. That is a very different thing. A colony of Great Britain belongs to England.

Mr. Calhoun. As they belong to the United States, they must have exclusive authority over them; and as this government is the sole representative of the United States, it of necessity must possess whatever legislative power can be exercised over the territories. It is, then, as belonging to the United States that we derive, under the constitution, the power of legislating over the territories. Now, as the constitution creates the United States, and as it is the bond of Union which makes the United States, it is manifest that the authority of the United States cannot be extended to the territories unless the constitution extends to them. The opposite view would be absurd, as it presupposes that the government of the United States could legislate over a territory which does not belong to the United States.

The senator has again alluded to the courts of the United States in illustration of the position which he has taken. He has taken, in this respect, substantially the same ground which he did when he was previously up; and I am content with the answer which I made in reply to it when last up, without undertaking to combat it with any other. In order to show that there is a difference between the power of Congress in the States and in the Territories, he has referred to the subject of internal improvements, and asserted that there is not a member of this body, however opposed to internal improvements within the States, who hesitated to vote for internal improvements in the Territories. I admit there is a great difference as to the power of Congress in legislating within the States, and within the Territories. The senator is surely mistaken in asserting that while many objected to the exercise of the power referred to, none objected to its exercise in the Territories. I, myself, although I admit that this government, considered as a proprietor, might contribute to improvements made through its lands, to the extent they are benefited, deny that we have any more right to appropriate money in Territories than we have in the States. The question, however, of appropriating money for internal improvements, turns upon the interpretation of the provision in the constitution relative to laying taxes and appropriating money, and of course comes under an entirely different category. But there are many of my friends on this side who take a much more restrictive view of the power of internal improvements in Territories than I do, and who believe them to be unconstitutional in all cases.

Upon review of this discussion, I feel that I am justified in asserting that the proposition that the constitution does not extend to the Territories is so utterly indefensible, that all the ingenuity and powers of the senator has not been able to to maintain it, or render it even plausible.

I conclude by adding, as a sum total of the argument, that the South cannot be deprived of the rights she claims in the Territories, without being deprived of the protection which the constitution throws about her.

From the Washington, D.C., *Daily Union*, February 27, 1849, pp. 1–2. Variant in the Washington, D.C., *Daily Union*, February 26, 1849, pp. 2–3; the New York, N.Y., *Herald*, February 28, 1849, p. 4. Another variant in *Congressional Globe*, 30th Cong., 2nd Sess., pp. 273–274; the Washington, D.C., *Daily National Intelligencer*, February 26, 1849, pp. 2–3; the Boston, Mass., *Daily Advertiser*, March 2, 1849, pp. 1–2; the Charleston, S.C., *Mercury*, March 3, 1849, p. 2; Crallé, ed., *Works*, 4:535–541; Benton, *Abridgment of Debates*, 16:309–312; *Writings and Speeches of Daniel Webster*, 18 vols. (Boston: Little, Brown & Co., 1903), 14:323–335 (part). Another variant in the Baltimore, Md., *Sun*, February 24, 1849, p. 2; the Charleston, S.C., *Mercury*, March 1, 1849, p. 2; the Greenville, S.C., *Mountaineer*, March 9, 1849, p. 2. Note: The report presented above is the most detailed version of the debate. It was presented by the Union as "a corrected and revised portion of the interesting debate last Saturday between Mr. Calhoun and Mr. Webster. We . . . request that the following sketch may be substituted for that which appeared in the daily Union yesterday [2/26], by all those papers which may think proper to publish the same."

From S[usan Wheeler] Decatur

GeorgeTown D.C., Feb. 25th 1849

My dear Mr. Calhoun, I was *totally* ignorant that a claim had been laid before Congress, in behalf of the captors of the Frigate Philadelphia, until a person brought me a news paper, five days since, to show, me the proceedings of the Senate, upon the subject, and the passage of *their Extraordinary* Bill! which I will venture to say, is the most *Extraordinary* Bill that has ever pass'd that honorable Body!– In the most common Court of Justice it is necessary to hear both sides of the question before a decision can be given!– But in this *case* the Honorable Senate thought it proper to *violate* my belov'd Husband [Stephen Decatur's] *Will*; and to *throw imputations* upon my character without affording me a *chance* to say a *single* word in my defense!

My Husband *never* had any more idea of *adopting* the ladies in question than he had of adopting you and they were in much more *limited* circumstances when he made his *Will*, than they have *ever been since*!—They were at that time *all* unmarried!—When the Claim in relation to the Frigate Philadelphia, which I had by my belov'd Husband's direction laid before Congress, Miss MacKnight presented *awful* charges against me; which I instantly refuted!—and neither herself, nor either of her Sisters have ever intimated to me, in any manner, that they had any claim either upon myself, or upon my belov'd Husband, which had not been fulfill'd—and from that time to this, whenever they have call'd upon me they have always address'd me as "*dear aunt*"—and it is only from their *constant* detraction of me to other persons, that I have come to the knowledge of their pretentions! !

I take the liberty to transmit a *certified* Certificate which I hope you will have the goodness to read! I remain, My dear Mr. Calhoun very Sincerely & Respectfully Yours, S. Decatur.

[Enclosure]

Georgetown D.C., February 13th 1849

I hereby certify that my beloved, and lamented Husband the late Commodore Stephen Decatur, never, during the whole course of our married life (*fourteen* Years) communicated to me a *thought*, a *word*, or a *desire*, that I would in the event of his death make provision, for the Ladies, who have been brought forward by the Honorable Senate, as his *adopted Children*!– Ladies termed the *Miss McKnights*; the *youngest* of whom was married [*"nineteen" canceled and* "twenty seven" *interlined*], or *twenty* [*"eight" interlined*] years since to Lieutenant Twiggs, of the Marine Corps!—and a man of fortune. Another of them was married *nineteen*, or *twenty*, years since, to Doctor Klappe of Philadelphia, a man of fortune also! After his death she married Mr. Stockton, a purser in the Navy; and he is *sole* Heir to a considerable fortune in Philadelphia! The eldest of those Ladies, is a woman upwards of *fifty years* of Age! She has never been married, and has *ample funds* of her *own*, for all her personal expenses; and she has always, since the death of her mother, resided, *Gratuitously*, with her connexions. She ["has" *canceled*] received her due proportion of her mother[']s estate; and in the year eighteen hundred, and thirty Seven under ["under" *canceled*] the Naval pension act, then passed, She received a *thousand* dollars, as pension, from the day of her Father[']s death (Captain of the Marines) until she became of age! Her Sister (now Mrs. Stockton) received *fifteen* hundred dollars. And Mrs. Twiggs being the youngest, received *two Thousand* dollars, which she (being many years married) Invested! All these facts were communicated to me by the *present Miss* [M.H.] *McKnight*; who also informed me that her *half-brother* W[illia]m D. Hurst, so soon as, he was appointed Midshipman, gave her one *hundred* and *fifty* dollars a year; and when made a Lieutenant, he allowed her *Six hundred dollars* a year, so that she has never Suffered for want of money!

I never heard my beloved Husband express any Sentiment of *attachment* towards those Ladies beyond the ordinary feeling of regard which a man should have for his female relatives. He never lived in the same house with them, for more than a few days at a time! He never kept up any correspondence with them! He never did any thing for them after I became acquainted with him except in making them, a present of some small articles of *dress*, which he directed me to do in my *own name*. Wishing all his connexions to understand *distinctly*, that whatever his fortune might be it was *all mine*; That he did not consider any thing as his own but his *Sword* and his *Ship*! Although we had been so many years married he never once invited those Ladies to his house. After we had resided one, or two years in Washington, he had occasion to visit Philadelphia, on some matter of business. I proposed to him to bring with him, when he returned, one, or two of the Miss McKnights to let them see the Seat of Government. He brought one of them with him, and when she returned home, I *invited* the others; and it so happened that the *eldest* of those Ladies the present Miss McKnight, at that time a woman *twenty two* years of age, had been my Guest (for the first time in her life) *two months*, when my beloved Husband expired! Almost *twenty nine* years since!

While the claim which ["was pen" *canceled and* "I had" *interlined*] laid before Congress by my beloved Husband[']s direction, was pending and the House then in Session, the present *Miss McKnight* addressed a letter signed with her own *name*, to one of the Hon. Gentlemen, claiming a portion of the Prize Money for herself, and Sisters, (they both being married) stating that I had treated the Memory of their Uncle with the *greatest disrespect*! That the *Swords*, and other Articles, presented to him by the Government for his *public Services*, I had given to *Indians*! The Gold Box, ["pr" *canceled*] which had been presented to him by the Corporation of *New York*, ["I had" *canceled*] for the Capture of the *British Frigate Macedonian*, I had given to the *British Minister* who had recently returned to England! (A *pretty* present for the *British Minister*!)

These charges were followed, by others of Similar Character, and *all false*! A person of my acquaintance was in the House of Representatives, when the letter to which I have alluded ["to" *canceled*], was read to the House, and came immediately to inform me of its contents. I then wrote a note to the Hon. George C. Washington who was ["then" *interlined*] a member of the House, and resided in Georgetown, requesting him to call on me, and take charge of *all the Articles*, about which I had been so *maliciously* calumniated!—and to place them on the Speaker[']s Table, asking every Hon. Member to examine them and see, how malisciously, I had been traduced! Mr. Washington executed my wishes, and the Articles were examined by the whole House! I at the same time wrote a letter to be read to the House, and which was read either by Mr. Washington, or the Hon. Edw[ard] Everett (who was also a member of the House), refuting the whole *fabrication*! I stated to them the *fact*, that I had given *all the Swords* to my brother-in-law, Col. Jno. P. Decatur, a few weeks after my ["beloved" *interlined*] Husband[']s deplorable fate! That he packed them up in the presence of *Miss McKnight*, and, *Sister* (now Mrs. Stockton) who were at that time my Guests: and that he took them home, with their *full knowledge*; they are now in possesion of Lieutenant Stephen Decatur, the God son, and, name-sake of my beloved Husband. He resides in New-York!

Two, or three years Subsequent, when those Ladies, were *again* my Guests, A party of Indians, came to my House and informed me, through their Interpreter, that as my Husband, had been a *Warrior*, they wished to have something that had belonged to him! I had some *old* and *broken Swords* and, *Foils* (for fencing) and some worn out *Epaulettes*, unfit to be offered to any Gentleman, and these I gave the Indians! So that those Ladies made use of my hospitality to themselves (for they were *present* when the Indians received the Gifts) to *traduce* me before the Congress of the Nation! (and the whole *foreign* Diplomatic Corps)!

I have not been able to ascertain a Single Sentence of the charges, which they have now brought forth, and which have induced the Honorable Senate to pass so *extraordinary* a Bill! which though intended as may be presumed to honor the memory of him whose acheivements have induced it is still ["left" *canceled*] the *only* individual whose memory has been treated with disrespect by the violation of his most ardent wishes, as will be plainly seen by his last *will*, and *testament*, and his *widow* the object of his devoted Affection, *charged* and *condemned*, with, *she knows not what!*

If my beloved Husband had entertained such an *excessive attachment* to those Ladies, he would not have concealed it from me, who was ever ready to adopt all his partialities, and whose greatest delight, was to see him pleased, and happy! and I do not *beleive* that he ever expressed any such Sentiment ["of" *canceled*] to any person whatever! There was no *double-dealing* about him! whatever he wished to do, and thought it right to do, he had courage enough to do it, at all hazards! And I cannot help thinking that the Ladies in question have manifested very little respect, for his memory, by casting *imputations* on his *moral* character, and defaming the person who they know full well, was the object of his devoted affection!

This is only a *question of Character*! as nothing could induce me to receive a dollar, from any sum appropriated (which I consider) under circumstances, disrespectful to my beloved Husband[']s memory!

I have in my possesion the testimony of one, of the most respectable *Gentlemen* in Philadelphia, who has been intimately acquainted, with the present Miss McKnight, from her earliest childhood, (and which testimony I am ready to show) that she does not hesitate to depart from the truth, whenever she thinks it will be for her interest, to do so; and I have had many proofs of it from my own knowledge! If Congress is desirous to show the *Generosity* of the Nation, it appears to me that the three Miss Decaturs, the daughters, of the late Jno. P. Decatur, are women over twenty years of age, unmarried, and in much more limited circumstances than the Ladies, who have been given to my beloved Husband, as his *adopted* Children, ["and" *canceled and* "except those nam'd in the Bill" *interlined and then can-*

celed] are greater objects of Charity! They are his only female relatives ["except those nam'd in the Bill," *interlined*] their elder brother Stephen Decatur, is a Lieutenant in the Navy, and lost his sight in the discharge of his official duty; he is totally blind, and of course cannot do much for them! [Signed,] Susan Decatur.

District of Columbia
County of Washington

to Wit: On this twenty fourth day of February 1849, personally appeared before me the subscriber a justice of the peace in and for said County, Mrs. Susan Decatur, the widow of the late Com[modor]e Stephen Decatur, and made oath in due form of law, that the facts set forth in the foregoing certificate or statement signed by her, are just and true as therein set forth, to the best of her knowledge and belief. Sworn to before me, Lewis Carbury, J.P.

ALS with En (in another hand) in ScCleA.

From C. C. Kelly

Springfield Ky., 25 Febr[uar]y 1849

Sir, Though personally a stranger to you, I hope you will excuse me for this intrusion. Kentucky in the present year will elect delegates to remodel her constitution—the question of emancipation, I fear, will be agitated, and as I am decidedly opposed to any such measure present, or prospective, and am besides a candidate for delegate in this County, I wish to be armed to meet any attempt of the kind with facts.

Believing that you Sir, afford the most reliable source of information, I have ventured to trespass on your valuable time, by asking of you a suggestion, or so.

I wish if possible to obtain a condensed history, of a reliable kind, of slavery in the U.S. Can you inform me of one? I have an impression how derived, I do not know that the last persons engaged in ["the" *interlined*] importation of slaves to the U.S. were Yankees—is this true? Any suggestions you can find time to give me will be received with pleasure & remembered by Your ob[edien]t Serv[an]t, C.C. Kelly.

[P.S.] Northern fanaticism as yet has made no impression on Kentucky except perhaps in some two or three river Counties—and I feel confident that during this summer the last spark of that pharasaical philanthropy, which seeks the negroes emancipation, that the white man of the north may take his place will be quashed. Kentucky[']s position, with a great natural barrier on the north, like the Ohio must determine her place. She is southern—and must be so. C.C.K.

ALS in ScCleA. NOTE: An AEU by Calhoun reads, "Mr. Kelly, Send doc[umen]t."

J[OHN] C. CALHOUN, JR., to Z[achary] Taylor, [President-Elect]

Milledgeville [Ga.], Feb. 26th 1849

Sir, Although I have not the pleasure of a personal acquaintance with you, I must beg your indulgence, for thus taking the liberty, of infringing upon your valuable time.

When the Mexican war commenced—before war had been declared by Congress—I was in Mobile, and was among the first to subscribe my name, as a volunteer, to fly to your rescue. Unfortunately, a severe attack of sickness and subsequent feeble health, prevented me from fulfilling my wishes.

I have been advised, to visit the southern portion of Europe[,] for my health, although much improved, requires a change to a more genial climate. It is for this reason that I now address you, to ask you as a favour, to give me the appointment, of Chargé d'Affaires, to one of the southern European, or South American Capitals. For referrence, I give you the names, of [former] Gov. [John] Gayle [of] Alabama, Hon. David [Levy] Yulee [of] Florida, F[ranklin] H. Elmore [of] So. Ca., Gen. E[dmund] P. Gaines U.S. A[rmy], Hon. J.C. Calhoun, &c, &c.

If you are disposed to pay any attention to my communication, you will much oblige me, by directing your reply, to Dr. J.C. Calhoun, Jr., Milledgeville, Georgia. Please to accept the assurances, of the highest regard and esteem of, respectfully your Ob[edien]t S[er]v[an]t, J.C. Calhoun, Jr.

ALS in DNA, RG 59 (State Department), Letters of Application and Recommendation during the Administrations of James K. Polk, Zachary Taylor, and Millard Fillmore, 1845–1853 (M-873:12, frames 537–539).

From ROBERT WICKLIFFE

Lexington [Ky.], Feb[ruar]y 26th 1849

My Dear Sir, I thank you for your draft of the address to the South upon the subject of the aggressions of the North upon the rights of the South[.] I had before, read it with instruction & pleasure[.] ever since the second marriage between [John Quincy] Adams & [Henry] Clay (in forty one) I have trembled for the condition of the South & in my feeble way warned the South that nothing but unanimity could save them, but still the South is not and I fear never will present the undivided front which brave men, should do[.] Time was when I could keep Kentucky straight but the President Makers have sealed her fate, I fear, for while there is not a man in the whole Legislature that dare avow himself an emancipator or a free soiler Still, every ["which" *altered to* "Whig"] ["votes" *altered to* "voter"] of the Legislature voted for, Clay one of the champions of free soilism[.] Without union the South is to be used up in the next six years. The house is already prepared for all & every outrage upon The slaveholder & the majority in the Senate is melting away. The moment they secure the Senate, They will go it with a rush (as the vulgar is) untill the South will have ["been" *canceled*] to chose between fighting the negroe stealers & the the [*sic*] negroes themselves[.] I am from position and age unable to aid in averting the black crisis which the South has brought on herself by her divisions & Clay delusions beyond the feeble voice which I have long extended to rally the whole South particularly my own State against the Combination of Whiggery & Negrory—but while nineteen twentieth of the slaveholders are violent against negroe stealers, none but the Democrats vote against negroe stealing & the Combination of the negroe party of the North & the Whigs of the South. What Southern can look a man in the face & cry out I am no abolitionist that voted for [Millard] Fillmore & there are miriads that do it expecting the Conservatives of both parties to protect them. May you live to open the Eyes of the South In time to save her—from—her greatest & worst enemy herself[.] Yours Truly, Robert Wickliffe.

ALS in ScCleA; PC in Boucher and Brooks, eds., *Correspondence*, p. 499. NOTE: Wickliffe was the son of Charles A. Wickliffe, who had been a colleague of Calhoun's in John Tyler's cabinet. Robert was to be Governor of La., 1856–1860.

From RICH[AR]D K. CRALLÉ

Lynchburg [Va.], Feb[ruar]y 27th 1849

My dear Sir: I have just reached home after an absence of three weeks, and find your favour of the 10th inst. on the table. It affords me much gratification to hear that you have recovered from your late indisposition, which I ["was" *interlined*] prepared to hear had been greatly exaggerated by the papers; many of which rely, in their statements, on rumour only.

It was my purpose, when I left home, to have gone on to Washington merely for the gratification of seeing you for a short time; but a relapse of fever, attendant on a severe attack of the prevailing influenza, confined me to my room during the period I had set aside for this purpose. This was a sad disappointment to me; for I know not when I shall again have an opportunity to visit the City. Messrs. [John?] Goode and [Thomas S.] Bocock, I suppose, you have seen, as they were both on their way to pay you a visit when I parted with them in Richmond. They will, doubtless, have given you an account of matters and things, so far, at least, as the Legislature is concerned. As far as I could ascertain the state of public opinion, the tone of the members is higher and sounder than it has been for many years past, so far as the slavery question is concerned. The course of the Southern Whig Members in Congress is very generally condemned even by the Whigs themselves, and I am inclined to think that [William B.] Preston, [Thomas S.] Flournoy, [William L.] Goggin, and, *perhaps*, [James] McDowell will be made to feel their responsibility. Certain it is that they have not acted in accordance with the popular feeling or sentiment of the state—a fact of which they must have been aware from the proceedings of the Legislature. Preston's attempt to shelter himself behind his new California Bill will not avail him. It is but a second edition of that introduced by [Stephen A.] Douglas; and the Laudations of the Northern Press will only lead to a more rigid scrutiny of his conduct. Had the Democrats brought out a proper man, he would undoubtedly be left at home in April. As it is, I think it highly probable he will be defeated.

The fate of Flournoy is certain, as I am informed; and McDowell will have strong opposition in his own ranks. [John S.] Pendleton represents the most infected District in the State, and, (though ex Gov. [William] Smith is spoken of as likely to run against him,) will probably be again re-elected. By the bye I intended before to have notified you of one of the misrepresentations of this fellow during the late Presidential Canvass. He stated publicly, as I am told, that

Gen. [William F.] Gordon had designed, nay, avowed his determination to vote for Gen. [Zachary] Taylor, until he received a letter from you informing him of a Party arrangement by which, if your friends should sustain [Lewis] Cass, you were to be the nominee in 1852. I publicly pronounced the statement to be a falsehood—an unnecessary labour, for I do not believe that a single individual believed it to be true; no, not even the bitterest of your political opponents.

We have no definitive intelligence as to the new Cabinet. [John M.] Clayton's appointment [as Secretary of State] is the only one which has, as yet, reached us. Others have been named in the Papers, but this is the only one which will give any general satisfaction. [George] Evans, [Caleb B.] Smith, & the others named (with the exception of [Thomas B.] King,) would be unpopular. I much fear, from certain indications, that Taylor will disappoint many who voted for him. If the Course of the Southern Whigs shadow forth his own feelings, or the policy of his Administration, I shall regard his election as more calamitous than that of [Andrew] Jackson himself. He cannot, indeed, do much worse than his mean, cowardly and perfidious predecessor [James K. Polk]; but great evils must arise if he attempt to sustain the Whigs of the South in the course they have adopted. The result will be a division amongst ourselves—attended with a bitterness of feeling, a violence of action compared with which the past will be peace. I hope, however, for the best, but am prepared for the worst. I did not think that he would have formed an entire Whig Cabinet; and wrote some time since to Mr. [Isaac E.] Holmes, urging him to remonstrate against it. An administration composed of grave and moderate men, without respect to Parties, seemed to me to be not only practicable but highly expedient. But it seems that his repudiation of "*ultra-Whiggery*", was but an idle thing. I should be glad to know whether he has offered to any of the State Rights Party a place in his Cabinet.

What does the election of Mr. [Henry] Clay, and the reputed course of Mr. [John J.] Crittenden mean? Does the former intend to play the same game he played with [William H.] Harrison & [John] Tyler—and is the latter afraid of the consequences? The conduct of both seems to me very mysterious; for I take it for granted that the one *desired* to be returned to the Senate, and that the other has been offered a Cabinet appointment.

You will, I suppose, leave Washington soon after the 4th prox. Can you not visit Virginia during the ensuing summer? Would it not be of great service to you to spend the sultry season at the White and Blue Sulphur Springs? If you would make my House your headquarters, you might ride every day to the latter; and what with our mountain air, exercise and waters, I make no doubt you would derive great benefit. You know how much pleasure it would afford us to have you as a guest. Besides I have been so much pressed to *write a Book* in reference to you, that I should like much to consult you on the subject. It has long been my purpose to arrange some materials in my possession, *for the benefit of my Son*, or my family if I had no son. I promised poor [Dixon H.] Lewis to do this years ago, and to dedicate it to him. I did not contemplate immediate publication, but designed it to be a posthumous work. This, if my life is spared, I shall certainly do, but so many persons from different sections have urged me to do this now, that if it did not conflict with your feelings—and further, if I will persuade myself that I could do the subject anything like justice, I believe I should attempt it. I never contemplated any connected or elaborate work, but rather leading *incidents and anecdotes* illustrative of *life* and *character*, written in a free and familiar style. In recounting some of these, (for I have many recorded,) I have frequently had occasion to observe how deeply they affected others. In a very recent conversation, when I was lead to speak of some of these incidents, in the company of intelligent gentlemen, the whole—*political opponents all*, earnestly requested that I would make them public *now*; and not, as I told them was my purpose, to wait for some future day. A nephew of [Daniel] Webster's in Boston, three years ago, begged me to allow him to publish some which he had heard from me. But I never felt at liberty to indulge my own feelings in this respect—knowing your fixed aversion to the ordinary arts of politicians and their biographers—and seeing how liable such a work would be to misconstruction on the part of friends and misrepresentation on the part of enemies. Your fame is not of that *four year's copy-right*, which distinguishes your cotemporaries; and I am, by no means, emulous of the honors of [Amos] Kendall, [William M.] Holland, [George Dennison] Prentice, [George W.?] Curtis, and that forgotten biographer who was sent by Tyler to the Sandwich Islands. Thier [*sic*] objects enter not into my mind. To expose vice and to vindicate virtue is a duty which every man owes to himself, to his family, and to his country. These would be the *motives* and the *objects* of action, if I act at all—and at all events I shall do this, whether you approve of it or not, should I be the longer liver.

But I am taxing your time too far. In this matter I shall venture to do nothing without further reflection. I hope you will be enabled to pass the summer months in our mountains; and that we shall have you as a guest in our mountain home, whither we expect to remove in the early part of July. Mrs. [Elizabeth Morris] Crallé–(Mary [Crallé] is absent in the Country) begs to be most affectionately remembered to you, and to Mrs. [Floride Colhoun] Calhoun and Miss [Martha] Cornelia [Calhoun], should they be with you. With highest regard and respect I remain ever truly yours, Richd. K. Crallé.

ALS in ScCleA.

Remarks on the Patent Renewal Law

[In the Senate, February 27, 1849]

Mr. Calhoun said, as he understood it—for he had not listened very attentively to the discussion—that the bill proposed to vest the Commissioner of Patents with the power to renew any patents, at his discretion, within three years after their expiration. He greatly doubted the legality or constitutionality of such a measure. The constitution simply provided that patents for invention should extend for a limited time. After the expiration of that time they became public property. Every citizen had a right to use them; and he would ask, where was the right to divest them of that privilege? This was the stipulation: the public was to forbear the use of the invention for fourteen years. That was the stipulation between the community and the patentee—Congress fixing the time; and after that time, it seemed to him that the invention was the common property of the people of the United States, and they had no right to interpose. He would not insist upon that; but what he would insist upon was, the great discretionary power given to the Commissioner of Patents. How many patents, he would ask, were now in existence that would, within that time, run out? [*After further debate*:]

Mr. Calhoun resumed. The power was much more limited than he had supposed from the argument. With that limitation, it was a new patent to all intents and purposes. The old patent had gone to the benefit of the people of the United States who had the common use of it, and the power originally granted to the patentee was the only power that could be given by the constitution. He trusted that no more time would be consumed upon the bill. We were now near the close of the session, and bills of this kind were of too much moment to be introduced at so late a period, unless under some pressing exigency, which did not in that case exist. He would therefore move to lay it on the table [*which was agreed to*].

From the Washington, D.C., *Daily Union*, February 28, 1849, pp. 2–3. Variant in the Washington, D.C., *Daily National Intelligencer*, February 28, 1849, p. 2; *Congressional Globe*, 30th Cong., 2nd Sess., p. 601.

Remarks on Diplomatic Appropriations

[In the Senate, February 27, 1849]

[*John P. Hale of N.H. moved an amendment to raise the salaries of the U.S. Ministers to Great Britain, France, and Russia.*]

Mr. Calhoun. I rise to say a very few words. My impression is, that a revision of the whole of the subject is necessary. I think there ought to be a special salary for each court, because there are a great variety of circumstances that serve to increase the expenses; but this is a thing which ought to be done after a very careful examination of the subject. It ought to be examined by a special committee—a committee raised for that express purpose. Under these circumstances I cannot vote for the proposition. It has been presented without a particle of information, as far as I can learn—taken up I suppose barely upon individual assertion, at a late period of the session, when there is no time to examine it here or in the other House. I hope the proposition will not receive the sanction of the Senate.

[*Hale withdrew his amendment.*]

From *Congressional Globe*, 30th Cong., 2nd Sess., p. 603. Also printed in the Washington, D.C., *Daily National Intelligencer*, February 28, 1849, p. 3.

From F[itz]w[illiam] Byrdsall

New York [City,] Feb[ruar]y 28th 1849

Dear Sir, I congratulate you for many reasons—one because I perceive by your usual ability in the Senate that your health is restored; another, because I never saw a prettier or more conclusive point brought out by a debate than your reply to Messrs. [William L.] Dayton [of N.J.,] [John P.] Hale [of N.H.,] and [Daniel] Webster [of Mass.]. It was so triumphant that it struck my mind with the force of an electric flash as I read it. It proved to me that you were yourself again—the only man who *fully* comprehends our Constitution and system of Government.

We stand now more clearly where we have *always stood* upon the platform of Constitutionality. I might go further & say upon the platform of morality of patriotism and the well being of the White and negro races. I hold that the day of abolition of the subjection of the latter to the former, would be the darkest[,] worst and most fatal to both that the human mind could conceive. The region of our most valuable exports upon which the commerce and business of our whole country mainly depends, would become a desert ever after, and the contest in the labor market would ensue between the white and Black to be only terminated by the extermination or exodation[?] of the latter.

We stand therefore upon *better* ground than the Constitution, and are bound to maintain our stand because nothing so bad could happen as an abandonment of that ground by us. Comparatively we are probably as strong now as we ever can be, and for the sake of all that is dear and sacred we "fight the good fight["]. If the injustice and the law of force of an infatuated majority should compel sectional separation of the confederacy, much as I would deplore it, yet it would be preferable to colonial subjection to the northern section and positive ruin to the Southern.

Any and every attempt to make Indian or negro people a portion or part of the *political people* of these United States is monstrously repulsive to every sense that God has given to me. I would not want any of my kith or kin or posterity to inhabit ["such" *interlined*] a country. May Heaven and its providence save us from such a National deterioration, from such an abasement of our race—from the disgrace of deserting that superiority over all existences upon this earth, which our Creator has given to us! Every consideration of race—of country—of morality of fitness—of wise benevolence—of true christian charity to say nothing of self preservation, all unite in favor of preserving the institution of slavery as it now exists in this country, both as consistent with the Constitution of the Union and the Constitution of Nature itself.

All the means of creating a false public opinion are in the hands of the physical majority of those who are opposed to us in Christendom. A crusade is got up against us in which truth and right are alike disregarded and every misrepresentation of us and our sentiments is disseminated in every direction against us. It was a part of the policy of the evil workers to spread over the world that your health had failed that you had broken down &c &c. no doubt with the fiendish intention of impressing this on the minds of yourself and friends knowing that if successful in this, it would hasten your dissolution. I would not allude to this but for the purpose of excusing the advice I now presume to offer—namely to beg you to be careful of your health—to avoid late sessions—fatigue of body or mind—to eat at regular intervals, and to use the temperate Bath and the flesh Brush. You have a frame of Body and mind calculated with proper care to last many years, for which, for the sake of our country and its well being, that you may be preserved, is the heartfelt wish of Dear Sir, Yours with all Respect, F.W. Byrdsall.

ALS in ScCleA.

From M[ARIA] D[ALLAS] CAMPBELL

349 Chest[nut] St., Philadelphia
Thursday Feb: 28th [1849]

My dear Friend, I had so earnestly hoped to have seen you, before the close of your labors this session, that I have reluctantly yielded to the necessity of my disappointment, but I cannot let you leave Washington without recalling to you, that you have a friend in this direction who is ever watching with deep interest all public events in which you are so prominent a participator and so eminently distinguished. Your indisposition has caused me much anxiety for I knew the deep concern you felt in the great & agitating questions would both produce & continue ["continual" *altered to* "constant"] anxiety & excitement, but I trust with the *scene*, will vanish the *evil*, & that the pure breezes of Fort Hill, & the repose you ever enjoy there will restore that physical strength which is prostrated by mental energy. Before you leave your post, do give me a few lines to tell me "alls well" & what your hopes are of the present rulers. As to those now leaving us, I think *we* have thought alike, although *circumstances* have compelled me to avoid coming within their vortex, or indulging in any expression of opinion. I almost wish an extra session could be called for then I should see you once more, for every year makes my *old* friends *more few* & more precious. I think Ye Conscript Fathers will never recede and in that case, what can be done[?] May I not tell you with what deep interest & conviction I have traced all your views, badly as they are transmitted to me through the reports of the news papers; & more especially may I not tell you how gratified I have been at your *recent* triumph keen encounter with [Daniel Webster] the Giant of the North[?], (who I insisted today in conversation with some of his Whig worshippers, you had effectually *cornered*[)].

I will not intrude longer on your *fully* employed moments, but beg you will attribute this intrusion to its true source, an unwillingness that you should forget me—& a disappointment at not seeing you[,] for I fear *three years*, at our time of life, may not very well be spared—& I have not been in Washington since the first winter of the Polk administration. I rejoiced to see your daughter [Anna Maria Calhoun Clemson] looking so well. I wish you could be induced to pay a visit this way, no motive unworthy of your dignity could now be imputed to you and you would find many many admirers, & some warm friends to greet you. Mr. [Alexander] C[ampbell] & my son [St. George T. Campbell] unite with me in kind regards to you. It gives me great pleasure to say my son's health appears to be gradually improving.

With cordial good wishes for your present & future health & prosperity I am now as ever your most trusted & trusting friend, M:D: Campbell.

ALS in ScCleA.

Remarks on the Purchase of James Monroe's Papers

[In the Senate, February 28, 1849]

[*Under consideration was an appropriation of $20,000. A similar appropriation for George Washington manuscripts had just passed.*]

Mr. Calhoun. I have steadily voted against all appropriations of this kind, but if the first part of the amendment is to prevail, I think the second ought also to prevail, for I believe the papers of Mr. Monroe will be found to be of considerable value. I believe further, from information which has been imparted to me—I speak only on the authority of such information—that a great act of injustice has been done to the heirs of Mr. Monroe, inasmuch as the other papers that have been ordered to be printed, and are printed in connexion with the correspondence of those distinguished men, Mr. [Thomas] Jefferson and Mr. [James] Madison, very nearly deprived the heirs of Mr. Monroe of the benefit of his whole correspondence. I shall vote for retaining this part of the amendment, although I shall vote against the whole.

From the Washington, D.C., *Daily National Intelligencer*, March 1, 1849, p. 4. Also printed in the Washington, D.C., *Daily Union*, March 9, 1849, p. 1.

From Calhoun and many others, [*ca.* 3]/1849. A printed invitation to the forthcoming inaugural ball contains Calhoun's name as one of the many Managers. Printed document (addressed to Miss Mary E. Edwards) in DLC, Decatur House Papers.

Receipt from Ann [Mathewes] Ioor, Greenville, S.C., 3/1. "Received of Mr. John C. Calhoun Four hundred and twenty Dollars ($420.00) being the balance due for Interest on his Bond to John R. Mathewes as Trustee for myself and Children, up to the above date." DS in ScU-SC, John Raven Mathewes Papers.

Remarks on the Census Bill

[In the Senate, March 1, 1849]

Mr. Calhoun. Mr. President, there is a great deal of truth in what has been said by the Senator from Florida [James D. Westcott, Jr.]. If I had been called upon for illustrations of the tendency of the action of this Government towards a concentration of power, I would have submitted the operation of this census law as one, and the progress of the Patent Office as another. The Constitution requires Congress to provide for taking the census, for the purpose of fixing the ratio of representation, every ten years. It requires the mere enumeration of the people, and nothing more. But we have carried it from minutia to minutia, down, down, down, until we have come to the price of labor, and all that. Why are we to collect all these statistics? Is it to supersede the labor of the States? Are not the States competent to take their own census, and manage their own affairs? Why not leave it to them? Why do we undertake to do their work for them? Sir, I know that when, under the census law of 1840, the agents began to inquire of people the number of eggs and hens, and all that, which they possessed, they did not understand what it all meant. They instinctively resisted the operations of the law, and their instincts were right.

So it is in regard to the Patent Office. Under the simple power of granting patents for a limited time, we have gone on until we have reared up a great agricultural institution, with voluminous reports, which cost us thousands of dollars a year to print them. Sir, it is time that we should stop. Ours is a Federal Government, not a National Government. It is a Government of States. As we depart from the original rules of action in regard to all these subjects, the census included, we tend to concentrate and consolidate the power of the Government, and as we go to consolidation, we go to our certain ruin. It is time to arrest this tendency. There will be ample time at the commencement of the next Congress to pass a simple bill of this kind, providing merely for the enumeration of the inhabitants. I understand that it has never been customary to pass a bill until the commencement of the year in which the census was to be taken.

[*Joseph R. Underwood of Ky. stated that the last census bill had been passed earlier.*]

Mr. Calhoun. Be that as it may. Here, in the last week of the session, when other business is crowding upon us, we have a bill going beyond all former bills, and which will require much attention. I had no idea that the bill would be taken up at this time. I had not looked at it, and therefore I was compelled, though reluctantly, to ask the indulgence of the Senate to have it read, in order that I might understand it. I move that the bill be laid upon the table.

[*Calhoun's motion was rejected. Simon Cameron of Pa. urged immediate passage of the bill as "necessary, in order to give the State Department time to prepare the forms and send them abroad."*]

Mr. Calhoun. The only necessity for preparing these forms in such a complicated form, and in a manner which will take up a great deal of time, is because we are going beyond what we ought to do. If we adopt the bill for taking the first census it will take but a short time to prepare the forms. And one reason why I prefer that the bill should go over to the next session is, that it will be compelled to take a simpler and better form.

[*There was further discussion during which John Davis of Mass. argued that the expanded census was "essential to all our great interests. . . . this information is found to be constantly useful in the progress of our legislation here, and useful to the country in a thousand ways." He pointed out that the government collected extensive statistics on foreign commerce and should do so on internal commerce as well.*]

Mr. Calhoun. Mr. President, a very few words in reply. The Senator asks, why do we collect information in relation to the [external] commerce of the country, and upon what principle are the reports of our custom-houses made? My answer is, because it is the duty of the Federal Government to regulate external commerce. That is wholly within the power of Congress. The regulation of commerce at home, as far as respects commerce between the States, and no further, is also in the power of Congress. To that extent information may be collected, and no further. There is undoubtedly some reason why the Government should have information to that extent, because they control that branch of our industry; but all the internal commerce and internal productions belong to the States, and let every State provide for itself. I object to this on account of its tendency to absorb the interests of the whole country. I object to it on that ground, and because I think it is taking upon ourselves the proper business of the States.

From *Congressional Globe*, 30th Cong., 2nd Sess., pp. 627–628. Also printed in the Washington, D.C., *Daily National Intelligencer*, March 10, 1849, p. 2. Variant in the Washington, D.C., *Daily Union*, March 2, 1849, p. 2. Another variant in the New York, N.Y., *Herald*, March 4, 1849, p. 3.

Sam[uel] Houston, Washington, "To My Constituents," 3/2. Houston [Senator from Texas] replies to remarks made by Calhoun at a public meeting at Charleston that Houston and Thomas H. Benton had abandoned the South when they supported the bill to organize a government for the Oregon Territory. Houston denies that allegation and accuses Calhoun of inconsistency and disunionism. He claims that Calhoun is a spokesman solely for South Carolina and is not a guardian of Southern interests. PC in the Washington, D.C., *Daily National Intelligencer*, March 8, 1849, p. 2.

Remarks on a Bill to Remit Customs Duties on Goods Destroyed by Fire at New York City

[In the Senate, March 2, 1849]

Mr. Calhoun. I have not read this bill, nor do I know what its provisions are. I understand, as the bill now reads, that the insurer is not to be paid, but the indemnity is limited to the goods insured. I am not prepared to vote for the bill. As I understand it, sir, all dealers sell their goods at a price sufficient to pay for the insurance, freight, expenses, and the general hazards they are liable to incur, and among these is the hazard of fire. They charge a price to make the business profitable, everything considered. If that be so, the dealer, who is not insured, stands in very much the same position with him who is insured. The latter are self-insured. They charge an additional price to cover the risk of fire. The very argument against insurers applies to these dealers, for they are the insurers of their own property. They charge an additional price; retaining, in this manner, the premium charged by other insurers. I have never seen my way clear in attempting to distinguish between this and other cases of fire. I know that when an evil falls upon large masses, our sympathies are so powerful that we can scarcely resist them. But it seems to me that we should look at the facts and bearings of our legislation. This bill is to make the Government an insurer of goods. Now, sir, I hold that the proper way is to consider each man who is not insured by others as self-insured. Under this impression, unless it shall be removed, I shall feel constrained to vote against the bill.

[*Robert M.T. Hunter of Va. disputed Calhoun's interpretation. "This was the only Government in the world that charged duties on goods lost by fire."*]

Mr. Calhoun. The view of my friend does not seem to me to be correct. I will propound to him a question. Suppose the goods have been insured, would you refund the amount to the merchant which you are paid for the duties?

Mr. Hunter. Being insured, this bill does not give him any indemnity.

Mr. Calhoun. That is the very point to which I wish to call your attention. That is just and right; he should not be twice indemnified. But why should not the insurance company be indemnified? True, they have received their premium; but so with the merchant, who is self-insured. Does he not lay a general charge upon what he sells to cover the expense of insurance? And does he not, by retaining that amount instead of paying it to an insurance company, virtually insure his own property, and receive the premium upon that insurance?

Mr. Hunter. They do lay this general charge, and will do so, unless the Government saves them from it by this bill.

Mr. Calhoun. Precisely. Then the Government would become the insurer. It seems to me to be a great deal better that each man should be made to have his goods insured, or to insure himself by making this general charge.

From *Congressional Globe*, 30th Cong., 2nd Sess., p. 645. Also printed in the Washington, D.C., *Daily Union*, March 3, 1849, p. 2.

Remarks on the Distribution of Books to New Senators

[In the Senate, March 2, 1849]

[*Under consideration was a resolution to give to new Senators the collection of published historical records that had been distributed to members in 1847.*]

Mr. Calhoun. If I understand the object of the resolution, it is to give to every new Senator that comes in the same number of copies as the old members have had, for the purpose of distribution. It appears to me that the proposition made by the Senator from New York [Daniel S. Dickinson], now supported by the Senator from Tennessee [Hopkins L. Turney], is perfectly fair, to give to the members of the new States, who have not received their proper quota, and to give to each new member, as they come in, one copy. That is the whole affair. The resolution, as it stands, will make a perpetual job of it. Now, we know that unless we publish an edition far beyond our capacity, we cannot give to all the people of the United States. The copies that are now distributed go to few. But if the resolution, as it stands, is adopted, you will be giving book upon book to every newly-elected member, and there will be no end to it. It must, then, stop somewhere; and, in my opinion, this is the proper place for it to stop, as proposed in the amendment.

From *Congressional Globe*, 30th Cong., 2nd Sess., p. 647.

Remarks in the Senate, 3/3. Calhoun made barely reported and unsuccessful remarks against suspension of the Senate rule which prevented sending of bills to the House of Representatives or the President during the last three days of the session. From *Congressional Globe*, 30th Cong., 2nd Sess., p. 668; the Washington, D.C., *Daily National Intelligencer*, March 26, 1849, p. 1.

Further Remarks on the Census Bill

[In the Senate, March 3, 1849]

Mr. Calhoun said: Census bills have not heretofore passed at the short session, but early in the next succeeding one. If it is the desire of the Senate to go back to the primitive practice of the Senate, and adopt that simple mode by which we first commenced, it can be passed in the course of one week. The object of this bill, however, looks at a different result; it is at least as complicated as the one the Senate voted down the other day. It is to refer the subject to the Executive departments. They will be surrounded by men who will wish this to be extended, and it will be very difficult for them to resist their influence. Sir, I always object to referring our duties to the department. We have always performed this duty ourselves, and we are abundantly capable of performing it. This is a simple question, and I will not discuss it. I will merely say, that I hope we shall not transfer to the executive departments our own duties.

From the Washington, D.C., *Daily Union*, March 23, 1849, p. 1. Variant in *Congressional Globe*, 30th Cong., 2nd Sess., p. 669.

Remarks on a Bill to Create an Interior Department

[In the Senate, March 3, 1849]

Mr. Calhoun. I am aware that the Senate is impatient, and I do not intend to trespass upon their time beyond what I deem it my duty upon this occasion. This, Mr. President, is a very important bill, and I exceedingly regret that I am so imperfectly acquainted with its details, and the principles upon which it has been urged at this time. I have had no further opportunity of knowing its contents than hearing it read, and hearing the discussion, disturbed and broken in upon by so much noise, that the greater part of it escaped my ear. I also regret exceedingly that we have so short a period to consider it. I have noticed, sir, as the result of my experience, that a measure, however important, is scarcely ever urged or opposed to any purpose at this late period in the session. Sir, no man can hope to get the attention of the Senate now, when there is one continual bustle, agitation, and moving to and fro. Attention cannot be commanded, and it is useless to expect it. And, sir, is it fair to urge a bill of this magnitude upon us at this time?

I concur entirely, sir, in what has been said by the Senator from Virginia (Mr. [James M.] Mason.) The fact that a bill of the character of this has been urged upon Congress, I believe, from the first administration of Washington, and repeated at intervals down to the present time, while it has never been favorably acted upon by Congress, and there has been no particular effort to get it through, is a strong evidence that there is a deep sense in the people against it. Sir, there is something ominous in the expression, "interior." This government, as so well said by the senator from Virginia, was made to take charge of exterior relations. Had there been no exterior relations, this government would never have existed; it was founded upon the exterior relations of the Union with foreign courts, and exterior relations of States with States; and that, perhaps, to a very limited extent. And now, to offer to create an interior department, is to introduce a great change in the very principles of our government.

What is the cause? We are told that the business of our government now has become so great, the departments have become so overloaded, that we require a new department, *ipso facto*. What evidence have we of that fact? Has a committee been appointed to call upon the several departments and ascertain the facts? I understand not. We have a single communication—volunteer so far as I know, perhaps called for by the other House—from a single department; and on that authority alone, on this, the last day of the session, when but a few hours remain for legislative action, we are to have this measure urged upon us as coming recommended by the department. Those professing opposite political principles, and friends of the incoming administration, are its supporters here, and that is a very important and significant fact.

If the departments are overcharged, what has been the cause? Has it not resulted from the overaction of our government? Is it not a strong admonition to us to check, to hold in, to retrace many of our steps, instead of giving new impulse to the government? Or, sir, suppose that this increased labor has not been the result of overaction and overburden: is there no other way to remedy it than by creating a new department, a "Department of the Interior?" May it not be corrected in a much more simple and safe form, by increasing the strength of the departments themselves, by adding assistants? You have already set the example in one of your departments, the Post Office Department, where there are three Assistant Postmasters General. Why not introduce the same machinery here, and confine the labors of the department to their own sphere? What answer can be given to that. I lay it down as a rule, founded upon experience, that it is far better that large classes of business analogous to one another should be under one general head, instead of being divided off artificially under several independent heads. All that relates to revenue, should be under the charge of the Secretary of the Treasury. All that relates to officers of the army and military operations, should be under the control of the War Department; and so on.

Now, sir, I do not know that I am correct about the facts in this case; but if I state them incorrectly, I hope some one will correct me. I understand it is proposed to make this new department take charge of our Indian affairs. Well, sir, who does not see that our Indian affairs are immediately connected with the War Department? Who does not see that the preservation of peace and harmony on our frontier, both in our own and the Indian towns, depends upon the action of the War Department? There is an intimate relation between our Indian affairs and the War Department, and you cannot separate them without doing great injury to both.

Next, it is proposed to create in this new department a Commissioner of Customs. Who does not see that this will greatly embarrass the unity of the operations of our Treasury Department? Then there is to be the Land Office connected with it. Who does not see that there is an intimate relation between that office and the Treasury Department? It is from the sales of the public lands that the Secretary of the Treasury looks for a considerable portion of the revenue; and there is, therefore, a connexion between that office and the Treasury Department which cannot be disturbed without materially deranging the affairs of the government.

Now, sir, it appears that we are to take one bureau from the Treasury Department, another from the War Department, and others from other departments; we are to have a new commissioner, called the Commissioner of Customs; and thus we are to create a new department, with new machinery, under a new Secretary, who is to take charge of all these various offices.

[*William Allen of Ohio remarked that "It will be another Secretary of the Treasury."*]

Mr. Calhoun. Yes, sir, another Secretary of the Treasury. Why, sir, the thing is entirely unexampled. The Patent Office is to be connected with it also, and taken from the department of the Secretary of State. To be sure, there is not a very intimate relation between the Patent Office and the State Department; but I think it is quite as intimate a relation as between the Patent Office and the Indian bureau, and a little more so. But I wish to ask a question of gentlemen who advocate this bill. The Patent Office now has charge of the agriculture of the country, and submits a regular annual report, and a very extensive one it is. It has charge of all the statistics of the agricultural operations of the country. Now, sir, is it proposed to transfer that branch of the duties of the Commissioner of Patents to this Home Department? I put that question, whether this agricultural portion of the Patent Office bureau is to be transferred to the Home Department also?

[*Jefferson Davis of Miss. stated that under the new organization there would be less interference with the country's agriculture. The head of the Patent Office would no longer have to gather statistics "to build his reputation."*]

Mr. Calhoun. I am very glad if that will be the effect, but that is now so strongly connected with the Patent Office that I fear it will not avail anything to attempt to remove it by such means. Congress has tried for four years to my certain knowledge to limit that power, but without success. We have got a bureau connected with the agriculture of the country; and there is now another institution of the government connected with the education of the country—the Smithsonian Institution.

[*An unnamed Senator remarked that the Smithsonian Institution had "no connexion with the government."*]

Mr. Calhoun. I think it has great connexion. The government is the trustee of that institution, and five years will not pass before it will be still more intimately connected with the government. Then there is a penitentiary connected with the department. It seems as if everything on the face of God's earth was to be put together in this one department—Indians, patents, lands, public buildings, are all thrown together without the slightest connexion.

Sir, this thing ought not to be. This is a monstrous bill. Its power is immense, and is to extend over the whole interior. It is one of the greatest steps which has ever been taken in my time to absorb all the remaining powers of the States. This ought to be stopped. Ours is a federal government. The States are constituents of this federal government. It has created a supervisory power, and now, step by step, we are concentrating and consolidating this power in the general government by a new plan, under the name of the Interior Department. Sir, I cannot believe that if this bill had been taken up sufficiently early, if there had been eight or ten days for consideration and deliberate discussion, that it would have found favor here. But it is useless now to oppose it; there is barely time to touch upon the subject. I know the impatience of the Senate, and I do not purpose to throw myself in the way of its action, if it has determined to take this step.

From the Washington, D.C., *Daily Union*, March 23, 1849, p. 2. Variant in *Congressional Globe*, 30th Cong., 2nd Sess., pp. 672–673; the Washington, D.C., *Daily National Intelligencer*, March 26, 1849, pp. 1–2; Benton, *Abridgment of Debates*, 16:337–339. Other variants in the Boston, Mass., *Daily Advertiser*, March 5, 1849, p. 2; the New York, N.Y., *Herald*, March 6, 1849, p. 1.

Further remarks on the Interior Department Bill, 3/3. Henry S. Foote of Miss. suggested that Calhoun had favored such a department when a member of James Monroe's cabinet. "Mr. Calhoun. It is so long since the termination of Mr. Monroe's administration that I will not undertake to assert from memory whether the measure then proposed was similar to this; but I will say this, that I have never been in favor of such a measure." From *Congressional Globe*, 30th Cong., 2nd Sess., p. 676. Also printed in the Washington, D.C., *Daily National Intelligencer*, March 28, 1849, p. 1.

From Hilliard M. Judge

Eutaw [Ala.], 8th March 1849

Dear Sir: I take the liberty of transmitting by to day[']s mail, a newspaper, containing an article on the subject of "Slavery in the territories," to which, I beg leave to call your attention.

The views correspond with those entertained by you; in fact, they were elicited by the debate in the Senate last year on that subject. The article, is from the pen of the Hon. H[arry] I. Thornton of this place.

I am happy to tell you, we are united to a man, in a determination to resist further aggression upon the rights of the South.

The constituents of [Henry W.] Hilliard, will no doubt repudiate his course in refusing to sign the Address; but I fear, we cannot hope so much, from those of [Williamson R.W.] Cobb and [George S.] Houston.

If your time will permit, I would be very much pleased to receive a letter from you.

I sincerely hope your health is entirely restored. I have the honor to remain, Your friend, & ob[e]d[ien]t Serv[an]t, Hilliard M. Judge.

ALS in ScCleA.

From Ja[me]s & C. Lillybridge

Pine[,] Oneida Co[unty] N.Y., March 8th/49

Sir, We have taken the liberty to address this letter to *you*, for the reason that we are unacquainted with any one at the *present time* at the

City of Washington, and can think of no one there, who would be more likely to aid us in effecting the object we have in view.

Upon the Slavery question which is now agitating the public mind and creating sectional jealousies, our sympathies are entirely with the South. Being extensively acquainted with the institutions of the South, one of us having spent some twenty years in that section of the Union, we take a lively interest in whatever may tend to effect the interest, rights or happiness of our southern friends.

We have recently seen accounts of certain transactions, by Southern gentlemen, at Washington City, both in and out of Congress, in regard to the agitating movements of the North, and are desirous of benefiting ourselves and others by the perusal of their addresses, speeches &c. We wish for a copy or two of the address of the Southren Delegation, addopted at a meeting at the Capital. Also a few Copies of Gov. [James] McDowel[l']s speech in the House of Rep[resentative]s on the Slavery question, of which we see reported a large edition in pamphlet form; and any others pertinent to the subject. On the northern side of the question we get a full supply without the trouble of asking.

Could you make our object known to some one, whose youth, leisure, and inclination would enable him to attend to our request, and if possible forward to us the Documents, without the inconvenience we fear it might cause yourself, you would confer a favour, which we assure you is reluctantly asked: and if the documents are received our honour for it, they will ["be" *interlined*] placed where they will tell for the object they were designed.

A Pamphlet ["on slavery" *interlined*] published by Gov. [James H.] Hammond of S.C. was sent us, but was destroyed by accident. We would like to get that and the one published by Gov. [George] McDuffie.

Could our address be placed with a proper person who would from time to time forward to us such Documents as they come out, we should be gratified. But of yourself we ask nothing more than to make this known, if you know of such persons. In the mean time we assure you, sir, of our High Respect and Consideration, Jas. & C. Lillybridge, Pine, Oneida Co[unty,] N.Y.

P.S. We would refer to our Representative Hon. Tim[othy] Jenkins, but he probably is not there.

LS in ScCleA. NOTE: An AEU by Calhoun reads, "Messrs. Lillybridge."

From T[HOMAS] B. FRASER

Sumterville So. Ca.
March 12th 1849

Dear Sir, In accordance with a resolution passed at a Meeting of the citizens of Sumter District on Monday the 5th inst. I herewith transmit you a copy of its Proceedings. Respectfully Yours, T.B. Fraser.

[Printed Enclosure]

District Meeting.

A large and enthusiastic meeting of the citizens of Sumter District was held agreeably to a previous call on Monday, the 5th inst., in the Court House, for the purpose of responding in a suitable manner to the Address of the Southern Delegates in Congress, on the subject of Abolition.

Col. F[ranklin] I. Moses, on motion of F.M. Adams Esq., was called to the Chair, and having, in a few impressive and glowing remarks, portrayed the wrongs of the South, and explained the object of the meeting, appointed Messrs. R.M. Dyson and T.B. Fraser, Secretaries, and announced that the meeting was ready for business.

Major A[lbertus?] C. Spain moved "that a committee of twenty-five (25) persons be appointed to consider and report on the Address of the Southern Delegates in Congress." The motion being seconded and passed, the Chairman appointed the following gentlemen to constitute the committee.

Maj. A.C. Spain, Col. Wm. Nettles, Maj. Wm. Haynsworth, Dr. J[ohn] B. Witherspoon, J[ames] M. Nelson Esq., Capt. J[ohn] D. Ashmore, S. Mayrant Esq., Col. J.B. Miller, Capt. J.W. Rrownfield [*sic*; John W. Brownfield], Capt. F[rancis] Sumter, Capt. J[ames] D. Blanding, F[rancis] H. Kennedy Esq., Dr. J.L. Mellett, Col. Jas. E. Rembert, Saml. E. Wilson Esq., Col. M[ontgomery] Moses, Robt. Bradford Esq., Gen. S[amuel] R. Chandler, Capt. W.A. Muldrow, Dr. J.E. Dennis, Rev. J[ohn] S. Richardson, Rev. C.P. Elliott, Rev. H. Spain, Hon. L[evy] F. Rhame, Rev. H.D. Green.

The Committee retired and after deliberation returned and made through their Chairman the following Report.

The Committee appointed to consider and report on the Address of the Southern Delegates in Congress beg leave to make the following Report.

"The Address of Southern Delegates in Congress to their Constituents" is an impressive warning from those, whose position enables them to detect the immediate approach of danger to the continued and peaceful existence of the Federal Union, and requires them to sound the note of alarm. It was made "in discharge of what *they* believed to be a solemn duty, on the most important subject ever presented for *our* consideration." "The acts of aggression and encroachment," on the part of the North, "in reference to the relation existing between the European and African races at the South," form the basis of that Address. Should the acts of aggression, therein too truthfully detailed, prove successful, (of which there is a certainty, without *prevention*) we are told, "the blacks, and profligate whites in union with them, would become the principal recipients of federal offices and patronage, and would in consequence, be raised above the whites of the South in the political and social scale"—that "*we* would change *conditions* with *them*." This surely is a frightful picture, and such a condition would, indeed, be "a degradation greater than has ever yet fallen to the lot of a free and enlightened people." That such is the gloomy prospect ahead, we have the written declaration of forty-eight faithful and vigilant sentinels from the South. They have admonished us of the danger, and, to avoid it, entreat us "*to be united*" and, for that purpose, to adopt all necessary measures.

With such a warning and such a prospect before us, what is the duty of the South?

Unquestionably, the day for argument has passed, and remonstrance is no longer heeded. The Constitution, the grand Charter of our rights, no longer constitutes a barrier to the progress of fanaticism and pseudo-philanthropy. The unblushing effrontery, with which Congress violates the sacred compromises of the Constitution, and the unmanly subterfuges, to which individuals, associations and even State Legislatures resort to render inoperative its plainest, and yet to us, its most important provisions, foreshadow, without mistake, the approach of anarchy—the reign of the law of force and numbers. We have the evidence of all this plainly, yet ably detailed in the Address to the South.

Will we stand idly by and see the supreme law of the land violated by overt acts of aggression on the part of Congress, and nullified by subterfuge and indirection on the part of Northern citizens and Legislatures? Will we parley whilst Southern Citizens are ostracised from the common territory, purchased, in part, at least, by Southern blood? Will we consent to our own bondage and degradation and to become "hewers of wood and drawers of water" to our own slaves? The firm and unalterable response of every man of Sumter is an indignant negative. If the aggressive steps be not retraced and further assaults upon the Constitution do not cease, the citizens of Sumter are ready to join the whole Southern people in *action* for the supremacy of the established law. They are ready to adopt, as their own, the language of McDuffie, and to declare that "absolute submission and passive obedience to every extreme of tyranny are the characteristics of slaves only,"—that, rather than submit, like slaves, to their own degradation, they are willing to strike in defence of the Constitution and permanent equality,—that they are unwilling to leave the redress of their own greivances as a legacy to their posterity,—that they prefer to transmit to their children, their own inheritance, a stable government and equality of rights.

The Committee recommend the adoption of the following Resolutions.

1st. *Resolved,* That the proceedings of the Southern Delegates in Congress, whose names are subscribed to the Address to the South, meet our cordial approval.

2nd. *Resolved,* That no greater degradation could befal us, as freemen, than submission to the fate, which Northern fanaticism is preparing for us, in its measures for the restriction and Abolition of our domestic institutions.

3d. *Resolved,* That whilst we cherish the Federal Union, and would deplore its dissolution, we can only remain as we were left by our forefathers, equals in privileges and rights,—that, with the North and not with the South, will rest the responsibility of its of its [*sic*] overthrow.

4th. *Resolved,* That the citizens of Sumter District are prepared to unite with the citizens of the other Districts of this State and of the other Southern States in any measure necessary for the preservation of our common institutions,—that the time has arrived, in which union of action and effort is necessary to avert our own degradation, and to teach the enemies of law and order, that there are bounds, beyond which forbearance ceases to be a virtue.

5th. *Resolved,* That a Committee of Safety be appointed, whose duty it shall be to correspond with the citizens of the other Districts in this State and other Southern States for the purpose of devising the means for united action for the common safety; and that they have authority to call a meeting of the citizens of this District, when, in their judgment, proper and necessary.

The meeting was then addressed in eloquent and patriotic language by Maj. A.C. Spain, Gen. S.R. Chandler, Maj. R.M. Dyson and

Mr. F.H. Kennedy, who vindicated the course which the South has been called on to pursue and pointed out the degradation which is preparing for us, and which inevitably awaits us if we should now shrink from the assertion of our rights.

The report and resolutions were unanimously adopted and the Chairman appointed a committee under the 5th resolution to consist of the following gentlemen:

Hon. J[ohn] L. Manning, Wm. E. Richardson, O[rlando] S. Reese, L. White, Wm. H.B. Richardson, Dr. T.W. Briggs, Gen. S.R. Chandler, Col. F.M. Mellett, Col. J[ohn?] C. Rhame, L.H. Dinkins, Col. Wm. A. Colclough, Hon. J[ohn] P. Richardson, Rev. G.C. Gregg, Dr. J.B. Witherspoon, J[ames] M. Nelson, J.D. Ashmore, Dr. S[amuel?] W. Witherspoon, Dr. J.J. [*sic*; John I.?] Ingram, J[ohnson?] J. Knox, Capt. L.L. Belser, Capt. F. Sumter, Maj. T[homas] M. Baker, J.W. Stuckey, J[ames] S.G. Richardson, W.H. Burgess, H[enry] J. Smith, Hugh Wilson, J[ohn?] H. Ragin, J[ohn] N. Frierson, Richard Ragin, Capt. C.S. Mellett, R.B. Cain, Rev. H.D. Green, W[illiam] J. Reynolds, John Ballard, R.B. Muldrow, Dr. J.C. Haynsworth, Capt. Wm. M. Scott, J.D. McFaddin, A.C. Spain, Dr. W.W. Anderson, E. Keels, Maj. E.M. Anderson, Wm. Nettles, Willis Ramsay, F.M. Adams, Hon. J.J. [*sic*; John I.] Moore, J.R. Brock, Anthony White, Harvey Skinner, M. Moses, Dr. C.S. Crane, J.N. McLeod, Rev. T[homas?] R. English, M[oses] M. Benbow, T.J. Dinkins, G.W. Lee, Capt. J.B.N. Hammet, T[homas] J. Coghlan, E.J. Pugh, J[ohn] T. Green, R[ichard] R. Spann, Isaac Lenoir, Capt. L.P. Loring, Capt. J. Thompson Green.

On motion of T.B. Fraser the following resolution was passed by the meeting.

Resolved, That the Sumter Committee of Safety be and hereby is authorised and requested immediately to invite similar committees in this State, to unite with them in the selection of two members from each District committee, to meet and organize themselves as a *Central Committee of Safety*, at the Capital of this State, to meet as often as they may deem necessary—to correspond with similar committees in the *Southern States* and the District committees of this State, and to take measures whenever occasion may require for a convention of the *People of South Carolina*, with a view of promoting "firm, united and concerted action" at the *South*.

The following resolutions were offered by Capt. J.D. Blanding, and adopted.

1st. *Resolved*, That we, the citizens of Sumter District, return to our immediate Representative in Congress [Joseph A. Woodward] our hearty thanks for the firm course he has pursued in opposition to the aggressive acts of the North; that, as his constituents, we give him his meed of "well done, thou good and faithful servant."

2d. *Resolved*, That this meeting would most respectfully request His Excellency, the Governor, to convene the Legislature of South Carolina, to determine upon the immediate and proper steps to be taken, upon the passage of any bill by Congress, to which may be attached any Proviso, excluding slavery from newly acquired Territories.

3d. *Resolved*, That the proceedings of this meeting be transmitted to His Excellency, the Governor, also to our immediate Representative and Senators in Congress, to be laid before that body.

On motion of F.M. Adams, Esq.,

Resolved, That the Chairman of this meeting be added to the Committee of Safety.

On motion of Gen. S.R. Chandler, the meeting adjourned *sine die*.

F.J. Moses, *Chm'n.*

T.B. Fraser, *Act. Sec'y.*
R.M. Dyson, *Sec'y.*

ALS with En in ScCleA; PC of En in the Charleston, S.C., *Mercury*, March 10, 1849, p. 2. NOTE: An AEU by Calhoun reads, "The Sumter proceedings." The Charleston *Mercury* in various issues from March 8 through May 2, carried reports of similar meetings in Barnwell, Colleton, Lexington, Abbeville, Laurens, Marlboro, Union, Spartanburg, Beaufort, Williamsburg, Georgetown and Darlington Districts and St. James Santee Parish.

From LEM[UEL] TOWERS

Washington, March 13, 1849

Dear Sir: The proposition I made for printing a newspaper for you needs some explanation, as it is a mere calculation as to amount of subscription, and number of subscribers, without regard to "editor." The proposition embraces the pay of an editor, at the follow rate, which, I think, is not too much to ensure the time and talent that will be required.

The editor to receive for the "Daily," (if you conclude to have the Daily) $3000 per annum. If a "Triweekly," $1500 per annum; if "Twice a week" $1250 per annum; If "weekly" $1000 per annum.

I ask nothing more from you than the assurance that the number of subscribers will be got, at the prices named. If more subscribers are procured I propose to print a paper as large as the "Daily Globe" and on as good paper, and in as good style. Respectfully, yours, Lem: Towers.

ALS in ScCleA.

Remarks on the Seating of James Shields

[In the Senate, March 14, 1849]

[*Shields had been elected Senator from Ill., but had not been, apparently, a citizen of the U.S. long enough to qualify. A select committee had proposed a resolution which would delay his seating until the next December, when he presumably would be eligible.*]

Mr. Calhoun, who said: Mr. President, I hold nothing to be more certain than that if General Shields is not now a senator of the United States of right, he never can become so. The constitution is explicit that no person shall be a senator unless he has been nine years a citizen of the United States. If, then, he is not a senator now, there is a vacancy; Illinois would have but one senator, and the vacancy must be filled according to law. That proposition I hold to be conceded by every one in advance.

That he is not a senator is clear, because he cannot perform one duty belonging to the senatorial office, unless the nine years have expired previous to the time of the commencement of the senatorial term. Thus thinking, Mr. President, I think it is due, in the first place, to the State of Illinois, that the question should be now settled. And if General Shields shall allege that he has evidence, which will in all probability be satisfactory to the Senate, that the term of nine years had expired before the 4th of March—upon such an allegation upon the part of General Shields, it would be the duty of the Senate, in my opinion, to postpone it, but not otherwise. No such allegation having been made, in my opinion, as the thing now stands, it is the duty of the Senate to decide this question—a duty that we owe in the first place to the State of Illinois. I understand that the Illinois legislature will not be in session until January twelvemonth. If, then, the decision shall be adverse to General Shields, it is proper that the governor of Illinois shall know it in due time, to assemble the legislature to elect a senator to take his place on the first Monday in December next. I hold it, in the next place, to be due to Gen. Shields himself; because in so clear a case as this, I think he would gain by the course he has intimated that he will pursue, but would lose by the course which his friends are so anxious to adopt. For these reasons, Mr. President, unless General Shields will make the allegation I have stated, I shall feel myself bound to vote for the resolution properly amended.

Now, sir, I come to a point which I think of some little importance; that the question involved here should be definitively settled, not only to our satisfaction, but the satisfaction of all future time. In my opinion the resolution is not exactly correct. It would seem to assume that in all cases the election is void, unless the nine years should run out previous to the election. I do not think that is the constitution. According to my conception, if the nine years are consummated previous to the 4th of March, it is good, and the election is not void. But if the nine years terminate after the 4th of March, when the term commences, I hold the election to be void, according to the language of the constitution. I will therefore suggest to the Chair an amendment which I propose to offer at the proper time—to add the following words; which I ask to be read for the information of the Senate: "At the commencement of the term for which he was elected."

The resolution, as thus amended, would read as follows:

Resolved, That the election of James Shields to be a senator of the United States was void, he not having been a citizen of the United States the term of years required as a qualification to be a senator of the United States at the commencement of the term for which he was elected.

From the Washington, D.C., *Daily Union*, March 15, 1849, p. 2. Variant in *Congressional Globe*, 30th Cong., 2nd Sess., Appendix, p. 338; the Washington, D.C., *Daily National Intelligencer*, March 15, 1849, p. 2; the Charleston, S.C., *Mercury*, March 19, 1849, p. 2. Other variants in the New York, N.Y., *Herald*, March 15, 1849, p. 2; the Petersburg, Va., *Republican*, March 16, 1849, p. 3; the Charleston, S.C., *Courier*, March 19, 1849, p. 2. NOTE: The resolution was tabled until the next day, and shortly afterward the Senate was informed that Shields had resigned.

To J[OHN] M. CLAYTON, [Secretary of State]

Senate Chamber, 15th March 1849

Sir, I understand T[homas] L. Jones Esq. is an applicant for the place of Chargé de Affairs to some European Court.

I take pleasure in stating, that from my acquaintance with Mr.

Jones, I believe him to be well qualified from his character, standing and acquirements to fill the place for which he applies. With great respect I am & &, J.C. Calhoun.

ALS in DNA, RG 59 (State Department), Applications and Recommendations during the Administrations of James K. Polk, Zachary Taylor, and Millard Fillmore, 1845–1853, Thomas L. Jones (M-873:46, frames 680–682).

Further remarks on the seating of James Shields, 3/15. (Yesterday's discussion continued on the select committee resolution with Calhoun's amendment, a substitute resolution, and a motion to table the whole matter.) After a few parliamentary remarks Calhoun said, "If the motion be to lay the whole upon the table, I desire to say a few words." The presiding officer said that the pending motion could only table the substitute resolution. James M. Mason of Va. spoke in favor of Calhoun's amendment to the original resolution, stating that Calhoun's language had clarified and made explicit what the committee intended. Calhoun said, "That was my impression," and later said, "That is the whole object of it." (Eventually, the Senate agreed only to notify the executive of Ill. of Shields's resignation.) From *Congressional Globe*, 30th Cong., 2nd Sess., Appendix, p. 36. Also printed in the Washington, D.C., *Daily National Intelligencer*, March 17, 1849, p. 1; the Washington, D.C., *Daily Union*, March 17, 1849, p. 1.

From F[ITZ]W[ILLIAM] BYRDSALL

New York [City,] March 16th 1849

Dear Sir, As a citizen of the United States I consider it a duty at the close of another Session of Congress to express my high appreciation of your arduous patriotic efforts during the last two Sessions, to preserve intact the Constitution of the Confederacy. No man living has labored so much in defence of its principles—add to which your expositions and analytical groupings of its sacred provisions, all tending to shew that it has been the subject of your long anxious and careful thought. I observe that members of Congress from all sections of the Country declare great veneration for it, but when their votes are noticed and their greater regard for party ["is" *interlined*] considered, I hold their professions of adherence to be really nothing more nor less than political twaddle. He who truly esteems the Constitution as ["the" *interlined*] palladium of the Republic, as the wisest and best result of human society that has ever governed in any Country, would dread to infringe it, and still more to suffer it to be infringed. The fundamental principle of it is—the political Equality of the States and of the Citizens. Certainly, Wilmot provisoism strikes at the foundation of the whole system. The Northern man who supports any such provision, or the Southern man who does not at once, regardless of all party obligations, repel indignantly by word and deed such an outrage upon the rights of his State and himself, has really no adequate regard for the Constitution.

I judge that the address of the Southern members of Congress to their Constituents is doing its work well from the fact that [Samuel] Houston of Texas has come out with a pronunciamento; so has the other Southern members who voted against the adoption of the address, and so has Mr. [James D.] Westcott [Jr.] with an explanation in the Senate Chamber. It is the fear of the address and its consequences that brought out Houston, and not your Charleston speech nearly a year old. His production has the features of demagogueism upon its front; his artful conjuration of his reminiscency of Andrew Jackson is intended to evoke the prejudices of the past as aids to his enmity. There is a spirit of rancorous ambition that speaks not well for his head or heart.

I have seen an extract of the address of the Southern members in opposition to yours—in vindication of themselves. It seems like a petitioning appeal to the north and South rather than a statement of wrongs, or a declaration of Rights. These men must have read history to little or ["un" *interlined*]profitable instructions. When did a sense of justice or the dictates of magnanimity restrain popular majorities from exercising power where prejudice fanaticism or sectional interests led the way? The history of all democracies, aristocracies and even of our ["own" *interlined*] Country, all prove that those who know they have power will exercise it justly or unjustly as it appears most advantageous to themselves. There is no other safety for rights but this—that they must not, shall not be infringed. A union of Southern Democrats & Whigs in Congress against Wilmot provisoism would have killed it for ever and commanded the respect of the north. As it is I deplore it.

With Mr. Westcott's course generally I have no great fault to find but his defence that the address did not go far enough in denunciation is not cogent. If it did not go far enough he could not deny with reason his acquiescence to as far as it did go. He should have signed it.

It is in the power of Gen[era]l [Zachary] Taylor to reorganize the political parties of the country different from, and better for constitutional doctrines than they now are. Here again it is bad that the South is not united, for union amongst Southern members against encroachments upon Constitutional rights, would aid and strengthen him in the only course that would eventually, because of such union, make his administration popular and do good to the Country[.]

My best hopes are in him and you. I shall further hope that your health & strength will be renovated during the Summer ["And"(?) *canceled*] for the sake of our Country and yourself. For health and happiness merited by a life of usefulness and patriotic devotion you have the sincere wishes of Dear Sir, Yours with all Respect, F.W. Byrdsall.

ALS in ScCleA; PEx in Boucher and Brooks, eds., *Correspondence*, pp. 500–501.

To Lewis S. Coryell, [New Hope, Pa.?]

Washington, 18th March 1849

Dear Sir, I regret to say, that our friend Gen[era]l [John] Davis has been superceded, & that before I could make effort to save ["him" *interlined*], though I doubt not, it would have been all in vain. Such was the crowed of expectants that surrounded the Departments, & so constantly was the Cabinet in session, except one hour in the morning, that it was next to impossible to see the secretaries, from a few days after the 5th Inst., and in that short period Gen[era]l Davis['s] case was acted on. I called to see Mr. [William M.] Meredith [Secretary of the Treasury] as soon as I suppose[d] he would be accessible. I failed to see him ["at" *interlined*] my first called and at my next, I found it was too late. Had I known, that his term expired so soon, I would have made an earlier effort to see the Seceratary. I was under the impression that it was a case that required a removal to make a vacancy. From what I hear, I infer, that ["in" *interlined*] all cases under the 4 year's law the incumbents, if of opposite politicks, will be superceded, in States ["where" *interlined*] the proscriptive policy prevails. If so, no effort could have served our friend.

It is uncertain when the Senate will adjourn. It is thought it will not to the last of the week. Your's truly, J.C. Calhoun.

ALS in ScU-SC, John C. Calhoun Papers. Note: John Davis, a former Representative from Pa., was Collector of Customs for Philadelphia.

To Ja[me]s Ed[ward] Calhoun, Ju[nio]r, [Columbia, S.C.]

Washington, 19th March 1849

My dear James, As the session approaches its close, my time becomes more & more occupied, & I am compelled to make my letters breifer [*sic*].

Your senior year is really crow[d]ed with studies—quite, in my opinion, to excess. I am not surprised, that you should have no leisure left, in your endeavour to make yourself acquainted with them all. The absence of Col. [William C.] Preston must be a serious loss to the class.

As soon as I can get the drawings of the battles in Mexico, I will send them to you.

You write that you think of taking as a subject for a speech the "Benefit of Domestick Slavery"; and desire me, if I know of any work bearing on the subject to send it to you. I would suggest to you to modify the subject, and instead of the "Benefit of Domestick Slavery," to take "African Slavery as it exists in the Southern States." It will give you much more scope, both in portraying its character & showing its beneficent effects. I would also suggest, that you should reserve it for your Commencement speech, if you should be appointed one of the Orators. You would have the leisure of the vacation for preparing it.

I know ["of no" *interlined*] book of the kind you refer to; but there are many excellent pamphlets ["in" *canceled*] vindicating slavery as it exists with us. Among them, one has just appeared in the form of a lecture by Ellwood Fisher of Cincinnati. I will send you a copy as soon as I can get one. The late Chancellor [William] Harper published an able defence some years since; a copy of which you can no doubt get in Columbia. Gov[erno]r [James H.] Hammond also defend[ed] the institution with great ability in a letter some years ago, which you can also get in Columbia. Besides these, there are many others, of which I have among my papers at home a large portion.

I enclose a check for $20, as you request. Acknowledge the receipt.

With love to your brother [William Lowndes Calhoun] & kind regards to James Rion. Your affectionate father, J.C. Calhoun.

ALS in NcD, John C. Calhoun Papers. Note: The Pendleton, S.C., *Messenger*, March 9, 1849, p. 2, reported: "Mr. Calhoun sent us a few days since, a copy of an address delivered before the 'Young Men's Mercantile Library Association of Cincinnati, Ohio, by Elwood Fisher,' which is the most powerful vindication of the Southern principles and people and their institutions that we have seen." Fisher's lecture, delivered on 1/16/1849, was printed that year as a pamphlet by John T. Towers in Washington, J.B. Colin in Richmond, and A.J. Burke in Charleston, as *Lecture on the North and the South* . . . .

From Francis Wharton

Philadelphia, March 19, 1849

My dear Sir, I came across to day a very curious pamphlet just published by a committee of the (orthodox) society of friends, which from the conscientious accuracy of those from whom it emanates is entitled to the fullest confidence so far as its statistics are concerned. Of course its inferences are mere matter of opinion; and in sending it to you, you will be good enough to understand me as inviting your attention to it in no controversial spirit, but for the purpose of bringing to your view a series of very curious & authentic tables. Indeed I rather question whether the committee[']s conclusions may not be safely discarded as discordant with their facts.

I shall take the liberty of sending to you in a few days a sketch of the administration of Mr. [John Quincy] Adams which with a collection of state [*ms. torn; word or partial word missing*] I am just putting through the press.

[*Ms. torn*; P]ermit me to say that in one point in your late [*ms. torn*; Southern? Ad]dress you have done injustice to the northern people [*ms torn; half of next five lines missing*] any case, as[?] we would be far from disposed [*ms. torn*] the feeling to them is one of [*ms. torn*]re you the northern population [*ms. torn*] to which you think it sends [*ms. torn*] of the Potomac, at least [*ms. torn*] from hatred to the blacks, I think the partisanship of the north would be sufficiently decided & vehement. I have just returned from a visit to South Carolina, a plantation visit, & I can say with great confidence that the worst feelings exhibited there to the slaves are friendship compared with those which they receive with us. With great respect I am yours &, Francis Wharton.

ALS in ScCleA.

From Henry Young

New York [City,] March 19/49

Dear Sir, Some weeks since I called your attention to matters interesting to the South. I have been an attentive observer of the sighns of the times and such as are calculated to affect the interests of the South to an alarming extent.

Among the most prominent is the intended an[n]exation of Canada and Nova Scotia to the Union. While in Canada a few years since most that I conversed with appeared loyal. Among them the citizens who had settled there from the United States appeared to be uniformly so. They said the gover[n]ment protected both person and property and they saw no need of change. Not unfrequently they said they were better protected than in the U.S.

The Editor of the N.Y. Herald [James G. Bennett] often stated that there were designs in embryo for an ultimate separation from the parent Gover[n]ment and an[n]exation to our Union. Such were not my own conclusions and as very little credit was due the man who edits that sheet I paid little or no attention to. But since a change has taken place in the Revenue laws of England so that the Canadas have but little protection on their trade with the Mother country a change has taken place in the minds of the people in her Majesties possessions.

They apply for a free trade with the States in agricultural productions, timber lumber ores &c &c. That arrangement they confidently expect to take place. Next they expect a separation from England and an[n]exation to the Union. Within the last 4 weeks I have accidentally met with two intel[l]igent gentlemen from Nova Scotia (one from Newbrunswick.) and some 20 from differ parts of Canada. All assure me that the public sentiment is becoming set[t]led in favor of this change. They think it would contribute to their improvement. They are growing in favor of republican institutions. That we are about having very intimate connections by means of Rail Ways &c. That the inducement to continue a connection with England is greatly lessened by late commercial arrangements. That the receiving a governor from a place so remote is distasteful to them. That however good the intentions of the magistrate may be he is but illy acquainted with the country and its necessary gover[n]ment.

A gentleman of the State of Ohio an honorable and reliable member of the Barr of that State told me last fall that he chanced to be a travelling companion with a member of the Canadian gover[n]ment, who stated to him that these changes in the public mind in

Canada had taken place and that in a few years he confidently expected a Union of the British Provinces with the U. States. This measure appears to be popular with the commercial community here and in Boston and I think would meet the ap[p]robation of the citizens of this State.

I was in the south at the time of the unconstitutional invasion of Mexico by order of Mr. [James K.] Polk. There was as you will recollect much rejoicing. It was thought that the measure would add strength to the South and extend our peculiar Institutions to the territory we might acquire from Mexico. I viewed it as the most unfortunate move the South ever made. We have little if any prospect of any addition to the Slave States. The territory acquired from Mexico is filling us with a crowd of emigrants from the free States that is beyond all example. In addition the extraordinary discovery of gold is bringing a host of foreigners in all to a man opposed to the Institutions of the Southern States. I would ask what is to be the condition of the South when placed between the free States growing up on her Southern and Western borders and the rapidly multiplying free States of the North. The policy is already avowed of connecting these two sections of the Country by Rail Roads thus drawing a line of Connection around the interior of the South. Funds will be asked of the Congress to make this immence Railway through the wilderness. You had the wisdom and foresight to oppose the aggressions on Mexico which by the way your future historians will record as one of your wisest acts. I trust you will oppose the commercial connections with the British provinces as but the prelude to a political connection. You may at least delay or defeat the measure tho my fears are that you cannot for any very long time. What is to be our fate as a nation I cannot tell it is only known to *Him who controls Empires.* I have fears that it may be a gloomy ["one" *interlined*]. The spirit of aggression is aroused a disposition to acquire the surrounding territory. Once acquired and an[n]exed to us, the immence extent becomes to[o] unwieldy to hold together long—dissentions would soon arise and divisions take place. A crusade would be made against the Institutions of the South. Could the South maintain her ground against such immence odds.

Many were of opinion that the Free Soil excitement was transient. That it was a measure in the main of Mr. [Martin] Van Buren[']s to retaliate on Mr. [Lewis] Cass for a real or supposed injury done him in 1844 but the indications are that it is to be a test for future party contests. The late Elections in Massachusetts have ["in part," *inter-*

lined] given place to *Free Soil* Candidates. The indications are equally in favor of this agitating question in most of the Northern States. And what is most extraordinary—Individuals whom I knew to be engaged but a few years since in *mobbing* the *Abolitionists* are now the most fiery leaders of the *free soil Party*. They are more severe in their denunciations of the Southern Institutions than the Abolitionists ever were as a body. They carry these feelings into the Social relations. In one of the village papers that I happened to get hold of of late I saw a notice of a *free Soil Tea party*—where it was distinctly intimated that *Pro Slavery Gentlemen* would not be invited.

I have gone into these remarks much beyond what I anticipated. They have been hastily compiled but I was lead to bring the subject to your attention by the somewhat alarming indications that Canada was to be an[n]exed to our northern border, and a belief that you would if duly apprised of the danger take early means to prevent it. I add an article cut from the Herald—republished from the Globe. I am my Dear Sir with Great respect Yours, Henry Young.

ALS with En in ScCleA. Note: An AEU by Calhoun reads, "Mr. Young. Relates to Canada." Enclosed is a newspaper clipping headed "Annexation of Canada."

Remarks on printing extra copies of a Supreme Court decision annulling laws of N.Y. and Mass. in regard to immigrant passengers, 3/20. "Mr. Calhoun thought that 5,000 copies would be ample, but finally withdrew his opposition to the amendment." From the Baltimore, Md., *Sun*, March 21, 1849, p. 4. Also printed in the Petersburg, Va., *Republican*, March 23, 1849, p. 2; the Charleston, S.C., *Mercury*, March 24, 1849, p. 2.

To A[ndrew] J. Donelson, [Berlin?]

Washington, 23d March 1849

My dear Sir, The Senate unexpectedly adjourned today; and as I have overstayed my time all ready, I am busy preparing to get off tonight. Under such circumstances you must excuse the brevity of my letter.

I have seen both the President [Zachary Taylor] & Secretary of State [John M. Clayton] in reference to the contents of your letter. They are both very kindly disposed toward you, and you may calculated [*sic*], I think, with certainty on being continued in your Mission to Frankfort. You are, I supposed [*sic*], already informed, that the Mission to Berlin was filled by the late administration by the appointment of Mr. [Edward A.] Hannegan.

I fear the slavery question has gone so far, that it will be very difficult, if not impos[s]ible to adjust it. Gen[era]l Taylor, I doubt not, is well disposed to settle it. I shall be well disposed to aid him in any feasible plan for accomplishing it. Nothing short of the greatest skill, prudence & firmness can succeed, ["whether" *canceled and* "if" *interlined*] even that can.

I enclose a copy of the Southern Address in pamphlet form. It has made a strong impression on the South, & done much to unite the two great parties there in opposition to the aggression of the North. Nor has it been without salutary effects on the North.

Nothing yet has occurred to indicate the line of policy the administration intends to persue. My impression is, that they have fixed on none, & that their course will be determined by circumstances. I wish them well, & shall give them my support, whenever I can consistently with ["my" *interlined*] principles & views of policy.

The Democratick party is divided & distracted by the slave question. It will weaken them much, as an opposition party. Indeed, I do not see how they can regain power as a party, without a firm & united return to the principles & policy that brought Mr. [Thomas] Jefferson into power & adopting the principle of an entire non interference, as far as the federal government is concerned, in reference to the slave question. Yours truly, J.C. Calhoun.

ALS in DLC, Andrew Jackson Donelson Papers.

To [Thomas] Ewing, Secretary of the Interior

Washington, 23d March 1849

Dear Sir, I have long been acquainted with Gen[era]l [Robert] Wallace[,] Marshall of this District [of Columbia,] and am very favourably impressed as to his character both as a man and a citizen. I understand that he has performed his duty with fidelity & in a satisfactory manner; & that he has abstained from taking any part in the recent presidential contest.

With these impressions, I would be gratified, if he should be continued in his present ["office" *interlined*] & hope you will find it consistent with the course of policy which the administration has prescribed to itself, to retain him. Yours truly, J.C. Calhoun.

ALS in DNA, RG 59 (State Department), Applications and Recommendations during the Administrations of James K. Polk, Zachary Taylor, and Millard Fillmore, 1845–1853, Robert Wallace (M-873:90, frames 219–221).

MARCH 24–JULY 31, 1849

Calhoun reached Charleston in the Wilmington boat on March 26. The Pendleton, S.C., Messenger *reported on April 13 that "The Hon. J.C. Calhoun and family, arrived at their residence in this neighborhood last week, in good health." On April 10 he wrote to son Andrew in Alabama about the family business affairs. To Anna Clemson, who was slowly en route back to Brussels, he wrote on the same day more gently, about flowering plants and family. To both he wrote cheerful remarks about his own health. In May the Clemsons sailed for Europe, Thomas Clemson having been assured that the new Whig administration would not make him a victim of spoils.*

The summer was spent mostly at Fort Hill, taking care of the farm and working on his treatises on government, which were nearing completion. A significant private event was the marriage on July 3 of John C. Calhoun, Jr., to Miss Anzie R. Adams, daughter of the late Rev. Jasper Adams. The ceremony took place at the bride's home near Pendleton and was conducted by the Rev. Andrew H. Cornish, Episcopalian. (Pendleton, S.C., Messenger, *July 6, 1849, p. 3.)*

The most significant public event of the summer was what would be Calhoun's last important public statement outside of the Senate, a letter of July 5 to the people of the South, giving his opinion on their present situation, in reply to a vitriolic personal attack made by Thomas H. Benton at Jefferson City, Missouri, on May 26. Calhoun seemed, in much public opinion, to have the best of the argument. Benton's fortunes were on the way down. Having defied instruction by the Missouri legislature, he would be defeated for reelection to the Senate next year on exactly the issues upon which he had attacked Calhoun.

J. C. Calhoun, A[ndrew] P. Butler, and R[obert] B. Rhett to William Meredith, Secretary of the Treasury

Charleston, March 26t[h] 1849

Sir, We understand that an effort is being made to eject ["from office" *interlined*] Mr. John M. Clapp the Inspector of Drugs at this Port. We are acquainted with Mr. Clapp—and cannot doubt his entire competency to discharge the duties of this office. He was a graduate of Yale College—studied chemistry under Professor [Benjamin] Silliman—and is a man of fine Classic and literary attainments. He has been in this office for nine months, and we learn and believe that he has been laboriously preparing himself for its proper discharge. If competency, character and education are [*one word canceled*] grounds for retaining an officer in his office, Mr. Clapp in our opinion ought to be retained. J.C. Calhoun, A.P. Butler, R.B. Rhett.

LS (in Rhett's handwriting) in DNA, RG 56 (Treasury Department), Applications for Appointment as Customs Service Officers, 1833–1910, John Clapp.

Proceedings of a Public Meeting in Accomac County, Va.

[Accomac Court House, March 26, 1849]

A call having been made upon the people of the county of Accomac to respond to the appeal addressed by the late convention of Senators and Representatives in Congress, from slave-holding States to their constituents, they met at their Court House on Monday, the 26th of March, it being the first day of the quarterly session of the county court, in large numbers.

Henry A. Wise then rose and appealed to all, of all parties and of all sects, political and religious, to unite with him in certain resolutions, which he had prepared for the occasion. He addressed the people for a few minutes, and commenced reading the "Appeal" of the Convention at Washington. This having been generally read and understood, its reading was suspended; and, on motion of Mr. Wise, the meeting proceeded to organize.

Wm. P. Moore, Sr., and Henry A. Wise, were appointed Chairmen, and John B. Ailworth and John S. Dix were appointed Secretaries of the meeting.

Mr. Wise, thereupon read the following resolutions, and moved that they be referred to a committee to consider and report upon them, to wit:

Resolved, That the time for action, to resist the movements of "Abolition," made not only in the North, but by some in the South has arrived; and that the danger which threatens Southern institutions is so imminent, and the insult to the Southern States and people is so offensive, that no time should be lost in preparing for the impending crisis, lest the moment for efficient and successful action will have passed away.

Resolved, That we approve the late resolves of the Virginia Legislature on this subject; that we will maintain them by all the means in our power, to the utmost extent of constitutional and legal right; that we tender our grateful acknowledgements to the Delegates and Senators who passed these resolves, whilst we indignantly reprobate the sentiments and votes of those members who sided with fanaticism in opposing resistance to the grossest violation of the Constitution of the United States—who were for submitting to the most degrading inequality proposed between the slave States, and those which claim to be the only "*Free* soil" States in the Confederacy; and who advocated a "passive obedience" and "non-resistance" to an oppression, the inevitable consequence of which would be to engender and establish a tyranny, or dissolve the Federal Union.

Resolved, That we will defend the "*Union,*" by maintaining our own rights of *Sovereign Equality* in it, to the last extremity of argument, of reason, of remonstrance, of appeal, of moral resistance, in all its forms; and, finally, if compelled to do so, *by force of arms.*

Resolved, That we eschew all connection on this subject with party politics; that, in respect to it, all of all parties and sects who are with us are friends; all who are not with us are against us, and all who are against us are foes; foes to our rights, to our honor, to our peace, to our safety, to our Federal equality, to our Federal Constitution, and to our Federal Union. And this we solemnly resolve in respect to all men, but more especially in respect to men in the South, citizens in our midst, whether they be in private or public life, in the service of the State or of the United States.

Resolved, That such at this period is the *necessity,* actual and imperious, of *union amongst ourselves,* that we are not allowed, even by the rules of toleration and charity, to view any portion of the Southern and slave State population who would separate from us in this struggle, in any other light than as only legally less than traitors to the State and to the security of her citizens; and we will endeavor to cause the crime of inciting division, whenever and by whomsoever it may manifest itself, to be punished by all the penalties provided by statutes, and by all the odium and reproach to be cast upon it by that public opinion which is the supreme law of every free country, and in every well regulated society.

Resolved, That we have received the appeal of a late Convention of Senators and Representatives in Congress from slaveholding States, held in the Capitol at Washington, without alarm, because we have been prepared by the forbearance of years to await it with patience and composure; but not without the most painful apprehension, nor without a solemn sense of its importance, of its truth, of its justness, of its moderation, of its patriotism, of its devotion to the best interests of the United States, as well as of its faithfulness to our interests; nor without the consciousness of our duty to respond to it in the most decided tone and temper of our minds, as men summoned to defend their inalienable rights and sacred honor, attacked by those who are brethren descended from the same sires, of the same Revolution, who are citizens of the same Republic, subjects of the same Constitution and Laws, bound by the same bond of political and conventional faith, sworn under the same Christian covenant with us to support, maintain and defend all the institutions guaranteed by the Federal compact, and who profess to be friends as well as fellow citizens and patriots.

Resolved, That the expression of our gratitude be tendered to John C. Calhoun, a Senator from the State of South Carolina, for the conception and authorship of this appeal, and to those with him in the Convention who voted to adopt it and to reject all temporizing substitutes which were proposed by some whose *extreme moderation* has ever heretofore yielded and will forever hereafter "*yield the question,*" and whose proposed action would have committed the fate and fortunes of the minority in the action to that ruthless *majority* which has never yet been touched by the tenderness of an appeal, and the pride and passion of which have always been more haughtily emboldened *by the humility of imprecation and protest.*

Resolved, That the danger of the State and the safety and welfare of the people of Virginia, call for a Convention, to be assembled as soon as the Legislature can pass a bill for that purpose, to determine upon the whole question of encroachment by the Federal Government, and by the "Free soil" States and the people of the North, on the institution of Slavery in the States, Territories and Districts of the United States; that it is full time for the State to decide what will be its sovereign action, finally, on this subject; and to inform its citizens and subjects whether they will be authorized to resist, if they are required by Federal Legislation to submit to the oppression of a majority in Congress; and that a State Convention, organized according to law, can best settle the rule of conduct for the citizen.

Resolved, therefore, That Mease W. Smith, John W.H. Parker, Richard P. Read, John H. Custis, Zadock Knock and Richard J. Ayres, be a committee to prepare a petition to the Legislature, at its coming session in May next, for a law to organize a State Convention, to be assembled at the earliest convenient period; and that Dr. Thomas P. Bagwell, Dr. John Bowdoin, Dr. James Savage, Daniel Wallop, James J. Ailworth, and William P. Moore, Jr., be a committee at this place to correspond with the several counties in the Commonwealth, to induce a concurrence in arresting the encroachment of Abolition, or of ascertaining "the mode and measure of redress."

Resolved, That a copy of these resolutions be transmitted to the Hon. John C. Calhoun, and to his coadjutors in the late Convention at the Capitol in Washington, a copy to the Governor of the State of Virginia, a copy to the President of the Senate, and one to the Speaker of the House of Delegates of Virginia at Richmond, one to each of the Senators and Representatives of Virginia in Congress, one to the Vice President or President of the Senate, and one to the Speaker of the House of Representatives in Congress, and one to the clerk of each county in this State, with a request to post the same at the Court-house door of his county.

On motion, the foregoing resolutions were adopted unanimously and by acclamation, without the appointment of a committee to consider and report upon them. And it was further

Resolved, That the Chairman have power to nominate persons, without distinction of party, to fill the blanks of the two committees, six to each committee. And that these proceedings be published in all the newspapers of Norfolk, Richmond and Washington City, and that the Chairman shall cause to be printed a sufficient number of copies for the use of the Committee of Correspondence.

The persons named as committeemen were appointed. And, thereupon, the meeting, on motion, adjourned sine die.

Wm. P. Moore, Sr. }
Henry A. Wise } Chairmen.

John B. Ailworth, }
John S. Dix, } Secretaries.

PC in the Alexandria, Va., *Gazette and Virginia Advertiser*, April 10, 1849, p. 2.

From J[OHN] H. MEANS

Buckhead, Fairfield [District, S.C.] March 28th [1849]

My Dear Sir, I hope you will find an excuse for the liberty I take in addressing a letter to you, in the importance of the subject. The citizens of our District and I hope those of the State generally, have come to the conclusion that we have *talked* enough about the wrongs and insults heaped upon us by the North, and that the time has arrived for *action.* The spirit of resistance has been lighted up and I trust will spread with a rapidity commensurate with the magnitude of the wrongs which has excited it.

You have probably noticed that the different committees of correspondence are appointing Delegates to meet in Columbia on the 1st of May, to agree upon some course of effectual resistance. Amongst other remedies that will be proposed, is a nonintercourse with the North in commerce and trade. This I think will be impracticable, for reasons which will readily suggest themselves to you, and inefficient even if it could be ["made" *interlined*] practicable. It will be only throwing a tub to the whale. It seems to me, that the only efficient remedy will be to get up a Southern Convention, and if that is not possible, for the States to act alone. The latter plan would make an issue at once and force the rest of the Southern States either to take sides for, or against us. The nature of the case, would force them to side with us. As anxious as we all are to rid ourselves of the grievances with which we are encumbered, we are unwilling to do any thing that might tend to prejudice our cause, and as restive as we are under our wrongs, we are desirous to act with that prudence and caution which are necessary to ensure success. I have therefore taken the liberty of writing to you knowing your ardent devotion to the interest of the South, and having the profoundest respect for your sagacity and foresight, to advise what will be the prudent and effective course to pursue at the meeting in May. If you are not too much engaged at present, you will confer a particular favor upon me, and perhaps a benefit upon your country by letting me know your views upon this subject. If we were to follow the dictates of a virtuous indignation, we should feel like going at once for a dissolution of the Union, but we are anxious to act with that prudence, which will ensure success to the great cause of Southern rights and Southern institutions. With much respect Your ob[edien]t Serv[an]t, J.H. Means.

ALS in ScCleA. Note: This letter was addressed to Calhoun at Pendleton. Calhoun's AEU reads, "Mr. Means. Relates to the Meeting at Columbia[,] also a rough draft of my answer."

From Samuel S. Mills

Charleston So. Ca., 29th March 1849

Dear Sir, If this is too early an encroachment on a quiet retirement, for a season, which you must have yearned for; I beg you will lay it by for a more suitable hour. But I must take care not to make it worse by a long apology. I wish to submit to you my project for an "Atmospheric Mail Conveyance." It is to lay a Continuous Tube or Cylinder between the principal seaport & inland Cities & Towns, of a diameter of bore proportioned to the bulk of mail between each place—with Engines placed at proper distances for the purpose of exhausting, as perfectly as possible, the air from the tube between such points, as the mail is to pass. I shall attach a little diagram which ["may assist" *interlined*] to explain. The right hand end of the tube, please consider the point the ["point the" *canceled*] mail is to start from. I shall attempt to represent *two* mail Bags in this end of the tube. It will probably be as well to consider the tube & bags as cut Longitudinally & vertically thro' their centers. The Bags may be put in at the end of the tube, or the top part of the tube, between valve no. 1 & valve no. 2, may come off, in sections, & when on to fit snugly. The mail bags being in, these top covers properly on, and the air in the tube, between no. 1 & no. 2 Engines (or any more distant Nos.) where the bags may be intended to stop) having been extrated, we will then withdraw the valve no. 2, and immediately after, that of no. 1, when the atmosphere, pressing in at this end of the tube & not being able to pass the ["piston" *canceled*; "mail Bag" *interlined and then canceled*] head of the mail bags, will drive them forward with the force of 14 @ 15 lbs., to the square inch, but as it is probable ["this pressure" *interlined*] will, in some degree, diminish, as the distance of the bags from the end of the tube increases, & moreover for the purpose of applying a force in the Bags *beyond* that of the natural atmospheric pressure—I propose to close valve no. 1 as soon as the Bags have passed Engine no. 1 & to set this Engine in motion, forcing air into the tube, with such number & construction of pumps, as to employ near the whole power of the Engine. In this way it is thought the bags may be made to move at the rate of 150 @ 200 miles an hour; provided they can be so lubricated as to prevent setting themselves on fire. ["A" *interlined*] small gutta penha tube could be laid with the cast Iron one; and by putting a suitably sized air pump in play a few moments, at the time the bags started; a signal could be transmitted, by means of a whistle or *otherwise*, to the point where the mail was to stop, so that they might be ready for its reception. The Bags could be made of thick stiff sole leather; or a new manufacture, called, I believe, metalic packing. It could be made of any required width or thickness. Either would be stought or stiff enough for a bag of 8 @ 10 feet long, (especially when filled with letters) to force on other bags, tho it were the last in a train of 4 or 5 Bags. The first cost of this mail conveyance would be considerable: But it is confidently believed that the average expense of the first five years, including cost, would show a great reduction from the present mode; besides proving incalculable additional advantage to all the great interests of the country. There would be little danger of the mail being robbed during its transmission from delivery to delivery. The Bags being made of either of the substances named, would readily accommodate themselves to vary [*sic*] considerable deviations, in the tube, from a strai[gh]t line. The Bags should have ["two or more" *interlined*] bands of packin[g] around them, made [*diagram here*] so as gently to press against the tube & they should be saturated with the most desirable kind of lubricating substance. When the Bags have passed engine no. 2 (which of course can't appear on my *short* diagram) they close the valve on the side next no. 1 & give the signal; when no. 1 reverses its motion & withdraws the air in the tube between it & engine no. 2. The same will be done by all the other engines successively—as also is the case in forcing air into the tube, after the mail Bags have passed them.

I have not as yet made any move towards securing a patent. I wished first to get your opinion of its practicability & expediency. And should you find a leisure & convenient moment, which you could devote to this purpose, I shall be Yours Very much obliged, Samuel S. Mills.

ALS in ScCleA.

From Rose [O'Neal] Greenhow

Washington, April 3rd 1849

My dear Sir, Your great and unvarying kindness releives me from any hesitation, in making my present request to you, for a letter addressed to General [Zachary] Taylor, in my husband's behalf. Mr. [Robert] Greenhow['] s health is such, that it will be impossible for him to hold his situation [in the State Department] here, any longer.

Under this conviction, he had, this morning, a long conversation with Mr. [John M.] Clayton [Secretary of State], who seems most kindly disposed towards him. Mr. Clayton referred to the conversation which you held with him, in my husband's behalf, and told him, that he must get from you a letter, addressed to General Taylor, in as strong terms as possible, which Mr. Greenhow must present in person to Gen. Taylor, and that he (Clayton) would *back it*, as far as he could.

From what I can learn of the feelings existing towards you, I shall have but little doubt of the success of my husband's application—for I beleive that the Administration is fully alive to the necessity of looking to the South for support, in the trying times which are approaching; and *you* as the representative of that *needful support*, would have all deference paid to your wishes.

Do not understand me, my kindest and best friend, as wishing you, in any way to trammel yourself, by your kindness to us. You told me, in conversation, upon one occasion, that you could write a letter to Gen. Taylor &c. and hence, I caught with avidity, at Mr. Clayton['] s suggestion of a letter from you.

Mr. Greenhow's situation is one, which admits of no temporary measures—it is alarming in the extreme; the irritability of the nervous system is greater than at any previous time, together with intense pain in the head and eyes—I am haunted by the fear of paralysis or blindness, and my first feeling in the morning is to ascertain if he is worse than on the previous day.

Turin or some place in southern Europe is where we desire to go. Mexico is where my husband would desire to go, as he feels that he could be of great use there; but that we conclude to be out of the question.

I saw Mr. [Thomas] Ritchie [editor of the Washington *Daily Union*] a few days since. He has been very ill, and I think is much changed by it—he is confident in being able to maintain himself here—says that his position with the Democratic party is stronger than ever—confesses that he may have injured himself by his devotion to Mr. [James K.] Polk. He speaks of you in terms very different from what I ever heard expressed before, but like all old sinners, tryed to fix the burden of blame upon you—but said fra[n]kly, had he not been seized by illness, that he should have made overtures of reconciliation.

Reynold's letter gives him great trouble[;] he trys hard to cast discredit upon the charge made in it of want of confidence [*ms. torn*; in Mr. James] B[uchanan]—by Polk—and predicates his positive denial of it upon a conversation which Mr. Buchanan held with Mr. Ritchie to the effect that he was sorry Reynolds made the assertion as he Mr. B[uchanan] was not aware of it.

My dear friend I must claim your indulgence for this long letter—and trust that I shall hear from you with as little delay as practicable.

Mr. Greenhow joins me in kindest love to yourself and Mrs. [Floride Colhoun] Calhoun and family. With most affectionate Regard I remain dear Sir Yours, Rose Greenhow.

ALS in ScCleA. NOTE: "Reynold's letter" apparently refers to John Reynolds, a close friend of Buchanan, Clayton's predecessor as Secretary of State.

From [JAMES P.] CARROLL and Others

Edgefield C[ourt] H[ouse, S.C.]
April 4th 1849

Dear Sir, A public Dinner is intended to be given by the citizens of this vicinity to the Hon. A[ndrew] P. Butler, on thursday, the 12th of this month. It is their earnest wish that you, also, should be their guest on that occasion, as they desire to avail themselves of every opportunity of manifesting their high sense of the distinguished public services which you have rendered the country through a long series of years, and in especial, during the late session of congress.

In performing the duty which has been assigned to us as the organ of our Fellow citizens, we have the honor to offer you the assurances of our highest personal regard. Carroll, [William C.] Moragne, [Preston S.] Brooks, [Simeon] Christie, [George A.] Addison, [Milledge L.] Bonham, Committee.

LS (with signatures in one hand) in ScCleA. NOTE: An AEU by Calhoun reads, "Invitation to Edgefield." A second AEU is Calhoun's draft of a toast [to Edgefield District] for the meeting: "ever ["heretofore" *interlined*] among the fo[re]-

most to meet ["the call of the State" *canceled*] in the hower [*sic*] of danger, she will be found in the front rank should the south be compelled to ["tak"(?) *canceled*] make ["a" *canceled and a partial word interlined*] stand ["up" *interlined*] in defence of her rights & equality."

From W. Pinkney Starke

Charleston S.C., April 4–49

Dear Sir, I found in the Hamburg [S.C.] Post Office the other day a package addressed to me bearing your frank upon its envelope. I have also to acknowledge with many thanks the receipt of the Southern Address in pamphlet form. The Address I read with the attention claimed by every thing coming from under your pen. The careless indifference manifested by the South to open and repeated assaults upon rights so solem[n]ly guaranteed is to my mind pregnant with vast mischief not only to her, but to the Union. What means this moral paralysis? While pain lasts there is always life and hope, but in the mortification which brings relief to the patient his physician detects the premonitions of death. It is time for the people of the South to look the crisis boldly in the face. It will not do for us to hide our heads in the sand and imagine the danger is gone. We have tried tolerance long enough and it will be criminal folly to look ["longer" *interlined*] for salvation from others. We have thrown grass at those who wantonly invade our rights with none effect and like the man in the Fable we must ["now" *interlined*] try "what virtue there is in stones."

I wrote on the subject of giving the election of Electors to the people but did not print. In preparing for my examination for admission to the bar I had not the time to finish my investigation in a manner to suit me. Whenever the question arises again I shall endeavor to be at my post. Our Legislature did not seem to have a right conception of the importance of the question. I am afraid I don't misrepresent them when I say, there was hardly an advocate of the existing mode ["who" *canceled*] would have risked the loss of his dinner upon the event. Everything seems to be preparing for Carolina her day of little things.

Your son [John C. Calhoun, Jr.], whose acquaintance I lately made at Milledgeville with much ["satisfaction to myself," *canceled and* "pleasure" *interlined*] will be able to give you the latest tidings of Mr. [George] McDuffie's state. In placing the General under hydropathic treatment his friends had two objects in view: the first and by far the most important was to relieve him from pain and make life tolerable; and then if possible to restore to health his entire system—to carry life to long palsied nerves—to raise and place him once more on his feet. The first end has been fully accomplished—the last, if it can ever be, ["it w" *canceled*] will require long time to ["be" *interlined*] effected.

I should have been greatly pleased to witness the passage at arms betwixt you and Mr. [Daniel] Webster—your advantage was very decided. If I had known of your arrival at Hamburg I would have come down from [James H.] Hammond[']s, where I was passing the night, to see you.

If I thought you had the time to read them I would send you up some volumes of [Emanuel] Swedenborg, who among his vast accomplishments was not a little eminent as a statesman. I am certain your mind would feel an affinity for his whose Philosophy is as far & above all others as his Religion is above the patched and thread-bare system which bigots call the handywork of God.

I would request of you, my dear Sir, to leave ["behind" *interlined*] as did Mr. [Thomas] Jefferson some memorial of yourself at least of those earlier days of your life which if not, like the sources of the Nile, entirely unknown are at ["least" *canceled and* "yet but" *interlined*] little known. Leave such a memorial to me and I will give the ["length of" *interlined*] time required by the English Poet for the construction of his Epic, to the recording of a life whose image has indeed been stamped upon the age. Of the young men of the State ["I believe" *canceled*] no one I think understands you better or appreciates you more highly. I am not playing the flatterer to Mr. Calhoun, which would be as unnecessary as unbecoming.

Be pleased to present my name to the Doctor's [John C. Calhoun, Jr.'s] recollection from whom I should always be glad to hear.

Hoping that your health is improving and that you will be able to begin your senatorial duties in December entirely restored I am with great respect Your Obliged & humble Servant, W. Pinkney Starke.

ALS in ScCleA; PEx in Boucher and Brooks, eds., *Correspondence*, p. 501.

To [James P.] Carroll and Others

Fort Hill, April 7, 1849

Gentlemen: I regret exceedingly that my engagements, will not permit me to accept your invitation, to be present at a Public Dinner, to be given to the Hon. A[ndrew] P. Butler, on the 12th inst., by the citizens of Edgefield and its vicinity.

Had circumstances permitted, I would have been happy to be your guest on the occasion, and to have an opportunity, not only to express, in person, the high regard I have for my able and distinguished colleague, but to make my grateful acknowl[e]dgement to the citizens of your District, for the early confidence they bestowed on me, and the constant support I have received from them, through a long and trying period of public service, now nearly of forty years continuance.

I avail myself of the occasion, to offer the following sentiment:

Edgefield District—Ever heretofore, among the foremost in the hour of danger, she will be found in the front rank, should the South be compelled, by continued aggression and injustice, to stand up in defence of her rights, and equality in the Union. With great respect, I am, &c., John C. Calhoun.

PC in the Edgefield, S.C., *Advertiser*, April 18, 1849, p. 2; PC in the Charleston, S.C., *Mercury*, April 23, 1849, p. 2 (misdated 4/7/1848); PC in the Charleston, S.C., *Courier*, April 25, 1849, p. 2. Note: Other members of the committee were [William C.] Moragne, [Preston S.] Brooks, [Simeon] Christie, [George A.] Addison, and [Milledge L.] Bonham.

To A[ndrew] P[ickens] Calhoun, [Marengo County, Ala.]

Fort Hill, 10th April 1849

My dear Andrew, I wrote you before I left Washington. I hope you have got my letter.

I arrived here yesterday week, and found all well; the place in good order, & my business well advanced, considering that all my negroes, with few exceptions, had the measeles in my absence. I will finish planting cotton to day, & all my crop this week. The spring is advanced about ["as" *interlined*] usual with us, & has been quite seasonable.

On my return, I found that Mr. [Robert A.] Maxwell & Dr. [Ozey

R.] Broyles had deposited with Mr. [John S.] Lorton $4980 of the sum they propose to loan us. I have applied it in the following manner: in discharge of our bond to Mrs. [Placidia Mayrant] Adams $2369.59; to the payment of my note to Mr. [Thomas R.] Cherry $1899.26 & in payment of a note of mine to J. Lorton $712.63. ["There" *canceled.*] There was due on Mrs. Adams' bond on the 7th Aug[us]t 1847, when the last preceding settlement was made, $2508.32. There has been paid ["since" *interlined*] on the bound [*sic*], including principal & interest $2789.54, being all that was due, when I settled with her day before yesterday, & took her receipt in full. The payment consisted of the $2369.59 above stated; $302.95, advances I had made to her during the last winter, & a due bill, I gave her in our joint name for $117, which I will take up out of the first funds received from Dr. Broyles or Mr. Maxwell. It is, I think, probable ["that" *interlined*] considerable payments will be made by both of them during the summer & fall—possibly sufficient to meet our debt to the bank of the State [of South Carolina], or even that to Mr. [Thomas G.] Clemson. I am of the impression, that we had better apply it to the former. It is very uncertain, whether he will wish to have what is due to him. He can make no better investment of it; and, I think, he looks only to the punctual payment of the interest. But should he ["need" *canceled and* "want it" *interlined*], by paying the debt to the bank, we can readily raise ["it" *canceled and* "the sum" *interlined*] from the bank, should we ["need" *canceled and* "require" *interlined*] it. With this impression, I will so apply it, if you should not take a different view.

I endorsed your note to the bank. It will have to be renewed on the 14th of next month, & you must send your name in blank for the purpose in time. You must also send your name in blank for bounds, or notes, as they may prefer, for the money to be loaned by Dr. Broyles or Mr. Maxwell. Let it be on large sheets, to suit the former, if required.

The debts I now owe are small, & such as I hope to be able to meet out of my own funds, notwithstanding the heavy expense, to which I am subject by the education of John [C. Calhoun, Jr.], James [Edward Calhoun] & Willie [William Lowndes Calhoun]. Indeed, I hardly know how I have got along, ["with it," *canceled*] without being much more involved. The debt to Cherry was altogether for the purchase of land.

My health still continues to improve; &, I hope, it will continue even more rapidly, with the process I have just commenced. John ["has" *canceled*] returned a few days since from Milledgeville, very much improved, and with a thorough conviction of the superior efficacy of the water cure process. Even Mr. [George] McDuffie has been wonderfully benefitted by it, as he states. I have long thought it would be of service to me carried to a certain point; and this morning, under John's superintendence, I commenced with the wet sheet. The process was very agreeable & soothing. It has effectually cleansed the skin, and done much, I doubt not, to open ["my" *canceled and* "its" *interlined*] pores—a thing in my opinion, I much needed. I already feel its good effects & shall continue it daily, until I give it a fair trial.

I hope you had a pleasant journey home & found all well. Write me soon & fully. My love to Margaret [Green Calhoun] & the children [Duff Green Calhoun, John Caldwell Calhoun, Andrew Pickens Calhoun, Jr., and Margaret Maria Calhoun]. Your affectionate father, J.C. Calhoun.

[P.S.] John thinks that the water cure would certainly & effectually cure little Andrew. He says it is a certain remedy in scrofolous cases.

ALS in NcD, John C. Calhoun Papers.

To Anna [Maria] C[alhoun] Clemson, [Philadelphia?]

Fort Hill, 10th April 1849

My dear daughter, I had a safe & pleasant journey home. The weather was pleasant & spring was rapidly advancing. The Jessamine & dog-wood were in bloom, & the forest had just commenced cloding [*sic*] itself with green. The contrast was great between being pent up in a boarding house in Washington & breathing the pure fresh air of the country, made fragrant by the blossoms of spring.

Patrick [Calhoun] accompanied me to your Uncle James [Edward Colhoun's], where we met your Mother [Floride Colhoun Calhoun] & Sister [Martha Cornelia Calhoun]. They, with your Uncle, were well. I remained there four days, when we took our departure for Fort Hill, leaving Patrick with his Uncle. We found all well on our arrival ["here" *canceled*], & the place in good order & business forward, considering that the measeles had passed through the negro quarter during the winter, and that none, but a few had escaped, but with ["the" *interlined*] loss of only one, an infant of a constitution too feeble to survive the attack. I shall finish planting cotton to day, & the whole of ["my" *interlined*] crop this week. The small grain looks well, & the place ["bears" *interlined*] the appea[ra]nce of good order.

We have no local news, in which you would take interest.

John [C. Calhoun, Jr.] returned from Milledge Ville by the last stage but one. He looks well & I think his health is much improved by the water cure. His cough is much better. He is quite a convert to the system. I advise ["him" *interlined*] to visit the establishment at B[r]attleborough in Vermont, both to complete his cure & perfect himself in the practise. He says, that Gen[era]l [George] McDuffie has improved wonderfully under the process. He is entirely releived from the Dy[s]pepsia & his nerveos affections, & has recovered the free use of his arms, is cheerful, sleeps well, and eats heartily. With the exception of his paralized leg may be said to be well.

I have for some time believed, that the process, carried to a certain extent, would be of service to me; and have determined, under John's superintendence, to make a trial. I began this morning with what is called the wet sheet, or rather the damp sheet, which in effect is no more nor less, than a safe & effecint form of the vapour bath. I remained wrapt round with the sheet, & covered with 8 or 9 blankets for 1½ hours, & ended in a warm bath, & ["an" *interlined*] effec[t]ual rubbing dry. The process was soothing & pleasant. It has cleansed the skin effectually, & I doubt not, done much to open the pores—the one thing, in my opinion, needful to me. I shall presist [*sic*] in it until I give it a fair trial; & if I find it as beneficial as I expect, I shall fix up a complete bathing establishment. I am pleased with the first essay; and I hope it will prove a substitute for brandy tod[d]y & hot punch. They have, I doubt not done me good; but, I think, the water cure will do me still more.

All join their love to you, Mr. [Thomas G.] Clemson & the children [John Calhoun Clemson and Floride Elizabeth Clemson]. Kiss them for their grandfather & tell them how much I miss them. Your affectionate father, J.C. Calhoun.

[P.S.] You see I substitute a C for an M in your name. I hope you will adopt the change.

ALS in ScCleA; PC in Jameson, ed., *Correspondence*, pp. 763–764. Note: By his P.S. Calhoun meant he had addressed this letter to "Mrs. Anna C. Clemson," rather than to "Mrs. Anna M. Clemson," as usual.

To J[ohn] H. Means, [Fairfield District, S.C.]

Fort Hill, 13th April 1849

My dear Sir, I am glad to learn by your letter [of 3/28] and from other sources, that a meeting is to be held next month in Columbia, to be composed of delegates from the different Committees of correspondence. I regard it as a step of much importance & responsibility.

You ask my opinion as to the course the Meeting should take. Before I give it, I deem it due to candour & the occasion to state, that I am of the impression, that the time is near at hand, when the South will have to choose between disunion, and submission. I think so, because I see little prospect of arresting the aggression of the North. If any thing can do it, it would be for the South to present with an unbroken front to the North, the alternative of dissolving the partnership or of ceasing on their part to violate our rights & to disregard the stipulations of the Constitution in our favour; and that two [*sic*] without delay. I say without delay, for it may be well doubted, whether the alienation between the two sections has not already gone too far to save the Union; but, if it has not, there can be none, that it soon will, if not prevented by some prompt & decisive measure. It has been long on the increase and is now more rapidly increasing than ever. The prospect is as things now stand that before four years have elapsed, the Union will be devided into two great hostile sectional parties.

But it will be impossible to present such a front, except by means of a Convention of the Southern States. That and that only could speake for the whole, & present authoritatively to the North the alternative, which to choose. If such a presentation should fail to save the Union, by arresting the aggression of the North and causing our rights & the stipulations of the Constitution in our favour to be respected, it would afford proof conclusive, that it could not be saved, and that nothing was left us, but to save ourselves. Having done all we could to save the Union, we would then stand justified before God & man to dissolve a partnership which had proved inconsistent with our safety and, of course, distructive of the object which mainly induced us to enter into it. Viewed in this light, a Convention of the South is an indispensible means to discharge a great duty we owe to our partners in the Union; that is to warn them in the most solemn manner that if they do not desist from aggression, & cease to disregard our rights & the stipulations of the Constitution, the duty we owe to ourselves & our posterity, would compel us to dissolve forever the partnership with them. But should its warning voice fail to save the Union, it would in that case prove the most effecient of all means for saving ourselves. It would give us the great advantage of enjoying the conscious feeling of having done all we could to save it, & thereby free us from all responsibility in reference to it, while it would afford the most effecient means of United & prompt action, and thereby of meeting the momenteous occasion without confusion or disorder, & with certainty of success.

Thus thinking, my opinion is, that the great object to be aimed at by the Meeting is to adopt measures to prepare the way for a convention of the Southern States. What they should be the Meeting can best decide. It seems to me, however, that the organization of our own and the other Southern States is an indispensible step and & [*sic*] for that and other purposes there ought to be an able Committee appointed having its center in Charleston or Columbia & vested with power to take such steps as may be deemed necessary to carry into effect that and the other measures which may be adopted by the Meeting.

I agree with you as to a non intercourse with the north in commerce & trade. Passing over the objection that it would be below the dignity of the occasion, it would be neither prudent nor effecient, most certainly as preceeding the meeting of a Southern Convention. With great respect I am & &, J.C. Calhoun.

Autograph draft in ScCleA; PC in Jameson, ed., *Correspondence*, pp. 764–766. NOTE: The above transcription omits dozens of cancellations and interlineations made by Calhoun in his rough draft and attempts to approximate the letter that was sent, which has not been found.

From ANNA [MARIA CALHOUN] CLEMSON

Philadelphia, April 15th 1849

My dear father, You may think me a little negligent, in delaying so long to write you, but I had been owing sister [Martha Cornelia Calhoun] a letter for sometime before leaving Washington, & of course wrote her first.

I was very anxious about you, knowing what a fatiguing journey you had before you, till I received a letter from Pat[rick Calhoun] at Charleston, giving such excellent accounts, that I was entirely relieved. The complete establishment of your *strength*, (for I am happy to think your health is as good as ever,) now depends upon yourself, & you must be careful for all our sakes. To aid in this good work, Mr. [Thomas G.] Clemson begs me to tell you, that he has sent you some of the best Port Wine, & Brandy, Philadelphia contains. The Brandy, in particular, he says is as old as (I forget what,) but "as old as the hills" will do. In short he speaks of it as something extraordinary, which I hope it will prove. Dont forget the miracles I performed with the warm toddy on going to bed, & stick to it. Take exercise, but dont fatigue yourself. Study, but dont worry yourself, & dont write too much, (*except to me*). Live generously, & go to bed early. There are some "golden rules" for you! I am sure no doctor could better them, & if you follow them I shall know you love me.

We are all well, & Floride [Elizabeth Clemson] in particular has not had a single headache, since we left Washington. They enjoyed the country extremely, & did nothing all day long, but make gardens, & plant trees, which [John] Calhoun [Clemson] manured very highly, for he said he "had heard grandpappa say, manure made things grow fast." He is a very singular child. He takes great pride in being thought like you; I hope it will cause him to desire to imitate you in all things.

While in Virginia Mr. C[lemson] took four portraits. Three were excellent, & his sister's, (Mrs. [Louisa Clemson] Washington's,) was one of the best he has ever done. Is it not too much he should have failed in you? I saw in Virginia a Mr. Davenport, a neighbour of Mrs. Washington's, & an old friend of ours. He is quite wealthy, & devotes much of his time to his vineyard, & the making of wine. In the course of conversation he expressed a great desire to procure the genuine Scuppernong grape. I told him I thought you had it, & I would beg you to bring on some cuttings, when you came to Washington, as he said that was a good season. You might send them to Mrs. Washington, or get Senators [James M.] Mason, or [Robert M.T.] Hunter, to send them for you. He would be much gratified.

We have had our portraits [from Europe] opened since we came. They are perfectly safe, & every one says they have never seen such likenesses & such paintings. The director of the Academy of Fine Arts, has laid violent hands on them, & insists on placing them in the Academy for a month that persons may see what good paintings are. We have consented, as we know the artist who painted them [Jacob Joseph Eeckhout] is anxious to come to America, at least for a time, & if they are seen, he may receive encouragement to do so. He promises at the end of that time to see them sent to Charleston himself, so the delay will not be long, & they may perhaps get to Pendleton as soon as if they went now, as there are perhaps but few waggons at this busy season.

Tell mother [Floride Colhoun Calhoun] Mrs. [Elizabeth Clemson] Barton will put my velvet bonnet, with the things she was to have fixed for her, in a box, & send them by steamer, to Mr. [John E.] Bonneau. I hope she will get them safe.

We have heard since our arrival here, that Gen. Jolly has arrived in this country. Mr. C[lemson] says he knows it is to buy his place, & I fear it is. If so, Mr. Clemson will have to go south he says for ten days, or two weeks, but we have not heard from the general, so cannot speak with certainty. This would delay us till nearly the middle of May. I will write mother shortly, & I shall then be able to tell with more certitude, what our movements will be. It is really cold to-day, as one must sit without fire, so I must stop, to put on gloves to keep my hands warm.

Calhoun & Floride send "as much love as the letter will hold, & a heap of kisses to grandpapa[,] grandmama & auntie & howdye to Duke." Mr. C[lemson] sends love. Your devoted daughter, Anna Clemson.

ALS in ScCleA.

To [W. Pinkney Starke, Charleston]

Fort Hill, S.C., April 15, 1849

My Dear Sir—The paralysis of the South to which you refer, and which you justly say threatens so much mischief to her and the whole Union, is to be attributed, not to any indifference to her interest or safety, but to the deluding and blinding effects of party devotion and attachment. The Federal Government is no longer under the control of the people, but of a combination of active politicians, who are banded together under the name of Democrats and Whigs, and whose exclusive object is to obtain the control of the honors and emoluments of the Government. They have the control of the almost entire press of the country, and constitute a vast majority of Congress, and of all the functionaries of the Federal Government. With them a regard for principle, or this or that line of policy, is a mere pretext. They are perfectly indifferent to either, and their whole effort is to make up on both sides such issues as they may think for the time to be the most popular, regardless of truth or consequences. It has been the aim of both to keep the great question which divides the North and the South out of their party issues, from the fear that it would separate the Northern and Southern wings of each. To avoid what each would consider so great a calamity, every device has been resorted to by each to keep the South in a state of profound ignorance of what is going on at the North in reference to this, the most vital of all subjects, and of the consequences that must follow if nothing be done in time to avert them. The few solitary voices which have been raised to warn the South, have been by both parties charged to faction. The only authoritative movement that has ever been permitted to be made to warn the South of its danger, was the address of last winter, and that had to encounter the almost entire opposition of the party coming into power in Congress, and the entire opposition of the party going out of power. It is that which has paralysed the South and debased the whole Union, and which is rapidly preparing the way for a terrific revolution. I rejoice that Mr. [George] McDuffie's health is so far restored as to make life comfortable. It is a great point gained. Nothing I feel confident could ever have effected so much but water cure. With great respect, I am yours truly, J.C. Calhoun.

PC in *Testimonials* (n.p., n.d.), pp. [1]–2; PEx in Wilson, ed., *The Essential Calhoun*, p. 348. NOTE: A copy of the 10-page pamphlet entitled *Testimonials* can be found in ScU-SC, William Pinkney Starke Manuscripts. A footnote added, evidently by Starke, to Calhoun's final sentence in this letter reads: "Having persuaded Mr. McDuffie to try the water cure, I had taken him to Milledgeville, Ga."

From Walker & Bradford, Hamburg [S.C.], 4/17. They enclose an account indicating about a dozen charges for household goods, commission, freight, and interest from 8/27/1847 to date. The total amount due from Calhoun is $241.64. Within a few days they will issue a draft against Calhoun for the amount, payable at sight to J[ohn] S. Lorton. Calhoun's AEU reads: "Walker & Bradford[.] The order on the paper[?] of John Lorton." LS with En in ScU-SC, John C. Calhoun Papers.

From F[itz]w[illiam] Byrdsall

New York [City,] April 20th 1849

Dear Sir, I have long felt it as a pleasurable duty to transmit such political matters and to write of such passing events as I deemed might be useful or interesting to the only living man from whom I have derived ["the best" *interlined*] instruction not only as regards our constitutional system of Government, but as regards every subject he has discussed in our whole range of politicks, and whom I now deeply venerate as the last of our Republican patriarchs. In all that I have written in this direction, I do not assume that I have enlightened you upon any principle, but only that I have expressed myself freely[,] frankly and I believe truthfully. I have looked to you for many years as my political guide with an interest in your behalf which I never felt for any other public man, hence you were and are still my preference for the Presidency. I can recollect on reverting to the past, that often when your star seemed to shine less brightly in the political firmament than at other times, it was then the more brilliant to my view, for it illustrated the beautiful sentiment of the antients that "the Gods could not behold a more sublime spectacle than a ["great" *canceled and* "virtuous" *interlined*] man struggling with adverse circumstances. From the above hasty grouping of ideas you will perceive the reason of my writing to you so often and unbidden.

I enclose you [*not found*] the description of the [Henry] Clay birth day Festival, in which the unmistakable evidences of the Whig feeling towards General [Zachary] Taylor are manifested. I do not blame those Whigs who are faithful in their devotion to Henry Clay, and I certainly like the conduct of those who declare their devotion to him. They are honester men than the Taylor Whigs of the North who are using Taylor as they would an Orange—squeeze the juice out and then throw away the rind. Such Yankee Whigs as [Horace] Greel[e]y detest the idea of a slaveholder being President. They hate him too as a military man, as well as a Southerner. They are making much of him now for the sake of the official patronage in his gift, and they (his advisers), are holding up the administration of [John] Tyler to him as a president without a party, thus weaning him off the platform he erected ["before his election" *interlined*] for himself to stand on subsequently. According to his voluntary pledges and declarations of being President, not of a party—but of the whole people—of carrying out the schemes of no party—of having no enemies to punish &c &c Democrats so called have as much reason and right ["under his pledges" *interlined*] to be applicants for office as Whigs. It was upon ["his" *interlined*] pledges of party neutrality and independence that he obtained the suffrages of a majority of the people, and I deny the right of any man to make professions calculated to win votes to be afterwards falsified. What is this but obtaining the Presidency and all its concomitants, on false pretenses?

I enclose you also an article [*not found*] of the New York Tribune setting forth that the Barnburners should be spared from removals—because they defeated [Lewis] Cass and were not opposed to Taylor; in other words, only those who opposed Abolitionism and Wilmot provisoism should be removed from office. Truly we have fallen upon evil times if those men who have stood ["in the north" *interlined*] as defenders of the ["dearest" *interlined*] rights of the Southern people, the rights of property and constitutional rights of General Taylor himself and his children after him, are to be proscribed under his administration, the presidency of a Southern man. The apparition of John Tyler, as a President without a party may be placed in ter[r]orem before President Taylor, and although Tyler was not commended ["or as popular" *interlined*] as he deserved, yet we can imagine an Executive of a far worse reputation before mankind, that of faithless declarations and broken pledges.

For myself I hold a small office [of Inspector in the Customs House] which small as it is I regret that I need. Through the secret work of ["the" *canceled and* "some" *interlined*] Van Buren men I was removed from a better one in 1845 and I can conceive the political reason that has prevented my restoration since. I have as many friends in this city as any officer ["or citizen" *interlined*] of my rank. I might say more—but the old leaders of the Van Buren faction like me no better than I do them, and the Whigs here are free soilers (I know not a single exception) to all of which root & branch Mr. Clay[']s Lexington speech platform and that of [the] Buffalo [Free Soil Convention], I am a well known opponent ["and have no mercy to expect as such" *interlined.*] In this, as a States right Republican, I take pride. The cause is not the less dear to me that ["it" *interlined*] is not triumphant; by me it shall never be deserted. If I am struck down for my principles, I can then say that the ["Taylor" *interlined*] Whigs finished what the ["Polk" *interlined*] democrats began. On looking back over this paragraph I would rather I had not written it—there is too much of self in it, but I hate to draw black lines of erasure as much as I do to write the whole letter over again as I have not time.

In our recent [city] Charter Election the Barn burners vote fell off far beyond ours. They led the Hunkers to believe that the nomination of Van Schieck [*sic*; Myndert Van Schaick] their candidate for the Mayoralty would induce union against the Whigs. This was done, and notwithstanding this concession on the part of the Hunkers, the Barnburners run candidates in opposition both for county and ward officers, whereupon the Hunkers did not support Van Schaick generally. As there were three tickets for county Judges the relative strength of the parties are ascertained thereby to be as many thousands for the Hunker side, as there are hundreds for the Barnburners or free soil. Last fall we stood as nearly four votes to their one, now we stand as nearly ten to their one. But the whole vote of the county nearly twenty thousand less this spring than last fall.

[Ellwood] Fisher's Lecture on the North and the South for the two copies of which I beg you to accept my thanks, is calculated to do much good. I have had them read pretty extensively already, and we are trying to get it in one of the papers of largest circulation. I like it because it shews cause for citizens of the slave States to be well satisfied with their social condition and that slavery is not detrimental to their to their [*sic*] moral[,] political or temporal welfare; and it proves to the people of the free States, that Equal and exact justice has not been done to the south neither by congressional legislation nor public opinion.

I should be much pleased to see a similar production in print shewing the thousand rills of abstraction of profit drawn ["by the North" *interlined*] from the South annually in the shape of freights on goods from the north to the south—the profits on the sale of the goods at the south, the freights of cotton[,] rice & sugar to the north in payment for the goods—the Insurances both ways—the commissions &c &c all of which ultimately reach the north. Why does not some able man shew up in a popular form the value of the southern to the Northern States—as producers of the most valuable exports and as consumers of northern products of industry. Talk of it as the world may—it is demonstrable by facts that Southern slavery is at this day [*one word canceled*] the most profitable institution to the whole United States and the greatest blessing to the whole world. What human being is not benefitted by the cheap production of cotton which now contributes to the comfort of every human being in the bounds of civilization! Is it not the greatest article in the world's commerce?

I sat down to write a short letter but I see I have written a long one, for the fact is we are in the midst of a world of crowded events that you can hardly touch on any ["part" *canceled*] of those events without taking hold of more. Moral[,] religious and political revolutions seem to be the order of the day, men do not understand the philosophy of masterly inactivity, they must be in active excitement, they cannot understand that the failure of revolutions in nations is owing to the fact that each people has actually the government they are fitted for, and that when they are qualified for Liberty and the best forms of government, these will be at hand.

I will close with this remark that you need not be surprised if the men who defeated the nomination of Henry Clay in 1840—who effected the nomination of General Taylor in 1848, shall effect the nomination of W[illia]m H. Seward in 1852. Much will depend upon the future whether Clay & Seward shall prove friends or foes in the Senate. Yours with increased respect, F.W. Byrdsall.

[P.S.] Free soilism is going down fast in the Democratic party.

ALS in ScCleA; PEx's in Boucher and Brooks, eds., *Correspondence*, pp. 501–502.

From Richard M. Young, [Commissioner, General Land Office]

Washington City, April 24, 1849

My Dear Sir, I send to you by the mail of to day, my annual Reports for the years 1847 and 1848, with Doct. David Dale Owen's late Geological Report, all bound together in one volume, with your name lettered on the back. Also an "appendix" in tabular form, also bound up seperately. Will you please accept them, as the best testimonial of respect I have at present to offer, from your old political and personal friend.

The "appendix" especially, you will find to be a document of great value, to such as take, as you have always taken, an interest in the subject of the public lands. It is in fact, a comprehensive, and well digested tabular history of the public domain, from the commencement of the land system, down to the 1st of January 1849. These Reports, and the appendix I now send you, embody the sum of my labors during the time I have had the control of the Land Office. Whatever my political enemies may choose to say of me in other respects, they cannot say that I have been idle. But my labors here will now very soon be brought to a close, as whether removed or not, by those now in power, I have made up my mind to resign with the close of the present fiscal year (i.e., June 30, 1849). As I will have gone home to Illinois, before your return to Congress, I think it more than probable that I will never see you again.

With many thanks for your kindness to me, on many occasions, since I first had the pleasure of making your acquaintance, I bid you farewell, with the kindest wishes for your present, and future happiness. Your obliged friend, Richard M. Young.

ALS in ScCleA.

To A[NDREW] P[ICKENS] CALHOUN, [Marengo County, Ala.]

Fort Hill, 28th April 1849

My dear Andrew, This is the fourth letter I have written to you since I received your's dated at Charleston, and which I answered before I left Washington, without having a line from you. I know not how to account for it, unless mine have miscarried; and I write now principally to inform you of the fact, that I have not heard from you.

I have been the more anxious to hear from you, in consequence of the severe spell of weather we had a short time since; & which, I see has done much damage in the South & West. I am, of course, anxious to learn, whether we have been sufferers, or not; &, if we have been, to what extent. It has done much damage in this State below this, & will certainly shorten the cotton crop, for as far as I can learn all was killed that was up. In this vicinity, it has done less. We had little snow. Not enough to whitten the ground. The frost was severe; but did less damage than below. The peaches are killed, but the apples, ["peaches" *canceled and* "pears" *interlined*] & plumbs have in a great measure escaped. The corn was cut down, but did not require replanting, & what cotton was up was killed, but there was suffecient seed left in the ground for a stand. The wheat is slightly injured. I hope we have escaped as well with you; & that our cotton is safe. I think the prospect of a favourable market for the crop is good.

The Wheather for the last week has been as fine as could be desired. Fine showers and moderately warm. [*Partial word canceled.*] Every thing is reviving & beginning to look well. My crop & place are in a fine condition. We have begun hoeing our cotton.

Before I close, I must remind you, that our note in the State bank must be renewed on the 14th next month. If you have ["not" *interlined*] sent your name in blank for renewing it, you have no time to lose, and I hope you will transmit it, in that case, as soon as you receive this.

["We" *canceled.*] My health continues good; and I have regained in a great measure my strength. I hope you are all well. My love to Margaret [Green Calhoun] & the children [Duff Green Calhoun, John Caldwell Calhoun, Andrew Pickens Calhoun, Jr., and Margaret Maria Calhoun]. I hope little Andrew continues to improve in health. Your affectionate father, J.C. Calhoun.

ALS in NcD, John C. Calhoun Papers.

From Hilliard M. Judge

Eutaw [Ala.], 29th Ap[ri]l 1849

Dear Sir: Your favor of the 15th ultimo has just been received, and I regret, you did not receive the paper, I sent you. If I can procure another copy, I will send it to you, as I desire very much, that you should see the article alluded to.

The immediate object of this letter is, to inform you of an attempt, which is being made, to destroy your influence in this State, by secretly circulating an abominable falsehood, well calculated to deceive the unwary and produce the most injurious effect upon the great Southern question. I have it, not directly, but through the most undoubted authority, that Mr. [George S.] Houston of this State, defends himself for not signing "the Southern Address," by stating, that the Slavery question is agitated alone for party purposes and party effect, and in evidence of that fact, says, you told Mr. [Stephen A.] Douglass of Illinois, during the discussion of the California bill—"that it would never do to settle this question of slavery—that its agitation, was necessary to the success of the Democratic party in the South." He referred his hearer (Judge [James B.] Wallace of Tuscaloosa) to the Hon. Mr. [Henry W.] Hilliard of Montgomery, in corroboration of what he stated.

The object of this statement is clear—those Southern Whigs and democrats, who betrayed their constituents, seek to defend themselves, by assailing you, in whom, the whole South, without distinction of party, have the most unlimited confidence.

It is part and parcel of the attack made upon you by that base sot and demagogue, Senator [Samuel] Houston, urged on, doubtless, by Senator [Thomas H.] Benton, whose sympathies, are wholly with the Abolitionists. Those Whig members of Congress, who have betrayed their constituents and the South, from love of party and spoils, have united in the attack, as evidenced by Mr. Houston of this State referring to Mr. Hilliard for support & corroboration. Whether or not, this statement ought to be contradicted, you best know, but I can say to you, it has gained no credence from any person of intelligence, with whom I have conversed, of either party, yet, at the same time, ignorant persons in other portions of the South may be deluded by it.

Almost all the Counties of South Alabama have responded most emphatically "to the Southern Address" without distinction of party—North Alabama is much less interested and will be slow in her action, yet I think she will follow the lead of the Southern portion of the State. A favorable omen of public opinion there, is furnished by Houston's refusal to be a Candidate for reelection. Hilliard will be beaten [for Representative] in his District, by a Whig or Democrat, who is sound, as may seem best calculated, to accomplish this result.

Judge [Henry M.] Goldthwaite of Montgomery is arousing public attention to this great question, in the best manner that it can possibly be done, viz.—by charging the grand-jurys in his Circuit, in an able manner, upon the subject. The effect, is most admirable upon the ignorant portion of the people, from the color of authority under which it is done. The great difficulty is, to make the masses, see beyond their noses—they do not see and feel, that the necessary consequence of allowing all the outposts of Slavery to be carried, involves the certain destruction of the Citadel itself.

The public mind, is rapidly being prepared for what must come at last—the dissolution of the Union, but *we must have time.* Let the Legislatures speak out in support of Va., as they will all do—let them all be *committed* to the principle of resistance, and then, when the time does come for action, they will be prepared to defend their rights to the last extremity. Let South Carolina hold back—a little, until her more slothful sisters can be equally well instructed in their rights & duty under the present emergency, the whole South will then present an unbroken front, and thus accomplish peaceably, what we desire! This delay, is not so necessary for Alabama, as for the more western States, for next to South Carolina, Alabama is better prepared for resistance than any other Southern State.

Your suggestion, as to the necessity of a convention of the Southern States, is perfectly obvious. We cannot get along in any other way—the North, will not be deterred from her course of wanton aggression, by resolutions of the State Legislatures, but let the Legislatures first declare the principle and the people of the States can give them force and effect in Convention.

Our corn & cotton crops were destroyed entirely by a frost on the 15th ultimo, also all the wheat north of this county. This is the second time our cotton has been killed during this spring, which has caused an unusual demand for cotton seed—the next crop cannot possibly be a full one. I have the honor, to remain, your friend & ob[e]d[ien]t Serv[an]t, Hilliard M. Judge.

ALS in ScCleA; PC in Jameson, ed., *Correspondence*, pp. 1195–1197.

From Ro[bert] Greenhow

Washington, April 30th 1849

My Dear Sir, I received your kind letter, with its most kind enclosure, in due course of mail; and on the following day, when I was about to answer it, my little boy—my only boy, whom you may remember as a strong and merry baby, was seized with convulsions. A fever followed, which continued with slight intermissions until last evening, when he expired. His brain was probably injured, during the convulsion, as he never after exhibited any farther sign of consciousness, than a preference for his mother [Rose O'Neal Greenhow]. All that could be done by ["the" *interlined*] courage and watchfulness of his mother, and the skill of his physician, was vain, as the symptoms constantly became worse, until the close.

I can only say, at present, that your letter [*not found*] was presented to the President [Zachary Taylor], who read it with attention. He was evidently pressed by business, and though his manner was most kind, and even flattering, he said nothing from which I could infer anything whatsoever, either favourable or unfavourable, to my object. He spoke of the great pressure of the applications, and of the complaints made by some parts of the country, that their claims had been overlooked, while others were specially favoured—that he could not remove without cause—and that he should make no appointments of diplomatists, until the end of the fiscal year. On reporting the particulars of my interview, to Mr. [John M.] Clayton [Secretary of State], he said that the answer which I received, was the only one which the President gave, or could give at present. I have since been so painfully absorbed, by the condition of my child, that I have been unable to think of any thing else.

Mrs. Greenhow is much reduced in flesh and strength, by her unwearied attentions; never have I seen more courage, and perseverance displayed, than by her. She is only able at present, to express to you, through me, our grateful recollection of your kindness, so promptly rendered. *Your caution had been anticipated by us.* To this moment, no one is aware of your communication to the President, so far as We know, except Mr. Clayton, the President and Col. [William W.S.] Bliss; nor shall any one hear of it from us. It is proper for me to add, that the President on reading your letter, which he seemed to have read *twice* with extreme care, did not mention your name. I told him, that I should not produce any other recommendations; upon which, he observed, that this, holding the letter, was amply sufficient—or words to the same effect.

I am sorry that I have nothing whatsoever to communicate to you, of an interesting nature, in consequence of my afflictions of the last fortnight, from which I have had no refuge, except in constant labour in my business. In Europe, there seems to be every prospect of a grand convulsion, during this summer. [Guillaume T.L.] Poussin [French Minister to the U.S.] says, that his Government is resolved, at all hazards, to remain neutral, with regard to Italy, and that its warlike preparations are all purely precautionary.

With my best wishes for yourself, and family—and particularly that you will do no work with your mind, during this inter-session—I remain most respectfully Your Obed[ien]t Serv[an]t, Ro. Greenhow.

ALS in ScCleA.

To J[ohn] M. Clayton, [Secretary of State]

Fort Hill, April 1849

My dear Sir, I take pleasure in repeating in a letter, what I stated [to] you in conversation, before I left Washington, as to Mr. [Francis] Markoe's qualifications to fill the place of Chargé to some European court.

While I was in the State Department, I had a good opportunity of forming an opinion, as to his qualifications, and am of the impression, that few could be found more suited. He is well informed, possessed of good sense and good manners & is familiar with all the duties appertain[in]g to such offices. I found him very attentive & competent in performing the duties of the office he fills in the Department.

Under these impressions & with my feelings towards him personally, I would be gratified should he succeed in his application. With great respect yours truly, J.C. Calhoun.

ALS in DNA, RG 59 (State Department), Letters of Application and Recommendation during the Administrations of Franklin Pierce and James Buchanan, 1853–1861, Francis Markoe (M-967:29, frames 680–681).

From L[EWIS] WARRINGTON, Acting Secretary of the Navy

Navy Department, May 2nd 1849

Sir, In reply to yours of the 4th ult[im]o [*not found*] I have the honor to state, that the name of Richard Cook does not appear in the Rolls of the Constitution, nor on those of the Marine Corps, nor has he enlisted at any Naval Rendezvous since June 1846, the date of the Register of recruits, kept at the Department.

He might (as is often the case) have entered under an assumed name. I am respectfully Your ob[edien]t Serv[an]t, L. Warrington, Acting Secretary of the Navy.

FC in DNA, RG 45 (Naval Records), Miscellaneous Letters Sent by the Secretary of the Navy, 1798–1886, 41:384 (M-209:15).

From CITIZENS OF MEMPHIS

Memphis Ten[nesse]e, May 4th 1849

Sir, From the enclosed Pamphlet you will perceive a convention is to be held in Memphis on the 4th day of July next for the purpose of aiding—by the expressed will of citizens from every part of the country—the project of constructing a Rail Road from the Valley of the Mississippi to the Pacific ocean.

With much pleasure we have witnessed that the people of the Country are sanctioning the proposed measure by their deliberate approval.

We are aware Sir, that this great enterprize, to be successful must be assisted by the Prominent men of the Union, whose elevated position enables them to direct public sentiment and control public action.

Duly solicitous to avail the Country of your aid and influence, we invite you, very earnestly, to be present at the proposed convention. Assuring you in behalf of our Citizens a cordial welcome—very respectfully, A.B. Warford, Henry Van Pelt, H[enry] G. Smith,

R.J. Yancey, James Penn, Seth Wheatley, Robertson Topp, M[arcus] B. Winchester, Jno. T. Trezevant, David Looney, David Park, R[obert] C. Brinkley, John Pope, B.R. Teryman, Corresponding Committee.

LS in ScCleA. NOTE: An AEU by Calhoun reads, "Memphis Convention."

From TOMLINSON FORT, [former Representative from Ga.]

Milledgeville, [Ga.,] 5th May 1849

D[ea]r Sir, Three days ago I sent you by mail a medical book, which I hope will have come to hand in safety. You will percieve by its title that it is intended as a popular work, while it shall not be unworthy of a place with books of science.

I tender to you this book, in testimony of the high regard I have long entertained, and with a hope that you may find in its contents something worthy of your attention. Should you find time to read a few of its leading articles, you will find that the work is intended to fill a place in literature which is almost vacant, there being no work of the kind entitled to much confidence. As far as I can yet judge the work has proven satisfactory, and the notices published of it by the Augusta Medical Journal, the [Augusta] Constitutionalist, Milledgeville Federal Union and others, are highly complementary. Intending to offer this book for sale in your State, it has been suggested to me that you might not think it wrong to signify your approbation of it, in a way that I might render it available in satisfying any doubt which might rest on the minds of those who might desire such a work. In contemplation of a more extended field, as my bookseller will have it "from Delaware to the Rocky Mountains" a word from you would be the more important.

Mrs. [Martha Fannin] Fort unites with me in the expression of the highest regard for yourself & family. Y[ou]r ob[edient] Serv[an]t, Tomlinson Fort.

ALS in ScCleA. NOTE: Fort had published at Milledgeville a work called *The Practice of Medicine.*

From F[ITZ]W[ILLIAM] BYRDSALL

New York [City,] May 7th 1849

Dear Sir, Virginia has set an example to all the ["States" *interlined*] South and Southwest of Mason & Dixon's line, which if they follow, will secure their just and constitutional rights, will revolutionize public opinion in the northern States, preserve the confederacy from dissolution, and consequently the worst of all intestine feuds, the war of races. I rejoice over the defeat of [John S.] Pendleton [as Representative from Va.], as there was a great principle involved, for I hold a Southern traitor in these days, in perfect abhorrence, as a traitor to the whole Union. He who is elected in his stead [Jeremiah Morton], is, I learn, a Brother of the recently chosen U.S. Senator of Florida [Jackson Morton], who was supported in the Legislature of that State by the Democratic Members. An old friend of mine the member from Jefferson County wrote to me on the first of Jan[uar]y last, "We have just elected a successor to Mr. [James D.] Westcott—and in this matter we the Democratic party claim we have accomplished *Something.* The Whig nominee [George W.] Ward is defeated by our running Morton. On the first balloting Ward got 27 votes—Morton 29—blank 2. On the second Morton 30—Ward 27—blank 1—necessary to a choice 30—we, the democrats 22, voting for Morton." All things considered, I am inclined to believe that both these Mortons are only half Whigs—at all events they are republican upon the subject of free soilism.

Wilmot Provisoism would not have made such headway against the South if it had not been for certain fools and traitors from the Slave States as [Thomas H.] Benton, [Samuel] Houston, [Alexander H.] Stephens, Pendleton and others in Congress and Henry Clay out of Congress. Had the Southern Democrats and Whigs stood together as a firm phalanx in the common cause of the sacred rights of all their constituents, Northern members would have collected around them anxious to be foremost in standing by the rights of the South and public opinion would have been shaped accordingly. The ["open" *interlined*] desertion of these fools or traitors—the cold shoulder of other Southern men was deemed by the rest of the world as an acknowledgement that the Southern cause was a bad one; hence popular opinion against the South accumulated to a tremendous extent, the few northern men who dared to stand for the ["right" *interlined*] were proscribed and persecuted—the press is not open to our vindication not for love, and only for money when the amount is large, and thus does there exist a Crusade more becoming the dark ages than one of civilization.

And there are other fruits growing out of this state of things which Southern men should know. The Clay Whigs [Vice-President Millard] Fillmore & Co. and the anti Clay Whigs Seward & Co. are becoming united in this State for the contest of 1852 under the master spirit ["of" *canceled*; William H.] Seward. They are united in the projet of obtaining from the [Zachary] Taylor administration—the controll and dispensation of the Executive patronage of the General Government in this State, to be divided between both sections of Whiggery, but to be allotted only to those who will use their position and influence to elevate him whom the calculating Whigs believe can carry this State against any competitor under the present condition of parties. Seward is a most able political tactitian, as well as Demagogue. It was he who when Governor of this State on a fourth of July addressed the Sunday school children en masse of New York assembled on Staten Island and said to them "that it was true we had attained political equality—but not that social equality of condition without which our system of Government would prove a failure." I quote from memory and am certain of being correct in meaning and substance. It was this Governor too who recommended to the State Legislature that in our public schools the German[,] the Celtic, the Dutch, the French and other European languages should be taught in order that Emigrants could have their children trained to speak their mother tongue. It was this Wm. H. Seward who defeated in 1840 the nomination of Henry Clay for the Presidency, and although the latter knows all this and has hated him accordingly, yet such may be the event of the future however strange now, (unless some intervention of Providence occurs in the mean time) that the mighty Henry Clay may live to discover that the impressions made ["amongst" *canceled and* "upon" *interlined*] the Whigs of the North by his Lexington Speech & Resolutions—his recent abolition movements—that in fact himself as well as strongest friends will be all useful and even used for the elevation of Seward a competitor he probably never contemplated. But these are not all, for [Martin Van Buren] the Sage of Lindenwald—his Buffalo platform and dough head Barnburners have been contributing to this result, together with the hero of Buena Vista, if he ever *surrenders* the Executive patronage to ["the" *canceled*] Seward Fillmore & Co. These are the materials which the master hand of the politician has to shape to the end in view, and when we add to these the fact that he has gained the approbation of the naturalized citizens especially the Irish and German Catholics and [John J. Hughes] their Bishop, a mighty Ally; that he has the Abolitionists or semi Abolitionists—free soil men of all parties—the anti masons, anti renters, Socialists, Fourierists and majority of the Whig party with [Thurlow] Weed, [Horace] Gree-l[e]y &c &c—the denouement of the political drama now commenced may be calculated. Oh it is a spectacle to excite the mockery of a Mephistophiles to behold the great men of this day heretofore the principal characters on our political stage, becoming knowingly or unknowingly subordinates to Wm. H. Seward.

The preservation of our Republic depends upon the South maintaining their rights, with a proper regard for their Institutions and that self respect to induce union which will command respect every where. By proper regard for their Institutions, I mean a patriotic pride in the mighty incontrovertible fact that no where on this habitable globe is there as little pauperism[,] destitution[,] suffering and crime, in proportion to population, as in the Slave States of this Union.

The speculations which I have sketched in this letter respecting the political schemes of parties here are by no means only visible to me. They are as well or better understood by many others. In conversation with Mr. [J.H.] Hunt, brother of the Comptroller of this State [Washington Hunt], a few days ago, a democrat and author of the anti Wilmot Proviso tract, he expressed himself so much to the point that I requested him to put the same in writing for your perusal. I enclose you what he wrote though it is much more brief and goes not into the numerous particulars upon which his views are founded.

It is lamentable that General Taylor was taken up for the presidency because he was popular in the first instance, but really ["afterwards" *interlined*] because he declared he knew nothing about the questions which divided political parties—that he had not voted in his life (if I recollect rightly)—that he would yield to the majority in Congress &c &c and therefore the designing politicians conceived he would be a plastic tool in their hands. For so far they appear to be gradually using him to perform their wishes instead of his own declarations and pledges of independence. It will require a mighty effort to regain the ground he has already surrendered.

In short my dear Sir, I am satisfied that the salvation of this confederacy from the evils which now beset it, depends entirely upon the Southern States and therefore I write to you as the man having pre-eminently the wisdom and virtue to meet the crisis. I once had enthusiastic faith in the intelligence and virtue of the people but experience has taught me to have faith in the intelligence of the Intelligent, and the virtue of the virtuous. Popular opinion under the influence of a vicious public press is often erroneous. Our only trust therefore is in a benign providence and the wise and good men of our country. Yours with the highest Respect, F.W. Byrdsall.

[Enclosure]

J.H. Hunt to F.W. Byrdsall

New York [City,] May 5/49

D[ea]r Sir—The opinions you asked me a day or two ago to repeat in writing are—

That there has long been an understanding between the leaders of the Barnburners in this State & Seward—

That Bishop Hughes and the bulk of the Irish Catholics are to be reckoned among the political chattels of Seward—

That the Custom House of this Port is to be the exclusive property of the above coalition, and all the offices belonging to the establishment will be used to promote its designs and reward Seward & V[an] Buren's instruments—They ["(Seward & Co.)" *interlined*] may however leave a few democrats, partly by way of a blind—partly to purchase their silence.

That the greatest danger to the south is from the weakness of southern fools and southern traitors. If the south can be united, and true to itself for 4 or 5 years to come, all is safe—if not, — — — — The abolition faction at the north, notwithstanding its immense noise and bulk, is but a monstrous mushroom, and will perish like a mushroom if the south stand firm till the battle is fought. The power of wisdom and courage is greater than the power of Impudence and of Numbers. ["The trial will be severe, but if" *canceled.*] Y[ou]rs &c, J.H. Hunt.

ALS with En in ScCleA; PC in Boucher and Brooks, eds., *Correspondence*, pp. 502–505.

From [James B. Longacre, Chief Engraver of the U.S. Mint]

Philad[elphi]a, May 8, 1849

Dear Sir, The small gold coin enclosed is one ["of" *interlined*] the coinage of this day of the gold dollar, and this day is the first on which the coin ["was" *canceled*] has been made at the Mint of the United States.

[“It is” *canceled.*] This being the first opportunity I have had since my appointment as Engraver of the Mint, of executing a coining die of my own design and modelling—I do but execute a long cherished purpose, and at the same time obey the prompting of my own feelings, in presenting you with the first impression from it, of which I have been enabled to possess myself.

It is a very small token of remembrance it is true, but it may serve to inform you, that I have not forgotten the partiality, on your part to which I am proud to attribute my first appointment to the place I now occupy.

Draft (unsigned) in PPL, Longacre Collection. NOTE: An engraving from a Longacre drawing of Calhoun was published in volume 2 of Longacre’s *National Portrait Gallery of Distinguished Americans* . . . . 4 vols. (New York: M. Bancroft, 1834–1839).

TO FRANCIS WHARTON, [Philadelphia]

Fort Hill, 8th May 1849

My dear Sir, I am much obliged to you for the copy of your introduction to your collection [of] American Political Trials. It is well executed, and contains much interesting matter. I have read it with pleasure. Yours truly, J.C. Calhoun.

ALS in ScU-SC, John C. Calhoun Papers. NOTE: Wharton in 1849 published *State Trials of the United States during the Administrations of Washington and Adams.*

TO R[ICHARD] M. YOUNG, [Commissioner, General Land Office, Washington]

Fort Hill, 8th May 1849

My dear Sir, I am much obliged to you for the valuable Documents you were so kind [“as” *interlined*] to send me, bound up in forms so convenient. The Appendix I had looked over before I received the copy you sent me. It is a complete and most valuable document, in reference to a very interesting subject, & will stand as a lasting monument of your administration of the Land Department.

I greatly regret, that your valuable & faithful services will be lost to the government by your resignation. It will be difficult to fill your place by one combining all the qualifications requisite to discharge its important duties. I shall ever recollect with pleasure our acquaintance & shall ever be happy to hear of your health & prosperity.

With my kind regards to Mrs. [Matilda James] Young I am yours truly & sincerely, J.C. Calhoun.

ALS in DLC, Andrew Jackson Donelson Papers; CC in IHi, Richard M. Young Paper; CC in DNA, RG 48 (Secretary of the Interior), Appointments Division.

From C[OLLIN] S. TARPLEY

Jackson Mi[ss.,] 9th May 1849

Sir, I take the liberty of forwarding to you the proceedings of a public meeting recently held [on 5/7] at the Capitol of this State. The subject is one of vital interest to the South, and demands the united eneregies [*sic*] of her people by *firm* yet temperate action to resist the repeated encroachments upon rights regarded as sacred by the Constitution[.] You will perceive Sir from the resolutions adopted by the meeting that a State Convention is called to assemble on the first monday in October next to take into consideration the the [*sic*] appropriate remedies that the South should use in order to m[a]intain her constitutional rights and stay the hand of aggression. This is a grave question and may be attended with results more important in their character than any that have transpired since the formation of the Constitution, and it becomes necessary that we should have the benefits derived from admitted talents and enlarged political experience to enable us to take such steps as are compatible with the dignity of the question, and at the same time such as will meet a cordial support from the other States of the South. In view of this momentous question, permit me Sir as a private Citizen identified in all things with the South, and warmly attached to the institutions of our common Country, to request your opinion as to the proper course to be pursued at our October Convention. We desire to take a position that will awaken the North to the danger of further agitation of the Slave question in the Halls of Congress, that ["that" *canceled*] shall not only assert our constitutional rights, but prescribe a mode of redress in the prosecution of which we pledge all that is sacred and dear to us. We intend to *say* nothing more than we mean *to do*[,] but to act with dignity and efficiency we must be careful to take no step that will not meet with the sanction of the whole South. Nothing Sir but the importance of this all absorbing question would excuse the liberty I have taken, but in times of common danger when the whole South is in emminent peril, the necessity for wisdom in counsel, and harmony in action must supersede the rules of established etiquette; and the South has so long looked to you as its great Champion, that in the hour of danger we naturally turn our eyes to you and claim the benefit of your wisdom and experience.

The Address which you will find in the proceedings of our meeting was drawn by Chief Justice [William L.] Sharkey, confessedly the most talented and eminent Whig in our State and will meet a hearty response in the bosoms of our people without regard to party[.]

May I respectfully request an answer to this to be used if necessary in the Convention. I have the honor to be with great respect Your Ob[edien]t S[er]v[an]t, C.S. Tarpley.

ALS in ScCleA. NOTE: Tarpley was a prominent stock breeder, planter, and lawyer of Hinds County. Calhoun's AEU reads, "Relates to the proposed convention in Miss[issipp]i." The copy of "proceedings" forwarded to Calhoun has not been found. However, they are published in full in the Jackson, Miss., *Mississippian* (weekly), May 11, 1849, p. 3. Resolutions called for every county to elect delegates to meet in Jackson in October to consider the State's position on slavery in the Territories.

To T[homas] G. Clemson

Fort Hill, May [*ca.* 15?] 1849

My dear Sir, The mail of the day before yesterday brought me yours of the 5th Inst. [*not found*], from which I learn, that you will sail on the 24th Inst. for London. I transmit this by the return mail, in the hope, it may reach you before you sail; but to guard against accident, I have put it under cover to Mr. [James Edward] Boisseau to forward it to Brussels, if it should arrive too late to reach you in New York.

I fear the letter I wrote to Anna [Maria Calhoun Clemson] and her mother's [Floride Colhoun Calhoun's] to her have not been received, as neither your letters to me, [n]or hers to her mother make any mention of them. Mine was address[ed] to Philadelphia, to the care of Mr. [George W.] Barton, & her Mother's to Virginia, on the supposition you would not leave your sister[']s [Louisa Clemson Washington] before its arrival.

I am greatly obliged to you for ordering the old Port & Brandy. They will, I doubt not, be very fine and of service to me. I continue to drink a little Brandy & water after dinner. I think it is of service to my health. When the Port arrives I will substitute that, for a while, and will adhere to that, which I finds [*sic*] suits me, or take them alternately, if I shall find that best. I am in all respects fully as well, as I was this time last summer. I still have some cough, but it is much abated, & hope to get (in a great measure at least) free of it, when summer fairly sets in. I can take, ["without fatigue," *canceled*] my usual walk, morning & evening over the place without fatigue. I will substitute riding, when the weather becomes warmer.

I left special instructions with Mr. [John Ewing] Bonneau, in Charleston & Mr. [Gollothun] Walker in Hamburgh [S.C.] about the pictures. We are gratified to hear that they are so much admired, and anticipate their arrival with pleasure.

I very much regret that circumstances make your return to Europe necessary; and I hope the necessity for your remaining there will not continue long. The place of superintendent of the mint would suit you admirably. Should there be a vacancy your friends in Philadelphia ought to make an effort to obtain it for you. Whatever I can do in that case, shall be done, but I do not know whether I can have any influence with those in power. I shall do all I can in aid of Col. [Francis W.] Pickens toward disposing of your property in Edgefield. Whether you will be able to sell or not at the prices you have affixed, will depend much on the price of cotton. If it should rise to 8 or 9 cents I have no doubt you could realise the prices & perhaps exceed them. It is wonderful that prices hold their own so well, considering the low prices of our staples. It indicates the commencement of a more prosperous state of things in the South, of which I think there are many signs. How far the growing crop of cotton will be influenced by the severe cold weather during the ["last" *interlined*] month is uncertain. It is certain, that all that was up was killed, but there was a good deal not up, especially on the Northern limits of its growth. How far seed could be had for replanting where it was thoroughly killed, is also uncertain. The article was certainly very s[c]arce. Our crop in Alabama was twice destroyed, once in March & the other in April. We fortunately had ample seed for replanting; but that was not the case ["of" *canceled and* "with" *interlined*] our neighbours. My crop here was but partially up. It has since come up finely, &, with the exception of some light sandy land, the stand and the plant looks remarkably well. Indeed, my whole crop of corn, cotton, & small grain is fine; as good as I ever had at this season. The place is in fine order. My lands, instead of washing & exhausting, are in a regular course of improvement. But taking the whole cotton region together, my impression is, that the prospect is, a short crop will be made, & that there will be a rise of price.

I hope the accident to which you allude, will not deprive the country of a pure breed of goats, as I regard them as a valuable animal. The few I have are wonderfully prolifick. If you should think proper to order your she goat up here, I shall have her carefully attended to.

We are all well. There has been in the upper part of the State very little of the disease which has proved so fatal in the lower parts of Edgefield. You have been fortunate in escaping its attacks. It speaks well for the health of your place.

All join their love to you, Anna & the children [John Calhoun Clemson and Floride Elizabeth Clemson], with their wishes for a short & pleasant voyage.

Kiss the children for their Grandfather, & tell them how happy I am that they are so well & doing so well. Your affectionate father, J.C. Calhoun.

ALS in ScCleA.

From John P. Norton

Tisbury, Mass[achuse]tts, May 18th 1849

Sir, Permit me to take the liberty to enclose you a copy [*not found*] of my petition to the Legislature of this State for liverty to import Slaves, &c.

I was sincere in my movement and thought that if I could get one or two steady negros and use them kindly they would stay with me in spite of Gov. [George N.] Briggs and his associates. at any rate I would risque it[.] I will enquire of you Sir, if you can think of any method that will be proper for me to pursue to obtain a steady man, I would go to Washington City could I be assured to obtain my designs.

I on[c]e had an introduction to by Mr. [David] Henshaw of Boston. I do most sincerely hope the time will come when you will be the President of the U.S.—but it now takes *five* to make one President. I have the honor to be Sir, Very Respectfully your Ob[edien]t Servant, John P. Norton.

ALS in ScCleA. Note: Calhoun's AEU reads, "J.P. Norton[,] relates to his petition."

To A[NDREW] P[ICKENS] CALHOUN, [Marengo County, Ala.]

Fort Hill, 19th May 1849

My dear Andrew, I received your letter & the blanks in time to attend to the renewal of our note with the bank of the State [of South Carolina].

You must have been, indeed, hard pressed, having to plant your cotton three times & your corn twice. I suffered much less. Only a small part of my corn was hurt; & although what cotton was up was killed, there still remained in the ground ample seed for a good stand. Since the severe spell, we have had much wet weather. Every thing has come up well, but there has not been sufficient warmth to push the crop forward. Still my entire crop[,] corn[,] cotton & small grain looks well, and though backward, I think it very promising. I hope such also is the case with you. I shall be anxious to hear, whether it is or not; as I am of the impression the cotton crop will be short & the price high the next year. If so, & we can succeed in making a good crop, it would be a great relief to us. My place was never in such good order. It is, I think, yearly increasing in its productive powers. I hope with not an unfavourable season to avarage between 800 & 1,000 pounds of cotton to acre.

I very greatly regret to learn, that little Andrew's health continues so bad. He appeared to me to be one of the stoutest & most healthy of your children, and I sincerely hope this prescription of Dr. [Josiah C.] Nott may relieve him, but I fear the disease is one hard to overcome.

My own health is good & my strength is, I think nearly fully restored. I have always trusted much to nature to relieve me from indisposition. My constitution is a good one; but I am of the impression, that I do not throw off the morbid matter of the system sufficiently freely by the skin. In such cases, I believe what is called the wet sheet, but which really is a wrung out sheet, is highly serviceable. It is a great cleanser of the pores; and is in reality but the vapour bath judiciously applied. I have as yet taken it but once. The effects, I think have been decidedly good. When the weather becomes warm and settled, I will try it again, & repeat it at intervals & with caution, if I find it serviceable. I have much less cough than I had, & no return of the attack, which gave such uneasiness to my friends last winter.

We are all well. I hope little Andrew is better and all the rest are well with you. I hope you will write at least once a month, as I shall be desireous of hearing how you all are & what is the prospect of our planting interest.

With love to Margaret [Green Calhoun] & the children. Your affectionate father, J.C. Calhoun.

ALS in NcD, John C. Calhoun Papers. NOTE: Andrew's living children at this time were Duff Green Calhoun (1839–1873), John Caldwell Calhoun (1843–1918), Andrew Pickens Calhoun, Jr. (1845–11/12?/1849), and Margaret Maria Calhoun (1847–1910).

To Dr. TOMLI[N]SON FORT, [Milledgeville, Ga.]

Fort Hill, 19th May 1849

My dear Sir, I am greatly obliged to you for your "medical practise." I have not had leisure to examine the whole volume; but have read with attention several of its chapters, and am so well pleased, that in future, it will be our guide in our family practise.

You have in my opinion done well in devoting so large a portion of the work, in giving the result of your practise. Most diseases seem to be modified by climate & local causes, of which a knowledge can only be acquired by practise & experience. You have had great advantages in coming to a correct understanding of the modifications they have undergone in our climate & locality. Besides your sound judgment & powers of discrimination, of which I can speak from personal knowledge, few have had a practise so long & widely extended.

With these impressions, I am of the opinion that our portion of the Union is under obligation to ["you" *interlined*] for the work. It is, I believe, the first of the kind, ever publish[ed] by our professional men; and I hope it may be extensively patronised in this & the adjacent States. With great respect Yours truly, J.C. Calhoun.

ALS in GEU, Tomlinson Fort Papers; microfilm copy of ALS in NcU, Tomlinson Fort Papers; transcript in Chattanooga-Hamilton County, Tenn., Public Library.

To JAMES B. LONGACRE, [U.S. Mint, Philadelphia]

Fort Hill, 19th May 1849

My dear Sir, I accept with a great deal of pleasure, the dollar gold coin, coming as it does from an esteemed freind [*sic*].

The design and modelling are beautiful and do you much credit. I wish you much success & long continuance in the office you hold. Yours truly, J.C. Calhoun.

ALS in PPL, Longacre Collection.

To [William B. Sprague, Albany, N.Y.]

Fort Hill, May 19, 1849

Dear Sir: I comply with pleasure with your request to give you a brief statement containing a summary of the character of the late Rev. Dr. Moses Waddel. I knew him well. Under his tuition I prepared myself for College.

His character as a man was good. He discharged punctually and faithfully the various duties attached to all his private relations. He was sociable and amiable; but not without a due mixture of sternness and firmness. As a minister of the Gospel, he was pious, zealous, and well versed in Theology generally. His style of preaching was plain, simple and earnest. He addressed himself much more to the understanding than to the imagination or passions.

It was as a teacher that he was the most distinguished. In that character, he stands almost unrivalled. Indeed, he may be justly considered as the father of classical education, in the upper country of South Carolina and Georgia. His excellence in that character depended not so much on extensive or profound learning, as a felicitous combination of qualities for the government of boys, and communicating to them what he knew. He was particularly successful in exciting emulation among them, and in obtaining the good will of all but the worthless. The best evidence of his high qualities as a teacher is his success. Among his pupils are to be found a large portion of the eminent men of the State of Georgia. In this State it is sufficient to name [George] McDuffie, [Hugh S.] Legaré, [James L.] Pettigru [*sic*], and my colleague in the Senate, [Andrew P.] Butler. To these many others of distinction might be added. His pupils in Georgia who have distinguished themselves are numerous. In the list are to be found the names of W[illiam] H. Crawford, [Augustus B.] Longstreet, &c. It is in the character of a teacher especially that he will long be remembered as a benefactor of the country. With great respect, I am your obedient servant, John C. Calhoun.

PC in William B. Sprague, *Annals of the American Pulpit; or Commemorative Notices of Distinguished American Clergymen of Various Denominations, from the Early Settlement of the Country to the Close of the Year Eighteen Hundred and Fifty-Five. With Historical Introductions.* (New York: Robert Carter & Brothers, 1857–[1869]), 4:67.

From WHITEMARSH B. SEABROOK, [Governor of S.C.]

Executive Department, Charleston, May 21, 1849

Dear Sir: Having been invited by many of the most respectable citizens of South-Carolina to appoint Delegates to the Convention at Memphis, I hereby request the attendance of the following gentlemen at that town, on the 4th day of July, to confer with their brethren of the States interested in the enterprize, on the expediency of constructing a Rail-Road to connect, at the most suitable point, the valley of the Mississippi with the Pacific Ocean. Respectfully yours, &c., Whitemarsh B. Seabrook.

PC in the Charleston, S.C., *Courier*, May 22 and 23, 1849, p. 2; PC in the Columbia, S.C., *Tri-Weekly South-Carolinian*, May 24, 1849, p. 2; PC in the Greenville, S.C., *Mountaineer*, June 15, 1849, p. 1. NOTE: This invitation was addressed to Calhoun and 119 other prominent S.C. businessmen, attorneys, planters, and politicians.

From ANNA [MARIA CALHOUN] CLEMSON

New York [City,] May 22d 1849

My dear father, We start [for Europe] day after tomorrow [*ms. mutilated; several words illegible*] lest I should not find time in the bustle & confusion of leaving to write, I scribble a few lines now. We arrived here three days ago, & as usual, cousin [James] Edward Boisseau, with his constant kindness, has kept us going from morning till night. Even now, he has taken the others to Hoboken [N.J.], but I begged off, in order to have a few moments to devote to you. I feel, indeed, but little inclination to go about, & had it not been for my sisters-in-law Mrs. [Elizabeth Clemson] Barton, & Mrs. [Louisa Clemson] Washington, who accompanied us, & who have never seen New York, I should have remained at home.

I feel very sad as the time approaches again to leave my country & friends, & undertake such a long & dangerous voyage. I have not even the pleasure of anticipation to sustain me. I know all I am to see & expect, & how little there is in that all, to recompense me for my separation from my family. But enough of this. I know you all suffer at parting from me, & why should I enhance your suffering, by telling of my own. Let us rather think of the pleasure of meeting once more & hope that it may be sooner than we anticipate.

Dont be uneasy about us while at sea. They say this is the most favourable season to make the voyage, & at least we will hope for the best. I will write immediately on our arrival[?; *ms. mutilated; several words illegible*], & hope you will all write regularly, that I may find several letters when I reach Brussels. I will get Mrs. Barton to write mother [Floride Colhoun Calhoun] a few lines when we are fairly off.

Do, dearest father, take care of yourself, for my sake. When disposed to be imprudent think of the pain it would give me to hear of your illness when so far away. I do not like to hear of this water cure business. It may be good, but I am sure you require nothing but rest & quiet to restore you entirely, & I dont like tampering with the system. I asked a very intelligent physician here, what he thought of this water cure. He said he thought the effects sometimes excellent, but also frequently most injurious.

We are all well particularly the children [John Calhoun Clemson and Floride Elizabeth Clemson] who regret much leaving America & send grandpapa, grandmama, & auntie [Martha Cornelia Calhoun] a thousand kisses & good bye's. Mr. [Thomas G.] C[lemson] sends much love & Mimi begs to say everything kind & respectful to all.

I have been several times interrupted, & must stop, for it is getting dark, & besides my heart is too full to write.

God bless you all, & keep you in good health. Tell mother not to fret about us. We shall do well, I am sure.

Good bye dear father & do write me often I intreat you. Your devoted daughter, Anna Clemson.

[P.S.] I put in the box Mrs. Barton sends some of these new fashioned envelopes which are convenient when one has not time to wait for sealing wax & also some elastic bands for your papers.

ALS in ScCleA. Note: "Mimi" was the Belgian nursemaid to the Clemson children.

From JAMES C. JONES, [former Governor of Tenn.]

Memphis, May 24th [18]49

My dear Sir, In compliance with the wishes of your friends of this place I sit down to join my personal solicitude with the publick manifestations you have received that you honour us with your presence at the Convention to assemble here on the 4th of July. Of the magnitude and importance of the objects sought to be advanced by this Convention I need not speak to you—they are such as I think commend themselves to the favourable consideration of every patriot; and ought to secure the favourable regards of our National Legislature. But it is not my purpose to say one word in behalf of this enterprize great and important as it may be—my object is to offer my entreaties that you will be with us on that occasion. We remember with much pleasure the honour you did us on a former occasion and if there be anything in the recollections of that ["occasion" *canceled*] event of a pleasurable character I can assure you your presence at this time would be hailed with increased pleasure and delight. We feel that we have a personal interest in you and some sort of claim upon you—you have been the long tried constant friend of such improvements as this Convention contemplates; at least as far as a connexion of the Southern Atlantic with the valley of the Miss. Give us then I beg you; the aid of your presence and counsel on this to us deeply interesting occasion. Come let us greet you once more on the banks of this great *inland sea.*

Pardon me if I seem importunate on this subject; our people look to you more than any other man to stand by them on this important subject. You know Mr. [Thomas H.] Benton is urging forward his particular project; which with all proper respect for him I think whol[l]y impracticable. We look to you to parry his blows and vindicate the superiority of our project over his. Come amongst us we are ready to receive you with open hearts and give you a cordial welcome. With highest respect I am dear Sir your friend and servant, James C. Jones.

ALS in ScCleA. NOTE: An AEU by Calhoun reads, "Mr. Jones[,] relates to Memphis Con[ventio]n."

From F[ITZ]W[ILLIAM] BYRDSALL

New York [City,] May 26th 1849

Dear Sir, When I take a review of your past political life, singularly distinguished by an independence beyond all your cotemporaries, which no Executive however much an object of popular idolatry could either bend or subdue—by a purity which in the midst of Government patronage, contracts, jobs, land speculation and other incentives of corruption, still survives unstained and even above suspicion, I cannot but feel deeply sensible of the friendly sentiments of your letter of the 13th inst. coming from such a source. Your expressions in reference to your position are consistent with that course which every true friend should encourage you to persevere in, even unto the end. I should feel myself lost to a generous consideration of the circumstances in which you are placed, were I to desire you to sacrifice for my behoof, one iota of that "perfect Independence," so sacred to you and so essential to our cause at this crisis, the very quality of all others, which has won most upon my confidence[,] esteem and veneration.

In making you acquainted hitherto with matters relating to myself personally and politically, I did so because I felt a perfect confidence in my own mind, that in any case of proscription of your friends, you would, when in possession of the facts, do all that you could with honor and propriety and without any solicitation. No friend however near to your heart, should wish more than this, and he who comprehends the nature of your mind will rest confident that when you see just cause and a proper way to serve your friends, you will avail yourself of the most blessed of all human enjoyments, the opportunity of doing good.

It was the purpose of the late [James K. Polk] administration at its commencement to appease and conciliate the friends of [Silas] Wright and [Martin] Van Buren, hence so far as yourself or friends could be reached, they were struck. In this city you had many admiring friends, preferring you, but not *hostile* to Van Buren whilst I for years was known as his indefatigable adversary, distinct in this respect, from all the Democrats I knew. I had got up political addresses—circulated through the Northern and Western States documents and written and printed circulars and furnished facts and arguments for the Newspapers against that most artful of unprincipled Demagogues. When therefore Mr. [Cornelius Van Wyck] Lawrence came into the collectorship of this Port, the partizans of Van Buren conspired for my removal and the tools of Polk were not loath to gratify them. After the deed was done, I wrote to Mr. Lawrence some letters which worried him, and besides some friends of mine of the highest respectability called on him and remonstrated. At length I was advised by *his* confidential friend Gen[era]l [Prosper M.] Wetmore then Navy Agent to go with him and see Mr. Lawrence.

It was at this interview that Mr. L[awrence] spoke of you and your abilities in the highest terms and disavowed that he had removed me as charged in ["the" *interlined*] Newspapers, for "Calhounism," though he owned up that Mr. Van Buren was his preference for the presidency. He was in a dilemma, he was sorry that he had removed a friend of yours, as you were in the Senate, (the office was then worth from ten to twenty thousand Dol[lar]s per annum) and he liked not the appearance of restoring me in opposition to Van Buren's partizans here, for John A. Dix & Co. were also in the Senate. But something must be done to make amends if possible, therefore after making some enquiries as to the business I had been engaged in, *he formally proposed to loan me capital to recommence it.* I knew his motives for making the proposition and at once declined it.

He promised to give me the first vacancy of equal grade, ["but" *interlined*] *that* he did not keep. Afterwards he promised the first vacancy that occurred among the Measurers, *that* ["too" *interlined*] was broken. He adhered to no promise that he made to me before his confirmation by the Senate, and he disregarded one made since then. Finally I brought influences to bear upon him and when an Inspector died, I wrote him a note for that vacancy, which he granted ["the" *canceled*] with all the grace of an animal of the Bear species. He did not like it, but he could not avoid it, for he was cornered. I was so far satisfied.

I was not the only friend of yours he removed from Office while I know of but one friend, little known as such, that he appointed: all his appointments were Van Buren men & Whigs. Because the one I allude to Mr. [Patrick J.] Devine, had a letter from you in his favor, I took considerable interest in his case—prevailed on Hon. John McKeon [Representative from N.Y.] to go with him to Lawrence and to urge his appointment. I also contrived to have Mr. Wetmore as his auxiliary and finally after a long siege of many months he was appointed ["and without my aid and advice he would not have succeeded" *interlined*]. He had also a letter from Gen[era]l [Lewis] Cass.

During the late presidential canvass—The General Committee of the Dem[ocratic] party at Tammany hall took ground for the removal of the Free soil-Wilmot proviso men holding office in the customs, and he was furnished with the names of nearly one hundred co-operators of Benjamin F. Butler & Co. The Committee sent delegations to him on the subject and the friends of Cass urged the matter strongly but Lawrence resisted. But he removed a Cass man named Scott for taking part in a meeting in the first Ward upon that subject.

Recently a measurer resigned and I wrote a note to Mr. Lawrence quoting his promise to me in his own words—but he answered that he could not grant it. Ex Governor [William L.] Marcy when informed of the vacancy enclosed me the enclosed letter [*not found*] in my favor *which I never handed to Lawrence.* A Whig was appointed. After you read the enclosed please destroy—only another person has seen it.

Hugh Maxwell the new Collector intends I learn to make removals in this way—On the fifteenth of June those officers who are doomed will be notified that on the first of July they shall go out of Office. In this way removals & appointments will take place simultaneously, and I expect to be ousted. This I regret because it is undeserved, because I like not to share the fate of those who are enemies of the constitution, and because I will not then have the time & means to devote to the cause that is dear to me. This wrong to come to me under the presidency of a Southern man [Zachary Taylor] who if he does not detest Wilmot provisoism in any ["and all" *interlined*] of its features ought to be himself detested. Such proscription in face of his voluntary pledges is vile as vile can be—the profit may be to the Whig party, but the infamy of duplicity and deception will be all his own.

It was in the papers of Wednesday that the Hon. I[saac] E. Holmes of Charleston was in Washington as one of the pall bearers at the funeral of Mr. [Daniel] Duncan [Representative from Ohio]. Mr. Henry D. Cruger wrote to him requesting him to call on the Secretary of the Treasury [William M. Meredith] to prevent my removal. If the letter reached Mr. Holmes before he left Washington something may have been done in the matter.

The [New York] Tribune has published two articles against E[l]lwood Fisher[']s Lecture on the North & South. We have tried to get it published in the New York Herald and [James Gordon] Bennett has promised to do so but keeps putting it off. We should like to get that Lecture spread abroad.

The anti free soil Democracy have concluded to go on the even tenor of their way, making no concession to the Barn burners. We will stand firm on the old Republican platform ["our" *interlined*] calculation being that the rank & file will desert the Van Buren or Buffalo standard ["and Leaders" *interlined*] by and bye. There are indications of fraternity between the Whigs & Barnburners. There is little or none of difference between Van Buren, [William H.] Seward, [Benjamin F.] Butler, [Horace] Greel[e]y, [William Cullen] Bryant and Thurlow Weed on the Wilmot proviso. God bless and preserve you many years Is the fervent invocation of yours truly, F.W. Byrdsall.

ALS in ScCleA.

To Citizens of Memphis

Fort Hill, 26th May, 1849

Gentlemen: I have received your invitation [of 5/4] in behalf of the citizens of Memphis, to be present at a meeting of the citizens of every part of the country to be held there on the 4th of July next, for the purpose of aiding, by expressing public opinion, the project of constructing a railroad from the valley of the Mississippi to the Pacific ocean.

I would be happy to accept your invitation, and to be present on the occasion, but regret to state, that I have an engagement with which I cannot dispense, and which will not permit me.

The object of your meeting I regard as very important. Of all the projects of the age, I consider it as one of the greatest magnitude, viewed either in its commercial or political aspect. It would do more than any other to facilitate intercourse between the two great oceans of the globe—the Atlantic and the Pacific—and thereby unite, commercially and politically, the western coast of this continent and the eastern coast of the old, with the eastern coast of this and the western coast of the old, far more intimately than they have ever heretofore been. The valley of the Mississippi would become the common centre of the intercourse between the two oceans and the extremes of both continents, with all the great benefits it would confer.

Thus far, there can be no division of opinion; but it remains to be determined whether a railroad is practicable; at what point, if it is, should it commence on the Mississippi and terminate on the Pacific? and what intermediate tract should it take between? what will be its cost? and what plan should be adopted for its execution? All these questions should be deliberately and carefully settled before the work is undertaken. Nothing ought to be hastily or precipitately done in a case of such magnitude. A careful recognizance [*sic*] and an actual survey, where necessary, ought to be made by able and faithful engineers of all the routes, preparatory to determining the question of practicability; and, if found to be so, to determine what would be the shortest, the most easily constructed, the cheapest, and the most open and readily passed over at all seasons, and what the actual cost of constructing each would be. All this information would be necessary to determine the point at which it should commence on the Mississippi and terminate on the Pacific. But in determining on these points, other considerations would have to be taken into the estimate. In determining the former, it will have to be considered, first, what point on the river will best suit its valley, and in the next, what will best suit the rest of the Union, all things considered? The former would involve the question, what point will, at all seasons, be most easily, cheaply and certainly approached by its waters, including its great tributaries? And the latter, the question, what point would, in like manner, be approached by railroad from other portions of the Union? These are questions which will demand, at the proper time, grave and careful examination. The selection should be made in reference to the general good of the whole Union, and not in reference to any particular portion.

The selection of the point of terminus on the Pacific will be less complicated. The goodness of the port, its position in reference to the general trade of that ocean, and the facility of reaching it by railroad, should be considered in determining it.

But candor compels me to state, there still remains another and graver question for us of the South to determine, before *we finally decide* what course we should take in reference to this great project; and that is, what portion we are to occupy in reference to our territories on the Pacific acquired from Mexico by the late treaty with her? Are we to be excluded from them? Are we, after having spent so much of our blood and treasure for their acquisition, to be deprived, contrary to the provisions of the Constitution, and in violation of every principle of equity and justice, of our equal right in them? Are they to be made the means of our humiliation and subjection to the rest of the Union, instead of our prosperity? And, if so, shall we still go on, and spend millions on millions, in addition to what we have already, in aggrandizing the rest of the Union at our expense and for our subjection? I trust not. I trust we shall pause until it is ascertained how we are to stand, as to those territories and the rest of the Union, before we decide finally on our course in reference to the subject of the meeting. In the meantime, steps may be taken to obtain information preparatory to a decision; but let us *reserve that until we can see what interest we are to have in the work.*

With great respect, I am, &c, J.C. Calhoun.

PC in the Memphis, Tenn., *Daily Eagle*, June 5, 1849, p. 2. PC's in the Charleston, S.C., *Courier*, June 13, 1849, p. 2; the Charleston, S.C., *Mercury*, June 14, 1849, p. 2; the Richmond, Va., *Enquirer*, June 19, 1849, p. 1; the Edgefield, S.C., *Advertiser*, June 20, 1849, p. 2; the Washington, D.C., *Daily Union*, June 20, 1849, p. 2; the Spartanburg, S.C., *Spartan*, June 21, 1849, p. 2; the Washington, D.C., *Daily National Intelligencer*, June 21, 1849, p. 3; the Pendleton, S.C., *Messenger*, June 22, 1849, p. 1; the Pickens, S.C., *Keowee Courier*, June 23, 1849, p. 3; the Nashville, Tenn., *True Whig and Weekly Commercial Register*, June 29, 1849, p. 204; the Greensborough, Ala., *Alabama Beacon*, June 30, 1849, p. 2. NOTE: Calhoun addressed this letter to "Messrs. Robertson Topp, M[arcus] B. Winchester, J[ohn] T. Trezevant, and others of the Committee of Correspondence." Because of a June outbreak of cholera in Memphis, the proposed convention was postponed from July 4 to October 15. (Greenville, S.C., *Mountaineer*, June 22, 1849, p. 2.)

William L[yon] Mackenzie, [former leader of a Canadian rebellion,] New York [City], to Duff Green, Washington, 5/26. Mackenzie read some time ago in the [New York] Herald that Green had accused him of betraying Green's confidence [about the Collectorship of Customs there]. Mackenzie denies that he has ever betrayed any confidence. "You never told me a secret—never sent me a line marked *private* or *confidential*—you asked me to tell you where I wanted a favor and you would try to get it for me—I never till now asked ["for" *interlined*] one. Of your relative the justly distinguished John C. Calhoun I have written much and in his praise wherever I could conscientiously do so. From him neither, any more than ["from" *interlined*] you, have I had any marks of favor or confidence. How then could I betray it?" Mackenzie discusses his pamphlets, which he suggests have aided politically Zachary Taylor's cause, and from which Mackenzie has received no money. Party feeling still runs high in Canada, and Mackenzie has no hope for reimbursements from the British government for his losses. The party that he has aided is now in office, and Mackenzie wishes from Green a letter of recommendation for a clerkship in the customs service. ALS in NcU, Duff Green Papers (published microfilm, roll 9, frames 217–220).

From J[AMES] H. MCBRIDE

Springfield Mo., June 2nd 1849

Sir, Herewith I forward you a paper, containing the proceedings of a meeting held here on Monday. Though small, I offer it as a tribute, due your patriotism and your profound devotion to the peculiar institutions of the South & part of the western States.

In the spring 1845 with others from this State I had the pleasure of an introduction to you & listening for a few minutes to your conversation in Washington, while you were yet acting as Sec[retar]y [of State] under Mr. [John] Tyler. It is one to which I frequently recur with feelings of deepest gratification. That your life & health may be long spared, to enable you to defend the South & the federal Constitution & that your setting sun may be as calm & happy as your midday one was brilliant is the fervent hope of your ob[edien]t Ser[van]t, J.H. McBride.

[Enclosure]

At a meeting of the citizens of Green county, held at the court house, in Springfield on Monday, the 28th day of May, 1849, for the purpose of expressing their opinions on the subject of the Wilmot Proviso, Col. J[ohn] W. Hancock was called to the chair, and C.E. Fisher and Wm. C. Price requested to act as Secretaries.

Col. Wm. C. Jones was called on by the Chairman to state the object of the meeting, which he did in a few brief and pertinent remarks.

On motion of Col. Wm. C. Jones, a committee of fifteen was appointed by the Chairman, to report a preamble and resolutions expressive of the sense of the meeting. The following gentlemen were appointed said committee. Wm. C. Jones, Marcus Boyd, Joel H. Haden, Washington Merrit, Wm. Parish, Howard Broome, John S. Waddill, S.H. Owens, Wm. G. Roberts, B.C. Chapman, D.A.W. Morehouse, James H. McBride, Joseph Farrier, Edmund Turner and B.S. Lane.

During the absence of the committee, the Southern Address and the instructions passed at the last session of the Missouri Legislature were read.

The committee then reported through their chairman, Col. Wm. C. Jones the following preamble and resolutions.

Whereas, It hath ever been the custom of the people of the United States, when a question of great import is, agitating the public mind, to hold primary meetings and express their opinions, touching the same; and whereas, it is probable that at the next session of Congress, in organizing the territories of California and New Mexico, an effort will be made by the Abolitionists of the North to interdict the institution of slavery in said territories; and whereas, a portion of the delegation in Congress, at the last session thereof, from the South and West, published an address, and that last General Assembly of the State of Missouri, adopted resolutions and gave instructions to our Senators in Congress, on the same subject, therefore we, the people of Greene county and State of Missouri, without distinction of party, in accordance with said custom, to the end that our feelings may be known in the premises, have therefore

Resolved, 1st. That the question of domestic slavery, rising high above all party considerations, is paramount to every other question which now agitates the people of the United States, and that a crisis has arrived in which the citizens of the slave holding States, should break down all party distinctions, and rallying on the broad platform of the constitution, upheld by right, justice and their common interests, present a firm and unyielding bond of Union, against the further encroachments of northern fanaticism, and with the weapons of reason and truth await the coming struggle.

2d. That the constitution of the United States never would have been ratified by the Southern States, if the full recognition of the rights of citizens to their property in slaves, in the slave holding States, had not been admitted and guaranteed in that instrument, for being indispensibly necessary to the security of the rights of the South, and so vital to the preservation of their interests and institutions; it constituted a great fundamental provision, without the adoption of which the Union could not have been formed.

3d. That the foundations of the national government are laid and rest on the right of property in slaves, and that the northern fanatics, by their usurpations, and encroachments, are disturbing the corner-stone and endangering the whole structure.

4th. That the States, as distinct and independent sovereign communities, and as members of the Federal Union, are the joint owners of the territories belonging to the United States; that the equality of the States in right and dignity constitute the basis of their union, power and government, and that to deny to the Southern States, and their citizens, a full share in the territories declared to belong to them in common with the other States, would destroy the basis of equal rights on which the bond of union rests, break down the equality and independence of the Southern States as members of the Federal Union, and sink them into a condition, where they would be subordinate to, and swayed at the mercy of the non-slaveholding States.

5th. That every citizen of the U. States, under the constitution, possesses equality of right and privilege, and that Congress cannot pass any law making odious and unjust discriminations among our citizens, without a violation of that instrument; therefore they possess no power to enact a law which prohibits a portion of our citizens from removing or emigrating to any territory of the United States with their slaves, or any other description of property; for to imply the power to prohibit one species of property, would warrant a license to prohibit property of every description, and thus make every citizen's right to his acquisitions or property the mere sport of Legislative will. In short, no one could have an absolute right in any property, or call any thing his own. If they can usurp power to deprive us of our slaves, they can, under the same constitution, usurp power to deprive us of every thing.

6th. All territory acquired by the United States is the joint property of the several States, in and to which the several States have the same constitutional rights, privileges and immunities, except so far as the institution of slavery is restricted by the compromise act of 6th of March, 1820, and this act if it ever had any constitutional force and effect has been violated and annulled by the action of the Northern States, and leaves the South free to insist on her rights in all territory, without regard to latitude; still for the sake of peace and harmony, if the North will adhere to said act of compromise, and desist from further encroachments on the rights and equality of the slave States, we are willing to abide by the same; but if the North persists in disregarding the said compromise, then we hold that the slave States owe it to their interest and sovereignty to insist on their whole rights, and any act of Congress, to prohibit the introduction of slaves into any territory of the United States, or to affect the title to such property, is in derogation of the federal constitution, and subversive of the equality and sovereignty of the slave States, and has a direct tendency to alienate the affections of the people of those States from the government of the United States.

7th. That our forefathers, by their valor, achieved our independence, by their patriotism and forbearance, accomplished an union of the States, by their wisdom, spirit of compromise and concession, framed and adopted our federal constitution, all of which they bequeathed to us; and it is a solemn and sacred duty we owe to their memory and future prosperity, to guard, maintain and defend inviolate this glorious legacy—that the Union and constitution are one and indivisable, and as such we are willing to defend them with our property and lives.

8th. That the resolutions of the last General Assembly of this State on the subject of slavery, and the address of a portion of the Southern and Western delegation from the slave States on the same subject, are entitled to our most cordial approbation. The former we believe, expresses the feelings of the people of Missouri, and the latter we regard as a plain, temperate and candid recapitulation of the injuries and insult inflicted on the South, and is a solemn and dignified admonition to the slave States, that their rights, their sovereign equality, and the constitution of the United States are in imminent peril, and that it is necessary for the people of those States to reflect what action may be necessary to defend themselves from further aggression.

9th. That the question of slavery in the territories is one which belongs exclusively to the people thereof, and it is for them alone, in organizing a State government, to determine whether they will tolerate or prohibit slavery therein.

10th. That we have seen and read with surprise the appeal of Col. [Thomas H.] Benton, a Senator in Congress, from this State, from the instructions of the last General Assembly on the subject of slavery. We hold that all Senators are the creatures of legislative action, and as such are bound to obey the power that created them.

11th. That we will support no man for any office, State or national, who is not totally opposed to the Wilmot Proviso, nor any one who will hesitate to use all means, moral, legal, and constitutional, to defeat said Proviso, and rebuke and put down northern fanaticism.

12th. That the foregoing preamble and resolutions be signed by the Chairman, and Secretaries of this meeting, and a copy thereof furnished the two papers printed here, and the "Metropolitan," at Jefferson City, for publication, and that the "Republican" and "Union," at St. Louis, be requested to copy the same.

A motion being made that the above resolutions be adopted, Burton A. James rose and offered an amendment to the same, and supported his amendment by a speech, in opposition to the remarks made by Col. Jones at the opening of the meeting.

He was replied to by Col. Jones in a speech of some length. Col. Jones thought the time had arrived when the people of the South should put a stop to the aggressions of the north, and that now was the time to adopt such resolutions as the above, and any other resolutions or amendments couched in milder language would not be consistent with the feelings of the true friends of the South.

Hon. John S. Phelps then rose and addressed the meeting, in opposition to Col. Jones, and at the close of his speech offered a set of resolutions, as a substitute for the resolutions reported by the committee, Mr. James having, at the suggestion of Mr. P[helps], withdrawn his amendment.

Mr. Phelps was answered by James H. McBride, Esq. Mr. McB[ride] took the same grounds as did Col. Jones.

The resolutions offered as a substitute by Mr. Phelps were then taken up, and the vote being taken, they were rejected.

Mr. James then again offered his amendments, and the vote was then asked, which resulted in the rejection of the same.

Mr. Phelps then moved to strike out all the first part of the tenth resolution, down to the word "We," in the fifth line, which was rejected.

The vote was then taken on the resolutions reported by the committee, and they were adopted by a vote of nearly two to one.

On motion, the meeting adjourned.

J.W. Hancock, Chairman.

C.E. Fisher }
Wm. C. Price, } Secretaries.

ALS in ScCleA; PC of En in the Springfield, Mo., *Advertiser*, June 2, 1849, p. 3. Note: An AEU by Calhoun reads, "Mr. McBride, meeting at Springfield Mo. Send Speech." James Haggin McBride (1814–1864), a native of Ky., was a lawyer, judge, banker, member of the Mo. legislature, and later a Brig. Gen. of the Missouri State Guard in Confederate service.

To T[homas] G. Clemson

Fort Hill, 3d June 1849

My dear Sir, The mail of yesterday brought me your letter, written just before you went on ship board, and the preceeding Anna's [Anna Maria Calhoun Clemson's] written a day, or two earlier.

I hope you may have a safe & pleasant voyage. We shall be exceedingly anxious to hear of your arrival. If you do not write from London, I hope you will not fail to do so immediately on your arrival at Brussels.

We are all well, and the spring, as far as feelings are concerned, delightful, since the cold spell. The rains have been moderate & frequent, but the weather too cool to push the cotton crop. It looks, however, well, but is backward. My other crops are very good. I have just commenced my wheat harvest.

My health continues good, and my strength is equal to what I ought to expect at my time of life. I walk 3 or 4 miles every day; and write 6 or 7 hours on an avarage. I am making good progress, in the work I have on hand & hope to be able to take ["it" *interlined*] with me, if I go to Washington next winter, to place it in the hand of the publisher.

I have received the wine & brandy you were so kind as to send from Philadelphia. I find both to be excellent, and doubt not will be of service to me.

I received a letter from Col. [Francis W.] Pickens some 8 or 10 days since, informing me that Mr. Harris has made you an offer for your place [in Edgefield District]; lands, negroes and all, which he thought you ought to accept, and requested me, if I concur[r]ed, to write to you, and advise you to accept. Before complying with his request, I wrote to him, and among other things, enquired as to the time delivery was to be made of the possession. To that, I received an answer by the mail before the last. I enclose both, which will put you in full possession of the terms offered, & his opinion.

My opinion is, that the offer is a fair one; and that you ought to accept. It is possible, that you might get more by holding back & selling the property seperately; but that is not so certain, & would be accompanied by a good deal of trouble. The place in consequence of your absence has failed to make good crops; &, I fear, from what I learn it will again fail this year. The overseer has been sick and there has been a good deal of sickness among the negroes; and the cold wet spring ["is" *interlined*] unfavourable ["has been" *canceled*] to making a good crop, on a soil of a cold nature. I think, besides, having the amount of the sale of your entire possessions there well secured by bond & mortgage in a single responsible hand & your gang of negroes kept together on the place with a kind master to superintend & take care of them, are considerations, that should not ["over" *canceled*] be overlooked. I feel confident you will never get a more advantageous offer for the whole.

With this impression, I give it as my decided advice to accept the offer, & give possession forthwith, for the reasons assigned by Col. Pickens. If you concur, you ought not to delay in transmitting to him the requisite power to act for you. To get clear of it will releive you from much anxiety & trouble, & secure you a regular income of $2,100, which, with your other sources, will give you a han[d]-some income for your small family. As to the goat, or any other property you might wish to except, we will take care of them until you return; but I would advise you, not to make any exception, that was not dependent on Col. Picken[s]'s discretion, as it might be made a reason for not closing the bargain.

I will write to Col. Pickens, that I have advised you to accept the offer, and to enclose a power to ["you" *canceled and* "him" *interlined*] to act for you.

All join their love to you, Anna & the children [John Calhoun Clemson and Floride Elizabeth Clemson]. Kiss them for their grand-father and tell them how much I love them. May God bless you all.

Say to Anna I will write to her next week. Your affectionate father, J.C. Cahoun.

ALS in ScCleA.

From John Custis Darby

Lexington Ky., 4th June 1849

Dear Sir, Enclosed [*not found*] is an article on slavery & abolition of which I am the author. I beg leave to call your attention to it. The articles were first published in the Louisville Chronicle; & I requested the Editor to send them to you. I have twice before taken the liberty to write to you. This is the most important subject upon which I have ever addressed you. The Slave States are reduced to two alternatives; either to demand a dissolution of the Union, or to carry out the Plan which I have proposed. If Maryland, Virginia, Kentucky & Missouri, the border slave States, would incorporate my plan into their Constitutions, the question between the North & South would soon be settled: we would effectually have carried the war "into Africa." The question as to whether Kentucky, for instance, has the right to make my Plan a part of her organic Law, in the face of the article in the Constitution of the United States, to the contrary, is one in which I think you must agree with me. The greatest dif-ficulty in the way of the reception of my plan is plainly this; that the great men of the nation are unwilling to acknowledge that a man utterly unknown to the people of the United States should [*ms. torn; word missing*] the credit of settling this qu[estion; *ms. torn*]t it must be so. I sincerely & honestly believe that unless the Almighty Ruler of the Universe intends to wipe away as with the besom of destruction every vestige of good Government & of true religion from the face of the Earth, he will preserve the institution of African slavery in the United States, intact; & I as honestly & as fully believe that the plan which I have developed is the way in which it is to be done. To carry my plan into immediate adoption, it is only necessary that you approve it. All eyes are now turned to you; the eyes of those who have not been bewildered by the spectral illusion of modern philanthropy, the yet sane men of the world; as well as the eyes of those who first objecting in their hearts to God[']s Government of the World, would next make for him a better government: these look to you with fear & hatred; those with confidence & hope. If you endorse "The Ohio River Plan" then all men, both friends & foes will think it a thing of some importance. The Plan is no sudden ebulition of thought. I wrote out the same plan in substance in the spring of 1847, just after seeing in the newsPapers that the Legislature of Pennsylvania had passed an act which virtually nullified the Article of the Constitution of the U.S. which I [*ms. torn*]ope that the States of Maryla[nd, Virgin]ia, Kentucky & Missouri shall for themselves repeal. I sent my article through a friend to the Editor of the Union. That friend told me in Washington City as I passed through there in July that Mr. [Thomas] Ritchie seemed to be pleased with the plan, but was unwilling at that time to introduce the question into his columns. I could not see Mr. Ritchie. The manuscript of the original article is still in the Union office.

I shall be pleased my dear Sir to hear from you on this subject; but much better pleased to see in the news Papers your endorsement of a measure which is to perpetuate the Union of the United States of America. With sentiments of the highest regard Your ob[edien]t serv[an]t, Jno. Custis Darby.

ALS in ScCleA. NOTE: An EU on the address page reads, "P. Master at Charleston please forward to Mr. Calhoun's address." An AEU by Calhoun reads, "Mr. Darby, about slavery & abolition."

From F[ITZ]W[ILLIAM] BYRDSALL

New York [City,] June 5th 1849

Dear Sir, If the political memoirs up to a few years ago—of Henry Clay, Martin Van Buren, Thomas H. Benton, and William H. Seward, were presented to the consideration of any good or wise man, ignorant of what has occurred in latter years, he would deem it improbable that these four men could ever be brought to stand on the same political platform. Yet there they are, the first with his Lexington speech and Resolutions—the second with his letters and Buffalo nomination platform, the third with his recent speech at Jefferson City in defence of Wilmot provisoism, and the fourth with his speech at Cleaveland Ohio last year. They are engaged in a most unholy crusade against the Constitution of the Union, to subvert its fundamental principles, while at the same time with Macchiavellian wickedness and Jesuitical duplicity, they are charging "dissolution of the Union" upon those who from the circumstances of the case, can only act upon the defensive. And yet these four men are not equals in wickedness, in my opinion Van Buren and Benton are much the worst; but they are all willing and anxious to do battle against you, particularly as if you were an impediment to the march of their ambition. It is certainly an involuntary homage to you that every demagogue seeking popularity, every Aspirant to the presidency acts as if he deemed it an indispen[s]able preliminary to do battle, or to be in opposition to you in some way or other.

The magnetic Telegraph announces that Benton's recent pronunciamento at Jefferson City is out and out in favor of Wilmot provisoism as Jeffersonian Doctrine and that the positions taken by you and the Instructions of the Missouri Legislature are in tendency dissolution of the Union. (I will forward you the first copy of this speech I see in the papers.) Since its delivery, [Representative from Ill.] John Wentworth's paper at Chicago [the *Daily Democrat*] recommends him for the next presidency. The Brooklyn Freeman puts up his name at the head of its columns for that Office; and the New York Evening Post mentions these movements most approvingly. I have long believed that Benton was in [Andrew] Jackson's time designated to come in the regular line of succession, and now his turn has come later than was intended owing to unforeseen interruptions—the campaign of 1840—and the Baltimore convention of 1844 when Van Buren was deprived of his second term. That he will be the candidate of the free soil Van Buren men of the North in 1852 nothing but his own excentricity or death can prevent.

Wm. H. Seward has made his bid for the presidency by his Cleaveland speech which ensured him a triumphant election by the Whig Legislature to a seat in the U.S. Senate. He is among the Whigs what Van Buren has been among the Democrats, adroit circumventing and a superior demagogue. He was the master spirit of those who defeated the nomination of Clay in 1840 and 1848 and although the latter is to some extent aware of all this, yet as the former stands now upon Clay's platform or will do so, I should not be surprised to see the mighty Henry Clay unwittingly to himself, worked[,] managed and used by the wiley Seward. As regards yourself—the free soil men of both parties are calculating that he will distinguish himself in the Senate as an antagonist of yours—not by superior intellect for that they admit he is not possessed of—not by abler constitutional views, or greater powers of analysis, or profounder political philosophy, but by cool adroitness—never losing temper in argument—expert in annoyances of that kind most chafing to those who are most ingenuous in spirit and generous in motive. I trust he will be used up in the Senate nevertheless.

[*Two paragraphs inserted on attached slip*:] In consequence of the vast accessions to our population from Europe, the naturalized citizens have for many years past had the casting vote in our presidential Elections, and as they are mostly Catholics in religion, or Socialist Fourierites in politicks, It has long been the effort of such Whig Politicians as Seward, [Horace] Greel[e]y, [Thurlow] Weed & Co. to woo the naturalized citizens by paying court to their religious and other prejudices. As far back as 4th July 1839 Mr. Seward delivered himself to a large gathering of Sunday School Children ["on Staten Island" *interlined*] as follows—which is an extract from his speech Published in the [New York] Courier & Enquirer 9th July of that year.

"Our Institutions excellent as they are, have hitherto produced but a small portion of the benevolent results which they are calculated to bestow upon the people. The chief of these benefits is Equality of civil rights. But we have ["not" *interlined*] yet ["attained" *canceled*] attained—we have only approximated toward what is even more important—*Equality of social condition.*"

The predictions of your Charleston speech have been more than verified and it is easily discerned that the South has to go through a struggle which the longer it is put off or postponed, will be the harder. It is not alone for equality of rights under the Constitution, for if discomfited in this, the rights of property will not be safe. I care not about theories of Government so much as I do about practical results, and I do hold that social system to be the best which produces the least pauperism, poverty, suffering and crime, and such is the social system of the Slave States; add to which the mighty consideration that negro Slavery is of absolute vitality to the Southern States. It is a natural law of Climate and of races that white people could not have ["have" *canceled*] a desirable existence in those

States without negro Slaves—and if in the hands of negroes only, those ["States" *interlined*] would ["soon" *interlined*] become the most wretched countries on earth, without white people. In short the Southern States are in jeopardy, and nothing but Union among themselves can save them and hardly that, for with the state of public opinion in the north and some portions of the West, if the annexation of the Canadas takes place it will be ominous of more danger to the South.

I have lately conversed with an intelligent German, a merchant or business man who travelled over upper and Lower Canada and he states that both the Loyalists (British) and the Liberals (French Canadien) are in favor of annexation to the United States. I have seen Americans from various parts of the Canadas who inform me that annexation is the general sentiment. Three days ago I was at a wholesale establishment where two Canadien merchants purchasing goods were in warm controversy upon the politicks of Canada. They agreed in no one point but annexation as the only mode of making peace in Canada. On my expressing surprise that both the Tories and Republicans, for so they openly designated the opposite parties, should wish for annexation, he who called himself Republican replied that the Tories were not sincere in going for annexation, that it was only to alarm the British Government. The tory answered that the people of Upper Canada did mean it because they were much the same as the people of the U. States—speaking the same language &c. better fitted for annexation and above all they would be an independent state to manage their own local concerns, untrammelled by the French race of Lower Canada.

When I survey the past legislation of Congress—Tariffs, Banks[,] appropriations of public money, all generally for the especial benefit of one section of the Union, I arrive at the conclusion that the other section has no cause to rely upon the sense of justice or sentiment of magnanimity of the north. It is idle to expect that the rights of the South will be regarded any longer than power exists sufficient to deter aggression, therefore union amongst the Southern people is a necessity. The proverb that "it is a base bird that befouls its own nest" applies with all its force to the conduct of [Samuel] Houston, Benton, [John S.] Pendleton, [Alexander H.] Stephens and such Southern men as acted with them. They have caused the golden opportunity ["to" *interlined*] pass when they could have had justice done to their home-land, when they could ["have" *interlined*] sustained the constitutional rights of their constituents. Their course was consistent neither with patriotism[,] political rights, nor moral courage, for certainly there was no gallantry in going with the strongest side. And when they saw Northern Democrats & Whigs united against the South, their desertion was all the baser and more unpardonable.

I cannot forget that the Whigs, though for different and unworthy reasons, hated the Mexican war worse than you did, who foresaw the evil consequences of it some of which have already taken place, yet they had not the moral courage to oppose the declaration of war, and not untill you alone stood forth ["its" *interlined*] antagonist did they dare to speak a word against it, and then they could extoll you for virtue of which they were destitute themselves. Now, one of those who extolled you most highly is premier of the present Cabinet [John M. Clayton] and yet so hollow hearted are the professions of respect of such men, that with those in power you have no influence. This will prove all the better for you—for I foresee that in the next session of Congress you will have power, and I trust you will make yourself felt. General [Zachary] Taylor is fast sacrificing his popularity by doing too small a business for an independent "president of the whole people." It is said by some that he obtained the presidency by false pretences, by others that he won their suffrage by sentiments not his own, by affixing his name to the declarations of Colonel [William W.S.] Bliss. Be this as it may, he is sinking in the popular estimation.

It occurs to me at this moment that it might possibly be of use to me to use your letter to me with our new Collector. Would it be in any respect incompatible with your feelings so to do? Were it headed *Confidential* or *private*, or if it contained any matter that might in the least affect you disadvantageously, I certainly should not ask this permission.

Be careful of your health—brace your nervous system as much as possible—and avoid mental exertion. You will have ["to contend with" *interlined*] those ill disposed men Benton, Houston, Seward, and possibly Clay—but, I fear not for you in the contest—if you will devote as much attention to your bodily health as Benton does, and will not overtask yourself. There is more thought—more condensation in one of your efforts than in a hundred of theirs. Yours with best wishes, F.W. Byrdsall.

ALS in ScCleA. NOTE: Bliss was Taylor's son-in-law and active partisan during the Presidential campaign.

To Ja[me]s Ed[ward] Calhoun, Jun[io]r, [South Carolina College], Columbia, S.C.

Fort Hill, 5th June 1849

My dear James, I enclose a draft on Mr. [John Ewing] Bonneau for $30 agreeably to your request. You had better not negotiate it, until you want the money, as it will not draw interest until Mr. Bonneau pays the money. I will remit William's [i.e., William Lowndes Calhoun's] in time to be there by the 24th Inst. I do not know whether James Rion, will want a remittance before he leaves. He had better write me & let me know, if he should need a remittance.

We are all well. The weather has been very cool, but is now warm. My crop looks well.

All join their love to you & your brother [William], & kind respects to James Rion. Your affectionate father, J.C. Calhoun.

ALS in ScU-SC, John C. Calhoun Papers.

From H[enry] S. Foote, [Senator from Miss.]

Washington, June 5th, 1849

My dear Sir: I have just read one half of Colonel [Thomas H.] Benton's Wilmot Proviso speech just delivered in Missouri. I would send the paper containing it to you, but for the fact that there is only a single copy in town, & that belongs to the [Daily National] Intelligencer office, which ["they" *canceled and* "the Editors" *interlined*] are reserving until the other half shall arrive, designing to publish the whole speech in their paper. It is the most labored speech of his life, full of fierce invective and coarse appeals to the worst passions of human nature. The whole speech, so far as I have read it, is devoted to a review of your course upon the question of Slavery in Territories. I am decidedly of opinion, my dear Sir, that it is calculated to do us much harm, if it is not seasonably counteracted. I am further of opinion that no man ["can" *interlined*] do this but yourself. He is intrinsically beneath your notice, in my judgment, a traitor to his country, & to the South in particular, a base unprincipled man. And yet he has ["much"(?) *canceled and* "it in his" *interlined*] power, owing somewhat to accidental circumstances, and somewhat to his extraordinary energy of character, to do us deep injury at this crisis. You cannot, as I think, refrain from responding to him, without much peril to the Union and the South. But in what mode do you prefer doing it? Will you deliver a speech, or publish an *Exposé* in your own State? Or would you prefer being written to from Washington requesting you to make an immediate reply? Either of these courses, it seems to me, would be sufficiently eligible.

I had intended last week, at the Richmond dinner, expected to have come off in honor of the recent democratic victory achieved ["the"(?) *canceled*] in Virginia, & to which I had the honor of being invited, to review Mr. Benton's whole course on the subject, & to prefer special charges in addition. The Editors of the [Washington Daily] Union desired that I should do so, & certain enlightened friends in and about Richmond. I had looked into his whole political life for the right kind of material & flatter myself that I have collected ["them" *interlined*] in rich abundance. But the Cholera broke out at Richmond, & my speech was not delivered, as the dinner expected was postponed. I may, & probably shall, in a few days, address the people of Mississippi in defence of myself against the accusation of being unfriendly to the Union, which Mr. Benton has dared to prefer against all of us who participated in the Southern movement. But this will be a merely *local* affair; I have no *national* character, nor the high powers of discussion requisite for dealing with this momentous question in all its bearings & aspects. Let me earnestly insist upon your throwing aside all feelings of *delicacy* in regard to this matter, & coming out without delay in defence of our rights & our honor.

Whatever you choose to write will be at once published in the Union, with approbatory comments.

When I shall obtain ["I" *canceled*] a copy of Mr. B[enton]'s speech in *extenso*, I will cause you to be supplied with it. I remain, my Dear Sir, your true friend, H.S. Foote.

ALS in ScCleA; PC in Boucher and Brooks, eds., *Correspondence*, pp. 505–506.

From Henry Young

New York [City,] June 6/49

My Dear Sir, Some days since I wrote you giving you my opinion on the *Signs of the Times*[.] You will recollect that I then said that appearances indicated that Col. [Thomas H.] Benton was to be the next Free Soil Candidate for the Presidency[.]

My acquaintance with some of the leading members of that party enables me to judge with tolerable accuracy. That question may be regarded as now settled. Col. Benton will come fully up to the Standard of the party. He may even be a little Ultra and will the more certainly rely on being elected.

The Whig party are alarmed throughout the whole Northern States. The only chance they have in the opinion of the most intel[l]igent leaders of the party is to come fully up to the Free Soil Standard[.] In the late Congressional Election in Connecticut they ventured to put up Candidates that were suspected of being unfriendly to the exclusion of Slavery in the new territory and were defeated even where they were known to have a large majority if they could[?] bring all out. How far Col. Benton will be able to get the support of the Southern States may be uncertain even of the democratic ones but his nomination will compel the Whigs to select a candidate equally opposed to the institutions of the South and the most [*ms. torn*; ultra?] will be apt to command the greatest number of votes. Col. Benton is supposed by his Free Soil friends to be a man who will not be behind his opponent in coming up to the Standard[.]

You will see by the movements in California that we have but little to hope for there and if we may credit the knowing ones here that our prospects are little if any better in New Mexico. Large sums of money and able men have been entrusted with the especial care of the matter in that Territory. The next movement will be to drive the Institution out of the District of Columbia[.] Those interested there will be very glad they say to compromise by agreeing to exclude the slave trade and to a prohibition of the introduction of any more slaves into the District, and a provision that all born after the passage of the law shall be free at 21. On this Col. Benton will be expected to speak soon and next under any and all circumstances to admit no more slave States into the Union. The next prominent movement will be to an[n]ex the British [Canadian] Provinces. There is a Company or association of an[n]exationists in this City where the matter is watched with great care. The leaders are men who were connected with the rebel[l]ion in Canada in 1837–8[.] They there administered an oath to such as were called Patriots. One man told me he administered the oath to 43,000, most of whom were provided with arms. Recently he told me that about the same number were provided with arms, and would be ready to act by the 4th of July. I saw him a few days since and asked him if such a matter was now in contemplation he said no. The seperation from England and an[n]exation to us would be bloodless. All could be effected by amicable arrangement[.]

There are Canadian merchants here frequently and with few exceptions all agree that an[n]exation is certain and not remote. It would seem that such is the fact[.] So many States are directly interested that they can command a majority at any time and no effective opposition is feared[.]

What a pity that the South should have been deluded into the miserable policy of setting an example and getting up an excitement for an[n]exing foreign territory[.] While such as we have got is turned directly against us. With the certainty of having so much more an[n]exed as will render the very existence of our Institutions precarious, if not a speedy destruction of them[.]

It was much easier to see the evil than to provide a remedy. Some may remonstrate but their influence will be powerless. For it must be evident to all who are acquainted with the Signs of the Times, that any opposition to the further extension of Territory must be unavailing.

I have remarked in conversation with these men that the South would not willingly submit to such a state of things. They say in reply that with Col. Benton they shall have a part of the South or rather the South West, that the most determined opposition will be in South Carolina, and that she has no strength of her own and none worthy of notice when united with such as choose to befriend her[.]

It is certainly deeply mortifying to my feelings to hear the State where I have lived so many years spoken of so lightly and not unfrequently with derision, and by the more candid as superan[n]uated and feeble.

I assure you my dear Sir that come what may, *Weal or woe* I shall ever respect you for the noble stand you took in opposing these untoward measures, and while I assure you of my respect I unite with you in my expressions of mortification and regret that you were not successful[.] Very sincerely yours, Henry Young.

[Marginal P.S.] Attached I send you a slip from the [New York] Courier & Enquirer.

ALS in ScCleA; PC in Boucher and Brooks, eds., *Correspondence*, pp. 506–508.

From J[OHN] T. TREZEVANT

Memphis, June 7th 1849

D[ea]r Sir, I am just in receipt of your favor. By the time this reaches you, you will have seen, that, owing to facts stated, we have deemed it best to postpone our Convention till the 16th Oct. next; at which time I trust the Southern & S. Eastern States will attend in commanding force. This I deem all important, if but to hasten a connection between this point & the South Atlantic Seaboard; and really, no portion of country designed to be benefitted by the Atlantic R.R. will be so much so, as that into whose lap our trade is poured, & to which, as a common centre, our rays of commerce are directed. Private enterprise, or State energy will accomplish it; but the sooner it is done, the better; for it will direct public Sentiment towards it, and will be regarded, at once, by Southern men, as an item (and an important one), in the chain of events that may be invoked to render us less dependent upon the North. The sooner the route from this point to the S.E. is finished, the sooner we begin to catch a great deal of trade that now goes by us, & secure a great deal that will soon go *directly east from the Ohio valley* to N.Y. if the grand system of R.R. projected from St. Louis to N.Y. be completed first. Once direct ["Southern" *interlined*] travel & trade from the Northern rivers & northern Cities, & direct them South, and the blow is felt; for 'tis a trade & travel of no small moment. Then I look upon a grand turn out from Va.[,] N.C.[,] S.C.[,] Geo. & Ala. as all important to beget & push up, a proper spirit of enterprise, in reference to connecting our great valley with the Atlantic.

But, lamentable as it is, there is a large party in our own State, disposed to cater for Northern support. Mr. [John] Bell stands at the front, having, in his debate with Mr. [John M.] Berrien, last winter, made a bold & politic bid or [*one word illegible*] bid for Northern votes, in 1852. Admitting ["in that debate" *interlined*] the constitutionality of the Wilmot proviso, his position was caught up by the [Baltimore?] North American & the [New York] Tribune, as being orthodox, and his move, in making such admission, though a Southerner, complimented as deserving more than ordinary reward. Bell carries with him nearly all of the leading Whigs of the State—[Meredith P.] Gentry, [James C.] Jones, [Neill S.] Brown (Gov.) &C. and those who dare not go quite so far, ["admit" *canceled*] place the whole matter in charge of the Supreme Court; and own, openly and before hand, that they will *submit* when they cannot *do any better.* This is their defence; and all those who are for *preventing* the passage of such a law as the Wilmot proviso—who contend that the Constitution shall *not* be violated; who say that they will *resist* the infraction of it, "at all hazards & to the last extremity," are called "disunionists"—"agitators" &C.

'Tis a serious affair, to see, in Tenn., two parties, upon this question, and shows evil influences are at work somewhere.

But the question with me has been, is it a matter with which Congress has aught to do? If not, can the *Supreme Court* take jurisdiction of it?

Will you allow me to say that your name has often been quoted here lately, by *Northern Whigs* ["in spirit" *interlined*], as Sanctioning the appeal they are willing to make to the Supreme Court? They allege that the compromise bill reported by you & Mr. [John M.] Clayton recognized that right. I did not look upon that as your view, so far as I could judge from the territorial bill reported. If I am in error, will you correct me?

I will also thank you for a copy of your speech on this question (the power of Congress to exclude slavery &C) as I am satisfied you denied that power, in some speech within the past two years.

It is a delicate question; and rendered still more so here, by a division among ourselves, of which the North will take all advantage, in her future legislation.

In conclusion, my dear sir, I hope to see you and many others of your State, with us, in Oct. We want help, & that help must come from S.C.[,] Va. & Geo.

Nashville & its influence are for St. Louis. Most of ["her" *interlined*] leading men have large interests in St. Louis, and she has, for several years, had a foolish jealousy of the Commercial advantages of this point.

I again repeat, that we shall look for a large delegation from the South E. and an impetus may be given to things that may yet render the South more potent than at present. With resp[ec]t, J.T. Trezevant.

ALS in ScCleA; PC in Boucher and Brooks, eds., *Correspondence*, pp. 508–510.

F[RANKLIN] H. ELMORE to R[ichard] K. Crallé, [Lynchburg, Va.]

Charleston, 8 June 1849

My Dear Crallé, It gives me pleasure to see your name once again. What are you doing & how beats your pulse? Are you up with Virginia & what will she be up to on the Slave question? What are you for? And how long are we to be trampled on before we take some overt step for redress? demand & have some guaranty for the future?

We are ready *now* & we stand ["only" *canceled*] to our arms, waiting only on Old Virginia. Yours truly, F.H. Elmore.

ALS in ScCleA, John C. Calhoun Papers.

From JAMES G. BENNETT

New York [City,] 9th June 1849

Dear sir, The Bearer of this note is Mr. [Joseph A.] Scoville, an acquaintance of yours in former years. I have engaged him to go to the South as a correspondent to give me for publication correct statements of the condition of your region on the great question so vital to the South. On that point there is great ignorance in this section. The recent movements of Mr. [Henry] Clay and Mr. [Thomas H.] Benton tend also also [*sic*] to complicate the southern question. Any information or advice you can give him will be duly appreciated. I am Dear Sir Yours Truly, James G. Bennett, Herald Office.

ALS in ScCleA.

To F[ITZ]W[ILLIAM] BYRDSALL, [New York City]

Fort Hill, 9th June 1849

My dear Sir, I enclose a letter to Mr. [Hugh] Maxwell [newly-appointed Collector of Customs at New York City] in your favour, which I hope may reach you in time and may be of some aid. I would have address[ed] Mr. [William M.] Meredith [Secretary of the Treasury], but am very slightly acquainted with him. I regard with abhor[r]ence the spoils doctrine, which has so deeply infected the country. If there were no other causes, it, of itself, would corrupt the people & destroy our system of Government. Yours truly, J.C. Calhoun.

ALS in DLC, Duff Green Papers. NOTE: Calhoun's letter to Maxwell has not been found, but Byrdsall mentioned it in a letter of 4/27/1850 to Duff Green (ALS in NcU, Duff Green Papers, published microfilm, roll 10, frames 380–382).

TO GEO[RGE] P. A. HEALY

Fort Hill, 9th June 1849

Dear Sir, It will afford me pleasure, when I arrive at Washington next winter, to comply with your request in reference to the da[g]u[e]rreotype likeness you desire to have taken of me.

I will endeavour to obtain a likeness of Mrs. [Floride Colhoun] Calhoun for you, should she not accompany me to Washington. If she should, it can be taken there. Yours truly, J.C. Calhoun.

ALS in ICHi, George P.A. Healy Collection. NOTE: In his memoirs, *Reminiscences of a Portrait Painter* (Chicago: A.C. McClurg, 1894), Healy left accounts of several occasions when Calhoun sat for him.

FROM JOS[EPH] J. SINGLETON

Dahlonega [Ga.,] 10th May [*sic*; June] 1849

My Dear Sir, It has been so long since I heard from you, that it really seems that I have either neglected my business as an Agent, or you have neglected yours as principal. Be this however as it may, on your part, perhaps it is more excusable, than on my part.

Hence I write now under a sense of duty only, the principal object of which is to ap[p]rize you of the am[oun]t of toll Gold coin in my hands subject to your order, which is one hundred & ninety three dollars & 37 cents—& Robert B. Lewis request[ed] me to inform you that he had about sixty dollars ready for you.

Your Lessees are working the Obarr Mine to the best advantage for their own interest, (as they think) which is the common practice of this part of the country at least, among Lessees of every description. They have repaired your old pounding mill, and think they will now do better business.

Can we not have the pleasure of your company over here this summer[?] No visit would give us more pleasure, especially, if you would, (I won't say if you could), bring Mrs. [Floride Colhoun] Calhoun with you. We will try to make her comfortable at least, if she should not be pleased with her visit. I do not ["believe in" *interlined*] burying our Wives alive. They certainly are entitled to a portion of the recreations of this life. Especially when they take a deep interest in the domestic affairs of their Husbands, while absent either for his Countries good, his personal ag[g]randisement, or his pleasures.

I shall expect you at my House whenever you may make it convenient to visit this part of the country. Very respectfully I have the hon[or] of being yours &c, Jos. J. Singleton.

ALS in ScU-SC, John C. Calhoun Papers. NOTE: This letter was marked "June 11" by the Dahlonega postmaster. Calhoun's AEU reads, "Mr. Singleton[.] Has $193.37 of toll gold in his hand & Mr. Lewis about $60. Rec[eive]d 15th June. Rece[ive]d through Mr. [William] Sloan."

From H[ENRY] S. FOOTE

Washington, June 11th, 1849

My dear Sir: According to my promise, made a few days since, I enclose you herewith a copy of the speech of that *Arch-Traitor*, Mr. [Thomas H.] Benton. The conclusion of the speech is, if possible, more objectionable than the commencement. He seems to have had you in his eye throughout this strange harangue. I hope you will pardon me for again urging upon you a full response to this villainous attack upon the South. However spicy you choose to make it, I will secure its appearance in the [Washington Daily] Union.

Should it be desirable to you to receive any particular documents from this City which you have not with you, I need not say how gladly I ["will" *canceled*] will assume any amount of trouble in order to supply you. Your own familiarity with Mr. B[enton]'s public course is such ["that" *canceled*] I suppose, ["that" *interlined*] it can hardly be necessary to refer you to certain speeches of his in former days which are directly at war with his present attitude. I do hope though that you will not spare him. His offences are indeed most rank, and call for speedy and signal punishment.

I sent you the Union the other day. I hope you are satisfied with its present attitude. Most truly & fully, Your friend & obedient servant, H.S. Foote.

ALS in ScCleA.

From RICH[AR]D POLLARD

Alta Vista, near Warren, Albemarle County, Va.
June 11th 1849

Dear Sir: You are justly looked upon as the most prominent Sentinel of Southern rights—the most efficient advocate of our interests. Viewing you in this character, I address this letter to you.

Since Mr. [Thomas] Ritchie has formed a connexion with Mr. [Edmund] Burke, in the editorial management of *the Union*, it would appear from the Prospectus published by the two, together with the communication of Senator [Henry S.] Foote, to the Editors, accompanying the proceedings of a meeting in Mississippi, upon the subject of Southern rights, and the continued aggressions of the North upon our ["Constitutional rights" *canceled and* "institutions" *interlined*], that the *Union* is henceforth to be neutral upon the subject of the Wilmot Proviso, and its kindred associations. In this state of things ought we not to have a press at the Capitol to advocate fearlessly our Constitutional ["guar" *canceled*] guarranties—our rights by the primary ["and" *canceled*] laws & legislative enactments? and can you not engage some suitable person in South Carolina to take charge of such a press? I think it would have the fullest support from all the Southern States.

Excuse me in the liberty I take in addressing to you these few lines. It is time the South should be aroused to its principles, and adopt measures to maintain them. I have the honor to be with great respect y[ou]r Friend & Serv[an]t: Richd. Pollard.

[P.S.] A *true* paper at Washington could doubtlessly do much for us and would certainly be liberally and generously supported.

ALS in ScCleA; PC in Boucher and Brooks, eds., *Correspondence*, p. 510. NOTE: The writer was the father of Edward A. Pollard, later a notable Richmond editor and author.

From F[ITZ]W[ILLIAM] BYRDSALL

New York [City,] June 12th 1849

Dear Sir, Having forwarded to you the two previous portions of the speech of [Thomas H.] Benton, I herewith send you the third and last installment.

The main points of the speech—its sum and substance are two—namely anti-Calhoun and anti-Slavery. He proves the truth of the very antient saying of a Greek philosopher that men are very apt to charge upon others those faults which lie at their own doors or in modern phraze, they judge others by themselves. Benton is evidently not aware of his own gross egoism.

He fancies or sees you in every thing moral social and political to which he is opposed and his hostility is such that he opposes you in every thing. You are ["too" *canceled and* "so" *interlined*] really great in his eyes that he throws the responsibility of every administration with which you have been connected much or little upon you and your influences.

His enmity to you carries him so far that he has gone over to abolitionism avowing himself wholly opposed to slavery. He is a traitor to the people of the Slave States—their constitutional rights—and even their rights of property.

A grave question now arises respecting yourself, as ["to" *interlined*] what you should do respecting Benton's speech against you and the rights of the South. This is a matter of great delicacy for any friend to advise you about; I dare not undertake it. Yet every friend to the cause should sustain you as much as he can, you have a right to his support—I will drop a few words.

I believe it would gratify him to draw you into a personal controversy. You cannot go into this without some loss of personal dignity. Yet perhaps something should be said—if so the *manner* and the *time* of doing this are proper considerations. As to the abolitionism of his speech that is easily got at, and upon this point as he has gone over to North—he is a double traitor to the South. Here you have him in your power if you decide to use it.

Were it not for such Southern traitors as Benton [Samuel] Houston [Alexander H.] Stephens [John S.] Pendleton & Co. we would ["have" *interlined*] gained the Victory.

The harping that is kept up about the Declaration of Independence—Thomas Jefferson and the Ordinance of 1787 is an absurdity of the worst kind. At best they were but simple acts of Congress—superceded in a great degree by the Constitution subsequently—

which being our Governmental Compact of the States and the people is of course infinitely more solemn[,] obligatory and stationary. Yours in haste and with the greatest Respect, F.W. Byrdsall.

ALS in ScCleA.

To A[nna Maria] Calhoun Clemson, [London]

Fort Hill, 15th June 1849

My dear daughter, I do hope by this time, you are all safe in London, after a pleasant voyage. I shall be on the look out for a letter dated at London in about two weeks from now.

I wrote Mr. [Thomas G.] Clemson subsequent to the receipt of your letter [of 5/22], and addressed to Brussels, where I hope he will find it, on his arrival. I stated in it, that I would write you the next ["week" *interlined*], which would have been Sunday last, but when I was about commencing to write, [Martha] Cornelia [Calhoun] brought me ["one" *canceled and* "a letter" *interlined*] to you, to be put under cover, which I did & forward[ed] it to the State Department, to be sent by the first opportunity. You will probably find it at Brussels on your arrival. Cornelia gave you, I doubt not, all the news.

In consequence of her writing, I postponed my letter for a week, which will give it the opportunity to go by the next ["steamer" *interlined*] after that which took yours.

We all felt, my dear daughter, as you described your feelings to be, at your departure. It is, indeed, distressing to be so far off & for so long a time from those so dear to us; but let us rather look forward, ["to" *interlined*] when we shall again meet, than indulge in unavailing sorrows. I trust two years, at the utmost, will terminate your residence in Europe, & return you all again safe to our country. It is due to the children, that your stay should not be longer. Their habits & mode of thinking will, by that time, begin to be formed; and it is important, that they should be such, as to conform to the condition of the country, which is [to] be their home. I often think of them, & how much delighted they would be, to be enjoying themselves in our green & shady yard. The season has been wet, and ever thing looks beautiful. Even the old feild [*sic*] beyond the yard looks as green as a meadow. In the feild beyond it, (Speeds feild), now containing 125 acres, by the addition of clearing, has a fine crop of oats, just fully shot out, which completely covers the whole ground, ["that" *canceled*; "presents" *changed to* "presenting"] an unbroken mass of green in that direction. The big bottom ["on the other side" *interlined*] is covered, with a superb crop of corn, the best at this season, I ever had on it, which covers the whole with a deep green. Back of it, lies fort hill, with its harvested wheat in shocks. The spring has been too cool & wet for cotton, but mine looks well, &, with my hill side drains & serpentine rows, really looks han[d]some. The place is altogether, ["is" *canceled*] in fine order. I ride or walk, according to the weather twice a day, morning & evening, over it, for the double purpose of exercise and superintendence. I have no trouble, as Fredericks has become a first rate overseer, & takes as much interest ["as I do" *interlined*] in every thing about the place. I would be delighted to have you & the children ["with me" *interlined*] occasionally, in my walks. It would be wearomsome [*sic*] to take them, as often as I do.

My health & strength are as good, as I could expect at my time of life. I take all necessary care of ["it" *canceled and* "them" *interlined*], except being rather more over tasked, than I could wish. I devote all the time left me, to finishing the work, I commenced three years ago, or more; but which I had to suspend the last two years. I ought not to delay its execution any longer, & aim to put it to press, if I can finish it in the recess, next spring, or summer. I finished yesterday, the preliminary work, which treats of the elementary principles of the Science of Gover[n]ment, except reading it over and making final corrections, previous to copping [*sic*; "and publishing" *interlined*]. It takes 125 pages of large foolscap closely written for me. I am pretty well satisfied with its execution. It will be nearly throughout new territory; &, I hope, to lay a solid foundation for political science. I have written, just as I thought, ["& told the truth" *interlined*] without fear, favour, or affection.

After a few days of relaxation, I shall commence to treat of the Gover[n]ment of the United States. It will be more than twice as voluminous as the elementary work, but not near so difficult of execution. It will take me four, or five months, I suppose. I have got a good deal of it blacked out. I should like to read both to you & Mr. Clemson before I publish, & regret that I shall not have the opportunity to do so.

You need not fear, that I shall make any experiment, the least hazardeous, in reference to my health. I know my system too well, to tamper with it. Nor did I venture to resort to the wet sheet, until

I was perfectly satisfied of its safety & that it would suit me. But, I ["proceed" *changed to* "proceeded"] with caution. I have gone through the process, as yet, but twice, with, I think, decided benefit. My pores needed opening, & for that purpose, the skin required a thorough cle[a]nsing; & for that, nothing can be better, or safer than the process of the wet sheet. It is, in fact, but a vapour bath ["of" *canceled*] in the most effective & safe form. John [C. Calhoun, Jr.] is very expert in putting me through the process.

James [Edward Calhoun] return[ed] home from Columbia day before yesterday, looking thin, but quite well. He got off earlier, as a Senior. William [Lowndes Calhoun] is expected to be home about the 24th. He is most anxious to get home. He [*one word altered to* "as"] well [as] James stand[s] well ["in" *interlined*] College. Cornelia, of course, has written you and informed ["you" *interlined*] of John's intended marriage, & arrangement after he is. They leave immediately after for Battlebo[ro]ugh in New York, & will be absent about 3 months. She is a sensible, han[d]some girl, &, I doubt not, will make a good wife.

I had a letter [*not found*] from Patrick [Calhoun] yesterday, informing me of Gen[era]l [Edmund P.] Gaines' death by the Cholera. It was short, as he was busy preparing for his funeral; & said he would write, in a few days, more fully. I am very uneasy about him. I urged him to the last, not to go to N. Orleans, and have several times by letter urged him strongly to leave it. He, of course, will now; &, I trust, it will not be too late. He has had three attacks of it, two light & one pretty severe. I urged him in my last letter to come directly to Fort Hill, & spend the summer with us. I now think it probable, he will do so. He will be at a loss what to do ["hereafter" *interlined*]. It will be difficult to get another staff appointment, & he will be very much disinclined to join his regiment. I trust, it may lead to his leaving the army, & changing his condition in life.

I had a letter from Andrew [Pickens Calhoun] a few days since. He had a good prospect of corn & cotton, notwithstanding he had to plant the latter three times & the former twice, & had, had, but one light season from the mid[d]le of March to the 3d of June, the date of his letter. The place stands both drought & wet wonderfully. We fear nothing from the former, & nothing but overgrowth & worms from the latter. They are all well, except poor little Andrew, who is no better, & I fear his case ["is" *interlined*] hopeless. I wish you would write to him. I am sure he would be glad to hear from you. He feels wounded in consequence of the conduct of his mother towards him, which was not in the least deserved. I regret it profoundly.

We are all well. There has been no sickness on the place, except bowel complaints & colds from the cold damp spring, & summer, thus far. All join their love to you & Mr. Clemson & the children. Kiss them for their grandfather & tell them how glad I would be to have them with us.

Tell Mr. Clemson he must write me fully & frequently his opinion of the course of events in Europe. From indications, the year is destined to be a fearful one for that portion of the globe. To my mind, the signs of war & convulsions never were stronger. I can see no immediate termination to the present state of disorder. All appear to be apt at pulling down existing political institutions, but not one able architect has risen in all Europe to reconstruct them. Your affectionate father, J.C. Calhoun.

[P.S.] You see I drop the M & put the C for your mid[d]le name.

ALS in ScCleA; PEx in Jameson, ed., *Correspondence*, pp. 766–768. NOTE: John C. Calhoun, Jr., married Anzie Adams on 7/3/1849. She died on 9/15/-1850.

From SAM[UE]L TREAT, "Private"

St. Louis, Mo., June 17, 1849

Dear Sir: I forward to you by to-day's mail a copy of Col. [Thomas H.] Benton's tirade against you and the constitutional rights of the slaveholding States. I should have done this sooner, if I had not been absent from home. The design of the speech is manifold—to get up a personal issue with you in order to withdraw public attention from his own faithlessness—to bid for Abolition and Barnburner votes in the North—to secure once more the ascendency of the [Martin] Van Buren, [Francis P.] Blair and Benton faction. A determined effort is now made, and will grow more resolute each day, to hurl Benton from his seat in the Senate. On his return from Washington he published an "Appeal" from the Legislature to the people, and this speech is the opening one in the case. Mr. [Claiborne F.] Jackson (the author of the resolutions) has published a statement, denying the allegations of Benton concerning their origin. Two-thirds of the Democratic papers in Missouri have denounced the Col.; and of the many public meetings held in the State, only one has gone with him. By Whig aid, which he is receiving, he may endanger the

State, for the population is a strange one in many respects. Were the contest among Democrats alone, he would be beaten two to one.

Although my ill-health has forced me to leave the editorial chair, I take just as lively an interest now, as ever, in the great questions of the day. A new journal will be commenced in this city in a few weeks, devoted to the Constitution and Southern rights. Benton is canvassing the State, haranguing the people about your alleged movement to dissolve the Union, and seeking thus to arouse sympathy and assistance for himself. He quotes largely from some of the imprudent and unwise resolutions passed in S. Carolina, to give the appearance of truth to his imputations—and without such imprudence in S.C., he would have no ammunition whatever. The people of Missouri are devoted to the Union, and it is on that devotion, he seeks to play.

Several Democrats here have desired me to write to you, with the suggestion that a calm *exposé* of Col. Benton's errors and of Southern rights under the Constitution, coming from you now, would be of vast moment. His speech is ostensibly an assault upon you and your views, and as he has chosen to assail you whilst absent, it may be well for you to vindicate yourself. The tone and temper of the "Southern Address" suit Missouri at this time. If it be consistent with your views, I hope to hear from you at an early day; but desire, whether you prepare any thing for the public or not, that you will favor me with ["a" *canceled*] private information, so that it can be used ["by our Editorial friends by" *canceled*] (not as coming from you) in meeting the Col.'s attacks. With the hope of hearing from you soon, I am Yours truly, Saml. Treat.

ALS in ScCleA; PEx in Boucher and Brooks, eds., *Correspondence*, pp. 511–512. NOTE: Calhoun's AEU reads, "Mr. Treat[,] relates to Col. Benton's speech."

From R[ICHARD] O. DAVIDSON

Columbus, Mi[ssissippi], June 18th, 1849

Sir—I have addressed a letter, within the last few weeks past, to Lady Jane Franklin, London, acquainting her ladyship of the fact, that I have discovered the true *principle* and, theoretically, ["constructed" *canceled and* "devised" *interlined*] a machine by means of which the air may be traversed at the rate of 100 miles per hour; and, respectfully suggested, that if she will assist me in carrying the plan into practical operation, ["and it should" *canceled*] I will employ it in making diligent search for her husband, Sir John Franklin, and his missing party. And in order to assure her ladyship of the sincerity of my purpose, I took the liberty of refer[r]ing her to ["yourself" *altered to* "you"] *with reference merely to my character as a man*, suggesting at the same time, that you would not ["be" *interlined*] likely to entertain any more favorable opinion of the success of my project, than others who are not thoro[u]ghly acquainted with it.

And, as it has been nine years since I was introduced to you in Washington, and which circumstance you may have entirely forgotten, I deem it but just to you, in the event ["that" *canceled and* "of" *interlined*] Lady Franklin's writing to you as suggested, to state that T[haddeus] Sanford, P[ercy] Walker, Daniel Chandler, C[harles] C. Langdon, Judge [Alexander B.] Meek, J[ohn] A. Campbell and Chancellor Lesane [*sic*; Joseph Lesesne] of Mobile, where I have resided a considerable portion of the time since I saw you in washington, are among my friends and acquaintance, and would cheerfully give you suitable assurance of my character as a man. I could refer you to many ["other" *interlined*] respectable and distinguished gentlemen in Ala.; and New Orleans among ["whom" *interlined*] is Col. S[amuel] Inge, Representative in Congress, ["friend"(?) *canceled*] from [*illegible word canceled and* "4th Dist." *interlined*] if deemed necessary. But, I trust, that these will be sufficient to induce you to endorse my character as a man, should the abovementioned lady call upon you as suggested.

Permit me to add, sir, that I have persued my darling project, aerial locomotion, with unceasing devotion and growing confidence every hour since I had the honor of making your acquaintance in 1840; and confidently believe now, that I am on the eve of a glorious triumph. But "there is a time for all things", and this case forms no exception to the general rule.

With great respect for you as a man of spotless purity of life, and the most exhalted admiration of your truly great intellectual powers, I have the honor to be, most sincerely, Your humble servant, R.O. Davidson.

ALS in ScCleA. NOTE: Richard Oglesby Davidson published at least two works on flight. Although it was not yet known, Franklin had apparently perished in the Arctic in 1847.

ADVERTISEMENT for a Lost Horse

[Pendleton] June 19 [1849]

A Sorrel Filly. Strayed about four weeks ago from my plantation. It is about two years old, has a star in her forehead, and a small white spot near the end of her nose. Liberal compensation for his trouble and expense will be made to any one, who may return her to me, or inform me where she may be found. J.C. Calhoun.

PC in the Pendleton, S.C., *Messenger*, June 22, 1849, p. 3, June 29, 1849, p. 3, and July 6, 1849, p. 3.

TO J[OHN] R. MATHEWES, [Clarkesville, Ga.]

Fort Hill, 20th June 1849

My dear Sir, I am glad to learn, that a better state of feelings begins to disclose itself in Georgia. It is high time, that they should merge their contests for the spoils, and begin to look to their safety and equality as members of the Union. Mississippi, you will see by the enclosed, has set, in this respect, a noble example. There both parties have united, like true patriots against the aggressions of the North. I regard the call of a convention to meet at Nashville, in June next, as the most important movement, that has yet been made. It is to be hoped, that every Southern State will respond to the call. Should that be the case, it may be still hoped, that the Union will be saved; but if that should prove impossible, it will certainly save ourselves. For that purpose, we want only concert & unanimity of action. But, if the convention should fail from the want of a response, gloomy, indeed, would be our prospect. Nothing can be done without concert, & that can be had only by a convention.

I trust, Georgia will not lag behind, where she has so much at stake; & that both parties will agree to merge their old differences to save her and the other Southern States. Her example, added to Mississippi, could be decisive. Her Legislature will soon be in session, which will give her an early opportunity for acting. The members in their individual capacity might respond to the call, by appointing delegates, to consist ["I hope" *interlined*] of the ablest and most experienced of both parties.

Would it not be well to have, in the mean time, the Mississippi report & resolutions widely circulated through your papers?

There is no foundation for the report to which you al[l]ude. My health is as good as usual.

With best respects to Mrs. [Elizabeth Jenkins Whaley] M[athewes] & family. Yours truly, J.C. Calhoun.

ALS in DLC, John C. Calhoun Papers.

From James Cooch

Post Office Larne [Ireland]
21 June 1849

Sir, I beg leave to acknowledge the receipt of your note [*not found*] of the 18 May last—believe me that Mrs. Cooch is very much Obliged for all the trouble you have taken indeed her application to you was without my Knowledge which I hope you will excuse the liberty of a mother's feelings for a son I may say a child as my son *Richard* was only in his fifteenth year when he left home.

I have now the pleasure to inform you that Mr. George McHenry of Philadelphia called with me last Week and informed me that my son called at their office about Twelve months ago at Philadelphia and mentioned that he was Three years on Board the Constitution Frigate during the Mexican War, that he was Earning 10 p per day he enquired if we were all well at home and desired Master Smyly who was writing a letter to mention that he was well, but that he w[oul]d not write as he had left home without consent, until he had realis'd some money. When a Boy he was very anxious to get forward and always said he w[oul]d go abroad and make a fortune. God has been very good to him that has spared him through all the War. I think he might likely go to California. He was an excellent English scholar and a fine looking Boy he was nearly six foot high when left home.

It appears that the Caldwell Family Emigrated from Scotland in the year 1587 to the neighbourhood of *Colerain.* The[y] were Old light Presbyterians. Some of the Family still resides there. Part of said Family settled in the locality of Larne at Ballycraigy & Ballygally the[y] had large Tracts of Land and a Tanyard and also had the Greatest portion of Larne which they held for ever in Perpetuity. Nearly 100 years ago James Caldwell[,] John Caldwell & W[illia]m Caldwell, John Torbert, Piden Caldhoun [*one word altered to* "Murdogh"] Smyly & Familys Emigrated to Virginia in

Carolina and was involved in the American War—leaving part of the Family in this Neighbourhood (leaving) Robert Caldwell & Abraham Caldwell ["who" *canceled*]. Robert was my Wife's Grandfather & Abraham was her Father[']s Unkle. Mrs. Murdogh was her Father[']s full Cousin & Mrs. Calhoun was also her father['s] full Cousin and was a Daughter of John Caldwell. The Family still retains old coins that was sent over as Keep Sakes at the birth of any Child about 60 years ago to Ballycraigy (*as tokens*).

Colonel *Caldwell* Muir of Caldwell is a Member of Parliament for Renfrew in Scotland and is Lord Rector of the University of Glasgow for the present year. He is one of the same Family. The Caldwell of Caldwell is now extinct and Colonel Muir has the Property through his mother Caldwell, (he is a near Relative).

I will by first safe opp[ortunit]y send you the Caldwells coat of arms. Mr. John Caldwell my Brother in law who is Proprietor of the Drains[?] Dromain[?] & Tobergell has promised to furnish a Copy for his Friends in America.

You were quite correct respecting the name as my son wrote this name Richard Caldwell Cooch, however as he has turned up I am in hopes to hear from himself. Mean time I beg to return you my most grateful thanks and service that I or any Friend here Could render you will give me much happiness. I am Sir Yours very Respectfully, James Cooch.

ALS in ScCleA.

To A[ndrew] P[ickens] Calhoun, [Marengo County, Ala.]

Fort Hill, 23d June 1849

My dear Andrew, I was gratified to learn by yours of the 3d Inst., that the crop looked well, under so many adverse circumstances. While you have been dry, we have had an excess of cold wet weather. As the season passes from North to South, I suppose you have had since the date of your letter, your share of wet weather, but I hope it may not be in such excess as we have had.

My crop looks ["well" *interlined*]. The corn & oats are remarkably fine. Nearly one half of the wheat crop was destroyed by the rust. The cotton looks well. It is of good size & has a fair stand.

I read the account of your proceedings in reference to the slave question with pleasure. Both tone & substance are good. The time is rapidly approaching when we shall have to take our stand, and we must begin to prepare for it. You see that [Thomas H.] Benton has openly deserted & that ["he" *interlined*] pours out his venom against me. I am averse to touching him, and, if his aim had been against me exclusively, I would not notice him. But such is not the fact. He strikes at the South & its cause through me; and I have concluded to repel his attack against myself, to the extent that it is necessary to repel it against the South. My communication will be ["addressed" *interlined*] to the people of the South. His whole speech is a mass of false statements, illogical conclusions and contradictions. I expect to appear in the [Pendleton, S.C.,] Messenger, in the number succeeding the next. Neither he, nor his cause will gain anything by the attack.

We are all well. I deeply regret that poor little Andrew is in so bad a condition. I hope all others are in health. If there be any truth in the sulphur remedy, you will have nothing to fear from the cholera, but I fear that there is nothing in it. I am very anxious about Patrick [Calhoun]. He wrote me immediately after the death [on 6/6] of General [Edmund P.] Gaines, & said he would soon write again, but I have not heard from him yet, & am at a loss to ["ad" *canceled*] know where to address him. I do hope he will be induced now to leave the Army.

You must not forget that our note in bank, will have to be renewed on the 14th ["of July" *interlined*] & you must not fail to send your name in ["on the receipt of this" *interlined*; in] blank. It will ["besides" *interlined*] have to be renewed twice ["after" *interlined*] before I leave for Washington and you had better send at once ["three" *interlined and* "two" *canceled*] blanks. Of the three sent before, one was intend[ed], for the last renewal & the other two to meet the ["deposite in our hands" *canceled*] loans of Dr. [Ozey R.] Broyles & Mr. [Robert A.] Maxwell.

Write me soon & fully.

The family join their love to you all. Your affectionate father, J.C. Calhoun.

ALS in NcD, John C. Calhoun Papers; PEx in Jameson, ed., *Correspondence*, pp. 768–769.

From F[ITZ]W[ILLIAM] BYRDSALL

New York [City,] June 25th 1849

Dear Sir, Your favour of the 9th inst. has been gratefully received together with the letter addressed to Hugh Maxwell Esqr. in my behalf, the latter one to say the least, was quite unexpected, but this only enhances the obligation so considerately conferred by you. The friendly interest expressed towards me both in manner and concise fulness, is gratifying to all my feelings, and should be the more deeply appreciated as it comes from one who "rarely ever interferes in matters connected with either appointments or removals from office." Add to these considerations, the further gratification that your interposition will probably place me beyond the fanatical influences of those who would proscribe me for my political principles & preferences—that it has enabled me to decline, for I will not now accept, the aid of any friends here because you have done all that I could wish in the case, and I would rather be under such obligation to you, than to any other Being except the God that created me.

My business qualifications are such, that friends of mine the proprietors of the Croton Steam flour mills, one of the most prosperous establishments in this State, proposed to me months ago to take me into their partnership, when removed from office or at any time I would choose to accept. I verily believe that I could attain affluence in that concern, but I am not avaricious, have no expensive habits or tastes, and my salary, in addition to my other means, is commensurate with my pecuniary desires. A crisis is at hand in our history as a confederacy of Republican States, my whole mind is [so] engrossed in the contemplation of our future that I cannot devote it to any other pursuit of mere personal welfare; and as my private means are not sufficient for the decent support of myself and those who have claims upon me and as I am too deeply interested in the mighty struggle at hand to go into any business whatever, my office is necessary to me in more than one point of view. It appears to me that the pre[sent] sectional contest must result in the establishment of the perfect equality of all the members of this Union or else its dissolution must be the alternative, rather than the subjection of one sec[tion] to the injustice of the other. And should such a calamity as a [se]paration of northern and Southern States take place, it will be inevitably followed by a separation of the east and west.

It sometimes seems to me that many of the Southern people are not aware of the dangers that environ them. Not many years ago when no State legislature in the Union could have been induced to come out for abolitionism—Look at the following from the State of Maine. [*Attached newspaper clipping*: "The Maine Legislature on Slavery in the District of Columbia—In the Maine House (of) Representatives on Wednesday last, the following (re)solve was passed by 112 yeas to 14 nays:

'Whereas the people of Maine regard slavery w(ith) feelings of profound abhorrence as conflicting with (the) great principles of freedom and free government, de(tri)mental to political progress and ought not to be uph(eld) or sanctioned in the capital of our glorious Union, (the) very sanctuary of liberty; therefore,

'Resolved, That our Senators and Representati(ves) in Congress be requested to use their utmost influe(nce) to abolish slavery and the slave trade in the Distric(t of) Columbia, by all constitutional means.'"] To this same complexion will free soilism come at eventually—As well might the legislature of Maine propose the abolition of Slavery in Maryland and Virginia.

In addition to the foregoing and as an item in the history of the times, I attach the last political move of Benjamin F. Butler. [*Attached newspaper clipping*: "At a meeting of the Democratic Republican Committee (of) the city and county of New York, held at their Headquarters, corner of Broadway and Lispenard street, June 8, 1849, Mr. B.F. Butler, from the Committee previously appointed for that purpose, reported the following resolutions, which, after consideration, were unanimously adopted, and ordered to be signed by the Chairman and Secretaries, and published in the Evening Post, and the Globe, and New Yorker Demokrat.

1. Resolved, That the sweeping and indiscriminate exercise of the power of removal, by the present Executive [Zachary Taylor], clearly verifies the sage remark of the 'virtuous and indignant' Roman Consul, quoted by President [William Henry] Harrison, 'that a most striking contrast is observable in the conduct of candidates for offices of power and trust before and after obtaining them;' and that this new instance of 'violated confidence' is in no wise excused, however it may be accounted for, by the fact, that the hero who never surrendered to a Mexican commander, is now a prisoner at discretion, in the hands of 'an ultra whig' cabinet.

2. Resolved, That after the experience referred to in the foregoing resolution, it would be idle to expect, that in matters of national policy, the Executive will venture to oppose the schemes of his 'ultra whig' advisers; and that it therefore behooves the Democracy of the Union to be vigilant and active in the maintenance of their principles.

3. Resolved, That President Taylor, by allowing his name and

influence to be used for the benefit of the slave power, at the close of the late session of Congress, has not only violated the spirit of his pledge not to interfere with the action of Congress, but by threatening, through his official organ, to visit the 'free soil party' with his indignant frown, in case they should do what southern members of Congress have done without incurring any such frowns, has abundantly shown that the cause of freedom in the now free territories of New Mexico and California, has nothing to hope, but much to fear, from the present national Administration.

4. Resolved, That to protect this great interest, and to ensure, in other respects, a sound administration of public affairs, it is indispensable that there should be a re-union of the democratic party on the great principles of human rights, promulgated in the Declaration of Independence, and set forth in the Inaugural Address of its author; and that we hail with unmingled satisfaction, the beginnings of this re-union in the measures lately taken in Wisconsin, Vermont, and several other States.

5. Resolved, That we have observed, with pleasure, various indications, through the press, and in other forms, of a general desire for such a re-union in the democratic masses of this State; and while, as a Committee, we disclaim all authority or right, to propose, or to receive terms of union, to or from our former political associates—no such power having been delegated to us by our constituents—we think it proper, on the present occasion, to declare our readiness, as individuals, cordially to co-operate in all just, equal and honorable measures to promote this end.

6. Resolved, That to make the proposed union permanent and effectual, it must come spontaneously from the people themselves, and must be founded in a clear recognition of fundamental principles; and that paramount among these, in the present state of our national affairs, is the Jeffersonian policy, of prohibiting, after the manner of the ordinance of July 13th, 1787, the existence of human servitude, except as a punishment for crime, in the new free territories of the United States.

7. Resolved, That unless some other provision shall be made by our constituents, in connexion with their and our democratic associates throughout the State, it will be the duty of this Committee, and of all kindred bodies, to adhere to, and abide by, the State organization with which it is connected, and, at the proper time, to take measures for electing Delegates to the democratic State Convention, regularly called, in pursuance of ancient usage, for the 12th of Sep-

tember next, and then to be held at the city of Utica, for the nomination of State officers and of a Judge of the Court of Appeals.

8. Resolved, That in his late appeal, from the disorganizing resolutions of the Legislature of Missouri, to the sources of authority—the people themselves—Thomas H. Benton has taken a course, which, under the circumstances in which he is placed, this Committee deem perfectly consistent with the right of instruction; and that the boldness and ability with which he has vindicated the true principles of the Constitution, and the sacred interests of Humanity, give him a new title to the confidence and affections of the American people. In our just admiration of this great service to his country, and to mankind, we almost forget the differences of opinion which yet exist between us; we quite forgive the ill-timed visit, of 1848, to our State and city; and we tender him, with our hearty 'God speed,' the right hand of fellowship. Anthony J. Bleecker, Chairman.

Charles I. Bushnell, Robert A. Adams, Secretaries."]

I am informed that John Van Buren is doing and writing to the free soil Editors and partizans ["to" *canceled*] all he can to promote the reunion of the Democratic party. With these unprincipled Demagogues whatever issue they may present to gull the people their real object is the public plunder and nothing else. Yours with grateful esteem & veneration, F.W. Byrdsall.

ALS in ScCleA.

From H[ERSCHEL] V. JOHNSON, [former Senator from Ga.]

Milledg[e]ville, Ga., June 28, '49

My Dear Sir, I have read Mr. [Thomas H.] Benton's great St. Louis speech; and I have read it with mortification, but not with surprise. I am mortified at the exhibition which it furnishes of his profound personal and political depravity. Was such arrogance, such vanity, such impudence, such falsehood, such base treachery ever before compressed, in so great abundance, in so short a compass? As a specimen of these qualities, it is indeed multum in parvo [much in little]. I was not surprised however, because I was prepared for almost any thing from Mr. Benton. I knew he was prepared for treason; but I confess I would have supposed, it would have been more covert. For few men have the temerity, to perpetrate that offence in open day light. I knew his hostility to you and that no assault would be too malign for him to attempt. Your purity, your inflexible firmness, your unwavering devotion to the constitution and republican principl[e]s have been a standing, living rebuke to him, for more than twenty years. With such coals of fire heaped upon his head, it is not ["to be" *canceled*] strange, that, in his ravings, he should speake [*sic*] from the "abundance of his heart."

Now what I desire to say is, that I sincerely hope it will comport with your views of propriety, to reply reply [*sic*] to his attack. But my dear Sir, do not suppose from this suggestion, that I believe your fame requires it. I believe no such thing; I believe it is far out of the reach of any poisoned arrow from the quiver of Mr. Benton. I desire you to reply to it, because I solemnly believe, that in so doing, you will render important service to the South. He is not alone in his effort to bring the Southern Address into odium, by ascribing to you the authorship of the whole movement. In this ["he" *interlined*] cannot succeed, except with a few who cherish unfounded and foolish prejudices against you. You know the extent and origin of these prejudices. They have been alluded to by Gen. Foot [*sic*; Henry S. Foote, Senator], of Miss. in his letter to Mr. [former Representative Henry A.] Wise of Va. And by the bye, Gen. Foot has exonerated you from the charge of having originated the Southern meeting very handsomely. His letter will do good in Georgia, and I doubt not in all the slave States. It will neutralize the slang by which the non-signers are seeking to throw ridicule on that movement. A reply from you, I believe will do much good in the same way.

This is a crisis with the South. Those who signed the Address, are those who are emphatically her friends and on whom she is to rely in the hour of peril. Those who failed to sign are seeking to avoid censure by expressing great devotion to the union, and insinuating, in no concealed terms that we are looking to a disruption of the confederacy. Now is a most favourable occasion to set the public mind at perfect ease on this subject and show that we are the true friends of the Union.

When I speak ["of" *interlined*] your being *charged* as the author of the Southern Meeting, you will not understand me as Countenancing the idea, that it is a political sin. I really regard it as a compliment; for I believe it was a patriotic movement & I glory in the fact of having signed the address. I use the language only as adapted to the state of the case.

Our Democratic Convention comes off on the 11th of July. From present indications, I believe we shall meet no difficulty in adopting the Va. resolutions in full. The non-signers are alarmed and will raise no opposition. They will be very quiet, unless assailed, which will not be done.

Mrs. [Ann Polk Walker] J[ohnson] sends her very kind regards to you[rs]. Very truely &c, H.V. Johnson.

ALS in ScCleA; FC in NcD, Herschel V. Johnson Papers, Letterpress Book, pp. 20–23; PC in Percy Scott Flippin, ed., "Herschel V. Johnson Correspondence," *North Carolina Historical Review*, vol. IV, no. 2 (April, 1927), pp. 182–184; PEx in Boucher and Brooks, eds., *Correspondence*, pp. 512–513.

From JOSEPH PORTER

Independance Jackson County Missouri
June the 28th 1849

Mr. John C. Calhoun, Sir this must appear as obtrusion for one who must bea a stranger to you, therefore I beg you to accept ["it" *interlined*] as it is from one of your Longest and warmest friends, the warm and ardient attachment which I entertain for you and the cose which you support, is my apology for this obtrusion, and if you should doubt my cincerity, I will reffer you to C.F.M. Nolan[d] of Arkansas[,] Thomas S. Drew Ex Governor [of Ark.]—or to John G. Millar of Boon[e]ville Mo., the consum[p]tion of space precludes the mention of ["numers" *altered to* "numbers"], besides many articles which I have wrote and published which have doubtles[s] escaped of your notice. Thomas H. Benton is now canvassing the Stat[e]; he has maid you the Base of all his spe[e]ches the many fals[e] charg[e]s, which he has attempted to alledge against you, has fiered my mind with indignation and it is owing that which has gave rise to this communication as things ar[e] turning favourab[le] to you and the cose which you support. I Exult in having some thing good to communicate, I stood by you although ["upon" *canceled*] remote, ["from you" *interlined*] upon the Tariff question growing out of the Bill of abominations of [18]28, against the proclamation and the Bludy force Bill, against the arbitrary streach of Power By Majorritys, and in defence of reserved Rights garenteed to the States; your Exposition of Executive influence ["and" *canceled*] of [18]35 you[r] stand against the Removial of the deposits, and your remedy to prevent the consummation of the purse and sword, your defence against [Daniel]

Webster and [Henry] Clay at the Extra cession of [18]38. That defence I consider one of your master efforts upon that occasion, you proved by Webster that you had resisted party ties and party con-[n]ections, and that you had taken your stand in advance upon all great questions, such as the Bank of 1816[,] the war with Great Britton[,] the Embargo[,] Non Intercourse, the Navy, as an important arm of national defence. Upon all ["of" *interlined*] these questions Mr. Webster admit[t]ed that you had took the Lead and that time had proved your wisdom. He then claimed the Honor of followinng you, your Retort upon Henry Clay his Want of beaing metaphysical, owing to the want of which as you told him then, that he was always mounted upon som[e] popular and favorite measure which he whip[pe]d a long cheer[e]d by the Shouts of the multitude and would never dismount untill he had rode it down and that he was then mounted upon the Back of a Bank which would shurley shire the same fate, never was their a prediction more completely varafied. Your defeating [Martin] Vanburen['s] nomination in 1844—has proved a bles[s]ing to the nation which has br[o]ught to Publick v[i]ew Van[']s deformity; your southern address, has maid strong inrodes upon Colonel Benton, it has with othar coses arraid the Best Tallent of this State against him. He has the Boldness to accuse the State Legislatur[e], of beaing disunionist for pas[s]ing Resolutions, beaing prototype of those ["past" *canceled*] introduced in the Senate chamber February 1847 by you[r]-self and to Back which Benton & [David R.] A[t]chison was instructed to vote against the Wilmot proviso—those resolutions mentained nuthing more than what the Constatution guarentees to the States equality in the use and appropriation of new Territorys, which are the common property of all the States; and they alsoe denie the right of Congress to interfer[e], with the question of slavery and such interference is a danger[ou]s infringement upon the Rights of the State ["States" *canceled*]. He is often met with retorts of this kind, that it is him with his northern confederates who ar[e] strikeing the blow of Disunion of the States by assuming for Congress powers which the Constatution has never granted. Senator A[t]chison has defined his position he submits to the right of instruction and endorses the sentaments of the Southern address With ability, and repudiates the North ["for" *interlined*] stir[r]ing up the seeds of discord and disunion. You may re[a]d[i]ly conc[e]ive the dilemma in which Mr. Benton is plaist that he has not onely you to op[p]ose but he has his colleagues, nearly the whole Legislative Body, to consiliuate much less to convert, becose he has accused them With ignorrence for vote-ing for those Resolutions. He now appeals from thier instructions, to the people, he ["will" *canceled*] seems to forget that saim Body is desiminated with the peopl[e], eaqually zealous to sustain them selves, against his attacts, fortunate for the people of this State that Mr. Benton has devised the agent of his one disstuction his eagotism has betrayed him, he came with his Rail Road progect as beaing a balm sufficient, to heal up the soars, which his Rath has inflicted, ["but" *interlined*] it has proved inefficacious. It seems that you ar[e] desdined ever to bea the obgect of attact by such men as Benton and Vanburen. They mount Hobys irrespective of national good, for the sake mearly of individually advantages; overlooking publick duty and publick good, ["for" *interlined*] the want of foresight, or ["the" *interlined*] love of patriotism which is wanted in demagogues like them—who ar[e] always pushing ["forward" *interlined*] measur[e]s without looking to consequences or regarding the wisdom of others; hence their want of foresight often impels you to interpose measur[e]s, which throws obstacles in their way. Hence their sp[l]een and hence their [*one illegible word*]. It is your penetration, they hate, it is fortunate for the American peo[ple] that they have you in hir councils, although, they know little how to appreciate your worth. I close, With great Respect yours, Joseph Porter, June 28th 1849.

[P.S.] John C. Calhoun Porter wishes you to remember him. Your note bearing date September the 7th 1844 [*not found*] was received.

ALS in ScCleA. Note: An AEU by Calhoun reads, "J. Porter, Mo."

From Augustus Mitchell

Portland [Maine,] June 30th 1849

My dear sir, No doubt you will say that a yankee is a strange sort of a compound, just so I have been thinking for some years, from the fact of thus liberally bestowing his thoughts and advancing his opinion when not asked. Therefore at a venture we will make a few ethnical remarks on a subject which has for sometime been a matter of interest and study, hoping you will excuse me for thus obtruding my opinion. The subject under consideration is exclusively confined to observations and characteristics of the Ethiopian Species in the Genus Homo; much has been said—and more has been written on this subject we will allow. But thus far in my studies of nature connected with the intellectual and physical developement of mankind, I have strictly followed-up and carefully observed the wonderful and undeniable designs of our Great Creator; there are no proofs so powerful and convincing than those—which is legibly stamped and indelibly written by the Maker of all things. In everything whether of animate or inanimate nature, in the moral and social condition of man, from the mollusca, to the most intellectual animal on earth, His designs are apparent to every reflective mind. In the first place you will consider, that after strict investigations and anatomical observations of the negro, I ["do" *interlined*] conscientiously believe him to be—without borrowing from others, *a distinct species of mankind.* Such I believe is the opinion of Prof. [Louis] Agassiz the successor of [Georges Leopold, Baron] Cuvier, now in our country. It may be asked—where is the authority to sustain such an opinion. It could as well with propriety be asked—on what grounds—can we seperate and subdivide the various animals and plants which inhabit the earth so abruptly and obviously bounded by lines that cannot be mistaken. We have no room here to descant at large—and enter comparatively into the physical developements configuratively of animals, on minutely observing every particular connected with this matter. And therefore shall confine our remarks to the simple fact of the true state of the Ethiopian species from time immemorial as designed by our Creator. It will be seen that our species with its varieties are progressively and designedly making rapid strides towards the acme of their glory—which will soon be ["the" *interlined*] highest attainable point of human perfection. The negro species for over four thousand years have never perpetuated their ideas beyond the rude hut, and simple canoe, although in contact with the most civilized nations of ancient and modern ages during that period of time, with all the advantages of the early dawn of light and literature among the Arabians they have been in no manner tinctured with thought or sentiment expressing a social[,] moral or intellectual condition, and the only existing proofs to the contrary of this is where there has been an anomalous elevation of character in their ancient relation to mankind of a more elevated intellect. Can we fathom the mystery which shrouds this peculiar species of mankind in darkness, have we not the greatest proofs of its being the apparent design of our Creator; has He not by the most wonderful laws, closed all the avenues against the introduction of civilization, its shores are pestilence and death to the European, its languages and dialects almost in[n]umerable—into which the Bible and other books must be translated for the diffusion of knowledge among them.

Added to this their perfect inaptitude[,] their debased stupid and gross sensuality, prefering darkness rather than light—all designed by our Great Creator for purposes we know not—as His ways are just—and we know them not; and when He with His mighty power shall design their regeneration it will be done. The cloud which hangs over them and shrouds their future ["in darkness" *interlined*] will be dispelled and they will be snatched from that thraldom of ignorance, superstition and barbarism which are the predominant traits of their character. And in no instance from the remotest periods have they attained so high a degree of social[,] religious and moral enjoyment as under the system and care of humane and kind masters of our own happy country. And we will close this subject by asking, when will men become more rational—how long will they push their fanatical opinions beyond the boundaries of human reason, shall this happy country be agitated to the centre by a band of pseudo-philanthropist[s], who are regardless of all sacred ties, save their own foolish and maniacal ideas, "doubt and darkness" you may well say—yet I hope we shall be banded together as brothers, until time be no more with strict adherence to our constitution and love to the Southern brethren. I am dear sir with the highest considerations of esteem your ever faithful friend and Obedient Serv[an]t, Augustus Mitchell, M.D.

ALS in ScCleA. NOTE: An AEU by Calhoun reads, "A. Mitchell." Samuel Augustus Mitchell (1792–1868) published many works of science. His *A System of Modern Geography* went through numerous editions.

From CHA[RLE]S N. WEBB

Halifax, N.C., July 2, 1849

My Dear Sir, I send you the "Raleigh Register," containing a long Editorial upon the subject of slavery, in which the Editor speaks unkindly of you.

The War has just commenced and I should like to have your views in relation to the subject of Slavery, and a defence of yourself, against the charges made by the Editor of the "Register," which I shall substitute as my own, in the "Republican."

I send you the last "Republican," containing some of my views upon this subject; in which I have taken the occasion to pay you a just and merited compliment. I am sir, very faithfully yours with the highest regard, Chas. N. Webb, Editor of the "*Roanoke Republican.*"

ALS in ScCleA.

To the People of the Southern States

Fort Hill, July 5th, 1849

Several reasons would have prevented me from taking any notice of Col. [Thomas H.] Benton, if his attack in his late speech [of 5/26] delivered in the Capitol of Missouri had been directed exclusively against me. The line of conduct I have prescribed to myself, in reference to him is, to have as little to do with him as possible, and, I accordingly, never notice what comes from him, even in his character as Senator, when I can avoid doing so consistently with my publick duties. I regard him in a light very different from what he seems to regard me, if we may judge from the frequency and violence of his attacks on me. He seems to think, I stand in his way, and that I am ever engaged in some scheme to put him down. I on the contrary, have never for a moment thought of raising him to the level of a competitor, or rival, nor considered it of any importance to me, whether he should be put down or not. He must think he has something to gain by assailing me; I on the contrary feel, that I have nothing to gain by noticing him, and when compelled to do so am satisfied, if I escape without some loss of self respect. I have another reason for not desiring to notice him on the present occasion. All his charges against me, with few and trifling exceptions, are but the reiterations of those often made heretofore by himself and others, and which I have met and successfully repelled in my place in the Senate. That they made no impression against me at the time, either in the Senate or community, there can be no better proof, than is afforded in the laborious and tiresome effort he made in his present speech to revive and give them circulation.

Under the influence of these reasons, I would have remained silent had I alone been concerned. But such is not the case. His blow is aimed much more at you, than me. He strikes at me for the double purpose of weakening me in your confidence, and of striking at you and your cause through me, which he thinks can be done more effectually indirectly, than directly. Thus regarding his attack, I feel it to be a duty I owe you and your cause to repel it.

The effort of Col. Benton, from the beginning to the end of his speech, is to make out that I have ever been unfaithful to your cause and true to that of the free soilers and the abolitionists; while, on the contrary, you had in him an unknown but faithful friend on all occasions. He assumes, that you and they have been both mistaken in reference to my course; you in regarding me as a friend and supporter of your cause, and they in regarding me as hostile to theirs. Judged by appearance, his object would seem to be to expel this delusion, while in truth it is, to give you and your cause what he hopes will prove deadly blows. This the abolitionists and free soilers well understand. The disguise was not assumed to deceive them, but to deceive you. They understand him, and have hailed with acclamation his speech, and published it and circulated it far and near, and glorified it and its author to the skies. They rejoice in the belief, that it has demolished me, and this too, while it holds me up as the truest and best friend to their cause. It remains to be seen, whether you will understand him as perfectly as they do, and will meet the speech, so lauded by them, with the reprobation due to effrontery and desertion. It is not the first time that a deserter has had the assurance to address those he deserted, and while professing regard for their cause, denounced those who remained faithful to it. The history of our revolution furnishes a notorious instance of the kind. The deserter in that instance, failed to deceive those whom he addressed, or to shake their confidence in those who remained faithful to them, and in return for his effrontery and desertion, [they] have sent his name down to posterity with reprobation. It remains to be seen, whether such will be the fate of the deserter in this instance.

He commenced his speech with attacking the resolutions I offered to the Senate the 19th February, 1847, and charges that they were introduced for the purpose of disunion. That you may judge for yourselves, whether they are liable to the charge or not, I insert them.

"*Resolved*, That the territories of the United States belong to the several States composing this Union, and are held by them as their joint and common property.

"*Resolved*, That Congress, as the joint agent and representative of the States of this Union, has no right to make any law, or do any act whatever, that shall, directly or by its effects, make any discrimination between the States of this Union, by which any of them shall be deprived of its full and equal right in any territory of the United States, acquired or to be acquired.

"*Resolved*, That the enactment of any law which should, directly or by its effects, deprive the citizens of any of the States of this Union from emigrating with their property into any of the territories of the United States, will make such discrimination, and would, therefore, be a violation of the Constitution, and the rights of the States from which such citizens emigrated, and in derogation of that perfect equality which belongs to them as members of the Union, and would tend directly to subvert the Union itself.

"*Resolved*, That, as a fundamental principle in our political creed; a people, in forming a constitution, have the unconditional right to form and adopt the government which they may think best calculated to secure liberty, prosperity and happiness; and that, in conformity there to, no other condition is imposed by the federal Constitution on a State, in order to her admission into this Union, except that its constitution be republican and that the imposition of any other by Congress, would not only be in violation of the Constitution, but in direct conflict with the principle on which our political system rests."

They are, as you see, confined to asserting principles appertaining to the nature and character of our system of Government, and making inferences clearly deducible from them; and which are of vital importance, in the question between you and the North, in relation to the Wilmot Proviso. If the facts be, as the resolutions stated, there is no denying the inference; and if both be true, then your right to emigrate with your slaves into the territories becomes unquestionable under the Constitution. This he felt, and hence his bitter denunciation of them. But he has confined himself to denunciation without making an effort to refute the resolutions by showing they contain error, either as to the facts asserted, or inferences deduced. He knew that to be beyond his power and prudently avoided it. But, if the resolutions be true as he is compelled to admit they are by his silence; How can they be a firebrand, as he calls them, or be justly chargeable with disunion? Col. Benton has his own way of proving things, which appears to be very satisfactory to himself, but to no one, who will take the pains to examine his assertions and reasons.

Despairing of finding any thing like disunion in the resolutions themselves, he seeks for it in the motive, which he gratuitously assigns to me for introducing them. He first asserts, that they are the prototype of those adopted by the Legislature of Missouri at their late session, and then asserts that the only difference between them is, that mine aim directly at disunion, and theirs ultimately at the same thing, for which he offers no reason, except that theirs pledge the State to co-operate with the other slaveholding States. He thus assumes, that your aim as well as mine, is disunion; and this, while he is exerting himself to the utmost to discredit me with you, as a disunionist; for it is apparent his speech was intended to have its effects on you generally as well as his own constituents particularly. He then drags in the Accomack [County, Va.,] resolutions to prove, that the object is a Convention of the Southern States, and that he assumes to be proof conclusive, that disunion is intended by my resolutions. He is quite horrified at the idea of your meeting in Convention, in order to consult on the best mode of saving both yourselves and the Union; if indeed the madness of fanatics, and the treachery of deserters should not make the latter impossible. He next asserts, in order to prove that disunion is their object, that they render the adjustment of the territorial question impracticable, and that, that was my motive for introducing them. He makes this assertion, in the face of facts perfectly well known to him; that the Northern members, with a very few honorable exceptions, had rejected every effort at compromise, and had declared their fixed determination not to accept of any. It was against this arrogant and uncompromising course, that I offered my resolutions. It was, then, they and not me, who took ground against compromise, or adjustment. So far from this being true, I have ever been in favor of any fair adjustment, which was consistent with your constitutional rights. Of this I gave very strong proof at the very next session, by supporting the bill reported by Mr. [John M.] Clayton, which left the decision to the adjudication of the courts. The Bill would have passed but for his [Benton's] associates, the abolitionists and free soilers, and the question in controversy between the two sections, in reference to territories finally adjusted; and yet, he knowing all this, has the effrontery (to call it by no harsher name) to charge me, and not them, as opposed to any adjustment, and that too for the base purpose of destroying the Union.

But all these assumptions were but preliminary to a charge, still more audacious; that I am the real author of the Wilmot proviso. He calls it the Calhoun proviso, and says that I am better entitled to its paternity, than [David] Wilmot himself, which he accompanies by strong denunciations of the proviso, and a long enumeration of the many and great evils it has inflicted on the country. What effrontery! He, the avowed advocate of the Wilmot Proviso, accuses me of being its author, and denounces it in the most unmeasured terms in the same speech, in which he praises it and declares himself to be in its favor! He would seem to be perfectly indifferent of the recoil on himself, when his object is to assail me. There is no term in the language, by which such a combination of insincerity, inconsistency, and brazen effrontery can be characterised. The way, in which he attempts to make out his assertions, are in keeping with their character.

He first assumes that the Wilmot Proviso and the Missouri Compromise are identically the same, and then undertakes to prove, that I am the author of the latter, and, of course, also, of the former. This must be a piece of strange intelligence to Mr. [Henry] Clay and his friends and admirers. I had supposed there was no doubt whatever as to his being the real author of the Missouri Compromise. It was he who devised the measure, introduced it into the House of Representatives, carried it through, by his address, and gloried in the reputation of being its author. It is a little cruel to strip him of the honor of being its author at this late date, and to bestow it upon another, who no one ever suspected of being so until Colonel Benton discovered it.

But, if he could really make out, that I am the author of the Missouri Compromise, he must go one step farther to make me the author of the Wilmot proviso. He must prove the two measures to be identical; this he has not done or even attempted. Instead of that, he has adopted his usual course of assuming what he is incapable of proving. It is a very easy way to reach a conclusion that is desired. In this too, he has disclosed his wonderful aptitude to see what no one ever before saw, or suspected. Heretofore all had supposed that they were very different things—that a compromise was essential to one, while the other necessarily excluded it—that one pre-supposes a conflict of opinion between parties, on a question of right or expediency, to have been adjusted on ground, in which neither surrendered its rights or opinion. The other, on the contrary, presuppose a positive assertion of right, or opinion, to the exclusion of all compromise. Thus in the case of the Missouri Compromise, the north and the south differed on the constitutional question, whether Congress had the right to prohibit the introduction of slaves, as a condition of admitting a State into the Union. One contended, that Congress, had the right to impose whatever condition it might think proper on a territory, about to become a State, and the other, that it had no right to impose any, except, that prescribed by the Constitution; that its government should be republican. The North in that case waived the claim of power, on the proposal made by Mr. Clay to fix the northern limits of the territory, into which slaves might be introduced, at 36.30. This proposal, although made by a Southern member, was taken up and carried by the vote of the north, and thus became, in fact, their offer to compromise. The South acquiesced, without, however, yielding her principles or assenting, or dissenting, as to the power of Congress, to exclude slavery from the territories. It was a compromise, in which both waived, but neither yielded its opinion, as to the power of Congress.

Very different was the case in reference to the Oregon bill, passed at the session preceding the last. There the north contended for the absolute right to exclude slavery from all the territories, and announced their determination to do so, against the efforts of the south to compromise the question, by extending the Missouri Compromise line to the Pacific Ocean. The offer was scornfully refused, and the bill passed, without any compromise. It was intended indeed to be the practical assertion of the naked principle, that Congress had the power to claim for it, by the Wilmot proviso. It was the first act of the kind ever passed, and was carried by the desertion from your cause by Col. Benton and Gen. [Samuel] Houston. It is not surprising that the former should be desirous of confounding this far more odious measure, with the Missouri Compromise, a much less odious one, in the hope of mitigating your deep indignation, occasioned by his betrayal of you, on a question so vital to the South. But he had another motive which will be explained, hereafter, and which makes it still more desirable to him, that the two should be confounded and regarded as identical. When it comes to be explained, it will be seen, that it was necessary that they should be, in order to extricate him from a very awkward dilemma in which he has placed himself. Job exclaimed "Oh that mine adversary had written a book"; and well might I have exclaimed oh that my adversary might make a speech. His adversary must have been very much like mine. We have never heard whether his had the folly to accommodate him as mine has had to accommodate me.

I have now effectually repelled his preposterous charge, that I am the author of the Wilmot Proviso; for it is utterly impossible that he ever can show that I am the author of the Missouri Compromise, or that, that compromise and the Wilmot Proviso are the same. But as he has made it the position from which to assail me with the charge of disunion, and thro' me you, including his own constituents, I shall follow him step by step, through the long process, by which he makes the desperate endeavor to establish his preposterous charge, by attempting to show, that I have changed my opinion, as to the powers of Congress over the territories. But my purpose is more to expose his inconsistency, contradictions and absurdities, than to refute what he advances as argument. If he could prove to a demonstration, that I have changed my opinion, it could have no weight whatever, towards showing that my resolution[s] aimed at disunion. Nor do I deem it a matter of any importance, in this connection, whether my opinion has or has not undergone a change, in the long period of 30 years, since the adoption of the Missouri Compromise. At that time, the power of Congress over the territories had received but little consideration, while for the last few years it has been a subject of vital interest to you, and, as such, has been thoroughly investigated by myself and others, whose duty it has been to defend your rights in the councils of the Union, in reference to it.

To substantiate the charge of a change of opinion, he introduced a copy of what purports to be a draft of a letter found among the papers of Mr. [James] Monroe. It is said to be in his hand writing. It is without date, not signed, or addressed to any person by name, but contained expressions, which leave no doubt, that it was intended for General [Andrew] Jackson. This paper was found filed away with another endorsed "Interrogatories–Missouri–March 3th 1820." "To the Heads of Departments and Attorney-General." It contained two questions, of which the one pertinent to the present subject is in the following words: "Has Congress a right under the powers vested in the Constitution to make a regulation prohibiting slavery in a territory?" The only material sentence in the draft of the letter, in reference to the point under consideration is in the following words: "I took the opinion in writing of the administration, as to the constitutionality of restraining territories, which was explicit in favor of it." These are the exact words of the sentence as finally corrected by its author. It is explicit as to the statement, that the administration, as a body, was in favor of the constitutionality, but furnishes no proof whatever of its members being unanimous, and of course no evidence that I or any other particular member of the Cabinet, was in its favor.

This deficiency Col. Benton undertakes to supply, first from the interlining and next a statement purporting to be from the diary of Mr. [John Quincy] Adams. First as to the interlining: instead of the expression, which was "explicit" as it now stands, it read in the original draft, "and the vote of every member was explicit." These words were all struck out except "explicit," and in their place the following words were interlined in the first instance, "which were unanimous and," afterwards the words "unanimous and" were struck out, which left the paper as it now stands. Now I hold it to be clear that the interlining and striking out, so far from strengthening the inference that the Cabinet were unanimous, as Col. Benton contends, it strengthens and sustains the very opposite. So far then it is certain, the draft of the letter, standing by itself, instead of furnishing proof, that the Cabinet were unanimous, furnishes proof directly to the contrary. Even Col. Benton himself seems to have been conscious, that it furnished no satisfactory proof, as to the unanimity of the Cabinet, and endeavors to supply this defect from statements purporting to be taken from the diary of Mr. Adams. From these, it would appear, that a meeting of the Cabinet was held on the 3d of March for the first time to consider the compromise bill, and that, according to the statement of Mr. Adams the Cabinet were unanimous upon the question of constitutionality. It also appears that the President [Monroe] sent him the two questions, on the 5th of March, informing him at the same time that he desired answers in writing from the members of the Cabinet, and that the answers would be in time if received the next day. Such is the substance of the statement purporting to be taken from his diary.

Connecting this with the draft as it originally stood, and the subsequent alterations including the date of the memorandum filed with it, the natural interpretation of the whole affair is, that Mr. Monroe drew up interrogations, and the draft of his letter intended for General Jackson, on the 4th of March, the date of the memorandum. It could not have been earlier according to the diary of Mr. Adams, nor probably later. He did not date the draft because the letter could not be finished and transmitted to General Jackson, until after he had signed the bill. The draft was drawn up as it stood, in all probability on the basis of the opinion expressed on the third of March, the first day of the meeting of the Cabinet, and which, at the time as the diary states was "unanimous," and the doubts and uncertainty of opinion were expressed by some of the members on the two subsequent days (the 5th and 6th of March,) which caused the interlining and the first modification of the draft, as it now stands. It is difficult to give any other explanation.

I turn now to Col. Benton's reasoning upon the subject. He alledges that the words ["]and vote of every member was explicit["] were struck out, and "explicit" inserted, evidently to avoid violating the rule of Cabinet secrets not to tell the opinion of members which the word "unanimous" would do. His statement contains two errors, as to fact. "Explicit" was in the original draft and never struck out. ["]Unanimous["] made no part of the original draft, as he supposes. It was a part of the interlining at first; but subsequently struck out. All this is apparent from a certified copy of the paper now before me. Thus his reasoning falls to the ground. He carries the rule of Cabinet secrets very far, much farther than he does the same rule applied to the secrets of the Senate. Who ever heard that it was a violation of any rule of Cabinet secrets, to say the administration was unanimous or divided? It is constantly said in reference to their meetings, and yet he would have you believe, that it would have been a breach of confidence in Mr. Monroe in writing a confidential letter to a friend of high standing, to say that his Cabinet were unanimous; and especially, as the question was one of constitutionality, and not of policy. What member of any Cabinet would be so base and cowardly, as to desire to conceal his opinion on a constitutional question? Who, accordingly, did not know at the time, that the opinion of the Cabinet of General [George] Washington was divided, on the question of chartering a bank and what side every member took? Col. Benton's explanation is destitute of even plausibility, and leaves the draft to speak for itself, as it stands; and that clearly is against the Cabinet being unanimous. The diary of Mr. Adams furnishes the only opposing evidence. Now, I hold it to be a sound rule, that a diary is no evidence of a fact against any one, but he who keeps it. The opposite rule would place the character of every man at the mercy of whoever keeps a diary. It is not my object to call in question the veracity of Mr. Adams, but he was a man of strong prejudices, hasty temper, and much disposed to view things as he desired. From his temperament, he would be liable to notice and mark what fell within his own views, and to pass unnoticed what did not. I venture little in saying that if his diary should be published during the lifetime of those who were on the stage with him, its statements would be contradicted by many, and confirm all I have stated. But few statements from it have yet been brought to the notice of the public, but even [of] these few two have been contradicted; (one, if my recollection serves me,) related to General Jackson, and the other, to a Mr. Harris of Philadelphia, during the administration of Mr. Monroe.

Opposed to the statement of Mr. Adams, stands the fact, that no opinions as is is [*sic*] admitted by Col. Benton, are to be found on the files of the Department of State, nor any evidence that any such opinions were ever filed; although the statement purporting to be from the diary of Mr. Adams says, that Mr. Monroe directed them to be filed. One of two things would seem to be clear; either he fell into an error, in making the entry, or that he failed to place them on file, in consequence of some subsequent direction from the President. It is hardly possible, if they had been placed on file, but that they would still be there, or some evidence, in existence, that they had been there. My own recollection is, that Mr. Monroe requested the opinion of the members of his Cabinet in writing; but that in consequence of want of time to prepare a written opinion or some other cause, none was given, and this I stated in the Senate, when General [John A.] Dix brought up the question as to the opinion of the Cabinet of Mr. Monroe, before the fact was disclosed, that there was no written opinion on the files of the department. I have entire confidence, that if any was given, it amounted to no more, than the simple affirmation, or negation of the power. The time did not admit the preparation of an elaborate opinion, and if any such had been given, it is impossible that I should forget it; and next to impossible, that it should so long have remained concealed from the public. As to the insinuation, that I am the only member of the Cabinet of Mr. Monroe, who has since been secretary of State, and all others of like character, I pass them with the silent contempt due to their baseness, and the source whence they came.

There is besides, a fact which clearly shows, that there had been a considerable change of views from the 4th to the 6th of March; I allude to the fact, that the draft of the letter intended for General Jackson was never sent. It is inferable from the fact, that there is no such letter to be found among his papers, after the most diligent search. It is not improbable that the same change of circumstances which caused the striking out and inserting, and which induced him not to finish and transmit the letter to General Jackson as intended, induced him, also, finally to dispense with a written opinion, and will account why no such opinion is found on file.

But suppose the case to be as Col. Benton contended; of what importance is it, or how does it enable him to make out his charge, that the resolutions which he so vehemently denounces, were introduced for the purposes of disunion? The opinion of the cabinet, whether for or against, whether unanimous or divided; whether written or unwritten, were given under circumstances, which would entitle them to but little weight. In the first place, there was no time for consideration. But one day elapsed from the time the questions were put and sent to the members of the Cabinet, until a final decision was made. In the next place, the subject was little understood and had at that time received little consideration. The great point in the discussion of the Missouri question; whether Congress had a right to impose any other limitation on the admission of a State into the Union, than that prescribed by the Constitution. The question of its power over the territories did not come up until near the end of the discussion; and, according to my recollection, was scarcely noticed, much less discussed. So loose, indeed, was the prevailing opinion at the time, that the power of legislating over them was believed to be derived from that portion of the Constitution, which provides "that Congress shall have power to *dispose* of, and to make all needful rules and regulations respecting the territories and *other property* belonging to the United States." Such it would seem to have been the opinion of Mr. Monroe, judging from his manner of propounding the question. He puts it in language borrowed from the provision "to make *a regulation* prohibiting slavery in the territories" and not to make *a law* to prohibit. But since then, a more careful examination has established beyond all reasonable doubt, that this provision was intended to be limited to the disposition and regulation of the territories, regarded simply as land or property, and that it conferred no power whatever beyond, much less, that of prohibiting slavery under circumstances, even if it could be made out beyond a shadow of doubt that the cabinet was unanimous, and that its members gave written opinions in the affirmative, it could have little right in settling the constitutional question; and yet Col. Benton in his zeal to strike at me, and through me at you and your cause, insists that the opinion of Mr. Monroe's cabinet forever foreclosed the question against the South. To establish a doctrine so absurd he, by implication lays down a rule, that the opinion of Congress, or any department of the government, once expressed on a constitutional question settles it forever; and this too when it is well known that it was in direct contradiction to the course he pursued in reference to the Bank of the United States. The right of Congress to charter such a bank had again and again been sanctioned by Congress, and every department of the government. That he did not consider all this as settling the constitutional question, the long war he waged against the institution proves conclusively.

It is his fate to involve himself in dilemmas at every step he takes and which he is either too blind to see, or too reckless to regard. He has labored through many columns to prove, that the cabinet of Mr. Monroe was unanimous in favor of the power of Congress to exclude slavery from the territories, and that they gave written opinions to that effect, in order to prove, that I am the real and responsible author of the Wilmot proviso, without apparently perceiving, that if he could succeed, it would destroy his conclusion; for if the cabinet was unanimous, how could I alone be responsible. He seems to have felt the dilemma after he got into it and has made a desperate effort to escape from it. For that purpose, he had to falsify the Constitution, and to assert, that the veto power was vested in the Cabinet, and not in the President, when that instrument expressly provides, that "the

Executive power shall be vested in the President"; and that every bill shall be presented to the President for his approval or disapproval; and that, if he approves of it, it shall become a law, and, if he disapproves it, shall not, unless passed by two thirds of both houses of Congress. He follows up this false assertion by another, that I had one-fifth of the veto power in my hands, when, in fact, I had no part, and when the paper, on which he relies to make out his charge, shows on its face, that the cabinet consisted of six and not five, and of course, if it had the veto power, but one sixth part was vested in me. But this double mistake is not sufficient of itself to support his charge. The question would still remain. How could I be solely responsible, when according to his own showing, I had but a fifth of the power? Upon what principle of justice could I be made responsible for the acts of the other three, or as the fact really is—the other four? To escape from this dilemma, he attributes to me the most commanding influence over the Cabinet—so commanding as to be able to draw over to my side, a sufficient number of members to make a majority; and this too, when it is apparent from the paper from which he draws his statement, that Mr. Monroe had no doubt as to the power of Congress. I then, in order to command a majority would have had to control three other members against him, which Col. Benton seems to think I could have done very easily, if I had thought proper. He seems to have a most exalted opinion of my abilities, far more so than I have of his. Wherever I am placed, whether in Mr. Monroe's, or Mr. [John] Tyler's cabinet; whether in the Senate, or the House of Representatives, or in the chair of the Vice-President, I alone, in his opinion, am responsible, on all questions.

I have now traced him through the long process by which he attempts to prove that I am the author of the Wilmot proviso, and, by consequence, of all the mighty evils, that have followed in its train, and which he exhibits with so much parade; but after all, mighty as he represents them to be, they are not so much so, as to prevent him from declaring himself to be a Wilmot proviso man. He follows up his charge, by asserting that the effects of disclosing the opinion of the cabinet by Mr. Dix, introducing the paper, compelled me to close my lips, abandon my resolutions, and to give up my intention of making them the subject of a general debate at the next session, with the intention[,] to use his own language, to make a chance for myself at the next Presidential election, by getting up a test which no northern man could stand. All this is just as erroneous, both as to facts and inferences, as are his statements and reasons, in his vain attempt to make me the author of the Wilmot proviso.

If by abandoning my resolutions, he means, that it compelled me to abandon their principles, on a single position taken by them, or to be silent, as to the constitutional power of Congress over the territories, his assertion would be false throughout. The resolutions were introduced, as he states, the 19th day of July, 1849 [*sic*; February 19, 1847], near the close of the short session. So far from abandoning them, or from keeping silent, I discussed the principles on which they rest in the debate, on the bill to establish the Territorial government of Oregon at great length, at the next session, and established them by arguments that have never yet, and, I will venture to say, never will be refuted. Few have undertaken to refute them, and those, who have undertaken it signally failed. Others like Col. Benton, have taken the more prudent course, to cry out firebrand–disunion–instead of attempting to refute them.

But if he means, that I was deterred from introducing my resolutions at the next session, by the cause which he assigns, a simple statement of facts will give his assertion a flat contradiction. He has made his statement so as to make the impression, that Mr. Dix introduced the paper at the same time that I introduced my resolutions, or at farthest, early in the next session; for otherwise, it would not suffice to show, that it was owing to its introduction, and the disclosures it made, that I was deterred from introducing them, as he states. The fact is not so. The session commenced the first Monday of December, 1847, and Mr. Dix did not introduce the paper until the 26th of July, 1848, nearly eight months subsequent, and one month after I had fully discussed the principles of my resolutions. Did he see, that all this would have been manifest at once without a word from me, if he had given the dates? and was not that his reason for not giving them?

Colonel Benton seems to be conscious, that it was necessary for him to explain why he had not assailed my resolutions and the base and corrupt motives he attributes to me for introducing them, long before, and in his place in the Senate; and accordingly, he has attempted to make one. He asserts, that "Mr. Calhoun's resolutions are those of the Missouri Legislature. They are identical. One is copied from the other. When the original is invalidated, the copy is of no avail. I am answering his resolutions, and choose to do it. It is just and proper that I should do so. He is the prime mover and head contriver. I have had no chance to answer him in the senate, and it will not do to allow him to take a snap judgment upon me in Missouri, in carrying disunion resolutions in my own State, which he has been forced to abandon in the Senate. Duty to the country requires me to answer him, and personal reasons re-inforce that public duty."

His explanation, then is that notwithstanding his burning zeal to defend the Union and his own character against these wicked resolutions, "he could get no chance before to answer them." What! could get no chance from February, 1847, until June 1849 [*sic*; May] (the date of his speech) a period of upwards of two years! Could get no chance, when they were first introduced and discussed? None, during the long session which followed, and which lasted more than eight months! None, during the long and full discussion on the Oregon Territorial bill, when the principles of the resolutions formed the basis of the argument on the side of the South? None, to reply to me, who fully discussed, and I may say established them beyond controversy? None, during the discussion of the report of the select committee, of which Mr. Clayton was chairman? None, on the discussion of the bill from the House of Representatives, which applied the Wilmot proviso to the Oregon territory, and which was passed by his vote and his friend General Houston's? None, during the whole of the last session, and still more wonderful, none in making his last speech? I say none, for he confined himself to denunciation and abuse of the resolutions, without even attempting to answer them. No, he never could get, and never can get a chance to answer them. For every other purpose, he can get a chance whenever he pleases. No one is better at getting a chance when he is disposed. He had no difficulty in getting a chance to pour out a torrent of abuse, to empty seats, against the late General [Stephen W.] Kearney, day after day for the greater part of a week, and that too just at the close of a session, to the utter disgust of the Senate, and at the hazard of defeating many bills then ready for final action. I might go on and repeat similar questions, until they would fill pages, but enough has been said to prove, that his explanation is puerile and hollow.

He had many and fair chances to answer the resolutions and could have made one, if he desired it at any time, but there were two reasons which prevented him. The first is, that although he had made up his mind to desert you and your cause before the introduction of the resolutions, he saw the hazard, and was unwilling to take that step hastily. The Missouri Resolutions forced him to disclose his intentions, and to proclaim his desertion before he was fully prepared to execute his design, and hence the depth to which they have excited his ire. The other is, that he had too much discretion to address such a farrago to a body too well informed to be imposed upon by old, stale and oft repeated charges. He knew besides, that they would have been promptly met, and repelled, and that the antitode [*sic*; antidote] would go with the poison. He knew this from experience. He had tried it before. It failed most signally.

It was in the session of 1847, a few days after I had introduced the resolutions. In that attack he paraded nearly in the same words, all that he has charged in this, about the Florida treaty, Texas, and almost every other subject. He had taken time and prepared deliberately. It was given out, that he would demolish me. The Senate was crowded by those, who wished to witness the sacrifice. I rose and repelled off hand his charges. I leave those who were present to decide, with what effect. It was certainly not to his gratification or satisfaction. He did not even attempt a rejoinder. But what becomes of his apology, that he had no chance to reply to my resolution[s]? They had been introduced but shortly before, and then he had a full chance to answer them. He then assailed every act of my life, which he thought he could distort, so as to make a plausible charge against me. Why then omit to answer resolutions which he now holds up as the worst and most objectionable of all? Can any answer be given, except that he is either not sincere, in what he now asserts, or that the time had not then arrived, at which he could safely venture to betray you?

But, according to his own statement, he is impelled, in making his attacks, by private grief, as well as public considerations. He says I instigated attacks on him for twenty years. I, instigate attacks on him! He must have a very exalted opinion of himself. I never thought of such a thing. We move in different spheres. My course is, and has been, to have nothing to do with him. I never wanted his support, nor dreaded his opposition. He took the same ground in his speech, just referred to, and endeavored to establish the charge by what purported to be an extract from a letter, which he states was delivered to him by some person unnamed, and was written by an unknown person to an unknown person. He introduced it into the Senate, in a manner to make the impression that I was its author. I arose and asked him, if he intended to assert that I was. He stood mute at first, but was forced to admit I was not. I then repelled his charge with a scorn, which the base insinuation, that I had any knowledge or connection with it whatever, deserved. He was covered with confusion; and yet he has the effrontery to introduce it again to the public, accompanied with the same insinuation which covered him with disgrace at its first introduction.

But the deepest wound, it seems, was inflicted by a statement in my address to the people of Charleston on my return home after the session of [18]47 and [18]48, that he voted for the bill establishing the territory of Oregon, containing the principle of the Wilmot proviso, and that he and General Houston were the only two Southern members, who voted for it; that without their votes, it would not [*sic*] have been defeated, followed by the expression of an opinion, that for so doing, they deserved the reprobation of the whole South. Neither of them have ever denied the truth of my statement, nor ever can. Every word is true, as the journals of the Senate show. The statement itself is in plain language and free from distortion, or exaggeration. The fact stated, related to official acts, which it was important my constituents should know. In expressing my opinion, I abstained from impeaching motives. All was done within the rules of decorum, and those that govern parliamentary proceedings. Wherein then consists the offence? I am at a loss to perceive, except the principle be adopted, that the greater the truth the greater the libel. It may be, that it was regarded as an offence because it was calculated to embarrass him, and thwart what he then meditated, and has since carried into execution; an open desertion to the abolitionists.

I pass now to his next charges. He asserts that I gave away Texas, and to make it out, he asserts, that Texas belonged to the United States, when the treaty with Spain was made, by which she ceded Florida to us. He claims that Texas was a part of Louisiana, and that its boundary extended to the Rio Grande; that it was all slave territory, and looked to as the natural outlet for their great increasing slave population, and finally, that it was surrendered by the treaty of Florida, made in 1819, during the administration of Mr. Monroe, of which I was one of the members. On this statement, he rests his charge that I gave away Texas.

It is difficult for one, who lacks sincerity and is actuated by violent passions, to escape the greatest inconsistency and contradiction in defending himself or assailing others, in making a long speech. Benton furnishes a strong illustration of the truth of this position, and never more so, than in making the above statement. In order to aggravate the act of giving away Texas, which he charges me with, he has made assertions entirely inconsistent with the grounds he took, and the course he pursued while the question of the annexation of Texas was before the Senate. He now asserts that the boundary of Texas as part of Louisiana extended to the Rio Grande; when the treaty of Florida was made, in the very teeth of the assertions, he made, when the ques[tion] of annexation was before the Senate. In the speech he made in May 1844, on the treaty for annexing Texas, he asserted, that "The Texas which we acquired by the treaty of 1803, (that of Louisiana,) never approached the Rio Grande, excepting near its mouth." To show that by "near its mouth!" he did not mean that it touched the river, he said speaking of Tamaulipas, one of the states of Mexico, that "it covered both sides of the river from its mouth for some hundred miles up." He asserted in the same speech that all New Mexico, Chihuahua, Coahuila and Tamaulipas made no part of the Texas which we acquired by the treaty of Louisiana. He estimates the part belonging to Mexico lying on the east side of the Rio Grande to be 2000 miles long, (the whole length of the river,) and some hundred broad, and concluded by saying "he washed his hands of all attempts to dismember the republic of Mexico by seizing her dominions in New Mexico, Chihuahua, Coahuila and Tamaulipas."

These were his assertions, solemnly made, and as he states after the fullest examination, when his object was to defeat the treaty which I negotiated with the commissioners of Texas for its annexation. For that purpose he attempted to show, that the treaty covered a large part of Mexico, which never belonged to Texas, although the treaty specified no boundary, and left the boundary open on the side of Mexico, intentionally, in order to settle it by treaty with her. But now, when his object is to show, that I gave away Texas by the treaty of Florida, he holds a very different language. He does not, indeed, say in so many words, that Texas covered the whole region from the Sabine to the Rio Grande, for that would have been too openly and plainly a direct contradiction to what he contended for when his object was to defeat annexation; but he does the same thing, in a more covered and objectionable way, by using language that could not fail to make that impression on all who heard him, or who may read his speech.

He goes further. In order to aggravate the charge against me he becomes apparently a warm advocate of slavery extension, as he calls it, and uses strong language to shew the value of Texas to the South, in that respect. He says, it was all slave territory; that it was looked to as the natural outlet of the Southern States with their increasing slave population, and it was large enough to make six large States, or ten common ones. Such, is his language, when his object is to prove that I gave away Texas. You would suppose from this language, that he was a slavery extensionist, as he calls all those, who defend your rights and that he placed a high value on Texas, as an outlet for your slave population, and to preserve your just influence and weight in the Union. One would conclude, that with these feelings and views, he would have been a strong advocate of the treaty, that was rejected by the Senate, which proposed to annex Texas without any restriction whatever in relation to slavery so as to leave it, to use his own language, as the outlet to your increasing slave population. Instead of that, he made the most strenuous effort to defeat it, and contributed not a little towards it. He went further. After its defeat, he moved a string of resolutions, containing provisions for its admission, and among others, one which proposed to divide Texas into two parts, as nearly equal as possible by a line running North and South, and to allot the eastern to you, and the western to the abolitionists, to the entire exclusion to your "*increasing slave population.*" It can hardly be, that he forgot all this in delivering his speech; but, if not, what matchless effrontery and inconsistency to make the charge he does against me? There would indeed seem to be no limits to his audacity and inconsistency, and he appears to have selected Texas as a proper field to make the greatest display of them. As, if to cap the climax, after having so deliberately asserted, and so strenuously maintained, that the western boundary of Texas, did not extend to the Rio Grande, he placed, a short time afterward, his vote on record, that it did—by voting for the bill declaring war against Mexico. The bill assumed it did in asserting that the blood shed on the eastern bank, was blood shed on the American soil, which could not be, unless Texas extended to the Rio Grande. If it did not, the war stands without justification. If it did not, the march of our army to the Rio Grande was an invasion of a neighboring Country, unauthorized by Constitution or law; and yet Colonel Benton, who had but a short time before declared solemnly, after full investigation, that all the east bank of the river for some hundred miles wide, belonged to the Mexican republic; and emphatically declared, he "washed his hands of all attempts to dismember the Mexican Republic, by seizing her dominions, New Mexico, Chihuahua, Coahuila, and Tamaulipas," voted for the bill! He went further. He reported it as the Chairman of the Committee on military affairs, in total disregard of his own motion made the day before to refer so much of the Message of the President [James K. Polk], as related to declaring war, to its appropriate Committee—that on Foreign relations. Comment is unnecessary.

But I am not yet done with Texas, nor with the effrontery and absurdity of the charges he made against me, in reference to it. He says I gave it away—gave it away by the Florida treaty. How could

I give it away by that, or any other treaty? The power to make treaties belongs to the President, and never was invested in me. It was at the time, invested in Mr. Monroe, as President of the United States. Nor did I negotiate it. I was only one member of the Cabinet, and the youngest of the whole. How could I, then, give away Texas? To prove the charge, he resorts to his old patent reasoning; but I was all powerful—so much so, as to make the President and all the members of his Cabinet mere cyphers. He would have it, that they were but tools in my hands; and I alone was responsible for all that was done. Well—if he will have it so, I meet the charge directly. It is not true, that the Florida treaty gave away Texas. I did not believe, when the treaty was made, that Louisiana extended, or ever did extend to the Rio Grande, or even to the Nueces, and that it was uncertain, whether it extended beyond the Sabine. I knew it was claimed to extend far beyond, even to the Rio Grande; just as we claimed the whole of Oregon, and with just about as little title. I have seen nothing to change this opinion: On the contrary, if my informant is correct, there are now documents in the State Department, obtained within the last few years, which conclusively prove, that Louisiana never extended an inch beyond the Sabine.

In reply to Col. Benton's assaults as to the treaty, I annex an abstract from a speech in answer to him, when he made the same charge, in 1847. It was an offhand reply to a premeditated attack.

> "The Florida Treaty, forming another subject of attack, figured also on that occasion, in connection with annexation; and what he said now is but a repetition of what he said then. He then, as now, made me responsible for that treaty, although I was but one of six members of Mr. Monroe's Cabinet, and the youngest of its members—responsible, without advancing a particle of proof that I even gave it my support or approbation. He rests the charge on some disclaimer, as it seems, that the then Secretary of State (Mr. Adams) has, at some time, made, that he was not responsible for the treaty. The Senator may be right as to that; but how can that, by any possibility shew that I was responsible? But I am prepared to take my full share of responsibility, as a member of Mr. Monroe's Cabinet, without having any particular agency in forming the treaty, or influence in inducing the cabinet to adopt it. I then thought, and still think it a good treaty; and so thought the Senate of the United States; for, if my memory does not deceive me, it received every vote of the Senate. (A Senator: 'yes—every vote.'[)] It then received the unanimous vote of the Senate, promptly given. Of course, if that treaty was the cause of the war with Mexico, as the Senator seems to suppose, this body is as much the author and

cause of the war, as the individual on whom he is now so anxious to fix it.

I have said it is a good treaty, not without due reflection. We acquired much by it. It gave us Florida—an acquisition not only important in itself, but also in reference to the whole southwestern frontier. There was, at that time, four powerful tribes of Indians, two of whom the Creeks and the Choctaws were contiguous to Florida, and the two others—the Chickasaws and Cherokees were adjoining. They were the most numerous and powerful tribes in the United States, and from their position, were exposed to be acted on and excited against us from Florida. It was important that this state of things should terminate, which could only be done by the obtaining possession of Florida.

But there were other and powerful considerations for the acquisition. We had a short time before, extinguished the Indian title to large tracts of country in Alabama, Mississippi, and Georgia, lying upon streams and rivers which passed through Florida to the Gulf—lands in a great measure valueless, without the right of navigating them to their mouths. The acquisition of Florida gave us this right, and enabled us to bring into successful cultivation a great extent of fertile lands which have added much to the increased production of our great staple, Cotton. Another important point was effected by the acquisition. It terminated a very troublesome dispute with Spain, growing out of the capture of St. Marks and Pensacola by General Jackson, in the Seminole war; and, finally, it perfected our title to Oregon, by ceding to us, whatever right Spain had to that territory."

Nor is his next charge, in reference to the tract of land lying west of Arkansas and south of 36.30, less baseless. He asserts that this strip of land, as he calls it, was enough to form two States, and that I "required this strip of land to be given up to the Indians, as a permanent abode; and that it was lost to the slave States." This, like his other assertions, is without foundation. He makes no attempt to establish it, but leaves it to be inferred from the mere statement that "I was at the time Secretary of War, and member of Mr. Monroe's administration." He knew it would not do to go into details, as they would refute his charge, and hence the vagueness of the language, in which it is couched. What he omitted, I shall supply. The history of the affair may be told in a few words.

The Choctaw tribe of Indians, at the time, inhabited the State of Mississippi, and occupied almost its entire territory. General Jackson and General Hines [that is, Thomas Hinds] of Mississippi were appointed by Mr. Monroe to treat with them, for the purpose of obtaining a cession of a portion of their lands. They succeeded in obtaining a large tract, lying in the very centre of the State, and extending from Pearl river to the Mississippi, in exchange for all the territory lying between the Red river, and the Arkansas, west of a line drawn from the point of the Arkansas, opposite to where the lower line of the Cherokee Indians struck it to a point on Red River, three miles below the mouth of Little river, and westwardly to the source of the Canadian fork of the Arkansas, and a line drawn due South to Red river. But the treaty, in making the exchange, made no provision to change the character of the Indian title to the land given in Arkansas in exchange for that, which we received in Mississippi. Nor did it make it the permanent abode of the Indians, as he asserts. They hold it just as they held the land they ceded in Mississippi. Nothing was lost by the slaveholding States, but a great deal gained by the treaty. A large and valuable tract in the very heart of the cotton region, and lying convenient to market was acquired by Mississippi; without the loss of a single acre to her sisters of the slave holding States. So that the great sympathy which he professes for the slave States, in this case is misapplied. If he chooses to consider me responsible for the treaty, instead of Mr. Monroe, and the commissioners who made it, and the Senate, that approved of it, he is welcome to do so, however contrary to the truth of the case.

Another, and only another treaty was made with that tribe, while I remained in the War Department. I was the commissioner on the part of the United States, and, of course, acknowledge my responsibility for its provisions. Instead of requiring a strip to be given to the Indians for their permanent abode, the Indians receded to the United States by treaty a part, and a most valuable part without our ceding an inch to them. The entire line was moved westward, as far as fort Smith, on the Arkansas, and thence by a line due South to Red river. Nor did it make the slightest change in the title to what remained to the Indians, or provided a permanent home for them, as he would have you believe. So much for this charge and its author.

The next is of a kindred character. He states it still more vaguely; so much so, that I am at a loss to know, to which one of the many treaties made with the Indians, about the region in question, he refers. He speaks of a slice forty miles wide and three hundred long, "cut off from Arkansas and given to the Indians;" "that it was done by Indian treaty—treaty made by a protege [James Gadsden] of Mr. Calhoun's;" and adds that I was Vice President at the time, but gives no boundary and avoids naming what treaty it was, with what tribe of

Indians made, or the name of the person he calls my "protege." It is an indictment, without specification of time, place, or circumstances, to which it is impossible to make a specific answer. But, fortunately such an one is not necessary to repel it effectually, without descending into details, which it is fair to presume, were omitted, because they could not be given without exposing the absurdity of the charge. His admission that the treaty was made while I was Vice President, furnishes me with ample means for that purpose.

It is sufficient to repel it, to state, that during the whole period, that I filled the office of Vice President, that of President was filled, either by Mr. Adams or General Jackson, and that it was my fortune to be in opposition to both, and the object of their strong dislike, as must be well known to all. I not only had no influence with either, but was the object of their persecution. My support of any measure or recommendation of any individual, was sufficient to defeat the one, and reject the other; and yet Col. Benton, who is familiar with all this, assumes, in making his charge, that I am responsible, for a treaty made by either one or the other of them, it matters not which. It was going far to make me solely responsible for the acts of administration, of which I was no member; but it makes me responsible, not only for them, but for the acts of those, that were deadly hostile to me, is a piece of extravagance beyond the reach of any individual, but the author of the charge. Even he, in this instance, seems to have a mis-giving, that he has gone too far, and in order to give some colour to so wild a charge, adds, that the treaty, was negotiated by a protege of mine. He must have been a fortunate man bearing that relation to me, to have got an appointment from either of the two administrations. I have examined all the Indian treaties, relating to the region in question, made during their administrations, in order to ascertain, who this lucky individual could be, but have been unable to discover him. There is not a single treaty negotiated, during the period, that was negotiated by any individual, who had any claim to be called a protege of mine.

But why charge me with being the author of a measure, by which these large tracts, sufficient, as he says, to make two States, were lost to the slave States, and given away to the Indians, when the authors of the measures by which they were given away, are known to all, and to none better than Col. Benton. They were the measures of Mr. Adams and General Jackson and their administrations. One or the other made all the treaties by which the old merely possessory titles, of the Indians to their lands, were converted over the whole territory, into a permanent right of possession, and property, and made the permanent home of the Indians, to use his own expression. There was no treaty made while I filled the War Department, in Mr. Monroe's administration, which made any such alterations in the title of Indians to lands west of the Mississippi, or any where else to my knowledge. The making of Indian treaties, containing stipulations for permanent titles, and their removal west of the Mississippi, constituted a large portion of the doings of those administrations, and much of that, on which they rested their reputation. Much the greater part was the work of General Jackson's administration, with which Col. Benton was intimately associated and over which he had sufficient influence to make himself responsible for no small share of its doings, especially as to what related to the West. In attempting now to shuffle off his portion of the responsibility, and that of the administration, and to place it on me, who was hostile to it, speaks badly for his manliness, or regard for the character of the administration of General Jackson, for which he professes so much attachment and admiration. He would hardly have ventured in the lifetime, of "the old Hero," to make the heavy charge he has, against measures, of which he was the author, and on which he so much prided himself.

In his eagerness to assail me, he has lost, not only his discretion, but his memory. In order to make out that the anti-slavery party of the North duly appreciated the great service that I had done their cause, he says "that they gave proof of their gratitude, that I was then a candidate for the Vice Presidency, and became the favorite of the North, beating even Mr. Adams himself on the free soil track," forgetting what he had said just before, that I was Vice President at the time, when he well knew, that I was elected for the first time Vice President with Mr. Adams, and of course, the vote of the North could not have been given me for the reason he assigns.

His next charge is that I supported the abolition of slavery in a State. Among his other traits, Col. Benton is distinguished for charging on others, what he knows he is guilty of himself. Most men from prudence and a sense of propriety, cautiously abstain from assailing others for what they know they may in turn themselves be justly assailed. Not so with him. He is one of the few who are ever more fierce in their assaults when they know they can be assailed for the same thing. They seem to delight in dragging down others to their own level, and to have a concealed joy in thinking that others partake of their own deformity. It is a trait so detestable that those who are distinguished for it are usually likened to a notorious personage reproving sin. Col. Benton has strikingly displayed this trait of character in the present charge. He well knows how utterly false he was to you throughout on the Texas question. He took, as has been stated, an active part to defeat the treaty of annexation, negotiated by me on the part of the United States. He knows that it contained no provisions that countenanced the abolition of slavery in any portion of Texas. I was strongly urged during the negotiation to insert a provision to extend the Missouri compromise line [a]cross Texas to its western boundary, and was informed that it would aid in securing a constitutional majority in the Senate, in its favor. I peremptorily refused. He knows, that he offered a proposition to abolish it in one half of the whole of Texas, and that by a line, not drawn east and west, but north and south, so as to hem in the south on all sides, by surrounding her with abolition States. He also knows, that his friend and supporter, on the occasion, Mr. Hayward [that is, William H. Haywood, Jr.], of North Carolina, went still farther, and offered resolutions to extend the ordinance of 1787, not only over all of Texas, but even all the Territories lying west of Arkansas, and Missouri, and south of 36. 30., with however a proviso excepting the portion of Texas lying south of a line drawn east and west in the 34th degree of parallel of latitude. The presumption is strong that in offering his resolutions, he acted with his friend Colonel Benton, to whose course he adhered on the Texian question. But, be that as it may, certain it is, he sat mute. He raised no voice of indignation, against a measure which proposed to exclude slavery forever from that very region, which he charges me with having given away to the Indians, and losing it to the South. As bad as the policy of Mr. Adams and Gen. Jackson may be, in reference to that region, they did not exclude slavery. The Indians, who occupy it, are slaveholders and having an interest in common with you, may be regarded as faithful allies on that vital question. The resolutions of his friend Mr. Hayward were designed to deprive you of this advantage; and yet Col. Benton now raises his voice in loud denunciation against me upon the false charge of giving away the territory to the Indians, while he approved, at least by his silence of excluding you entirely from the territory, and one half Texas to boot and to extend the principle of the ordinance of [17]87 over the whole, including Texas and the territories. So much for his own position, in reference to the subject of the charge.

It now remains to show that it is, like all his other charges, destitute of foundation. He rests his charge that I abolished slavery in Texas, on the fact that I was then Secretary of State, and that I selected the resolution, as it passed the House of Representatives, instead of the amendment originally proposed by him, as the basis on which to annex Texas. Thus far, he has departed from his usual rule, and stated the facts correctly. I shun no responsibility. I am willing to take the whole on this occasion; but it is due to the President [Tyler] and the members of his administration to say—they were unanimous in favor of the selection made. I not only selected it, but assigned my reasons for making it, in a despatch to our then Minister to Texas, Mr. Donaldson [that is, Andrew J. Donelson]. I assigned them, because I anticipated that there would be an attempt to undo what was done, after the expiration of Mr. Tyler's administration. This I was resolved to prevent, by stating reasons for the selection, that could not be overruled. The attempt, as I suspected, was made, and the late President [James K. Polk] has since been arraigned before the public by two friends and associates of Col. Benton, ([Francis P.] Blair and [Benjamin] Tappan,) because he could not be forced to overrule, what his predecessor had done. The following is an extract from the despatch.

> "It is not deemed necessary to state at large the grounds on which his decision rests. (The President). It will be sufficient to state, briefly, that the provisions of the resolution, as it came from the House, are more simple in their character, may be more readily, and with less difficulty and expense, carried into effect and that the great object contemplated by them is much less exposed to the hazard of ultimate defeat.
>
> That they are more simple in their character a very few remarks will suffice to show. According to the resolution as it came from the House, nothing more is necessary than that the Congress of Texas should be called together, its consent given to the provisions contained in it, and the adoption of a constitution by the people in Convention, to be submitted to the Congress of the United States for its approval, in the same manner as when one of our own territories is admitted as a State. On the contrary, according to the provisions of the Senate's amendment, the Congress of Texas must, in like manner, be convened; it must then go through the slow and troublesome process of carving a State out of a part of its territory; afterwards it must appoint agents or commissioners to meet similar agents or commissioners, to be appointed on our part, to discuss and agree on the terms and conditions on which the State shall be admitted, and the cession of the remaining territory to the United States; and after all this, and not before, the people of the said State must call a convention, frame a constitution, and then present it to the Congress of the United States for its approval, but which cannot be acted on, until the terms agreed upon by the Negotiators, and which constitute the conditions on which the State is to be admitted, shall have been ratified.

That they may be more readily, and with less difficulty and expense carried into effect, is plain from the fact, that the details are fewer and less complex. It is obvious that the numerous and complicated provisions contained in the amendment of the Senate must involve much time and difficulty in their execution; while as to the expense, the appropriation of $100,000 provided for by it, is a clear additional cost, over and above that attendant on the execution of the resolution of the House.

But the decisive objection to the amendment of the Senate is, that it would endanger the ultimate success of the measure. It proposes to fix by negotiation between the Governments of the United States and Texas, the terms and conditions on which the State shall be admitted into our Union, and the cession of the remaining territory to the United States. Now, by whatever name the agents conducting the negotiation may be known—whether they be called commissioners, ministers or by any other title—the compact agreed on by them in behalf of their respective governments, would be a treaty, whether so called or designated by some other name. The very meaning of a treaty is a compact between independent states founded on negotiation, and if a treaty, (as it clearly would be) it must be submitted to the Senate for its approval, and run the hazard of receiving the votes of two-thirds of the members present; which could hardly be expected; if we are to judge from recent experience. This of itself, is considered by the President as a conclusive reason for proposing the resolution of the House, instead of the amendment of the Senate, as the basis of annexation."

The above extract will place you in possession of the leading reasons for making the selection. Events prove that the selection was judicious. Texas was annexed against every effort of open enemies and treacherous friends, both here and there, and the most strenuous efforts to defeat it by England and France, and by it, your weak and most exposed flank was protected against danger from without, and the machinations of abolitionists and their abettors at home. It was a great victory, both for your cause and the country and was felt to be so at the time. That it was due to the selection made, I have the highest authority. Mr. Donaldson, in his letter to me after annexation was achieved, said that any other course, but that pursued, would have defeated it.

But Col. Benton now objects, that the House resolution contained a provision to extend the Missouri Compromise line to the western boundary of Texas, and asserts, that this extension abolished slavery in the State; meaning, as I suppose, that it prevented the introduction of slaves in the portion north of the line, when at the time there were no settlements or slaves. It was not, it seems, the resolution or those who voted for it, and passed it, and among them himself, whose vote could have defeated it, that abolished slavery, as he calls it, but I, who made the selection of the House resolution, in preference to his amendment. The slightest agency it seems on my part, in reference to any measure, makes me solely responsible for the whole. It would be better at once for him to take the ground, that I only am responsible for all the misdeeds of the government, since I came into public life, whether of commission or omission. But what could I do? The President had to act, and to select one or the other resolutions—His or the House. The selection was left to him. If that of the House was tainted by the Missouri Compromise with abolitionism, as he states, his resolution was much more deeply infected. I have his own words for the assertion. He declared, that his amendment, as adopted by the Senate, was the same with the string of resolutions he had introduced at the preceding session, and renewed at the then session. He also declared, that they were generalized and comprised in one, to avoid objections to details. One of this string of resolutions thus covered under general terms, was to divide Texas into two equal parts, by a line drawn North and South, of which the western part was to be subject to the ordinance of [17]87. A measure, coming from a quarter so hostile and accompanied by such a declaration, was justly suspected, as intending mischief. It was so considered, generally, by the friends of annexation in the Senate, and was assented to reluctantly and only because he had a few supporters, who with himself held the balance, and refused to vote for the resolution of the House without the amendment. Among them, if my memory serves me, was his friend Hayward, who was for covering all Texas and the whole region North of 36°30′ with the ordinance of [17]87. *Timeo Deanaos et dona ferentes.*

I come now to the last of his charges; that I abandoned the South, and left him and a few others alone by the side of the ill-fated owners of the [ships] Comet, Encomium, Enterprize, and Creole. He does not state by what act, I abandoned you, but leaves it to be inferred from his remarks, that it was by voting in favor of the Ashburton treaty, which contained no stipulation in favor of the owners of those vessels. It is a trick of his to make his charges very vaguely, so as to make it difficult to detect his errors and repel his slanderous attacks. I admit that I voted for the Ashburton treaty. I did more, I delivered a speech in its favor, which, in the opinion of its friends, saved it from rejection. Its fate was doubtful. The opposition headed by Col. Benton was violent, and it required two thirds to confirm the treaty. I am willing to take whatever share of responsibility he may think proper to allot to me for voting it. I look with no little satisfaction to my course on the occasion, from the belief that I rendered then great & permanent service to the country. For its adoption was the first link, in that series of causes, by which war between Great Britain and us was averted. Who is there now so blind, as not to see, that if the treaty had been rejected, war could not have been avoided? The two countries, were in truth, on the very eve of a rupture, the way events were moving at the time, without either being aware of it. At the very next session the Oregon question for the first time assumed a dangerous and menacing aspect. A bill was introduced immediately after its opening, which covered the whole of that territory, the object of which was to commence systematically, the work of colonization and settlement on our part. I took my seat in the Senate two or three weeks after the commencement of the session, and found the bill on its passage, without opposition, and apparently without division of opinion. I saw the danger to the peace of the two countries, and that the time had come to take a stand to save it. I determined to do my duty, regardless of consequences to myself. I arose, and opposed it, and thereby exposed myself to the opposition of the entire west, which was strongly in its favor. My name then, as well as when the Ashburton treaty was pending in the Senate, was before the people for the highest honor in their gift—placed there, not by myself, but by my friends. Did I then permit the low motive of aiming at the Presidency, to which he attributes my course on the treaty, to sway me from the path of duty?

My stand prevented the bill from becoming a law, and that constituted the second link, in the series of causes, by which we were enabled to avert war between the two countries. Col. Benton then went for the bill, and was I believe for the whole of Oregon. Had the treaty been rejected at the preceding session, the stand I took and the resistance I made to the bill, would have been all in vain. It would have passed, and the country precipitated into war; but as it was, time was gained, which was all important. The agitation, however, was kept up about Oregon, and similar bills were introduced the two succeeding sessions, which failed by small majorities. In the meantime, negotiation was commenced and the claim to the whole of Oregon made. The cry was "all or none," and so strong was the current in its favor, that both parties yielded to it in the early part of the session. I had resigned my seat in the senate, but was re-elected a short time before the session commenced, and took my seat several weeks afterward. I saw and felt the strength of the current, but resolved to breast it, and save the peace of the country if possible.

It was arrested and a counter current created. Col. Benton himself yielded to the counter current, and delivered a speech after the battle was won in which he belabored those who stuck to "all or none" after he found that they were in a minority. It was this chain of causes, of which the Ashburton treaty was the first and indispensable link which averted war, and by it saved the two countries from one of the greatest calamities which could have befallen them, and, I might add, the civilized world. I shall ever remember with proud satisfaction, that I took a prominent lead and a highly responsible part on the side of peace throughout the whole.

I also admit, that the treaty contained no stipulation in favor of the owners of the vessels, nor any to prevent similar outrages in future. It was an objection, and I admitted it to be so in my speech in favor of it, not a sufficient one to induce its rejection. But, although the treaty contained no stipulations to guard against like outrages thereafter, much, nevertheless, was done in the negotiation to prevent them, and to place the south on much more elevated ground in reference to the subject, than where it stood, when the negotiation commenced. To understand how much was done towards this, a brief statement of facts, connected with the case of those reports [*sic*; vessels], is necessary.

They were all coasting vessels having slaves on board, and were all either stranded in their voyage from the Atlantic ports to those on the Gulf on the British possessions, Bermuda and the Bahama Islands, or forced to put into their ports by stress of weather to save themselves from shipwreck, or were carried in by the rising of the slaves and taking the vessel into port. Their fate was the same. The slaves were liberated, under circumstances of more or less violence and indignity, by the local authority. The outrage was enormous, and the insult to the American flag great. The first occurred as early as the year 1830, and all under the administration of General Jackson or Mr. [Martin] Van Buren, except the Creole. Application was made to the Executive by the owners for redress. After a feeble and tame negotiation of many years, the British Government agreed to compensate the owners in the case of the Comet and Encomium, but refused to make any in that of the Enterprize, on the ground, that the two first occurred before her act of abolishing slavery had gone into operation, and the other after it had. The Administration (Mr. Van Buren's) accepted the compensation and acquies[c]ed in the refusal, in the case of the Enterprize, without remonstrance or protest, and thus waived our right and admitted the absurd and dangerous principle, on which the refusal was placed.

What the Administration shamefully omitted to do, I resolved to do through the Senate, if possible, and with that view, and in order to perpetuate our claim of right I moved in the Senate, in 1840, the three following resolutions, and succeeded in passing them by a unanimous vote, with some slight amendment, Col. Benton voting for them, but not standing by me, as he says, for he never uttered a word in their support:

> "*Resolved,* That a ship or a vessel on the high seas, in time of peace, engaged in a lawful voyage, is, according to the laws of nations, under the exclusive jurisdiction of the State to which her flag belongs; as much so as if constituting a part of its own domain.
>
> "*Resolved,* That if such ship or vessel should be forced by stress of weather, or other unavoidable cause, into the port of a friendly power, she would, under the same laws, lose none of the rights appertaining to her on the high seas; but, on the contrary, she and her cargo and persons on board, with their property, and all the rights belonging to their personal relations, as established by the laws of the State to which they belong, would be placed under the protection, which the laws of nations extend to the unfortunate under such circumstances.
>
> "*Resolved,* That the Brig Enterprize, which was forced unavoidably by stress of weather into Port Hamilton, Bermuda Island, while on a lawful voyage on the high seas, from one part of the Union to another, comes within the principle embraced in the foregoing resolutions; and that the seizure and detention of the negroes on board by the local authority of the Island, was an act in violation of the laws of nations, and highly unjust to our own citizens to whom they belong."

Such was the condition in which the administration of Mr. Van Buren left these outrageous cases. They never were brought to the notice of the public, and the principle first contended for was surrendered, and that maintained by Great Britain in the case of the Enterprize acquiesced in; and, of course, all claims of compensation on the part of the owners rendered hopeless. The following administration had nothing to stand on, but my resolutions and the vote of the Senate in their favor. If then "the ill fated owners" were sacrificed, it was not by me. Their case was rendered hopeless by the preceding administration, with which Mr. Benton was intimately associated, and in which he acquiesced; for he never raised his voice in their favor, in the long period of ten years, during all which time his voice might have been potential. I turn now to explain what was done in reference to this subject by the negotiation, which ended in the Ashburton treaty, and how much the South, which he accuses me as having abandoned, has gained by it. For that purpose I insert an extract from my speech on the treaty.

> "Such was the state of the facts, when the negotiations commenced in reference to these cases; and it remains now to be shown in what state it has left them. In the first place, the broad principles of the law of nations, on which I placed our right, in my resolutions have been clearly stated and conclusively vindicated in the very able letter of the Secretary of State, which has strengthened our cause not a little, as well from its intrinsic merit, as the quarter from which it comes. In the next place, we have an explicit recognition of the principles for which we contend, in the answer of Lord Ashburton, who expressly says that, "On the great general principles, affecting this case," (the Creole) "they do not differ["]; and that is followed by "an engagement that instructions shall be given to the Governor's of her Majesty's Colonies, on the Southern borders of the United States, to execute their own laws with careful attention to the wishes of their government to maintain good neighborhood; and that there shall be no officious interference with American vessels driven by accident or violence into their ports. The laws and duties of hospitality shall be executed." This pledge was accepted by our Executive, accompanied by the express declaration of the President, through the Secretary of State, that he places his reliance on those principles of public law which had been stated in the note of the Secretary of State."

Here we have a positive acknowledgement of the principle, which the administration of Mr. Van Buren had abandoned[,] and a pledge that necessary measures would be taken to prevent similar occurrences in future, and the laws and duties of hospitality be executed. Now when I add, that all this, thus far, has been faithfully executed, I may assert with truth, that you gain much, far more than I had hoped, considering the state, in which the subject had been left by the preceeding administration. So much for the charge, that I had abandoned you on the occasion, and the assertion of Col. Benton that he had stood by "the ill fated owners."

I have now repelled all the charges, intended to shake your confidence in my fidelity to you, in reference to the most vital of all subjects to the South. I have shown that they all rest either on statements that are utterly false, or conclusions that are entirely erroneous or inconclusive. I have also shown, that Colonel Benton has involved himself at every step, in false statements, contradictions, inconsistency and absurdities. I will not say, that he made his charges knowing them to be false; for that would brand him as a base calumniator and slanderer; But I will say he ought to have known they were. It may be, however, that he was too much blinded by his passions and prejudice or lacked the discrimination to perceive they were.

I have passed over all that was directed against me personally, and not intended to impeach my fidelity to you and your cause; because it did not fall within the reasons, which induced me to notice him at all. I have also passed over the torrent of abuse, he has poured out against me; not only for the same reason, but because I deem it beneath my notice. He doubtless thinks differently, and regards it, as the finest portion of his speech; for he had used expressions, which pretty clearly indicate, that he anticipates, it will raise him to the level of the great Athenian orator, for indignant denunciation. He mistakes his fate. He will be fortunate, should he escape sinking to the level of Thersites. He seems, not to apprehend, that the difference is wide between the indignant eloquence of patriotism and truth and scurrilous defamation. I also pass over his attack on the Southern Address, because it has been too generally read, and is, too well understood, by you for him to do any mischief by assailing it. The wonder is, that he should venture to make an attack in open day light. The remote twilight region of the past, lying between truth and fiction best suits his taste and genius.

Passing all these by, I am brought to where he throws off his disguise, and enters the camp of the enemy and openly proclaiming himself an abolitionist, endorses all their doctrines, and steps forth as their champion. In that character, he assumes a dictatorial air, and pronounces that it is absurd to deny the power of Congress to legislate as it pleases, on the subject of slavery in the territories; that it has exercised the power from the foundation without being questioned, until I introduced my resolutions; that slavery is local in its character; that it must be created by law, and cannot be carried an inch beyond the limits of the State that enacted it; that slaves cannot be carried into New Mexico or California because the Mexican laws abolished slavery there and are still in force, and concludes, that it is a mere abstract question of no importance, because the people there, and especially the foreigners, are opposed to it and will not permit you to emigrate into the territory with your slaves.

I do not propose to enter into a formal repetition of assertions so ostentatiously pronounced. It is not necessary. They were the same that were put forth and relied on by those opposed to you in the discussion on the Oregon territorial bill, during the session preceding the last; and which were then fully met and refuted by me and others, who took your side of the question. What I now propose is a very summary and brief notice of these several assertions.

I begin with that which asserts, that Congress has the power to do, as it pleases, upon the subject of slavery in the territories. I deny the assertion and maintain that Congress has no such power over slavery there or elsewhere, or over any other subject. I deny that Congress has any absolute power whatever; or that it has any of any description except, such as are specifically delegated, or that are necessary and proper to carry them into execution. I maintain, that all its powers are delegated and trust powers, and not positive and absolute, and that all of the latter description, belongs exclusively to the people of the several States in their sovereign character. I also hold, that Congress is but their representative and trustee, and that in carrying into execution its powers, it cannot rightfully exercise any inconsistent with the nature and object of the trust, or with the character of the party who created the trust, and for whose benefit it was created. I finally hold, that instead of having the absolute power over the territories of doing as it pleases, that Congress, is restrained by all these limitations, and that its power to exclude you from emigrating with your slaves into them, cannot be maintained without denying that ours is a government of specific powers; that it is a Government of which States and not individuals are the constituents, and that Congress holds its powers as delegated and trust powers. Nor can it be maintained, without assuming that ours is a consolidated Government, and holds its powers absolutely in its own sovereign right of doing as it pleases.

I also deny, the truth of his next assertion, that it has exercised the power over the territories, as it pleased, without being questioned until I introduced my resolutions. I maintain on the contrary, that such power never was exercised by Congress, until he and his associates, passed the Oregon territorial bill. That was the first bill containing the Wilmot Proviso, that ever passed, as has been stated—passed solely to assert the the [*sic*] absolute right of [Congress] doing as it pleases. All others, including the ordinance of 1787 were passed as compromises which waived the question of power, as has been frequently shown. Nor is his assertion more correct, that the power never was questioned, until the introduction of my resolutions. It was questioned from the start, beginning with the ordinance of 1787. Mr. [James] Madison pronounced that it was adopted without a shadow of right. Since then, it has been acquiesced in not as a right, but as a compromise until the North refused all compromise, and forced the South to stand on its rights, where it should have stood from the first.

The next assertion, that slavery is local in its character; that it must be enacted by law, and cannot be carried an inch beyond the limits of the State, that enacted it is, equally unma[i]ntainable. It is clear that in making it, he intended to affirm, that in these respects, property in slaves stands on very different ground from every other description of property.

I deny the fact, and ma[i]ntain that there is no distinction between it and other property, in that respect. It no more requires to be enacted by law, or to express it more specifically—to have a positive enactment for its origin, than property in land or any thing else. The relation of master and slave was one of the first and most universal forms in which property existed. It is so ancient, that there is no record of its origin. It is probably more ancient than separate and distinct property in lands, and quite as easily defended on abstract principles. So far from being created by positive enactment; I know of no instance, in which it ever was, or to express it more accurately, in which it had its origin in acts of legislatures. It is always older, than the laws which undertake to regulate it, and such is the case with slavery, as it exists with us. They were for the most part slaves in Africa, they were bought as slaves, brought here as slaves, sold here as slaves, an[d] held as slaves, long before any enactment made them slaves. I even doubt, whether there is a single State in the South, that even enacted them to be slaves. There are hundred[s] of acts that recognize and regulate them as such, but none, I apprehend[,] that undertake to create them slaves. Master and slaves are constantly regarded as pre-existing relations.

Nor is it any more local in its character, than other property. The laws of all countries, in reference to every thing, including property of every kind, *are local* and cannot go an inch beyond the limits to which the authority of the country extends. In case of property of every description, if it passes beyond the authority of the country where it is, into another, where the same description of things are regarded as property, it continues to be so there, but becomes subject to the laws and regulations of the place in reference to such property. But, if it be prohibited, as property, in the country into which it passes, it ceases to be so, unless it has been forced in, under circumstances which placed it under the protection of international laws. Thus, one and the same principle apply in this respect to all property; in things animate or inanimate, and rational or irrational. There can be no exception; as property every where, and of every kind, is subject to the control of the authority of the country. Thus far, I hold, that there can be no reasonable doubt.

Nor can there be any, that the same principle applies between the several States in our system of government. Slaves or any other property carried into a State where it is also property continues still to be so; but if into one, where it is prohibited, it ceases to be property. This is admitted too, by all. It is also admitted by all, that the general government cannot overrule the laws of a State, as to what shall or shall not be property, within the limits of its authority. The only question then is, what is the power of the general government where its authority extends beyond the limits of the authority of the States, regarded in their separate and individual character? or to make it more specific; can it determine what shall, or shall not be property in the territories, or wherever else its authority extends, beyond that of the States separately? or to make it still more so, can it establish slavery in the territories? can it enact a law providing that any negro or mulatto found in the territories of the United States shall be a slave and be liable to be seized, and treated as such by whoever may choose to do so? According to Col. Benton's doctrine that Congress may legislate as it pleases, upon the subject of slavery in the territories, it would have the power, but I doubt whether there is another individual, who would agree with him. But, if it has not the power to establish slavery in the territories, how can it have the power to abolish it? The one is the counterpart of the other, and where is the provision of the Constitution to be found which authorizes the one and forbids the other?

The same question may be propounded as to public and private vessels belonging to the United States and their citizens on the high seas; for the principle, which applies to the territories, equally applies to them, and to all places, to which the authority of the general government extends, beyond the States regarded separately.

It is, indeed, a great misconception of the character and object of the general government, to suppose that it has the power either to establish or abolish slavery, or any other property, where its authority extends beyond the limits of the States regarded individually. Its authority is but the united and joint authority of the several States, conferred upon it by a Constitution, adopted on mutual agreement, but by the separate act of each State, in like manner in every respect, as each adopted its own separate constitution, with the single exception, that one was adopted without, and the other on mutual agreement of all the States. It is then, in fact, the Constitution of each State, as much so as its own separate Constitution, and is only the

Constitution of all the States, because it is that of each. As the Constitution made the general government, that too is, in like manner, as much the government of each State as its own separate government, and only the government of all, because it is the government of each. So likewise are its laws, and for the same reason. Its authority, then, is but the united and common authority of the several States, delegated by each to be exercised for the mutual benefit of each and all, and for the greater security of the rights and interest of each and all. It was for that purpose, the States united in a federal union, and adopted a common Constitution and government. With the same view, they conferred upon the government whatever power it has of regulating and protecting, what appertained to their exterior relations among themselves and with the rest of the world: Each, in brief, agreed with the others, to unite their joint authority and power to protect the safety and rights and promote the interest of each by their united power.

Such is clearly the character and object of the general government, and of the authority and power conferred on it. Its power and authority, having for its object the more perfect protection and promotion of the safety and rights of each and all, it is bound to protect by their united power the safety, the rights, the property, and the interests of the citizens of all wherever its authority extends. That was the object for conferring whatever power and authority it has, and if it fails to fulfil that, it fails to perform the duty for which it was created. It is enough for it to know, that it is the right, interest, or property of a citizen of one of the States, to make it its duty to protect it whenever it comes within the sphere of its authority; whether in the territories, or on the high seas, or anywhere else. Its power and authority were conferred on it, not to establish or to abolish property, or rights of any description, but to protect them. To establish or abolish belongs to the States, in their separate sovereign capacity—the capacity in which they created both the general and their separate State governments. It would be, then, a total and gross perversion of its power and authority to use them to establish or abolish slavery or any other property of the citizens of the U. States, in the territories. All the power it has, in that respect, is to recognize as property there, whatever is recognized as such by the authority of any one of the States, (its own being but the united authority of each and all of the States,) and to adopt such laws for its regulation and protection as the state of the case may require. Nor is there the slightest danger, that the recognition of the property of citizens of each and all the States within the territories, would turn them into a babel, as Col. Benton contends. All may co-exist without conflict or confusion, by observing the plain and simple rule of duty and justice.

There is another error akin to this, that the Mexican law abolishing slavery is still in force in New Mexico and California when not a particle of its authority or sovereignty remains in either. Their conquest by us & the treaty that followed extinguished the whole, and with it, annulled all her laws applicable to them, except those relating to such rights of property and relations between individuals, as may be necessary to prevent anarchy; and even these are continued only by *sufferance* and on the implied *authority of the conquering country and not the authority of the conquered,* and only from the necessity of the case. Her laws abolishing slavery, are not embraced in the exception; and if it were, it would be taken out of it, as the assent of Congress could not be implied to continue a law, which it had no right to establish.

But still higher ground may be taken. The moment the territory became ours, the Constitution passes over and covers the whole with all its provisions, which, from their nature, are applicable to territories, carrying with it, the joint sovereignty and authority of each and all the States of the Union, and sweeping away every Mexican law, incompatible with the rights, property, and relations, belonging to the citizens of the United States, without regard to what State they belong, or whether it be situated in the northern or the southern section of the Union. The citizens of all have equal rights of protection in their property, relations and person in the common territories of each and all the States. The same power, that swept away all the laws of Mexico, which made the Catholic religion, the exclusive religion of the country, and which let in the religion of all denominations, which swept away all the laws prohibiting the introduction of property of almost every description, some absolutely and others under the condition of paying duties, and letting them in duty free until otherwise provided for, swept that which abolished slavery, and let in property in slaves. No distinction can be made between it and any other description of property or thing consistently with the Constitution and the equal rights of the several States of the union and their citizens.

But we are told by Col. Benton, that the question has become a mere abstraction of no importance; that few have gone into either territory, except citizens of the north and foreigners; and that they are all opposed to us. What insult! What? taunt us by telling us we cannot go into them, because foreigners and others who have been let in freely, and we kept out by the threat of confiscating our property by himself and his associates, have become sufficiently numerous to keep us out, without the intervention of Congress to aid them! He knew that "property is timid" and could be kept out by threats, and that to keep us out for a short time was one of the ways to exclude us ultimately. What a comment on the equity and justice of the government, that we, who have so freely spent our blood and treasure to conquer the country, should be excluded from all its benefits, while it is left open for the use and enjoyment of all that rabble of foreigners, which he enumerates with such zest, as the efficient means of our exclusion. Is there another instance of such an outrage to be found in the history of any other government that ever existed?

His avowal of the doctrines of the abolitionists, will have an effect, he little suspected, when he made it. It furnishes ample evidence to show that he used deception in assigning his reasons for declining to obey the instructions of his [Missouri] legislature. It will be remembered, he offered as his reasons, that their resolutions instructing him were borrowed from mine, and that mine were introduced for disunion purposes, and that there was no difference between them, except that mine aimed directly at disunion, and theirs ultimately at the same thing. He added in effect, that his devotion to the Union would not permit him, to vote for resolutions so deeply tainted with disunion. That was at the commencement of his speech. We now have in its conclusion conclusive evidence from himself, that all this was a mere *fetch*, a stratagem to conceal his real motive for declining to obey them. His real motive, as it now appears was that he could not vote for them under any circumstances, for how could an abolitionist as he avowed himself to be, possibly obey resolutions, which are utterly at variance with their doctrines. To obey would have involved him in palpable contradiction, so much so, that it could not fail to prostrate, and to overwhelm him with shame if he is not to shame invulnerable. This he saw, and that he had no alternative left, but to resign or disobey. He determined in favor of the latter; but this of itself, did not relieve him of his dilemma. He knew well, that it would defeat his object to come out boldly, and say that he had abjured his former creed and adopted that of the abolitionists. And hence, he was forced to adopt some other expedient; and for that purpose, adopted the miserable pretext of slanderously charging me and my resolutions and his own legislature and their resolutions with disunion, and of assigning that as his reason for not obeying them, when he knew that his position made it impossible for him to obey them. But these are not the only resolutions adopted by the Legislature of his State to instruct him. The previous Legislature adopted two others, of which he says, that they truly express the sense of the State, and that he obeyed them, not only in their letter, but spirit. They are in the following words:

> "*Resolved,* That the peace, permanency and welfare of our national Union depend upon a strict adherence to the letter and spirit of the 8th section of the act of Congress of the United States, entitled, 'an act to authorise the people of the Missouri territory to form a constitution and State government for the admission of such State into the Union on an equal footing with the original States, and to prohibit slavery in certain territories;' approved March 6th 1820."
>
> "*Resolved,* That our Senators in the Congress of the United States are hereby instructed, and our representatives requested to vote in accordance with the provisions and the spirit of the said 8th section of the said act, in all the questions which may come before them in relation to the organization of new territories or States, out of the territory now belonging to the United States, or which hereafter may be acquired either by purchase, by treaty, or by conquest."

It is proper to observe, that the 8th section to which they refer contains the Missouri compromise, which established 36.30., as the dividing line between the slave-holding and non-slaveholding States, drawn between the western boundary of the State of Missouri and the western boundary of Louisiana. These resolutions he says he obeyed, in letter and spirit, when in fact he flagrantly violated them, by his vote for the Oregon territorial bill, prohibiting slavery in that territory, without any compromise annexed; and that too to assert, the principle of unlimited power of Congress over the territories, and in open defiance of all compromise. He calls that bill *his* proviso, and well he may, for he passed it, when it was in his power to defeat it. A very few remarks will suffice to show that I have not expressed myself stronger than truth warrants.

The first resolution asserts "that the peace, harmony [*sic*], and welfare of our national Union depends upon a strict adherence to the letter and spirit["] of the Missouri compromise, and the last instructs their Senators and representatives *to vote in accordance with its provisions and spirit in all questions which may come up before them* ["]*in relation to the organization of new territories or States*, out of territories now belonging to the United States, or which hereafter may be acquired." No instruction could be more full or explicit, or assign stronger motives for obeying them, especially to one professing so great a devotion to the Union. There is no mistaking the meaning. He is instructed to vote for all bills in reference to the territories which may conform to the letter and spirit of the Missouri compromise, and against all that do not; that is, to vote for all that extend the line westward from its terminus on the western boundary of Texas, for that is its letter; and to secure to the South that portion of the territory lying on the Southern side of the line, as effectually as that compromise did in fact, all, the territory which lay on its southern side, and to vote against all bills, that did not, for that is meant by its spirit. There was good reason to put in "spirit," for it was understood then, that the doctrine began to be broached, that the laws of Mexico abolishing slavery would continue in force, unless they were repealed, if not prevented by some effectual guard. No additional remarks can make his disobedience more clear, and he now stands condemned for disobeying the instructions of his legislature, which he himself praises, and which he does not even pretend to charge with disunion.

I notice in the progress of this communication, that Col. Benton evinced unusual solicitude to confound the Missouri compromise and all other compromises of the kind, with the Wilmot Proviso. I attribute it, in part, to a desire to screen himself from the odium of having voted for the Wilmot Proviso, by confounding it with other measures, that were far less offensive; but I said, that there was another more powerful reason, which would be explained in the sequel. That reason was to shelter himself, if possible, against the charge of violating instructions, which he acknowledged to be above exception. If he could possibly establish that the Missouri compromise and the Wilmot Proviso were identical, as he would have his constituents believe, to obey the one would be to obey the other. But I have shown that was impossible, and thus he is left, without the possibility of escaping the charge of disobeying them.

With a few additional remarks, I shall close this long communication.

Col. Benton assigns devotion to the Union as his motive for taking the course he has; and by implication, charges yours, as being the side of disunion, and his and the abolitionists' that of union. In this, he but follows the example of all who have betrayed you; or intend to betray you. It is so common, that it has become notorious, that a strong profession of attachment to the Union and condemnation of what is called the violence and ultraism of the South, accompanied by a volley of abuse of me, and the absence of all censure or condemnation of your assailants are certain signs, that he who utters them is ready to seize the first opportunity to desert your cause.

To these signs may be added another—an appeal to that portion of the farewell address of the Father of his country [George Washington], quoted by Col. Benton, under circumstances, which make its application apply to you, and not to those who assail you. I respond to every word it contains, with a hearty amen. It is indeed deeply to be deplored, that parties should be designated by geographical position, and I regard whatever party or individual may have caused it, as deserving of public reprobation. But to avoid geographical designation of parties, it is indispensable that each section of the Union, should respect the rights of the others and carefully abstain from violating them. Unless that is done, it will be impossible to avoid it—aggression will, and ought to lead to resistance on the part of those whose rights are trampled upon and safety endangered. Sectional assault on one side and sectional resistance on the other, cannot fail to lead to sectional designation of parties. The blame and responsibility rightfully falls on the section that assails, and not that which repels assaults. Which that is in the present case, admits of no doubt. The South has been on the defensive throughout, and borne for a long series of years, indignities and encroachments on its rights and safety with a patience unexampled, and yet she is basely charged with disunion, and the North lauded as its advocate. We must learn to disregard such unfounded and unjust charges, and manfully do our duty, to save both the Union and ourselves, if it can be done consistently with our equality and our safety; and if not, to save ourselves at all events. In doing so we should but follow the example of our Washington in the great struggle, which severed the union between the colonies and the mother country. He was ardently attached to that Union, struggled hard to preserve it by resisting the encroachments of Parliament on the old and established rights and privileges of the colonies, but the folly and infatuation of Parliament, and the vile machinations of tories among ourselves, rendered all his efforts and those of the patriots of his day, unavailing. The world knows the consequence. My sincere prayer is, that those who are encroaching on our rights—rights essential to our safety, and more solemnly guarantied than those of the colonies may, as well for their sakes as ours, profit by the example. J.C. Calhoun.

PC in the Pendleton, S.C., *Messenger*, July 13, 1849, pp. 1–4; rough autograph draft in ScCleA; PC in the Columbia, S.C., *Daily Telegraph*, July 16, 17, 18, 19, 1849; PC in the Charleston, S.C., *Courier*, July 17, 1849, pp. 2–3; PC in the Charleston, S.C., *Evening News*, July 17, 1849, pp. 2–3, and July 18, 1849, p. 2; PC in the Charleston, S.C., *Mercury*, July 17, 1849, p. 2, and July 18, 1849, p. 2; PC in the Camden, S.C., *Journal*, July 18, 1849, p. 2, and July 25, 1849, pp. 1–3;

PC in the Greenville, S.C., *Mountaineer,* July 20, 1849, pp. 1, 4, and July 27, 1849, pp. 1, 4; PC in the Laurensville, S.C., *Herald,* July 20, 1849, pp. 1–3, and July 27, 1849, pp. 1–2; PC in the New York, N.Y., *Herald,* July 21, 1849, pp. 1–2; PC in the Washington, D.C., *Daily National Intelligencer,* July 21, 1849, pp. 2–3; PC in the Washington, D.C., *Daily Union,* July 22, 1849, pp. 1–2; PC in the Richmond, Va., *Enquirer,* July 24, 1849, pp. 2, 4; PC in the Edgefield, S.C., *Advertiser,* July 25, 1849, pp. 1–2; PC in the St. Louis, Mo., *Republican,* July 28, 29, 30, 1849; PC in the Jackson, Miss., *Mississippian,* August 3, 1849, pp. 2–3; PC in the Springfield, Mo., *Advertiser,* August 11, 1849, pp. 1, 4, and August 19, 1849, pp. 1–2; PC in *Mr. Calhoun's Address to the People of the Southern States* [Charleston: A.J. Burke, 1849?], a 15-pp. pamphlet; PC in *Mr. Calhoun's Reply to Col. Benton* [Pendleton, S.C.: printed by Pendleton *Messenger*?, 1849], a 25-pp. pamphlet; PC in *Address of the Hon. John C. Calhoun, to the People of the Southern States; and Letter of Gen. Lewis Cass to Mr. [Thomas] Ritchie* ([St. Louis]: St. Louis Union Job Printers, n.d.), pp. 1–20; PEx's in the Alexandria, Va., *Gazette and Virginia Advertiser,* July 21, 1849, p. 2; PEx's in the *National Era,* vol. III, no. 30 (July 26, 1849), p. 119; PEx in the Spartanburg, S.C., *Spartan,* July 26, 1849, pp. 1, 4, and August 2, 1849, pp. 1, 4; PEx in the Vicksburg, Miss., *Tri-Weekly Sentinel,* August 7, 1849, pp. 2–3.

From Rose [O'Neal] Greenhow

Washington, Friday July 6th 1849

My dear Sir, I cannot resist the desire to write to you although I have in truth scarcely an excuse for trespassing upon your time—but having had contradictory accounts of your health I feel very anxious to hear directly from yourself. I trust that your healthful and pure pursuits may invigorate you for the arduous duties of the coming season. Indeed I wish that the crisis did not demand your presence in our National Councils, I always feel anxious about you in a stormy and exciting session, such as the next bids fair to be from present indications.

'Tis said here that the [Zachary Taylor] Administration will support the Wilmot Proviso, their policy so far as regards the exercise of the appointing power favors such a conclusion. Their papers all support [Thomas H.] Benton and ["publish" *altered to* "republish"] everything laudatory in regard to him. The [Washington] Union has decidedly improved of late, and the change is no where more perceptible than in regard to yourself. In publishing Benton[']s speach, they omitted the part most offensive towards you—that was it is true caused by the advice of Mr. [James] Buchanan who was here at the time, he said that you and himself had been seperated upon some points but he had no doubt that you would both be together upon the trying questions of the day and spoke very handsomely of you. Mr. [Thomas] Ritchie is now disposed to defer to your wishes and views in a great measure, he told me that his paper was open to you in any way. But at the same time said, that his position was a delicate one, that although he was thoroughly aroused to the importance of the present political crisis, that though all his sympathies were in the cause of the South—he had been advised that it would defeat his usefullness to the cause, by taking too decided a partizan part in the questions at issue, as the other portion of the ["Democratic" *altered to* "Democracy"] are only waiting the moment to establish an out and out free soil paper here; [Edmund] Burke so far seems to lean to the Southern side, Mr. Ritchie says that he is decidedly so in his feelings.

Mr. Ritchie addressed me a note last evening wishing to know whether I had heard from or could give him any information in regard to your views or wishes. My devotion to you and the interests ["to" *canceled and* "you" *interlined*] sustain may pardon my presumption in offering myself as a medium of communication, should you desire it, indirectly, or otherwise, with the Union or others—the same feelings being a guarantee for discretion.

Mr. [Isaac E.] Holmes has been here and I think discovers that he has committed a blunder in his unqualified devotion to the no party President, as yet the phials of his wrath are poured out upon the Cabinet or Regency for it is nothing else. H[is] E[xcellency, Taylor] declares that he was elected by the Whigs to carry out Whig measures—so far he certainly has respected most faithfully his obligations to that party for no one has received an appointment for other than brawling party service while they do not even attempt to play the farce any longer of requireing qualifications. Their Organs openly justify such a policy and proclaim the intention to act upon it. For my part I long to escape from this infected political atmosphere—else to plunge more deeply into it. Nothing would please me better than that my husband [Robert Greenhow] should be connected with a newspaper at this time. I cannot say what our prospects are in regard to the appointment. [John M.] Clayton [Secretary of State] appears very favorable towards Mr. Greenhow—commends his great talents and acquirements[,] says that he has a right on account of his services &ca but I cannot bring myself to give faith to the sincerity of this just appreciation. It is said that the Premier[']s aspirations are already directed towards the Presidency hence all his patronage will be used for that end.

Our City continues healthy there are as yet no certain cases of

Cholera—it has been very fatal in Richmond almost causing an entire cessation of business—we have been greatly injured by it Mr. Greenhow's property being in the centre of the town has been deserted by the tenants—tis extending on the James River. Mr. Carter has been obliged to abandon his harvest which was never finer. Mr. Greenhow has been quite ill but is somewhat better, his has been an affection of the head attended with great prostration. Mr. Greenhow joins in best wishes to yourself & family. I remain dear Sir with affectionate regard, Rose Greenhow.

ALS in ScCleA; PC in Boucher and Brooks, eds., *Correspondence*, pp. 513–515.

[To George W. Crawford, Secretary of War], 7/9. An entry in a register of letters indicates that Calhoun's letter of this date presenting "the application of I.M. Holmes a Sapper & Miner at West Point for his discharge," was received. The letter was referred to the Engineer Office. Entry in DNA, RG 107 (Secretary of War), Registers of Letters Received by the Secretary of War, 1800–1870, 70:C-143 (M-22:70).

To "Col." C[OLLIN] S. TARPLEY, [Hinds County, Miss.]

Fort Hill, July 9, 1849

Dear Sir: I am greatly obliged to you for a copy of the proceedings of your (Mississippi) meeting [sent with your letter of 5/9]. I have read it with a great deal of pleasure.

You ask me for my opinion as to the course which should be adopted by the (Mississippi) State Convention, in October next. I have delayed answering your letter until this time, that I might more fully notice the developments at the North before I gave it. They are more and more adverse to us every day. There has not been a single occurrence, since the rising of Congress, which does not indicate on the part of the North a fixed determination to push the abolition question to the last extreme.

In my opinion there is but one thing that holds out the promise of saving both ourselves and the Union; and that is a Southern Convention, and that, if much longer delayed, cannot. It ought to have been held this fall, and ought not to be delayed beyond another year. All our movements ought to look to that result. For that purpose, every Southern State ought to be organized, with a central committee, and one in each county. Our's is already. It is indispensable to produce concert and prompt action. In the mean time, firm and resolute resolutions ought to be adopted by your's and such meetings as may take place before the assembling of the Legislatures in the fall. They, when they meet, ought to take up the subject in the most solemn and impressive manner.

The great object of a Southern Convention should be, to put forth in a solemn manner the causes of our grievances in an address to the other States, and to admonish them, in a solemn manner, as to the consequences which must follow, if they should not be redressed, and to take measures preparatory to it, in case they should not be. The call should be addressed to all those who are desirous to save the Union and our institutions, and who, in the alternative, should it be forced on us, of submission or dissolving the partnership, would prefer the latter.

No State could better take the lead in this great conservative movement than yours. It is destined to be the greatest of sufferers if the abolitionists should succeed; and I am not certain but by the time your Convention meets [in Oct.], or at farthest, your Legislature, that the time will have come to make the call. With great respect, I am, &c., J.C. Calhoun.

PC (from the Jackson, Miss., *Southron*) in the Washington, D.C., *Daily National Intelligencer*, June 4, 1850, p. 3; PC in the Nashville, Tenn., *Republican Banner and Nashville Whig*, May 27, 1850, p. 2; PC in the Nashville, Tenn., *Daily Union*, May 28, 1850, p. 2; PC in the Alexandria, Va., *Gazette and Virginia Advertiser*, June 5, 1850, p. 2; PC in the *National Era*, vol. IV, no. 24 (June 13, 1850), p. 96; PC in the Sumterville, S.C., *Black River Watchman*, July 13, 1850, p. 1; PC in *Congressional Globe*, 32nd Cong., 1st Sess., Appendix, p. 52; PC in *Publications of the Southern History Association*, vol. VI (September 1902), pp. 415–416; PEx in H. von Holst, *John C. Calhoun* (Boston: Houghton Mifflin & Co., 1882), pp. 326–327; PEx in Cleo Hearon, "Mississippi and the Compromise of 1850," *Publications of the Mississippi Historical Society*, vol. XIV (1914), p. 62; PEx in Dunbar Rowland, *History of Mississippi, the Heart of the South* (2 vols. Jackson, Miss.: 1925), 1:712. NOTE: This letter later became the object of controversy concerning the motives behind the Nashville Convention of June, 1850. In a speech in the Senate on 12/18/1851, Henry S. Foote of Miss. charged Calhoun with instigating the movement for a Southern Convention and with hiding its ultimate purpose–disunion–from the Miss. delegation. As proof, Foote referred to the letter to Tarpley which he had placed on record. For a rebuttal, see Tarpley's letter of 5/16/1850 to the editors of the Jackson, Miss., *Mississippian* (weekly), May 17, 1850, p. 2.

To Sam[ue]l Treat, [St. Louis]

Fort Hill, 9th July 1849

My dear Sir, Your letter found me engaged in preparing a communication in reference to Col. [Thomas H.] Benton's speech. It is in the hands of the editor of our Village paper, & will appear Friday next. It is addressed to the people of the South, and is confined to repel such of his charges, as are intended to impair their confidence in my fidelity to them & their cause; but I have used the occasion to turn his battery against himself, not, I trust, without effect. I will transmit a copy to you as soon as it appears, and hope it will be published in all your sound papers. It would be impor[tant] for it to appear in one, or two of the leading whig papers, if admittance can be had. It is, I would say, about as long as his speech.

I greatly regret your retiring from your editorial duties, & still more, the cause that made it necessary. Never before were there such momenteous events approaching. I am glad to learn, that the Democratick press of your State is so sound, and to learn, that one will be shortly established in St. Louis.

I am of the impression, that Benton's calculation on the whigs will fail him. Insuperable difficulties, as it strikes me, stand in the way of union between them; & among them, not the least, is the jealousy, which will be excited against him on the part of their leaders. They play with him & laud him for a time; but his will be the fate of traitors. He will find to his sorrow, that they love the treason, but hate the traitor. It is well, that he has left us. He has been false to the South for the last ten years, and can do us much less injury in the camp of the abolitionists, than he could in our camp.

He does not believe a word he says about disunion. The South, I mean the slave holding States, are the only portion of the country, that has a real & sincere attachment to the Union—the Union established by the Constitution. There is no better proof, that this is understood, than is afforded by the strong appeal made to it by Col. Benton & all other traitors to our cause, who hope to conceal their treason by the cry of disunion. With great respect yours truly, J.C. Calhoun.

ALS in MoSHi, Judge Samuel Treat Papers. Note: Treat left an undated memorandum with this letter: "The enclosed letter from John C. Calhoun in 1849 shows his views . . . . Struggle at that time was to suppress the causes of conflict between the North & South. . . . He was no disunionist or Secessionist . . . . His prognostication failed and the Civil Conflict came." (DU in MoSHi).

From D[avid] L[evy] Yulee, [Senator from Fla.]

St. Augustine [Fla.,] July 10, 1849

My Dear Sir, The overt treason of [Thomas H.] Benton & [Henry] Clay, and the coalescing process going on in the Northern States between the Free Soil & Democratic organizations, added to the now manifest indifference of the President [Zachary Taylor] & probable hostility of his Cabinet, brings ["us" *interlined*] to a point at which it seems to me the Southern States must decide their course without further delay. To palter any longer with the question is to surrender—and surrender involves not disgrace only, but ruin also.

It would ["appear" *interlined*] from the indications upon the political surface that as far as California is concerned, it ["seems" *canceled*] is expected by our enemies and the idea is said to be encouraged by the administration, that a State organization in that territory, & the presentation of a State constitution and Representation at the next session will settle all differences—and that the South will accept this evasion as an adjustment. For one I cannot. It is but one of the modes, and a most effective one, of sealing our exclusion from these territories, before our immigrants have had time to reach their destination and establish their due influence in the direction of affairs there. But if even the South was willing to fall asleep in the lap of the Delilah of the North, and allow her locks to be shorn and her power dissipated by the addition of a new free State, and the consequent irreversible supremacy of Northern power in the Union—there are other issues preparing against us which we must meet. Nothing can be more plain than that the extinction of slavery in the District of Columbia, and of the inter State Slave migration, and, if Northern politicians can arrange it, Canadian annexation, are to rise into the consequence of distinct political issues. The North I fear is to be embodied against us. We can only meet her by embodying the South in unmistakable unity of action. How is this to be done? We have treacherous influences in our midst to subdue, and an indifference amounting to apathy to be overcome. Yet I believe the mass of the South is prepared for the course of duty. Some mode of eliciting the manifestation of public mind, & of concentrating its purpose & efforts, is essential—and that before the next meeting of Congress. I doubt if the occasional meetings which occur in the Southern States having reference to the subject (& far different from the organized movements in your State) will answer the purpose. They have probably done all the good which can be expected from isolated action.

Some movement of a more systematic and pervading character it seems to ["me" *interlined*] ought now to be resorted to. Are you prepared to advise? What ought the South to do? To what point should we direct our steps?

A convention of this county will meet next month to consider our Federal relations—and it is not unlikely its proceedings will have some share in influencing the tone of the rest of the State. It seems like a vain vaporing to meet & resolve what our rights are, unless we at the same time resolve to resist ["their" *canceled*] ag[g]ression ["of them" *interlined*], and proceed *to do so*—for the aggression is impending! Besides I think the people can best be aroused by a *call to action.* But how to act? What to do? That is the point to be considered. Shall we shape our action to the contingency of a convention of the Southern States, or of a Convention of the United States. If the first shall it be a convention based upon popular appointment, or regular State appointment—that is to say, by primary meetings, or the more imposing ["form of" *canceled*] act of the ["State" *canceled*] Legislatures of the States. If to the last (a convention of the United States) shall we move it at this or a later stage of the issues. Or is there any mode of action which is to be preferred. For myself, convinced that the inevitable alternative, if our honor is to be preserved, is an amendment of the compact of Union, or its dissolution, I am quite prepared to meet the issue in this shape at once. As I once before remarked to you there is an elementary antagonism in the social structure of the two sections which will render their continued political connection as equals impracticable, unless by some amendment of the Constitution a check can be provided against the aggressions of the more powerful northern section of the States. I am willing to try if such an amendment is practicable, but failing in this, I think the truest and best policy is to take steps at once for a separation. We must have domestic security, and fireside peace. We must hold and enjoy our customs and property in tranquility. If the Govt. of the Union cannot exist consistently with these primary necessities, it fails of one of the first purposes of Govt. and should be abandoned. Our institutions or the Union must yield, if the North presses her advantage under the compact. We must change our social or political structure. We must abandon Slavery or the Union at once (unless the terms of compact can be amended)—for the attempt to maintain both will only be to whet a knife for the throats of our families & selves.

The Independence of the Pacific States might solve the difficulty, so far as the accession of those States to the Northern Power is concerned—and I am nearly prepared to say I w[oul]d recommend & sustain them in an independent organization. This w[oul]d relieve us of the Wilmot Proviso question for the time and by crippling the Northern Power and arresting its unrestrained ascendancy in the Federal Legislature, postpone any dangerous collision, until by the division of Texas, and the possible acquisition of ["Texas" *erased*] Cuba, we might be in a position to check any such increase of free States as would settle their preponderance in the Government.

These are very crude reflections—thrown out hastily. To return to the object of this letter. We rest upon your wisdom to advise the South properly in this our great emergency. Are you prepared to advise—or would you prefer more time.

Perhaps preliminary to a Southern Convention, or to Southern action, a consultation between the States should take place. Several modes occur to me for effecting this. The Governors of the several Southern States might be recommended by their several constituencies to assemble at some convenient point to consult and advise a course—or a convention in each State might as in So. Ca., organise a central committee of vigilance—and these committees from the several States might assemble together for ["general" *interlined*] consultation—or a few leading spirits ["in" *canceled and* "from" *interlined*] each State might meet by private arrangement to confer together, & devise some systematic movement—or we might organise a State Rights Republican party, and hold a National Convention—admitting all States from which Representatives subscribing to our tenets might come, for the purpose of erecting a platform of State Rights as antagonist to the Buffalo platform. ["All" *canceled and* "Most of" *interlined*] the Southern Democrats, a large part of the Southern whigs, and a considerable strength from the free States might thus I think be embodied in what would eventually become the renovated Republican party. We *must* have some distinctive organization by which we may *be seperated* from the enemies of the Rights of the States, whether those enemies claim to be democrats, whigs or abolitionists.

Mrs. [Nannie Wickliffe] Yulee desires to be kindly remembered to your family, and with assurance of my esteem I am Respectfully Y[ou]r friend & Serv[an]t, D.L. Yulee.

ALS in ScCleA; PEx in Boucher and Brooks, eds., *Correspondence*, pp. 515–517. NOTE: An AEU by Calhoun reads, "Mr. Yulee."

From H[ENRY] S. FOOTE, [Senator from Miss.]

Washington, July 16th 1849

My dear Sir: I have just received your very gratifying letter. To receive communications from *such* a quarter, is worth more to me than golden treasures. Every day, for the last week, I have gone over the City in quest of your letter, ["in reference to (Thomas H.) Benton" *interlined*] but as yet it has not come to hand. The [Washington] Union has agreed already to publish it; & I shall visit the [Daily National] Intelligencer office in person and demand its publication so soon as I know it to be in town. All here are looking for it with the most intense eagerness; & I am of opinion that it will be just in season. Last mail brings me three letters from [David R.] Atchison; he is in high spirits, & says, "old Bullion" will be beaten; but they are to have a hard struggle. I hope your letter will render the [*sic*; *one word and* "of" *canceled*] it a more easy task than he anticipates, to overthrow this Arch-Traitor & crush him for ever.

I have a letter from Gen. [Lewis] Cass denouncing Benton in the strongest terms, & renewing his pledge to stand by us in defeating the Wilmot Proviso & all kindred measures. Never, in my time, has the South been so united; thanks to the much-denounced Southern Address!

I shall go to Mississippi, by earnest request of some of my constituents, in time to attend our October Convention. Meanwhile, I have received letters from leading Whigs & leading Democrats, desiring advice as to what it will be most wise for them to do in Convention, & urging me warmly to consult with you in regard to this matter, & let them know what you counsel without delay. If your mind is made up in reference to ulterior movement, & you ["to" *canceled*] choose to communicate to me freely on the subject, either confidentially or otherwise, I will not fail to convey information to those desiring it. If you judge it best, to defer coming to a definite conclusion in regard to *ultimate* measures, you will of course pursue that course. I hope though, at all events, you will in some shape or form, put me fully in possession of your views, at an early moment, so that no blunder may be committed in my own State.

If you will do me the honor to look over my poor eulogy upon Mr. [James K.] Polk, delivered here a few days ago, you will find some allusion to the pending struggle between Northern *factionists* & Southern *patriots* with which I hope you will not be displeased. Most cordially, your friend, H.S. Foote.

ALS in ScCleA.

From H[ENRY] S. FOOTE

Washington, July 17th 1849

My dear Sir: So soon as I received your letter, that is to say, on the same day, I made a courteous but pointed application in writing to [Joseph] Gales [Jr.] & [William W.] Seaton, desiring[?] the publication in their columns of your address immediately on its reception. I received the enclosed reply [*not found*]. Your address has not yet arrived. We are all impatient to see it. I fear very much that I shall have to loose a very early perusal of it, in consequence of a flight from the Cholera to the mountains of Virginia, which I contemplated making on Friday next.

I hope, at your earliest leisure, you will give me your views touching the course to be pursued in our [Mississippi] Southern Convention which will assemble in October. If you could accompany me to our Capitol of Jackson & see our people face to face I would gladly be your escort. At any rate I must be possessed of your views touching the ultimate action of the South, in certain events, before I go to Mississippi. *Harmony*, & absolute *concord* on this subject, are of the highest importance.

If you write to me, shortly, direct to Warrenton, Va. I remain most cordially, H.S. Foote.

ALS in ScCleA.

From F[RANKLIN] H. ELMORE

Charleston, July 19, 1849

My Dear Sir, I have this moment rec[eive]d yours of the 16th & the inclosure from Dr. [Daniel] Drake [*not found*].

I also rec[eive]d yours [*not found*] covering the letter from Mason[?], & immediately set afoot inquiries for such a man as would suit, intending to write to you as soon as any thing definite could be ascertained. I was so unsuccessful that I have waited longer than I had any idea of—in fact my Dear Sir, the Bank Committee have so absorbed me that I have been forgetful & inattentive to a degree that I must really ask your indulgence for.

Your reply has satisfied every body. It is most happy & conclusive. We shall publish a great many pamphlet copies of ["(Thomas H.) Benton's speech" *canceled*] your reply & a statement of [James] Gadsden (the "Protegee") who made the Creek treaty he ["Benton" *interlined*] denounces. Gadsden['']s statement will be as strong against Benton, as most of your own.

It was most unfortunate that Mr. [Joseph A.] Scoville['']s letter to me & his package for the [New York] Herald, were by some unhappy mistake, sent through Charleston, to Washington, & then returned here. They were only received when the [Pendleton] Messenger reached us with your reply. Mr. Head the agent here for the Herald, offered the Telegraph $200 to send it on a-head of the papers, which they declined—indeed they could not have done it.

23d [July]

The Committee arrested me at this point of my letter & I was unable to resume it—not being able in my present state of health to do half my usual work. I cannot write at night, except occasionally & always suffer from it after.

We had at first thought of publishing Benton['']s speech along with your reply, but I am not sure we shall do it. There is much of his, attacking you on points which you have disposed of by former refutations that might be misunderstood by those who have not read those refutations or have forgotten them, that it is perhaps better to omit his speech & I think that will be our conclusion.

I rejoice very much that you have sent out this paper. It is not only good for yourself but for the Southern cause & comes at a good time—just before the summer & fall elections.

It will especially come in happy time to the aid of [David R.] Atchison [Senator from Mo.], who will want all the help he can get. I feel most anxious for his success in Missouri. If the slave States continue as they have begun &[,] like Virginia, sweep off the faithless Representatives whose timidity or treason abandoned you in the Southern Address, we may hope for justice. Otherwise I see little hope except in actual resistance—sooner or later.

The visit of Mr. Scoville was a surprise to me & an agreeable one. I saw in it evidence that our movements were producing impressions & that through him & the Herald a great deal might be accomplished in bringing Northern men to their senses. I write to him today but not knowing where he is I send my letter under cover to you, as he requested. In my letter I have briefly touched some points with a view to attract his attention & in hope they may serve as heads for him. Pray read my letter & forward it if he has left you & you know where to send to him.

I have been so intirely occupied in my own affairs & those of the Bank, since I saw you that I have neither had time or spirits for any other than the work of absolute necessity—and of that I have had enough in my disabled condition, to work me down. Had it not been so I would have written to you before the meeting at Columbia & asked your views. I would be glad now to hear what you think of what we did. I regretted the call was made—and yielded reluctantly to its being held. I went to it with fear & anxiety—but I believe no harm has come of it.

The Bank Committee, engaged in investigating it, has been in session since the middle of May, sifting & searching into every thing—weighing every paper & security & submitting all the[m?] to the severest tests. Of course I do not know their conclusions, except in a general way, that they admit that the debts are good & the Bank sound. My own summing up is that there are not $50,000 of bad debts & scarcely $50,000 more for doubtful. In any judicious mode of winding up its affairs, there would not I think be so much lost. To balance this there are arrears of interest perfectly good to probably all that would be lost in the above estimate, while there are gains on lost circulation to full $250,000. To establish this we have the tables of circulation showing the issues of every plate & denomination & the amount of each issue returned & cancelled. One of these will illustrate. The issue of small change, under $1. This begain [*sic*] in 1815, & was suppressed in Dec[embe]r 1833 by Act. All were called in & as rec[eive]d cancelled. There are now unredeemed $78,000. That these are lost & therefore a gain we have the evidence, that we do not get in one a month—for several years they have almost intirely ceased to appear.

The objections against the solvency of the Bank & its profitableness must go by the Board. So far it has paid every cent of public debt charged on it to $5,000,000, for prin[cipal] & int[erest] besides $590,000 into the Treasury & it has yet to pay prin[cipal] & int[erest] $4,000,000 charged on it by *contract with the public creditors.*

There seems to me a madness in Mr. [Christopher G.] Memminger[']s scheme of winding up this bank, which, in the present condition of our Federal Relations, to say nothing of the domestic bearing of the question & its effect on the character & faith of the State, is most mischievous. If the South, if our State is driven to resistance[,] how is she [to] stand up without her finances in order & her people with a stable condition in their affairs? If this Bank is put in liquidation, who, that knows the course of such things, can fail to see, that it will necessarily produce vast derangement[?] It will not be the settling up of one Bank but of all; & of all credits to a great degree. It will, too, occur, just when the State will most want confidence & resource for her struggle. Where is she to go for aid in such an event? In the nullification contest every Bank in the State was against her—and will they be otherwise if a collision were to come with the Gen[eral] Gov[ernmen]t? Will they not rather anchor under the guns of the greater power & not merely with[h]old aid but actually join the enemy?

The Bank of the State alone stood true to the Palmetto Colors—and would be alone or nearly so, if such another issue came. It would seem to me, to destroy it now would be as wise as it would be to burn one[']s house at the beginning of winter or to draw our shot when going into battle.

But I had no intention of throwing this subject before you & don[']t know how I have got into it, except that my mind is just now filled with the Bank on one side & the Southern questions on the other. But as I have touched it, allow me to send you a compilation of the Bank Laws, Reports &c. You may find occasion to think on the subject & desire to examine the documents.

If you write me soon, please direct to Columbia—& if not before the 1 Aug[us]t to Limestone Springs. Yours truly, F.H. Elmore.

P.S. I had forgotten Dr. Drake[']s letter. Col. Gadsden & myself have consulted & think we can venture to publish extracts—in such way as not to commit the Doctor to any disagreeable notori[e]ty.

ALS in ScCleA.

From R[OBERT] B[ARNWELL] RHETT

July 19th 1849

My Dear Sir, I congratulate you on your successful vindication of yourself from the malignant aspersions of [Thomas H.] Benton, in connexion with the Southern Address and your still more successful conviction of Benton himself of his long practical treason to the South. His hatred of you, I really believe arises more from the conviction, that your influence in the South was adverse to his schemes of self-exaltation at the expense of our honour and safety than from any other cause. But whether his ambition or his enmity has drawn him in opposition to your course, his influence in the South must now be gone—or the South is gone. If an avowed enemy to our institutions can keep himself in the confidence of the Southern People they are self-destroyed. But I hope for far better things. Benton as a

Southern Statesman, is killed. Congress will not pass the Wilmot Proviso or any kindred measure, altho' there will be no end to anti-slavery aggressions in some form or other. The expedient which we will next have to meet, to master us will be admitting Free-States and excluding Slave-States from the Union. Here they will act within the Constitutional competency of Congress, and if submitted to with fatal effect. On the present issues, the South will triumph—but all such victories, only shift the ground of battle, with encreased strength to our foes, and encreased weakness to us. On this account, I am sorry to come to the conviction that there is no chance for the Wilmot proviso, or the abolition of Slavery in the District of Columbia at the approaching Congress. Would to God, they would do both, and let us have the contest, and end it once and for ever. It would then accomplish our emancipation, instead of that of our Slaves. But the Northern Statesmen will commit I am satisfied no such blunder. We are put off to another and more formidable contest.

I had determined to write something exposing Benton[']s inconsistency & treason, but you have done it so much better than I could do that I shall attempt nothing. I wrote however the Editorial in the Charleston Mercury recommending and commending your Reply.

Wishing you a happy summer, Believe me Dear Sir, Yours most truly, R.B. Rhett.

ALS in ScCleA; PEx in Boucher and Brooks, eds., *Correspondence*, pp. 517–518.

From H[ERSCHEL] V. JOHNSON, [former Senator from Ga.]

Milledgeville, Ga., July 20th, 1849

My Dear Sir, The perusal of your reply to Col. [Thomas H.] Benton has afforded me the most heartfelt satisfaction. It is so lucid, so simple and yet so powerful, and so overwhelming, that it will produce a deep impression upon the country, and consign your insolent assailant to that infamy which traitors deserve. I have read it, and thrice read it; and there is but a solitary remark which I would be willing to see stricken from it. That is[,] "If it did not," (i.e. Texas did not extend to the Rio Grande) ["]the war stands without justification. If it did not, the march of our army to the Rio Grande was an invasion of ["a" *interlined*] neighbouring country unauthorised by the Constitution or Law." I have always differed with you on this subject. I believe the war can be triumphantly vindicated, even admitting that Texas did not extend to the Rio Grande. Still your remarks on this point, in exposition of Benton's inconsistency are strictly true and unanswerable. The only reason I have for feeling any regret at the expressions above quoted, is, that I fear there may be those so very sensitive of Mr. [James K.] Polk's reputation, that they will seize hold of it, with the view, if possible, of arraying the prejudices of that class of politicians against you. I feel nothing of this myself, and I can fully appreciate the honesty, with which you entertain your opinions, in reference to the war. But who can satisfy captious faultfinders? No one need attempt it. Your reply will win its way to victory, against all prejudice and silly hypercriticism. Truth is mighty and will prevail. The press, thus far, has spoken of it in terms of unqualified approbation. I trust the South will be awakened from her lethargy.

Our Democratic State Convention came off, according to appointment on the 11th, inst. It was ["a" *interlined*] very large assemblage and distinguished for weight of character and intelligence. For the sake of harmony, the subject of the Southern Address was not touched. It would have torn us to atoms, without giving us any strength. We adopted the Virginia Resolutions unanimously; and I think we went a little further on the doctrine of non-interference, than any other Convention in the South (except Carolina) has gone. We not only denied the power of Congress to establish or prohibit slavery in the territories, but denied also the power to ratify any act of a territorial legislature having such an object. There is much excitement in the Democratic party of this State upon the slavery question. The great mass is obviously with the signers, and in order to remove the distrust, which the non-signers feel is felt towards them, there was no hesitation in adopting the Virginia Resolutions.

But notwithstanding these demonstrations, I entertain gloomy forebodings. I seriously fear, that the people of the South are not properly awake to the danger—not thoroughly nerved to united resistance.

What do you think will be the course of the next Congress? It is said that Gen. [Zachary] Taylor has sent on a Commissioner to California to urge and assist the people to make a Constitution preliminary to admission into the Union. If this be true, it shadows forth pretty distinctly, the policy of the administration. It will be to bring in California & thus avoid the Wilmot Proviso. In the consummation of this policy the non-signing Democrats will vigorously co-operate. This is but a circuitous mode of cheating the South out of her rights and gaining the object of the Provisoists. But how can we help ourselves? Suppose California presents her Constitution at the next session and demands admittance, how can the South object? We admit the right of the people in forming a State Constitution to establish or eschew slavery. Then, ought we to oppose and how? But California being admitted, what becomes of New Mexico? It still leaves the question all open. It seems to me, that before the South consents to the admission of California, we ought to demand a just compromise as to New Mexico, and a total abandonment on the part of the North, of their aggressions in respect to the District and slavery in the States. Now is the time for a settlement in full. If we yield now, we are gone. Concession will invite further insult; and we shall ultimately lose our self respect & become worthy of our degraded fate. How dark the future looks! If you have time drop me a word on these points. I want light and desire to know the views of our sage statesmen. Very Sincerely Yours &c, H.V. Johnson.

ALS in ScCleA; FC in NcD, Herschel V. Johnson Papers, Letterpress Book, pp. 47–50; PC in Jameson, ed., *Correspondence*, pp. 1197–1199; PC in Percy Scott Flippin, ed., "Herschel V. Johnson Correspondence," *North Carolina Historical Review*, vol. IV, no. 2 (April, 1927), pp. 190–192; PEx's in Flippin, *Herschel V. Johnson of Georgia*[,] *State Rights Unionist*, pp. 24–25.

From F[itz]w[illiam] Byrdsall

New York [City,] July 23d 1849

Dear Sir, I have just read your Address to the people of the Southern States, to the gratification of both heart and mind. While it will command the attention and consideration of the World, it is at this crisis peculiarly precious to the Southern patriot. There is not a weak point in it that I could discern, nor one that is not of interest not only as a masterly vindication of yourself, but also as throwing great light upon our political history and therefore of especial importance to the Historian, which in my view is one of its greatest merits.

The opening of the address is so correct in feeling, so expressive of gentlemanly propriety that I cannot convey my appreciation of it. Never was a shameless traitor, an overweening egotist more properly dealt with, or his misrepresentations and effrontery more effectively exposed. When I read his Jefferson speech, it presented to me so much personal abuse, so much evidence of his own baseness of feeling that I did not see how you could handle so much rubbish without going into the same channels and becoming soiled. In frankness, ["for your sake," *interlined*] I felt chagrined that his attack upon you was not better and decenter, so that you ["could" *interlined*] answer him as a decent antagonist. This was my misconception. The result shews that a base enemy can be overthrown without any sacrifice of self respect or loss of personal dignity.

The New York Herald and Ev[ening] Post has published the address entire—the Courier—the Express—the Commercial give numerous extracts. The Post announces it also in pamphlet form, if I like the form, I shall send you a few Copies for your own use. There is every prospect of its being extensively read in whole or in part all over the United States. It cannot do otherwise than good any where.

If you could travel incognito in this part of the world, you would find more inconsistencies in politicks and religion, than is reconcileable with rationality. Men who consider their right to lands and other property as perfectly sacred, entertain a species of holy horror at the idea of slave holding, wholly unaware that both kinds of property are held by the conventional arrangements of society. They prate about the declaration of Independence and bring up the plea of natural rights not aware that the phraze natural rights expresses a compound of physical force and moral principle, in other words Natural might and moral right. It is the biggest fact in the history of man that every people or nation has as good a government—as much life[,] liberty and pursuit of happiness as it is fit for, or qualified to ["attain" *canceled and* "exercise" *interlined*]. I admit that our system of Government is wiser and better than ourselves, because the founders who had the political power of the country in their hands, were more virtuous[,] more enlightened than the bulk of the people who wield by suffrage the political power in these days. It is with individuals as it is with nations—shew me the man who is mentally inferior to his fellows and I will shew you that he is a slave to others in some form or other. Who can deny that it is not naturally right that he should be governed by those whose mental and moral attributes are greater than his? It is by the same right that God himself governs.

The religious world is as full of inconsistency and error as the political. The peaceful teachings of the Gospel are abandoned to get up a crusade of falsehood[,] slander[,] dissention[,] disunion throughout the confederacy, in short the press[,] the pulpit[,] the monarchists[,] the aristocrats[,] the demagogues of Europe and the

Northern States are as zealously engaged in the work of wickedness as if they were serving both God & man. And yet they are no friends of the negro—Dogs[,] cats[,] any kind of animal may ride in stages & rail cars with white people here but not the negro. He has no real friends but in the Southern States—and the records of our courts and prisons here—the census prove that his condition South is the best for him on this Earth untill his Creator shall bestow upon him higher endowments.

Never had a people so much to contend for as those of the Southern States at the present time. There is not an interest[,] a consideration[,] a right dear to the heart of man that is not endangered. Every right of property, family, race, home, country is involved in the contest of Equality of constitutional right. If this Equality cannot be maintained there remains no alternatives but separation of the confederacy, or Abolition of Slavery.

You have argued the matters of rights of property and of the Constitution in a manner not thought of by the northern mind. It ["the northern mind" *interlined*] is rapid and ready but not profound and unfortunately has little deep seated regard for principle, but it seems to me that your address must tend to give it a right direction upon the points you have treated. Such an Exposition was much needed and it has come at a good time. I have the gratification to be Yours with all respect, F.W. Byrdsall.

ALS in ScCleA.

To A[NDREW] P[ICKENS] CALHOUN, [Marengo County, Ala.]

Fort Hill, 24th July 1849

My dear Andrew, I have not heard from you since I received your letter of the 3d June [*not found*]. I wrote you several weeks since informing you that our note in bank (State bank) would have to be renewed on the 14th Inst., and requested you to send me your name in blank for the purpose. I have got no answer, but fortunately Mr. [Robert A.] Maxwell has not applied to me to give any[?] note for the sum deposited with me to be applied to our engagements, & I used the remaining blank, reserved for him, to the renewal of our note. Without it, I would have been left in an awarked [*sic*; awkward] condition, and our credit [have] been exposed at at [*sic*] a critical moment, when an enquiry was going on into the condition of the bank. I have received nothing since I wrote you originally from Dr. [Ozey R.] Broyles, or Mr. Maxwell, and had to advance the sum necessary for the two last renewals. You must not fail to send your note in blank on the [first opportunity] as I know not when Mr. Maxwell may ["wish" *canceled and then interlined*] to have our note for what he advanced. You had better send three at once; One for his; and two for the two renewals in Charleston of our note, one on the 14th Sep[tembe]r & the other on the 14th Nov[embe]r. By that time, or at least before I ["go" *canceled*] start for Washington, I trust I may be in funds from him & Dr. Broyles, to apply ["to the pa" *canceled*] towards the payment of the note. The latter speaks with confidence as to being in funds.

I fear you have had an excess of rain and that cotton is, in consequence, overgrown. We have had incessant & often heavy rains, since the last of April; & I see no prospect of its termination. It is now clowdy & misting, with a fair prospect of the continuance of the wet spell. My corn is very fine, where not injured by excess of moisture. It is the best I ever had. It will go round[?], I think, fully 40 bushe[l]s. The cotton is large & looking well, except on sandy soil & low places. Much of it is nearly breast high & is bolling well. The prospect is good; but from all I can learn it is far from being the case in the State. The prospect is good, I think, for a fair price. I would not be surprised, if cotton average 10 cents next year, unless the prospect is better in the West, than we are lead to believe.

I hope your prospect is good. Let me hear, as I am anxious to learn, both as to that & the health of the place. We all remain very healthy.

I sent you a [Pendleton, S.C.,] Messenger, containing a copy of my communication in reference to [Thomas H.] Benton's speech. I hope you have received it; and trust it will be extensively circulated in the South West. It will be published in all our papers.

It is high time the South should begin to prepare. I see no hope of bring[ing] the North to a sense of justice, but by our united action, and for that purpose, a Convention of the South is indispensable. To that point our efforts should be directed. The first step towards it ["is" *interlined*], to put an end to the old party divisions; which might be effected by an understanding between ["the" *canceled*] a few prominent leaders ["on both sides" *interlined*], and short & well written articles throug[h] the leading presses of both parties, showing the folly & danger of continuing [*one word or partial word canceled*] our party warfare when our existence is at stake. The next step is an organization of all the Southern States as has been done in this State. The convention ought to be held before the meeting of Congress, but that, I take it, is impracticable. It ought to [be] called before the year ends, to meet next summer. The call ought to be addressed to the people of the South, who are desireous of saving the Union and themselves, if the former be possible; but who, at the same time a[re] prepared, should [the] alternative be forced on us, to resist rather than submit. ["Should" *canceled and* "Such" *interlined*] a call could not fail to secure a large delegation from every Southern State, & what is important, a harmoneous one, on the essential point. The call might be made by the members of the Legislatures of one or ["two" *canceled and* "more" *interlined*] Southern States, or by the members of Congress from the South, when they meet in Washington. The call itself would have a powerful effect on Congress. Could not Alabama be induced to make the call[?] Atlanta would be a good point for the meeting.

I am making good progress in the work I have on hand. I have finished the ["elementary" *canceled*] Discourse on the elementary principles of Gov[ernme]nt and have made considerable advance in the Discourse on our system of Govt. The work ["will" *interlined*] hit the lines both here & in Europe; and, I think, cannot fail to make a deep impression. I hope to have it completed before I leave home; and intend to take it with me to put to press in New York [City], early next year. I would ["be" *interlined*] glad to show it to you & have your opinion ["on" *interlined*] it before I publish.

John [C. Calhoun, Jr.] was Married on the 3d to Miss [Anzie] Adams, as I suppose you have seen by the papers. He & his wife & William [Lowndes Calhoun] left for Battleburgh [*sic*; Brattleboro, Vt.] shortly after; he to obtain a more thorough knowledge of the water cure prospect, & William to try its effects on his health, which is not good. He has never fully got over the attack & the affect of the medicine he took during ["his" *canceled*] the ["severe" *canceled*] attack two years ago. It affects his studies, though he in spite of it, stands at the head of his class. James [Edward Calhoun] is with us. He stands high in College, & seems to be very study [*sic*] & economical.

All join their love to you, Margaret [Green Calhoun] & family. Your affectionate father, J.C. Calhoun.

ALS in NcD, John C. Calhoun Papers; PEx in Jameson, ed., *Correspondence*, pp. 769–770.

From John D. Hyman

Milwaukee Wis. July 24th 1849

Sir, The subscriber is not acquainted with you personally—but he adores your name. He is a citizen of Wisconsin, but is a Southerner in birth, education, & feeling: having been borned in N. Carolina & educated in her University. He is a young man just of age, & is desirous of making the best use of his time. Will you do him a favor by hinting what law books are best, as also those extraneous to his legal studies. He has read [Joseph] Story on constitutional law, but is loth to subscribe to all his tenets. Should the undersigned be favored by a few hints from you, as he trusts he may, he will prosecute them to the letter, as emanating from the highest authority in the Union. With Profound Respect & Reverance, Jno. D. Hyman.

ALS in ScCleA. Note: An AEU by Calhoun reads, "Mr. Haymond."

To Prof[esso]r [Francis] Lieber, [Columbia, S.C.]

Fort Hill, 24th July 1849

My dear Sir, I am of the opinion it would be better to delay application in favour of your son [Hamilton Lieber] until I go on to Washington.

Drop me a line about the time I will arrive there, to remind me of it, as it might possibly escape my recollection.

I have not yet received the opinion of the Jud[g]es in the case you refer to. When I get it I will send you a copy. Truly, J.C. Calhoun.

ALS in MH.

From J[ames] F. Simmons

Office of the Weldon Herald
Weldon North Carolina, July 24th 1849

Honored Sir, I cannot permit the opportunity to pass without, offering my hearty congratulations on the able & forcible manner in which you repelled the attack of the Missouri Senator [Thomas H.

Benton]. I send you (directed to Fort Hill S.C.) a copy of my paper in which you will see my opinion pretty plainly expressed. Though occupying a position in a different political party from that with which you have been identified, I have ever regarded you as one of the purest men of the times & I see nothing to cause me now to change that long cherished opinion; on the contrary, the eminently able document which has called forth this letter has greatly *strengthened it.* Till within the last twelve months I have never had the honor of an acquaintance with, or even a sight of you, but it has not been for the want of the desire. I have read all your speeches that I could get (& I regret to say they were far from all you have delivered) and whilst following your beautiful, forcible & patriotic thoughts of course I could not but feel the strongest desire to see & know him who gave them utterance.

You know me Mr. Calhoun, & when you come to know me better, ["which I hope you will," *interlined*] you will be satisfied that I speak only what I feel & think. I know that the good opinion of one so humble as myself is too small a thing to be prized by a great man, but I still desire to make it known to you at the same time that I offer my congratulations for your able & successful refutation of Benton's charges.

Could I receive a letter from you in reply I should be happy to know that mine was not deemed entirely unworthy of notice. With sentiments of high regard Sir: Y[ou]r most ob[edien]t s[er]v[an]t, J.F. Simmons.

N.B. If you have any copies of speeches delivered by you, *old or new*, I would thank you for *all* you can spare & will have them bound in a volume. J.F.S.

ALS in ScCleA. NOTE: James Frederick Simmons (1826–1905) founded the Weldon *Herald* in his native N.C. while in his early twenties. He was subsequently a planter in Miss., a Major in the Confederate Army, and had two collections of his poems published by J.B. Lippincott & Co. of Philadelphia in 1881 and 1885.

From W[ILLIA]M PINKNEY STARKE

Charleston S.C., July 24, [18]49

Dear Sir, It was perhaps my duty to have answered your last favour. Two circumstances restrained me from doing so, the first was that I had nothing worth communicating to you, and secondly, I feared to intrude myself upon your labours by what might have been regarded as an attempt to force you into a correspondence. I cannot however restrain the expression of my gratification at your castigation of the Missouri Apostate. Had the contest been between equals, either in character or reputation I should have commenced by congratulating the victor in a controversy so entirely unsought for on his part. As it is, the rejoicings of all true Southern men at the issue must be tempered by regret that at this imminent crisis so few should be found wil[l]ing and capable of effectually seconding you. It does appear to me that each last effort of yours always excels whatever before had come from under the same pen.

This attempt of [Thomas H.] Benton to poison the minds of the people of the South against you is so natural that its ["prof" *canceled*] prototype may easily be found: indeed it has been generalized in the expressive wisdom of ancient fable. The wolf in order to seize the sheep had first to breed in their minds a distrust of their long-tried and natural protector.

On every side we have notices of critical action about to take place in the body politic—signs of an effort being made to throw off disease. It may be for our ultimate good. The human system never gives way under fever—as ["so" *canceled*] long as there is febrile action (to follow the simile) there is hope: death is only to be ["feared in" *canceled*] dreaded in the deceitful quiet of incipient mortification.

I called on your son Dr. John C. Calhoun on his way to the North. He looks improved.

If my brother shall not have left home on my arrival there I shall propose to send him on to Brattleboro [Vt.]. I saw myself in the [Charleston] Mercury, a fortnight since, in some articles on steam navigation between Charleston and Liverpool. The careless typographer, however, marred the image so much as to make me look somewhat distorted. I hope you continue to improve and with high regard as ever Am Sir Your obedient & humble Serv[an]t, Wm. Pinkney Starke.

ALS in ScCleA.

From R[ICHARD] K. CRALLÉ

Lynchburg [Va.], July 25th 1849

My dear Sir: I received last night, and read with great pleasure your reply to [Thomas H.] Benton. An extract from it had previously reached us; and expecting the residue, a large number of persons gathered around the Post Office on the arrival of the mail on yesterday. Curses, deep and bitter were uttered against the Traitor; and some who, for years, have been your steady enemies, came up to congratulate me on the triumphant defense. It seems to me that it must surely overwhelm the scoundrel even in Missouri. In this State I am sure he will not have an advocate, whatever may be the effect of his desertion in the free States. But even there it seems to me his piratical cruise will not be rewarded with a single prize. It is obvious that neither [Lewis] Cass nor [Martin] Van Buren are prepared to give way—especially in favour of one who, in the effort to intrude on their own peculiar territory, hazards if do not sacrifice his title to his own. He has undoubtedly overreached himself; and his fate will be as you predict; tho' from present appearances, it is to be feared he will carry his own State. What effect your reply will have there remains to be seen. It will certainly weaken him no little.

I was at first inclined to think that you should not dignify him with a notice; but subsequent reflection convinces me you have pursued the right course—*placing the reply on the grounds you do.* In this aspect the subject is divested, in a great measure, of its mere personal character and bearing, and brings up to view more distinctly to the public the true issue which lies behind the gauze-work of the scoundrel's malignity. I think it will, more than any other Paper the public has yet seen, bring the People to consider the true question which is pending—a question not between Whig and Democrat, but between the *North* and the *South.* I hope it will tend no little to unite and consolidate public sentiment in the latter; tho' this, in the present state of Parties, seems almost impracticable. As to Virginia, I am almost hopeless. The *interests* of the leaders of both Parties are indissolubly connected with the Federal *Treasury*—and, of course, opposed to the assertion of any principles, or the adoption of any course of action which, by hazarding what they call "*the Union,*" put in jeopardy their hopes of preferment and plunder. It is not their *patriotism,* but their *love of pelf* which would prompt them to submit to any and every usurpation and outrage, rather than hazard their chances of advancement. These, through the machinery of Party, have got the People under absolute controul. The course of the last Legislature was, I fear, a mere *ruse de guerre*—a manouvre of Party. Neither Party acted in good faith; and neither I fear will venture to come up to the principles avowed in the Resolutions. Indeed, had the action on the Resolutions been postponed until after the result of the meetings in Washington were known, I am sure they would not have received the votes of a dozen Whigs. On the other hand the design of the Democrats was to ["through"(?) *canceled*] force their opponents into a false position, while they covered their own past treachery to the South. In short, Sir, should the Wilmot Proviso be passed—nay, should Congress next proceed to abolish slavery in the District, and the trade between the States, I am compelled to say, with feelings of deep mortification, that Virginia, after a few patriotic groans, will submit. She is already deeply infected with the spirit of abolitionism, much more deeply than most persons think; and I have no doubt our Leaders—who, for the most part, are mere Pensioners of the Federal Gover[n]m[en]t in *esse* or in *fieri*, will take advantage of the circumstance to make such *compromises* hereafter as they have made heretofore. The result of the last elections affords no fair criterion of popular sentiment, except in some portions east of the mountains. [John S.] Pendleton, [John M.] Botts and [Thomas S.] Flournoy may show that sentiment in their respective districts, but [James] McDowell, by far the most unsound and dangerous of the whole Delegation, reflects but too faithfully the sentiments of the west generally.

With these opinions I fear that when the occasion shall call for decisive action, South Carolina will have to look to the States still further South for support; for, with the lights at present before me, she will not be sustained by Virginia; and, *if not sustained*, she will be hunted down, as is usual in such cases, with the tiger vengeance that always characterizes the Traitor. At this moment I am sure the leading Editors of the two Parties in Virg[ini]a hate the People of S. Carolina with a more intense spirit than [William Lloyd] Garrison, [Benjamin] Tappan or [Joshua R.] Giddings, and for the obvious reason that their conduct is a standing reproach on their own venality and treachery. They are, as they have always been, only looking to President making. Does not the late letter of Cass to [Thomas] Ritchie show that, under the rose[?], the game of delusion is still going on? Is it not manifest that ancient political jockey is still rubbing down his spavined steed for a second heat? And will he or those whom he controuls ever stop to inquire about rights or principles, when place and plunder to the amount of millions per. an. depend upon the result of a Presidential election?

Still, if some State do not act we are irretrievably lost; we and our children. There are yet seven thousand men in Virginia who have not bowed the knee to Baal, and I am certain that in what ever course S. Carolina may determine to take, in the last resort, she will find a cooperation which will render it no easy matter to crush her.

Should the Wilmot Proviso pass, or any kindred measure, I am clear that a Convention of the People should be called immediately, to recommend a General Convention of the Southern States at an early day to take the whole matter into consideration; and on failure to procure such concurrence, to take steps for their own individual safety. But I am digressing far from the matter which lead me to take up the pen.

I wrote to you at some length two months since in reply to your favour written on the eve of your departure from Washington. On reflection however, I determined to retain it until I could find time to draw your attention to some transactions in Congress between the years 1812 & 17 on which I wished some more exact information. This, owing to a multitude of engagements, and arrangements preparatory to a removal to the mountains I have not been able to command. I am collecting materials in regard to that period of your history; and find that, as you suggest, it will be necessary for me to see you in person. To visit Washington however, should I remove to my farm this year, will be almost impossible; but if I remain here until next spring, (which my business almost compells me to do,) this may readily be done. But passing events embarrass me no little. There are if not strong probabilities, at least growing indications of popular sentiment that you will be before the Country as a Candidate in 1852. If so I would not, with my present views, be willing to publish such a memoir as I design to draw up, lest it might give offence to any individual, party or section—for I shall speak as freely as [Thomas B.] Macauley himself, and must needs give offence. Nay, I design, if God spare my life, to use a whip of scorpions when the occasion calls for it—and to make those who destroyed their Country feel what is the truth of History. I will spare neither the living nor the dead. This, however, in the event alluded to, would be injudicious. It would in such case be better to draw up a brief memoir for circulation amongst the masses, containing the leading events of your public & private history, written in a plain Style and conciliatory temper. This I would do—leaving for future publication a more matured and elaborate work. I shall, I trust, after the present year, be able to be master of my own time for the remainder of my life; and though I am fully aware, notwithstanding your flattering estimate of my qualifications, of my defects both as respects information & ability, yet I feel a stern pleasure in undertaking the task of vindicating truth, honor, virtue, and patriotism—recklessly assailed, as they have been, in your person. This, with God's blessing I will do; if not to the satisfaction of my head, to the relief of the heart. Some financial difficulties—the results of extensive improvements of Town property, demand now so much of my time and attention that I can do little more than collect and arrange materials at present. But having put in the way of collection some $25,000 long due me, I hope in twelve months to collect enough at least to discharge some $6 or 7,000 I owe here; and to secure me that exemption from pecuniary cares so well calculated to disturb and distract the attention of a student. So anxious, indeed, have I been to effect this at once, and to retire to the seclusion of my mountain home, that I have offered to one of our Capitalists here a lien on real estate to quintuple the amount for a loan for eighteen months; but those scoundrels are all *shavers* and demand unlawful interest, which I am resolved not to pay. I shall, therefore, probably remain here some twelve months longer; employing such leisure as I can command, in collecting and arranging materials. I much wish to have a brief abstract of the life of your Father [Patrick Calhoun]; and fully intended, years ago, when more with you, to obtain this—as I do not know what reliance is to be placed on the accounts I have read. Connected with this, it is essential to my purpose to have a fuller account of your own early life from birth to the end of your college life, than I have yet seen published—even supposing that to be authentic. Perhaps Mr. [Armistead] Burt might aid me in this during the next session. Many illustrative anecdotes I have taken the care to preserve, but I want something like a connected history as the public—the present and the future, will desire to know something of that system of *moral* as well as *mental* culture; which, to say the least, has so wonderfully *individualized* you. I have read all, I believe, that has been written; but the accounts are jejune—the facts, few as they are, being mixed[?] and without connection. A brief account of your brothers and sisters, too—their pursuits and connection, might be woven into the staple of the work to gratify the public interest; somewhat after the manner adopted by [Sir Walter] Scott in his life of Napoleon. Have you ever met with the memoir of Dr. [E.L.] Magoon? It is far more to my taste than any I have yet seen; but saving the political part of it, I do not know what reliance may be placed on his facts.

I find, on referring to my Diary that I did not, as I thought I had, recorded an anecdote you once told me of Gen. [Andrew] Jackson and some old and worthy officer, during the administration of Mr. [James] Monroe, which presented the character of the former in no way enviable, because in its *true* light. I wish I could recall it to your recollection; but my own is so imperfect, (arising no doubt from the belief that I had reduced it to writing,) that I cannot, perhaps, distinguish it from others in your mind. It turned, I think, on a promise of office—or a removal from office, involving the treble crimes of hypocrisy, falsehood and ingratitude.

But this is a small loss in comparison of some others. We once walked in the open fields towards Col. [George] Bomford's, when the subject of conversation was the *influence of the selfish principle*—on the essential *individuality of man*, which you traced in all the relations he bore to his fellows, socially, civilly, economically and politically. The subject carried you into the establishment of the Banking system, as well as other institutions—and I well remember to have regarded the views as the most original and interesting I ever listened to. I have often attempted, in select companies, to give a sketch of them; and as often had the general wished expressed that I could obtain them more in full for future use. If you can ever have the leisure to think of the subject again and can go through the manual labour, you would confer a great favour on me by putting your thoughts, no matter how carelessly, on Paper. It will enable me to complete a chapter which must ever remain defective without it.

But I am obtruding too long on your time. Other points present themselves but I will not trouble you with them now. Should your Reply be published in Pamphlet form, I would be much obliged to you for a copy. The tone, style and manner in which it is executed are admirable; better even than your last letter to Jackson; and equally conclusive. The single sentence in reply to the vile insinuation in respect to the draughts alledged to have been filed in the Department, is as withering, in every sense, as the language is susceptible ["of" *interlined*]—while that which, exempting him from ["the" *interlined*] charge of asserting what *he knew to be false*, gives him three inches of steel in the stern, quick conclusion that *he ought to have known it to be so*, might well compare with the best passage of like character in Junius. Taken as a whole it is one of most triumphant arguments—the most tremendous Phillipics ever published. The scoundrel will reply of course; but it seems to me you need not notice him further.

Mrs. [Elizabeth Morris] Crallé and Mary unite with me in affectionate regards to Mrs. [Floride Colhoun] Calhoun and Miss [Martha] Cornelia [Calhoun]. Say to Mrs. C[alhoun] I fear that the name of our youngest, has made her too much a favourite with all of us—if it has not made us believe that she is almost a prodigy. She certainly is ["the" *canceled*] most extraordinary child—parental partiality aside. With the highest regard and esteem, I am, dear Sir, Truly yours, R.K. Crallé.

ALS in ScCleA; PEx in Jameson, ed., *Correspondence*, pp. 1199–1202. NOTE: In a public letter of 7/10/1849 Cass, late nominee of the Democratic party for President, complained to editor Ritchie that the Whig press had misrepresented his positions on internal improvements and the Wilmot Proviso.

From D[AVID] L. YULEE, [Senator from Fla.]

St. Augustine [Fla.,] July 25, 1849

My Dear Sir, Your response to the speech of Col. [Thomas H.] Benton came to us by the last mail. I have read it with *very great satisfaction*, and cannot refrain from the expression of my grateful sense of the service you have done the southern cause. As a response it is demolishing and as a manifesto of southern feeling & duty, it will meet acceptance in the South & respect in the North. In the condensed summary of the principles belonging to the issue, with which you conclude your address, the true platform is presented. I think that the tone you adopt, altho' harsh beyond your habit, is justified by the occasion, and is that which was best calculated to render your address effective. A colder paper w[oul]d have vindicated yourself, without inspiring the South, or sinking Mr. Benton. ["which" *canceled*] He can scarcely recover the blow. If the Democratic party still hold him in embrace, it will be evidence of too much abolitionism in its texture for southern interest.

Mrs. [Nannie Wickliffe] Yulee, who has a fine son of a fortnight old at her side, desires to be respectfully remembered to yourself & y[ou]r family. Very truly Y[ou]r friend & ob[edien]t s[ervan]t, D.L. Yulee.

ALS in ScCleA.

From GEO[RGE] W. CRAWFORD, Secretary of War

War Department
Washington, July 26th 1849

Sir, I have the honor to acknowledge the receipt of your letter of the 9th instant forwarding certain papers sent to you by Private I.M.

Holmes of the Company of Sappers and Miners with a view to procure his discharge from the service.

The report of [Bvt. Brig.] General [Joseph G.] Totten, Chief of the Corps of Engineers, herewith enclosed, contains an explanatory statement from the officer commanding the company, which appears to disprove the existence of various grievances complained of by Private Holmes, as well as his allegation that he was induced to enlist through false representations made by the recruiting officer. It will be perceived that if Private Holmes wishes to obtain a discharge on the ground of ill health which appears to be his true reason for desiring to leave the service, he should apply to the Surgeon for a certificate of his unfitness for his present employment. Very respectfully Your Ob[edien]t Serv[an]t, Geo. W. Crawford, Sec. of War.

FC in DNA, RG 107 (Secretary of War), Letters Sent by the Secretary of War Relating to Military Affairs, 1800–1889, 29:265 (M-6:29).

From R[APHAEL] J. MOSES

Columbus Ga., July 26 1849

Dear Sir, As I do not propose to tax your time with an acknowledgment of this I trust that I will not be deem'd unduly obtrusive, in expressing to you the pleasure I received from a perusal of your reply to the Missouri Senator—it is regarded by both parties in this region as a triumphant vindication of your own course, and with it the rights of the South, the two being so identical, that to repel an attack upon one necessarily involves a defence of the other. The recent letters of Mr. [Henry] Clay, Col. [Thomas H.] Benton, Mr. [Martin] Van Buren and the speech of his son John [Van Buren] at the Free-Soil Convention, have tended to arouse both parties in Western Geo. and while the Democracy try to ["make" *canceled and* "prove" *interlined*] Gen[era]l [Lewis] Cass'[s] letter more acceptable to Southern feeling—(which it is not) and the Whigs still pretend to hope for better things from the present administration (which they can scarcely from the indications *expect*) yet there is evidently an excited feeling in the masses of both parties which has not been heretofore evinced and the impression is gaining ground rapidly, that the issue may be postponed but cannot be averted, and therefore the sooner it comes the better.

The Whig *politicians* evidently desire to keep matters quiet least the Harmony of the party may be disturbed, while the Democrats have no such wish, but for this I do not accord to the Democrats any more "patriotism" than the Whigs, they have only changed places since ["the Baltimore Convention" *canceled*] Presidential election. At the Baltimore Convention the Democrats shew'd as much party fealty, and were as willing to make sacrifices for harmony as the Whigs are now. The safety of the South depends less upon the patriotism of her politicians than it does upon the boldness of her opponents. The North is becoming reckless and will ere long place signs on the political horizon that the *people* will be able to *see with their own vision* and not through the partial lenses of political partisans. Whenever this state of things arrives I judge from the tone of public feeling among the masses of both parties, that despite of all influences they will stand by their rights under the Constitution. ["And still" *interlined*] If South Carolina were not a State of the Union, I should be less confident, for I do not feel certain that even Virginia would break the chains. The *people might be deceived by politicians* into a false security until the time for resistance had passed but I have no such fears for Carolina, and when she takes her stand, an attempt to co-erce her *cannot* be concealed from the people of the other Southern States, and in a confidence that they will not stand by passively, is my great hope, that vassalage will not be our ["children's" *interlined*] heritage.

I have taken no active part in Politics since last summer. My whole soul is absorbed in "the Southern question" and for that I have but three arguments; myself and two Sons! They are young—but old enough to die, if the price of a protracted life is to be submission to an uncontroll[e]d majority.

My present residence is in Columbus Georgia. My resting place shall be in my native State whenever she requires her sons to defend her soil.

Excuse this, but I write from the heart. I have forborne this pleasure for several days, not wishing to encroach upon your valuable time. Believe me, with the most sincere respect and admiration for Y[ou]r character Y[ou]r obe[dien]t Serv[an]t, R.J. Moses.

ALS in ScCleA; PEx in Boucher and Brooks, eds., *Correspondence*, pp. 518–519. NOTE: For information about Moses' sons, see *Last Order of the Lost Cause, the Civil War Memoirs of a Jewish Family from the "Old South"* (Lanham, Md., New York, London: University Press of America, 1995).

"A VISIT TO FORT HILL" by "A Traveller"

[Published July 26, 1849]

A Visit to Fort Hill, the Residence of the Hon. John C. Calhoun, Near Pendleton, S.C.

In paying a visit to the great statesman of America in his secluded home at the South, the visiter is so struck with both him and his home, that he is at a loss which to admire most—the far-seeing sage, or the magnificent scenery by which he is surrounded.

Few Northerners have had the pleasure of seeing Mr. Calhoun at home. On his plantation, in the bosom of his family, and surrounded by scenes familiar to him for so many years, he is the same, and yet he is in some respects a different person from the Senator at the capital. He is more at his ease, more sociable and familiar, and far happier.

His residence is about four miles from Pendleton, an old town in Picken's district, about 250 miles from Charleston.

I reached Pendleton about mid-day, and no sooner had I landed from the mail stage, than I made inquiry of the landlord of the hotel in regard to the distance to Fort Hill. He replied, "Yonder is Mr. Calhoun himself." My eyes followed the direction to which his finger pointed, and sure enough I saw, seated under the shade of a large tree, that stately head, whose features if once seen are scarcely if ever forgotten, and I had seen Mr. Calhoun before in the Senate, and recognised him at once. He rose as I approached to where he was seated, surrounded by a group of gentlemen, his neighbors, and when I delivered him my letter of introduction, he asked me to a seat. When he had read the letter, he introduced me to his neighbors, and then kindly invited me to return with him to his residence and spend two or three days. It is needless to say, that I at once accepted his invitation, so cordially given, and in the course of an hour I was seated by his side in his carriage, and on the way to Fort Hill.

Soon after leaving Pendleton, the carriage entered a forest, in which we continued until we reached the gate, which opened into the grounds in the immediate vicinity of the mansion. This is so concealed that you hardly notice it, until you are within a very short distance of the white pillars of the north and east fronts of his house.

The door yard is filled with trees and shrubbery—oaks that have stood there at least two hundred years, locusts, elms, willows, wild orange, and fig trees innumerable, the latter loaded with fruit; attached is a very large garden, filled with fruits, flowers, plants, and vegetables of every description, and not far distant are large apple and peach orchards. The mansion itself is a plain, unpretending-looking building relieved by wide piazzas, and, on each side, rows of columns. As I said before, the oak trees standing close to the house are very old, large, and lofty, and their immense tops are of great service, not only in presenting an impenetrable shade, but in protecting it in a thunder storm, as I had occasion to witness, for, during my short stay, Fort Hill was visited by one of the most severe thunder storms I had ever witnessed, and I should do the thunder injustice were I not to state that it was of the regular Calhoun order, and exactly what I should have expected in this region. It was tremendous, and the lightning was very brilliant. Flash and crash followed each other, it being difficult to distinguish which came first, for some fifteen minutes, when the performance, to my extreme satisfaction, came to a close, with a remark from Mr. Calhoun, who was seated in the room, that thunder was unusually loud in our neighborhood. I made some casual remark in reply, as though I was used to it in the North, but it was no such thing. We have no such scaring thunder in the North, and I have been nervous and down on such thunder and lightning ever since.

We reached Fort Hill about two o'clock, P.M. It was nearly the dinner hour. I was introduced to his family, which, at that time, consisted of Mrs. [Floride Colhoun] Calhoun, his youngest daughter [Martha Cornelia Calhoun], and the three youngest sons [John C. Calhoun, Jr., James Edward Calhoun, and William Lowndes Calhoun]. Mr. Calhoun has seven children—the eldest, Andrew [Pickens Calhoun], is a planter in Alabama; the next, Patrick [Calhoun], is a captain in the army, and stationed near New Orleans; the eldest daughter [Anna Maria Calhoun Clemson] is in Europe, the wife of our *Chargé* at Belgium [Thomas G. Clemson]. Mrs. Calhoun is just such a wife as a man like Mr. Calhoun should have—sensible, domestic, and industrious. She governs her household in a style that no Roman matron, in the old times, ever surpassed. Cornelia, the daughter at home, is a most affectionate companion for the mother. Of the three sons who were at home, I must make some mention. John is a physician, and was married, shortly after I left, to [Anzie Adams] the daughter of a near neighbor [Placidia Mayrant Adams]. He will make a leading physician wherever his destiny leads him to settle. James, the next, is a calm, quiet, thinking young man, of 20, and, in many respects, strongly resembles his father.

Willie is the youngest of all Mr. Calhoun's children, about 18 years of age, and the pet of all. The two last are students in the South Carolina College, and at home during the vacation.

I dressed for dinner, and when I sat down to the table I was soon at home, and felt as much so as if I had known every member of the family for the last twelve years.

Everything that is to be had in the South is raised or found on Mr. Calhoun's estate, and on his table. He is a very spare eater, and his temperance is so well known, that I need not allude to it. During the dinner, Mr. Calhoun asked me if there was anything very new at the North in the political world. To which I replied, that [Thomas H.] Benton's speech was very much talked about, and that it was evidently making a sensation. I was curious to hear what he would say to this, and asked him if he had read it?

"Some one has sent me a copy, which I have read. He has said many things of me which he well knew were false. I do not yet know whether I shall notice it or not. Should I do so, I should avoid anything like personalities. Mr. Benton is a man with whom I care to have little intercourse in any shape; and though his career and character are such, that they leave him very much exposed to be completely torn to pieces, I should only reply to such statements of his speech as are injurious to the South, and confine myself simply to refuting them, without touching his own deformities."

After dinner we went out on the north piazza; there is not another such view in the world as is to be seen at Fort Hill, from the front door. There are a range of mountains—both the Alleghany and Blue ridge—which extend from west to north, where they are lost in the distance, which can be distinctly seen, with their tops and peaks coming up into the sky, forty or sixty miles distant; and the scope of your eye, in the instant, embraces mountains in the four States of North Carolina, Georgia, Tennessee, and South Carolina. The view from his residence is as striking as his own views. He can look far ahead into the distant future, and events and results are clear to his vision long before they can be seen by others, who have not his advantages in point of view. These lofty mountains and changing appearance with changing seasons, and changing atmosphere—storm and sunshine—are a glorious sight. I can only give you a faint idea, and an imperfect sketch of the scenery—its wildness and softness—mountain and valley—forest and cultivated field—which surround him. Nature is here most bountiful; and I cannot but believe that the associations by which Mr. Calhoun is surrounded have had a great bearing in making him the illustrious man he is.

Directly south of the mansion, distant, perhaps, twenty steps, is his study. It stands alone, a plain white building, with but one room, a piazza, and four pillars, and one door, or entrance. In it is his library, not large, but choice; and most of the books are in some way connected with the great study of his life—the Union and her interests. He is not a reader. His book is nature, and practical experience. His theories, or doctrines, as the world calls them, are all based on these, and they never fail him; always correct, and he always will be, as long as he lives. The key of this building he always keeps under his immediate control when he is at home. No one enters it but him, unless he is there.

The view to the southward of his house is very beautiful, extending over hill and dale; the Seneca river passes through his plantation, and forms the principal branch of the Savannah river, by which the produce of his plantation is sent to Hamburg, opposite Augusta. His house itself stands 1,000 feet above the level of the sea, and about 200 feet above the Seneca river. In sight of the house and office is the negro quarter, on a hill 100 feet above the valley, and one-eighth of a mile from the mansion. The houses are built of stone, and joined together like barracks, with garden attached, and a large open space in front. There are, perhaps, seventy or eighty negroes on and about the place. The largest part of his negroes are in Alabama, where Mr. Calhoun owns a large plantation, and which is under the management of his son Andrew, (alluded to as his eldest son,) who has the reputation of being one of the best cotton planters in Alabama.

Towards sunset Mr. Calhoun gave me an invitation to walk over his farm. I gladly accepted. After leaving the mansion, we proceeded towards the valley at the south of it. We descended to the valley, passing by the negro quarter. Here Mr. Calhoun stopped a few moments, making inquiries in regard to some who were sick; among them, seated under a cherry tree, was an aged negro man, who was, as he informed me, the oldest on the place, and enjoyed some particular privileges. He was allowed to cultivate some four or five acres of land for cotton and other things; the proceeds of which became his property, and sometimes produced $30 to $50 a season. This is a privilege, however, that Mr. Calhoun allows his slaves and all have a patch containing more or less acres of cotton. These patches are near the negro quarter, for their convenience. The negroes cultivate the cotton at their leisure. Mr. Calhoun has it ploughed for them by his horses and ploughs, and they hoe it in their spare time. These darkies are as shrewd in getting the highest price for their little crops as white planters, and are as perfectly conversant with the fluctuations in the cotton market in Liverpool and New York as a cotton broker. Mr. Calhoun has no drivers. He has an overseer, Mr. Fredericks, who superintends his planting interest—a very intelligent and faithful man. Leaving the quarter, we passed down to a mill, at the foot of the hill on which the negro houses are built. From the mill we passed into a large field of Indian corn, and I assure you I do not exaggerate when I say that I never saw such a splendid agricultural sight in my life. The field is in the low ground or bottom, and covers one hundred and twenty acres. The average height is twelve to fourteen feet!—a sea of dark green, waving with tassels and glossy silk of every hue and color, and is grand beyond description. From this we passed into a cotton field, which is as large or larger, covering over one hundred and twenty acres, and extending over hill and flat, high and low ground. It was the first time I had ever seen cotton growing, and it was a new and novel sight to me. Mr. Calhoun explained to me the process of its cultivation. It is planted like Indian corn, and cultivated with even greater care; it is hoed four times. He pointed out to me the blossoms; the first day after the blossom appears, the flower is white; the next day red; and the third it drops off, and the cotton boll begins to form. It was in this stage I saw it. It is a pleasant mode of farming. There is nothing wanting on the farm; fields of oats, of wheat, of potatoes and of rice, and all in a forward state. The rice field occupies a part of the low land, near the Seneca river, and its pale green was in striking contrast with the dark green of the corn. The farm is a model farm, it consists of about one thousand acres, four hundred and fifty of which are in cultivation. Mr. Calhoun's striking method and arrangements are seen everywhere. His system of drainage, of ditching, and manner of planting on the side hills—so that the furrows carry off the water without allowing the land to wash—is novel; and so useful is it found, that his neighbors copy his plan. They have the advantage of his example constantly before them; and his crops are far ahead of any one else in this region. There is not anything which escapes him. After an hour had been spent in passing through these fields, we returned towards his outbuildings, cotton press, barns, granaries, &c. I was surprised. His whole heart and soul seemed absorbed in the farm. Had I not known with whom I was conversing, I should have set him down in my mind as the most thorough-going practical farmer I had ever met with. There is no detail connected with it, with which he is not perfectly familiar, and as he carries you along with him, he points out to you, and explains every thing in the most simple manner possible. You wonder, knowing the man, where he got his information from, and when he had time to get it, and still more when he had time to carry it into operation. But people cannot understand Mr. Calhoun; he is a perfect Napoleon in his system and power of combinations. He has a time and place for every thing; in a word, to give a vulgar quotation, "what Mr. Calhoun don't know about any and every thing, aint worth a man's while to look after." Say what you please about Mr. Calhoun's other qualifications, dispute about them as much as you please, whether he is this, that or the other, I care not—but this assertion I will make, John C. Calhoun is the best practical farmer in the United States, and if any man doubts this assertion, let him make a pilgrimage to Fort Hill, and his doubts will be left there.

By the way, while walking in the large corn field, I asked Mr. Calhoun what gave the name of Fort Hill to his place. He answered my query by pointing out to me a long hill about a mile from the mansion, and west of the corn field, above the Seneca, and remarked: "There was a fort stood there, built, I believe, during the war of the revolution; it was used during that time by the Americans, and called Fort Hill. It was dismantled with peace, but its name has been given to my farm, on which the old fort stood." His conversation is ever instructive and while giving me the history of Fort Hill, of which the above is but an abrupt summary, he gave a most interesting narration of the Indian war, long before the time of the French war of the Six Nations, of whom the Senecas extended down South as far as this region, and gave their name to the river near us; of their power and greatness, their war with the Cherokees; and when the Cherokees had driven them back to the north, he came down to the history of the Cherokees themselves—their alliance with the French against the English colonists. Then again the Cherokees, in the revolution, sided against the Americans, and with the English; and during the war Fort Hill was fortified more against the Indians than against the English. By this time we had passed through the tall corn and had reached the bank of the river, a narrow but a rapid and very deep stream, whose head waters were found not forty miles from him, in fact, in sight of his house in the mountains. There was a long scow tied to a tree on the bank, swung out into the stream. We both entered it, and I took a seat. The sun had just set, and all was still and quiet; there was a silence which was really solemn, connected as it was with the mossy and dense green foliage and trees which overhung the Seneca on both sides, down to the water's edge. Not a word was spoken for some moments, and an impression was made on my mind which I shall not soon forget. Mr. Calhoun's clear voice for a moment broke the spell. "The Seneca must be about two-thirds of the size of the Jordan." I looked up, and he described the resemblance, probably, with as much accuracy as if he had seen both. Again, I thought with what is he not familiar. The history of an empire or republic, or the history of the cotton plant or Indian corn; these rivers and brooks, or Jordan and Euphrates, and Texas rivers. While he was gazing up that placid stream, I gazed at him, and I have felt an irresistable love come over me, and a consciousness of irresistable power in him, which I never have felt before in the presence of any created being. I have stood in sight of emperors and kings in the old world, at reviews, amid the rolling of artillery, the peals of music from hundreds of bands, and the marching of thousands, and yet I never was so impressed with a feeling of the one man power, as in the presence alone of John C. Calhoun, in a boat on the Seneca river, and during that brief period a hundred things flashed across my mind, which I will recall again. One conviction was this: that but for ignorance, downright stupid ignorance, on the part of the people of the United States, made so and kept so by still more stupid, hack party papers, contented with the interest of selfish, aspiring party leaders, whose interest it is to keep the mass of the people ignorant of the real character of John C. Calhoun, of his glorious and god-like intellect, his lofty patriotism, and love for country, which is only bounded by that country, and not by any one State or section—he wishes but justice to all—of his unswerving devotion to the constitution, his supreme contempt for dishonest, time serving politicians, tricksters, and lickspittles; and his love for all that is good, useful, and patriotic; above all, his honesty and incorruptibility or his sagacity—his long experience of forty years in the highest seats in the councils of the Union—and his deep thought and foresight, which all make him what he is, the greatest man in the federal Union—but for this, the people, as one man, would have arisen and placed him at the head of affairs at Washington, long ago; and he would have stamped the impress of his mighty mind, for years to come, for good. With so pure, so lofty and patriotic a President, how would our government now stand before the struggling European nations? He would mark his administration by acts and policy that would cause it to be blessed for a century to come. As it is, what has he not done, for the last twenty years only? He has originated and carried more measures, which have become law, and defeated more which he believed to be bad, than all the Presidents during that period. Is it not true, and are not the people of the United States fully conversant with these facts? He has no press to trumpet forth and blazon his great actions, as every other little great man has, and who consequently become quite honored and carressed. These men, and that class of men, every one of them, know what John C. Calhoun is, and what he has done, and feel that to him they are the pigmy to the giant. Mr. Calhoun stands alone. He is like the mighty chain of the Alleghanies, which loom up into the clouds, 40 or 60 miles from his mansion; when time has passed with him, when 40 or 60 years intervene, then, and not till then, will the people of our country look back, and then in that distance—above all, will tower the memory of the acts of Calhoun. He is like the mountain—the grandeur of his mind and its conceptions cannot be seen by those in his time. Distance will mark his outlines with distinctness and do him justice—better for him—too late for us.

What experience has been his—how long and how varied! Six years a member of the lower House of Congress—eight years Secretary of War—seven years Vice President—one year Secretary of State—eighteen years Senator in Congress! For forty years, without intermission, in the public service, and during periods fraught with the greatest excitement and interest to the Union. I thought what a burning shame that party subserviency should be able to obscure in our own land an intellect which would shine brilliantly in any other; and the sage of experience never occupy his true position in our estimation, until after he leaves us; and what does he think of this or of the Presidency? I asked him, and as near as I can recollect, I will give his reply.

"What could I gain to be President? Care and anxiety that I am free from now. I am not ambitious. The only reward I seek, is the approbation of my own conscience. I neither ask nor desire any other reward than that. I would not accept the office of President, on any other terms than the most entire freedom to reform abuses, abolish this system of removals, and break up the spoils and plunder system, and restore the government to a healthy and vigorous action, and this without any trammel or pledges, except those which the constitution imposes upon the President."

And what American in his senses doubts that fact? What could Mr. Calhoun gain by being President, except the power to do more and greater good than a more limited sphere has yet allowed him to do?

After leaving the river, we walked back towards the mansion. On our way, he spoke of the beautiful Indian names still retained in this section. I asked if any of those Indians yet remained in the neighborhood? He replied that about 1,200 Cherokees yet remained in the North Carolina chain of the Alleghany, about 40 miles from Fort Hill, "and are," says Mr. Calhoun, "a very well behaved, peaceful and industrious people; there is sufficient land in that chain to form two mountain States." We returned to the mansion about dark. Soon after, tea was served to the family, on the piazza. Afterwards, we adjourned to the drawing-room. Mrs. Calhoun played several favorite tunes upon the piano, and at ten P.M. all separated for the night, and I retired to bed, and dreamed of the extraordinary individual whose guest I was for the time being.

The next day I arose at daybreak, and found that Mr. Calhoun was up before me, and had rode on to the plantation. He was absent about an hour. When he returned breakfast was served in the dining room. After breakfast he retired to his library, and left me to amuse myself as I pleased. His habits are very regular, and I presume they are the same one day as another, when at home. He rises at four to five o'clock; exercises on horseback or in a long walk over the farm for an hour; he then returns and writes until breakfast, which is about eight o'clock, he then retires again to his library, and writes or reads until one or two o'clock. Dinner is then served. After dinner, he converses until towards sunset, when he goes on the farm and remains until dark. After tea, he spends the evening in conversation with his family or friends. On Friday he generally rides to the village, it being the great mail day, meets those with whom he has business, converses with his friends and neighbors, and returns home in time for dinner. The mail reaches his house every day about one P.M. The newspapers, of which a large number are sent him, are laid upon the table in the hall, to be read by any one who has a fancy for them. He is very hospitable, has large numbers who come to see him and he is always glad to see those who come, friends or strangers. He is as much of a curiosity to people outside of a circle of five miles, as he would be were he to go to New York. Very few in this State, I fancy, have seen him. He keeps a very large number of horses, which are at the service of his visiters.

Left to myself, I took a stroll over the farm, and called at the snug cottage of his overseer, Mr. Fredericks, a most estimable man, and I should judge he took as much interest and pride in the high state of cultivation to which the plantation has arrived as Mr. Calhoun. He gave me every information I desired. Not a death has occurred on the place in four years, and I should judge that it was the healthiest location in the State. I went down to the slave quarter, and saw them at work also in the field. I had heard so much said in regard to Mr. Calhoun and his slaves, that I was anxious to see them with my own eyes. The slaves are certainly as happy and contented as it is possible for them to be. They love their master, and he is kind to them. On Sunday they go to church, or do as they please. They have their holidays. There seems to be as much aristocracy among the negroes of Mr. Calhoun as among white folks. The marriage of his young male or female slaves with a slave on another plantation, creates as much excitement as a marriage in Astor place would do. The matter requires a great deal of arrangement and proper settlement. These matches are generally made up between parties residing on different plantations. A very intelligent house servant of Mr. Calhoun was married (the second night I was at his house) to a female slave on an adjoining plantation. The marriage ceremony was performed in the evening, and in the mansion of the proprietor of the plantation. I listened to the fiddles and the happy songs of the negroes, on their way to and from the wedding, from this and all the neighboring plantations, until nearly daylight. The ceremony was performed by the oldest negro, who was a sort of authorized, or rather recognised parson of the Methodist order. Mr. Calhoun has some very old slaves on his plantation. One old negress that I saw, Monemi Calhoun, (by the way, all the negroes on his estate are called by his name in the neighborhood,) is over 112 years old. She has 63 living descendants on this plantation, who take care of the old dame. Her husband lived to a very old age; his name was Polydore. Both were brought from Africa, and have lived with the Calhouns for a century. The negroes on this place pay as much respect to the old negress as if she was a queen. Directly in front of the negro quarter is a field containing several acres of the sweet or Carolina potato. They grow to be very large. I did not notice any of the Seward kind on this farm. I don't think they could flourish this side of Washington.

The second morning I took my departure for Pendleton, very much gratified and delighted with my visit. The personal appearance of Mr. Calhoun is very imposing, he stands fully six feet. His features are very marked; he has an eye as clear and piercing as an eagle's; his hair stands up falling backward from his forehead and is quite gray. He is full of life, energy, and activity, and bids fair to live thirty years yet. He is a man that, I think, will live to a very great age. I should judge him to be 62 or 63 years old now. The longer such men live, the better for mankind and the human race. A TRAVELLER [Joseph A. Scoville].

PC in the New York, N.Y., *Herald*, July 26, 1849, p. 1. Extracts and abstracts in the Edgefield, S.C., *Advertiser*, August 8, 1849, p. 1; the Pendleton, S.C., *Messenger*, August 10, 1849, p. 2; the Greenville, S.C., *Mountaineer*, August 17, 1849, p. 1; the Washington, D.C., *Daily Union*, August 18, 1849, p. 3; the Philadelphia, Pa., *Pennsylvania Freeman*, August 23, 1849, p. 4. NOTE: A more intimate description of Calhoun at home was given by Anna Maria Calhoun Clemson in a letter of April 8, 1867, in reply to an inquiry: ". . . . my fathers actual life, except as connected with the history of the country, was singularly uneventful, & simple & unaffected goodness, & a daily discharge of every duty, tho presenting a rare & beautiful subject of contemplation, offers no salient points of interest, to the general reader. It is this which renders it so difficult, nay almost impossible to do the character of my father justice, in the eyes of those who knew, & loved him, as all did who knew him. His habits were simple, & regular, especially when at home. He practised a wise moderation in all things, mingling in due proportions intellectual effort, physical exertion, & relaxation, often saying that by so doing we preserved our capability of usefulness, & enjoyment, for a much longer time. He was peculiarly pleasant & cheerful in his every day intercourse. To say I never saw him angry, would but feebly express his rare equanimity. I never *saw him out of humour even*, or heard him use an expression, or do an action, I should not have been proud the whole world should hear or see. This may seem exaggerated, but it is simply the truth, & in him was plainly proved, that even in this world virtue is its own reward, for as he was the best, so was he the most contented—I may even say the happiest person, (so far as happiness is possible in this world), I ever knew. Not from stoicism did this proceed, for he had the tenderest heart, & the readiest sympathy with all around him. He is commonly called a stern man, but no one who saw the lovely smile which lit his countenance, when with those he loved, or enjoyed the delight of daily intercourse with him, ever thought him stern. In trouble or in joy all turned to him, certain of sympathy, & counsel. He has been also called a stoic—"a cast iron man." This was equally untrue. Where principle was involved, or duty required, no one was firmer or more self reliant but no one enjoyed the simple pleasures of life more than he did, or was more ready to promote the happiness of those around him. My earliest recollection, when he was Secretary of War, are of the eagerness with which we children listened for his return from the office, & the rush to be first to meet him & be taken in his arms for our usual *game of romps*, & all who visited Ft. Hill can testify to his geniality, & ready participation in all that was going on. He was very fond of music, particularly songs, in which the words were expressive. Appreciated highly *good* poetry, often repeating his favorite passages, & took intense delight in the beauties of nature. He was early in life a keen sportsman, & a fine shot, & often carried his gun when going around the plantation, but it is characteristic of the man that as soon as his failing eye sight rendered him less certain, he laid aside his gun & never used it again, tho always taking interest in the hunting exploits of his sons. Tho never humourous himself, he had a keen sense of humour, & laughed readily & heartily when that sense was appealed to. I found him, one day, reading The Pickwick Papers, (then just out) to his eldest brother [James Calhoun], whose sight was bad & both of them enjoying, with the greatest zest, Mr. Pickwick's adventures. He was the most affectionate husband, father, brother, & friend, & the kindest of masters. His brothers were equally devoted to him, & no shade ever marred their intercourse."

(*Leverett Letters: Correspondence of a South Carolina Family, 1851–1868*, Frances Wallace Taylor, et al., eds., Columbia, S.C.: University of South Carolina Press, 2000, pp. 424–425).

From John Reese

New York [City,] July 28th 1849

Dear Sir, The accompanying extract [*not found*] with regard to your late noble vindication of the rights of the South, and your own high political character, is only one of the many tributes to your exalted patriotism and long tried political integrity with which our presses at the North are daily teeming—be assured dear Sir you have as many warm and devoted friends in the Empire State, as in your own long cherished Carolina where you are known and loved so well. Esteeming you as I do the truest Patriot, and purest Public man in our country, I cannot withhold the expression of the deepest respect and admiration for you as a Statesman[,] a Patriot[,] and a Man. With the highest respect your fellow Countryman, Jno. Reese.
N.Y. City, 191 Broadway.

ALS in ScCleA.

To J[oseph] H. Hedges, [Philadelphia, Pa.]

Fort Hill, 30th July 1849

Sir, I return the enclosed [*not found*]. The Writer [John Ewing Colhoun] was an eminent lawyer. He died, when a member of the Senate of the United States [from S.C.], in 1802. He was my cousin. Respectfully, J.C. Calhoun.

ALS in Eugene S. Farley Library, Wilkes College, Wilkes-Barre, Pa.

From Francis Lieber

Columbia S.C., 30 July 1849

My dear Sir, I must again express my acknowledgments for the kind interest you show in behalf of the warrant desired for my son [Hamilton Lieber]. I received your favour of the 24th only last night. I am sorry that I have sent my application long ago. I think I wrote you already that I hesitated troubling you with the matter because it seemed to me out of proportion with the prominent place of so distinguished a statesman, nor had I any claim upon you for any private affair. At least this appeared to me so when the question was whether I should take the liberty of writing to you. Had I had the pleasure of seeing you I might easily have brought the matter verbally before you.

I shall not omit writing to you when at Washington, as you direct me to do.

I am afraid that Mr. [William C.] Preston's health is not much improving and that those who are most directly concerned, will be obliged to cast their looks about, with reference to a successor, should the president resign, whatever apparent indelicacy there may be in so doing notwithstanding. I feel sure that you consider with me the College [South Carolina College] one of the most essentially important institutions of our State, and the appointment of a presiding officer of proportionate importance. With this view I donot [*sic*] hesitate to beseach you deeply to impress every leading man with whom you may come in contact, with the great necessity of taking the best man that can be got. Secondary considerations are all the world over but too apt to sway, but the difficulty is much increased in the U.S. by an otherwise most convenient and, in general, beneficial fact—the general adaptability of the American mind. This leads people to suppose that a man, once clever and efficient must be in all situations so, and persons are but too frequently appointed for offices, not because they are fit or have shown themselves so, but because they are expected to fit themselves for them. This will do no doubt in many cases, but not in this. I write this without having any name in my mind as to who would be the best individual; but I have heard of late so many names suggested, some of whom are so palpably [*partial word canceled*] ill adapted, that my fears have become somewhat roused.

I hope that the very great importance of the subject will serve as an excuse for having written to you on ["the subject" *canceled and* "it" *interlined*]. I feel most thouroughly [*sic*] convinced that the choice for no office requires more unhesitating conscienciousness [*sic*] and deliberate wisdom as the one I have spoken of. I am with the greatest regard Your most obedient, Francis Lieber.

ALS in ScCleA. NOTE: An AEU by Calhoun reads, "Prof[esso]r Lieber."

From Willis L. Williams

St. Louis, Mo. 31 July 1849

My dear Sir; The first time I remember seeing you, was at Milton N.C. if my memory serve me aright, where you attended a small dinner party—in company I believe with Gen[era]l [Romulus M.] Saunders. I may be wrong, for I was quite a boy. Whereever it was, I was then taught to respect and admire you. Your acquaintance, I first had the honor and pleasure of forming at Washington during the winter of 1832–3, when you will well remember your thoughts were too much engrossed with momentous matters of State, to retain in any great degree the recollection of young men. That was, however, a proud epoch in my then existence of comparative youth, when I felt the influence of your matured intellect and pure mind, operating to make me, almost daily, a wiser and better man. Thrown by Providence, in the far west, I saw you not again till the winter of 1845–6, when I had the rich pleasure of ["again" *canceled*] seeing you at the Capitol, and renewing an acquaintance under such favorable circumstances, as afforded me opportunity of spending several most delightful evenings with you and your family, and listening to that once familiar voice and wisdom, which, as a Son of the South, I had long before learned to reverence and love. During every succeeding session of Congress, I have had frequent occasion to be kept in remembrance of you; for in none of the many exciting scenes that have transpired, have you been a silent spectator, but in all of them an active and conspicuous participant. But recent events have brought you most prominently before our whole public and private gaze—and it is to say a word or two on these events, that has induced me to address you this letter. When Mr. [Thomas H.] Benton made his undignified and malicious assault upon you, and through you upon the interests of the whole South, I, in common with all who knew you, felt that, if you could consent to notice him at all, we should be favored with a communication, which, while it should vindicate your own honor, would furnish those of us who are your personal and political adherents, with arguments on the exciting subject that now agitates the nation, and I fear will continue to do so, till agitation is swallowed up by a much deeper and more intense emotion. And, Sir, your address has reached us, and is just what was predicted of it—dignified—severe—full of self respect—and as an argument, most beautiful and conclusive. Scattered over this great country, there are thousands who admire you, and it will have a wonderful effect whereever it is read—and to insure its reaching the huts of all, many of us here, who are Southern born and with you heart and soul, now and forever, intend publishing it in pamphlet form and circulating it. It is almost a pity that you did not address it to the Citizens of the slaveholding States—for in that case, all such, would have felt that it included them. It is capital, and must stand always, a proud monument of your genius and patriotism. God bless you, and spare you to live till all the exciting questions about which you have thought so much, may have been settled as you desire; and the South, as an integral part of this glorious union, shall rejoice in the full and perfect belief that her brethren of the north & northwest, are ever ready to protect and defend her against all aggressions made upon her smallest right or interest, whether by an invader from abroad or a pretended friend nearer by her home. But if her doom is to be different, there are thousands here, who will gather round her flag in the darkest storm, and die amid its honored folds.

Benton is west of us still, addressing the dear people—and although he ought to be put down, and with proper management might be, yet it is hard to bring those who have lauded and feared him so long, to act independently against him. Our population is hardly enlightened enough—but still, he is surrounded with much more powerful opposition & more numerous too, than he has had to encounter here for twenty years. Large numbers of the most prominent men in different portions of the State, are fully committed against his course, both on the Wilmot proviso question, and his appeal. Until your address came here, no one had thought of his disobedience of the former resolutions, which will no doubt be now pressed home upon him with some effect. If Atcherson [*sic*; David R. Atchison] had the ability to meet him in debate, and would do it, he could fix his fate. If [James S.] Green of the House, would stick close to him, he might put him down—but you can[']t conceive of the cowardice of his constituents, when they are called upon to act against him. I was in our Legislature in 1844–5 when his last election came on, and we whigs wanted only eleven votes wherewith to defeat him, but not a man in the State could be found to oppose him. I mean, of course, not a democrat. It is still too much the case, but we have hopes that by a union of the disaffected democracy and whigs, at the next session, he may be defeated—a consummation most devoutly to be wished. And yet there will be another difficulty. Many of our whigs are northern men, or Kentuckians, and by means of their intelligence occupy seats in the legislature, and they are generally *proviso* men—So that no one can divine the result of matters. I trust something may turn up at Washington this winter and Session, that may lead him to take a leap that shall destroy him. "Quem Deus vult peredere &c"—[Henry S.] Geyer, [Edward] Bates and others, old whigs and able men, have long since given up all effort to put him down with the ingorant [*sic*] Jackson populace here—and those of us who are younger, and less talented, but more ardent and sanguine, are generally too poor to spare the time.

You see that I am a Whig—but I am a Southerner in all that concerns her peculiar institutions. Born in Williamsboro', a little town in Granville Co[unty] settled by my ancestors, when I desert the land of my nativity and whatever is calculated to advance her to prosperity and renown, may my tongue cleave to the roof of my mouth. I wish you were a Whig too—but perhaps then, you might not wield the influence so necessary in this heated hour to attach to your honored name. No party as such merely can claim you—for you have ever been above its shackles that bind to the earth both soul and body. I too so far bolted in the late election as to prefer [Lewis] Cass to [Zachary] Taylor, feeling afraid, as I did and still do, that the latter would sanction even the Wilmot Proviso were it presented for his signature. If it come to him in an honest, plain, unsophisticated way, and I trust it may if it come at all, and he should sanction it, it would be well for him to change his domicil. I presume Louisiana would prove quite too warm a climate after that for his comfort.

Excuse me Sir, for assuming the privilege of writing to you. I only desired to thank you for your vindication of the Constitution of my Country, especially when struck at directly through those interests dear to all the rightminded of our liberty and union loving region. Can it be possible that Judge [George E.] Badger will misrepresent his people on this subject? I feel confident that his associate Judge [Willie P.] Mangum will not—and if Badger should, I do hope old Rip Van Winkle will wake up long enough to teach him his duty. But there again, the ignorance of the masses is so impenetrable as to form a shield to a public servant like the Judge, who can talk well about nothing. I trust you will help manage matters so as to keep him before his Constituents in a proper light.

Your address has been published here, in all of our prominent papers of both castes—and must be circulated extensively and read by thousands, unless the high priests shall interdict its perusal.

Remember me most kindly to Mrs. [Floride Colhoun] Calhoun & your niece whom I met at your rooms in 1845–6, and for yourself accept of the highest considerations of Sir, Your obedient Servant, Willis L. Williams.

P.S. It would delight this City and surrounding country, if you would visit us. Much good would result from a mere passing visit of a day or two, which you might make by coming this way; and by the lakes on your next trip to or from Congress. It would seem accidental, and you almost owe it to us and yourself to come & See us.

If you have a copy of your speech on the Oregon Territorial bill, I would like to see it—and during the coming session, will thank you to send me any thing that will help us along in this great struggle for liberty & right.

ALS in ScCleA; PEx in Boucher and Brooks, eds., *Correspondence*, pp. 519–520.
NOTE: Badger and Mangum were the Senators from N.C.

SYMBOLS

The following symbols have been used in this volume as abbreviations for the forms in which documents of John C. Calhoun have been found and for the repositories in which they are preserved. (Full citations to printed sources of documents can be found in the Bibliography.)

Abs	—abstract (a summary)
ADS	—autograph document, signed
ADU	—autograph document, unsigned
AES	—autograph endorsement, signed
AEU	—autograph endorsement, unsigned
ALS	—autograph letter, signed
ALU	—autograph letter, unsigned
ArU	—University of Arkansas, Fayetteville
CC	—clerk's copy (a secondary ms. copy)
CSmH	—Huntington Library, San Marino, Cal.
CtY	—Yale University, New Haven, Conn.
DLC	—Library of Congress, Washington
DNA	—National Archives, Washington
DS	—document, signed
En	—enclosure
Ens	—enclosures
EU	—endorsement, unsigned
FC	—file copy (usually a letterbook copy retained by the sender)
GEU	—Emory University, Atlanta, Ga.
Ia-HA	—State Historical Society of Iowa, Des Moines
ICHi	—Chicago Historical Society, Chicago, Ill.
IGK	—Knox College, Galesburg, Ill.
IHi	—Illinois State Historical Library, Springfield
LS	—letter, signed
M-	—(followed by a number) published microcopy of the National Archives
MH	—Harvard University, Cambridge, Mass.
MoSHi	—Missouri Historical Society, St. Louis
Nc-Ar	—North Carolina Department of Archives and History, Raleigh
NcD	—Duke University, Durham, N.C.
NcU	—Southern Historical Collection, University of North Carolina at Chapel Hill
NjP	—Princeton University, Princeton, N.J.
PC	—printed copy
PDS	—printed document, signed

PEx	—printed extract
PPL	—Library Company of Philadelphia, Pa.
RG	—Record Group in the National Archives
ScC	—Charleston Library Society, Charleston, S.C.
ScCleA	—Clemson University, Clemson, S.C.
ScU-SC	—South Caroliniana Library, University of South Carolina, Columbia
TxU	—Barker Texas History Center, University of Texas, Austin
Vi	—Virginia State Library, Richmond
ViU	—University of Virginia, Charlottesville

BIBLIOGRAPHY

This bibliography is limited to sources of and previous printings of documents published in this volume.

The Address of Southern Delegates in Congress, to Their Constituents. [Washington:] Towers, Printer, [1849].

Address of the Hon. John C. Calhoun, to the People of the Southern States; and Letter of Gen. Lewis Cass to Mr. Ritchie. [St. Louis:] St. Louis Union Job Printers, [1849].

Aderman, Ralph M., ed., *Letters of James Kirke Paulding.* Madison: University of Wisconsin Press, 1962.

Alexandria, Va., *Gazette,* 1808–.

Ambler, Charles Henry, ed., *Correspondence of Robert M.T. Hunter, 1826–1876,* in the *American Historical Association Annual Report* for 1916 (2 vols. Washington: U.S. Government Printing Office, 1918), vol. II.

American Quarterly Register and Magazine. Philadelphia: 1848–1851.

Anderson, S.C., *Gazette,* 1843–1855.

Athens, Ga., *Southern Banner,* 1831–?.

Baltimore, Md., *Sun,* 1837–.

Barbee, David Rankin, ed., "A Sheaf of Old Letters," in *Tyler's Quarterly Historical and Genealogical Magazine,* vol. XXXII, no. 2 (October, 1950), pp. 77–102.

Benton, Thomas H., ed., *Abridgment of the Debates of Congress.* 16 vols. New York: D. Appleton & Co., 1854–1861.

Boucher, Chauncey S., and Robert P. Brooks, eds., *Correspondence Addressed to John C. Calhoun, 1837–1849,* in the *American Historical Association Annual Report* for 1929. Washington: U.S. Government Printing Office, 1930.

Boston, Mass., *Advertiser,* 1813–1929?.

Camden, S.C., *Journal,* 1826–1891?.

Charleston, S.C., *Courier,* 1803–1852.

Charleston, S.C., *Evening News,* 1845–1861.

Charleston, S.C., *Mercury,* 1822–1868.

Charleston, S.C., *Southern Baptist,* 1846–1860.

Columbia, S.C., *Palmetto State Banner,* 1846–1853?.

Columbia, S.C., *South-Carolinian,* 1838–1849?.

Columbia, S.C., *Telegraph,* 1847–1851.

Congressional Globe . . . 1833–1873 . . . . 46 vols. Washington: Blair & Rives and others, 1834–1873.

Crallé, Richard K., ed., *The Works of John C. Calhoun.* 6 vols. Columbia, S.C.: A.S. Johnston, 1851, and New York: D. Appleton & Co., 1853–1857.

Edgefield, S.C., *Advertiser*, 1836–.

Flippin, Percy Scott, ed., "Herschel V. Johnson Correspondence," in *North Carolina Historical Review*, vol. IV, no. 2 (April, 1927), pp. 182–201.

Flippin, Percy Scott, *Herschel V. Johnson of Georgia, State Rights Unionist.* Richmond: Dietz Printing Co., 1931.

Greensborough, Ala., *Alabama Beacon*, 1843–1851.

Greenville, S.C., *Mountaineer*, 1829–1901.

Hearon, Cleo, "Mississippi and the Compromise of 1850," in *Publications of the Mississippi Historical Society*, vol. XIV (1914), pp. 7–229.

Holst, Hermann von, *John C. Calhoun.* Boston: Houghton, Mifflin & Co., 1882.

Jackson, Miss., *Mississippian*, 1832–1865.

Jameson, J. Franklin, ed., *Correspondence of John C. Calhoun*, in the *American Historical Association Annual Report* for 1899 (2 vols. Washington: U.S. Government Printing Office, 1900), vol. II.

Laurensville, S.C., *Herald*, 1848–1933.

Liberator, The. Boston: 1831–1865.

Memphis, Tenn., *Eagle*, 1843–1851.

Mr. Calhoun's Address to the People of the Southern States. [Charleston: A.J. Burke, 1849?].

Mr. Calhoun's Reply to Col. Benton. [Pendleton, S.C.: printed by Pendleton *Messenger*?, 1849].

Nashville, Tenn., *Whig*, 1838–1855.

National Era. Washington: 1847–1860.

New Orleans, La., *Daily Picayune*, 1836–1914.

New York, N.Y., *Herald*, 1835–1924.

Niles' Register. Baltimore: 1811–1849.

Oliphant, Mary C. Simms, Alfred Taylor Odell, and T.C. Duncan Eaves, eds., *Letters of William Gilmore Simms.* 6 vols. Columbia: University of South Carolina Press, 1952–1982.

Pendleton, S.C., *Messenger*, 1807–?.

Perry, Thomas Sergeant, ed., *The Life and Letters of Francis Lieber.* Boston: James R. Osgood and Co., 1882.

Petersburg, Va., *Republican*, 1843–1850.

Philadelphia, Pa., *Pennsylvania Freeman*, 1843–1850.

Pickens, S.C., *Keowee Courier*, 1849–1868.

"A Pro-Slavery Letter by John C. Calhoun," in *Annals of Iowa*, 3rd series, vol. II (1894), p. 235.

Richmond, Va., *Enquirer*, 1804–1877.

Richmond, Va., *Whig*, 1824–1888.

Rowland, Dunbar, *History of Mississippi, the Heart of the South.* 2 vols. Jackson, Miss., and Chicago: S.J. Clarke, 1925.

St. Louis, Mo., *Missouri Republican*, 1836–1919.

Segal, Charles M., "Isachar Zacharie: Lincoln's Chiropodist," in *American Jewish Historical Quarterly*, vol. XLIII, no. 2 (December, 1953).

Spartanburg, S.C., *Spartan*, 1843–1853.

Sprague, William Buell, *Annals of the American Pulpit* . . . . 9 vols. New York: Robert Carter & Brothers, 1857–1869.

Springfield, Mo., *Advertiser*, 1844–1861?.

Sumterville, S.C., *Black River Watchman*, 1850–1855.

Testimonials. No place: no date.
Tuscaloosa, Ala., *Independent Monitor*, 1837–1872.
Tyler, Lyon G., *Letters and Times of the Tylers.* 3 vols. Richmond: Whittet & Shepperson, 1884–1896.
U.S. Senate, *Senate Documents*, 30th Cong.
U.S. Senate, *Senate Journal*, 30th Cong.
Vicksburg, Miss., *Sentinel*, 1838–1851?.
Washington, D.C., *Daily National Intelligencer*, 1800–1870.
Washington, D.C., *Union*, 1845–1859.
Wilson, Clyde N., ed., *The Essential Calhoun: Selections from Writings, Speeches and Letters.* New Brunswick, N.J., and London: Transaction Publishers, 1992, 1999.
Writings and Speeches of Daniel Webster. 18 vols. Boston: Little, Brown & Co., 1903.

INDEX